James W.

INTRODUCTION TO THE BUDDHIST TANTRIC SYSTEMS

F. D. Lessing and A. Wayman

INTRODUCTION TO THE BUDDHIST TANTRIC SYSTEMS

Translated From

MKHAS GRUB RJE'S

Rgyud sde spyiḥi rnam par gźag pa rgyas par brjod

With Original Text and Annotation

MOTILAL BANARSIDASS
Delhi :: Varanasi :: Patna

Indological Publishers and Booksellers
Head Office : BUNGALOW ROAD, JAWAHAR NAGAR, DELHI-7
Branches : 1. CHOWK, VARANASI-1 (U.P.)
2. ASHOK RAJPATH, PATNA-4 (BIHAR)

First Edition : The Hague, 1968
Second Edition : Delhi, 1978
Price : Orient-Book $12.95

Printed in India
BY SHANTILAL JAIN, AT SHRI JAINENDRA PRESS, A-45, PHASE-1, INDUSTRIAL AREA, NARAINA, NEW DELHI-28 AND PUBLISHED BY NARENDRA PRAKASH JAIN FOR MOTILAL BANARSIDASS, BUNGALOW ROAD, JAWAHAR NAGAR, DELHI-7

INTRODUCTION TO THE SECOND EDITION

May I first explain that the brevity of introduction to the first edition of Mkhas-grub-rje's tantra survey was because Professor F. D. Lessing had passed away prior to the final preparation of the manuscript. I had collaborated throughout with him on the translation, but had to supply all the notes myself. Doubtless if Professor Lessing had lived, he would have provided a fine introduction. Since that time I have published two works myself on the Buddhist Tantras: *The Buddhist Tantras; Light on Indo-Tibetan Esotericism* (Samuel Weiser: New York, 1973), and *Yoga of the Guhyasamājatantra; the Arcane Lore of Forty Verses* (Motilal Banarsidass: Delhi, 1977). Being more familiar now with the background of Mkhas-grub-rje's work, I shall clarify this background by the following considerations, necessarily brief.

The editor of the Kanjur and Tanjur (the Tibetan canon) was Bu-ston (b. 1290), who broke off from the Sa-skya-pa sect to found the celebrated school of Zha-lu. His collected works have been reprinted by Dr. Lokesh Chandra in New Delhi, who kindly presented me with a set during my visit to his International Academy of Indian Culture in December 1976. From this edition I have perused Bu-ston's three survey works of the Buddhist Tantra, as well as his survey work on the Yogatantra (the third branch of Tantra). This enables me to say definitely now that Mkhas-grub-rje must have had these works of Bu-ston as a source from which he summarized various materials for his own introduction to the subject, also incorporating a number of the reform Gelugpa positions of his immediate teacher, Tsoṅ-kha-pa. For example, Mkhas-grub-rje's first chapter on "How the Teacher Bhagavat became Abhisambuddha" is simply drawn from the somewhat more extended account in Bu-ston's works.

It is well known that Bu-ston had classified the Kanjur Tantra section of authoritative Tantras under the headings of four Tantra classes, Kriyā, Caryā, Yoga, and Anuttarayoga. His three survey works cite various explanations for these four classes. Of special significance is the passage, repeated in all three—in the "small-sized" (Pha, 'bsdus po,'

27b), in the "large-sized" (Ba, 'rgyas pa,' 45a-b), in the "medium-sized" (Ba, 'ḥbriṅ po,' 44a-b), classifying the four Tantra classes by the four theory-systems (*siddhānta*), which are the Vaibhāṣika, Sautrāntika, Yogācāra, and Mādhyamika, as I translate:

1. According to the theory of the Vaibhāṣikas that external entities (e.g. the four elements) are true and have a wordless nature, one attracts the knowledge being onto the cloth one has arranged in front, and disposes a mantra-garland in his heart, then with bathing and ritual purity, reciting mantras, one takes *siddhi* (i.e. from that deity in front)—so the Kriyā Tantra.
2. According to the theory of the Sautrāntikas that all appearances are cognition and that there are the pair, apprehending and apprehended object, one generates oneself into the 'symbolic being, attracts the knowledge being in front and disposes the mantra (garland) in his heart and incants it, then takes *siddhi* from the god like a friend—so the Caryā Tantra.
3. According to the theory of the Yogācāras that while external entities are not true, still introspection is true without the pair, apprehending and apprehended object—one generates oneself into the 'symbolic being' and draws in the 'knowledge being'; one recites the mantra and in conclusion dismisses the 'knowledge being'—so the Yoga Tantra.
4. According to the Mādhyamikas accepting in a conventional sense the pair, apprehending and apprehended object, while completely denying them in the absolute sense—one generates the 'symbolic being', draws in the 'knowledge being'; and omits the ritual of dismissing (the knowledge being)—so the Anuttarayoga Tantra.

Bu-ston mentions that while the foregoing description was set forth by certain Tanjur authorities, such as the tantric Nāgārjuna, and repeated by some Tibetan gurus, his own school finds no supporting information for it. Observe that this correlates the two 'Hīnayāna' systems with the first two Tantra classes, and the two 'Mahāyāna' systems with the last two Tantra classes. The Gelugpa rejects the correlation, preferring to include the entire Tantra system in the Mahāyāna, with the 'Prajñāpāramitā' portion of the Mahāyāna as a basis. When Mkhas-grub-rje refers to this fact as the Prāsaṅgika Mādhyamika position underlying all the Tantra, he probably means simply the Mādhyamika emphasis on voidness, especially of all the natures (*dharma*) arising dependently, avoiding the extremes of existence and non-existence.

The correlation of the four theory-systems with the four Tantra classes may well have been a reason for the neglect by the older Tibetan gurus of the first two Tantra classes (the 'Hīnayāna' two) as cults to be followed in their own right, and the emphasis instead on the last two Tantra classes (the 'Mahāyāna' two), since Tibetan Buddhism was prevalently of the Mahāyāna variety. A further circumstance fostering this preference was the fact that the main Tantras of the first two classes were translated in the first period of Tibetan Buddhism, with lineages of these works largely lost during the period before the revival which became known as the Second Diffusion of Buddhism in Tibet. In contrast, most of the third and fourth Tantra classes and their voluminous commentaries were translated in the second period along with continuation of lineages of 'permission' to evoke the deities, and initiations that prepare for study and practice of the individual Tantras. A third reason, taken from Bu-ston's writings and incorporated into Mkhas-grub-rje's first chapter, is that only the Yoga Tantra and the Anuttarayoga Tantra have the traditions of how the Buddha obtained his full enlightenment. For those various reasons it was thought that the Yoga and Anuttarayoga Tantra were alternate ways of becoming a Buddha in this life (the quick path of the Tantra), while all four divisions of the Tantra could be used for evocations of deities for inferior *siddhis*. Thus, among the older Tibetan lamas there was a tendency to downgrade the Kriyā and Caryā Tantras. The restoration of these two 'lower' Tantra divisions to their justified importance was begun in Bu-ston's tantric surveys and editing of the tantric portions of the Kanjur and Tanjur by way of the four Tantra classes. Bu-ston, while himself an auhority on the Yoga Tantra (the third class) and the *Kālacakra-tantra* (in the fourth class), has numerous and long citations from the Kriyā Tantra work *Mañjuśrī-mūla-tantra* and from the Caryā Tantra work *Vairocanābhisambodhi*. The Gelugpa further promoted the importance of these two Tantra classes in Tsoṅ-kha-pa's *Sṅags rim chen mo*. That is why Mkhas-grub-rje has a generous treatment of the Kriyā Tantra and refers to "the steps of the path of becoming a Buddha by way of the Kriyā Tantra."

Another topic that needs introduction is that of initiation (*abhiṣeka*). Bu-ston treats the matter in the 'medium-sized' survey (Ba, going from 21a to 25b), discussing especially remarks of Atīsa in his *Bodhipatha-pradīpa* and Self-commentary, e.g. Ba, 25a: There are two kinds of 'initiations'—those based on homelife, and those based on the pure life (*brahmacarya*. The ones based on the home are all of them, to the extent stated in the Tantras. The ones based on the pure life omit among them the Secret Initiation and Insight-Knowledge Initiation (see herein Chapter Nine). The question is raised: Why omit those two ? Atīśa's answer is that only the pure life is consistent with the Buddha's Dharma, while those two initiations violate the pure life; and he adds that there is no fault in knowing the situation. Bu-ston mentions that some persons understood from Atīśa's remarks that one could understand the lower and higher Tantras, listen to them and explain them to others, without 'initiation' (*abhiṣeka*); that it suffices to have taken the vow of enlightenment and have entered the Bodhisattva path. Bu-ston takes this as an insult to Atīsa, and a complete misreading of his position. It would mean, for example, that one would recite mantras that were personally chosen, not imparted by the guru during initiation; that this is said to lead to disaster. But Bu-ston did not clarify an important issue, which can be stated this way: The morality of Buddhism requires the stipulations of conduct to be accepted literally. But read literally, the higher initiations appear to violate morality. Did Atīśa allow all initiations to be taken by lay persons, who would read the Tantra in a literal way, while persons in the 'pure life' could take the higher initiations of the Anuttarayoga Tantra, provided the Tantra be read in a non-literal manner according to precepts of the gurus ? In this connection, the Gelugpa insists that the fourth Tantra class, the Anuttarayoga, is preeminently inner *samādhi*; and so the references to male and female are understood as combinations of forces within the yogin or yoginī.

Then, what does this teaching of Buddhist Tantra, especially the Anuttarayoga Tantra, have to do with the mysterious force called Kuṇḍalinī on which Pandit Gopi Krishna has written at length ? The Buddhist tantric teaching set forth herein (Chapter Nine) in the treatment of the 'Secret Initiation' concerns making the 'winds' enter, dwell, and dissolve in the central channel of the body, in fact the 'subtle body'. This process would presumably arouse forces loosely referred to as 'Kuṇḍalinī' in the Hindu tantric books. The meaning of the Buddhist tantric method is stated at length in my new book *Yoga of the Guhyasamājatantra*. Here may I say only briefly that the method is attended with the dangers made clear in Gopi Krishna's writings as long as the candidate has not first strengthened the subtle body so that it can withstand the unusual forces that are thus aroused.

Finally, what can be said of Mkhas-grub-rje's book as a whole ? It seems that in preparation for writing his large commentary on the *Kālacakra-tantra*, he first wrote this survey work on the Tantras and then his commentary on the *Hevajra-tantra*. The survey work reveals his striking ability to seize the main points of a vast literature and present them in orderly fashion. On the other hand, it should be conceded that he has accordingly so abbreviated as to afford scant intimation of the actual involved ritual in its true amplitude. To see this, one must resort to the specialized treatises, for example, as he himself recommends at the conclusion, Tsoṅ-kha-pa's *Sṅags rim chen mo*.

April, 1978, New York City ALEX WAYMAN

CONTENTS*

Introduction 11

Chapter One 17

I. How the Teacher Bhagavat became Abhisaṃbuddha (1b-2) 17

A. Position of the Śrāvakas (1b-3) 17

B. Position of the Mahāyāna (2b-5) 21

1. Teaching of the Pāramitā school (2b-5) 21

2. Teaching of the Mantra school (4a-1) 25

a. Teaching of the Yoga school (4a-2) 25

(1) Position of the Śākyamitra and Buddhaguhya (4a-3) 27

(2) Position of Ānandagarbha (4b-4) 27

(3) The Five Abhisaṃbodhi (5a-2) 29

b. Teaching of Anuttara school (7a-2) 35

Chapter Two 41

II. The method of setting the Wheel of the Law into motion (8b-2) 41

A. The method of setting the Wheel of the Law of the Pāramitā-yāna into motion (8b-3) 41

1. The Promulgations (9b-6) 43

2. Assembling the Promulgations (14b-1) 53

a. The first council (14b-2) 59

b. The second council (16b-5) 63

c. The third council (18a-1) 67

[d. A note concerning the Mahāyāna scriptures] (19a-3) 69

3. Commentaries on the Promulgations (19b-2) 71

* The contents, under each chapter, show the folio numbers of the Labrang edition where the respective material begins.

a. The four outer sciences (20a-1) 73
b. Inner science (23a-3) 81
(1) Commentaries on the First Wheel of the Law (23a-5) 81
(2) Commentaries on the Intermediate Wheel of the Law (24b-5) 85
(3) Commentaries on the Last Wheel of the Law (28a-1) 95

Chapter Three 101
B. The method of setting the Wheel of the Law of the Mantra-yāna into motion (29b-4) 101
1. Fundamentals of the Kriyā Tantra (29b-4) 101
a. Fundamentals of the various varieties of the Kriyā Tantra (29b-5) 101
(1) The Tathāgata Family (30-5) 103
(2) The Padma Family (37b-2) 123
(3) The Vajra Family (39a-1) 129
(4) Mundane Families of the Kriyā Tantra (40a-5) 133
(5) General Kriyā Tantra (41-5) 135

Chapter Four 141
b. Fundamentals of Initiation and holding of vows in the Kriyā Tantra (42a-6) 141
c. Fundamentals of studying the path, after having received initiation and taken vows (47a-6) 157
(1) Meditation with muttering (48a-1) 159
(a) Preliminary acts (48a-1) 159
(b) The main part of the four members of muttering (48a-3) 159
α. Generation of Self into Deity (first member) (48a-4) 159
β. Generation of Deity in Front (second member) (52a-6) 175
γ. The four members, general (56b-1) . . 187
(c) Terminating acts to the four members of muttering (58b-6) 193
(2) Meditation without muttering (59b-4) 195
(a) Meditation of dwelling in the flame (59b-5) 195
(b) Meditation of dwelling in the sound (60a-1) 197

(c) Meditation granting freedom at the limit of the sound (60b-1) 199
(3) Accomplishment of *siddhi* after appropriate service (61a-5) 201

Chapter Five 205
2. Fundamentals of the Caryā Tantra (62b-1) 205
a. The varieties of the Tantra (62b-1) 205
b. Method of studying the steps of the path (63a-2) 207
(1) Procedure of preliminary service after being committed to the pledges (63a-4) 207
(a) Yoga with images (63a-6) 207
(b) Yoga without images (64a-4) 211
(2) Manner of accomplishing *siddhis* after aptitude in the service (64b-1) 211

Chapter Six 215
3. Fundamentals of the Yoga Tantra (64b-4) 215
a. Method of setting the Wheel of the Law of Yoga into motion (64b-4) 215
b. Method of studying the steps of the path (68a-6) 229
(1) Meaning of the expression 'four seals' (68a-6) 229
(2) Varieties (68b-1) 229
(3) Sequence (69b-6) 235
(4) Requirement and benefit of seal execution (71b-1) 241
(5) Method of seal execution (71b-2) 241

Chapter Seven 251
4. Fundamentals of the Anuttara-Yoga Tantra (74a-6) 251
a. Division into two Tantras (74a-6) 251
b. Meaning of the several divisions (74b-5) 251
(1) Refutation of other schools (74b-6) 251
(a) Tripartition by enunciation of the promulgation (75a-1) 253
(b) Tripartition by meaning of the subject matter (75b-1) 253
(c) Tripartition by the petitioner (76b-4) . . . 257
(2) Establishment of our school (78a-4) 261

Chapter Eight 271

[c. Procedure in the meaning of the subject matter] (80b-2) 271
(1) The path of Initiation which produces maturation (80b-2) 271
(a) Characteristics of the *maṇḍala* in which Initiation is conferred (80b-4) 271
(b) Characteristics of the hierophant who confers Initiation (81a-4) 273
(c) Method by which the hierophant initiates in whatever *maṇḍala* (83a-2) 279
α. Method of initiation in the *maṇḍala* of powdered colors (83a-2) 279
I Method of drawing the *maṇḍala* (83a-3). 279
A′. Ritual of the site (83a-3) . . . 279
B′. Ritual of the preparatory acts (84b-2) 283
C′. The ritual of drawing the *maṇḍala* 291
II . Method of accomplishing the *maṇḍala* (87a-6) 291
A′. The school which makes them different 293
B′. The school which makes them identical 293
[β. Method of initiation in the *maṇḍala* painted on cloth] (90a-3) 301
[γ. Method of initiation in the body *maṇḍala*] (90b-6) 303

Chapter Nine 309
δ. Manner of conferring initiation (91b-6) 309
I′. Ritual of conferring initiation on the disciple (92a-1) 309
A′. Entering the *maṇḍala* (92a-1) . 309
B′. Conferring initiation after entrance (92b-5) 311
1 . Initiation of the flask (92b-5) 311
2′. The Secret initiation (94b-1) 317

3 . The insight-knowledge initiation (95b-1) 321
4′. The initiation of the syllable (96a-5) 325
[(2) The relation between steps and initiations along the path] (96b-4) 325
[(3) Vows and pledges] (97b-1) 329
[(4) Steps of Production and Steps of Completion] (98a-4) 331

Index of Works Cited 338

Index of Names and Subjects 352

INTRODUCTION

The author of the work herein translated is styled in the colophon Mkhas-grub-thams-cad-mkhyen-pa Dge-legs-dpal-bzaṅ po, from which the "thams-cad-mkhyen-pa" (S. *sarvajña*) is frequently omitted. The chief part of the name is Dge-legs-dpal-bzaṅ-po, but the honorific Mkhas-grub is ordinarily prefixed. He is often referred to as Mkhas-grub-chos-rje, which can be abbreviated to Mkhas-grub-rje. The title *chos-rje* (S. *dharmasvāmin*) is also honorary. He has also been called Mkhas-grub-smra-baḥi-ñi-ma Dge-legs-dpal-bzaṅ po. Born in Gtsaṅ-stod of Tibet and living from 1385 to 1438, he first met his great teacher Tsoṅ-kha-pa (1357-1419) in the year 1407 (*me mo phag*), and went on to become the latter's chief disciple in the Buddhist Tantras. Mkhas-grub-rje was the eldest of three brothers, whose father was named Bkra-śis-dpal-bzaṅ and mother Bu-ḥdren-rgyal-mo. The next younger brother, Ba-so-chos-kyi-rgyal-mtshan, called a *grub-chen* (*mahāsiddha*), attained a lesser eminence; born in 1402 A.D., the year Tsoṅ-kha-pa completed the *Lam-rim-chen-mo*, Ba-so wrote a commentary on the latter work. In the last parts of their lives, they were the 2nd and 6th Abbots of Galdan Monastery, which was founded by Tsoṅ-kha-pa. After the death of his teacher who had created a new school, later called the Gelugpa, Mkhas-grub-rje contributed to the success of this institution by his literary talent, employed to clarify and defend Tsoṅ-kha-pa's Tantric reform. Tibetan tradition (probably starting in the 17th century), traced Mkhas-grub-rje's anterior incarnations back to the Sthāvira Ṣubhūti (considered to be an immediate disciple of Gautama Buddha) and his subsequent ones in the series called the Paṇ-chen Lamas.[1]

[1] The material of this paragraph has been compiled from several sources: Giuseppe Tucci, *Tibetan Painted Scrolls* (Rome, 1949), to which the reader may refer for more information; Kloṅ-rdol-bla-ma, Section Ra, 6b-6, ff.; Blo-bzaṅ-ḥphrin-las' *Thob yig gsal baḥi me loṅ*, III, 80b-1, ff., which is referred to later as *Thob yig*; and a Tibetan work on astrology and dates with abbreviated title *Bstan rtsis*, by Blo-bzaṅ-tshul-khrims-rgya-mtsho, also named Mi-pham-tshaṅs-sras-dgyes-paḥi-rdo-rje.

The author's chief work in the field of the Tantras is his great commentary on the *Kālacakra-tantra*, assigned No. 5463 in *A Catalogue of the Tohoku University Collection of Tibetan works on Buddhism* (Sendai, 1953), devoted to native Tibetan works which are referred to hereafter by "Toh." followed by the number in this catalog. Also popular among Gelugpa Lamas are his *Stoṅ-thun chen-mo* (Toh. 5459), on the theory of the Void (*śūnyatā*), and his *Sdom gsum* (Toh. 5488), on the three vows — those of the Prātimokṣa, the Bodhisattva, and the Mantra (or Vajrayāna). Among other works on the Tantras noteworthy is his commentary on the *Hevajra-tantra*, the *Brtag ḥgrel* (Toh. 5483).

His "Fundamentals of the Buddhist Tantras" has the full Tibetan title *Rgyud sde spyiḥi rnam par gźag pa rgyas par brjod* (Toh. 5489) and the abbreviated form *Rgyud sde spyi rnam.* It is neither his chief nor his best-written work. It gives the impression of a semester or summer-session lecture course, ending just as precipitately. However, no other book of comparable size belonging to the Gelugpa school and known to the present translators can serve as well through translation to open up the subject of the Buddhist Tantras to Western readers. This is because it presents the fundamentals along with important bibliography of all four divisions of the Tantras and indicates the non-Tantric Buddhist topics which the disciples were expected to master in preparation for the Tantras; and it presents these fundamentals with a minimum of quotations and other complications. On the other hand, ordinarily it does not define basic terms, and the notes to the translation have had to fill the gap.

We may presume that Mkhas-grub-rje employed the following method for composing the work: He had before him one or more earlier works of this type, possibly those by Bu-ston (1289-1364), the redactor of the Kanjur and Tanjur, who composed three works (Toh. 5167-5169), elucidating with increased detail the four Tantra divisions. Into the outline suggested by such preceding works, the author poured various non-controversial topics and many ideas of his teacher Tsoṅ-kha-pa. This was done partly by direct reproduction of passages and partly by paraphrase; and for this purpose he used a number of Tsoṅ-kha-pa's works, but especially the latter's *Sṅags rim chen mo* (Toh. 5281) as well as his personal instructions gained from being a close disciple. He mentions among native works only a few by Tsoṅ-kha-pa. The bulk of references are to canonical Kanjur and Tanjur works, which again we identify with the signal "Toh." and numbers as given in *A Complete Catalogue of the Tibetan Buddhist Canons* (Sendai, 1934).

It will be noted that the Prāsaṅgika-Mādhyamika school is claimed to be the philosophical base of all four Buddhist Tantra divisions. Of particular interest is the work's presentation of the practices of initiation in both external and internal *maṇḍalas* and of the mystical experiences associated therewith. It also shows the theoretical association of these practices and experiences with the traditions about how Gautama attained the Complete Enlightenment. However, the full import of the ideas brought forward in the present work may best be clarified by special comparative studies that are beyond the scope of this introduction.

As to the translation itself, I should have preferred that Professor Lessing provide the details, and he certainly would have, had not destiny intervened by his peaceful passing on the night of December 30, 1961. During one of his return trips to China, probably the one of 1947, he secured two copies of the text in the Labrang edition and the modern translation into Chinese by Fa-tsun. By reason of his assiduous labors on Tibetan ritual texts connected with the iconography and cult of the Lamaist temple in Peking called the Yung-ho-kung, Dr. Lessing was convinced that many obscure literary allusions would be comprehensible once such a work as Mkhas-grub-rje's were translated. When in 1950 as a graduate student I became his research assistant in his Yung-ho-kung project, Dr. Lessing felt that the time had come to attempt the difficult project of translating this book. A heart attack, requiring his hospitalization, provided the initial leisure. In bed he began the draft translation on March 16, 1951, comparing the original Tibetan text with Fa-tsun's translation, and finished it during the rest of the year. As he proceeded, I transcribed the Tibetan text, bit by bit, interspacing with Prof. Lessing's draft. The Labrang edition has many textual problems, since the separating dots between syllables are hardly visible, and a number of places are badly smudged, presumably because the woodblocks were worn at those spots. Later, when the East Asiatic Library, University of California, secured the Lhasa edition of Mkhas-grub-rje's works, the different edition of the text made it possible for me to decipher the bad spots in the Labrang edition, which, however, is generally superior in text readings — as far as this work is concerned — to the Lhasa edition. With our identification in the Tohoku Kanjur-Tanjur catalog of most of the works alluded to by Mkhas-grub-rje, it became possible for me to consult a number of them as well as Tsoṅ-kha-pa's collected works accessible at the East Asiatic Library, and thus derive more information bearing on the points raised in "Fundamentals of the Buddhist Tantras". After several years, and as this new data began to clear up certain difficult points in the Mkhas-grub text, Prof. Lessing wished me to be a collaborator in the translation, especially since he had little time himself to consult those works, his energies being largely absorbed in the *Mongolian-English Dictionary* which he finally finished in 1960. It is difficult to explain the memorable experience of such collaboration: the elder, encyclopedic in philological knowledge, experienced in and appreciative of scholarship, generous to his students; the younger, eager to learn, with a modest talent at problem solving. It would be some years before I could begin to equal his initial contribution to the translation, a *tour de force* possible through his two decades of work with related materials and a phenomenal memory for words in Oriental languages. Working with his first translation was the way I learned to read the Tibetan language. My attention was also diverted to other projects in those years; and after two years as a Fellow of the Bollingen Foundation, for Tibetan researches, I moved from the Berkeley area in 1960 to embark on University teaching. Before that, we had many opportunities of discussing points and coming to decisions on final translation of passages. On some passages we had explanations from the Mongolian Lama Dilowa Gegen Hutukhtu; but, by reason of his vows — which Mkhas-grub's text will clarify — he was not communicative on many aspects of the Tantras. If Dr. Lessing had had the time, he would undoubtedly have added notes from his files. But eventually I was responsible for all the notes and adopted a principle of letting the tantrics speak for themselves.

The late Dr. Lessing and I believe that our way of translating is faithful to the original Tibetan. Some recent translations from this language contain modern psychological terms and give the unsuspecting reader the impression that the original Tibetan words carry such meanings. We have no objection to interpretations of these doctrines in modern terminology — indeed, this is useful — but feel such interpretations should be relegated to footnotes or to separate essays or books.

A word about the format: it was the suggestion by Prof. J. W. de Jong now at Canberra, to reproduce the Tibetan text in transcription opposite the English translation. There is little doubt of the convenience and scholarly advantage of this arrangement, which does, however, create publishing problems, completely solved by Mouton & Co., with some publishing aid from the American Council of Learned Societies. The indexes are based on the devoted labor of my wife Hideko.

Madison, Wisconsin, June, 1967 ALEX WAYMAN

MKHAS GRUB RJE'S
"FUNDAMENTALS OF THE BUDDHIST TANTRAS"

(Rgyud sde spyiḥi rnam par gźag pa rgyas par brjod)

Namo gurubhyaḥ /

/ rab yaṅs mkhyen paḥi spyan ldan pas /
/ rab ḥbyams śes byaḥi gnas kun gzigs /
/ rab maṅ legs bśad chu gter can /
/ rab mchog bla maḥi źabs la ḥdud //
/ de yi legs bśad ga-ṅgāḥi rgyun /
/ ḥdul byaḥi gliṅ du babs pa las /
/ bdag blo skra yi rtse mo yis /
/ blaṅs paḥi chu thigs brjed gsor bri //

/ de la theg pa goṅ ḥog gi lugs tha dad paḥi rnam par gźag pa rnams las / ston pa bcom ldan ḥdas mṅon par rdzogs par saṅs rgyas tshul gyi rnam par gźag pa la /

/ ñan thos sde gñis kyi lugs la raṅ reḥi ston pa ḥdi sṅon de bźin gśegs pa śākya thub pa chen poḥi druṅ du byaṅ chub tu sems bskyed de / tshogs kyi lam la źugs śiṅ bskal ba graṅs med gsum du tshogs gsog paḥi mgo brtsams so /

/ de nas de bźin gśegs pa rin chen gtsug tor can ḥjig rten du byon paḥi bar gyis graṅs med daṅ po rdzogs so / de nas de bźin gśegs pa mar me

[1] The two divisions are the Vaibhāṣika and the Sautrāntika, named by Mkhas grub later in the section. The former are the followers who stress commentarial tradition; the latter are the followers who stress the *sūtra* contents.

[2] As pointed out by Obermiller (Bu-ston, I, note 922), "This Buddha Śākyamuni is of course not the Buddha of our age, but an extinct Buddha of former times to whom the Teacher addressed his first Initial Vow." For more information and references, see Lamotte, *Le Traité*, I, 247-9.

[3] The path of equipment (*saṃbhāra-mārga*) is generally explained as gathering the equipment of merit (*puṇya*) and of knowledge (*jñāna*). It is the first of five paths mentioned in this section. The second through fifth are path of training (*prayoga-mārga*), path of vision (*darśana-mārga*), path of intense contemplation (*bhāvanā-mārga*), and path beyond training (*aśaikṣa-mārga*). In the Prajñā-pāramitā literature the Śrāvakas (disciples), Pratyekabuddhas (solitarily enlightened beings), and Bodhisattvas (beings intent on enlightenment) each have their five paths (as named above).

CHAPTER ONE

Homage to the guides!

I bow to the feet of the most excellent guide (*guru*),
Who, possessed of the eye of vastest knowledge,
Envisions all states of the far reaching knowable,
Who holds the ocean of the copious well expressed teachings.
His Ganges River of well expressed teachings
Has poured down upon the land of candidates;
With the tip of the hair which is my intellect,
I shall pick up water drops and write to cure forgetfulness.

I. HOW THE TEACHER BHAGAVAT BECAME ABHISAṂBUDDHA

Among the fundamentals of the different schools of the upper and lower vehicles (*mahāyāna* and *hīnayāna*) are the fundamentals of the method by which the Teacher Bhagavat became a Manifest Complete Buddha (Abhisaṃbuddha).

A. POSITION OF THE ŚRĀVAKAS

According to the schools of both divisions of the Śrāvakas,[1] our Teacher produced the Thought of Enlightenment (*bodhicittotpādika*) in the presence of the great former Tathāgata Śākyamuni,[2] and at that time entered the path of equipment,[3] thus starting to collect the equipment (*saṃbhāra*) of three incalculable aeons (*asaṃkhyeya-kalpa*).

Then, when the Tathāgata Ratnaśikhin appeared in the world, he had

All these paths are discussed by E. Obermiller, "The Doctrine of Prajñā-pāramitā as exposed in the Abhisamayālaṃkāra of Maitreya", *Acta Orientalia*, XI (1932), pp. 14, f.

mdzad ḥjig rten du byon paḥi bar gyis gñis pa rdzogs so / de nas de bźin gśegs pa rnam par gzigs ḥjig rten du byon paḥi bar gyis gsum pa rdzogs so /

/ de nas rgyal po zas gtsaṅ gi sras rgyal bu don grub tu ḥkhruṅs paḥi bar bskal pa brgyar mtshan bzaṅ po sum cu rtsa gñis daṅ / dpe byad brgyad cuḥi rgyur tshogs bsags par ḥdod de /

/ rnam gzigs mar me rin chen gtsug /
/ graṅs med gsum gyi tha mar byuṅ /
/ daṅ po śākya thub pa yin / źes so /

/ de la graṅs med gsum du tshogs bsags pa daṅ / srod la bdud btul baḥi bar ni byaṅ sems so skye tshogs lam pa mtshan ñid par ḥdod do /

/ dguṅ lo sum cu rtsa lṅa pa la / dpyid zla tha chuṅ skar ma sa gaḥi ña baḥi tshe bco lṅaḥi srod la bdud btul / guṅ la mñam par bźag paḥi tshe / sbyor lam mthoṅ lam sgom lam rnams mṅon du byas / tho raṅs skya reṅs daṅ po ḥchar ba tsam na / mi slob lam mṅon du byas te mṅon par rdzogs par saṅs rgyas so /

/ de nas źag bźi bcu źe dgu ḥdas nas Wā-ra-ṇa-sir chos kyi ḥkhor lo bskor ro / de ni bden pa bźiḥi chos kyi ḥkhor lo yin la / chos ḥkhor de las gźan bskor bar mi ḥdod de / theg pa chen po bkar mi ḥdod do /

/ de nas dguṅ lo brgyad cu pa la mya ṅan las ḥdas te mar me źi ba bźin du rig pa rgyun chad du soṅ bar ḥdod do /

/ lam gyi skabs su sa bcuḥi rnam gźag mi ḥdod / ḥbras buḥi skabs su loṅs spyod rdzogs paḥi sku mi ḥdod / chos kyi sku daṅ gzugs sku gñis las / mchog gi sprul skuḥi tha sñad kyaṅ mi ḥdod do /

[4] The 32 characteristics and 80 minor marks are listed in many Buddhist works, with varying entries. The most important of the characteristics are the *uṣṇīṣa* on the crown of the head and the *ūrṇa-kośa* in the center of the forehead.

[5] V. V. Gokhale, "The Text of the Abhidharmakośakārikā of Vasubandhu", *JBBRAS*, Vol. 22 (1946), p. 89:

...... asaṃkhyeyatrayā 'ntajāḥ /
vipaśyī dīpakṛd ratnaśikhī śākyamuniḥ purā // IV, 110 //.

Cf. de la Vallée Poussin, *L'Abhidharmakośa de Vasubandhu*, 4° chapitre, 227-8.

[6] Since dusk begins the first watch of night, the Māra he subdued at dusk is the "son-of-the-gods Māra" (*devaputra-māra*): de la Vallée Poussin, *L'Abhidharmakośa de Vasubandhu*, 1° et 2° chapitres, p. 124. In certain Buddhist Tantras, the Māras, four in number, are identified with Hindu deities. Thus Snellgrove (Vol. I, p. 80, n.) cites a commentary on the *Hevajra-tantra*: "The four Māras are: '*Skandhamāra* who takes the form of Brahmā, *Kleśamāra* who takes the form of a *yakṣa*, *Mṛtyumāra* who takes the form of Yama and *Devaputramāra* who takes the form of Indra'." For native Tibetan demonic personifications of the Māras (Tibetan: *bdud*), cf. Nebesky-Wojkowitz, *Oracles*..., p. 276. His Tibetan names may be identified with the Sanskrit ones above, as follows: lha'i bdud = devaputramāra; nyon mongs pa'i bdud = kleśa-māra; phung po'i bdud = skandhamāra; 'chi bdag gi bdud = mṛtyumāra.

[7] That is to say, the fifteenth day of the increasing phases (*śukla-pakṣa*) of the month

completed the first incalculable aeon. When the Tathāgata Dīpaṃkara appeared in the world, he had completed the second. When the Tathāgata Vipaśyin appeared in the world, he had completed the third.

Then, it is maintained, for one hundred aeons (*kalpa*) he collected the equipment that was the cause of his thirty-two characteristics (*lakṣaṇa*) and eighty minor marks (*anuvyañjana*)[4] and finally was born as Prince Siddhārtha, son of King Śuddhodana.

Vipaśyin, Dīpaṃkara, and Ratnaśikhin
[Each] appeared at the end of [one of]
the three incalculable aeons;
The first [Tathāgata he honored] was Śākyamuni.[5]

It is maintained that between the time when he had finished collecting equipment for three incalculable aeons and the time of subduing Māra at dusk,[6] he was characterized as a traveller with the equipment of a Bodhisattva who is an ordinary person (*pṛthag-jana*).

At the age of thirty-five, in the dusk of the fifteenth day of Vaiśākha,[7] when the moon was full, he subdued Māra. Midnight was the time of equipoise (*samāpatti*), and he [then] made manifest the path of training, the path of vision, and the path of intense contemplation. At the very first appearance of dawn, he made manifest the path beyond training and became manifestly completely enlightened (*abhisaṃbuddha*).

Then, after forty-nine days, he set in motion the Wheel of the Law at Vārāṇasī (the modern Benares). That is the Wheel of the Law of the Four (Noble) Truths. They do not maintain that he set in motion any other Wheel of the Law. Nor do they maintain the promulgation of the Great Vehicle (*mahāyāna*).

Then, they maintain, when he entered Nirvāṇa at the age of eighty, his knowledge (*vidyā*) was cut off, just as a lamp is extinguished.

They do not maintain the fundamental of ten stages (*daśa-bhūmi*)[8] in the phase of the path. Nor do they maintain the body of complete enjoyment (*saṃbhoga-kāya*) in the phase of the fruit [of the path]. Nor,

---

Vaiśākha: the *śukla-pakṣa* may have constituted the second half of the lunar month; the *kṛṣṇa-pakṣa*, or decreasing phases, the first half.

[8] For the ten stages, see Dayal, *The Bodhisattva Doctrine*, Chap. VI. The list of the *Daśabhūmika-sūtra* (ed. by J. Rahder) is as follows: (1) The Joyful (pramuditā), (2) The Pure (vimalā), (3) The Luminous (prabhākarī), (4) The Radiant (arciṣmatī), (5) The Hard to Conquer (sudurjayā), (6) The Turned-Towards (abhimukhī), (7) The Far-Reaching (dūraṅgamā), (8) The Immovable (acalā), (9) The Good Mind (sādhumatī), (10) The Doctrine-Cloud (dharma-meghā). As will be shown soon by Mkhas grub's discussion of the Pāramitā school, a basic division of these stages is into the first seven and the last three. While on the last three, the Bodhisattva is sometimes called "non-regressing" (*avaivartika*).

/ bye brag smra bas rgyal bu don grub kyi lus de so skyeḥi lus yin pas / las ñon gyis ḥphaṅs paḥi sdug bsṅal gyi bden pa yin la / saṅs rgyas paḥi tshe yaṅ lus deḥi rgyun ma brjes par sdug bsṅal gyi bden pa yin pas / gzugs sku saṅs rgyas ma yin par ḥdod do / mdo sde pas de bźin gśegs paḥi sku la ṅan sems kyis khrag phyuṅ baḥi mtshams med ni srid par ḥgyur ba sogs kyis dgag pa byed gsuṅ ṅo /

/ theg pa chen po la pha rol tu phyin pa daṅ / gsaṅ sṅags gñis las /

/ pha rol tu phyin paḥi lugs ni / tshogs sbyor gyi riṅ la graṅs med daṅ po rdzogs / sa daṅ po nas bdun paḥi bar gyis gñis pa rdzogs / sa brgyad pa dgu ba bcu pa gsum gyi riṅ la graṅs med gsum pa rdzogs te /

/ srid pa tha ma paḥi tshe ḥog min stug po bkod par phyogs bcuḥi saṅs rgyas thams cad kyis ḥod zer chen poḥi dbaṅ bskur nas /

/ sa bcu pa rdzogs mtshams kyi ye śes de la rgyun mthaḥi ye śes źes kyaṅ bya / rdo rje lta buḥi tiṅ ṅe ḥdzin źes kyaṅ bya ste / de rgyud la skyes paḥi skad cig gñis pa la chos kyi sku daṅ loṅs spyod rdzogs paḥi sku gñis brñes te mṅon par rdzogs par saṅs rgyas so /

/ loṅs spyod rdzogs paḥi sku de ni gnas ṅes pa ḥog min kho na las gźan du gśegs mi srid / chos ṅes pa theg pa chen poḥi chos kho na las theg dman gyi chos gsuṅs pa mi srid / rnam pa ṅes pa mtshan dpes brgyan paḥi skuḥi rnam pa las gźan du ḥgyur ba mi srid / ḥkhor ṅes pa sa bcuḥi byaṅ sems las so skye sogs kyi ḥkhor mi srid / dus ṅes pa ḥkhor

furthermore, do they maintain the designation "best apparitional body" (*parama-nirmāṇa-kāya*) for either the Dharma-kāya or the formal body (*rūpa-kāya*).

The Vaibhāṣika maintains that because Prince Siddhārtha's body is the body of an ordinary person, it is the truth of suffering (*duḥkha-satya*) cast by means of action (*karma*) and corruption (*kleśa*); and that even at the time of his becoming a Buddha, the truth of suffering was unaltered in the continuum of that body. For this reason, it maintains that the formal body is not the Buddha. The Sautrāntika say that [argument] is refuted by the fact that [in such a case] there is no immediate retribution (*ānantarya*) for making the Tathāgata's body bleed with an evil intention.

B. POSITION OF THE MAHĀYĀNA

In the Mahāyāna, there are the Pāramitā [school] and the Mantra [school].

1. TEACHING OF THE PĀRAMITĀ SCHOOL

He completed the first incalculable aeon while on the path of equipment and the path of training. He completed the second one between the first and seventh stages. He completed the third incalculable aeon while on the three stages, the eighth, ninth, and tenth.

At the time of the last existence (*carama-bhavika*), the Buddhas of all the ten directions in the Akaniṣṭha heaven [called] Ghanavyūha ('a dense array') conferred on him the initiation (*abhiṣeka*) of great light.

The final knowledge at the completion of the tenth stage is called "knowledge at end of stream" (*rgyun mthaḥi ye śes*) as well as "adamantine *samādhi*" (*vajropama-samādhi*). When the second instant (*kṣaṇa*) [of realization] arose in his stream of consciousness (*saṃtāna*), he obtained both the Dharma-kāya and the Saṃbhoga-kāya, thus being a Manifest Complete Buddha.

The Saṃbhoga-kāya has five certainties:

a. *Certainty of place.* It does not proceed to any place outside the Akaniṣṭha heaven.

b. *Certainty of doctrine.* It proclaims only the Mahāyāna doctrine (*dharma*), not the Hīnayāna doctrine.

c. *Certainty of form.* It does not appear in any shape other than that of a body adorned with the (32) characteristics and (80) minor marks.

d. *Certainty of retinue.* Its retinue includes only Bodhisattvas of the tenth stage, not ordinary persons and the like.

ba ma stoṅs kyi bar du mya ṅan las bzla tshul mi ston pa ste / ṅes pa lṅa ldan no /

/ ḥog min de gaṅ na yod ce na / lhaḥi gnas rnams kyi mthar thug pa ni gtsaṅ maḥi gnas kyi ḥog min te / deḥi goṅ na ḥog min stug po bkod pa źes bya baḥi saṅs rgyas kyi źiṅ de yod de / mdo las /

/ gtsaṅ maḥi gnas dag spaṅs pa na /
/ ḥog min gnas ni ñams dgaḥ ba /
/ yaṅ dag rdzogs saṅs der saṅs rgyas /
/ sprul pa po gcig ḥdir ḥtshaṅ rgya / źes so /

/ loṅs spyod rdzogs paḥi sku de ḥog min du bźugs nas / sprul paḥi skus miḥi yul du mdzad pa bcu gñis kyi tshul ston te /

/ de la rgyal ba śākya thub paḥi saṅs rgyas kyi źiṅ mi mjed kyi ḥjig rten gyi khams ḥdi la gliṅ bźi paḥi ḥjig rten gyi khams bye ba phrag brgya yod paḥi ḥdzam buḥi gliṅ bye ba phrag brgyar / rgyal ba śākya thub paḥi mdzad pa bcu gñis kyi tshul bye ba phrag brgya cig car du ston no / de yaṅ dgaḥ ldan gyi gnas nas ḥpho ba bye ba phrag brgya cig car du ston te / de bźin du yab rgyal po zas gtsaṅ ma bye ba phrag brgya daṅ / yum sgyu ma lha mdzes bye ba phrag brgyaḥi sras rgyal bu don grub sku bltams paḥi tshul bye ba phrag brgya dus cig car du ston no / de bźin du gźon nu rol rtsed mdzad pa daṅ / btsun moḥi ḥkhor gyis rol pa daṅ / ṅes par ḥbyuṅ ba daṅ / dkaḥ ba spyod pa daṅ / byaṅ chub kyi śiṅ druṅ du gśegs pa daṅ / bdud ḥdul ba daṅ / mṅon par rdzogs par saṅs rgyas pa daṅ / chos kyi ḥkhor lo bskor ba daṅ / mya ṅan las ḥdas paḥi tshul bye ba phrag brgya cig car du ston te /

/ źiṅ ḥdir mya ṅan las ḥdas paḥi tshul bye ba phrag brgya ston pa daṅ / źiṅ gźan du / la lar sku bltams pa daṅ / la lar ḥtshaṅ rgya ba daṅ / la lar ḥkhor lo bskor ba la sogs paḥi tshul bye ba phrag brgya cig car du ston te / de bźin du ḥkhor ba ma stoṅs kyi bar du ston no /

[9] This verse has not been traced. Similar verses occur in the *Laṅkāvatāra-sūtra* and the *Ghanavyūha-sūtra*; and a similar verse is quoted in the *Kosalālaṃkāra* (Toh. 2503), Vol. Yi, 8b-2. For example, *Laṅkāvatāra*, Sagāthākam, verse 774: / kāmadhātau tathārūpye na vai buddho vibudhyate / rūpadhātv akaniṣṭheṣu vītarāgeṣu budhyate // "Neither in the realm of desire nor in the formless realm does a Buddha become a full Buddha; but in the passionless Akaniṣṭha of the realm of form he becomes awakened." Also, *ibid.*, Sagāthākam, verse 39B: / tatra budhyanti saṃbuddhā nirmitās tv iha budhyante / "The complete Buddhas awaken there, and their apparitions are awakened here."

[10] Mkhas grub discusses, in his *Sdom pa gsum*, Peking ed., f. 2b-2, f., these multiple apparitions of the twelve acts in 100 myriads of world-systems. He points out that King Śuddhodana and so forth are all apparitions, and that the *Pradīpodyotana* quotes the *Mahāyoga-tantra*: "As follows: Mañjuśrī became the great King Śuddhodana; Lokeśvara (i.e. Avalokiteśvara) became the Mahādevī Māyā; Śrīdevī, Yaśodharā; Vajrasattva, Rahula; Sarvanivaraṇaviṣkambhin, Śāriputra; Samantabhadra, the

e. *Certainty of time*. As long as the cycle of life (*saṃsāra*) is not depleted [of suffering beings], it does not demonstrate the method of passing over into Nirvāṇa.

Where is that Akaniṣṭha heaven located? The last outpost of abodes of the gods is the Akaniṣṭha heaven, an abode of the pure gods (*śuddhā-vāsāḥ*). Beyond it is the Akaniṣṭha heaven that is the Buddha field called Ghanavyūha. The *sūtra* says:[9]

> Rejecting the pure abodes, he is rightly and completely awakened in the ecstatic abode of Akaniṣṭha;
> And, being a full Buddha there, his single apparition (*nirmita*) becomes a Buddha here.

The Saṃbhoga-kāya takes residence in Akaniṣṭha, and the Nirmāṇa-kāya demonstrates the method of the twelve acts in the world of men.

In the Buddha field (*buddhakṣetra*) of Śākyamuni, which is the world-systems of tribulation (*sahā-loka-dhātu*), there are 100 myriads of world-systems of four continents, hence 100 myriads of Indian continent (*jambudvīpa*), in which the method of the twelve acts of the victor Śākya-muni is simultaneously demonstrated 100 myriads of times. Thus, the descent from the place of Tuṣita is demonstrated 100 myriads of times simultaneously. Likewise, there are 100 myriads of father King Śud-dhodana and 100 myriads of beautiful mother Queen Māyā, and the method of rebirth of their son Prince Siddhārtha is demonstrated simul-taneously 100 myriads of times. Likewise the ways of making sport as a youth, enjoyment of the harem women, departure from home, arduous discipline, passage to the vicinity of the tree of illumination, subduing of Māra, the state of being Manifestly Completely Enlightened, setting in motion of the Wheel of the Law, and the passing into Nirvāṇa, are simultaneously demonstrated 100 myriads of times.[10]

In this field the method of passing into Nirvāṇa is demonstrated 100 myriads of times; and in other fields, somewhere there is rebirth, some-where the attaining of Buddhahood, somewhere the setting in motion

---

sthavira Ānanda; Devendra Śatakratu (i.e. Indra), the *sthavira* Devadatta; Mahāvai-rocana became Samyaksaṃbuddha Śrī-jina Śākyamuni" (... rnal ḥbyor chen poḥi rgyud sgron gsal du draṅs pa las / ḥdi lta ste / ḥjam dpal ni / rgyal po chen po zas gtsaṅ mar gyur to / ḥjig rten dbaṅ phyug ni / lha mo / chen mo sgyu ḥphrul du gyur to / dpal lha mo ni / grags ḥdzin no / rdo rje sems dpaḥ ni / sgra gcan zin to / sgrib pa thams cad sel ba ni / śa-riḥi-buḥo / kun tu bzaṅ po ni / gnas brtan kun dgaḥ bor gyur to / lhaḥi dbaṅ po brgya byin ni / gnas brtan lha sbyin no / rnam par snaṅ mdzad chen po ni / yaṅ dag par rdzogs paḥi saṅs rgyas dpal rgyal ba śā-kya thub par gyur to / źes gsuṅs so).

/ de skad du yaṅ theg pa chen po rgyud bla ma las /
/ thugs rje chen pos ḥjig rten mkhyen /
/ ḥjig rten kun la gzigs nas ni /
/ chos kyi sku las ma gYos par /
/ sprul paḥi raṅ bźin sna tshogs kyis /
/ skye ba mṅon par skye ba daṅ /
/ dgaḥ ldan nas ni ḥpho ba daṅ /
/ lhums su ḥjug daṅ bltams pa daṅ /
/ bzo yi gnas la mkhas pa daṅ /
/ btsun moḥi ḥkhor dgyes rol pa daṅ /
/ ṅes ḥbyuṅ dkaḥ ba spyod pa daṅ /
/ byaṅ chub sñiṅ por gśegs pa daṅ /
/ bdud sde ḥjoms daṅ rdzogs par ni /
/ byaṅ chub chos kyi ḥkhor lo daṅ /
/ mya ṅan ḥdas par gśegs mdzad rnams /
/ yoṅs su ma dag źiṅ rnams su /
/ srid pa ji srid gnas par ston / źes so /

/ gsaṅ sṅags kyi lugs la / bya spyod gñis la pha rol tu phyin paḥi lugs kyi ḥtshaṅ rgya tshul las logs pa med pas /

/ yo ga daṅ bla med kyi lugs gñis las / daṅ po ni rtsa rgyud de ñid bsdus pa daṅ / bśad rgyud rdo rje rtse mo gñis las gsuṅs śiṅ / de dag gi dgoṅs pa ḥgrel baḥi slob dpon śākya bśes gñen daṅ / saṅs rgyas gsaṅ ba daṅ / kun dgaḥ sñiṅ po gsum la yo ga la mkhas paḥi mi gsum źes ḥphags yul du grags so /

[11] The *Mahāyānottaratantra* has been edited by E. H. Johnston under the title *Ratnagotravibhāga Mahāyānottaratantraśāstra* (appendix to *JBRS*, Patna, 1950). The passage is in Chapter II:

mahākaruṇayā kṛtsnaṃ lokam ālokya lokavit /
dharmakāyād aviralaṃ nirmāṇaiś citrarūpibhiḥ // 53 //
jātakāny upapattiṃ ca tuṣiteṣu cyutiṃ tataḥ /
garbhā[va]kramaṇaṃ janma śilpasthānāni kauśalam // 54 //
antaḥpuraratikrīḍāṃ naiṣkramyaṃ duḥkhacārikām /
bodhimaṇḍopasaṃkrāntiṃ mārasainyapramardanam // 55 //
saṃbodhiṃ dharmacakraṃ ca nirvāṇādhigamakriyām
kṣetreṣv apariśuddheṣu darśayatyā bhavasthiteḥ // 56 //.

[12] By Mantra school, Mkhas grub means all four Tantra divisions-Kriyā Tantra, Caryā Tantra, Yoga Tantra, and Anuttara-yoga Tantra. Therefore, at the outset of this section he briefly alludes to the first two Tantra divisions.

[13] The *Tattvasaṃgraha* has the full title *Sarvatathāgatatattvasaṃgrahanāma-mahāyānasūtra*. It was translated into Tibetan by the Indian Śraddhākaravarma and the Tibetan Rin chen bzaṅ po (10th to 11th cent.). Śākyamitra, who wrote the commentary *Kosalālaṃkāra* (Toh. 2503), and Ānandagarbha, who wrote the commentary *Tattvāloka* (Toh. 2510), may be tentatively placed in the 10th cent., A.D., just prior

of the Wheel, and so on, the methods being demonstrated simultaneously 100 myriads of times. And they are demonstrated as long as the cycle of life is not depleted [of suffering beings].

Furthermore, along the same lines, it is said in the *Mahāyānottara-tantra* (Toh. 4024):[11]

The Knower of the World with great compassion
Surveys the whole world;
And without stirring from his Dharma-kāya,
With his Nirmāṇa, by means of diverse forms,
Displays in the unclean fields,
For the duration of the world's existence,
Origination in illustrious lives:
(1) The descent from Tuṣita; (2) Entrance into the womb;
(3) Rebirth; (4) Skill in worldly arts;
(5) Enjoyment of the harem women; (6) Departure from home;
(7) Arduous discipline; (8) Passage to the precincts of Illumination;
(9) Defeat of the Māra host; (10) Complete Illumination;
(11) The Wheel of the Law; (12) Departure into Nirvāṇa.

2. TEACHING OF THE MANTRA SCHOOL[12]

There is no discrepancy between the teaching of both the Kriyā and Caryā [Tantras] and that of the Pāramitā school concerning the method of becoming a Buddha.

a. *Teaching of the Yoga school*

In the schools of the Yoga and Anuttara [Tantras], the former sets it forth in two works, the fundamental tantra *Tattvasaṃgraha* (Toh. 479), and the explanatory tantra *Vajraśekhara* (Toh. 480). They have primary commentaries by three men who are famed in India as being learned in Yoga, namely, Śākyamitra, Buddhaguhya, and Ānandagarbha.[13]

---

to the translation of their works into Tibetan (in the second period of translation of Buddhist texts). Buddhaguhya belongs to the middle eighth century, A. D. This is shown by his letter (Toh. 4194) dispatched to the Tibetan King Khri sroṅ ldeḥu btsan, whose reign began 755 A.D. Buddhaguhya was a contemporary of Padmasaṃbhava and Śāntarakṣita, and furthermore worked together with the Tibetan translators. His fundamental commentary on the *Tattvasaṃgraha* is the *Tantrārthāvatāra* (Toh. 2501). This is relatively brief and is greatly expanded in the *Vyākhyāna* (Toh. 2502) by Padmavajra, who may well have been a personal disciple of Buddhaguhya.

/ slob dpon daṅ po gñis kyi lugs la / raṅ reḥi ston pa bcom ldan ḥdas ḥdi rgyal po zas gtsaṅ gi sras su ḥkhruṅs nas / chu bo ni-ra-ñdza-naḥi ḥgram du dkaḥ ba spyod paḥi bar / sa bcu paḥi byaṅ chub sems dpaḥ mtshan ñid par ḥdod la /

/ der lo drug tu dkaḥ ba spyod pa na / bsam gtan bźi pa chen poḥi chen po źes kyaṅ bya / bsam gtan bźi paḥi rab mthaḥ źes kyaṅ bya / mi gYo baḥi tiṅ ṅe ḥdzin źes kyaṅ bya / mkhaḥ khyab kyi tiṅ ṅe ḥdzin źes kyaṅ bya ba la sñoms par śugs so /

/ deḥi tshe phyogs bcuḥi saṅs rgyas thams cad ḥdus nas / se gol gyi sgras tiṅ ṅe ḥdzin de las bslaṅs te / khyod kyis tiṅ ṅe ḥdzin ḥdi tsam gyis mṅon par rdzogs par ḥtshaṅ rgya bar mi nus so / źes gsuṅs pa la / ḥog min tu khrid de / de yaṅ rnam smin gyi lus de chu bo ni-ra-ñdza-naḥi ḥgram de ñid du bźad nas / byaṅ chub sems dpaḥ don thams cad grub paḥi yid kyi lus de ḥog min du byon pa la /

/ phyogs bcuḥi saṅs rgyas thams cad kyis gos kyi dbaṅ ste / cod pan gyi dbaṅ bskur nas deḥi rjes la / mṅon par byaṅ chub pa lṅa rim can du sgom du bcug ste / mṅon byaṅ lṅa rdzogs paḥi mthar / loṅs spyod rdzogs paḥi sku rnam par snaṅ mdzad chen por mṅon par rdzogs par saṅs rgyas so /

/ saṅs rgyas nas cho ḥphrul rnam pa bźi mdzad de / ri rab kyi rtse mor byon nas yo-gaḥi rgyud rnams gsuṅs / de nas mi yul du byon nas chu bo ni-ra-ñdza-naḥi ḥgram du rnam smin gyi lus de la slar źugs te bźeṅs nas / bdud ḥdul ba daṅ / mṅon par rdzogs par saṅs rgyas pa la sogs paḥi tshul rnams bstan par bźed do /

/ slob dpon kun dgaḥ sñiṅ poḥi lugs la / bskal pa graṅs med gsum du tshogs bsags paḥi mthar sa bcuḥi byaṅ chub sems dpaḥ srid pa tha ma par gyur paḥi tshe ḥog min du mkhaḥ khyab kyi tiṅ ṅe ḥdzin la sñoms par źugs so /

/ deḥi tshe phyogs bcuḥi saṅs rgyas thams cad ḥdus nas se gol gyi sgras tiṅ ṅe ḥdzin de las bslaṅs nas / khyod ñid tiṅ ṅe ḥdzin ḥdi tsam gyis mṅon par rdzogs par ḥtshaṅ rgya bar mi nus so / źes gsuṅs pa la / ḥo na ji ltar bgyi / źes gsol pas / phyogs bcuḥi saṅs rgyas thams cad

[14] *Thob yig* II, 63b-6, when presenting the same story, uses instead the expression *ye śes kyi lus*, which equals Sanskrit *jñāna-kāya*, or *jñānamaya-kāya* (the knowledge body). This fact suggests that the Anuttara-yoga Tantra replaced the non-tantric concept of the "mental body" with a tantric concept, not necessarily equivalent, of the "knowledge body".

[15] *Thob yig* II, 64b-1, 2: "He performed the four kinds of marvel (*prātihārya, cho ḥphrul*) of Blessing (*adhiṣṭhāna byin gyis brlabs*), Initiation (*abhiṣeka, dbaṅ bskur ba*), Wondrous Act (*karma* [honorific], *ḥphrin las*), and Profound Concentration (*samādhi, tiṅ ṅe ḥdzin*)."

(1) POSITION OF THE ŚĀKYAMITRA AND BUDDHAGUHYA

The school of the first two maintains that our teacher the Bhagavat had the characteristics of a Bodhisattva of the tenth stage from the time he was born as a son to King Śuddhodana until the time of practising austerities at the bank of the Nairañjanā River.

After spending six years there in practising austerities, he was equipoised in what is called "the great [part] of the great Fourth Meditation" (*dhyāna*), the "unstirring *samādhi*" (*āniñjyo-nāma-samādhi*), and the "Space-filling *samādhi*" (*āspharaṇaka-samādhi*).

At that time, the Buddhas of all the ten directions assembled, aroused him from that *samādhi* by snapping their fingers, and said to him, "You cannot become a Manifest Complete Buddha by this *samādhi* alone." "Then how shall I proceed", he implored them. They guided him to the Akaniṣṭha heaven. Moreover, while his maturation body (*vipāka-kāya*) stayed on the bank of the same Nairañjanā River, the mental body (*manomaya-kāya*)[14] of the Bodhisattva Sarvārthasiddha proceeded to the Akaniṣṭha heaven.

After the Buddhas of the ten directions had given him garment initiation (*vastra-abhiṣeka*) and diadem initiation (*mukuṭa-abhiṣeka*), they bade him enter the intense contemplation in sequence of the five Abhisaṃbodhi [*infra*]. After completing the five Abhisaṃbodhi, he became a Manifest Complete Buddha as Mahāvairocana, the Saṃbhoga-kāya.

Having become a Buddha, he performed the four kinds of marvel (*prātihārya*).[15] He proceeded to the summit of Mt. Sumeru and pronounced the Yoga Tantras. Thereupon, he proceeded to the world of men and re-entered his maturation body on the bank of the Nairañjanā. Then he arose, defeated Māra, and taught the methods of Manifest Complete Buddhahood, and so forth, So they claim.

(2) POSITION OF ĀNANDAGARBHA

After collecting the equipment for three incalculable aeons, at the time when he was a Bodhisattva of the tenth stage in his last life, he became equipoised in the Akaniṣṭha heaven in the "Space-filling *samādhi*".

At that time, the Buddhas of all the ten direction assembled, aroused him from that *samādhi* by snapping their fingers, and said to him, "You cannot become a Manifest Complete Buddha by this *samādhi* alone." "Then how shall I do it?" he implored them. All the Buddhas of the ten directions conferred upon him the initiation of the diadem and bade

kyis cod pan gyi dbaṅ bskur nas / deḥi rjes la mṅon byaṅ lṅa rim can du sgom du bcug ste / de rdzogs paḥi mthar loṅs spyod rdzogs paḥi sku rnam par snaṅ mdzad chen por saṅs rgyas so /

/ saṅs rgyas nas cho ḥphrul rnam pa bźi mdzad de / ri rab kyi rtse mor byon nas yo-gaḥi rgyud gsuṅs / de nas mi yul du rgyal po zas gtsaṅ maḥi sras su ḥkhruṅs te mdzad pa bcu gñis kyi tshul bstan par ḥdod do /

/ mṅon byaṅ lṅa la sṅon byuṅ ston paḥi rnam ḥphrul gyi dbaṅ du byas paḥi mṅon byaṅ lṅa daṅ / rjes ḥjug gdul byaḥi ñams len gyi dbaṅ du byas paḥi mṅon byaṅ lṅaḥo /

/ de yaṅ phyogs bcuḥi saṅs rgyas thams cad kyis byaṅ chub sems dpaḥ don thams cad grub pa la cod pan gyi dbaṅ bskur baḥi rjes la / tsi-tta-pra-ti-be-dhaṃ kā-ro-mi / źes paḥi sṅags kyi don sgom du bcug ste / des kyaṅ bsgoms pas mñam gźag tu raṅ gi sems kyi chos ñid stoṅ pa ñid bcu drug raṅ bźin rnam dag mṅon sum du rtogs śiṅ / de las laṅs paḥi rjes thob tu raṅ gi sems kyi chos ñid raṅ bźin rnam dag de raṅ gi sñiṅ gar zla baḥi dkyil ḥkhor gyi rnam par mṅon sum du mthoṅ ṅo / des ni me loṅ lta buḥi ye śes mi bskyod paḥi ṅo bo brñes śiṅ / mṅon byaṅ ḥdiḥi miṅ ni so sor rtog pa las mṅon par byaṅ chub pa źes byaḥo /

/ de rjes ḥjug gdul byaḥi ñams len gyi rim pa la sbyar na / tsi-tta-pra-ti-be-dhaṃ kā-ro-mi / źes brjod nas raṅ gi sems kyi chos ñid stoṅ pa ñid bcu drug raṅ bźin rnam dag mtshon paḥi ā-li bcu drug yoṅs su gyur

[16] The Sanskrit equivalent *anuṣṭhāna* for Tib. *ñams su len pa* derives from the *Guhyasamāja-tantra*, p. 159, line 8: *anuṣṭhānam adhiṣṭhānaṃ*, translated into Tibetan: *ñams su len ciṅ byin rlabs pa*.

[17] In the *Uṣṇīṣavijaya-nāma-dhāraṇī-kalpa* (Toh. 598), sixteen of the thirty-three Uṣṇīṣavijayā goddesses on sixteen petals of a lotus are produced from the sixteen voidnesses, as follows: (1) voidness of the internal (*adhyātma-śūnyatā, naṅ stoṅ pa ñid*), (2) voidness of the external (*bahirdhā-ś°, phyi stoṅ°*), (3) voidness of internal and external together (*adhyātmabahirdhā-ś°, phyi naṅ stoṅ°*), (4) voidness of voidness (*śūnyatā-ś°, stoṅ pa ñid stoṅ°*), (5) voidness of the supreme goal (*paramārtha-ś°, don dam pa stoṅ°*), (6) voidness of the conditioned (*saṃskṛta-ś°, ḥdus byas stoṅ°*), (7) voidness of the unconditioned (*asaṃskṛta-ś°, ḥdus ma byas stoṅ°*), (8) voidness of the neither prior nor subsequent (*anavarāgra-ś°, thog ma daṅ tha ma med pa stoṅ°*), (9) voidness of non-elimination (*anavakāra-ś°, dor ba med pa stoṅ°*), (10) voidness of ground (*prakṛti-ś°, raṅ bzin stoṅ°*), (11) voidness of all the elements (*sarvadharma-ś°, chos thams cad stoṅ°*), (12) voidness of individual characteristics (*svalakṣaṇa-ś°, raṅ gi mtshan ñid stoṅ°*), (13) voidness of non-support (*anupalambha-ś°, mi dmigs pa stoṅ°*), (14) voidness of non-substantiality (*abhāva-ś°, dṅos po med pa stoṅ°*), (15) voidness of intrinsic nature (*svabhāva-ś°, raṅ gi ṅo bo ñid stoṅ°*), (16) voidness of non-substantiality and intrinsic nature together (*abhāvasvabhāva-ś°, dṅos po med pa raṅ gi ṅo bo ñid stoṅ°*). The list of sixteen voidnesses found in the *Yogaratnamālā* (Snellgrove, Vol. II, p. 131) contains two items not listed above, namely, *mahā-ś°* and *atyanta-ś°*, and consequently does not contain two, namely, *anupalambha-ś°* and *svabhāva-ś°*.

him enter the intense contemplation in sequence of the five Abhisaṃbodhi. Upon completing them, he became a Buddha as Mahāvairocana, the Saṃbhoga-kāya.

Having become a Buddha, he performed the four kinds of marvel. He proceeded to the summit of Mt. Sumeru and pronounced the Yoga Tantras. Thereupon, he was born in the world of men as the son of King Śuddhodana, and displayed the method of the twelve acts. So his school maintains.

(3) THE FIVE ABHISAṂBODHI

There are five Abhisaṃbodhi brought about by dint of the magical exploits (*vikurvāṇa*) of the teacher who appeared first, and there are the five Abhisaṃbodhi brought about by dint of the (laid-down) procedure (*anuṣṭhāna*)[16] for the candidates (*vineya*) who enter later.

The first Abhisaṃbodhi

Thus, all the Buddhas of the ten directions, after conferring upon the Bodhisattva Sarvārthasiddha the initiation of the diadem, bade him contemplate intensely the meaning of the *mantra*, "*cittaprativedhaṃ karomi*" ("I perform thought penetration"). Having done so, in equipoise (*samāpatti*) he comprehended directly the intrinsic purity (*svabhāva-viśuddhi*) of the sixteen kinds of voidness (*śūnyatā*)[17] of his own supreme state of thought (*citta-dharmatā*). In a subsequent attainment upon emerging from that [equipoise], he saw directly the intrinsic purity of his own supreme state of thought in the shape of a moon disk in his own heart. Thereby he attained the "mirror-like knowledge" (*ādarśa-jñāna*)[18] which is the essence of Akṣobhya. The name of this Abhisaṃbodhi is Revelation-Enlightenment resulting from Discrimination (*pratyavekṣaṇā*).

In addition, there is the procedure for the candidates who enter later. Muttering, "*citta-prativedhaṃ karomi*", they contemplate intensely the intrinsic purity of the sixteen kinds of voidness of their own supreme

---

[18] Lwa-ba-pa in his *Cakrasambaramaṇḍalavidhi* (Toh. 1444), mentions in a passage beginning Derge Tg., Rgyud, Wa, 265b-3: "Through the transmutation (*parāvṛtti*) of the 'store consciousness' basis (*ālayavijñāna-āśraya*), there is the 'mirror-like knowledge' (*ādarśa-jñāna*)" (kun gźi rnam par śes pa gnas gyur nas me loṅ lta buḥi ye śes so).

pa las / raṅ gi sñiṅ gar zla baḥi dkyil ḥkhor gyi rnam par bsgom mo /

/ deḥi rjes la phyogs bcuḥi saṅs rgyas thams cad kyis byaṅ chub sems dpaḥ don thams cad grub pa la / Oṃ bo-dhi-tsi-tta u-pa-da-yā-mi / źes paḥi sṅags kyi don sgom du bcug ste / des kyaṅ bsgoms pas mñam gźag tu raṅ gi sems kyi chos ñid stoṅ pa ñid glo bur dri bral mṅon sum du rtogs śiṅ / rjes thob tu raṅ gi sems kyi chos ñid stoṅ pa ñid glo bur dri bral de ñid raṅ gi sñiṅ gar zla baḥi dkyil ḥkhor yoṅs su rdzogs paḥi rnam par mṅon sum du mthoṅ ṅo / des ni mñam pa ñid kyi ye śes rin ḥbyuṅ gi ṅo bo brñes śiṅ / mṅon byaṅ deḥi miṅ ni byaṅ chub mchog tu sems bskyed pa las mṅon par byaṅ chub pa źes byaḥo /

/ de rjes ḥjug gdul byaḥi ñams len gyi rim pa la sbyar na / Oṃ bo-dhi-tsi-tta u-pa-da-yā-mi / źes brjod nas / raṅ gi sems kyi chos ñid stoṅ pa ñid glo bur dri bral de mtshon paḥi kā-li yoṅs su gyur pa las / raṅ gi sñiṅ gar zla baḥi dkyil ḥkhor yoṅs su rdzogs paḥi rnam par bsgom mo /

/ deḥi rjes la saṅs rgyas thams cad kyis / ti-ṣṭha ba-dzra / źes paḥi sṅags kyi don bsgom du bcugs nas bsgoms pas / sṅar gyi byaṅ chub kyi sems kun tu bzaṅ po de ñid raṅ gi sñiṅ gar zla baḥi dkyil ḥkhor gyi steṅ du rdo rje dkar po rtse lṅa pa gyen du ḥgreṅ baḥi rnam par mṅon sum du mthoṅ ṅo / des ni so sor rtog paḥi ye śes ḥod dpag med kyi ṅo bo brñes śiṅ / mṅon byaṅ deḥi miṅ ni brtan paḥi rdo rje las mṅon par byaṅ chub pa źes byaḥo /

/ de rjes ḥjug gdul byaḥi ñams len gyi rim pa la sbyar na / ti-ṣṭha-ba-dzra / źes brjod nas raṅ gi sñiṅ gar rdo rje dkar po rtse lṅa pa bsgom mo /

/ ḥdir daṅ poḥi rdo rje źes bya baḥi don brjod par bya ste / daṅ po ni thog maḥi don yin la / thog maḥi don yaṅ sṅar saṅs ma rgyas pa gsar

[19] The sixteen vowels are the theoretical fourteen Sanskrit vowels plus anusvāra and visarga: a, ā, i, ī, u, ū, ṛ, ṝ, ḷ, ḹ, e, ai, o, au, aṃ, aḥ. The *Sṅags rim* quotes (380a-5) Dīpaṃkarabhadra, "The (16) vowels are the source of the (32) characteristics (*lakṣaṇa*)" (dbyaṅs yig mtshan daṅ yaṅ dag ldan).

[20] The consonants are the 34 Sanskrit consonants. The *Sṅags rim* quotes (380a-5) Dīpaṃkarabhadra: "The (34) consonants radiate the (80) minor marks (*anuvyañjana*)" (ka sogs dpe byad ḥod zer can).

[21] Śākyamitra writes in the *Kosalālaṃkāra* (Toh. 2503), Derge Tg., 26a-3: "'Samantabhadra of the mind of all the Tathāgatas' means holding the entirely good (*samantabhadra*) mind. This shows the knowledge of the pledge (*samaya*)" (de bźin gśegs pa thams cad kyi thugs kun tu bzaṅ po ni kun tu bzaṅ poḥi thugs mṅaḥ ba ste / ḥdis ni dam tshig mkhyen pa ñid du ston to). This particular comment seems closely related to Mkhas grub's use of the expression 'Samantabhadra'. Here the 'pledge' is the former thought of enlightenment, and Samantabhadra is the unity of Taṭhāgata knowledge of that pledge.

state of thought under the symbols of the sixteen vowels,[19] and the transformation of the latter into the shape of a moon disk in their own hearts.

The second Abhisaṃbodhi

Thereupon, the Buddhas of the ten directions bade Sarvārthasiddha contemplate intensely the meaning of the *mantra*, "*Oṃ bodhicittam u(t)pādayāmi*" ("Oṃ, I generate the thought of enlightenment"). Having done so, in equipoise he comprehended directly the freedom from adventitious defilement in the voidness of his own supreme state of thought. In a subsequent attainment he saw directly that freedom from adventitious defilement in the voidness of his own supreme state of thought in the form of a completely-full moon disk in his own heart. Thereby he attained the "equality knowledge" (*samatā-jñāna*) which is the essence of Ratnasaṃbhava. The name of this Abhisaṃbodhi is "Revelation Enlightenment resulting from the resolve of highest enlightenment (*paramabodhicittotpāda*)".

In addition, there is the procedure for the candidates who enter later. Muttering, "*Oṃ bodhicittaṃ u(t)pādayāmi*", they contemplate intensely the freedom from adventitious defilement in the voidness of their own supreme state of thought under the symbols of the consonants,[20] and the transformation of the latter into the shape of a completely-full moon disk in their own hearts.

The third Abhisaṃbodhi

Thereupon, all the Buddhas bade him contemplate intensely the meaning of the *mantra*, "*tiṣṭha vajra*" ("Stand up, O thunderbolt!"). Having done so, he saw directly that Samantabhadra[21] of the former thought of enlightenment under the shape of an upright five-pronged white thunderbolt in his own heart. Thereby he attained the "discriminative knowledge" (*pratyavekṣaṇa-jñāna*) which is the essence of Amitābha. The name of this Abhisaṃbodhi is "Revelation-Enlightenment resulting from the firm thunderbolt (*dṛḍha-vajra*)".

In addition, there is the procedure for the candidates who enter later. Muttering, "*tiṣṭha vajra*", they contemplate intensely a five-pronged, white thunderbolt in their own hearts.

At this point the meaning of the expression "first thunderbolt" (*ādi-vajra*) should be explained. "First" means "original" (T. *thog ma*); and the meaning of "original" is that a previously awakened-not-expanded

du ḥtshaṅ rgya ba la mṅon byaṅ lṅa rim can du sgom paḥi tshe / raṅ gi sñiṅ gar mthoṅ paḥi rdo rje dkar po rtse lṅa pa de la daṅ poḥi rdo rje źes byaḥo / de rtse lṅa bar ṅes paḥi rgyu mtshan gaṅ źe na / ḥtshaṅ rgya baḥi tshe mṅon byaṅ lṅa rim can du bsgoms paḥi mṅon byaṅ re res / ye śes lṅa re re mṅon du gyur pa de mtshon paḥi phyir rtse lṅa paḥo /

/ de nas phyogs bcuḥi saṅs rgyas thams cad kyis byaṅ chub sems dpaḥ don thams cad grub pa la miṅ gi dbaṅ bskur te / don thams cad grub pa źes bya baḥi miṅ de brjes nas / byaṅ chub sems dpaḥi rdo rje dbyiṅs źes bya bar btags so / de nas / ba-dzra-ā-tma-ko 'haṃ / źes bya baḥi sṅags kyi don sgom du bcug nas bsgoms pas / phyogs bcuḥi de bźin gśegs pa thams cad kyi sku rdo rjeḥi dbyiṅs / gsuṅ rdo rjeḥi dbyiṅs / thugs rdo rjeḥi dbyiṅs thams cad raṅ gi sñiṅ gaḥi rdo rje dkar po rtse lṅa pa de la mṅon sum du źugs te / rdo rje de ñid de bźin gśegs pa thams cad kyi rdo rjeḥi rdul phra rab las bsgrubs par mṅon sum du mthoṅ ṅo / des ni bya ba sgrub paḥi ye śes don yod grub paḥi ṅo bo brñes śiṅ / mṅon byaṅ deḥi miṅ ni rdo rjeḥi bdag ñid las mṅon par byaṅ chub pa źes byaḥo /

/ de rjes ḥjug gdul byaḥi ñams len gyi rim pa la sbyar na / ba-dzra-ā-tma-ko 'haṃ / źes brjod nas raṅ gi sñiṅ gaḥi rdo rje dkar po rtse lṅa pa de las ḥod zer phyogs bcur ḥphros pas de bźin gśegs pa thams cad kyi sku rdo rjeḥi dbyiṅs gsuṅ rdo rjeḥi dbyiṅs / thugs rdo rjeḥi dbyiṅs thams cad raṅ gi sñiṅ gaḥi rdo rje dkar po rtse lṅa pa la źugs par bsgom mo /

/ de nas phyogs bcuḥi saṅs rgyas thams cad kyis byaṅ chub sems dpaḥ rdo rje dbyiṅs de la / Oṃ ya-tha sa-rba-ta-thā-ga-ta-was ta-tha a-haṃ / źes bya baḥi sṅags kyi don sgom du bcug nas bsgoms pas / raṅ gi sñiṅ gaḥi rdo rje zla ba yoṅs su gyur nas mtshan bzaṅ po sum cu rtsa

one (*buddha-avibuddha*) becomes newly awakened-expanded (**buddha-vibuddha*). Thus, the five-pronged, white thunderbolt, seen in one's own heart at the time of contemplating intensely the five Abhisaṃbodhi in sequence, is called "first thunderbolt" (*ādi-vajra*). Why are there exactly five prongs? At the time one becomes a complete Buddha each Abhisaṃbodhi is contemplated intensely in the sequence of the five Abhisaṃbodhi. Thus each of the five knowledges is manifested directly, and the five prongs symbolize them.

The fourth Abhisaṃbodhi

Thereupon, all the Buddhas of the ten directions bestowed upon the Bodhisattva Sarvārthasiddha the initiation of the name (*nāma-abhiṣeka*). Having removed the name Sarvārthasiddha, they gave in exchange the name Bodhisattva Vajradhātu. Then they bade him contemplate intensely the meaning of the *mantra*, "*vajrātmako 'haṃ*" ("I consist of thunderbolt"). When he had done so, all the elements of the thunderbolts of body, of speech, and of mind (*kāya-vajra-dhātu*, *vāg-vajra-dhātu*, and *citta-vajra-dhātu*) of all the Tathāgatas of the ten directions entered in direct view into the five-pronged, white thunderbolt of his own heart; and he saw directly that very thunderbolt as made of the finest atoms of the thunderbolts of all the Tathāgatas. Thereby he attained the "knowledge of the procedure of duty" (*kṛtyānuṣṭhāna-jñāna*), which is the essence of Amoghasiddhi. The name of this Abhisaṃbodhi is "Revelation-Enlightenment resulting from thunderbolt composition" (*vajrātmaka*).

In addition, there is the procedure for the candidates who enter later. Muttering, "*vajrātmako 'haṃ*" they contemplate intensely that beams of light emanate in all the ten directions from that five-pronged, white thunderbolt in their own hearts, with the result that the elements of the thunderbolts of body, of speech, and of mind of all the Tathāgatas enter the five-pronged, white thunderbolt of their own hearts.

The fifth Abhisaṃbodhi

Thereupon, all the Buddhas of the ten directions bade the Bodhisattva Vajradhātu contemplate intensely the meaning of the *mantra*, "*Oṃ yathā sarvatathāgatās tathā 'haṃ*" ("Oṃ, like all the 'Thus-come', so am I"). When he had done so, because of the transformation of the thunderbolt and moon in his own heart, Mahāvairocana, the Saṃbhoga-kāya, came

gñis daṅ / dpe byad bzaṅ po brgyad cus brgyan paḥi loṅs spyod rdzogs sku rnam par snaṅ mdzad chen por mṅon sum du gyur te mṅon par rdzogs par saṅs rgyas so / des ni chos kyi dbyiṅs kyi ye śes rnam par snaṅ mdzad kyi ṅo bo brñes śiṅ / mṅon byaṅ deḥi miṅ ni de bźin gśegs pa thams cad kyi mñam pa ñid las mṅon par byaṅ chub pa źes byaḥo /

/ de rjes ḥjug gdul byaḥi ñams len gyi rim pa la sbyar na / Oṃ ya-tha sa-rba-ta-thā-ga-ta-was ta-tha a-haṃ / źes brjod pas raṅ gi sñiṅ gaḥi rdo rje zla ba daṅ bcas pa yoṅs su gyur nas / rnam par snaṅ mdzad chen poḥi skur gyur bar bsgom mo /

/ saṅs rgyas nas cho ḥphrul rnam pa bźi mdzad de / loṅs spyod rdzogs paḥi sku de ḥog min du bźugs śiṅ / des sprul paḥi sku rnam par snaṅ mdzad źal bźi pa gcig sprul pa des ri rab kyi rtse mo byon nas yo-gaḥi rtsa rgyud de ñid bsdus pa gsuṅs pa sogs kyi mdzad rnams mdzad de / mi yul du byon nas bdud ḥdul ba daṅ / mṅon par rdzogs par saṅs rgyas pa la sogs paḥi tshul rnams bstan to /

/ bla med kyi lugs la ston pa bcom ldan ḥdas saṅs rgyas tshul ni / dus ḥkhor / kye rdor / bde mchog sogs rgyud gźan rnams las ma gsuṅs śiṅ / ḥdus paḥi skor nas gsuṅs la / de yaṅ ḥphags lugs daṅ / ye śes źabs lugs gñis ka las gsuṅs te / ḥphags lugs kyi a-rya-de-baḥi spyod bsdus nas gsuṅs / ye śes źabs lugs kyi ḥjam dpal gyi źal luṅ che chuṅ gñis kyi chen mo las gsuṅs te / gñis ka dgoṅs pa gcig tu yod gsuṅ ṅo /

/ de la sa bcu paḥi byaṅ chub sems dpaḥ skye ba gcig gi thogs pa daṅ / srid pa tha ma pa gñis kyi rnam gźag pha rol tu phyin paḥi theg pa daṅ / gsaṅ sṅags kyi rgyud sde bźi ga la yod gsuṅ ṅo / de la sa bcu paḥi byaṅ chub sems dpaḥ skye ba gcig gis thogs pa ni / byaṅ sems sa bcu pa tshe deḥi phyi ma la ḥtshaṅ rgya bar ṅes paḥo / srid pa tha ma pa ni sa bcu paḥi byaṅ sems tshe de la ḥtshaṅ rgya bar ṅes paḥo /

/ ston pa bcom ldan ḥdas śākya thub pa ḥdis pha rol tu phyin paḥi

[22] By reference to Snellgrove (Vol. I, pp. 128-9, Diagram V), one will see that the *Hevajra-tantra* interchanges the correspondences of the *dharmadhātu-jñāna* and *ādarśa-jñāna* with the Tathāgatas Vairocana and Akṣobhya. The reason is that the *Hevajra-tantra* has Akṣobhya as the chief Tathāgata, and so Akṣobhya is accorded the chief *jñāna*, the *dharmadhātu-jñāna*. The correspondences, given by Mkhas grub in the present chapter, of Tathāgatas and knowledges (*jñāna*); and the correspondences, given by him in the ninth chapter, of Tathāgatas and initiations of the flask, are consistent with *Advayavajra-Saṁgraha*, p. 36. The correspondences are summarized as follows:

Tathāgata	*Knowledge*	*Flask Initiation*
Akṣobhya	Mirror-like	Water
Ratnasambhava	Equality	Diadem
Amitābha	Discriminative	Diamond
Amoghasiddhi	Procedure of duty	Bell
Vairocana	Dharma-realm	Name

into direct view, adorned with the thirty-two characteristics and the eighty minor marks. [Bo. Vajradhātu] became a Manifest Complete Buddha. Thereby he attained the "Dharma-realm knowledge" (*dharma-dhātu-jñāna*) which is the essence of Vairocana.[22] The name of this Abhisaṃbodhi is "Revelation-Enlightenment resulting from equality with all the Tathāgatas (*sarvatathāgata-samatā*)".

In addition, there is the procedure for the candidates who enter later. Muttering, "*Oṃ yathā sarvatathāgatās tathā 'haṃ*", they contemplate intensely the transformation into the body of Mahāvairocana of the thunderbolt and the moon in their own hearts.

After becoming a full Buddha, he performed the four kinds of marvel. His Saṃbhoga-kāya remained in the Akaniṣṭha heaven. By means of the Nirmāṇa-kāya he performed various acts. For example, with the single apparition (*nirmita*) of a four-faced Vairocana, he proceeded to the summit of Mt. Sumeru and recited the fundamental Yoga Tantra, *Tattvasaṃgraha* (Toh. 479). Then he appeared in the world of men and displayed the methods of defeating Māra, the Manifest Complete Buddhahood, and so forth.

b. *Teaching of the Anuttara school*

The method by which the Teacher Bhagavat became a Buddha, according to the Anuttara school, is not discussed in such Tantras as the *Kālacakra* (Toh. 362), *Hevajra* (Toh. 417-418), and the *Saṃvara* (Toh. 368). The explanation according to the cycle of *Samāja* (Toh. 442 and 443) is given by both the Ārya school and the Jñānapāda school. The explanation in the *Caryāmelāpakapradīpa* (Toh. 1803) by Āryadeva is followed by the Ārya school; and that found in the larger of the two *Mañjuśrī-mukhāgama*, the larger (Toh. 1853) and the smaller (Toh. 1854), is followed by the Jñānapāda school. There is no divergences between the two schools.

Both the Pāramitā vehicle and all four Tantra divisions of the Mantra vehicle set forth two possibilities for the Bodhisattva dwelling on the tenth stage, namely, he is "bound to one more birth" (*ekajātipratibaddha*) or is "in his last existence" (*carama-bhavika*). It is certain that "the Bodhisattva of the tenth stage who is bound to one more birth" means a tenth-stage Bodhisattva who has decided to become a full Buddha in his next life, and that "the one in the last existence" means a tenth-stage Bodhisattva who has decided to become a full Buddha in that life.

The Teacher Bhagavat Śākyamuni, taking recourse to the Pāramitā

theg pa la brten nas / bskal pa graṅs med gsum du tshogs bsags paḥi mthar / sa bcu pa la gnas paḥi byaṅ chub sems dpaḥ srid pa tha ma par gyur paḥi tshe ḥog min du mkhaḥ khyab kyi tiṅ ṅe ḥdzin la sñoms par źugs so / deḥi tshe phyogs bcuḥi saṅs rgyas thams cad ḥdus nas / se gol kyi sgras tiṅ ṅe ḥdzin de las bslaṅs te / khyod ñid tiṅ ṅe ḥdzin de tsam gyis mṅon par rdzogs par ḥtshaṅ rgya bar mi nus so / źes gsuṅs pa la / ḥo na ji ltar bgyi źes gsol pas / phyogs bcuḥi saṅs rgyas thams cad kyis lhaḥi bu mo thig le mchog ma bkug nas / dbaṅ gsum pa śes rab ye śes kyi dbaṅ dṅos dbaṅ du skur te / deḥi rjes la mṅon par byaṅ chub paḥi rim pa rnams bstan nas sgom du bcug nas / mtshan phyed na stoṅ pa gsum rim gyis thim nas / thams cad stoṅ pa don gyi ḥod gsal mṅon du gyur te / de las dag paḥi sgyu maḥi skur laṅs pa la / saṅs rgyas thams cad kyis dbaṅ bźi pa bskur te spyod pa byed du bcug pas tho raṅs skya reṅs daṅ po ḥchar pa tsam na / rdo rje lta buḥi tiṅ ṅe ḥdzin gyis śes byaḥi sgrib pa phra źiṅ phra ba yaṅ spans nas mi slob paḥi zuṅ ḥjug rdo rje ḥchaṅ gi go ḥphaṅ brñes te / mṅon par rdzogs par saṅs rgyas so /

[23] Tilottamā (T. *thig le mchog ma*) is listed among the thirteen celestial courtesans (*divya-veśyā*) by the Kloṅ rdol bla ma (Collected Works, Ma, f. 4b-7 to 5a-1). She is cited this way: "She the Lightning Flash (*vidyut-prabhā*), or as called by another name, Daughter of the Gods 'Best of Drops' (Tilottamā)" (glog gi ḥod can maḥam / miṅ gźan lha yi bu mo thig le chog ma zer). In the lexicon *Abhidhānaśāstraviśvalocana* (Toh. 4453) by Dpal ḥdzin sde, the division of Gandharva (Derge ed., Vol. Po, 78b-4 to 79a-4) includes Thig le mchog ma among the Apsarasa, who are the consorts of the Gandharvas. Presumably she is the drop in the "drop of springtime" (*vasanta-tilaka*) mentioned later by Mkhas grub (near end of Chapter Eight) in the description of the Body *maṇḍala*, and hence also the Vajravārāhī ("Diamond Sow") of the Saṃvara Tantra. Cf. S. B. Dasgupta, *Obscure Religious Cults* especially p. 118, for an excellent description, where [the tilaka of] Vasanta-tilaka, or Caṇḍālī, is shown to have a lustre like the dazzle of lightning, and is also called the Goddess Nairātmyā. This goddess is discussed in the *Sṅags rim*, 444b-3, f. under the subject of Yoga of Heat (*caṇḍā-yoga, gtum moḥi rnal ḥbyor*). In fact, Tsoṅ-kha-pa, *ibid.*, 446a-6 to 446b-1 quotes the first two verses that Dasgupta, p. 118 note, quotes from the *Sampuṭikā*. Tsoṅ-kha-pa, *ibid.*, 447a-5 to b-1, says: "And that blazing passes from the middle (channel) and pervades the spaces of the hair pores, crown (of the head), and forehead. Having cremated the three 'wheels' (*cakra*) and the personality aggregates (*skandha*), etc., it passes out from the right nostril and from the orifice of the *ūrṇā-kośa*. Thereupon, it pervades the ten directions like a lightning flash and informs the retinue (*parivāra*), the Śrāvakas, the Pratyekabuddhas, and the Bodhisattvas that someone has been made a Buddha, ..." (de ḥbar ba yaṅ dbu ma nas soṅ ste ba spuḥi bu ga daṅ rtse mo daṅ dpral baḥi mtshams rnams khyab par byas śiṅ ḥkhor lo gsum daṅ phuṅ po la sogs pa rnams gduṅs nas sna bu ga gYas daṅ mdzod spuḥi khuṅ bu las byuṅ ṅo / de nas glog gi ḥod bźin du phyogs bcur khyab nas ḥkhor ba pa daṅ ñan raṅ daṅ byaṅ sems rnams la rig pas saṅs rgyas su byas te ...).

[24] By comparison with Mkhas grub's ninth chapter, it may be seen that the placement of the *abhisambodhis* after the third initiation means that they are included in what is called "steps of completion" (*saṃpanna-krama*). Presumably, then, Tsoṅ-kha-pa, in his *Sṅags rim* includes them in the "steps of production" (*utpatti-krama*) as part of

vehicle collected the equipment for three incalculable aeons, then became equipoised in the Space-filling *samādhi* as a Bodhisattva of the tenth stage in the last existence. At that time, the Buddhas of all the ten directions assembled, aroused him from that *samādhi* by snapping their fingers, and said to him, "You cannot become a Manifest Complete Buddha by this *samādhi* alone." "Then, how shall I do it?", he implored them. Thereupon all the Buddhas of the ten directions summoned the daughter of the gods Tilottamā[23] and bestowed concretely the third initiation, the Insight-Knowledge Initiation (*prajñā-jñāna-abhiṣeka*). After that they revealed the steps of Abhisaṃbodhi[24] and bade him contemplate them. At midnight he successively dissolved the three voids [into one another];[25] and the universal void (*sarvaśūnya*), which is the Clear Light of the [Absolute] Object (**artha-prabhāsvara*), came into direct view. He emerged from that [Clear Light] in the pure illusory body,[26] and all the Buddhas bestowed upon him the fourth initiation and bade him perform the acts [of a Buddha]. As a consequence, at the initial appearance of dawn, he shed, by means of the adamantine *samādhi* (*vajropama-samādhi*), the subtlest obscurations of the knowable (*jñeyāvaraṇa*). Thus he attained the rank of Vajradhara, the union beyond learning (*aśaikṣa-yuganaddha*), and became a Manifest Complete Buddha.

"the procedure for the candidates who enter later". On f. 365a-6, he quotes the *Vajrapañjarā* (Toh. 419) for the terminology of dividing up the "steps of production" into a *yoga* of six parts (*ṣaḍaṅga-yoga*); and his subsequent quotations and commentary show that the six parts are done by way of the six progenitors (*kula*), as follows: (1) Vairocana – generation of the palace, (2) Vajrasattva – attraction of the residents, (3) Akṣobhya – initiation, (4) Amoghasiddhi – offerings, (5) Ratnasambhava – praises, (6) Amitābha – enjoyment of the ambrosia. In this classification, the five *abhisambodhis* pertain to No. 2, attraction of the residents. They are required to cause the "knowledge being(s)" (*jñāna-sattva*) to enter the meditator. In Tsoṅ-kha-pa's discussion of the five *abhisambodhis*, beginning *Sṅags rim*, f. 379b-7, it is brought out that the moon of the second *abhisambodhi* differs from that of the first one in being red. This red moon is also called the "second moon".

[25] Cf. Alex Wayman, "Notes on the Sanskrit term *jñāna*", *JAOS*, Vol. 75, No. 4 (Oct.-Dec., 1955), p. 263, n. 40, for the dissolution of the voids into one another. But at that point the terminology is presented by *citta* being drawn into *caitta*, and the latter being drawn into *avidyā*. For the same process, using the terminology of the voids, see *ibid.*, pp. 259-60, where it is shown that void (*śūnya*) is a synonym of *citta*, further void (*atiśūnya*) a synonym of *caitta*, and great void (*mahāśūnya*) a synonym of *avidyā*.

[26] Tsoṅ-kha-pa shows in the *Sṅags rim* (410b-2, 3, 4) by quotation from the *Muktitilaka* (Toh. 1859) of Buddhajñāna and commentary that the body developed by the "steps of production" is the *mantra*-body (*sṅags kyi sku*), while the one developed by the "steps of completion" is the knowledge-body (*ye śes sku*). The latter body, in turn, is of two kinds, (also) knowledge-body (*ye śes sku*) and pure-body (*rnam par dag paḥi sku*). Of these last two, the knowledge-body is the impure illusory body; and the pure-body is that knowledge-body purified in the Clear Light.

/ de la bum dbaṅ ma bskur bar dbaṅ goṅ ma bskur bas cho ga pa daṅ / bskyed rim ma bsgoms par rdzogs rim bsgoms pas cho ga paḥi dmigs bsal ḥdi kho na gsuṅs kyi / gźan ma gsuṅs / źes gsuṅ ṅo /

/ de nas loṅs spyod rdzogs paḥi sku rdo rje ḥchaṅ chen po de ḥog min du bźugs nas / sprul paḥi skus mi yul du mdzad pa bcu gñis kyi tshul bstan te / rgyal po zas gtsaṅ gi sras su ḥkhruṅs nas chu bo ni-ra-ñdza-naḥi ḥgram du lo drug dkaḥ ba spyod pa na / rgya śug gi ḥbru gcig / til ḥbru gcig / ḥbras ñag ma gcig ste gsum las kha zas rags pa ma gsol bar mkhaḥ khyab kyi tiṅ ṅe ḥdzin la sñoms par źugs so / deḥi tshe phyogs bcuḥi saṅs rgyas thams cad ḥdus nas se gol gyi sgras tiṅ ṅe ḥdzin de las bslaṅs te / khyod ñid dkaḥ thub kyis gduṅs paḥi lus ḥdi lta bus bdud ḥdul bar mi nus śiṅ / khyod ñid tiṅ ṅe ḥdzin ḥdi tsam gyis śes sgrib phra źiṅ phra ba spoṅ mi nus so / źes gsuṅ pas / kha zas rags pa gsol nas byaṅ chub kyi śiṅ druṅ du gśegs pa la / saṅs rgyas thams cad kyis lhaḥi bu mo thig le mchog ma bkug nas dbaṅ gsum pa śes rab ye śes kyi dbaṅ dṅos dbaṅ du bskur baḥi tshul bstan / de nas mṅon par byaṅ chub paḥi rim pa bstan nas sgom du bcug pas mtshan phyed na stoṅ pa gsum rim gyis thim nas / thams cad stoṅ pa don gyi ḥod gsal mṅon du gyur paḥi tshul bstan / de las dag paḥi sgyu maḥi skur laṅs pa la saṅs rgyas thams cad kyis dbaṅ bźi pa bskur nas spyod par byed du bcug pas tho raṅs skya reṅs daṅ po ḥchar ba tsam na / rdo rje lta buḥi tiṅ ṅe ḥdzin gyis śes byaḥi sgrib pa phra źiṅ phra ba spaṅs nas mi slob paḥi zuṅ ḥjug brñes te mṅon par rdzogs par saṅs rgyas paḥi tshul bstan to /

/ de la saṅs rgyas paḥi tshul tsam źig bstan pas chog mod / dbaṅ gsum pa daṅ / bźi pa bskur ba sogs kyi tshul bstan pa la dgos pa ci yod ce na / pha rol tu phyin pa rkyaṅ paḥi lam gyis sa bcu paḥi bar du bgrod nus kyaṅ / mthar ḥtshaṅ rgya ba sṅags bla med kyi lam du źugs pa la ṅes par ltos dgos kyi / der ma źugs par ḥtshaṅ rgya ba mi srid do / źes par bya baḥi phyir ro /

[27] As Mkhas grub shows near the end of the present work, following Tsoṅ-kha-pa's reform, it is necessary to have the initiation of the flask before being conferred the higher initiations, and it is necessary to undergo the steps of production before undergoing the steps of completion.

It has been said, "That account [regarding the Teacher Bhagavat] mentions only an exceptional case of the rite because it confers the higher initiations without [previously] conferring the initiation of the flask, and because there is contemplation of the steps of completion (*niṣpanna-krama*) without [previous] contemplation of the steps of production (*utpatti-krama*); but does not mention the other [requirements]."[27]

Thereupon, Mahāvajradhara, the Saṃbhoga-kāya, took abode in the Akaniṣṭha heaven, and his Nirmāṇa-kāya displayed the method of the twelve acts in the world of men. He was born the son of King Śuddhodana, and for six years practised severe asceticism on the bank of the River Nairañjanā. Apart from one Jujube fruit, one sesame seed, one grain of rice, he partook of no solid food. He equipoised himself in the Space-filling *samādhi*. At that time all the Buddhas of the ten directions assembled and by the sound of snapping fingers aroused him from that *samādhi*. "You will not be able to vanquish Māra by those ascetic practices and mortified body; this *samādhi* alone will not suffice for you to eliminate the subtlest obscurations of the knowable." Thereupon, he partook of some substantial food and proceeded to the Bodhi-tree. All the Buddhas summoned the daughter of the gods Tilottamā and revealed the method of concrete initiation into the third, the Insight-Knowledge Initiation. Thereupon, they revealed the (five) steps of Revelation-Enlightenment and bade him enter their intense contemplation. When he had done so, at midnight they taught the method by which the universal void, which is the Clear Light of the [Absolute] Object, came into direct view after the successive dissolution of the three voids [into one another]. He emerged from that [Clear Light] in his pure illusory body, and all the Buddhas bestowed upon him the fourth initiation and bade him perform the acts [of a Buddha]. At the first appearance of dawn, by the means of the adamantine *samādhi*, he eliminated the subtlest obscurations of the knowable and attained the union beyond learning (*aśaikṣa-yuganaddha*). Thus he showed the method of Manifest Complete Buddhahood.

To be sure, it is sufficient to show only the method of [achieving] Buddhahood. Why is there any necessity to show the methods of [the higher] initiations, such as the third and the fourth? The point is that although one may be able to reach the tenth stage solely along the Pāramitā path, to become finally a complete Buddha, it is certainly necessary for one to enter the incomparable (*anuttara*) Mantra path. Otherwise it is impossible to become a complete Buddha.

/ chos kyi ḥkhor lo bskor baḥi tshul la / pha rol tu phyin paḥi theg paḥi chos ḥkhor bskor tshul daṅ / gsaṅ sṅags kyi theg paḥi chos ḥkhor bskor tshul gñis las /

/ daṅ po ni / bcom ldan ḥdas kyis byaṅ chub kyi śiṅ druṅ du mṅon par rdzogs par saṅs rgyas paḥi tshul bstan nas / źag bdun phrag bdun du chos ḥkhor ma bskor ro / de nas yul gyi dbus ma-ga-dha rgyal poḥi khab yod pa nas / byaṅ phyogs su chu bo ga-ṅgā brgal baḥi yul wā-ra-ṇa-si draṅ sroṅ lhuṅ ba ri dags kyi nags su byon te / ciḥi phyir draṅ sroṅ lhuṅ ba źes bya źe na / sṅon saṅs rgyas ḥod sruṅs ḥjig rten du ḥbyon du ñe ba na / ri de la raṅ saṅs rgyas lṅa brgya gnas pa las / de dag la lha rnams kyis sbran pa la brten nas saṅs rgyas ḥjig rten du ḥbyon par mkhyen te / rdzu ḥphrul gyis nam mkhaḥ la ḥphags nas meḥi khams la sñoms par źugs te / raṅ gi sku las byuṅ baḥi mes sku lus rnams bsregs nas riṅ bsrel rnams sa la lhuṅ ba las / draṅ sroṅ lhuṅ ṅo źes smras pas draṅ sroṅ lhuṅ ba źes byaḥo / ciḥi phyir ri dvags kyi nags źes bya źe na / sṅon wā-ra-ṇa-siḥi rgyal po tshaṅs byin źes bya bas ri ḥdi la gnas paḥi ri dvags rnams bsad par mi byaḥo / źes khrims bcas pas / phyogs gźan nas kyaṅ ri dvags maṅ po der ḥdus nas ḥphaṅs pas ri dvags kyi nags źes byaḥo /

/ de na lṅa sde bzaṅ po źes bya baḥi kun tu rgyu chen po lṅa gnas te / tshe daṅ ldan pa kun śes kauṇḍinya daṅ / tshe daṅ ldan pa rta thul daṅ / rlaṅs pa daṅ / miṅ chen daṅ bzaṅ ldan no /

CHAPTER TWO

II. THE METHOD OF SETTING THE WHEEL OF THE LAW INTO MOTION

It is divided into two sections: A, the method of setting the wheel of the law of the *Pāramitā-yāna* into motion; B, the method of setting the wheel of the law of the *Mantra-yāna* into motion.

A. THE METHOD OF SETTING THE WHEEL OF THE LAW OF THE PĀRAMITĀ-YĀNA INTO MOTION

After the Bhagavat had exhibited the method of [attaining] Manifest Complete Buddhahood at the Bodhi-tree, he did not set the wheel of the law into motion for seven times seven days. Then from Rājagṛha in Magadha in the middle country (*Madhyadeśa*) he proceeded north to Vārāṇasī across the Ganges to the Deer Park Ṛṣipatana. Why is the place called Ṛṣipatana? Formerly when the time approached for the Buddha Kāśyapa to appear in the world, there lived on that hill five hundred Pratyekabuddhas. They learned from a message given them by the devas that the Buddha was to manifest himself. By their magical power they soared up to the sky and equipoised themselves in the element of fire (*tejo-dhātu*). The fire that issued from their own bodies burned their material bodies, and the ashes fell to the earth. It was said, "The Ṛṣis have fallen", and for this reason the place is called Ṛṣipatana (the falling of the Ṛṣis). But why is it called the Deer Park (Mṛgadāva)? Once Brahmadatta, King of Vārāṇasī, issued an order prohibiting the killing of the deer living on this hill. As a result, many deer, from other places as well, flocked there, gaining security. Therefore, it was called "Deer Park".

At that place were staying the five great peregrinators (*parivrājaka*) known as "the happy band of five" (*pañcaka-bhadravargiya*), *āyuṣmat* Ājñātakauṇḍinya, *āyuṣmat* Aśvajit, Vāṣpa, Mahānāma, and Bhadrika.

/ de dag gis bcom ldan ḥdas rgyaṅ nas ḥbyon pa mthoṅ ste / tshe daṅ ldan pa goḥu-ta-ma bsam gtan las ñams pa / lhod pa / maṅ du za ba de ḥdir ḥoṅ gis / de la smra bar mi bya / bśes par mi bya / bsu bar yaṅ mi byaḥo / stan lhag po ḥdi la ḥdug na ḥdug tu chug cig / ces ḥog khrims bcas te stan lhag po gcig btiṅ ṅo /

/ de nas bcom ldan ḥdas phebs pa na / de dag gis gzi brjid ma bzod nas / thams cad kyis phyag ḥtshal te / la las źabs bkrus / la las stan btiṅ ste tshe daṅ ldan pa goḥu-ta-ma legs byon tam / byon pa legs so / źes gsol to / de nas bcom ldan ḥdas kyis gdan btiṅ pa de la bźugs so / de nas lṅa sde rnams kyis bcom ldan ḥdas sṅon las mdaṅs gsal bar mthoṅ nas / tshe daṅ ldan pa goḥu-ta-ma / khyod ñid dbaṅ po rnams ni śin tu gsal bags paḥi mdog ni yoṅs su dag na / ye śes mthoṅ baḥi khyad par mṅon du mdzad dam / źes gsol bas /

/ bcom ldan ḥdas kyis bkaḥ stsal pa / rigs kyi bu dag de bźin gśegs pa la tshe daṅ ldan pa źes ma zer źig / khyed yun riṅ por sdug bsṅal bar ḥgyur ta re / ṅa ni de bźin gśegs pa ste / mṅon par rdzogs par saṅs rgyas so / raṅ byuṅ gi ye śes khoṅ du chud do / ṅa ni thams cad mkhyen pa ste / slob dpon gźan la rag ma las so / źes gsuṅs paḥi mod la / lṅa sde rnams kyi skra daṅ kha spu raṅ byi ste / lus chos gos dur smrig gsum gyis g ogs śiṅ lag na bya ma bum thogs pa / bsñen par rdzogs nas lo brgya lon pa lta bu / skra daṅ kha spu bregs nas źag bdun lon pa lta bur gyur to /

/ de nas tshaṅs pa daṅ / brgya byin la sogs pa lhaḥi bu dpag tu med pas / bcom ldan ḥdas la gser gyi ḥkhor lo rtsibs stoṅ daṅ ldan pa phul te chos kyi ḥkhor lo bskor bar gsol ba btab pas / ston pas źal gyis bźes te / srod thun daṅ po la ḥchag par mdzad / guṅ thun bar pa la gzims / tho raṅs thun tha ma la bźeṅs nas ḥdas paḥi saṅs rgyas bcom ldan ḥdas rnams kyis chos kyi ḥkhor lo sa phyogs gaṅ du bskor / sñam du dgoṅs pa sṅon du btaṅ bas / sa phyogs de ñid du bskor bar mkhyen te / skad

[1] In Mkhas grub rje's biography of Tsoṅ-kha-pa (the latter's *Gsuṅ ḥbum*, Vol. Ka, *Rnam thar*, 66a-5, ff.) in the course of speaking of the magical transformations exhibited by Tsoṅ-kha-pa toward the end of his life, he mentions, "It is said in the sacred scriptures of the Bhagavat that in whomever's stream of consciousness there is aroused the path of vision, or there is produced directly Arhatship, and so on, thereby that person obtains the ambrosia (*amṛta*), and he has many transformations of his former bodily appearance, e.g. his senses are completely clear, the color of his face is delightful, the color of his skin is pale, and so forth" (bcom ldan ḥdas kyi gsuṅ rab dag las / gaṅ gi rgyud la mthoṅ baḥi lam skyes pa daṅ / dgra bcom pa mṅon du byas pa la sogs paḥi sgo nas bdud rtsi thob par gyur ba na / dbaṅ po yoṅs su gsal źiṅ / bźin gyi mdog ni

When they saw the Bhagavat approaching from afar, they made this agreement (*kriyābandham akārṣuḥ*, LV 407,18): "Because *āyuṣmat* Gautama is coming hither, after having broken off his meditation and become slack and well fed, we should neither speak to him, nor be friendly with him, nor even go to meet him. When he sits down on this spare seat, let him sit down [i.e. without paying him any attention]." And they spread a spare seat.

Now, when the Bhagavat arrived, they could not bear his radiance (*tejas*), and all bowed to him. Some washed his feet; others spread a seat, and they said, "*Āyuṣmat* Gautama, did you travel well? Be welcome!" Then the Bhagavat seated himself on the prepared seat. When "the happy band of five" saw that the Bhagavat's face was clearer than before, they said, "*Āyuṣmat* Gautama, your senses are so clear, and your complexion is so pure; have you realized something special in the perception of Divine Knowledge?"[1]

The Bhagavat spoke: "O sons of the (Buddhist) family (*kulaputra*), do not call a Tathāgata '*āyuṣmat*' (long living), for that will cause you long-enduring suffering. I am a Tathāgata, a Manifest Complete Buddha (*abhisaṃbuddha*). I have comprehended perfectly the spontaneously generated knowledge (**aupapāduka-jñāna*). I am omniscient, not dependent upon another instructor (*ācārya*)." He had hardly uttered these words when the hair and beards of "the happy band of five" fell out; their bodies were attired with the three yellow-red garments (*trikaṣāya-cīvara*) [of the monk]; in their hands they held the begging bowls (*pātra*). They appeared as though ordained for a hundred years (*varṣaśatopasaṃpanna*, LV 409.19) and their hair and beards as though shaven clean for seven days.

1. THE PROMULGATIONS

Thereupon, Brahmā, Indra, and the innumerable sons of the gods (*devaputra*) offered him a golden wheel with a thousand spokes, praying him to set the wheel of the law into motion. The Teacher accepted it. In the first watch of the night he trod about. In the middle watch of the night he rested. In the final watch of dawn he arose, and when he reflected concerning the site on which the Buddhas of the past had set into motion the wheel of the law, he knew that in former times it was set into

---

dgal [sic.: for *dgaḥ*] / pags paḥi mdog ni dkar ba la sogs pa lus kyi mdaṅs sṅar las gnas gyur pa ḥbyuṅ ba du ma źig gsuṅs te).

cig yud tsam de ñid la sa phyogs der rin po che sna bźi las grub paḥi khri stoṅ byuṅ bar gyur to /

/ de nas bcom ldan ḥdas kyis khri daṅ po gsum la skor ba mdzad de / khri bźi pa la bźugs nas / lṅa sde bzaṅ po daṅ / lhaḥi ḥkhor dpag tu med pa la chos kyi ḥkhor lo daṅ po bden pa bźiḥi chos kyi ḥkhor lo bskor te /

/ dge sloṅ dag ḥdi ni sdug bsṅal ḥphags paḥi bden pa ste / śes par byaḥo / ḥdi ni kun ḥbyuṅ ḥphags paḥi bden pa ste spaṅ bar byaḥo / ḥdi ni ḥgog pa ḥphags paḥi bden pa ste mṅon du byaḥo / ḥdi ni lam ḥphags paḥi bden pa ste bsgom par byaḥo /

źes gsuṅs pas / kun śes kau-ṇḍi-nyaḥi rgyud la mthoṅ lam skyes te / lha rnams kyis ched du brjod pa ched du brjod nas me tog gi char pus mo nub tsam phab ste / sa rnam pa drug tu gYos so /

/ de la bden pa bźiḥi chos kyi ḥkhor lo bskor baḥi mdo ni / ḥkhor lo daṅ poḥi mdo dṅos yin źiṅ / de daṅ brjod bya phyogs mthun gyi sgo nas / ḥdul ba luṅ daṅ / mdo dran pa ñer gźag daṅ / mdo rgya cher rol pa daṅ / mdo sde las brgya pa daṅ / mdo sde rtogs brjod brgya pa la sogs pa yaṅ ḥkhor lo daṅ poḥi mdor gtogs so /

/ de nas bcom ldan ḥdas kyis gnas bya rgod phuṅ poḥi rir / lhan cig spyod paḥi ḥkhor lṅa sde bzaṅ po la sogs pa dge sloṅ lṅa stoṅ ste ñan thos kyi tshogs rnams daṅ / ched du bya baḥi gdul bya byaṅ chub sems dpaḥi graṅs med pa daṅ bcas pa la / bkaḥ bar pa mtshan ñid med paḥi chos kyi ḥkhor lo bskor te /

[2] Certain divergences between the presentation here and that in Bu-ston's *History of Buddhism*, II, 45, show that Mkhas grub rje is using other sources, even if (as appears likely) he has read Bu-ston's work. Thus, Bu-ston, following the *Lalitavistara*, says that the 1000 seats were made of 7 kinds of jewels. He also says that the Teacher spoke at midnight, whereas in Mkhas grub's account the Teacher was resting at that time.

motion on this very site. Instantaneously, a thousand thrones, formed of four kinds of jewels, appeared on that site.[2]

The First Wheel

Then the Bhagavat circumambulated the first three thrones and seated himself on the fourth throne. For "the happy band of five" and the uncountable retinue of gods, he set into motion the first wheel of the law, the Wheel of the Law of the Four Truths. He said,

> O Bhikṣus, suffering (*duḥkha*) is a Noble Truth (*ārya-satya*),
> and is to be recognized (*parijñeya*).
> The source [of suffering] (*samudaya*) is a Noble Truth,
> and is to be removed (*praheya*).
> The cessation [of the source] (*nirodha*) is a Noble Truth,
> and is to be realized directly (*sākṣātkareya*).
> The path [leading to that realization] (*mārga*) is a Noble Truth,
> and is to be contemplated intensely (*bhāveya*).

The path of vision (*darśana-mārga*) arose in the stream of consciousness (*saṃtāna*) of Ājñātakauṇḍinya. The gods repeatedly expressed joy and praise (*udāna*), while a shower of flowers fell knee-deep, and the earth trembled in six different ways.

The *sūtras* which come from the setting into motion of the Wheel of the Law of the Four Truths are as follows: the basic one is the *Dharmacakra-sūtra* (Toh. 337). The following *sūtras*, because their subject matter is consistent with that basic *sūtra*, also are classified as *sūtras* of the First Wheel: the *Vinayavastu* (Toh. 1, in 4 vols.), the *sūtra Saddharmasmṛtyupasthāna* (Toh. 287), the *sūtra Lalitavistara* (Toh. 95), the *Karmaśataka* (Toh. 340) of the *sūtra* class, the *Avadānaśataka* (Toh. 343) of the *sūtra* class, and others.

The Intermediate Wheel

Thereafter the Bhagavat, while sojourning on the mountain Gṛdhrakūṭa, set into motion the Wheel of the Law concerning lack of characteristics [of all the *dharmas*], which was the Intermediate Promulgation, to his assembled retinue — "the happy band of five" and other bhikṣus numbering five thousand, throngs of Śrāvakas, and innumerable Bodhisattva candidates for the high goal (*uddeśa-vineya*).

/ de la śes rab kyi pha rol tu phyin pa rgyas pa stoṅ phrag brgya pa / ḥbriṅ gi rgyas pa ñi khri lṅa stoṅ pa / ḥbriṅ gi ḥbriṅ khri brgyad stoṅ pa / ḥbriṅ gi ḥbriṅ bsdus pa śes rab khri pa / bsdus paḥi rgyas pa brgyad stoṅ pa / bsdus paḥi bsdus pa ḥphags pa sdud pa rnams ni / bkaḥ bar baḥi mdo dṅos yin źiṅ / de daṅ brjod bya phyogs mthun gyi sgo nas tiṅ ṅe ḥdzin rgyal poḥi mdo / rdo rje gcod pa / saṅs rgyas phal po che / laṅ kar gśegs pa / ḥphags pa dkon mchog brtsegs pa chen poḥi mdo / phal chen la sogs pa yaṅ bkaḥ bar baḥi mdor gtogs so /

/ śes phyin gyi mdo la sras yum bcu bdun źes grags te / sṅar bgraṅs paḥi stoṅ phrag brgya pa nas / sdud paḥi bar drug ni mṅon rtogs brgyad tshaṅ ba brjod byar ston pas yum du ḥjog la / rab kyi rtsal gyis rnam par gnon pas źus paḥi mdo / śer phyin bdun brgya pa / śer phyin lṅa brgya pa / śes phyin tshul brgya lṅa bcu pa / śer phyin lṅa bcu pa / rdo rje gcod pa / śes rab sñiṅ po / koḥu-śi-kaḥi mdo / lag bzaṅ gis źus paḥi mdo / śer phyin yi ge ñuṅ ṅu daṅ / yi ge gcig ma ste / bcu gcig ni mṅon rtogs brgyad tshaṅ pa mi ston pas sras su ḥjog go /

/ kha cig lag bzaṅ gis źus paḥi mdoḥi dod la / sgo ñi śu rtsa lṅa pa ḥdren no / raṅ lugs śer phyin gyi mdo la sras yum bcu bdun du ma ṅes te / de las maṅ ba yod paḥi phyir ro /

/ bkaḥ tha ma legs par rnam par phye ba daṅ ldan paḥi chos ḥkhor ni gnas yaṅ pa can la sogs par / ched du bya baḥi gdul bya theg pa thams cad la yaṅ dag par źugs paḥi byaṅ chub sems dpaḥ graṅs med pa rnams la gsuṅs te /

/ mdo sde dgoṅs pa ṅes par ḥgrel ba ni ḥkhor lo tha maḥi mdo dṅos yin źiṅ / de daṅ brjod bya phyogs mthun paḥi mdo rnams ni / ḥkhor lo tha maḥi mdo ru gtogs so / yaṅ ḥkhor lo tha maḥi mdoḥi mtshan la kha cig gis don dam rnam par ṅes paḥi chos kyi ḥkhor lo źes zer ro /

[8] The eight *abhisamaya* are the eight subjects of the *Abhisamayālaṃkāra* (cf. Obermiller, Bu-ston, II, p. 49, n.).

The basic *sūtras* of the Intermediate Promulgation are as follows: the most expanded of the *Prajñā-pāramitā* works, the *Śatasāhasrikā* (Toh. 8); the medium expanded, the *Pañcaviṃśatisāhasrikā* (Toh. 9); the medium medium, the *Aṣṭādaśasāhasrikā* (Toh. 10); the condensed medium medium, the *Daśasāhasrikā* (Toh. 11); the condensed expanded, the *Aṣṭasāhasrikā* (Toh. 12); and the condensed condensed, the *Sañcayagāthā* (Toh. 13). The greater bulk of *sūtras* (T. *phal chen la sogs pa*), because their subject matter is consistent with those basic *sūtras*, also are classified as *sūtras* of the Intermediate Promulgation, e.g. the *Samādhirāja-sūtra* (Toh. 127), the *Vajracchedikā* (Toh. 16), the *Buddhāvataṃsaka* (Toh. 44), the *Laṅkāvatāra* (Toh. 107), and the *Mahāratnakūṭa* (Toh. 45).

It is customary to regard seventeen of the *Prajñ-āpāramitā sūtras* as "mothers and sons". Thus, the six works starting with the *Śatasāhasrikā*, down to the *Sañcayagāthā*, are "mothers" because they teach the complete subject matter of the eight *abhisamaya*.[3] Eleven works are set down as "sons" because they do not teach the complete eight *abhisamaya*; these are: the *Suvikrāntavikrami-paripṛcchā* (Toh. 14), the *Saptaśatikā* (Toh. 24), the *Pañcaśatikā-prajñāpāramitā* (Toh. 15), the *Naya-śatapañcaśatikā* (Toh. 17), the *Prajñāpāramitā-pañcaśatikā* (Toh. 18), the *Vajracchedikā* (Toh. 16), the *Prajñā-hṛdaya* (Toh. 21), the *Kauśika* (Toh. 19), the *Subāhuparipṛcchā-sūtra* (Toh. 70), the *Svalpākṣaraprajñāpāramitā* (Toh. 22), and the *Ekākṣarīmātā* (Toh. 23).

Some substitute the *Pañcaviṃśati-prajñāpāramitā-mukha* (Toh. 20) for the *Subāhuparipṛcchā-sūtra*. Our own school has not decided on seventeen "mother and son" works among the *Prajñāpāramitā sūtras*, because there are many more than those [to be considered].

The Last Wheel

The Last Promulgation, the Wheel of the Law which has a perfect and intensive analysis, was pronounced in such places as Vaiśālī to the innumerable Bodhisattvas rightly stationed in any of the vehicles of candidates for the high goal.

The *Saṃdhinirmocana* (Toh. 106) of the *sūtra* class is the basic *sūtra* of the Last Wheel. *Sūtras* that are consistent with its subject matter are classified as *sūtras* of the Last Wheel. Also, some characterize the *sūtras* of the Last Wheel as the "Wheel of Absolute Certainty" (**paramārtha-viniścaya-cakra*).

/ kha cig tiṅ ṅe ḥdzin rgyal poḥi mdo / saṅs rgyas phal po che / laṅ kar gśegs pa rnams bkaḥ tha mar ḥdren pa mi ḥthad de / spyir chos thams cad bden par grub pas stoṅ par ston paḥi theg chen gyi mdo yin na bkaḥ bar par gtogs śiṅ / mthar thug theg pa gcig tu ston paḥi mdo yin na yaṅ der gtogs la / ṅo bo ñid gsum las kun brtags bden par ma grub ciṅ / gźan dbaṅ daṅ / yoṅs grub bden par ston paḥi mdo yin na bkaḥ tha maḥi mdor gtogs śiṅ / mthar thug theg pa gsum du ston paḥi theg chen gyi mdo yin na yaṅ der gtogs pa las / tiṅ ṅe ḥdzin rgyal po sogs mdo gsum po de ni / chos thams cad bden par med pa daṅ / mthar thug theg pa gcig tu ston pa śa stag yin paḥi phyir ro /

/ yaṅ bde gśegs sñiṅ poḥi mdo / ḥphags pa gzuṅs kyi dbaṅ phyug rgyal pos źus paḥi mdo / mya ṅan las ḥdas pa chen poḥi mdo / sor moḥi ḥphreṅ ba la phan paḥi mdo / dpal ḥphreṅ seṅ geḥi ṅa ros źus paḥi mdo / ye śes snaṅ ba rgyan gyi mdo / ḥphel ba daṅ ḥgrib pa med par bstan paḥi mdo / rṅa bo che chen poḥi mdo / rnam par mi rtog pa la ḥjug paḥi gzuṅs / mdo dgoṅs pa ṅes par ḥgrel pa ste / bcu po de la jo mo naṅ pas sñiṅ poḥi mdo bcu źes zer te / bkaḥ ḥkhor lo tha mar ḥdod ciṅ ṅes don du ḥdod do / mdo de dag kyis bde gśegs sñiṅ po daṅ / rdzogs paḥi saṅs rgyas kyi ṅo bo ñid sku don gcig ciṅ / bden par grub pa / rtag brtan ther zug / ḥdus ma byas mtshan dpes brgyan pa / sems can thams cad kyi rgyud la ḥkhor ba thog ma med pa nas ñon moṅs paḥi sbubs na raṅ chas su yod pa de dpe dgu don dguḥi sgo nas bstan par ḥdod la / ḥkhor lo daṅ po daṅ bar pa draṅ don du ḥdod do /

[4] The Sanskrit title is as the work is quoted in the *Ratnagotravibhāga Mahāyānottaratantraśāstra*, edited by E. H. Johnston (Patna, 1950); cf. his foreword, viii. The work is included in the list of ten *sūtras* on the strength of the quotations in the *Mahāyānottaratantra*, or *Uttaratantra*, as the *śāstra* is referred to in Tibet through the Tibetan equivalents of these titles, especially *Rgyud bla ma*. So far there is no evidence that the *Anūnatvāpūrṇatvanirdeśaparivarta* was translated into Tibetan under a different title or as a section of a larger work.

[5] The nine examples are available in Sanskrit in Johnston, ed. (*op. cit.*), pp. 59-60 (verses I, 96, 97):

Like the Buddha in an ugly lotus, honey in bees,
Kernels in husks, gold in alluvium, a treasure in the earth,
The stages beginning with the sprout in a tiny seed,
The body of the Victorious One in sodden clothes;
Royalty in the womb of a vile woman,
And a precious image in clods –
So also does this element abide in the sentient beings,
Who are obscured by adventitious corruption and defilement.

/ buddhaḥ kupadme madhu makṣikāsu
tuṣesu sārāṇy aśucau suvarṇam /
nidhiḥ kṣitāv alpaphale 'ṇkurādi
praklinnavastreṣu jinātmabhāvaḥ //
/ jaghanyanārījaṭhare nṛpatvaṃ

Some classify the *Samādhirāja-sūtra*, the *Buddhāvataṃsaka*, and the *Laṅkāvatāra* under the Last Promulgation, but this is not valid. In general, when a *Mahāyāna sūtra* teaches that all entities (*sarvabhāvāḥ*) are void in the sense of real production (**tāttvika-siddhyā śūnya*), it belongs to the Intermediate Promulgation. Moreover, when a *sūtra* teaches the ultimate oneness of the vehicles, it also belongs there. On the other hand, when a *sūtra* teaches that, of the three characteristics (*lakṣaṇa*), (1) the imaginary one (*parikalpita*) is not really produced, (2) the dependency one (*paratantra*) and (3) the absolute one (*parinispanna*) are really produced, it belongs among the *sūtras* of the Last Promulgation. Moreover, when a *Mahāyāna sūtra* teaches that the vehicles are ultimately three, it also belongs there. But the three *sūtras*, the *Samādhirāja*, etc., show only that all entities do not really exist and that the vehicles are ultimately one.

The Tathāgata-garbha sūtras

Furthermore, the ten *sūtras*, *Tathāgatagarbha-sūtra* (Toh. 258), *Dhāraṇīśvararājaparipṛcchā* (alias for the *Tathāgatamahākaruṇānirdeśa-sūtra*, Toh. 147), *Mahāparinirvāṇa-sūtra* (Toh. 120), *Ārya-aṅgulimālīya-sūtra* (Toh. 213), the *Jñānālokālaṃkāra-sūtra* (Toh. 100), the *Śrī-mālā-devī-siṃhanāda-sūtra* (Toh. 92), *Anūnatvāpūrṇatvanirdeśa-parivarta*,[4] *Mahābherīhāraka-sūtra* (Toh. 222), *Avikalpapraveśa-dhāraṇī* (Toh. 142), and *Saṃdhinirmocana-sūtra* (Toh. 106), are claimed by the Jo-mo-naṅ-pa school to be the ten [Tathāgata-] Garbha *sūtras* which, they maintain, are in the Last Wheel Promulgation and which, they maintain, have final meaning (*nītārtha*). They maintain that those *sūtras* teach by way of the nine meanings of nine examples[5] that the Embryo of the Tathāgata (*tathāgatagarbha*) means the same as the Intrinsic-nature Body (*svabhāvakāya*) of a Complete Buddha, that it is really produced, permanent, steadfast, eternal, adorned with unconditioned (*asaṃskṛta*) characteristics and minor marks, and that it has been in the stream of consciousness of all sentient beings since beginningless "cycles of life", but was covered by corruptions (*kleśa*) which have had the appearance of a self; and they maintain that the First and Intermediate Wheels are of provisional meaning (*neyārtha*).

---

yathā bhaven mṛtsu ca ratnabimbam /
āgantukakleśamalāvṛteṣu
sattveṣu tadvat sthita eṣa dhātuḥ //

/ bu ston rin po ches mdo bcu po de bkaḥ tha maḥi mdo yin źiṅ / mdo de dag las jo naṅ pas ḥdod pa ltar du bstan paḥi dbaṅ du mdzad nas de dag draṅ don du bźed la / ṅo bo ñid kyi sku daṅ / bde gśegs sñiṅ po don gcig par mdzad nas / de sems can kyi rgyud la med par bźed ciṅ / bkaḥ bar pa kho na ṅes don du bźed do /

/ mdo bcu po de brjod bya phyogs mthun du ḥdod pa mi ḥthad de / mdo dgoṅs pa ṅes ḥgrel gyi ḥphags pa spyan ras gzigs dbaṅ phyug gis źus paḥi leḥu raṅs pos mthar thug theg pa gsum du bstan / byaṅ chub sems dpaḥ don dam yaṅ dag ḥphags kyis źus paḥi leḥu raṅs pos / gźan dbaṅ daṅ / yoṅs grub bden par grub par bstan / byams mgon gyis źus paḥi leḥu raṅs pos yid śes las ṅo bo tha dad paḥi kun gźiḥi rnam śes yod par bstan la / mdo gźan dgu po de thams cad kyis chos thams cad bden par med pa daṅ / mthar thug theg pa gcig tu bstan ciṅ / kun gźiḥi rnam śes med paḥi dbaṅ du byas nas bstan paḥi phyir ro /

/ yaṅ jo naṅ paḥi raṅ lugs la gźan dbaṅ ri boṅ gi rva daṅ mtshuṅs śiṅ / mthar thug theg pa gcig tu ḥdod pa daṅ / mdo dgoṅs pa ṅes ḥgrel ṅes don du byas nas raṅ lugs kyi śes byed du byed pa ḥgal pa yin no /

raṅ gi lugs ni / bde gśegs sñiṅ po sems can gyi rgyud la med na / sems can gyi rgyud la saṅs rgyas kyi rgyu med pas sems can ḥtshaṅ rgya ba mi srid par ḥgyur la / bde gśegs sñiṅ po daṅ / ṅo bo ñid sku don gcig ciṅ / de sems can thams cad kyi rgyud la yod na sems can thams cad saṅs rgyas yin par ḥgyur źiṅ / saṅs rgyas slar ḥtshaṅ mi rgya bas sems can ḥtshaṅ rgya ba mi srid par ḥgyur baḥi phyir lugs de gñis ka yaṅ mi ḥdod do /

/ ḥo na ji lta bu źe na / theg pa chen po rgyud bla ma las / bde bar gśegs paḥi sñiṅ po daṅ / bde bar gśegs paḥi khams don gcig tu gsuṅs śiṅ / deḥi ḥgrel par / khams kyi don ni ḥdir rgyuḥi don yin no / źes

[6] That work is especially concerned with the "element" (*dhātu*) of the Tathāgata[6] also called the "embryo" (*garbha*) of the Tathāgata, and the "species" (*gotra*) as is pointed out by Obermiller, with different translations for those terms, in the foreword to his translation from Tibetan (before the Sanskrit was edited by Johnston), "The Sublime Science of the Great Vehicle to Salvation", *Acta Orientalia*, Vol. IX, (1931), p. 89.

Bu-ston rin-po-che took the position that those ten *sūtras* are *sūtras* of the Last Promulgation. While he was influenced to teach concerning those *sūtras* [the interpretation] maintained by the Jo-naṅ-pa, he took them as having provisional meaning; and while he took the Svabhāva-kāya and the Tathāgata-Garbha as having the same meaning, he held it not to be in the stream of consciousness of a sentient being; and he held that only the Intermediate Promulgation has final meaning.

It is not valid to maintain that there is consistency of subject matter in those ten *sūtras*. All of the chapter "Asked by Ārya Avalokiteśvara" of the *Saṃdhinirmocana-sūtra* is devoted to teaching that ultimately the vehicles are three; all of the chapter "Asked by the Bodhisattva Paramārthasamudgata" teaches that *paratantra* and *pariniṣpanna* are really produced; all of the chapter "Asked by Maitreya-nātha" treats the store consciousness (*ālaya-vijñāna*) as different in essence from the mind-based perception (*mano-vijñāna*). But all the other nine *sūtras* teach that all the natures have no reality and that the vehicles are ultimately one, because they teach on the assumption that there is no store consciousness.

Moreover, according to the Jo-naṅ-pa's own school, *paratantra* is equivalent to a hare's horn (*śaśa-viṣāṇa*) [i.e. an impossibility] and the vehicles are ultimately one. But if we take the *Saṃdhinirmocana-sūtra* to be of final meaning (*nītārtha*) [as the Jo-naṅ-pa maintains], the contradiction is made obvious by their own school [which disagrees with a *sūtra* they say has 'final meaning'].

According to our own school.

(a) if there were no Embryo of the Tathāgata in the stream of consciousness of a sentient being, there would be no cause (*hetu*) of becoming "fully expanded" (*vibuddha*) in the stream of consciousness of a sentient being, and hence there would be no possibility that a sentient being could become "awakened" (*buddha*) and "expanded" (*vibuddha*);

(b) if Embryo of the Tathāgata meant the same as Intrinsic-nature Body (*svabhāva-kāya*) and were in the stream of consciousness of all sentient beings, all sentient beings would be "fully expanded"; and since what is "fully expanded" does not again become "awakened, but not expanded", there would be no possibility that a sentient being could become "awakened" (*buddha*) and "expanded". Therefore our school does not admit either one of those two theories.

Well then, what is the situation? The *Mahāyānottaratantra* (Toh. 4024) speaks of Embryo of the Tathāgata (*tathāgata-garbha*) and Element of the Tathāgata (*tathāgata-dhātu*) as identical.[6] The commentary (Toh. 4025) says, "The meaning of 'element' here is the meaning of

gsuṅs pas bde bar gśegs paḥi sñiṅ po ni / bde bar gśegs paḥi rgyu / źes bya ba yin no / de yaṅ saṅs rgyas kyi rgyu tsam la bde bar gśegs paḥi sñiṅ po źes ni mi byaḥo /

/ ḥo na ji lta bu źe na / sems bden par grub pas stoṅ paḥi stoṅ ñid de la sems kyi chos ñid raṅ bźin rnam dag ces bya ste / de yaṅ glo bur gyi dri ma daṅ ma bral baḥi gnas skabs kyi sems kyi chos ñid raṅ bźin rnam dag de la bde bar gśegs paḥi sñiṅ po ḥam / raṅ bźin du gnas paḥi rigs / źes byaḥo / glo bur gyi dri ma ma lus pa daṅ bral baḥi gnas skabs kyi sems kyi chos ñid raṅ bźin rnam dag de la / ṅo bo ñid skuḥam / ḥgog bden mthar thug gam / bral ḥbras mthar thug gam / dag pa gñis ldan gyi chos ñid dam / dag pa gñis ldan gyi chos sku źes byaḥo / glo bur gyi dri ma źes bya ba ni / ñon moṅs pa daṅ / śes byaḥi sgrib pa gñis so /

/ des na ṅo bo ñid sku yin na bde gśegs sñiṅ po ma yin dgos pa yin te / glo bur gyi dri ma daṅ bral ba yin na / ma bral ba ma yin dgos paḥi phyir ro /

/ raṅ lugs la yaṅ bde gśegs sñiṅ po daṅ ṅo bo ñid skuḥi rnam graṅs de dag / ḥdus ma byas śiṅ dṅos po med pa / rtag brtan ther zug yin gyi / bden par grub pa ni ma yin no /

/ ḥkhor lo gsum las daṅ po ni theg dman gyi sde snod daṅ / gźan gñis theg chen gyi sde snod do / de yaṅ ḥkhor lo daṅ pos ñan thos paḥi lta ba ston / bar pas dbu maḥi lta ba ston / tha mas sems tsam gyi lta ba ston la / des na ḥkhor lo bar pa ṅes don daṅ / gźan gñis draṅ don no /

/ saṅs rgyas kyi bkaḥ thams cad gsuṅ rab yan lag bcu gñis su ḥdu ste / bcu gñis gaṅ źe na / slob dpon śānti-pas brgyad stoṅ ḥgrel pa sñiṅ po mchog las /

/ mdo sde dbyaṅs bsñad luṅ bstan daṅ /
/ tshigs bcad ched brjod gleṅ gźi daṅ /

[7] Johnston, ed. (*op. cit.*), p. 72, line 10: / hetvartho ’tra dhātvarthaḥ /. This is immediately preceded by: / atas tat prāpyate hetus tathāgatadhātur iti /.

'cause'."[7] Therefore, the Embryo of the Tathāgata is a *cause* of the Tathāgata. On the other hand, not in every case is a cause of Buddhahood to be called Embryo of the Tathāgata.

Well then, what is the situation? The *citta* is void of real production, but in that voidness the supreme state of thought (*citta-dharmatā*) is called "intrinsically pure" (*svabhāvaviśuddhi*).

Furthermore,

(a) that supreme state of thought, intrinsically pure, when in conditions not free from adventitious defilements, is the Embryo of the Tathāgata or Species intrinsically abiding;

(b) that supreme state of thought, intrinsically pure, when in conditions completely free from adventitious defilements, is the Intrinsic-nature Body, also called "ultimate of the truth of cessation", "ultimate fruit of freedom [from fetters]", "the supreme state possessed of two purities", or "Dharma-kāya possessed of two purities". "Adventitious defilements" means the two obscurations (*āvaraṇa*) of corruption (*kleśa*) and of the knowable (*jñeya*).

Thus, it must be that the Intrinsic-nature Body (*svabhāva-kāya*) is not the Embryo of the Tathāgata, because if there is freedom from adventitious defilement, it must be that there is no lack of (such) freedom.

Moreover, in our school, the terms "unconditioned" (*asaṃskṛta*), "non-concrete" (*abhāva*), and "permanent, steadfast, eternal" pertain to [both] Embryo of the Tathāgata and Intrinsic-nature Body; but not the term "real production" (T. *bden par grub pa*).

Of the three wheels, the first is the Hīnayāna collection (*piṭaka*); the other two, the Mahāyāna collection. Furthermore, the first wheel teaches the Śrāvaka doctrine; the intermediate one teaches the Mādhyamika doctrine; the last one teaches the Cittamātra doctrine. Consequently, the intermediate wheel has final meaning and the other two have provisional meaning.

2. ASSEMBLING THE PROMULGATIONS

All the promulgations of the Buddha are comprised by the twelve groupings of the Sacred Word (*pravacana*). The preceptor Śānti-pā states them in his *Aṣṭasāhasrikāprajñāpāramitāpañjikāsārottamā-nāma* (Toh. 3803):

> Aphorisms (*sūtra*), [the preceding in] Mingled Prose and Verse
> (*geya*), Prophecies (*vyākaraṇa*), Verses (*gāthā*), Joyous

/ rtogs brjod de lta bu byuṅ daṅ /
/ skyes rabs śin tu rgyas pa daṅ /
/ rmad byuṅ gtan la phab paḥi sde /
/ gsuṅ rab yan lag bcu gñis yin /

źes gsuṅs pa rnams so /

/ de dag las gleṅ gźi / rtogs brjod / de lta bu byuṅ ba / skyes rabs daṅ bźi gcig tu bsdus pa ni / gsuṅ rab yan lag dguḥo /

/ yaṅ saṅs rgyas kyi gsuṅ rab daṅ bkaḥ don gcig ciṅ / de la dbye na źal nas gsuṅs paḥi bkaḥ daṅ / byin gyis brlabs paḥi bkaḥ daṅ / rjes su gnaṅ baḥi bkaḥ daṅ gsum mo / daṅ po ni / ḥphags pa sdud pa lta buḥo / gñis pa la gsum las / skus byin gyis brlabs paḥi bkaḥ ni mdo sde sa bcu pa lta bu / gsuṅ gis byin gyis brlabs paḥi bkaḥ ni ma skyes dgraḥi ḥgyod pa bsal baḥi mdo lta bu / thugs kyis byin gyis brlabs paḥi bkaḥ la gsum las / thugs tiṅ ṅe ḥdzin gyis byin gyis brlabs paḥi bkaḥ ni śes rab sñiṅ po lta bu / thugs thugs rjes byin gyis brlabs paḥi bkaḥ ni / gnod sbyin daṅ lha daṅ klu la sogs pa rnams kyis raṅ raṅ gi sṅags smras pa rnams saṅs rgyas kyi thugs rjes ḥbras bu khyad par can ḥbyuṅ baḥi sṅags su byin gyis brlabs pa lta bu / thugs bden paḥi stobs kyis byin gyis brlabs paḥi bkaḥ ni / bcom ldan ḥdas kyis bden paḥi stobs thugs kyis brjod paḥi mthus / ri daṅ / śiṅ daṅ / rtsig pa sogs las chos kyi smra byuṅ ba lta buḥo /

/ rjes su gnaṅ baḥi bkaḥ ni / bcom ldan ḥdas kyis chos yaṅ dag par sdud paḥi mdo las / dge sloṅ dag ṅaḥi gsuṅ rab rnams kyi thog mar ḥdi skad bdag gis thos pa dus gcig na / źes bya ba la sogs pa daṅ / bar bar du ḥtshams sbyor gyi tshig rnams chug la sdus śig ces gsuṅs pas / bcom ldan ḥdas mya ṅan las bzla baḥi tshul bstan paḥi rjes la / ñan thos rnams kyis thog mar ḥdi skad bdag gis thos pa dus gcig na / źes bya ba la sogs pa daṅ / bar bar du ḥtshams sbyor la sogs pa gsuṅ rab la bcug pa lta buḥo /

Impersonal Utterances (*udāna*), Instructive Personal Discourses (*nidāna*), Parables (*avadāna*), Legends (*itivṛttaka*), The Bodhisattva Lives of the Buddha (*jātaka*), Grand Scripture (*vaipulya*), the Marvellous (*adbhutadharma*), and Explanation (*upadeśa*), are the twelve groupings of the Sacred Word.

If, among those, the Instructive Personal Discourses, Parables, Legends, and Bodhisattva Lives of the Buddha be subsumed under one category, then there are nine groupings of the Sacred Word.

Moreover, the Buddha's Sacred Word and Promulgations being identical, the Sacred Word may be divided into three classes: 1. Promulgation expressed with his own mouth; 2. Promulgation through blessing (*adhiṣṭhāna*); 3. Promulgation by authorization (*anujñā*).

1. (Promulgation expressed with his own mouth) — for example, the *Āryasañcaya* (Toh. 13).

2. (Promulgation through blessing) — this is further divided into three:

a. Promulgation through blessing of Body — for example, the *Daśabhūmikasūtra* (a chapter of the *Avataṃsaka*, which is Toh. 44);

b. Promulgation through blessing of Speech — for example, the *Ajātaśatrukaukṛtyavinodana-sūtra* (Toh. 216);

c. Promulgation through blessing of Mind — this is further divided into three:

(1). Promulgation through blessing of Mind Samādhi — for example, the *Prajñāhṛdaya* (Toh. 21);

(2). Promulgation through blessing of Mind Compassion — for example, the individual *mantras* expressed by *yakṣas*, *devas*, *nāgas*, etc., which are blessed by the compassion of the Buddha into *mantras* that originate superior fruit;

(3). Promulgation through blessing of Mind Truth-Force — for example, the words of the Doctrine (*dharma*), which proceed from mountains, trees, walls, and so forth, through the force of having been uttered by the Bhagavat mentally with the power of truth (*satya-bala*).

3. Promulgation by authorization — for example, the Bhagavat said in the *Dharmasaṃgīti-sūtra* (Toh. 238): "Mendicants, my Sacred Words (*pravacana*) must be introduced with the phrase, Thus I have heard on a certain occasion" (*evaṃ mayā śrutam ekasmin samaye*)', and so on; and, "At intervals [appropriate] connecting phrases should be inserted." Therefore, after the Bhagavat had displayed the method of passing into Nirvāṇa, the Śrāvakas introduced the Sacred Word (*pravacana*) with "Thus I have heard on a certain occasion" and so on, and at intervals inserted connecting phrases.

/ yaṅ rgyal baḥi gsuṅ rab thams cad sde snod gsum du ḥdu ste / lhag pa tshul khrims kyi bslab pa brjod byaḥi gtso bor ston pa ḥdul baḥi sde snod / lhag pa tiṅ ṅe ḥdzin gyi bslab pa brjod byaḥi gtso bor ston pa mdo sdeḥi sde snod / lhag pa śes rab kyi bslab pa brjod byaḥi gtso bor ston pa mṅon paḥi sde snod do / lhag pa tiṅ ṅe ḥdzin gyi bslab pa daṅ saṅs rgyas kyi bstan paḥi źi gnas don gcig la / lhag pa śes rab kyi bslab pa daṅ lhag mthoṅ don gcig go /

/ de la yaṅ gsuṅ rab yan lag bcu gñis kyi daṅ po lṅa ni / theg dman gyi mdo sdeḥi sde snod daṅ / de nas bźi ni ḥdul baḥi sde snod de / de la theg pa gñis kaḥi ḥdul baḥi sde snod yod do / tha ma gsum ni theg chen gyi mdo sdeḥi sde snod do / de dag gi bar bar na chos rnams kyi raṅ daṅ spyiḥi mtshan ñid ston pa thor bu thor bur gnas pa rnams ni mṅon paḥi sde snod do / mṅon pa kun las btus pa ltar na / gtan la phab pa bstan paḥi sde / mṅon paḥi sde snod de / de la theg pa gñis kaḥi mṅon paḥi sde snod yod do /

/ yaṅ rgyal baḥi gsuṅ rab thams cad chos kyi phuṅ po brgyad khri bźi stoṅ du ḥdu ste / gdul byaḥi rgyud kyi ḥdod chags la śas cher spyod pa ñi khri chig stoṅ daṅ / źe sdaṅ la śas cher spyod pa daṅ / gti mug la śas cher spyod pa daṅ / de gsum cha mñam la spyod pa ñi khri chig stoṅ re ste / ñon moṅs pa brgyad khri bźi stoṅ gi gñen por gsuṅs so /

/ tshad ni ñan thos pa kha cig gis / mṅon pa sde bdun gyi ya gyal gyi chos kyi phuṅ po źes paḥi bstan bcos gcig yod pa de chos phuṅ gcig gi tshad de / de la ślo-ka stoṅ yod ces ḥdod do / yaṅ ñan thos pa kha cig gis phuṅ po daṅ skye mched la sogs paḥi don tshan re rdzogs par ston paḥi gsuṅ rab tshan pa re chos phuṅ rer ḥdod do / theg chen pa kha cig glaṅ po che rab brtan gyi rgyab khal non paḥi snag tshas chos phuṅ gcig ḥbri bar nus so / źes paḥo /

/ raṅ gi lugs ni / slob dpon dbyig gñen gyis ñon moṅs pa brgyad khri bźi stoṅ las / ñon moṅs pa re reḥi gñen po rdzogs par ston paḥi gsuṅ rab tshan pa re la chos phuṅ re rer gsuṅs pa ltar ḥdod do /

/ bcom ldan ḥdas mya ṅan las ḥdas paḥi tshul bstan paḥi ḥog tu bkaḥ bsdu ba rim pa gsum byuṅ tshul ni / bcom ldan ḥdas kyis chos kyi ḥkhor lo bskor baḥi mdzad pa zin nas bstan pa ḥod sruṅs chen po la gtad de /

Furthermore, all the Sacred Word of the Buddha is gathered into three collections. The one that teaches chiefly the Instruction in Higher Morality (*adhiśīla*) is the *Vinaya-piṭaka.* The one that teaches chiefly the Instruction in Higher Meditation (*adhisamādhi*) is the *Sūtra-piṭaka.* The one that teaches chiefly the Instruction in Higher Insight (*adhiprajñā*) is the *Abhidharma-piṭaka.* The Instruction in Higher Meditation is identical with calming (*śamatha*) as taught by the Buddha; and the Instruction in Higher Insight is identical with higher vision (*vipaśyanā*).

Moreover, the first five of the twelve groupings of the Sacred Word are the *Sūtra-piṭaka* of the Lower Vehicle (*hīnayāna*). The next four are the *Vinaya-piṭaka*; and it is the *Vinaya-piṭaka* of both Vehicles. The last three are the *Sūtra-piṭaka* of the Great Vehicle (*mahāyāna*). Within them, the passages scattered at random which teach the individual and universal characteristics of natures (*dharma-svalakṣaṇa* and *dharma-sāmānyalakṣaṇa*) constitute the *Abhidharma-piṭaka.* According to the *Abhidharmasamuccaya* (Toh. 4049), the section [of the Sacred Word] that teaches the Explanation (*upadeśa*) is the *Abhidharma-piṭaka,* and in it is the *Abhidharma-piṭaka* of both Vehicles.

Again, it has been proclaimed that all the Sacred Word of the Buddha is incorporated in the *dharma-skandha* of the 84,000 *dharmas,* which are antidotes for the 84,000 corruptions (*kleśa*) as follows: 21,000 practices in which passion (*rāga*) predominates in the stream of consciousness of the candidates; a like number of practices in which hatred (*dveṣa*) predominates; the same number for delusion (*moha*); and 21,000 of practising the three [poisons] in equal proportion.

In regard to its size, some Śrāvakas maintain that of the seven sections of the Abhidharma, alone the treatise (*śāstra*) called *Dharmaskandha* is the size of a single *dharmaskandha,* that in it are one thousand *ślokas.* Other Śrāvakas maintain that each section of Sacred Word that fully explains a department of meaning, such as "aggregates" (*skandha*) and "sensory bases" (*āyatana*), is a *dharmaskandha.* Some Mahāyānists assert that one *dharmaskandha* is the amount that can be written with all the ink one strong elephant can carry on his back.

Our own school follows Vasubandhu, who maintains that one *dharmaskandha* is tantamount to that portion of the Sacred Word which suffices to counteract one of the 84,000 corruptions.

After the Bhagavat's entrance into Nirvāṇa, there were three steps in the compiling of his Promulgations. When the Bhagavat had finished setting the wheel of the law into motion, he entrusted it to Mahākāśyapa. Then,

dpyid zla tha chuṅ skar ma sa gaḥi ña baḥi tshes bco lṅaḥi nub mo rtsva mchog gi groṅ khyer du mya ṅan las bzla baḥi tshul bstan to /

/ deḥi dbyar de rgyal poḥi khab kyi bde can maḥi phug tu rgyal po ma skyes dgras sbyin bdag byas nas / ḥphags pa ḥod sruṅs chen pos dge ḥdun gyi gnas brtan mdzad paḥi dgra bcom pa lṅa brgyas dbyar gnas par khas blaṅs so /

/ deḥi tshe dgra bcom pa lṅa brgyaḥi snam sbyar rnams brtsegs pa gdan du btiṅ baḥi steṅ du ḥphags pa kun dgaḥ bos ḥdzegs te / kha mñan yod du phyogs nas thal mo sbyar gdoṅ mchi ma daṅ bcas sñan paḥi gdaṅs daṅ bcas te / ḥdi skad bdag gis thos pa dus gcig na / źes bya ba la sogs pas / mdo sdeḥi sde snod bsdus so / deḥi don ni mdo sdeḥi sde snod ji sñed gsuṅs pa thams cad tshig gcig kyaṅ lhag chad med par blo las bton paḥo / de nas kun dgaḥ bo stan las babs te ḥkhod do / de nas ḥphags pa ñe bar ḥkhor gyis ḥdul baḥi sde snod bsdus so / de nas ḥphags pa ḥod sruṅs chen pos sṅa ma bźin du mṅon paḥi sde snod bsdus so /

/ de nas ḥod sruṅs chen po ḥdi sñam du bdag gis bstan paḥi bya ba cuṅ zad byas kyi / da ni mya ṅan las bzlaḥo dgoṅs nas / kun dgaḥ bo la bstan pa gtad de / khyod kyis kyaṅ bstan pa śa-naḥi gos can la gtoṅ cig ces gsuṅs nas / bcom ldan ḥdas kyi mchod rten brgyad la phyag ḥtshal du byon te / klu yul daṅ / lha yul du de bźin gśegs paḥi tshems mche ba re re bźugs pa la yaṅ phyag ḥtshal du byon nas slar byon te / rgyal po ma skyes dgra la sbron bu byon pas rgyal po gñid log par gzigs nas / ḥkhor rnams la / ṅa mya ṅan las bzla ba ḥdir sbron du byuṅ źes smras źig / ces gsuṅs te / lho phyogs kyi ri bya rkaṅ can źes bya ba / ri gsum ḥdus paḥi dbus su byon nas rdzu ḥphrul sna tshogs bstan te / rtsvaḥi stan la skyil mo kruṅ bcas / bcom ldan ḥdas kyis gnaṅ baḥi phyag dar khrod kyi snam sbyar de bsnams te / spur de ji srid rgyal ba byams pa ḥjig rten du chos ston par ḥgyur pa de srid du mi ḥjig ciṅ mdaṅs cuṅ zad kyaṅ ñams par mi ḥgyur par byin gyis brlabs te / mya ṅan las ḥdas so / de nas gnod sbyin rnams kyis ri gsum po de kha sbyar nas bźag go /

[8] The translation "asterism Viśākha" is due to Mkhas grub rje's *skar ma sa gaḥi ña ba*. If *skar ma* is omitted, or is considered superfluous, the translation should be "Vaiśākha month".

in the city of Kuśinagara, in the evening of the fifteenth day of the last month of Spring when the moon was full in the asterism Viśākhā,[8] he demonstrated the method of passing into Nirvāṇa.

a. *The first council*

During the summer season of the same year, with the sponsorship of King Ajātaśatru, the five hundred Arhats whom Kāśyapa had made Elders (*sthavira*) in the Saṃgha, took a promise to observe a summer session (*varṣa*) in the cave "She who holds bliss" (T. *bde can ma*) of the city Rājagṛha.

At that time the five hundred Arhats piled up their waist robes (*saṃghāṭī*) for a seat; the noble Ānanda ascended it, joined the palms of his hands in the direction of Śrāvastī, and with his face wet with tears spoke in a melodious voice, "Thus have I heard on a certain occasion", and so on. Thereby, the *Sūtra-piṭaka* was compiled. The meaning of this is that he recited every single word of the *Sūtra-piṭaka* from memory, without any additions or omissions. Having finished, he descended from the seat and took his (own) place. Then the noble Upāli compiled the *Vinaya-piṭaka*, and after him the noble Mahākāśyapa compiled in the same way the *Abhidharma-piṭaka*.

Thereupon, the noble Mahākāśyapa reflected, "I have already performed the requirements of the teaching in some degree; now I intend to enter Nirvāṇa." He entrusted the teaching to Ānanda with the words, "You, in turn, must entrust the teaching to Śāṇavāsa." Then he went to bow to the eight *stūpas* of the Bhagavat; and as in each country of the *nāgas* and *devas* there was a tooth of the Tathāgata, he went to those places to bow. Upon returning, he went to report to King Ajātaśatru, who happened to be sleeping. Therefore he said to the courtiers, "Tell the King I came here to report that I am about to enter *Nirvāṇa*." Then he went south to the Chicken-foot Mountain (*kukkuṭapāda*); and having entered [the valley] between the group of three mountains, he displayed various magical metamorphoses. Seated with folded legs on a seat of grass, he held up the waist robe patched with rags from rubbish heaps, which the Bhagavat had allowed him. Blessing his corpse so that it would not decompose, nor even its complexion deteriorate until the time when the Victor Maitreya shall appear in the world to teach the Law, he passed into *Nirvāṇa*. Thereupon, the Yakṣas merged the three mountains.

/ de nas śa-naḥi gos can rgya mtshor rin po che len du soṅ pa las ḥkhor te / bcom ldan ḥdas gaṅ na bźugs / lo lṅaḥi dus ston byaḥo / źes smras pa las / mya ṅan las ḥdas so / źes thos pas brgyal bar gyur to / brgyal ba saṅs nas ḥphags pa śā-ri-bu daṅ / moḥu-gal-gyi-bu daṅ / ḥod sruṅs chen po rnams dris pas kyaṅ mya ṅan las ḥdas so źes thos te / yaṅ brgyal lo / de saṅs nas / da lta su bźugs / kun dgaḥ bo bźugs so / de nas kun dgaḥ bo ḥkhor bcas spyan draṅs te lo lṅaḥi dus ston byas so / de nas kun dgaḥ bos śa-naḥi gos can rab tu byuṅ źiṅ bsñen par rdzogs nas / des kyaṅ sbyaṅs pas sde snod gsum la mkhas par gyur ciṅ dgra bcom par gyur to /

/ de nas ḥphags pa kun dgaḥ bos bstan paḥi bya ba rgya cher mdzad nas / dge sloṅ źig kha ton byed pa las /

/ gaṅ ni lo brgyar ḥtsho ba ni /
/ ṅes par chu la bya gag bźin /

źes ḥdon pa gsan te / bcom ldan ḥdas kyis de ltar ma gsuṅs kyi /

/ gaṅ na lo brgyar ḥtsho ba ni /
/ ṅes par skye źiṅ ḥjig pa yin /

źes ldogs śig ces gsuṅs pas / dge sloṅ des raṅ gi mkhan poḥi druṅ du phyin te ḥphags pa kun dgaḥ bo ḥdi skad gsuṅ ṅo / źes smras pas / mkhan po dge sloṅ de raṅ gis nor bar bstan pa de ma ḥdod nas / kun dgaḥ bo ni rgas gyur te / dran pa ñams pas brjod pa yin / źes smras so / de dge sloṅ des kun dgaḥ bo la smras pas / kun dgaḥ bo yid byuṅ ste / da ni saṅs rgyas kyi bstan pa yaṅ ḥdi ltar gyur pas mya ṅan las bzlaḥo sñam du dgoṅs te / śa-naḥi gos can la bstan pa gtad de / khyod kyis kyaṅ groṅ khyer bcom brlag gi spos ḥtshoṅ sbas paḥi bu ñe sbas la bstan pa gtod cig / de ni mtshan med paḥi saṅs rgyas su gyur nas saṅs rgyas kyi bya ba byed par de bźin gśegs pas luṅ bstan to / źes gsuṅs nas rgyal po ma skyes dgra la sbron du byon pa na rgyal po gñid log pas / ḥkhor rnams la kho bo ḥdir sbron du byuṅ źes smras śig ces gsuṅs nas / ḥkhor daṅ bcas te chu bo ga-ṅgāḥi ḥgram du gśegs so /

/ de nas rgyal po ma skyes dgra gdugs kyi yu ba chag pa rmis pa las / sad de smras pas / ḥkhor rnams kyis / ḥphags pa kun dgaḥ bo mya ṅan las bzla ba sbron du byon no / źes smras pas brgyal bar gyur to / brgyal pa saṅs nas glaṅ po che la źon te brgyugs nas chu bo ga-ṅgāḥi ḥgram du phyin to /

/ deḥi tshe yaṅs pa can gyi li-tsā-byi rnams lhas sbran pa la brten nas mchod paḥi yo byad maṅ po thogs te chu bo ga-ṅgāḥi ḥgram du lhags so / draṅ sroṅ źig kyaṅ ḥkhor lṅa brgya daṅ lhan cig tu lhags te / kun dgaḥ bo las rab tu byuṅ źiṅ bsñen par rdzogs par gsol bas / kun dgaḥ

Then Śāṇavāsa, having obtained jewels from the ocean, returned and said, "Where is the Bhagavat? He will be my teacher for five years." "Passed into *Nirvāṇa*", he heard and fainted. Regaining consciousness, he inquired after Śāriputra, Maudgalyāyana, and Mahākāśyapa, and when he learned that they too had entered *Nirvāṇa*, he fainted again. When he recovered, he asked, "Who now remains?" and was told, "Ānanda remains." So he invited Ānanda and his followers, and they taught him for five years. Thereupon, Ānanda made Śāṇavāsa a monk and ordained him. He applied himself and became expert in the three collections (*tripiṭaka*), and attained Arhatship.

After the noble Ānanda had performed on a large scale the duties of [spreading] the teaching, he heard a *bhikṣu* reciting the stanza.

He who lives a hundred years
Is certainly like a water fowl in water.

And so he said, "That is not what the Bhagavat has taught, but rather,

He who lives a hundred years
Certainly is born and dies."

The *bhikṣu* thereupon went to see his own master to report what Ānanda had said. The master, unwilling to admit to the *bhikṣu* his own error, said, "Ānanda has grown old and speaks with a deteriorated memory." When the *bhikṣu* repeated that to Ānanda, the latter, despairing, thought, "Now that the teaching of the Buddha has come to this, I should enter *Nirvāṇa*." Thereupon, he entrusted the teaching to Śāṇavāsa with the words, "You, in turn, must entrust the teaching to Upagupta, the boy who sells incense at Mathurā. Concerning him, the Tathāgata made a prophecy that, having become a Buddha without the (32) characteristics (*lakṣaṇa*), he will perform the duties of a Buddha." He then went to report to King Ajātaśatru, but it happened that the King was sleeping. So he told the courtiers, "Report to the King that I came here." And he proceeded with his retinue to the bank of the Ganges.

Meanwhile the King dreamed that the handle of his parasol had broken. When he awoke, he spoke about his dream, and the courtiers reported that the noble Ānanda had come to announce his imminent departure into *Nirvāṇa*. The King fainted. When he recovered consciousness, he mounted an elephant and hurried to the bank of the Ganges.

At that time having been apprised by a *deva*, the Licchāvis of the city of Vaiśālī, carrying many offering supplies, assembled on the bank of the Ganges. Also, a Ṛṣi and his retinue of 500 came there all together to ask Ānanda to make them monks and ordain them. Ānanda "mate-

bos chu bo ga-ṅgāḥi dbus su gliṅ źig sprul te / ñi maḥi guṅ la rab tu byuṅ źiṅ bsñen par rdzogs pas de ma thag tu dgra bcom pa thob ste / dgra bcom pa ñi ma guṅ ba ḥam / chu dbus pa źes byaḥo / de mkhan po mya ṅan las bzla baḥi sṅon du bdag bya ṅan las bzlaḥo sñam nas kun dgaḥ bo la źus pas / khyod de skad ma zer źig / de bźin gśegs pas kha che ni bsam gtan gyi gnas daṅ mthun pa ste / der dgra bcom pa ñi ma guṅ ba źes bya bas saṅs rgyas kyi bstan pa ḥjog par ḥgyur ro / źes luṅ bstan gyi / khyod der soṅ la saṅs rgyas kyi bstan pa źog cig ces gsuṅs te / des kyaṅ kha cher bstan pa rgya cher spel to /

/ de nas kun dgaḥ bo mya ṅan las ḥdas te / gduṅ cha gñis su bgos nas rgyal poḥi khab daṅ / yaṅs pa can du mchod rten re re byas so / de nas śa-naḥi gos can gyis saṅs rgyas kyi bstan paḥi bya ba rgya cher mdzad de / ñe sbas rab tu byuṅ źiṅ / bsñen par rdzogs te de la bstan pa gtad do / de nas ḥphags pa ñe sbas kyis bstan paḥi bya ba bsam gyis mi khyab pa mdzad do / slob ma dgra bcom pa re re byuṅ ba na brag phug ḥdom lṅa bcu pa źig tu so śiṅ sor lṅa pa re re dor bas de yoṅs su gaṅ bar gyur to / de nas des bstan pa dhi-dhi-ka la gtad / des nag po la gtad / des legs mthoṅ chen po la gtad de /

/ legs par gsuṅ mdzad thub paḥi dbaṅ po daṅ /
/ ḥod sruṅs kun dgaḥ śa-naḥi gos can daṅ /
/ ñe sbas dhi-dhi-ka daṅ nag po daṅ /
/ legs mthoṅ chen po bstan paḥi gtad rabs bdun /

źes so /

/ de nas bsdus gñis pa ni /

/ bcom ldan ḥdas mya ṅan las ḥdas nas lo brgya daṅ bcu ḥdas pa na yaṅs pa can gyi dge sloṅ rnams ruṅ ba ma yin paḥi gźi bcu spyod pas rñed pa daṅ ldan no / de na dgra bcom pa thams cad ḥdod ces bya ba rnam thar brgyad pa źig yod pa de sñiṅ las chuṅ ṅur gnas so /

/ groṅ khyer nor can źes bya ba nas / dgra bcom pa grags pa źes bya ba ḥkhor lṅa brgya daṅ bcas te yaṅs pa can du lhags so / yaṅs pa can gyi dge sloṅ rnams rñed pa ḥgod pa mthoṅ ste ciḥi phyir ḥdi dag rñed pa che bar gyur sñam du brtags pas ruṅ ba ma yin paḥi gźi bcu spyad pa las

rialized" (T. *sprul*) an island in the middle of the Ganges river; and when the sun reached the zenith, they became monks, were given ordination, and immediately afterwards attained Arhatship. They were called the "Noon Arhats", or the "Men of the middle of the river". Then the Ṛṣi reflected, "I should enter *Nirvāṇa* before my superior (*upādhyāya*)." He asked Ānanda, who replied, "Do not say that. The Tathāgata has prophesied that Kashmir, being a place fit for meditation, will be where the Arhat Madhyāntika ('Zenith of the Sun') will establish the teaching of the Buddha. That being the case, go there and establish the teaching of the Buddha." He then propagated the teaching far and wide in Kashmir.

Then Ānanda entered *Nirvāṇa* and his relics were divided into two portions and *stūpas* erected at both Rājagṛha and Vaiśālī. Śāṇavāsa performed far and wide the duties of the Buddha's teaching, received Upagupta into the order, ordained him, and entrusted the teaching to him. The noble Upagupta performed the duties of the teaching in a miraculous way. Each of his disciples became an Arhat; [they were so numerous that] a cave of fifty fathoms was completely filled by each of them throwing into it a five-finger breadth of toothpicks. Then he entrusted the doctrine to Dhītika, who in turn entrusted it to Kāla, who in turn entrusted it to Mahāsudarśana. It is said,

> The powerful one of the *munis* made the [teaching].
> well expressed (*subhāṣita*);
> And Kāśyapa, Ānanda, Śāṇavāsa, Upagupta,
> Dhītika, Kāla, and Mahāsudarśana,
> Are the seven hierarchs of the teaching.

b. *The second council*

One hundred and ten years after the *Nirvāṇa* of the Bhagavat, the *bhikṣus* of Vaiśālī were committing the ten transgressions, thereby amassing goods. At that place lived an Arhat by the name of Sarvakāmin who, having experienced the eight releases (*aṣṭau vimokṣāḥ*), abided with few desires.

An Arhat named Yaśas, together with five hundred followers, arrived at Vaiśālī from the town of *Dhanika. When he saw that the monks of Vaiśālī had built up great holdings, he wondered how it was done and learned that the monks committed the ten transgressions. The Arhat presented himself to Sarvakāmin, saluted him, and asked, "Noble one,

byuṅ bar mkhyen te / dgra bcom pa thams cad ḥdod kyi druṅ du phyin nas phyag ḥtshal te / ḥphags pa a-la-la źes bya baḥi gźi spyad du ruṅ ṅam / des smras pa / ci źig / mi mthun paḥi las byas nas mjug tu thams cad kyis a-la-la źes brjod pas las ḥchags źes zer ro / smras pa mi ruṅ ṅo / ltuṅ ba cir ḥgyur / ñes byas so / gaṅ du bcas / mñan yod duḥo / su la bcas / drug sde laḥo / ḥo na yaṅs pa can gyi dge sloṅ dag de ltar spyod na bzod dam / mi bzod do / ḥo na ji ltar bgyi / spaṅ bar byaḥo / de bźin du gźi bcu po thams cad brjod de yaṅs pa can gyi dge sloṅ rnams spaṅ bar bgros so /

/ de nas ḥphags pa thams cad ḥdod kyis yaṅs pa can gyi dge sloṅ rnams dbyuṅ bar bya yi / khyod phyogs tshal du soṅs śig / źes gsuṅs te / dgra bcom pa grags pas rdzu ḥphrul gyis dmar bu can la sogs paḥi yul so sor phyin nas dgra bcom pa rnams la yaṅs pa can gyi dge sloṅs rnams gźi bcu spyod pa brjod nas / kho bos ga-ṇḍi brduṅs pa na khyed so so nas byon cig / ces bskul te slar yaṅs pa can du byon nas / gtsug lag khaṅ sgo bcad de / ga-ṇḍi brduṅs pas ḥphags pa kun dgaḥ bos mkhan po mdzad paḥi dge sloṅ dgra bcom pa bdun brgyar gcig gis ma chog pa ḥdus so / yul dmar bu can du dgra bcom pa sgur skyog ces bya bas ḥgog pa la sñoms par źugs pas ga-ṇḍi ma thos so /

/ de nas dgra bcom pa grags pas dge ḥdun la phyag ḥtshal nas / gźi bcu brjod de / a-la-laḥi gźi spyod du ruṅ ṅam / mi ruṅ ṅo / ḥo na dge sloṅ kha cig gis de lta bu spyod na bzod dam / mi bzod do / ḥo na ji ltar bgyi / spaṅ bar byaḥo / de bźin du dge sloṅ so sor re re nas dris te / gźi bcu thams cad brjod nas thugs bstun no /

/ deḥi tshe dgra bcom pa sgur skyog ḥgog pa las laṅs pa na / lhas khyod daṅ mkhan po gcig paḥi dgra bcom pa bdun brgyar gcig gis ma chog pa yaṅs pa can du ḥdus so / źes smras pas / rdzu ḥphrul gyis yaṅs pa can gyi sgo druṅ du lhags te sgo brduṅs so / grags pas su yin źes smras pas /

/ gaṅ dag dmar bu can na gnas pa yi /
/ dge sloṅ maṅ du thos pa ḥdul ba ḥdzin /
/ de dag rnams las gźan źig ḥdir mchis te /
/ dbaṅ po dul źes bya ba sgo na ḥdug /

ces smras so / dbaṅ po dul ba gźan yaṅ yod na khyod su yin źes smras pas / sgur skyog go / źes zer pa thos pas sgo phyeḥo /

is it right to do the thing called '*alala*'?" The other Arhat asked, "What is that?" "It is claimed that after doing a wrong deed, all exclaim '*alala*'! and assume their deed has been confessed." [Sarvakāmin] said, "That is improper." "What kind of a transgression is it?" "It is an evil action" (*duṣkṛtam*). "Where was that decreed?" "In Śrāvastī." "For whom was it decreed?" "For the group of six." "May then these things, if practised by the *bhikṣus* of Vaiśālī, be tolerated or not?" "They may not." "What then should be done?" "They should be expelled!" Accordingly, it was decided that the *bhikṣus* of Vaiśālī who advocated the ten transgressions should be expelled.

Thereupon, the noble Sarvakāmin said, "As the *bhikṣus* of Vaiśālī have to be expelled, go and find those who are on your side." The Arhat Yaśas, using his magical power (*ṛddhi*), then went to Pāṭaliputra and various other places and informed the Arhats that the *bhikṣus* of Vaiśālī were practising the ten transgressions. He exhorted them, "When I strike the gong (*gaṇḍi*), you must come from every quarter." Returning to Vaiśālī, he shut the temple door and struck the gong. Thereupon, all but one of the seven hundred *bhikṣu* Arhats who had been made "superiors" by the noble Ānanda assembled there. In Pāṭaliputra, the Arhat named Kubjita did not hear the gong because he was in the [trance known as] cessation equipoise (*nirodha-samāpatti*).

Then the Arhat Yaśas made salutation to the Saṃgha and spoke of the ten transgressions. He asked if the [outcry of] *alala* was proper; the reply was, "It is not proper." He asked if some *bhikṣus* who were practising in that manner should be tolerated; the reply was, "They should not be tolerated." When he asked, "What should be done about it, then?" the reply was, "They should be expelled." In that way, having asked every *bhikṣu* individually, after all of the ten transgressions were set forth, their minds were unanimous.

At that time the Arhat Kubjita emerged from his cessation equipoise, and a *deva* said to him, "You are the one 'superior' missing from the seven hundred Arhats, less one, who are assembled at Vaiśālī." By his magical power he arrived at the gate of Vaiśālī and knocked. Yaśas asked, "Who is it?" Thereupon, he replied,

> There are *bhikṣus* dwelling in Pāṭaliputra
> Who are very learned and adhere to the Vinaya;
> One of them has arrived and stands at the gate;
> He is called 'tamer of the senses'.

Then it was said, "As others also have tamed the senses, who are you?" He replied, "I am Kubjita." Hearing that, they opened the gate for him.

/ de nas las byas te sgo phye nas ga-ṇḍi brduṅs te yaṅs pa can gyi dge sloṅ rnams naṅ du bcug nas / ruṅ ba ma yin paḥi gźi bcu sun phyuṅ ste yaṅs pa can gyi dge sloṅ rnams la gnas dbyuṅ byas nas dgra bcom pa bdun brgyas bkra śis kyi gso sbyoṅ byas pas / lha rnams kyis chos ma yin paḥi phyogs ni pham mo / chos kyi phyogs ni rgyal lo / źes ched du brjod pa ched du brjod do /

/ de la bsdu ba gñis pa źes bya ste / sbyin bdag chos rgyal mya ṅan med kyis byas so /

/ bsdu ba gsum pa daṅ sde pa gyes tshul ni /

/ slob dpon legs ldan ḥbyed kyis rtog ge ḥbar ba daṅ / slob dpon dul ba lhaḥi sde pa tha dad pa bklags paḥi ḥkhor lo daṅ / slob dpon padma ḥbyuṅ gnas kyis mdzad paḥi dge tshul gyi lo dri ba rnams las bśad do /

/ de la lugs gcig la ston pa mya ṅan las ḥdas nas / lo brgya daṅ sum cu rtsa bdun ḥdas pa na / groṅ khyer skya boḥi bu źes bya bar / bdud sdig can bzaṅ po kun gyi mi mthun paḥi phyogs su gyur pa źes bya bas dgra bcom paḥi cha byad du sprul nas / rdzu ḥphrul sna tshogs bstan te dge ḥdun lta ba tha dad du phye nas ḥkhrug loṅ du gyur te lo drug cur mi mthun par gyur to / de nas dge sloṅ gnas maḥi bu źes bya bas dge ḥdun bsdus te rtsod pa bzlums pas chos phyogs su źi bar byas pa la bsdu ba gsum pa źes bya ste / sbyin bdag rgyal po dgaḥ bo daṅ padma chen po źes pa gñis kyis byas so /

/ yaṅ lugs gcig la ston pa mya ṅan las ḥdas nas lo brgya daṅ drug cu ḥdas pa na / groṅ khyer me tog gis brgyan źes bya bar dge ḥdun gyi gnas brtan bźi / skad mi mthun pa saṃ-skṛ-ta daṅ / zur chag daṅ / tha mal pa daṅ / śa zaḥi skad kyis luṅ ḥdon pas slob ma rnams lta ba mi mthun par gyur pas / rtsa baḥi sde pa bźir gyes so / de dag kyaṅ naṅ gses kyis dbye ba so sor gyes pas sde pa bco brgyad du gyes so / de dag saṅs rgyas kyi bstan pa ḥdi kho na yin gyi / gźan bcu bdun po ma yin no / źes rtsod pa la / nam źig na kri-kriḥi rmi lta luṅ bstan paḥi mdo rñed nas bltas pas / ras yug dkar po gcig mi bco brgyad kyis so sor ḥthen kyaṅ / ras yug de mi ḥdral ba źig rmis pa de / saṅs rgyas ḥod sruṅs la źus pas / rgyal po chen po rmi lam de khyod la dge bar yaṅ mi ḥgyur mi dge bar yaṅ mi ḥgyur gyi / de bźin gśegs pa śā-kya thub paḥi bstan pa gyes pa bco brgyad du gyur kyaṅ / rnam par grol baḥi

[9] The Tōhoku catalog does not list an author for this work. Bu-ston (*History of Buddhism*, II, 98, 99) says "the author of the *Bhikṣu-varṣāgra-pṛcchā*" and "the author of the *Varṣāgra-pṛcchā*". The *Bhikṣuvarṣāgrapṛcchā* (Toh. 4133) immediately follows in the Tanjur the *Śrāmaṇeravarṣāgrapṛcchā* and also has no author listed.

[10] The name Bhadra, as the Tibetan *bzaṅ po* indicates, is preserved in the Tibetan tradition (cf. Étienne Lamotte, *Histoire du Bouddhisme Indien*, Louvain, 1958, p. 308)

Afterward, the religious observances were performed, the gate was opened, the gong was struck, and the *bhikṣus* of Vaiśālī were admitted. The ten transgressions were rejected; the *bhikṣus* of Vaiśālī were expelled, and the seven hundred Arhats celebrated an auspicious Poṣadha. The devas, with expressions of joy and praise, said, "The unrighteous side has been defeated; the righteous side has been victorious."

That is called the second council, sponsored by the King of the Law (*dharmarāja*) Aśoka.

c. *The third council and division into sects*

It is described in the *Tarkajvāla* (Toh. 3856) by Bhavya, in the *Samayabhedoparacanacakra* (Toh. 4140) by Vinītadeva, and in the *Śrāmaṇeravarṣāgrapṛcchā* (Toh. 4132) by Padmasambhava.[9]

According to the teachings of one school, one hundred and thirty-seven years after the Nirvāṇa of the Buddha, in the city of Pāṭaliputra Māra, the Evil One, transformed himself into the aspect of an Arhat named Bhadra,[10] thereby taking on a form inconsistent with himself. By all kinds of magical tricks he split and perverted the views of the Saṃgha so that the resulting quarrel lasted for sixty years without reconciliation. Then a *bhikṣu* by the name of Vātsīputra assembled the Saṃgha, reconciled the dispute, and allayed it in the direction of the Law (*dharma*). This is called the third council, sponsored by the Kings Nanda and Mahāpadma.

According to another school, one hundred and sixty years after the *Nirvāṇa* of the Teacher, four elders of the Saṃgha in the city called Kusumapura (= Paṭaliputra) recited the Scripture in four different languages, Sanskrit, Apabhraṃśa, Prakrit, and Paiśācika. Consequently, the disciples took on disparate views, and thus there arose a division into four basic sects. Those, in turn, by reason of individual sub-divisions, gave rise to the division into eighteen sects. Each of them contended that it alone had the teachings of the Buddha, and that the other seventeen did not. Once King Kṛkin obtained a prophetic *sūtra* in a dream; it read that a piece of white cloth could not be torn to pieces by eighteen men. When he asked the Buddha Kāśyapa for an interpretation of the dream, the Buddha said, "That dream forbodes neither good nor bad for Your Majesty. It presages that, although the teaching of [the future Buddha]

---

on the basis of a passage in the *Tarkajvālā* of Bhāvaviveka. Whether the name Bhadra was actually the original Sanskrit is another question.

ras yug ñams par mi ḥgyur baḥi sṅa ltas yin źes gsuṅs pa mthoṅ nas bco brgyad po thams cad saṅs rgyas kyis bstan par bsdus pa la bsdu ba gsum pa źes bya ste / sbyin bdag rgyal po a-śo-kas byas so /

/ rtsa baḥi sde pa bźi ni / gźi thams cad yod par smra baḥi sde pa daṅ / dge ḥdun phal chen paḥi sde pa daṅ / maṅ pos bkur baḥi sde pa daṅ / gnas brtan paḥi sde paḥo / de dag gi khyad par ni /

/ daṅ po skad saṃ-skṛ-taḥi skad du ḥdon / mkhan rgyud rgyal rigs las rab tu byuṅ ba / tshul khrims rnam par dag pa rnams kyi naṅ nas mchog tu luṅ bstan pa sras sgra gcan ḥdzin nas / snam sbyar snam phrin ñi śu rtsa lṅa pa nas dgu pa yan / grva rtags u-tpa-la daṅ / pa-dma daṅ / rin po che daṅ / śiṅ lo bźiḥo /

/ gñis pa ni skad zur chag du ḥdon / mkhan rgyud bram zeḥi rigs las rab tu byuṅ ba sbyaṅs paḥi yon tan daṅ ldan pa rnams kyi naṅ nas mchog tu luṅ bstan pa ḥod sruṅs chen po nas / snam phran ñer gsum pa nas bdun pa yan / grva rtags duṅ ṅo /

/ gsum pa ni skad śa zaḥi skad du ḥdon / mkhan rgyud dmaṅs rigs las rab tu byuṅ ba ḥdul ba ḥdzin pa rnams kyi naṅ nas mchog tu luṅ bstan pa ñe bar ḥkhor nas / snam phran ñer gcig pa nas lṅa pa yan / grva rtags me tog so-rtsi-kaḥo /

/ bźi pa ni / skad tha mal paḥi skad du ḥdon / mkhan rgyud rjeḥu rigs las rab tu byuṅ ba mthaḥ ḥkhob ḥdul ba rnams kyi naṅ nas mchog tu luṅ bstan pa ka-tya-ya-na nas / snam phran sṅa ma daṅ mthun / grva rtags ḥkhor loḥo /

/ kha cig theg chen gyi bkaḥ bsdu ba byuṅ tshul la bcom ldan ḥdas mya ṅan las ḥdas nas / rgyal poḥi khab kyi lho phyogs kyi ri bi-ma-la-sva-bhā-wa źes bya bar byaṅ chub sems dpaḥi ḥbum phrag bcu ḥdus nas / ḥphags pa ḥjam dpal daṅ / byams pa daṅ / phyag na rdo rje gsum gyis / rim pa bźin theg pa chen poḥi mṅon pa ḥdul ba mdo sdeḥi sde snod gsum bsdus / źes zer ro /

/ de na mi ḥthad de / gsaṅ ḥdus kyi rtsa rgyud kyi mgor ḥdi skad bdag gis thos pa dus gcig na / źes pa nas / rdo rje btsun moḥi bha-ga la bźugs so / źes bya baḥi bar gyi yi ge bźi bcu la / bcom ldan ḥdas rdo

[11] This is the position of Bu-ston, II, pp. 101-2.

[12] The forty syllables (*Guhyasamāja Tantra*, ed. by B. Bhattacharyya, Baroda, 1931, page 1 of the Sanskrit text) are: E-vaṃ ma-yā śru-tam e-ka-smin sa-ma-ye bha-ga-vān sar-va-ta-thā-ga-ta-kā-ya-vāk-cit-ta-hṛ-da-ya-va-jra-yo-ṣid-bha-ge-ṣu vi-ja-hā-ra.

Śākyamuni be divided into eighteen, deliverance is like that indestructible piece of cloth." This meant that all eighteen schools had been included by the Buddha in his doctrine. This is called the third council, sponsored by King Aśoka.

The four basic divisions were (1) Mūlasarvāstivādin, (2) Mahāsaṅghika, (3) Saṃmatīya, and (4) Sthavira. Their distinguishing characteristics were as follows:

(1) The first one recited in Sanskrit. Their line of "superiors" began with the son Rāhula, who, born in the Kṣatriya caste, was foremost among those of pure morality, and was singled out by a prophecy. Their waist robe had from 25 to 29 fringes, and its edge symbols were the blue lotus (*utpala*), the red lotus (*padma*), the jewel (*ratna*), and the tree leaf.

(2) The second recited in Apabhraṃśa. Their line of "superiors" began with Mahākāśyapa, who, born in the Brahmin caste, was foremost among those possessing the ascetic virtues (*dhūta-guṇa*, 12 or 13 in number), and was singled out by a prophecy. Their waist robe had from 23 to 27 fringes, and its edge symbol was the conch-shell.

(3) The third recited in Paiśācika. Their line of "superiors" began with Upāli, who was born in the Śūdra caste, was foremost among those adhering to the Vinaya, and was singled out by a prophecy. Their waist robe had from 21 to 25 fringes, and its edge symbol was the Sorcika flower.

(4) The fourth recited in Prakrit. Their line of "superiors" began with Katyāyana, who, born in the Vaiśya caste, was foremost among those who converted the border countries (*pratyanta-janapada*). Their waist robe was the same as that of the Saṃmatīya, and its edge symbol was the wheel (*cakra*).

d. *A note concerning the Mahāyāna Scriptures*

Some contend[11] that the collection of the Mahāyāna Scriptures took place after the *Nirvāṇa* of the Buddha on the mountain called Vimalasvabhāva, which is south of Rājagṛha. There, where one million Bodhisattvas were assembled, the noble Mañjuśrī, Maitreya, and Vajrapāṇi collected the *Abhidharma-*, *Vinaya-*, and *Sūtra-piṭaka* of the Mahāyāna, respectively.

That [theory] is not tenable, for the following reasons: Now, there are 40 introductory syllables at the beginning of the fundamental *tantra*, the *Guhyasamāja* (Toh. 442), from *Evaṃ mayā śrutam ekasmin samaye* down through *vajra-yoṣid-bhageṣu vijahāra.*[12] The Bhagavat Vajradhara has explained each syllable with a verse (*gāthā*), set forth in the explana-

rje ḥchaṅ ñid kyis yi ge re la tshigs su bcad pa re res bśad pa / bśad rgyud rdo rje ḥphreṅ ba daṅ / dgoṅs pa luṅ ston sogs las gsuṅs pa daṅ / rgyud kyi ston pa daṅ / ḥkhor rgyud tha mi dad du byas paḥi bśad pa thams cad daṅ ḥgal la / sgron gsal las / e baṃ gyi yi ge gñis kyi brda rdo rje ḥchaṅ ñid kyis bśad daṅ ḥgal źiṅ / khuṅs rnam dag gaṅ nas kyaṅ bśad pa med paḥi phyir ro /

/ bkaḥi dgoṅs ḥgrel gyi bstan bcos byuṅ tshul la / bstan bcos yaṅ dag daṅ / ltar snaṅ gñis te / sa sde las /

/ don med don log don daṅ ldan /
/ ṅan gYo brtse bral sdug bsṅal spoṅ /
/ thos rtsod sgrub pa lhur len pa /
/ bstan bcos drug bral gsum du ḥdod /

ces gsuṅs paḥi dgu po der phyi naṅ gi bstan bcos mthaḥ dag ḥdu ste / don med pa daṅ / don log pa daṅ / ṅan gYo daṅ / sñiṅ po daṅ bral ba daṅ / thos pa lhur len pa daṅ / rtsod pa lhur len paḥi bstan bcos te / drug ni phyi rol paḥi bstan bcos te / bstan bcos ltar snaṅ ṅo / don daṅ ldan pa daṅ / sdug bsṅal spoṅ ba daṅ / sgrub pa lhur len paḥi bstan bcos te / gsum ni bstan bcos yaṅ dag ste naṅ baḥi bstan bcos so / daṅ po bźi ni rim pa ltar bya rog so rtog gi bstan bcos lta bu daṅ / mu stegs kyi bstan bcos rnams daṅ / mu stegs kyi rig byed kyi bstan bcos lta bu daṅ / gcer bu paḥi bstan bcos lta buḥo / thos rtsod lhur len gyi bstan bcos gñis kyaṅ phyi rol paḥi bstan bcos so /

[13] The *Pradīpodyotana* (Derge Tanjur, *Rgyud*, Vol. Ha, 10a-7, ff.) quotes the 40 verses from the *Vajramālā*, with an alternate translation into Tibetan to the translation of the verses in the *Vajramālā*, Chap. 59 (Derge Tanjur, *Rgyud ḥbum*, Ca, 264a-3, ff.).

[14] Presumably Mkhas-grub-rje's mention of this is associated with the fact that the Bodhisattvas Mañjuśrī, Maitreya, and Vajrapāṇi are on the tenth stage of the Bodhisattva path and hence are in the retinue of the Sambhoga-kāya, the pronouncer of Mahāyāna doctrine (cf. Chapter I, above).

[15] The first two verses (explaining E and Vaṃ) are available in the original Sanskrit in the Bihar Society's photographic *Pradīpodyotanā* manuscript (Prof. J. de Jong of Canberra informs Wayman that he has transcribed this entire manuscript); an edition and translation of the two verses follow:

/ E / ekārāye satī prajñā virāmādikṣaṇātmikā /
etad mūlaṃ vinirdiṣṭaṃ parijñānaṃ bhavatraye //
/ VAṂ / vaṃśaṃ taṃ bhavad ābhāti rāgādiprasavānvitaṃ /
ālokābhāsa-vijñānam upāyam iti saṃjñitaṃ //

"E" signifies the Noble Wife (*satī*) Prajñā,
the moments of aversion and so on. The total
knowledge displayed in the three worlds has that source.
That ("Vaṃ") radiates like a bamboo shoot,
begetting desire and so on. It is the 'Spread-of-light'
vijñāna called 'Means' (*upāya*).

As those verses are translated in the Tibetan *Vajramālā* (Ca, 264a-3, 4), the T. *snaṅ*

tory *tantras Vajramāla* (Toh. 445), *Sandhivyākaraṇa* (Toh. 444), and so forth.[13] [The contention] is in contradiction with all these explanations which set forth that there is no difference between the stream of consciousness of the retinue and of the Teacher of the *tantra*.[14] According to the *Pradīpodyotana* (Toh. 1785), it is in contradiction with the explanation by Vajradhara about the symbolic meaning (*brda*) of the two syllables *E* and *Vaṃ*.[15] (Finally), it is not set forth in any pure (scriptural) source whatsoever.

3. COMMENTARIES ON THE PROMULGATIONS

There are two kinds of treatises (*śāstra*): *genuine* and *ostensible* treatises. The *Yogācārabhūmi* says:

> Meaningless, erroneous, and meaningful;
> Perverse, hard-hearted, and eliminative of suffering;
> Devoted to wordly learning, devoted to polemics, and
> devoted to accomplishment;
> Of these treatises, we reject six and adhere to three.

In those nine, all "outer" and "inner" treatises are included. The meaningless, erroneous, perverse, hard-hearted, devoted-to-worldly-learning, and devoted-to-polemics treatises are the six "outer" treatises and *ostensible* treatises. The meaningful, eliminative-of-suffering, and devoted-to-accomplishment treatises are the three *genuine* treatises and "inner" treatises. Illustrative of the first four, in the given order, are the treatise "Musing on the tooth of the raven", the treatises of the heretics (*tīrthika*), the Vedic treatises of the heretics, and the treatises of the Nirgranthas. And the treatises that are devoted to worldly learning and devoted to polemics are also "outer" treatises.

---

ba gsal ba is an alternate translation of *ālokābhāsa*, usually translated by T. *snaṅ ba mched pa*. The two verses posit the two elements, with correspondences in this system, namely: (a) *prajñā – āloka – citta – śūnya*; (b) *upāya – ālokābhāsa – caitta – atiśūnya*. See Chapter I, above, note 25. The *Vajramālā* (263b-3, ff.) gives various explanations of E-Vaṃ, of which this is the first: "Evaṃ has two syllables. E is explained as voidness; likewise Vaṃ is compassion; and the 'drop' (*bindu*) arises from the union of those two. That is the marvellously originated *yoga*. E-Vaṃ is the Buddha and, in short, the seal of the doctrine (*dharma-mudrā*)" (E-Baṃ źes bya ba yi ge gñis / E ni stoṅ pa ñid du bśad / de bźin Baṃ ni thugs rje daṅ / thig le de gñis sbyor ba las byuṅ / de ni rnal ḥbyor rmad mchog byuṅ / E-Baṃ gñis ni saṅs rgyas daṅ / mdor bsdus chos kyi phyag rgyaḥo). Mkhas grub rje apparently means by "no difference in the stream of consciousness" the compassion or means which is Vaṃ. He reverts to the subject of E-Vaṃ at the end of his present work.

/ rig paḥi gnas lṅa ste / gtan tshigs rig pa daṅ / sgra daṅ / gso ba daṅ / bzo rig pa daṅ / naṅ gi don rig paḥo / de dag ston paḥi bstan bcos kyaṅ lṅa ste /

/ gtan tshigs rig paḥi bstan bcos la / phyi rig par gyur pa daṅ / naṅ rig par gyur paḥi rtog geḥi bstan bcos gñis so /

/ sṅa ma ni phyi rol paḥi ston pa draṅ sroṅ gliṅ skyes kyis byas paḥi rtog geḥi bstan bcos daṅ / bram ze rkaṅ mig gis byas paḥi rtog geḥi tshig don brgyad ston paḥi bstan bcos lta buḥo /

/ phyi ma ni sde bdun mdo daṅ bcas pa lta bu ste / dpal ldan phyogs kyi glaṅ pos mdzad paḥi tshad maḥi mdo kun las btus pa la leḥu drug go / deḥi dgoṅs pa ḥgrel pa la dpal ldan chos kyi grags pas tshad ma sde bdun mdzad de / gtso bo lus lta buḥi bstan bcos gsum ni / rgyas pa rnam ḥgrel / ḥbriṅ rnam ṅes / bsdus pa rigs paḥi thigs pa ste / daṅ po la leḥu bźi / gñis pa la leḥu gsum / gsum pa la leḥu phye ba med do / ḥphros pa yan lag lta buḥi bstan bcos bźi ni / gtan tshigs thigs pa / rtsod paḥi rigs pa ḥgrel pa brtag pa / rgyud gźan bsgrub paḥo /

/ sgra rig paḥi bstan bcos la /

/ lha yul du lha thams cad mkhyen pa dzñā-na de-wa źes bya bas sgro mdo chen po gcig byas / de lha yul du dar nas mi yul du ma phebs par nub po / deḥi rjes la brgya byin gyis i-ndra-byā-ka-ra-ṇa źes bya ba brtsams te draṅ sroṅ phur bu la bslabs nas / lha rnams la slob tu bcug pas / draṅ sroṅ phur bu la lhaḥi bla ma daṅ sgra mkhan źes grags so / de ṅa rgyal daṅ ldan par gyur pa la brgya byin gyis rgya mtsho chen po nas chu bum pa gaṅ blaṅs te / de las rtsva ku-śaḥi rtse mos thigs pa gcig blaṅs nas sgra ni rgya mtshoḥi chu daṅ ḥdra / ṅas śes pa ni bum paḥi chu daṅ khyod kyis śes pa ni ku-śaḥi rtse moḥi chu daṅ ḥdraḥo źes smras pas / de sems khoṅ du chud nas slob par mi byed pa la / ḥo

[16] Bu-ston, II, 166, does not have the name Jñānadeva, which Mkhas grub rje presents in transcription. Obermiller may have taken the words *lha thams cad mkhyen pa* "an omniscient god" (perhaps to be found in Bu-ston's text) as indicating a proper name and so translated "a god named Sarvajñāna". In any case, this is another indication that Mkhas grub rje did not draw these accounts from Bu-ston's work; cf. note 2, above.

Of the sciences there are five: Logic (*hetu-vidyā*), Grammar (*śabda-vidyā*), Medicine (*cikitsā-vidyā*), Arts (*śilpa-karmasthāna-vidyā*), and Inner Science (*adhyātma-vidyā*). The treatises (*śāstra*) teaching them are also fivefold.

a. *The four outer sciences*

Logic

Among the treatises on logical science are the *tarka* treatises belonging to Outer Science (i.e. non-Buddhist) and those belonging to Inner Science (i.e. Buddhist).

The former are the teachings of the outsiders — for example, the Tarka treatise written by the Ṛṣi Gautama (T. read: *glaṅ skyes*), and the Tarka treatise expounding the eight meanings of words, written by the Brahmin Akṣapāda.

The latter are, for example, the "group of seven works" (*sde bdun*) together with the *sūtra*. The *pramāṇa-sūtra* is the *Samuccaya* (Toh. 4203) in six chapters, written by Śrī Diṅnāga. The seven logical treatises by Dharmakīrti are the primary commentary on that work. The three chief treatises are comparable to a trunk (i.e. main part of body). The extensive one is the *Pramāṇavārttika* (Toh. 4210); the intermediate one is the *Pramāṇaviniścaya* (Toh. 4211); the abbreviated one is the *Nyāya-bindu* (Toh. 4212). The first has four chapters; the second, three; while the third is not divided into chapters. The remaining four treatises are comparable to limbs: *Hetubindu* (Toh. 4213), *Vādanyāya* (Toh. 4218), *Sambandhaparīkṣā* (Toh. 4214), *Saṃtānāntarasiddhi* (Toh. 4219).

Grammar

In heaven an omniscient god named Jñānadeva composed a great *sūtra* on grammar.[16] It was widely disseminated among the gods but never known among men, and it disappeared. Later on, Śatakratu (i.e. Indra) composed a grammar called *Indravyākaraṇa* and taught it to the Ṛṣi Bṛhaspati, enjoining him to teach it to the other gods. Ṛṣi Bṛhaspati is renowned as the guide (*guru*) of the gods and as a grammarian. When he became proud, Indra filled a flask with water from the great ocean, took one drop from it with the tip of a Kuśa [blade of] grass, and said, "Grammar resembles the water in the ocean. I know as much as there is water in this flask, while you know no more than the drop on this tip of Kuśa grass." Bṛhaspati understood and forsook teaching. Then

na kyaṅ gaṅ śes de slobs śig ces smras pas / ḥo na dus bzaṅ la mi slob gźan du slob par bgyiḥo źes smras pas / dus bzaṅ bźi ni /

/ tshes brgyad la ni slob dpon ḥjoms /
/ bcu bźi la ni slob ma ḥjoms /
/ gnam stoṅ la ni rig pa ḥjoms /
/ tshes gcig la ni thams cad ḥjoms /

źes yar do mar doḥi yoṅs ḥjoms kyi dus bzaṅ bźi bsruṅ ba diṅ saṅ gi bar du sgra pa rnams la srol du dar ro /

/ de nas mi yul du bram ze pā-ṇi-na źes bya bas lag ris mkhan la lag ris bstan nas sgra śes par ḥgyur mi ḥgyur dris pas śes par mi ḥgyur zer pa la / sgra źes paḥi lag ris ji ltar dgos bris nas / mtshon rnon pos bris te bslabs pas śes par ma gyur pa la / phyi rol paḥi lugs ltar na ma-hā-de-wa ste dbaṅ phyug chen po bsgrubs pas ḥgrub ste sgra la mkhas paḥi dṅos grub źus pas / dbaṅ phyug chen pos / a i u źes smras pas de ma thag tu sgra la mkhas par gyur par ḥdod do / naṅ ba ltar na ḥphags pa ḥjig rten dbaṅ phyug bsgrubs pas grub ste / skad cig la mkhas par gyur ces te / ḥjam dpal rtsa rgyud las / sgra byed pa ni pā-ṇi-ni / źes sogs kyis luṅ bstan pa daṅ mthun no / des pā-ṇi-bya-ka-ra-ṇa źes bya ba ślo-ka ñis stoṅ pa gcig brtsams so / de la kluḥi rgyal po źig gis ḥgrel pa ma-hā-bha-ṣa źes bya ba ślo-ka ḥbum pa gcig byas so /

/ yaṅ rgyal po bde spyod ces bya ba btsun mo daṅ lhan cig khrus byed pa la / rgyal pos btsun mo la chu gtor bas / btsun mos saṃ-skṛ-taḥi skad du chu ma ḥthor źes smras pas / rgyal pos sgra mi śes pas phal paḥi skad la til gyi la du byin cig ces go nas / ḥbaṅs mo gcig la til gyi la du bskur te btaṅ bas / btsun moḥi blo la rgyal po blun po ba laṅ daṅ ḥdra ba ḥdi daṅ lhan cig sdod pa las śi ba slaḥo sñam nas lceb par brtsams pa rgyal pos rig nas khyod de ltar ma byed ci ñes dris pas / btsun mos rgyu mtshan smras pa la / rgyal pos khyod de ltar ma byed cig ṅas kyaṅ sgra la mkhas par slob bo / źes smras so / deḥi tshe btsun moḥi źaṅ po sa-rvā-wa-rma źes bya bas btsun mo la khyod de ltar ma byed cig / kho bos gźon nu smin drug bsgrubs nas sgra la mkhas par byas te rgyal po la slob bo / źes smras te / bsgrubs pas grub nas des lus ma bstan par

[17] In India these are called the "academic holidays" (*anadhyāya*), but the *Manusmṛti* authority (IV, 114), as follows, is not exactly consistent with the grammarian's verse:

/ amāvāsyā guruṃ hanti śiṣyaṃ hanti caturdaśī /
/ brahmāṣṭakāpaurṇamāsyau tasmāt tāḥ parivarjayet //

Moreover, instead of the "science", Manu's verse has the "brahman", here meaning the Veda.

[18] Actually, there are eight such days in all: the first day after the full moon, the eighth, fourteenth, and dark of the moon in the decreasing phases of the moon; and the first day of the young moon, the eighth, fourteenth, and full moon in the increasing phases of the moon.

Indra said, "Teach what you know!" He replied, "On auspicious days,[17] I shall not teach; on other days I shall." Therefore he related the four auspicious days:

> The eighth day destroys the teacher;
> The fourteenth destroys the pupil;
> The dark of the moon destroys [grammatical] science;
> The first day destroys everything.

This means, then, that one guards against the four auspicious days that destroy in the increasing and decreasing phases of the moon.[18] Up to present times, it has been customary for grammarians to observe this.

In later times there appeared in the country of men a Brahmin named Pāṇini. He showed the lines of his hand to a palmist and asked whether he would be able to understand grammar. The answer was "No." Thereupon, he asked the palmist how the lines of the hand should run if one is able to understand grammar. He took a sharp knife and incised them, but still his studying brought no understanding. It is maintained by the "outer" school, he then evoked the great god Maheśvara and asked for the magical power (*siddhi*) of skill in grammar. Maheśvara said, "A, I, U", and immediately thereupon he became skilled in grammar. According to the "inner" (i.e. Buddhist) [school], he evoked Ārya-Lokeśvara and became skilled immediately, thus conforming to the prophecy in the *Mañjuśrī-mūla-tantra* (Toh. 543), "the grammarian Pāṇini..." He composed the *Pāṇinīya-vyākaraṇa* in 2000 ślokas. On it, a Nāgarāja (i.e. Śeṣa = Patañjali) composed the commentary called *Mahābhāṣya*, in 100,000 ślokas.

Furthermore, a king by the name of Udayana was once bathing with his queen when he sprayed water on her. The queen said in Sanskrit, "Don't splash me" (*modakair siñca*). The king, who did not know this speech, understood her as saying in the vulgar language, "Give me some sesame pastry." Thereupon, he sent a maid servant for the pastry. The queen felt that she would rather die than live with a king who was as stupid as an ox and she threatened suicide. When the king became aware of her intention, he said, "Don't do that! What have I done wrong?" The queen told him the reason, and the king tried to dissuade her, promising that he, too, would study grammar. The queen's uncle, named Śarvavarman, said to the queen, "Don't do that! I will evoke the six-faced youth (Kārttikeya), and having become skilled in grammar, I shall teach the king. When he was evoked, the god, keeping his body hidden behind a curtain, explained the *sūtra* on grammar which he had composed. After fifteen chapters had been completed, the Brahmin

yol baḥi phag nas raṅ ñid kyis brtsams paḥi sgra mdo bśad de leḥu bco lṅa rdzogs pa na / bram ze sa-rvā-wa-rmas chog tshod bzuṅ ste / ka-lā-pa ṅes ḥtshal lo źes smras pas gźon nu smin drug rma bya la źon nas ḥgro baḥi rma byaḥi mdoṅs yol baḥi phag nas mthoṅ bas ka-lā-pa bzod par mdzod cig ces smras pas sgra mdo de la / ka-lā-pa-sū-tra cha bsags kyi mdo źes bya bar grags te ka-lā-pa ni cha bsags te rma byaḥi mdoṅs la ḥjug go / deḥi ḥphro de bram ze sa-rvā-wa-rma daṅ / bram ze mchog sred gñis kyis brtsams te / leḥu ñer bźi ślo-ka bźi brgya pa gcig byas so / de la ḥgrel pa bgrod ka seṅ ges byas pa daṅ / slob ma la phan pa źes bya ba gñis yod de /

/ yaṅ slob dpon tsa-ndra-go-mis kluḥi rgyal pos byas paḥi ma-hā-bha-ṣa la brten nas tsa-ndra-byā-ka-ra-ṇa źes bya ba / leḥu so gñis ślo-ka bdun brgya pa gcig mdzad do / de la slob dpon de ñid kyi źaṅ po chos kyi ḥbaṅs źes bya bas ḥgrel pa ślo-ka drug stoṅ pa gcig byas so / de la slob dpon rin po cheḥi blo gros źes bya bas ḥgrel bśad ślo-ka stoṅ phrag bcu gñis pa gcig byas so / de la ḥgrel bśad slob dpon zla ba gaṅ ba źes bya bas ślo-ka sum khri drug stoṅ pa gcig byas te /

/ de dag las rtsa ḥgrel gñis ma gtogs bod du ma ḥgyur ro / bod la ñe bar mkho ba la pa-ṇḍi-ta smri-tis mdzad paḥi smra baḥi sgo mtshon cha lta bu źes pa miṅ tshig yi geḥi tshogs gsum ston pa gcig yod do /

/ de dag thams cad phyi rig paḥi bstan bcos su gtogs so /

/ sgraḥi bstan bcos kyi źar la sñan dṅags kyi bstan bcos la / sñan dṅags daṅ / sdeb sbyor daṅ / mṅon brjod daṅ / zlos gar bźiḥo / dṅags źes bya ba ni tha sñad ces bya baḥi brda rñiṅ paḥo / deḥi bstan bcos la sñan dṅags kyi mtshan ñid ston paḥi gźuṅ daṅ / gźuṅ de daṅ mthun par sbyar baḥi sñan dṅags gñis te / sṅon ma ni sñan dṅags kyi gźuṅ yin źiṅ sñan dṅags ma yin la / phyi ma ni de las bzlog paḥo / sṅa ma ni phyi rig paḥi bstan bcos so / phyi ma la phyi rig naṅ rig gñis kaḥi bstan bcos yod do / mtshan gźi ni rim pa ltar me loṅ lta bu daṅ / dpag bsam ḥkhri śiṅ lta buḥo /

/ sñan dṅags kyi gźuṅ gi brjod byar sñan dṅags kyi lus / rgyan / skyon gsum ston te / lus ni tshigs bcad rkyaṅ pa daṅ / lhug pa rkyaṅ pa daṅ / de gñis spel ma gsum gaṅ rtsom yaṅ lus kyi ñams bcu las skabs su gaṅ

Śarvavarman, being satisfied with his knowledge, said, "Kalāpa, I know it." Thereupon, when Śarvavarman saw from behind the curtain the tail feathers of the peacook on which Kārtākeya had mounted and was riding away, he said, "Kalāpa, please forgive [me]!" Therefore, that grammar is called *Kalāpasūtra*. [Śarvavarman] applied to the eyes of the peacock feathers the word "*kalāpa*", meaning "collection of parts". With the remainder of the grammar composed by the Brahmin Śarvavarman and the Brahmin Vararuci, the whole came to twenty four chapters with four hundred ślokas (Toh. 4282). It has a commentary by Durgasiṃha (Toh. 4283) and the *Śiṣyahitā* (Toh. 4286) [by Ugrabhūti].

Furthermore, the *ācārya* Candragomin, taking recourse to the *Mahābhāṣya* composed by the Nāgarāja, prepared the *Candravyākaraṇa* (Toh. 4269) in thirty-two chapters with seven hundred ślokas. His uncle Dharmadāsa wrote a commentary on it in 6,000 ślokas. On this, in turn, the *ācārya* Ratnamati wrote a sub-commentary in 12,000 ślokas. This sub-commentary was expanded by the *ācārya* Pūrṇacandra into 36,000 ślokas.

Of those works, only the two basic commentaries (i.e. the ones by Durgasiṃha and by Candragomin) were translated into Tibetan. Useful to Tibetans is the work by Paṇḍita Smṛti, the *Vacanamukhyāyudhopama* (Toh. 4295), which explains the sets of names (*nāma-kāya*), of phrases (*pada-kāya*), and of letters (*vyañjana-kāya*).

All those works belong to the treatises of Outer Science.

Appendages to grammar

To the grammatical treatises are appended the treatises of poetry, which are of four types, Poetics (*kāvya*), Prosody (*chandas*), Lexicography (*abhidhāna*), and Drama (*nāṭya*). The word "*dṅags*" [in *sñan dṅags* = *kāvya*] is the obsolete equivalent to "*tha sñad*" ("expression"). Among those works are the manuals explaining the characteristics of poetry, as well as the poetry composed in conformity with them. The former are discussions of poetry, not poetry; the latter are the reverse. The former are treatises of Outer Science, while among the latter there are treatises of both Outer Science and Inner Science. Characteristic examples are, respectively, the *Kāvyādarśa* (Toh. 4301) [a manual on poetry] and the *Avadānakalpalatā* (Toh. 4155) [a poetical work].

The subject matter of manuals on poetry falls under three headings, the body (*kāya*), the embellishments (*alaṃkāra*), and the faults (*doṣa*). The body (*kāya*) consists of pure verse (*padya*), pure prose (*gadya*), or a mixture of the two (*miśra*); and whichever of those three is used, the

bab paḥi ñam thon paḥo / ñams ḥdon lugs rgya gar śar phyogs gau-ḍa-pa daṅ / lho phyogs bhai-dar-baḥi ḥdon lugs gñis yod do / rgyan ni don rgyan so lṅa / sgra rgyan so gñis / gab tshig gi rgyan bcu drug go / skyon ni bcuḥo /

/ me loṅ gi gźuṅ rtsom pa po ni pa-ṇḍi-ta dbyug pa can źes bya ba phyi rol pa źig go / ḥo na dbyaṅs can ma la mchod brjod byed pa ci yin źe na / de ni phyi rol pa ltar na rgya mtshoḥi ḥgram na bram ze sgra paḥam / taṃ-bu-ra źes bya ba źig yod paḥi chuṅ ma yin źes ḥdod la / naṅ bas ni ḥphags pa ḥjig rten dbaṅ phyug gi tshems mche ba las sprul par bźed de / gñis kas kyaṅ ṅag gi lha mo źes lhar ḥdzin no /

/ dpag bsam ḥkhri śiṅ la leḥu brgya rtsa brgyad yod paḥi brgya daṅ bdun rgyal po dge baḥi dbaṅ po źes bya bas mdzad la / leḥu tha ma ni deḥi sras zla baḥi dbaṅ po źes bya bas mdzad do /

/ sdeb sbyor gyi bstan bcos la / dmar ser can daṅ / rgyal baḥi lhas mdzad pa sogs bod du ma ḥgyur ro / rtsod dus kyi thams cad mkhyen pa ra-tna-a-ka-ra-śā-ntis mdzad paḥi sdeb sbyor rin chen ḥbyuṅ gnas źes bya ba bod du ḥgyur te / sñan dṅags rtsom pa na sñan dṅags la mkho ba yi ge lci yaṅ gi sdeb sbyor daṅ / sgra la mkho ba yi ge pho mo ma niṅ gsum gyi rab dbye ston no /

/ mṅon brjod kyi bstan bcos ni slob dpon ḥchi med seṅ ges mdzad paḥi ḥchi med mdzod ces bya ba ḥgyur te / sa ḥog sa steṅ sa bla gsum gyi miṅ gi rnam graṅs du ma bstan to /

/ zlos gar gyi bstan bcos ni slob dpon tsa-ndra-go-mis mdzad paḥi ḥjig rten kun tu dgaḥ baḥi zlos gar źes bya ba daṅ / sñan dṅags pa chen po dpal dgaḥ baḥi lha źes bya bas mdzad paḥi klu kun tu dgaḥ baḥi zlos gar źes bya ba ḥgyur ro /

/ gso ba rig paḥi bstan bcos ni / slob dpon dpaḥ bos mdzad paḥi sman dpyad yan lag brgyad pa źes pa /

/ lus daṅ byis pa gdon lus stod /
/ mtshon daṅ mche ba rgas ro rtsa /
/ gso dpyad gaṅ la gnas pa yi /
/ yan lag brgyad pa źes bśad do /

[19] Of course the *Aṣṭāṅgahṛdayasaṃhitā* is by Vāgbhaṭa. But this name was translated into Tibetan as Pha khol. The confusion with Ārya Śūra in Tibetan tradition can be seen by the fact that when Tsoṅ-kha-pa in his *Lam rim chen mo* (Tashilunpo ed., 266b-4) quotes from a work by Dpal ldan Ma khol, the annotator Ba so chos kyi rgyal mtshan (born 1402 A.D.) precedes that name with the note: "ma la gus pas ma khol źes daṅ de bźin du pha khol daṅ rta dbyaṅs daṅ ma-ti-tsi-tra". This asserts that the author is called Ma khol because of his devotion to his mother, for a similar reason is called Pha khol, and is Aśvaghoṣa and Mātṛceṭa. D. R. Shackleton Bailey, *The*

body also has sentiments (*rasa*), chosen from the ten sentiments, appropriate to the occasion. As to the sentiments (*rasa*), there is a difference between the Gauḍa style of East India and the Vaidarbha style of Southern India. As to the embellishments (*alaṃkāra*), there are thirty-five of meaning (*artha*), thirty-two of sound (*śabda*), and sixteen of riddles (*prahelikā*). As to the faults (*doṣa*), there are ten.

The author of the *Kāvyādarśa* (Toh. 4301), called Paṇḍita Daṇḍin, is an "outsider" (i.e. non-Buddhist). Then, who is the Sarasvatī to whom the invocation is made? She is claimed by the "outsiders" to be the wife of a Brahmin named Sgra-pa or Taṃbura, who lived on the shore of the ocean; but according to the "insiders", she was a metamorphosis of the great tooth of Ārya Lokeśvara. Moreover, both parties held her to be the goddess of speech.

The *Avadānakalpalatā* (Toh. 4155) contains 108 chapters, of which the first 107 are by king Kṣemendra and the last is by his son Somendra.

Textbooks on Prosody by Piṅgala and by Jayadeva were not translated into Tibetan. The *Chandoratnākara* (Toh. 4303 and 4304) composed by Ratnākaraśānti, "the omniscient one of the age of strife" (*kaliyuga*), was translated into Tibetan. It teaches the poet the rules of the heavy and light syllables, required for versification, and the division of letters into male, female, and neuter, required for grammar.

Concerning the treatises on Lexicography, there is a translation of the *Amarakośa* (Toh. 4299), written by Amarasiṃha. The words are arranged by such categories as *svarga* (heaven), *pātāla* (the underworld), and *bhūmi* (our world).

Concerning the treatises on Drama, there are translations of the *Lokānandanāṭaka* (Toh. 4153) by Candragomin and the *Nāgānanda-nāma-nāṭaka* (Toh. 4154) by the great poet Śrī Harśadeva.

Medicine

Concerning the treatises of Medicine, there is the *Aṣṭāṅga* (Toh. 4310) on therapeutic investigation by the *ācārya* Śūra.[19]

> Body (*kāya*), [diseases of] infants (*bāla*), demonic
> possession (*graha*), upper members (*ūrdhvāṅga*),
> [Wounds due to] sharp points (*śalya*) [and to] teeth (*daṃṣṭrā*)
> old age (*jarā*), and vigor (*vṛṣa*) —
> Are called the eight objects (*aṣṭāṅga*)
> On which rests therapy.

Śatapañcāśatka of Mātṛceṭa (Cambridge, 1951), p. 8, summarizes the later material by Tāranātha, who gives a string of names, including Śūra.

źes paḥi yan lag brgyad ston pa daṅ / deḥi ḥgrel chen kha che zla dgaḥ źes bya bas mdzad pa daṅ / ḥphags pa klu sgrub kyi mdzad paḥi sbyor ba brgya pa źes bya ba zas ḥdi spyad na nad ḥdi skyed ces pa ston pa rnams ḥgyur ro / ḥdi dag thams cad ni phyi rig paḥi bstan bcos so /

/ bzo rig paḥi bstan bcos ni / sku gzugs kyi cha tshad sogs ston paḥi bstan bcos te / ḥphags pa śā-riḥi-bus mdzad pa la sogs pa ḥgyur ro / ḥdi la naṅ rig par gtogs pa yaṅ yod do /

/ naṅ gi don rig paḥi bstan bcos ni /

/ naṅ sems kyi steṅ gi ñon moṅs pa daṅ śes byaḥi sgrib pa ḥdul baḥi thabs ston paḥi bstan bcos so / de la dbye na / bkaḥ daṅ po bden pa bźiḥi chos kyi ḥkhor loḥi dgoṅs pa ḥgrel paḥi bstan bcos daṅ / bkaḥ bar pa mtshan ñid med paḥi chos kyi ḥkhor loḥi dgoṅs pa ḥgrel paḥi bstan bcos daṅ / bkaḥ tha ma legs par rnam par phye ba daṅ ldan paḥi chos kyi ḥkhor loḥi dgoṅs pa ḥgrel paḥi bstan bcos so /

/ daṅ po la / bkaḥ daṅ po nas gsuṅs paḥi lta baḥi cha gtso bor ston paḥi bstan bcos daṅ / de las gsuṅs paḥi spyod paḥi cha gtso bor ston paḥi bstan bcos gñis so /

/ de la daṅ po ni / mṅon pa sde bdun daṅ / deḥi don bsdus pa bye brag tu bśad pa chen po / deḥi don bsdus pa mṅon pa mdzod rtsa ba raṅ ḥgrel daṅ bcas pa ste / de yaṅ bye brag smra baḥi lugs kyis mṅon pa sde bdun dgra bcom pas mdzad par ḥdod de /

/ chos kyi phuṅ po śā-riḥi bus /
/ gdags paḥi bstan bcos moḥu ḥgal bus /
/ rnam śes tshogs ni lha skyid kyis /
/ ye śes la ḥjug ka-tyaḥi bus /

Thus the eight objects are described. It has a large commentary by the Kashmirian Candranandana (Toh. 4312, 3 vols.). Also translated was the *Yogaśataka* (Toh. 4306) by Ārya-Nāgārjuna; it shows which food generates which illness. All these are treatises of Outer Science.

Arts

The treatises on the arts are those that teach the measurements of images (or icons), and so forth. The one composed by Ārya Śāriputra (presumably Toh. 4315, no author mentioned), and others, were translated. Among these are also works that belong to Inner Science.

b. *Inner Science*

The treatises on Inner Science are those which show the means of vanquishing the obscurations of corruption and of the knowable that are on the inner thought. They are divided into the treatises which are commentaries on the First Promulgation, the Wheel of the Law of the Four Truths; the treatises which are commentaries on the Intermediate Promulgation, the Wheel of the Law concerning lack of characteristics; and the treatises which are commentaries on the Last Promulgation, the Wheel of the Law concerning perfect and intensive analysis.

(1) COMMENTARIES ON THE FIRST WHEEL OF THE LAW

Here are the treatises that discuss principally the Doctrinal Part (*darśana-bhaga*) expressed in the First Promulgation, and the treatises that show principally the Practical Part (*caryā-bhaga*) expressed in that Promulgation.

(a) **The Doctrinal Part**

This includes the "Seven Sections of the *Abhidharma*", the condensation of their meaning in the *Mahāvibhāṣā*, and the condensation of the latter's meaning in the basic *Abhidharma-kośa* and its self-commentary. Furthermore, the Vaibhāṣikas maintain that the "Seven Sections of the *Abhidharma*" have all been written by Arhats, just as said:

> The *Dharmaskandha* (Aggregate of the Law) is by Śāriputra;
> The *Prajñaptiśāstra* (Treatise of Classification) is by Maudgalyāyana;
> The *Vijñānakāya* (Set of Perceptions) is by Devaśarman;

/ khams kyi tshogs ni gaṅ pos byas /
/ rab tu byed pa dbyig bśes kyis /
/ yaṅ dag ḥgro baḥi rnam graṅs ni /
/ gsus po che yis byas źes grags /

źes pa ltar ro / bye brag tu bśad pa chen po yaṅ dgra bcóm pa daṅ so so skye bo maṅ pos ḥthus nas byas par ḥdod do / mdo sde paḥi lugs kyis de dag thams cad so so skye boḥi pa-ṇḍi-tas byas par ḥdod do / mṅon pa sde bdun las gdags paḥi bstan bcos kyi naṅ tshan gyi ḥjig rten gdags pa daṅ / las gdags pa źes bya ba gñis bod du ḥgyur źiṅ gźan rnams ma ḥgyur ro / bye brag tu bśad pa chen po la ślo-ka ḥbum yod par grags te bod du ma ḥgyur ro /

/ mṅon pa mdzod kyi rtsa baḥi tshig zin kyis / kha che bye brag smra baḥi grub mthaḥ ston ciṅ / raṅ ḥgrel gyis mdo sde paḥi grub mthaḥ yaṅ rgyas par bstan to / slob dpon dbyig gñen ñid kyi slob dpon kha che mdun bzaṅ gis mdzad paḥi ḥgrel pa / slob dpon phyogs glaṅ gis mdzad paḥi ḥgrel pa / rgyal poḥi sras grags paḥi bśes gñen gyis mdzad paḥi ḥgrel bśad / slob dpon gaṅ ba spel gyis mdzad paḥi ḥgrel bśad rnams bod du ḥgyur ro /

/ tshad ma sde bdun mdo daṅ bcas pas kyaṅ gźuṅ gi cha maṅ po źig gis mdo sde paḥi grub mthaḥ ston no /

/ spyod paḥi cha gtso bor ston paḥi bstan bcos la /

/ slob dpon dul ba lhas mdzad paḥi luṅ rnam ḥbyed kyi ḥgrel pa daṅ / dge tshul gyi tshig leḥur byas pa la sogs pa daṅ / slob dpon dge legs bśes gñen gyis mdzad paḥi so so thar paḥi mdoḥi ḥgrel pa bam po lṅa bcu pa la sogs pa daṅ / dge sloṅ gi so sor thar paḥi mdoḥi ḥgrel pa brgyad daṅ / dge sloṅ maḥi so sor thar paḥi mdoḥi ḥgrel pa gñis te bcu daṅ / slob dpon yon tan ḥod kyis mdzad paḥi ḥdul na mdo rtsa ba gźi bcu bdun / rnam ḥbyed gñis daṅ bcas pa ston pa bam po dgu daṅ / de ñid kyis mdzad paḥi ḥdul ba ka-rma-śa-taṃ las brgya rtsa gcig pa bam po bcu gñis pa daṅ / mdo rtsaḥi raṅ ḥgrel ñid kyi rnam bśad / mdo rtsaḥi rgya cher ḥgrel slob dpon chos kyi bśes gñen gyis mdzad pa bam po bdun

[20] All the works listed are Vinaya texts of the Mūlasarvāstivādin school.
[21] The Derge Tanjur *Dkar Chag*, 449b-5, says 70 sections.
[22] The Derge Tanjur *Dkar Chag*, 450a-6, says 9 sections.

The *Jñānaprasthāna* (Entrance into Knowledge) is by Katyāyaniputra;
The *Dhātukāya* (Set of Elements) is by Pūrṇa;
The *Prakaraṇapāda* (Organized Presentation) is by Vasumitra;
The *Saṃgītiparyāya* (Well-sung Terminology) is by Mahākauṣṭhila.

Also, they maintain that the *Mahāvibhāṣā* was compiled collectively by many Arhats and laymen. In contrast, the Sautrāntikas maintain that all the [texts] were composed by learned laymen. Of the "Seven Sections of the *Abhidharma*", only a portion of the *Prajñapti*, namely the *Lokaprajñapti* (Toh. 4086, and presumably also the *Kāraṇa*°, Toh. 4087) and the *Karmaprajñapti* (Toh. 4088), has been translated into Tibetan. The *Mahāvibhāṣā*, said to contain 100,000 ślokas, has not been translated into Tibetan.

The basic stanzas (*kārikā*) of the *Abhidharma-kośa* (Toh. 4089) expound the tenets (*siddhānta*) of the Kashmirian Vaibhāṣikas; and the self-commentary (the *bhāṣya*, Toh. 4090) also teaches extensively the tenets of the Sautrāntikas. Translated into Tibetan were the commentary (Toh. 4091) composed by the Kashmirian Saṃghabhadra, who was the *ācārya* of the *ācārya* Vasubandhu himself; the commentary (Toh. 4095) composed by the *ācārya* Diṅnāga; the commentary (Toh. 4092, sometimes called the *vyākhyā*) by Prince Yaśomitra; and the commentary (Toh. 4093) by Pūrṇavardhana.

Moreover, many textual passages of the seven works of logic [by Dharmakīrti], together with the *sūtra* [by Diṅnāga], expound the tenets of the Sautrāntikas.

(b) **The Practical Part**[20]

All the following were translated into Tibetan: the *Vinayavibhaṅga* (Toh. 4114), the *Śrāmaṇerakārikā* (Toh. 4126), and so forth, composed by the *ācārya* Vinītadeva; the *Pratimokṣasūtraṭīkā* (Toh. 4106) in 50 sections (*bam po*),[21] and so forth, [including?] a *Bhikṣupratimokṣasūtra* commentary in 8 sections and a *Bhikṣuṇīpratimokṣasūtra* commentary in 2 sections, a total of 10 sections, by the *ācārya* Dge legs bśes gñen; the basic *Vinayasūtra* (Toh. 4117), which expounds 17 *pada*, together with the two *vibhaṅga* [i.e. the *bhikṣu-vibhaṅga* and the *bhikṣuṇī-vibhaṅga*], in 9 sections, the *Ekottarakarmaśataka* (Toh. 4118) in 12 sections,[22] and the *Vinayasūtravṛtti-svavyākhyāna* (Toh. 4119), by the *ācārya* Guṇaprabha; the *Vinayasūtraṭīkā* (Toh. 4120) in 70 sections, by Dharmamitra;

cu pa daṅ / dgra bcom pa sa gaḥi lhas mdzad paḥi ḥdul ba me tog phreṅ rgyud rnam ḥbyed gñis kho na ston pa bam po drug pa daṅ / slob dpon śākya ḥod kyis mdzad paḥi dge tshul gyi tshig leḥur byas pa sum brgya pa daṅ / deḥi raṅ ḥgrel ḥod ldan rnams te bod du ḥgyur ro /

/ spyir lta ba bkar btags kyi phyag rgya bźi khas len mí len gyis / saṅs rgyas paḥi lta ba khas len mi len du ḥjog pa las / ñan thos sde pa bco brgyad kyi maṅ pos bkur ba daṅ / gnas ma bu pa daṅ / bla ma pa daṅ / chos sbas pa daṅ / bzaṅ poḥi lam pa rnams / brjod du med paḥi gaṅ zag gi bdag khas len pas saṅs rgyas paḥi lta ba khas len par mi ḥjog kyaṅ / skyabs gnas daṅ tshul khrims sogs kyi sog nas saṅs rgyas par ḥjog go / bkar btags kyi phyag rgya bźi ni / ḥdus byas thams cad mi rtag / zag bcas thams cad sdug bsṅal / chos thams cad bdag med / mya ṅan las ḥdas pa źi źiṅ dben pa / źes bya ba rnams so / sde pa lhag ma rnams ni / bye brag smra ba daṅ mdo sde pa gaṅ ruṅ du ma gtogs pa med la / sde pa bco brgyad po thams cad kyaṅ theg pa chen po bkaḥ ma yin źes smraḥo /

/ slob dpon yon tan ḥod ni / kha cig ḥphags pa ñer sbas kyi slob mar ḥdod la / kha cig dgra bcom pa zla baḥi nor buḥi slob mar ḥdod mod kyaṅ / raṅ lugs la / slob dpon dbyig gñen gyi slob ma raṅ las mkhas pa bźi ste / mṅon pa raṅ la mkhas pa blo gros brtan paḥo / tshad ma raṅ las mkhas pa phyogs kyi glaṅ poḥo / phar phyin raṅ las mkhas pa ḥphags pa rnam grol sdeḥo / ḥdul ba raṅ las mkhas pa yon tan ḥod / ces bya ba yod pa de yin te / yul bcom brlag tu bram zeḥi rigs su ḥkhruṅs / ḥbum sde bco brgyad thugs la mṅaḥo /

/ bkaḥ bar paḥi dgoṅs ḥgrel la /

/ yoṅs su grags paḥi dkar chags ḥphaṅ thaṅ ma daṅ / ḥchiṅ bu ma daṅ / lhan dkar ma źes bya ba gsum daṅ / de dag gi rjes su ḥbraṅs pa maṅ po las / grub mthaḥi rnam dbye ma phyed par rnam gźag byas pa

[23] Of the three catalogs mentioned, only one is extant in the Tanjur. Mkhas grub rje speaks as though he had all three before him, but it may be that of the first two he had only citations in other works. The first two catalogs were prepared at the monastery Bsam yas, and presumably disappeared. Thus, in the work *Rje btsun ḥjam dbyaṅs bźad paḥi phar phyin gyi mchan ḥgrel bźad paḥi dgoṅs rgyan las skabs daṅ poḥi mchan* (Notes by Dkon mchog bstan paḥi sgron me on Ḥjam dbyaṅs bźad paḥi rdo rje's Mthaḥ dpyod of Chap. I of the *Abhisamayālaṃkāra*), it is said (8b-4, 5, 6): / dkar chag ḥphaṅ thaṅ ma ni / bod sṅa maḥi dus bkaḥ bstan ḥgyur ro cog gi dkar chag sṅa phyi mi ḥdra ba gsum byas paḥi gcig śos yin te / khri sroṅ sde btsan gyi dus su lo-tsā-ba dpal brtsegs sogs bkaḥ bstan ḥgyur ro cog gi dkar chag pho braṅ stod thaṅ lhan dkar du byas pa daṅ / bsam yas su byas paḥi ḥchiṅ bu ma daṅ / ḥphaṅ thaṅ ka med du byas paḥi dkar chag daṅ gsum yod paḥi gcig yin paḥi phyir / rgyun rnam las / yoṅs su grags paḥi dkar chag ḥphaṅ thaṅ ma daṅ ḥchiṅ bu ma daṅ lhan dkar ma źes

the *Vinaya-puṣpamālā-nāma* (Toh. 4123, also called *Vinayakārikā*), showing only the two *vibhaṅga* (see above), in 6 sections, by the Arhat Viśākhadeva; the *Śrāmaṇerakārikā* (Toh. 4124) in 300 stanzas (*kārikā*), and the self-commentary, the *Vṛtti Prabhāvatī* (Toh. 4125) by the *ācārya* Śākyaprabha.

In general, a doctrine, by upholding or not upholding the four Seals (*mudrā*) which define a Promulgation (*bkar btags kyi phyag rgya bźi*) is judged as upholding or not upholding the Buddhist doctrine. Of the eighteen Śrāvaka schools, the Mahāsammata (*or* Saṃmatīya), the Vātsīputrīya, the Uttarīya, the Dharmaguptika, and the Bhadrayānīya, are judged not to have had the Buddhist doctrine because they held to the unspeakable *pudgala-ātma*; nevertheless, they are judged as Buddhist because of having held to the Refuge, morality, and so forth. The four Seals which define a Promulgation are as follows:

1. The *saṃskāras* are all impermanent (*anitya*).
2. Everything with flux (*sāsrava*) is suffering (*duḥkha*).
3. All natures (*sarvadharmāḥ*) are devoid of self.
4. *Nirvāṇa* is tranquil and solitary.

The remaining schools belong either to the Vaibhāṣikas or to the Sautrāntikas. Moreover, all the eighteen schools say that the Mahāyāna is not a Promulgation [of the Buddha].

The *ācārya* Guṇaprabha is considered by some to be a disciple of Ārya Upagupta; and by others, a disciple of the Arhat Candramaṇi. According to our school, however, he is one of the four disciples of the *ācārya* Vasubandhu who were more learned than their master. Thus, Sthiramati in the *Abhidharma*, Diṅnāga in Logic, Ārya Vimuktasena in the *Prajñāpāramitā* texts, and Guṇaprabha in the *Vinaya*, were all more learned than their master [in their specialized fields]. Guṇaprabha was born in a Brahminical family in Mathurā. He knew by heart the eighteen schools of the Hundred Thousand [i.e., immeasurable teaching of the Buddha].

(2) COMMENTARIES ON THE INTERMEDIATE WHEEL OF THE LAW

As to the primary commentaries on the Intermediate Promulgation, there are the celebrated three catalogs, called *Ḥphaṅ-thaṅ-ma*, *Ḥchiṅ-bu-ma*, and *Ldan-dkar-ma* (Toh. 4364), with their numerous supplements.[23] Since many listings did not distinguish the varieties of tenets

---

bya ba gsum /. *Rgyun rnam* involves a misprint. The quotation is surely from Mkhas grub rje's *Rgyud sde spyi rnam*, and, in fact, the sentence we are now annotating.

maṅ po snaṅ pas / ḥdir de dag daṅ mi mthun pa cuṅ zad ḥbyuṅ ṅo / de la lta baḥi cha gtso bor ḥgrel pa daṅ / spyod paḥi cha gtso bor ḥgrel pa daṅ / gñis ka cha mñam du ḥgrel paḥi bstan bcos daṅ gsum las /

/ daṅ po ni / ḥphags pa klu sgrub kyis mdzad paḥi dbu ma rigs tshogs drug rjes ḥbraṅ daṅ bcas pa ste / dbu ma rtsa ba śes rab / rigs pa drug cu pa / stoṅ ñid bdun cu pa / rtsod bzlog / źib mo rnam ḥthag ste lṅa la mi mthun pa med ciṅ / sṅa rabs pa dag tha sñad grub pa / źes bya ba daṅ drug tu ḥdod la / raṅ reḥi bla ma dag tha sñad grub pa źes bya baḥi gźuṅ rigs tshogs kyi ya gyal źig yod na / ḥphags paḥi slob ma rnams kyi gźuṅ du ḥphags paḥi gźuṅ thams cad khuṅs su ma draṅs pa med pas / de dag tu draṅs ḥoṅ dgos pa las / de dag tu draṅs pa gcig kyaṅ ma byuṅ baḥi phyir daṅ / tshig gsal gyi gśam du rigs tshogs thams cad bgraṅs kyaṅ tha sñad grub pa ma bgraṅs paḥi phyir / med par śes gsuṅ ṅo / des na bla ma rje ni rigs tshogs lṅar bźed la / thams cad mkhyen pa tsoṅ kha pa rin chen ḥphreṅ ba daṅ drug tu bźed do /

/ de la rtsa ba śes rab / rigs pa drug cu pa / rin chen phreṅ ba daṅ gsum ni bstan bcos lus yoṅs su rdzogs pa daṅ / gźan gsum ni rtsa śes las ḥphros paḥi yan lag lta buḥi bstan bcos so / de la rtsa śe ni chos thams cad bden par grub pas stoṅ pa / rigs paḥi rnam graṅs mi ḥdra ba du maḥi sgo nas rgyas par ston la / thabs kyi cha mi ston no / gźan bźis kyaṅ stoṅ pa ñid kho na ston no / rin chen ḥphreṅ bas ni gaṅ zag daṅ chos kyi bdag med gñis rigs pas rgyas par gtan la ḥbebs śiṅ / thabs kyi cha yaṅ skyes bu gsum gyi lam gyi rim pa rags rim źig tshaṅ bar ston no /

/ rtsa śe la rgya gar na ḥgrel pa de-ba-śra-ma / gu-ṇa-ma-ti / gu-ṇa-śrī / sthi-ra-ma-ti / ḥog nas ḥbyuṅ ba bźi daṅ brgyad yod par grags śiṅ bod du bźi ḥgyur te / slob dpon saṅs rgyas bskyaṅs kyis mdzad paḥi ḥgrel pa bu-ddha-pā-li-ta bam po bdun daṅ / slob dpon zla ba grags pas mdzad paḥi tshig gsal daṅ / slob dpon legs ldan ḥbyed kyis mdzad paḥi

[24] The Bla ma rje is presumably Tsoṅ-kha-pa's teacher Rje btsun Red mdaḥ pa because Dkon mchog ḥjigs med dbaṅ po says in his *Rten ḥbrel rtsom ḥphro sogs ljags rtsom ḥphro can gyi skor* (Collected Works, Vol. Ja), 4a-5: / rje btsun red mdaḥ pa rin chen ḥphreṅ ba gtam gyi tshogs yin pas rigs tshogs su mi ḥdren par rigs tshogs lṅar bźed la ("The reverend Red mdaḥ pa held that the *Ratnāvalī* should not be included among the sets of reasons because it is a set of reports [to a king], and so held that there are five 'sets of reasons'").

(*siddhānta*), our exposition may be slightly inconsistent with those catalogs]. Among the works are the treatises which comment chiefly on the Doctrinal Part, those which comment chiefly on the Practical Part, and, finally, those which comment on both parts in equal proportion.

(a) The Doctrinal Part

There are the "six sets of Mādhyamika reasons" (*yukti*) (*dbu ma rigs tshogs drug*) composed by Ārya Nāgārjuna, and the later works written in conformity with them. There is no disagreement that the following constitute five of them: *Prajñā-nāma-mūlamadhyamaka* (Toh. 3824); *Yuktiṣaṣṭhikā* (Toh. 3825); *Vaidalya* (Toh. 3826); *Śūnyatāsaptati* (Toh. 3827); *Vigrahavyāvartanī* (Toh. 3828). The older generation of scholars maintained the sixth to be the *Vyavahāra-siddhi*. Our own Lamas say that if there were a single one among the "six sets of reasons" by the title *Vyavahāra-siddhi*, the disciples of the Ārya, who quote all his texts as authoritative sources, would have quoted this one, too. But there is not a single instance of such a quotation. Also, because all the "sets of reasons" have been enumerated in the course of the *Prasannapadā* (Toh. 3860), but not the *Vyavahāra-siddhi*, one therefore knows that there is no such text. Hence the Bla ma rje[24] assumes "five sets of reasons", while the omniscient Tsoṅ-kha-pa assumes six, including the *Ratnāvalī* (Toh. 4158).

Among them, the three treatises, *Prajñā-mūla*, *Yuktiṣaṣṭhikā*, and *Ratnāvalī* form the full-grown body, while the other three treatises are comparable to the limbs branching out from the *Prajñā-mūla*. The *Prajñā-mūla*, by way of a great number of diverse enumerations of reasons, shows extensively that all entities are void in the sense of real production; it does not show the part of the means (i.e. the practical part). The four others expound only voidness (*śūnyatā*). The *Ratnāvalī* establishes extensively, with reasons, the selflessness of personality (*pudgala-nairātmya*) and the selflessness of natures (*dharma-nairātmya*); moreover, it has the part of the means, which expounds completely the general outline of the steps of the path for the three [religious orders of] persons.

The *Prajñā-mūla* had eight Indian commentaries, those by Devaśrama, Guṇamati, Guṇaśrī, and Sthiramati; and the four following, which were translated into Tibetan: (1) the *Buddhapālita-vṛtti* (Toh. 3842) by Buddhapālita, in 7 sections (*bam po*); (2) the Prasannapadā (Toh. 3860) by Candrakīrti; (3) the *Prajñā-pradīpa* (Toh. 3853) by Bhāvaviveka, whose

śes rab sgron maḥi ḥphreṅ ba ni / de-ba-śra-mas mdzad paḥi ḥgrel pa dkar po rnam par ḥchar ba źes bya baḥi rjes su ḥbraṅ bar spyan ras gzigs brtul źugs kyis bśad / ga las ḥjigs med daṅ bźi ste / ga las ḥjigs med raṅ ḥgrel du sṅon gyi dkar chag rnams daṅ / deḥi rjes su ḥbraṅs pa maṅ pos ḥdod kyaṅ ma yin te / ḥphags paḥi slob ma rnams kyi gźuṅ du deḥi luṅ draṅs pa gcig kyaṅ ma byuṅ baḥi phyir daṅ / rab byed ñi śu rtsa bdun paḥi thad kyi ḥgrel par btsun pa ḥphags pa lhaḥi źal sṅa nas kyaṅ / źes bźi brgya paḥi luṅ draṅs paḥi phyir ro / rigs pa drug cu pa la slob dpon zla ba grags paḥi ḥgrel pa yod la / stoṅ ñid bdun cu pa / rtsod zlog / źib mo rnam ḥthag gsum la raṅ ḥgrel yod do /

/ ḥphags pa lhas bźi brgya pa mdzad de / rab byed bcu drug gi daṅ po brgyad kyis skyes bu chuṅ ḥbriṅ gñis kyi lam gyi rim pa daṅ / chen poḥi byaṅ chub sems sbyoṅ gi rim pa yan chad ston ciṅ / dgu pa man gyis bdag med gñis rigs pas rgyas par gtan la ḥbebs so /

/ de la slob dpon zla ba grags pas dbu ma la ḥjug pa raṅ ḥgrel dan bcas pa mdzad de / chos daṅ gaṅ zag gi bdag med gñis rigs pas rgyas par ston ciṅ thabs kyi cha yaṅ ston no / rtsa ḥgrel gñis ka la nag tshoḥi ḥgyur yod ciṅ / pa tshab kyi yaṅ gñis ka la yod do / gtsaṅ nag pas tshig rkaṅ thuṅ ṅu btaṅ nas / tshig bder btaṅ ba źig yod pa la ci rigs śig nag tshoḥi ḥgyur yin zer bar snaṅ ṅo /

/ slob dpon legs ldan ḥbyed dbu ma sñiṅ po raṅ ḥgrel rtog ge ḥbar ba daṅ bcas pa mdzad do / śes rab sgron meḥi ḥphreṅ ba la slob dpon spyan ras gzigs brtul źugs kyis mdzad paḥi ḥgrel bśad spyan ras gzigs brtul źugs źes bya ba / phyi rol paḥi ḥdod brjod daṅ / ñan thos sde bco brgyad kyi ḥdod pa sogs kyaṅ rgyas par brjod pa bam po brgyad cu pa gcig yod de / phyi rol paḥi ḥdod pa brjod pa de las rgyas paḥi bstan bcos bod du ma ḥgyur ro /

/ ḥphags pa lha ni siṅgalaḥi rgyal poḥi me tog gi ldum rar / me tog gi lba ba las rdzus te lhaḥi bu hdra ba źig ḥkhruṅs pa rgyal poḥi bur byas so / ḥphags paḥi slob ma gźan thams cad kyis slob dpon daṅ ḥdra bar tshad maḥi gnas su byed do / saṅs rgyas bskyaṅs ni rig ḥdzin gyi sa brñes par byed do / legs ldan ḥbyed ni sku tshe de la rdo rjeḥi gdan bsgrub par dam bcas kyaṅ / deḥi phyi ma la slob dpon rdo rje dril bu par gyur nas mchog brñes so / zla ba grags pa ni bod kyi dbu ma pa kha

work is explained (Toh. 3859) by Avalokitavrata, following the commentary composed by Devaśrama, the *Dkar po rnam par ḥchar ba*; (4) the *Akutobhaya* (Toh. 3829). This *Akutobhaya* is maintained by the older catalogs, and by many persons following them, to have been composed by Nāgārjuna; but that is certainly not so, because there is not a single instance of its being quoted in the works of his disciples, and while commenting on the twenty-seventh chapter [of the *Prajñā-mūla*] it says, quoting the *Catuḥśataka* (Toh. 3846), "Āryadeva also says." The *Yuktiṣaṣṭhikā* has a commentary (Toh. 3864) by Candrakīrti, while the three works, *Śūnyatāsaptati*, *Vigrahavyavartanī*, and *Vaidalya* have self-commentaries (Toh. 3831, 3832, and 3830).

Āryadeva wrote the *Catuḥśataka* (Toh. 3846) in sixteen chapters. The first eight chapters set forth the steps of the path for the lowest and middling orders of persons and teach the later steps of training of the great Bodhisattvas. From the ninth chapter on, the two kinds of selflessness (*nairātmya*) are defined in detail, with reasons.

Ācārya Candrakīrti wrote the *Madhyamakāvatāra* (Toh. 3861) and a self-commentary (Toh. 3862), which expound the two selflessnesses of natures and of personality, and also expound the part of the means (the practical part). Both the basic text and commentary were translated by Nag-tsho; and both were also translated by Pa-tshab. It is claimed that Gtsaṅ-nag-pa set the words in short verse lines and that whatever there be of felicitous expression is the translation of Nag-tsho.

Ācārya Bhāvaviveka wrote the *Madhyamakahṛdaya* (Toh. 3855) and its self-commentary, the *Tarkajvālā* (Toh. 3856). On his *Prajñā-pradīpa* (Toh. 3853), the *ācārya* Avalokitavrata wrote a commentary known as the *Avalokitavrata* (Toh. 3859, 3 vols.). Furthermore, in eighty sections, Bhāvaviveka explained in greatest detail the doctrinal positions of the "outsiders", those of the eighteen Śrāvaka schools, and so forth; but his extensive treatise on the doctrinal positions of the "outsiders" was not translated into Tibetan.

Āryadeva was born in a miraculous way from an excrescence of a flower in the garden of a King of Siṅgala [usually Ceylon]. Because he looked like a *devaputra*, he was adopted by the King. All the other disciples of Nāgārjuna considered him an authority equal to the Master himself. Buddhapālita held the rank of Vidyādhara ("wisdom holder"). Bhāvaviveka (also called Bhavya) had made a vow in that life to accomplish the diamond seat (*vajrāsana*); and in his next life, having become the *ācārya* Vajraghaṇṭa-pā, he obtained the highest [of siddhis]. Although some of the Mādhyamikas of Tibet assert that Candrakīrti was

cig gis ḥphags paḥi dṅos slob ma yin par ḥdod kyaṅ / ḥdus paḥi bla ma dag klu sgrub kyi dṅos slob yin par bźed ciṅ / luṅ rigs kyi sgrub byed kyaṅ maṅ la / mar lugs pa dag sku tshe de la mchog gi dṅos grub pa rñes par bźed ciṅ / dguṅ lo bźi brgya bźugs pa sogs kyi rnam thar maṅ po bla ma rdo rje gdan paḥi gsuṅ las byuṅ ba pa tshab lo-tsā-bas bsgyur ba na yod do /

/ slob dpon ye śes sñiṅ pos bden gñis raṅ ḥgrel daṅ bcas pa mdzad do / slob dpon źi ba ḥtshos dbu ma rgyan raṅ ḥgrel daṅ bcas pa mdzad ciṅ / deḥi ḥgrel bśad slob dpon ka-ma-la-śī-las mdzad zer ba na rdzun ma yin no / slob dpon ka-ma-la-śī-las mdzad paḥi dbu ma snaṅ ba bam po dgu ste / de dag la raṅ rgyud śar gsum źes zer ro /

/ slob dpon źi ba ḥtsho ni guṅ lo stoṅ du gcig gis mchog pa bźugs te / chos rgyal sroṅ btsan sgam pos bod du spyan draṅs / khri sroṅ lde btsan gyi sku riṅ la slob dpon pa-dma ḥbyuṅ gnas daṅ bcas pa spyan draṅs nas / bod kyi mi ma yin gdug pa can rnams btul źiṅ / sad mi mi bdun rab tu byuṅ / saṅs rgyas kyi bstan pa dar źiṅ rgyas par mdzad de bkaḥ drin śin tu cheḥo /

/ deḥi slob ma ḥphags pa rnam grol sdes mdzad paḥi ñi khri snaṅ ba daṅ / slob dpon seṅ ge bzaṅ pos mdzad paḥi brgyad stoṅ ḥgrel chen daṅ / ñi khriḥi ḥgrel pa leḥu brgyad ma daṅ / mṅon rtogs rgyan gyi ḥgrel chuṅ don gsal daṅ / sdud paḥi ḥgrel pa rtogs par sla ba daṅ / slob dpon chen po saṅs rgyas ye śes źabs kyis mdzad paḥi sdud paḥi dkaḥ ḥgrel rnams kyaṅ raṅ rgyud paḥi gźuṅ yin la / slob dpon de gsum ga yaṅ slob dpon źi ba ḥtshoḥi slob ma yin źiṅ /

/ slob dpon legs ldan ḥbyed kyi gźuṅ de dag ni dbu ma raṅ rgyud paḥi gźuṅ ṅo / slob dpon saṅs rgyas bskyaṅs / slob dpon zla ba grags pa / slob dpon źi ba lha rnams dbu ma thal ḥgyur ba yin la / slob dpon legs ldan ḥbyed / dpal sbas / ye śes sñiṅ po / źi ba ḥtsho dpon slob rnams dbu ma raṅ rgyud pa yin no /

/ dbu ma thal raṅ gñis la don dam ḥdod lugs la khyad par ji lta bu yod ce na / raṅ rgyud pa dag don dam par grub pa daṅ / bden par grub pa la khyad par med ciṅ de tha sñad du yaṅ mi srid la / de yod par bzuṅ

not a personal disciple of Nāgārjuna, the Lamas of the [Guhya-] Samāja maintain that he was a personal disciple of Nāgārjuna; and there is considerable confirmation from Scripture (*āgama*) and Higher Cognition (*adhigama*). The followers of Marpa say that he (Candrakīrti) obtained highest *siddhi* in that same life. There are many biographies which show that he lived for four hundred years, and so forth; the one based on the narration of *guru* Vajrāsana was translated by Pa-tshab *lotsāva* (translator).

Ācārya Jñānagarbha wrote the *Satyadvaya* (Toh. 3881) and a self-commentary (Toh. 3882). *Ācārya* Śāntarakṣita wrote the *Madhyamakālaṃkāra* (Toh. 3884) and a self-commentary (Toh. 3885). It is claimed that *ācārya* Kamalaśīla wrote a sub-commentary to the latter (self-commentary), but this is false. *Ācārya* Kamalaśīla wrote the *Madhyamakāloka* (Toh. 3887) in 9 sections. These texts are called "the three Eastern works of the Svātantrika".

Ācārya Śāntarakṣita lived a thousand years minus one. He was [first] invited to Tibet by the Dharmarāja Sroṅ-btsan-sgam-po. During the reign of Khri Sroṅ-lde-btsan, he was invited [again] together with *ācārya* Padmasambhava. They subjugated the non-human obnoxious spirits, ordained the "seven selected ones" (*sad-mi mi bdun*), and showed their compassion by spreading the teaching of the Buddha far and wide.

Three *ācāryas* who were disciples of *ācārya* Śāntarakṣita wrote these Svātantrika works: Ārya Vimuktasena wrote the *Ñi-khri snaṅ-ba* (Toh. 3787, the *Pañcaviṃśatisāhasrikāprajñāpāramitopadeśaśāstrābhisamayālaṃkāravṛtti*). Haribhadra wrote the great commentary on the *Aṣṭasāhasrikā* (Toh. 3791, the *āloka*), the commentary on the *Pañcaviṃśatisāhasrikā* (Toh. 3790) in eight chapters, the *Abhisamayālaṃkāra Sphuṭārthā* (Toh. 3793), and the *Pañjika* (Toh. 3792) on the *Sañcaya*, his *Rtogs par sla ba* (the easy to comprehend). Buddhajñānapāda also wrote a *Pañjika* (Toh. 3798) on the *Sañcaya*.

Those works of *ācārya* Bhāvaviveka are texts of the Mādhyamika-Svātantrika. Buddhapālita, *ācārya* Candrakīrti, and *ācārya* Śāntideva are Mādhyamika-Prāsangika, while the *ācāryas* Bhāvaviveka, Śrīgupta, Jñānagarbha, the teacher Śāntarakṣita and his disciple Kamalaśīla are Mādhyamika-Svātantrikas.

What is the difference between the Mādhyamika-Prāsangika and the Mādhyamika-Svātantrika with regard to their concept of the absolute (*paramārtha*)? The Svātantrikas maintain that there is no distinction between "absolute production" and "real production", not even in conventional terms (*vyavahāra*), and that holding such a distinction

na bdag ḥdzin du ḥgyur ba daṅ / raṅ bźin gyis grub pa daṅ / raṅ gi mtshan ñid kyis grub pa daṅ / raṅ gi ṅo bos grub pa gsum khyad par med la / de rnams tha sñad du yod de / dṅos po thams cad tha sñad du de ltar grub par bźed do / thal ḥgyur ba dag de ltar tha sñad du yaṅ med la / yod par bzuṅ na bdag ḥdzin du bźed do /

/ raṅ rgyud pa la yaṅ gñis las / slob dpon legs ldan ḥbyed daṅ / ye śes sñiṅ po sogs ni gzugs sgra sogs / sems las don gźan paḥi phyi rol gyi don / bem por bźed la / slob dpon źi ba ḥtsho rjes ḥbraṅ daṅ bcas pa ni / gzugs sgra sogs sems las don gźan ma yin te / phyi don nam / bem po gźi ma grub par ḥdod do / blun po dag chos thams cad raṅ gi sems yin / zer ba raṅ ni ches mi ḥdraḥo /

/ thal ḥgyur ba dag kyaṅ phyi rol gyi don bźed tshul slob dpon legs ldan ḥbyed daṅ ḥdraḥo / sṅags kyi rgyud sde thams cad kyi lta ba thal ḥgyur ro /

/ spyod pa gtso bor ḥgrel paḥi bstan bcos ni / ḥphags pa klu sgrub kyis mdzad paḥi sems skyed kyi cho ga daṅ / dpal ldan zla bas mdzad paḥi skyabs gsum bdun cu pa la sogs paḥo /

/ lta spyod gñis ka cha mñam du ḥgrel pa ni / ḥphags pa klu sgrub kyis mdzad paḥi mdo kun las btus pa daṅ / rgyal sras źi ba lhas mdzad paḥi bslab btus / spyod ḥjug sogs so /

/ spyir ḥphags pa klu sgrub kyis mdzad pa la goṅ du smos pa rnams daṅ / chos dbyiṅs bstod pa daṅ / ḥjig rten las ḥdas par bstod pa daṅ / rnam par mi rtog par bstod pa daṅ / sems kyi rdo rje la bstod pa sogs bstod tshogs daṅ / bśes spriṅ sogs gtam tshogs daṅ / gso ba rig pa daṅ /

[25] The tentative Sanskrit for the the three terms, and accordingly their translations, is based on the Sanskrit-Tibetan equivalences of the sixteen voidnesses in Chap. I, note 17.

amounts to *ātma-graha* (adherence to the view of self). They mean that being "produced by fundamental ground" (**prakṛti-siddha*), "produced by individual characteristic" (**svalakṣaṇa-siddha*), and "produced by intrinsic nature" (**svabhāva-siddha*) is not distinguishable,[25] that those are conventional terms, and that all entities are produced in conventional terms likewise. The Prāsangikas maintain that in such a case, they [i.e., the entities] are not [produced] even in conventional terms; and to hold that way [as do the Svātantrikas] is *ātma-graha*.

The Svātantrikas may, in turn, be divided into two [subschools]. The *ācāryas* Bhāvaviveka and Jñānagarbha, with others, maintain that form (*rūpa*), sound (*śabda*), and so forth, have an entity (*artha*) apart from thought (*citta*), an external entity: they posit unconscious substance (*jaḍā-svabhāva*). In contrast, *ācārya* Śāntarakṣita and his followers maintain that form, sound, and so forth, have no entity apart from thought, that there is no external entity, and that a substratum of unconscious substance is not demonstrable. But the assertion by the stupid that all natures (*sarvadharmāḥ*) are our own thought (*citta*) bears no resemblance to the Svātantrika position.

The Prāsaṅgikas, who also maintain an external entity, resemble Bhāvaviveka on this point. The doctrine (*darśana*) of all [four] sections of the *tantras* is Prāsaṅgika.

(b) **The Practical Part**

The treatises which comment chiefly on practice are the *Bodhicittotpāda-vidhi* (Toh. 3966) by ārya Nāgārjuna, the *Triśaraṇasaptati* (Toh. 3971) by Candrakīrti, and so forth.

(c) **Both Doctrinal and Practical Parts**

The treatises which give equal space to doctrine and practice are the *Sūtrasamuccaya* (Toh. 3934) by Nāgārjuna, and the *Śikṣāsamuccaya* (Toh. 3939, the *kārikā*, and Toh. 3940) and the *Bodhisattvacaryāvatāra* (Toh. 3871) by Śāntideva.

Compositions by Nāgārjuna have been mentioned previously. Among his other works translated into Tibetan are the following: the *Dharmadhātustava* (Toh. 1118), *Lokātītastava* (Toh. 1120), **Nirvikalpastava* (? Toh. 1119, *Nirupamastava*), *Cittavajrastava* (Toh. 1121), and so forth, in the "Collection of Eulogies" (*stava-kāya*); the *Suhṛllekha* (Toh. 4182), and so forth, among the "Letters" (*lekha*); his works on "Medical Sci-

gser ḥgyur gyi rtsiḥi bstan bcos sogs daṅ / bzo rig pa daṅ / ḥjig rten lugs kyi bstan bcos śes rab brgya pa daṅ / skye bo gso thigs la sogs pa yaṅ mdzad de bod du ḥgyur ro /

/ dbu ma phuṅ po lṅa pa zla ba grags kyis mdzad zer ba ni kha gYar ro /

/ sṅags phyogs kyi bstan bcos rnams ḥog tu ston no /

/ bkaḥ tha maḥi dgoṅs ḥgrel la / lta ba gtso bor ston pa daṅ / spyod pa gtso bor ston pa daṅ / lta spyod cha mñam du ston paḥi bstan bcos daṅ gsum mo /

/ de la spyir byams pa daṅ ḥgrel paḥi chos sde ñi śu źes grags te / byams mgon gyis mdzad paḥi mdo sdeḥi rgyan daṅ / mṅon rtogs rgyan te rgyan gñis / dbus daṅ mthaḥ rnam par ḥbyed pa daṅ chos daṅ chos ñid rnam par ḥbyed pa ste ḥbyed gñis / rgyud bla ma ste byams chos lṅaḥo / ḥphags pa thogs med kyis mdzad paḥi saḥi dṅos gźi daṅ / gźi bsdu ba daṅ / rnam graṅs bsdu ba daṅ / rnam par bśad paḥi sgo bsdu ba daṅ / rnam par gtan la dbab pa bsdu ba ste sa sde lṅa / bam po brgya ñer drug go / saḥi dṅos gźi la sa maṅ pos daṅ / ñan sa / byaṅ sa / saḥi go rim mo / theg pa thun moṅ paḥi sdoms mṅon pa kun las btus / theg chen thun moṅ ma yin paḥi sdoms theg bsdus te / sdoms rnam pa gñis so / slob dpon dbyig gñen gyis mdzad pa la / mdo sde rgyan / dbus mthaḥ rnam ḥbyed / chos daṅ chos ñid rnam ḥbyed gsum gyi ḥgrel pa / rnam bśad rig pa / las sgrub paḥi rab tu byed pa / phuṅ po lṅaḥi rab tu byed pa / ñi śu pa daṅ / sum cu paḥi rab byed de pra-ka-ra-ṇa sde brgyad do / kha cig chos daṅ chos

[26] This is, however, the possible ascription by Bhavya (Bhāvaviveka) in his *Madhyamakaratnapradīpa* (Derge Tg., *Dbu-ma*, Vol. Tsha, 266b-3, 4): "For the meaning of this *in extenso*, one should peruse the *Madhyamakapañcaskandha* composed by the *ācārya* Candrakīrti, the *Tarkajvālā* prepared by myself, and so on" (ḥdiḥi don rgyas par slob dpon zla ba grags paḥi źal sṅa nas mdzad paḥi dbu ma phuṅ po lṅa pa daṅ / bdag gis bkod pa rtog ge ḥbar ba la sogs par blta bar byaḥo). Since Candrakīrti takes up various of Bhāvaviveka's views in his *Prasannapadā* commentary on the *Mūla-Madhyamaka-kārikā*, the two men are exact contemporaries.

ence" (*cikitsā-vidyā*) [i.e., Toh. 4306-4308]; his treatise on making gold (necessarily Toh. 4314, *Rasāyanaśāstroddhṛti*, no author listed), and so forth, among the "Arts" (*śilpa-karmasthāna-vidyā*); the *Prajñāśataka* (Toh. 4328), the *Jantupoṣaṇabindu* (Toh. 4330), and so forth, among the treatises of "common prudent conduct" (*sādhāraṇa-nīti-śāstra*).

The ascription of the *Madhyamaka-pañca-skandha* (Toh. 3866) to the authorship of Candrakīrti is a spurious one.[26]

The treatises of the *mantra* category [i.e., the *tantras*] will be discussed further on.

(3) COMMENTARIES ON THE LAST WHEEL OF THE LAW

In regard to the basic commentaries on the Last Promulgation, there are three groups of treatises — those showing chiefly doctrine; those showing chiefly practice; and those showing doctrine and practice in equal measure.

Ranging over those categories are the famed twenty treatises of the Law (*chos sde ñi śu*) by Maitreya and associated commentaries. Maitreyanātha composed the two *alaṃkāra*, viz. the *Sūtrālaṃkāra* (Toh. 4020) and the *Abhisamayālaṃkāra* (Toh. 3786); the two *vibhaṅga*, viz. the *Madhyāntavibhaṅga* (Toh. 4021) and the *Dharmadharmatāvibhaṅga* (Toh. 4022); and the *Uttaratantra* (Toh. 4024); they constitute the "five Maitreya expositions" (*byams chos lṅa*). Āryāsaṅga composed the *Bhūmi-vastu* (Toh. 4035-4037), the *Vastusaṃgrahaṇī* (Toh. 4039-4040), the *Paryāyasaṃgrahaṇī* (Toh. 4041), the *Vivaraṇasaṃgrahaṇī* (Toh. 4042), and the *Viniścayasaṃgrahaṇī* (Toh. 4038); they constitute the "five *bhūmi* divisions" (*sa sde lṅa*), a total of 126 sections. The *Bhūmi-vastu* (*saḥi dṅos gźi*) comprises the *Bahubhūmika* (*sa maṅ pos*) (Toh. 4035, entered in Toh. catalog as *Yogācaryā-bhūmi*), the *Śrāvakabhūmi* (Toh. 4036), and the *Bodhisattvabhūmi* (Toh. 4037), in their *bhūmi* sequence [seventeen *bhūmis* in all]. He also composed the two collections, the collection common to the vehicles, the *Abhidharmasamuccaya* (Toh. 4049), and the uncommon collection of the Great Vehicle (*mahāyāna*), the *Mahāyānasaṃgraha* (Toh. 4048). *Ācārya* Vasubandhu wrote the three commentaries (Toh. 4026, 4027, and 4028, respectively) on the *Sūtrālaṃkāra*, the *Madhyāntavibhaṅga*, and the *Dharmadharmatāvibhaṅga*; the *Vyākhyāyukti* (Toh. 4061), the *Karmasiddhiprakaraṇa* (Toh. 4062), the *Pañcaskandhaprakaraṇa* (Toh. 4059), the *Viṃśatikā* (Toh. 4056), and the *Triṃśikā* (Toh. 4055); they constitute the "eight *prakaraṇa* divisions" (*pra-ka-ra-ṇa sde brgyad*). Some (scholars) do not include his commen-

ñid rnam ḥbyed kyi ḥgrel pa mi ḥdren bar rten ḥbrel gyi mdo ḥgrel ḥdren no. / raṅ lugs la brgyad du ma ṅes te / slob dpon dbyig gñen gyis mdzad pa la / rten ḥbrel gyi mdoḥi ḥgrel pa daṅ / sa lu ljaṅ paḥi mdoḥi ḥgrel pa daṅ / mdo sde sa bcu paḥi ḥgrel pa daṅ / theg bsdus kyi ḥgrel pa daṅ / rjes dran gsum gyi ḥgrel pa la sogs pa maṅ po yod paḥi phyir ro /

/ yum gsum gnod ḥjoms ni / daṃṣṭa-senaḥi yin źiṅ / ñi khri rnam ḥgrel bod na yod pa ni / rgyal po khri sroṅ lde btsan kyi yin par bźed pas gñis ka dbyig gñen gyi ma yin no /

/ de rnams las byams chos lṅaḥi mdo sde rgyan daṅ / ḥbyed gñis daṅ gsum po bkaḥ tha maḥi dgoṅs ḥgrel lta ba sems tsam ston pa ste / de yaṅ mdo sde rgyan gyis lta spyod cha mñam du ston / ḥbyed gñis kyis lta ba gtso bor ston te / de la mi mthun pa med do /

/ rgyud bla ma bkaḥ bar paḥi dgoṅs ḥgrel lta ba raṅ rgyud ston par sṅa rabs pa rnams bźed la / jo naṅ pas bkaḥ tha maḥi dgoṅs ḥgrel / lta ba khoṅ gi lta ba stoṅ par bźed do / bla ma rjes bkaḥ tha maḥi dgoṅs ḥgrel / lta ba sems tsam ston par bźed / bu ston rin po ches bkaḥ tha maḥi dgoṅs ḥgrel / yaṅ na dbu ma bstan / yaṅ na sems tsam bstan gsuṅ / raṅ lugs la rje rin po cheḥi bźed pas / bkaḥ bar paḥi phyogs mthun gyi mdo / bde gśegs sñiṅ poḥi mdo daṅ / gzuṅs kyi dbaṅ phyug rgyal pos źus paḥi mdo daṅ / ye śes snaṅ ba rgyan gyi mdo daṅ / sor moḥi phreṅ ba la phan paḥi mdo daṅ / ḥphags pa dpal ḥphreṅ gi mdo la sogs paḥi dgoṅs pa gtso bor ḥgrel la / dgoṅs pa thal ḥgyur du gnas śiṅ / ḥphags pa thogs med kyis kyaṅ thal ḥgyur du bkral bar bźed de / jo naṅ paḥi grub mthaḥ la ḥdi las gnod pa med gsuṅ ṅo /

/ mṅon rtogs rgyan ni / rgya gar du slob dpon dbyig gñen / phyogs glaṅ / śā-nti-pa sogs kyis sems tsam du bkral / ḥphags pa grol sde / btsun pa grol sde / seṅ ge bzaṅ po / saṅs rgyas ye śes źabs / a-bha-ya-

[27] The Tōhoku catalog gives Nāgārjuna as the author.

[28] The Tōhoku catalog gives Asaṅga as the author of these three commentaries.

[29] *Ñi khri* stands for the *Pañcaviṃśatisāhasrikā* version of the *Prajñāpāramitā*. However, there is no commentary on that version that can be in point here. *Ñi khri* must be a mistake for *Ḥbum*, and the large commentary on the *Śatasāhasrikā* version (Toh. 3807) must be meant here, because Dkon mchog ḥjigs med dbaṅ po says (*op. cit.*, idem): / gñis pa grub ste / gser ḥphreṅ las phyi ma ḥdi ḥphaṅ thaṅ gi dkar chag tu btsan po khri sroṅ lde btsan gyis mdzad pa ḥphags pa śes rab kyi pha rol tu phyin pa ḥbum gyi rgya cher ḥgrel źes ḥbyuṅ bas rgyal pos mdzad pa yin no / źes gsuṅs paḥi phyir ("And secondly it is proved because it is said in the *Gser ḥphreṅ* [Tsoṅ-kha-pa's commentary on the *Abhisamayālaṃkāra*]: 'Since the ancient *Ḥphaṅ thaṅ* catalog had the entry, *Ḥphags pa śes rab kyi pha rol tu phyin pa ḥbum gyi rgya cher ḥgrel* composed by His Majesty Khri sroṅ lde btsan, it was composed by that King'").

tary on the *Dharmadharmatāvibhaṅga*, but include instead his *Pratītyasamutpādasūtra* commentary (Toh. 3995, the *Pratītyasamutpādādivibhaṅgabhāṣya*). Our own school is not definite in regard to the eight, because there are other writings of Vasubandhu [to be considered as candidates for inclusion], such as the *Pratītyasamutpādasūtra* commentary (Toh. 3995), the *Śālistambaka-sūtra* commentary (Toh. 3986),[27] the commentary (Toh. 3993) on the *Daśabhūmika* of the Sūtras, the *Mahāyānasaṃgraha* commentary (Toh. 4050), the three *Anusmṛti* commentaries (Toh. 3981, 3982, 3983).[28]

We claim that the commentary (Toh. 3808) on the three *Prajñāpāramitā sūtras*, known as *Gnod ḥjoms*, is by Daṃṣṭrasena, and that the commentary on the *Ñi khri*,[29] which is in Tibet, is by Khri sroṅ lde btsan. Hence, neither of them is by Vasubandhu.

Of those [twenty texts], the two *vibhaṅga* and the *Sūtrālaṃkāra* among the "five Maitreya expositions" are examples of commentaries on the third and last Promulation; they show the "Thought Only" (*citta-mātra*) doctrine. The *Sūtrālaṃkāra* expounds doctrine and practice in equal measure; the two *vibhaṅga* expound chiefly doctrine. There is no disagreement in regard to those.

According to the older [Tibetan] scholars, the *Uttaratantra* is a commentary on the Intermediate Promulgation and teaches the Svātantrika position. The Jo-naṅ-pa school, however, maintains that it is a commentary on the Last Promulgation, presenting their own views; and the Bla-ma-rje maintains that it is a commentary on the Last Promulgation and teaches the "Thought Only" (*citta-mātra*) doctrine. Bu-ston rin-po-che holds that it is a commentary on the Last Promulgation and teaches either Mādhyamika or "Thought Only". In our own school, the Rje rin-po-che (i.e. Tsoṅ-kha-pa) states that it is a *sūtra* consistent with the category of the Intermediate Promulgation and explains chiefly the *Tathāgata-garbha-sūtra* (Toh. 258), the *Dhāraṇīśvara-rāja-paripṛcchā* (alias for the *Tathāgata-mahākaruṇā-nirdeśa-sūtra*, Toh. 147), the *Jñānālokālaṃkāra-sūtra* (Toh. 100), the *Ārya-aṅgulimālīya-sūtra* (Toh. 213), the *Śrī-mālā-devī-siṃhanāda-sūtra* (Toh. 92), and so forth. Tsoṅ-kha-pa maintains that its purport is Prāsaṅgika and that the commentary (Toh. 4025) by Āryāsaṅga is also Prāsaṅgika, notwithstanding the opinion expressed in the tenets of the Jo-naṅ-pa.

As to the *Abhisamayālaṃkāra*, in India the *ācāryas* Vasubandhu, Diṅnāga, Śānti-pa, and so on, explained it as "Thought Only". Ārya Vimuktasena, Bhadanta Vimuktasena, Haribhadra, Buddhajñānapāda, Abhaya, and so forth, explained it as Svātantrika; and Atīśa explained

sogs kyis raṅ rgyud du bkral la / jo bo chen po sogs kyis thal ḥgyur du bkral lo / bod kyi lo-tsa-ba chen po sogs kyi sṅa rabs pa thams cad daṅ / phyi rabs kyi phal che ba dag bkaḥ bar paḥi dgoṅs ḥgrel / lta ba raṅ rgyud du bźed la / jo naṅ pa bkaḥ tha maḥi dgoṅs ḥgrel lta ba dbu ma chen po bstan par bźed / ḥphags seṅ ges yum gyi dgoṅs ḥgrel du mdzad pa la skur pa ḥdebs so / bla ma rje sems tsam ston par bźed do / raṅ lugs la rje rin po cheḥi bźed pas mṅon rtogs rgyan raṅ lugs kyi dgoṅs pa mthar thug thal ḥgyur du gnas śiṅ / lta sgom gñis gtso bor ston la / bkaḥ bar paḥi dgoṅs ḥgrel du bźed do /

/ sa sde lṅaḥi lta ba ston paḥi cha rnams sems tsam ston ciṅ / bkaḥ tha maḥi dgoṅs ḥgrel yin la / byaṅ saḥi de kho na ñid kyi leḥus lta ba ston ciṅ / lhag mas spyod pa ston pas / deḥi leḥu gcig ma gtogs pa daṅ / gźan yaṅ spyod ston paḥi cha thams cad theg pa chen poḥi mdo sde spyiḥi dgoṅs ḥgrel lo /

/ sdoms rnam pa gñis ni bkaḥ tha maḥi dgoṅs ḥgrel / lta ba gtso bor ston paḥi bstan bcos te / sems tsam ston no /

/ pra-ka-ra-ṇa sde brgyad ni bkaḥ tha maḥi dgoṅs ḥgrel te / sems tsam ston no /

/ brgyad stoṅ don bsdus daṅ / yum gsum gnod ḥjoms kyis / yum gyi mdoḥi tshig zin gyis dbu ma bstan kyaṅ / de dgoṅs pa can yin / dgoṅs pa sems tsam du gnas / źes ḥgrel lo /

it as Prāsaṅgika. All the early and most the latter-day great Tibetan translators declare it to be a commentary on the Intermediate Promulgation, written from the standpoint of Svātantrika. The Jo-naṅ-pa say that it is a commentary on the Last Promulgation, and that it teaches the great Madhyamaka, thus casting aspersion on the commentaries by Ārya-Hari [bhadra] on the *Prajñā-pāramitā*. The Bla-ma-rje maintains that it teaches "Thought Only". Our school maintains, by the position of Tsoṅ-kha-pa, that the *Abhisamayālaṃkāra* is Svātantrika, but is Prāsaṅgika in its ultimate purport (*dgoṅs mthar thug*), that it chiefly shows both doctrine and intense contemplation (*bhāvanā*), and that it is a commentary on the Intermediate Promulgation.

The parts [of the twenty texts] which set forth the views of the "five *bhūmi* divisions", show "Thought Only", and constitute commentary on the Last Promulgation. The *tattva* chapter of the *Bodhisattva-bhūmi* teaches doctrine, while the remaining chapters teach practice. Apart from that one chapter, all the others, which set forth the practice, constitute a commentary on the general purport of the *Mahāyāna sūtra* section.

The two collections (i.e. the *Abhidharmasamuccaya* and the *Mahāyānasaṃgraha* by Āryāsaṅga) are commentaries on the Last Promulgation. They are treatises which chiefly teach doctrine; they teach "Thought Only".

The "eight *prakaraṇa* divisions" (by Vasubandhu) are commentaries on the Last Promulgation and teach "Thought Only".

The *Aṣṭasāhasrikā-piṇḍārtha* (alias for *Prajñāpāramitāsaṃgrahakārikā*, Toh. 3809, by Diṅnāga) and the commentary called *Gnod ḥjoms* (i.e. Toh. 3808, by Daṃṣṭrasena) on the three *Prajñāpāramitā sūtras* teach the Mādhyamika by the passages cited from the *Prajñāpāramitā sūtras*; nevertheless their purport is to explain those texts from the "Thought Only" standpoint.

/ gñis pa sṅags kyi chos ḥkhor bskor tshul la bźi / bya rgyud kyi rnam gźag / spyod rgyud kyi rnam gźag / rnal ḥbyor rgyud kyi rnam gźag / rnal ḥbyor bla med kyi rgyud kyi rnam gźag go /

/ daṅ po la gsum / bya rgyud kyi dbye ba so soḥi rnam gźag / bya rgyud kyi dbaṅ bskur ba daṅ sdom pa gzuṅ baḥi rnam gźag / dbaṅ thob ciṅ sdom pa bzuṅ nas lam la slob paḥi rnam gźag go /

/ daṅ po la / rigs so soḥi rgyud kyi dbye ba daṅ / bya ba spyiḥi rgyud kyi dbye ba ste / rim pa ltar rigs re re baḥi sgrub thabs daṅ cho ga ston paḥi rgyud daṅ / rigs thams cad kyi sgrub thabs daṅ cho ga spyir ston paḥi rgyud do /

/ ḥo na spyir rigs du yod ce na /

/ bla med la rnam snaṅ / rin ḥbyuṅ / ḥod dpag med / don grub / mi bskyod pa ste lṅa daṅ / rigs drug pa rdo rje ḥchaṅ ste drug go / de dag

[1] In Atiśa's commentary on his own *Bodhipathapradipa*, namely his *Bodhimārga-pradipapañjikā-nāma* (Toh. 3948), he classifies the Tantras into seven groups (Dbu-ma, Derge, Khi, 287a-4, ff.): Kriyātantra (*bya baḥi rgyud*), Caryātantra (*spyod paḥi rgyud*), Kalpatantra (*rtog paḥi rgyud*), Ubhayatantra (*gñis-kaḥi rgyud*), Yogatantra (*rnal ḥbyor gyi rgyud*), Mahāyogatantra (*rnal ḥbyor chen poḥi rgyud*), Anuttarayogatantra (*rnal ḥbyor bla na med paḥi rgyud*). From the examples which he lists under each group, it is obvious that the Mahāyogatantra group became the "Father Tantras" in the Kanjur classification of the Anuttarayogatantra, and that the Anuttarayoga-tantra group became the "Mother Tantras" in the Kanjur classification of the Anuttarayogatantra. He illustrates the Kalpatantra with the works, *Sgrol ma ḥbyuṅ baḥi rgyud* (possibly *Tārā-bhava-tantra*, Toh. 726), *Dam tshig gsum bkod paḥi rgyal po* (*Trisamayavyūharājā*, Toh. 502), and *Rtog pa kun las btus pa* (**Kalpasamuccaya*). He illustrates the Ubhayatantra with the works, *Sgyu ḥphrul dra ba* (*Māyājāla*, Toh. 466) and *Padma gar gyi dbaṅ phyug* (**Padmanarteśvara*).

[2] Mkhas grub rje mentions only this sixfold group to avoid complications. The "Mother Tantra" of the Anuttarayogatantra, in particular the *Śrī Cakrasaṃvara* cycle, may use either a sevenfold or a sixfold classification. Thus Tsoṅ-kha-pa in his *Sbas don* (Collected works, Vol. Ña) gives a way of classifying the Ḍākinīs into seven families (107a-2, ff.): Vajrasattva, Ratnasambhava, Śrī Heruka *drag poḥi rjes su ḥgro ba*, Amitābha, Akṣobhya, Amoghasiddhi, Vairocana; and mentions that these can be made into six by combining Vajrasattva (the causal Vajradhara) with Heruka (the

CHAPTER THREE

B. THE METHOD OF SETTING THE WHEEL OF THE LAW OF THE MANTRA-YĀNA INTO MOTION

There are four parts: fundamentals of the Kriyā Tantra, fundamentals of the Caryā Tantra, fundamentals of the Yoga Tantra, and fundamentals of the Anuttara-Yoga Tantra.[1]

1. FUNDAMENTALS OF THE KRIYĀ TANTRA

There are three parts: fundamentals of the various varieties of the Kriyā Tantra, fundamentals of initiation and holding to vows in the Kriyā Tantra, and fundamentals of learning the path after receiving initiation and holding to vows.

a. *Fundamentals of the various varieties of the Kriyā Tantra*

There are the varieties of Tantras according to the various Families (*kula*), and the varieties of Tantras according to the general Kriyā. Respectively, they are the Tantras which show the evocations (*sādhana*) and rites (*vidhi*) of the individual Families, and the Tantras which show in a general way the evocations and rites for all the Families.

Then, how many Families are there generally?

In the Anuttara, there are the five, Vairocana, Ratnasambhava, Amitābha, Amoghasiddhi, and Akṣobhya, to which Vajradhara is added as the sixth.[2] Of these Families, the sixth is the highest. After the latter,

---

fruitional Vajradhara). The sevenfold classification is the basis for the sevenfold series of correspondences as given, for example, by Padmavajra in his *Śrī-Ḍākārṇavamahāyoginītantrarājavāhikaṭikā-nāma* (Toh. 1419), Dza, 99b-3, ff. In this listing, the traditional five personality aggregates (*skandha*) are increased to seven by the addition of *jñāna-skandha* and *dharmadhātu-skandha* and identified with the seven mountains, the Himavat, etc.

las rigs drug pa mchog daṅ / deḥi ḥog nas mi bskyod paḥi rigs mchog go / de dag la rigs daṅ rigs can gñis gñis te / rgyal ba rnam snaṅ rigs daṅ / des rgyas ḥdebs paḥi lha rnams rigs can te / des gźan laḥaṅ ḥgreḥo /

/ yo-ga la de bźin gśegs pa / rin po che / padma / las / rdo rjeḥi rigs te lṅaḥo / de dag rim pa ltar rnam snaṅ gi rigs sogs daṅ don gcig go / rigs de dag las de bźin gśegs paḥi rigs mchog go /

/ bya spyod la ḥjig rten daṅ ḥjig rten las ḥdas paḥi rigs gñis las / phyi ma la de bźin gśegs paḥi rigs / padmaḥi rigs / rdo rjeḥi rigs gsum rim pa ltar mchog daṅ / ḥbriṅ daṅ / tha maḥo / bya rgyud kyi ḥjig rten paḥi rigs la / lṅas rtsen gyi rigs / nor can gyi rigs / ḥjig rten paḥi rigs te gsum mo/

/ de bźin gśegs paḥi rigs la sde tshan brgyad de / rigs kyi gtso bo / rigs kyi bdag po / rigs kyi yum / rigs kyi gtsug tor / rigs kyi khro bo khro mo / rigs kyi pho ña pho mo / de bźin gsegs paḥi rigs su gtogs paḥi byaṅ sems / der gtogs paḥi lha daṅ / klu daṅ gnod sbyin la sogs paḥi sde tshan no /

[3] This remark points to the classification of deities by grouping them into the Tantric families, with their existence stated in terms of seals (*mudrā*). They are, so to say, "sealed". The Sanskrit verb form is *mudryate* (T. *rgyas dgab paḥo*) in the *Guhyasamāja-tantra*, Skt. text, 157.9. Moreover, Indrabhūti writes in his commentary on the *Śrī-saṃpuṭatilaka* called *Smṛtisaṃdarśanāloka* (Toh. 1197), Derge Ca, 153b-3: "Besides, the expression 'complete universal *mudrā*' means that all the sentient beings of the three realms are 'sealed' by right knowledge" (yaṅ na kun du sna tshogs phyag rgya ni khams gsum gyi sems can thams cad yaṅ dag paḥi ye śes kyis rgyas btab paḥo).

[4] These Families are explained in the work *Ārya-Subāhuparipṛcchā-nāmatantra-piṇḍārthavṛtti* (Toh. 2673), Thu, 101b-2, ff.: The Tathāgata Family means knowing the intrinsic nature of all the natures in the same way as it is, and coming in the same way as the former Buddhas have come. It is accompanied by the Uṣṇīṣa and other *mantra* deities blessed by that (Family) (de bźin gśegs paḥi rigs źes bya ba ni / chos thams cad kyi raṅ bźin ji lta ba bźin du mkhyen ciṅ / sṅon gyi saṅs rgyas rnams ji ltar gśegs pa bźin du byon paḥi don to / des byin gyis brlabs paḥi gsaṅ sṅags kyi lha gtsug tor la sogs pa daṅ bcas paḥo). The Padma Family is Ārya-Avalokiteśvara who sees the sentient beings in the six times of day and night with the eye of compassion undefiled by corruption. It is accompanied by a retinue including Tārā, the *vidyā* blessed by that (Family) to rescue the world (padmaḥi rigs źes bya ba ni / ñon moṅs pas ma gos paḥi thugs rjeḥi spyan gyis ñin mtshan dus drug tu sems can rnams la gzigs pa ḥphags pa spyan ras gzigs dbaṅ phyug ste / des ḥgro ba bsgral bar byin gyis brlabs paḥi rig sṅags sgrol ma la sogs paḥi ḥkhor daṅ bcas paḥo). The Vajra Family has the purpose of protecting the Teaching and overcoming inimical elements. Therefore, it blesses into *vajra* (diamond *or* thunderbolt) that knowledge generated in the Bodhisattva Samantabhadra by the six perfections, and initiates him as Vajrapāṇi by way of the Tathāgatas. It is accompanied by the host of Wrathful Ones and other *mantra* deities given its blessing (rdo rjeḥi rigs źes bya ba ni / bstan pa bsruṅ ba daṅ / sdaṅ ba rnams gźom paḥi don du byaṅ chub sems dpaḥ kun du bzaṅ po la pha rol tu phyin pa drug gis bskyed paḥi ye śes de rdo rjer byin gyis brlabs nas / de bźin gśegs pa rnams kyis phyag na rdo rjer dbaṅ bskur te / deḥi byin gyis rlabs bstan paḥi gsaṅ sṅags kyi lha khro bo la sogs paḥi tshogs daṅ bcas paḥo).

[5] These Families are explained in the work of the preceding note, Thu, 102a-4, ff.: The Wealthy Family (*maṇi-kula*) means the dispelling of the evil of poverty among the sentient beings by Śrī Maṇibhadra and others after they have been blessed in the

Akṣobhya is the highest. Each of the Families includes a Progenitor (*kula*, abbreviation for *kuleśa* = *kula* "family" + *īśa* "lord") and the Progeny (*kulika*). The victor (*jina*) Vairocana is a Progenitor. The deities created by his seal (*mudrā*) are the Progeny, as are their transformations by him into other deities.[3]

In the Yoga, there are the five Families, Tathāgata, Ratna, Padma, Karma, and Vajra. In that order they coincide with the Vairocana Family and so on [of the Anuttara terminology]. Among those Families, the Tathāgata Family is the highest.

In the Kriyā and Caryā Tantras, there are both Mundane (*laukika*) and Supramundane (*lokottara*) Families, the latter comprising the three Families, Tathāgata, Padma, and Vajra. They are, respectively, the highest, middling, and lowest.[4] The Mundane Families of the Kriyā Tantra are these three: Pañcaka-kula (*lṅas rtsen*, "five who play with [dice]"), Maṇi-kula, and Laukika-kula.[5]

(1) THE TATHĀGATA FAMILY

There are eight sections to the Tathāgata Family, namely: Lord of the Family (i.e. the Progenitor), Master of the Family, Mother of the Family, Uṣṇīṣa of the Family, Male and Female Wrathful Ones of the Family, Male and Female Messengers of the Family, the Bodhisattvas belonging to the Tathāgata Family, and the group of gods (*deva*), serpents (*nāga*), secret folk (*yakṣa*), and the like, belonging there.

---

inexhaustible stream of wealth (nor can gyi rigs źes bya ba ni / dpal nor bu bzaṅ po la sogs pas nor gyi rgyun zad mi śes par byin gyis brlabs nas / sems can gyi dbul baḥi gnod pa sel źes bya baḥi don to). The Prosperity Family (*pauṣṭika-kula*) is the playing by five, because it is associated with five hundred gems and shows the play by five with dice. It is a term for making successful the prosperity rites which bring issue of sons and increase of wealth (rgyas paḥi rigs źes bya ba ni / nor bu lṅa brgya daṅ ḥgrogs śiṅ / cho lo lṅas rtse bar ston pas lṅas rtsen te / des bu tsha ḥphan pa daṅ loṅs spyod ḥphel ba rgyas paḥi las grub par byed ces bya baḥi tha tshig go). The Family of the Worldlings (*laukika-kula*) consists of the *devas*, *asuras*, and so forth, excepting those in the five Families (Tathāgata, Padma, Vajra, Wealthy, and Prosperity). They offer their individual *mantras* together with the *vidhis* (ḥjig rten paḥi rigs źes bya ba ni / lṅa po de rnams la ma gtogs paḥi lha daṅ / lha ma yin la sogs pas so soḥi gsaṅ sṅags cho ga daṅ bcas te phul baḥo). "They are rightly included in the three" means that the Wealthy one is included in the Padma Family, that the Prosperity one is included in the Vajra Family, and one should know that the Family of the Worldlings is also generally included under those two. Any not included in those two does not arise through the blessing of the Tathāgata (gsum du yaṅ dag par bsdus pa ston to źes bya ba ni / nor can ni padmaḥi rigs kyis bsdus so / rgyas pa ni rdo rjeḥi rigs kyis bsdus so / ḥjig rten paḥi rigs kyaṅ de dag gi bkab tu phal cher ḥdus par rig par byaḥo / de dag gis ma bsdus pa rnams ni de bźin gśegs paḥi byin gyi rlabs las byuṅ ba yaṅ ma yin la) ... The Skt. for T. *lṅas rtsen* is *pañcaka*, as found in the *Mañj.mūla*, Skt. text 417.18.

/ rigs kyi gtso bo ni bcom ldan ḥdas śā-kya thub paḥo / rigs kyi bdag po ni ḥjam dpal lo /

/ rigs kyi gtso boḥi rgyud kyi skor la / bcom ldan ḥdas gnas gtsaṅ maḥi gnas su sa bcu paḥi byaṅ chub sems dpaḥ seṅ geḥi gzugs su sprul paḥi seṅ geḥi khri la bźugs te / ḥkhor gyis ma źus par de bźin gśegs paḥi yi ge brgya paḥi cho ga phan yon daṅ bcas pa gsuṅs / de las ḥphros nas dam tshig gsum bkod paḥi rgyal poḥi rgyud gsuṅs te / de las rgyal ba śā-kya thub pas dkyil ḥkhor gyi gtso bo mdzad paḥi sgrub thabs bstan / sku gzugs thaṅ ga bya baḥi tshul daṅ / rdul tshon gyi dkyil ḥkhor bya baḥi tshul la sogs pa gsuṅs so / kha cig ḥdi las bdag bskyed bśad paḥi phyir bya rgyud ma yin spyod rgyud yin zer ba mi ḥthad de / sgrub byed de ma ṅes śiṅ / slob dpon A-bha-ya daṅ / jo bo chen po sogs kyis bya rgyud du bśad paḥi phyir ro /

/ bcom ldan ḥdas yaṅ pa can gyi groṅ khyer gyi khaṅ pa brtsegs pa na bźugs te / zla ba gsum na mya ṅan las bzlaḥo sñam du dgoṅs nas / moḥu gal gyi bu la stoṅ spyi phud kyi ḥjig rten gyi khams kyi dge sloṅ rnams sdus śig ces gsuṅs pas / moḥu gal gyi bus ri rab kyi rtse nas / bde gśegs slob mar gyur pa gaṅ su dag / ces sogs bsgrags pas dgra bcom pa bźi khri daṅ bcas paḥi stoṅ spyi phud kyi ḥjig rten gyi khams kyi dge sloṅ thams cad ḥdus so / de nas ḥphags pa śā-riḥu bus stoṅ gsum gyi stoṅ chen poḥi ḥjig rten gyi khams kyi dge sloṅ thams cad bsdus so / de nas byams pas phyogs bcuḥi ḥjig rten gyi khams thams cad kyi mos spyod nas srid pa tha ma paḥi bar gyi byaṅ chub sems dpaḥ thams cad bsdus so / de nas bcom ldan ḥdas kyis sgo mthaḥ yas pa sgrub paḥi gzuṅs phan yon daṅ bcas pa gsuṅs te / ḥdi las rgyal ba śā-kya thub pas dkyil ḥkhor gyi gtso bo mdzad paḥi dkyil ḥkhor gñis bstan par ḥgrel pa las bśad do /

/ yul ma-ga-dhaḥi dri ma med paḥi groṅ khyer źes bya bar bram ze dri ma med pa legs snaṅ źes bya bas saṅs rgyas ñan thos daṅ bcas pa gdugs tshod la spyan draṅs te / deḥi skyed mos tshal daṅ ñe bar na mchod rten brñiṅs pa phyag dar gyi phuṅ por soṅ ba źig las ḥod zer daṅ tshigs su bcad pa sogs byuṅ ba la bcom ldan ḥdas kyis phyag daṅ skor ba mdzad ciṅ spyan chab mdzad pa la ḥkhor rnams kyis rgyu rkyen źus pas / bcom ldan ḥdas kyis mchod rten ḥdiḥi naṅ na de bźin gśegs pa

[6] Ye śes sñiṅ po's *Anantamukhanirhāra-dhāriṇī-vyākhyānakārikā* and *Anantamukhanirhāra-dhāraṇī-ṭīkā*.

(a) **Lord of the Family**

The Lord of the Family is Bhagavat Śākyamuni. The Master of the Family is Mañjuśrī.

In regard to the cycle of Tantras of the Lord of the Family, when the Bhagavat in the pure abode (*śuddhāvāsa*) was seated on a lion throne formed by the Bodhisattvas of the tenth stage who had magically transformed themselves into lions, then without being asked by his retinue he expounded the rite of the hundred syllables of the Tathāgata (*tathāgata-śatākṣara-vidhi*) together with its benefits. Continuing, he pronounced the *Trisamayavyūharājā-nāma-tantra* (Toh. 502), in which he showed the *sādhana* of making Śākyamuni the Lord of the *maṇḍala* (*maṇḍala-nāyaka*), the method of making icons and images, the method of making the *maṇḍala* of powdered colors (*rajomaṇḍala*), etc. Some claim that it is not a Kriyā, but a Caryā Tantra, for the reason that it explains the "self generation" (*bdag bskyed*). That claim is not valid. Their argument is not convincing because *ācārya* Abhayākara, Atīśa, and others pronounce it to be a Kriyā Tantra.

When the Bhagavat was staying in the eaved building (*kūṭāgāra*) of the city of Vaiśālī, considering that in three months he would pass into Nirvāṇa, he said to Maudgalyāyana, "Gather together the *bhikṣus* of the *Sāhasracūḍika* world realms (*lokadhātu*)!" Then Maudgalyāyana proceeded to the summit of Mt. Sumeru and announced, "Whosoever is a disciple of the Tathāgata...", and all the 40,000 Arhats and all the *bhikṣus* of the *Sāhasracūḍika* world realms assembled. Thereupon Ārya Śāriputra called together all the *bhikṣus* of the *Trisāhasramahāsāhasra* world realms. Thereupon Maitreya called together all the Bodhisattvas of the world realms in the ten directions, beginning with those installed in faith (*adhimukticaryā*), and up to those in their last life (*caramabhavika*). Thereupon the Bhagavat pronounced the *Anantamukhasādhaka-nāma-dhāraṇī* (Toh. 525) and its benefits. In the commentary (Toh. 2695-2696),[6] it is said that the work teaches two *maṇḍalas* in which Śākyamuni is made the Lord of the *maṇḍala*.

In the city *Vimala of the Magadha district, a Brahmin named *Vimalaprabha invited the Buddha and his disciples to a noon meal. Near his pleasure garden there was an old *stūpa* which had fallen into the aspect of a heap of rubbish and from which light and verses proceeded. The Bhagavat bowed to it and circumambulated it, shedding tears. When his retinue asked him the cause (*hetu*) and condition (*pratyaya*) [for the phenomenon], the Bhagavat said, "It is through the power of the *dhāraṇī*

thams cad kyis byin gyis brlabs paḥi sñiṅ po / gsaṅ ba riṅ bsrel gyi za ma tog ces bya baḥi gzuṅs bźugs te deḥi mthu yin no / źes gsuṅs nas / deḥi cho ga phan yon daṅ bcas pa gsuṅs so /

/ byaṅ chub rgyan ḥbum da lta bod na tshaṅ ba mi bźugs / sṅon gyi mkhas pa dag gis de draṅs par de bźin gśegs paḥi chos skuḥi riṅ bsrel / sku gduṅ gi riṅ bsrel / sku bal gyi riṅ bsrel rnams / mchod rten du gźug par gsuṅs te / chos skuḥi riṅ bsrel ni gzuṅs rnams so / sku gduṅ gi riṅ bsrel ni sku gduṅ las byuṅ baḥi riṅ bsrel yuṅs ḥbru tsam mo / sku bal gyi riṅ bsrel ni sku gzugs te / de dag rim pa ltar mchog daṅ ḥbriṅ daṅ tha mar gsuṅs so /

/ bcom ldan ḥdas ser skyaḥi groṅ khyer na bźugs te / deḥi tshe ser skyaḥi groṅ khyer na bram ze ser skya zla ba źes bya ba bstan pa la ma dad pa źig yod de / de yid ches paḥi bram ze źig gi rmi lam du ser skya zla ba źig bdun na ḥchi bar luṅ bstan pa rmis te / de la smras pas / de ḥjigs skrag nas bcom ldan ḥdas la źus pas / khyod źag bdun na ḥchi bar ḥgyur te / mnar med paḥi sems can dmyal bar skye bar ḥgyur źiṅ / de nas dmyal ba chen po bcu drug tu rim gyis skye bar ḥgyur / de nas khyi daṅ phag la sogs par skye bar ḥgyur / źes luṅ bstan / des ston pa la skyabs źus pas / bcom ldan ḥdas kyis / de la ser skyaḥi groṅ khyer gyi lam gyi bźi mdor mchod rten brñiṅs pa źig yod pa de gsos la / deḥi naṅ du ḥod zer dri ma med pa rnam par dag paḥi ḥod kyi gzuṅs / źes bya ba ḥdi tshug cig daṅ khyod tshe nur nas riṅ du ḥtsho bar ḥgyur źiṅ / śi ḥphos nas de bźin gśegs pa mi bskyod paḥi saṅs rgyas kyi źiṅ du skye bar ḥgyur ro / źes gsuṅs pas / byaṅ chub sems dpaḥ sgrib pa thams cad rnam par sel bas źus te / gzuṅs chog phan yon daṅ bcas pa gsuṅs śiṅ / sgrib pa rnam par sel ba ñid kyis kyaṅ gsuṅs so / de nas phyag na rdo rjes źus nas mchod pa bya baḥi cho ga źib mo rnams gsuṅs so /

/ rten ḥbrel gyi mdo ni / bcom ldan ḥdas yul sum cu rtsa gsum gyi lhaḥi gnas kyi A-ra-mo-ni-ga lta buḥi rdo leb kyi steṅ na bźugs te / ḥphags pa spyan ras gzigs dbaṅ phyug gis lha rnams de bźin gśegs paḥi mchod rten bgyis te / bsod nams bgyi bar ḥtshal na de dag la phan gdags paḥi cho ga bśad du gsol / źes gsol bas / rten ḥbrel sñiṅ poḥi gzuṅs mchod rten du gźug paḥi cho ga phan yon daṅ bcas pa gsuṅs so /

[7] That work (Derge, Rgyud ḥbum, Na, 18a-7, ff.) explains the word *stūpa* as follows: A "*stūpa*" is a *maṇḍala* where all the Buddhas dwell. A "*stūpa*" is a tomb (monument, tumulus) for the corporeal relics of the Nirmāṇa-kāya of all the Buddhas. The Tathāgata, possessed of right speech, has so declared! (mchod rten źes bya ba ni saṅs rgyas thams cad kyi bźugs gnas dkyil ḥkhor yin no / mchod rten źes bya ba ni saṅs rgyas thams cad kyi sprul paḥi skuḥi sku gduṅ gi baṅ so yin no / de bźin gśegs pa yaṅ dag paḥi gsuṅ daṅ ldan pas de ltar gsuṅs so).

[8] The word *mūrtijā* occurs, e,g., *Mañjuśrī-mūla-tantra*, Skt. text, 596.19.

in this *stūpa*—the *Sarvatathāgatādhiṣṭhāna-hṛdayaguhyadhātukaraṇḍa-nāmadhāraṇī-mahāyānasūtra*" (Toh. 507), and then he explained its rite and the benefits going along with it.

In Tibet there is at present no complete text of the *Bodhimaṇḍa-lakṣālaṃkāra* (Toh. 508). When the former Pandits "invited" it, they said that there are three kinds of relics (*dhātu*) to put into a *stūpa* —[7] the relics of the *Dharmakāya* of the Tathāgata, the relics of his corporeal substance (*mūrtijā*),[8] and the relics of his garb. They said that the relics of his *Dharmakāya* are the *dhāraṇīs*, the relics of his corporeal substance are the relics derived from his corporeal substance, even when they are no bigger than a mustard seed, and the relics of his garb are the icons (*bimba* or *pratibimba*); and that in the given order, they are highest, middling, and lowest.[9]

Once when the Bhagavat was in the city of Kapila, there was a Brahmin in that city named Kapilacandra who did not believe in the Teaching. A trustworthy Brahmin dreamed a prophecy that the Brahmin Kapilacandra would die in seven days. Upon being informed of that (prophecy), the latter, frightened, asked the Bhagavat about it. The Bhagavat prophesied, "You will die within seven days and be reborn in the Avīci hell. Then you will be reborn successively in each of the sixteen great hells, and then you will be reborn as a dog, as a pig, and so on." He asked the Teacher to protect him, and the Bhagavat then said, "Now, at the cross-roads in the city of Kapila there is an old *stūpa*. Repair it and put into it this *Raśmivimalaviśuddhaprabhā-dhāraṇī* (Toh. 510); thereby your life will be prolonged, you will live a long time, and when you pass away, you will be reborn in the Buddha-field of the Tathāgata Akṣobhya." Therefore, at the request of the Bodhisattva Sarvanivaraṇaviṣkambhin, he expressed the *dhāraṇī* rite together with its benefits, and Sarvanivaraṇaviṣkambhin himself also expressed it. Then, at the request of Vajrapāṇi, he (the Bhagavat) expressed the fine points of the rite of the offerings to be made.

Concerning the *sūtra* on *Pratītya-samutpāda*, once when the Bhagavat in the Heaven of the the Thirty-three Gods (*trayastriṃśat*) was seated on the stone slab called "Like Aramoniga", Ārya Avalokiteśvara asked him, "Please explain the rite bringing benefit to those gods who seek to create merit by building *stūpas*." Therefore, the Bhagavat pronounced the *Pratītyasamutpāda-hṛdaya-dhāraṇī* (Toh. 519), including the benefit of the rite of placing it in *stūpas*.

---

9 The classification here is consistent with, but not stated in so many words in that work (Toh. 508), which is presumably the reason for saying "there is no complete text".

/ gzuṅs phyi ma bźi po ḥdi de bźin gśegs paḥi rigs kyi rgyud du gtogs par gaṅ gis ḥjog ce na / de dag las mchod rten du gźug paḥi gzuṅs daṅ / mchod rten bźeṅs paḥi cho ga la sogs pa bśad ciṅ / mchod rten de thams cad de bźin gśegs paḥi mchod rten yin paḥi rgyu mtshan gyis yin no /

/ de bźin gśegs pa bdun gyi sṅon gyi smon lam gyi khyad par rgyas paḥi mdo yaṅs pa can du kun dgaḥ bo la gsuṅs śiṅ / de nas ḥjam dpal daṅ / skyabs grol daṅ / phyag na rdo rje daṅ / tshaṅs pa daṅ / brgya byin daṅ / rgyal po chen po bźi daṅ / gnod sbyin gyi sde dpon bcu gñis sogs gyis raṅ raṅ gi cho ga smras pa daṅ bcas pa daṅ / de bźin gśegs pa sman gyi bla bai-dū-ryaḥi hod kyi rgyal poḥi sṅon gyi smon lam gyi khyad par rgyas paḥi mdo ḥphags pa ḥjam dpal gyis źus pa źiṅ bkod daṅ bcas pa gñis la kha cig mdoḥi phyogs su gtogs te sṅon gyi dkar chag rnams su mdor byas paḥi phyir / źes zer ro / kha cig sṅags kyi phyogs su gtogs te / slob dpon źi ba ḥtshos cho ga mdzad ciṅ de yaṅ sṅon du gso sbyoṅ blaṅ ba sogs bya spyod kyi cho gaḥi sgrigs daṅ mthun par mdzad paḥi phyir / źes pa daṅ / de bźin gśegs paḥi rigs su gtogs źes zer ro / raṅ lugs sṅags su gtogs so / gzuṅs thams cad kyi spyiḥi cho ga kun snaṅ gsal ba las kyaṅ sṅags su gtogs par bśad do / ḥon kyaṅ rigs gaṅ du gtogs ma ṅes so /

/ kha cig śer phyin yi ge ñuṅ ṅu sṅags su gtogs te der mu-ni mu-niḥi sṅags bśad pas so / źer zer pa ni sgrub byed ltar snaṅ ṅo /

/ yaṅ kha cig śer sñiṅ sṅags su gtogs zer te / ḥphags pa klu sgrub kyi mdzad zer baḥi ḥgrel par rgyal ba śā-kya thub pas gtso bo mdzad paḥi dkyil ḥkhor daṅ / slob dpon dha-ris mdzad zer baḥi ḥgrel par yum chen mo la phyogs bcuḥi saṅs rgyas kyis bskor baḥi dkyil ḥkhor daṅ / slob dpon padma ḥbyuṅ gnas kyis mdzad zer bar yaṅ de ltar bśad pa daṅ / mṅon rtogs brgyad kyi dbaṅ bskur sogs thams cad rdzun ma ḥbaḥ źig go / bdud bzlog byed tshul yaṅ ḥod gsal ma daṅ gleṅ gźi ma sogs yod de rtog bzoḥo /

/ kha cig su-rū-paḥi sṅags ḥdi de bźin gśegs pa gzugs mdzes kyi sṅags yin pas / de bźin gśegs paḥi rigs kyi rgyud du gtogs źes zer te / ḥdi khol phyuṅ las ma ḥgyur bas gaṅ du gtogs dpyad dkaḥo /

/ gser ḥod dam paḥi mdo la kha cig sṅags su gtogs śiṅ de bźin gśegs

Why are the preceding four *dhāraṇīs* included among the Tantras of the Tathāgata Family? It is because they explain the rites of *dhāraṇīs* placed in *stūpas*, the rites of *stūpa* erection, and so forth, and because all those *stūpas* are Tathāgata *stūpas*.

Some claim that the following two works belong to the *sūtra* category, because they are set down as *sūtras* in former catalogues:

1. the *Saptatathāgata-pūrvapraṇidhāna-viśeṣavistāra-sūtra* (Toh. 503) spoken to Ānanda in Vaiśālī, and including the voicing of their individual rites by Mañjuśrī, Skyabs grol (S. *Śaraṇamukta), Vajrapāṇi, Brahmā, Śakra, the four great kings, the twelve *yakṣa* generals, and so on;

2. the *Bhagavato bhaiṣajyaguru-vaiḍūryaprabhasya pūrvapraṇidhāna-viśeṣavistāra-sūtra* (Toh. 504), and including [a discussion of] the "field array" (*kṣetra-vyūha*) as requested by Mañjuśrī. Others claim that they belong to the *mantra* category, because the *ācārya* Śāntarakṣita has composed a rite [based on them] (Toh. 3133, no author listed). He composed it consistent with the structure of Kriyā-Caryā rites, in that he has the preliminaries of observing the Sabbath (*upoṣadha*), and so on. They claim, moreover, that the (two works) belong to the Tathāgata Family. Our own school places them in the *mantra* category. They are also explained as belonging to the *mantra* category in the *Sarvadhāraṇī-maṇḍala-vidhi* (Toh. 3136, by Ratnakīrti), called "Bright sun-rays". However, the Family to which they belong is not certain.

Some say that the *Svalpākṣara-prajñāpāramitā-sūtra* (Toh. 530 = Toh. 22) belongs to the *mantra* category, because it has the *mantra* "Muni-Muni". This claim seems reasonable.

Also, some assert that the *Prajñāpāramitā-hṛdaya* (Toh. 531 = Toh. 21) belongs to the *mantra* category. However, the following works are all spurious: the commentary ascribed to Ā*rya* Nāgārjuna (Toh. 2640), in which the *maṇḍala* makes the Jina Śākyamuni the Lord; the commentary ascribed to Dārika-pa (Toh. 2641), in which the *maṇḍala* surrounds the Great Mother with the Buddhas of the ten directions; the commentaries ascribed to Padmasambhava, viz. the one in which he explains that same way, and the one with initiation (*abhiṣeka*) of the eight *abhisamaya*. Likewise, the *Bdud bzlog byed tshul*, the *Ḥod gsal ma*, and the *Gleṅ gźi ma* are forgeries.

Some say that the *Surūpa-nāma-dhāraṇī* (Toh. 540) belongs to the Tantras of the Tathāgata Family because it is the *dhāraṇī* of the beautiful body of the Tathāgata; but since the translation is composed of selections only, it is difficult to determine where it belongs.

Some claim that the *Suvarṇa-prabhāsa-sūtra* belongs to the *mantra*

paḥi rigs kyi rgyud du gtogs zer / kha cig mdoḥi phyogs su gtogs źes zer ro / raṅ lugs la sṅags kyi phyogs su gtogs te / rgya gar ba maṅ pos kyaṅ sṅags su byas so / de la gser ḥod dam pa mchog tu rnam par rgyal baḥi mdo leḥu so gcig pa daṅ / gser ḥod dam pa mdo sdeḥi dbaṅ poḥi rgyal po leḥu ñer dgu pa daṅ / gser ḥod dam pa mdo sdeḥi dbaṅ poḥi rgyal po leḥu ñer gñis pa daṅ gsum yod de / gsum gaḥi gleṅ gźiḥi leḥu gcig tu snaṅ la / daṅ poḥi lha mo spobs pa can gyi leḥu daṅ / gźan gñis kyi dbyaṅs can maḥi leḥu gcig tu snaṅ źiṅ / leḥu de las dbyaṅs can maḥi sgrub thabs daṅ / śes rab blo ḥphel gyi cho ga daṅ bcas pa gsuṅs so / rgyal chen bźiḥi phyogs skyoṅ baḥi leḥu las rnam thos sras kyi sgrub thabs daṅ / yid bźin nor buḥi gzuṅs daṅ / ras bris la brten nas dṅos grub sgrub paḥi cho ga rnams gsuṅs so / lha mo chen mo dpal gyi leḥu daṅ / lha mo chen mo dpal gyis nor bsgrub paḥi leḥu gñis las lha mo deḥi sgrub thabs daṅ / de la brten nas nor sgrub paḥi thabs daṅ bcas pa gsuṅs so / gnod sbyin gyi sde dpon chen po yaṅ dag śes kyi leḥu las / deḥi sgrub thabs daṅ / ras bris la brten nas dṅos grub sgrub paḥi cho ga rnams gsuṅs so / de thams cad gsum ga la khyad med du snaṅ ṅo /

/ rigs kyi bdag poḥi rgyud kyi gtso bo ni ḥjam dpal rtsa rgyud yin te / de la leḥu sum cu rtsa drug yod ciṅ ḥjam dpal źi khroḥi sgrub thabs maṅ po bstan la / sku gzugs bya thabs kyaṅ bstan ciṅ / bcom ldan ḥdas mya ṅan las bzla baḥi tshul bstan nas sku gduṅ cha brgyad du bgo bar ḥgyur ba daṅ / bstan ḥdzin gyi skyes bu maṅ po ḥbyuṅ bar ḥgyur ba luṅ bstan to /

/ ḥjam dpal dpaḥ bo gcig tu grub paḥi rgyud ces bya ba leḥu bźi pa gcig yod de / de las ḥjam dbyaṅs A-ra-pa-tsa-na dkar po gtso ḥkhor lṅa ba daṅ / A-ra-pa-tsa-na gur gum mdog can gtso ḥkhor lṅa pa gñis kyi sgrub thabs chog daṅ bcas pa bstan ciṅ / rma bya chen mo la brten nas tshe bsgrub pa daṅ / thog bsruṅ ba daṅ / rmi lam brtag thabs rgyal ba śā-kya thub pa la brten pa daṅ / ḥphags pa spyan ras gzigs dbaṅ phyug

[10] Johannes Nobel, *Suvarṇaprabhāsa.* Sanskrit (1937).

category, and belongs among the Tantras of the Tathāgata Family. Others claim that it belongs to the *sūtra* category. According to our school, it belongs to the *mantra* category, and many Indian pandits also place it among the *mantras* [i.e. in the Tantra literature]. In connection with that *sūtra*, there are these three works: the **Suvarṇaprabhāsottama-vijayasūtra* (Toh. 555, no Skr. title given; apparently translated from Chinese) in 31 chapters; the *Suvarṇaprabhāsottamasūtrendrarāja* (Toh. 556) in 29 chapters; the *Suvarṇaprabhāsottamasūtrendrarāja* (Toh. 557) in 22 chapters. The three have identical introductory chapters. The chapter "Goddess *Spobs-pa-can* (**Devī Pratibhānavatī*)" of the first (recension) appears identical with the Sarasvatī chapter of the other two. Those chapters (No. VII in Nobel's edition)[10] set forth the *sādhana* of Sarasvatī, together with the rite of expanding insight and cognition (*prajñābuddhivardhana*). The chapters of the four great kings (*catur-mahārāja*, Nobel No. VI), protectors of the quarters, set forth the *sādhana* of Vaiśravaṇa, the *Cintāmaṇi-dhāraṇī*, and the rites of accomplishing *siddhis* by depending on paintings. Both the chapter of Śrī-mahādevī (Nobel, No. VIII) and the chapter of "Securing riches through Śrīmahādevī" (of the other recensions) set forth the *sādhana* of that goddess, together with the method of accomplishing riches by relying on her. The chapters on the great *yakṣa* general Saṃjñāya (Nobel, No. XI) set forth his *sādhana* and the rites of accomplishing *siddhis* in dependence on paintings. All those (chapters) reveal no difference between the three (recensions).

(b) Master of the Family

The chief Tantra of the Master of the Family is the *Mañjuśrīmūlatantra* (Toh. 543) in 36 chapters. It teaches many *sādhanas* of Mañjuśrī in his peaceful and angry aspects, and also the method of making icons; and it makes prophecies about the distribution of the eight parts of the relics of the corporeal substance after the Bhagavat had shown the method of passing into *Nirvāṇa* and about the arising of many persons who would be "holders of the teaching" (*śāsana-dhara*).

There is also the work, *Mañjuśrī-Siddhaikavīra-tantra* (Toh. 544) in four chapters. It teaches the *sādhana* of the white Arapacana-Mañjughoṣa, Lord and retinue amounting to five, and of the saffron-colored Arapacana-Mañjughoṣa, Lord and retinue amounting to five, together with their rites. It also shows the attainment of long life, protection from hail, and the way of interpreting dreams, through relying on

la brten pa daṅ / lhaḥi bu źig la brten pa la sogs paḥi las tshogs maṅ po bstan / deḥi leḥu gñis pa daṅ / ḥjam dpal rtsa rgyud kyi leḥu gñis pa ste / de gñis ka las sku gzugs daṅ / mchod rten gyi pad gdan du gźug paḥi dza-mbha-las gtso byas paḥi gnod sbyin pho dgu daṅ / nor rgyun du gźug paḥi dza-mbha-las gtso byas paḥi gnod sbyin pho dgu daṅ / nor rgyun mas gtso byas paḥi gnod sbyin mo dguḥi ḥkhor lo byed thabs rnams bstan to / a-ra-pa-tsa-na rigs gñis po ḥdiḥi bkaḥ da lta yaṅ ma chad par yod do / ḥdi khol phyuṅ yin pas gleṅ gźi daṅ rgyud gtad pa sogs med do /

/ rigs kyi yum ni ḥod zer can daṅ / gzuṅs grva lṅa la sogs pa ste /

/ ḥod zer can gyi gzuṅs źes bya ba gzuṅs phan yon daṅ bcas pa ston pa źig daṅ / ḥod zer can gyi rtogs pa źes bya ba gzuṅs kyi bśad pa daṅ sgrub thabs daṅ cho ga źib mo rnams ston pa źig ste gñis so / ḥdi bya rgyud du yid ches paḥo /

/ sgyu ma ḥbyuṅ baḥi ḥod zer can źes bya ba ślo-ka bdun brgya yod pa / ślo-ka stoṅ phrag bcu gñis pa gcig las phyuṅ ba yin zer ba źig yod de / de las lha ñi śu rtsa lṅa pa daṅ / bcu gcig pa daṅ / lha lṅa paḥi sgrub thabs daṅ cho ga ston la / de bya rgyud yin paḥi dbaṅ du byas nas zur bkaḥ daṅ / cho ga daṅ sgrub mchod byed paḥi lag len snaṅ ste / de las bskyed rim rdzogs rim sogs bla med kyi brda chad maṅ po bśad ciṅ / gźan yaṅ the tshom gyi gźi maṅ po snaṅ ṅo /

/ gzuṅs grva lṅa ni / stoṅ chen rab ḥjoms daṅ / rma bya chen mo daṅ / so sor ḥbraṅ ma daṅ / bsil baḥi tshal daṅ / gsaṅ sṅags rjes su ḥdzin ma rnams so /

/ de rnams kyi dgoṅs ḥgrel śānti-pas mdzad paḥi so sor ḥbraṅ maḥi sgrub thabs daṅ / bsruṅ ḥkhor bri thabs daṅ / lha mo lṅaḥi sgrub thabs daṅ gsum yod do /

/ slob dpon dze-tā-ri dgra las rnam par rgyal bas mdzad paḥi gzuṅs kyi cho ga daṅ / so sor ḥbraṅ maḥi sgrub thabs daṅ / deḥi bsruṅ ḥkhor

[11] The Tibetan term *zur bkaḥ* (specialized promulgation) contrasts with *spyi bkaḥ* (general promulgation) in the classification of Tantric works, for example in *Thob yig*, beginning Vol. I, 174b-2. Mkhas grub rje employs a comparable classification in his present work and chapter, where the final subsection "General Kriyā Tantra" is an illustration of *spyi bkaḥ*.

Mahāmayūrī. It also teaches a great set of rites based on the Jina Śākyamuni, based on Ārya Avalokiteśvara, based on a Devaputra, etc. Its second chapter, as well as the second chapter of the *Mañjuśrīmūlatantra*, teaches the means of making the circle (*cakra*) of the nine male *yakṣas* with Jambhala their Lord and of the nine female *yakṣas* with Vasuṃdharā their Queen, and of seating them on the lotus seat of the icon and of the *stūpa*. The promulgation of both these Arapacana families is still continued in our own times, but since they are merely excerpts, there are no introductory, admonitory, etc. sections.

(c) **Mother of the Family**

Here there are Mārīci, the five *Gzuṅs grva* [or five *viayā-rājñī*, also called the *pañcarakṣā*], etc.

The *Mārīci-nāma-dhāraṇī* (Toh. 564) expounds the *dhāraṇī* together with its benefits. The *Mārīci-kalpa* (Toh. 565) teaches the exposition of the *dhāraṇī* and the fine points of the *sādhana* and rite. These two are assuredly in the Kriyā Tantra.

There is also the *Māyāmārīci-saptaśata-nāma* [the one in 700 ślokas] (Toh. 566) said [in the full title] to be extracted (*uddhṛta*) from the one in 12,000 ślokas (*dvādaśasahasra*). It teaches the *sādhana* and rite of the 25 gods, 11 and 5 gods. That work appears to be a specialized promulgation (*zur bkaḥ*)[11] governed by the Kriyā Tantra and to show the techniques (*prakriyā*) of performing the rite, *sādhana*, and offerings (*pūjā*). However, it includes much terminology of the Anuttara Tantra, such as the Steps of Production (*utpatti-krama*) and the Steps of Completion (*niṣpanna-krama*), and there are many other doubtful spots.

The five *Gzuṅs grva* are: Sāhasrapramardanī (her *sūtra*, Toh. 558), Mahāmayūrī (her *sūtra*, Toh. 559); Pratisarā (her *sūtra*, Toh. 561), Śītavatī (her *sūtra*, Toh. 562), Mantrānudhāriṇī (her *sūtra*, Toh. 563).

Śānti-pa composed three basic commentaries on them: the *sādhana* of Pratisarā (possibly Toh. 3125, no author listed), the way of drawing the protective circle of Pratisarā (Toh. 3118), and the *sādhana* of the five goddesses (Toh. 3126, the *bsruṅ ba lṅaḥi cho ga* = *pañcarakṣā-vidhi*).

The *ācārya* Jetāri, "he who has been victorious over the enemy" (Dgra las rnam par rgyal ba), composed a rite of the *Gzuṅs* (*grva*) (possibly Toh. 3128, the *Pañcarakṣārcanavidhi*, no author mentioned), a *sādhana* of Pratisarā together with the method of drawing her protective circle (Toh. 3127, the *Mahāpratisarācakralekhanavidhi*), *sādhanas* of the five goddesses (probably Toh. 3119-3123 inclusive), and a work for enabling

ḥbri thabs daṅ / lha mo lṅa gaḥi sgrub thabs daṅ / mo gśam gyis srid bsgrub pa sogs yod do /

/ rigs kyi gtsug tor gyi rgyud ni / gtsug tor rnam rgyal / dri med / gdugs dkar la sogs pa ste / rnam rgyal la de bźin gśegs paḥi gtsug tor rnam par rgyal maḥi rtogs pa źes bya ba daṅ / ṅan soṅ thams cad yoṅs su sbyoṅ baḥi gtsug tor rnam par rgyal maḥi gzuṅs źes pa daṅ / de bźin gśegs paḥi gtsug tor rnam par rgyal maḥi rtogs pa ḥchi bdag gi dbyug pa ḥdzin pa źes bya ba daṅ / gtsug tor rnam par rgyal maḥi gzuṅs źes bya ba daṅ / gtsug tor rnam par rgyal maḥi rtogs pa źes bya ba daṅ lṅaḥo / de la daṅ po daṅ / gsum pa gñis ḥdra min cuṅ zad ma gtogs don gcig tu snaṅ bas ḥgyur khyad du mṅon gsuṅ ste / bde ba can gyi źiṅ gi chos yaṅ dag par sdud paḥi phug gi khaṅ bzaṅ du ḥphags pa spyan ras gzigs dbaṅ phyug gis źus na / rgyal ba tshe dpag med kyis gsuṅs śiṅ / gñis ka las lha dgu mar bstan to / ḥchi bdag gi dbyug pa ḥdzin pa źes bya ba yod pa de las gśin rje chos kyi rgyal pos gzuṅs gaṅ gis ḥdzin paḥi slad bźin ḥbraṅs nas bsruṅ bar źal gyis bźes par bśad do /

/ gñis pa ni bcom ldan ḥdas kyis yul sum cu rtsa gsum paḥi lhaḥi gnas su gsuṅs te / de yaṅ lhaḥi bu śin tu brtan pa źes bya ba la ḥchi ltas phog nas / źag bdun na śiḥi phos nas khyi daṅ / phag la sogs paḥi ḥgro ba bdun tu rim gyis skyes te / mnar med du skye bar mthoṅ nas lhaḥi dbaṅ po brgya byin la skyabs źus pas / kho bos skyabs mi nus so / źes bcom ldan ḥdas kyi druṅ du khrid nas źus pas / bcom ldan ḥdas kyi dbuḥi gtsug tor nas ḥod zer byuṅ ste gzuṅs kyi sgra byuṅ ṅo / de nas lhaḥi bu des źag drug tu gzuṅs kyi bzlas brjod byas pas ṅan ḥgror skye baḥi las sgrib thams cad byaṅ bar gyur to /

/ bźi pa las gzuṅs daṅ mchod rten du gźug paḥi rnam gźag tsam źig bstan to / lṅa pa las gtsug tor rnam par rgyal ma lha sum cu rtsa gsum gyi sgrub thabs bstan te / deḥi bkaḥ yaṅ da lta byed par snaṅ ṅo /

/ gtsug tor dri med kyi gzuṅs ni dgaḥ ldan gyi lhaḥi gnas su bźugs te / sum cu rtsa gsum paḥi lhaḥi bu nor buḥi sñiṅ po dri ma med pa źes bya ba la gnod sbyin skar mdaḥ gdoṅ źes bya bas khyod źag bdun na ḥchi baḥi dus byas nas mnar med par skye bar ḥgyur bas / de las skyob paḥi thabs la soms śig ces smras pas / lhaḥi dbaṅ po brgya byin la skyabs źus

[12] The work Toh. 3129 treats of offerings to the five goddesses preparatory to "inviting" the nine planets in order to accomplish mundane *siddhis*, hence to bring fertility to women.

[13] This expression occurs in Toh. 595, Derge Kanjur, Rgyud ḥbum, Pha, 238b-4.

barren women to accomplish fertility (probably Toh. 3129, the *Gzaḥ dguḥi mchod paḥi cho ga*).[12]

(d) Uṣṇīṣa of the Family

Here there are the Vijaya, Vimala, and Sitātapatrā Uṣṇīṣas. Five texts belong to Uṣṇīṣa-vijaya:

1. *Sarvatathāgatoṣṇīṣavijaya-nāma-dhāraṇī-kalpa-sahita* (Toh. 594),
2. *Sarvadurgatipariśodhanī-uṣṇīṣavijaya-nāma-dhāraṇī* (Toh. 597),
3. *Sarvatathāgatoṣṇīṣavijaya-nāma-dhāraṇī-kalpa-sahita* "holding the club of the Lord of Death" (Toh. 595),
4. *Uṣṇīṣavijaya-dhāraṇī* (Toh. 596),
5. *Uṣṇīṣavijaya-dhāraṇī-kalpa* (Toh. 598).

The first and third of these show slight differences which are, however, due merely to different translations of an identical original. They were pronounced by the Victor Amitāyus at the request of Avalokiteśvara in the hall of the Dharmasaṅgīti Cave of the field Sukhāvatī. Both texts set forth the nine deities. The one containing the expression "holding the club of the Lord of Death"[13] explains that the Dharmarāja Yama has personally promised to follow and protect those who hold this *dhāraṇī*.

The second text was promulgated by the Bhagavat in the Heaven of the Thirty-three Gods. When the omens of death appeared to the Devaputra *Susthira, he perceived that he would die within a week and would be reborn successively in seven lives as a dog, a pig, and other beings, and then would be reborn in the Avīci Hell. He implored the powerful one of the gods, Indra, for protection, but was told, "I cannot help you", and was led into the presence of the Bhagavat, whom he implored. From the Uṣṇīṣa of the Bhagavat's head rays of light issued forth, and the sounds of a *dhāraṇī* issued forth. Thereupon the Devaputra muttered the *dhāraṇī* for six days, and all the *karmic* hindrances which cause rebirth in an evil destiny were removed.

The fourth text teaches only the fundamentals of the *dhāraṇī* and of placing it in *stūpas*. The fifth one sets forth the *sādhana* of the 33 Uṣṇīṣavijaya goddesses. It is still promulgated in our day.

Regarding the *Vimaloṣṇīṣa-dhāraṇī* (Toh. 599), the Bhagavat was dwelling in the place of the Tuṣita gods. The *yakṣa* Ulkāmukha said to *Vimalamaṇisāra, the son of (one of the) thirty-three gods, "Within seven days you will die and be reborn in the Avīci Hell. Therefore, give thought to a means of rescue from that (fate)!" He implored the power-

pas / kho bos bskyab par mi nus / źes dgaḥ ldan du bcom ldan ḥdas kyi druṅ du khrid nas źus pas / bcom ldan ḥdas kyis / de śi ḥphos nas mnar med du skye źiṅ sdug bsṅal ḥdi lta bu myoṅ bar ḥgyur / źes paḥi tshul rnams bstan pas / thams cad ḥjigs skrag nas / de las skyobs par źus pas / bcom ldan ḥdas kyi dbuḥi gtsug tor nas ḥod zer dpag tu med pa byuṅ źiṅ / gzuṅs kyi cho ga rnams kyaṅ byuṅ ste / cho ga phan yon daṅ bcas pa gsuṅs so /

/ deḥi dgoṅs ḥgrel slob dpon lhan cig skyes paḥi rol pas mdzad paḥi gzuṅs kyi ḥgrel pa daṅ / mchod rten daṅ sa-tshva- bźeṅ baḥi cho ga daṅ gñis / slob dpon źi ba ḥtshos mdzad paḥi dri med kyi mchod cho ga rgyas pa daṅ gsum yod do /

/ rgyud ñid kyi tshig zin la mchod rten brgya rtsa brgyad bźeṅ baḥi spos chuḥi dkyil ḥkhor daṅ / mchod rten lṅa bźeṅ baḥi spos chuḥi dkyil ḥkhor gcig daṅ gñis bśad ciṅ / ḥgrel bas rigs so soḥi dkyil ḥkhor gsum / rigs bsdus paḥi dkyil ḥkhor lṅa ste / dri med kyi dkyil ḥkhor brgyad bśad do /

/ gdugs dkar la bźi yod de / de bźin gśegs paḥi gtsug tor nas byuṅ baḥi gdugs dkar po can gźan gyis mi thub pa phyir zlog pa chen mo źes bya ba daṅ / deḥi steṅ du mchog tu grub pa zer ba btags pa źig daṅ gñis yod pa ḥgyur khyad źiṅ ḥgyur phyi ma dag la / bcom ldan ḥdas kyis yul sum cu rtsa gsum paḥi lha gnas chos bzaṅ lhaḥi ḥdun sar gsuṅs so / de gñis las phyuṅ ba gleṅ gźi yod med gñis yod pa rim pa ltar lha yul ma chuṅ ba daṅ mi yul mar grags te / de dag gi naṅ nas brjod bya yoṅs su rdzogs pa ni mchog grub maḥo /

/ deḥi ḥgrel pa slob dpon śu-raṃ-ga-wa-rmas mdzad pa gzuṅs tshan pa bźir bcad paḥi rig sṅags daṅ / gzuṅs sṅags daṅ / sñiṅ po daṅ / ñe sñiṅ la brten paḥi dkyil ḥkhor bźi bśad pa źig yod do / deḥi lugs phal che ba gźir ḥjog ciṅ / mthaḥ gcig tu ḥkhrul med du mi ḥdzin no /

14 The translation "tile Buddhas" is after the Sino-Japanese of the title entry of Tōhoku Catalog No. 3080.

15 The *Ārya-Tathāgatoṣṇīṣasitātapatrāparājita-mahāpratyaṅgirāparamasiddha-nāma-dhāraṇī.*

16 The *Ārya-Tathāgatoṣṇīṣasitātapatrā-nāma-aparājitadhāraṇī.*

17 The *Ārya-Tathāgatoṣṇīṣasitātapatre aparājita-nāma-dhāraṇī.*

18 In Padmavajra's *Tantrārthāvatāravyākhyāna* (Toh. 2502), the first two of these terms are explained as follows (Ḥi, 273b-2, 3): 'Mantra' is a term for a male (deity) appearance as well as for the utterance associated with that form. 'Vidyā' is a term for a female (deity) appearance as well as for the utterance associated with that method (sṅags źes pa ni phoḥi tshul daṅ gzugs kyis smras paḥi tshig go / rig sṅags źes pa ni moḥi gzugs daṅ tshul ḥdzin pas gsuṅs paḥi tshig ste). For the use of these terms together with *hṛdaya* and *upahṛdaya*, one may study the *Vajravidāraṇā-nāmadhāraṇī* (Toh. 750) along with its commentaries. In this case, we deal with a *mantra* rather than a *vidyā*. In this *dhāraṇī*, the entire *mantra* section, starting with Namo ratnatra-

of the gods, Indra, for protection, but was told, "I cannot help ıd was led into the presence of the Bhagavat, whom he implored. ıgavat preached to him about the suffering he would have when d reborn in the Avīci Hell. The Devaputra was thoroughly and implored the Bhagavat to rescue him from that (fate). From şa of the Bhagavat's head innumerable light rays issued forth, of *dhāraṇī* also issued forth. Thereby the rite and its benefit ıounced.

re three basic commentaries on the *Vimaloṣṇīṣa-dhāraṇī*: the ry (Toh. 2688) on the *dhāraṇī*, and the rite (? Toh. 3080, *Sāccha ıḥi cho-ga*) on building *stūpas* and manufacturing tile Buddhas by *Sahajalalita; and the extensive rite of Vimala offerings or 3069) by Śāntarakṣita.

Eight Vimala *maṇḍalas* are set forth. The text of the Tantra itself sets forth the first and second, viz. perfumed-water *maṇḍala* of erecting 108 *stūpas*, and perfumed-water *maṇḍala* of erecting 5 *stūpas*. The commentary sets forth the third, which is a *maṇḍala* of the various families, as well as five concise *maṇḍalas* of the families.

There are four Sitātapatrā texts. There is the *Sarvatathāgatoṣṇīṣa-sitātapatrā-nāma-aparājitapratyaṅgirāmahā(vidyārājñī)* (Toh. 590), and the second text, which adds "*paramasiddha*" to the title (i.e. Toh. 591),[15] is a different translation. In those early translations, it is mentioned that the Bhagavat was in the meeting place of the gods "*Sudharma" in the Heaven of the Thirty-three Gods. There are extracts from those two, with introduction (Toh. 593)[16] and without introduction (Toh. 592),[17] which, in the given order, are not insignificant in the world of gods and of inferior renown in the world of men. Among those (four), the one with complete subject matter is the "*paramasiddha*" (Toh. 591).

Its commentary (Toh. 2689) by Śūraṃgamavarma expounds four *maṇḍalas* based on a division of *dhāraṇīs* into four kinds, *vidyā*, *mantra*, *hṛdaya*, and *upahṛdaya*.[18] His interpretation is usually taken as fundamental, but we do not hold it to be entirely infallible.

---

yāya / namaś caṇḍavajrapāṇaye / mahāyakṣasenāpataye / tadyathā / Oṃ truṭa truṭa, etc., down to the final hūṃ phaṭ, is called the basic mantra (*mūla-mantra*) or the long mantra (*dīrgha-mantra*). This entire *mantra*, regarded as sound or as letters, constitutes the Sound God and the Letter God among the Six Gods discussed in a subsequent chapter of Mkhas grub's work. Within the basic *mantra*, there occurs, first the mantra of the leading deity, Vajrapāṇi, and then the utterances expressing his magical acts of appeasing, etc. These are followed by the mantras of the immediate retinue, Vajrakīla, Vajradaṇḍa, Vajramudgara, and Vajracaṇḍa, and then the utterances expressing their magical acts of appeasing, etc. Thus, the individual *mantra* of Vajrakīla is *curu curu*

/ slob dpon tsa-ndra-gau-mis mdzad paḥi sgrub thabs / bsruṅ ḥkhor bri thabs / gzuṅs kyi cho ga / gtor maḥi cho ga / ḥkhrul ḥkhor la sogs pa dpe sna bcu bźi yod pa rnams ni tshad ldan kho naḥo /

/ bla ma rdo rje gdan pas mdzad paḥi ñe bar bśad pa źes bya ba daṅ / slob dpon rdo rje rnon pos mdzad paḥi sbyin sreg gi cho ga yaṅ yod do / slob dpon padma lcags kyu źes bya ba daṅ / slob dpon rdo rje go cha źes bya bas mdzad paḥi dkyil cho ga gñis yod de / rigs lṅaḥi sdom gzuṅs sogs bśad pas ma dag go / slob dpon tsa-ndra-gau-mis mdzad zer baḥi dkyil cho ga dbaṅ bźi rdzogs pa sogs bśad pa źig yod de / bod kyis byas paḥi rdzun ma yin no /

/ gdugs dkar las bśad paḥi legs ldan la bod dag / legs ldan spun gsum bya baḥi tha sñad byed kyaṅ mgon po beṅ yin no /

/ gtsug tor ḥbar ba ni ḥjam dpal rtsa rgyud kyi leḥu gcig las bkol ba yin la / gtsug tor nag mor grags pa ni bod kyi mi ma yin gyis byas par grags so /

/ sku gzugs kyi naṅ du gzuṅs gźug pa la bod dag gis gtsug tor skor gyi gzuṅs rnams gtsug tor gyi naṅ du gźug pa daṅ / mdzod spu nor buḥi gzuṅs mdzod spuḥi thad du gźug pa sogs kyi rnam gźag byas kyaṅ / raṅ lugs la rgyud sde goṅ ma goṅ maḥi gzuṅs goṅ du gźug par byed par bźed do /

/ rigs kyi khro bo khro moḥi gzuṅs ni / bcom ldan ḥdas gnas gtsaṅ maḥi gźal med khaṅ na bźugs paḥi tshe / de bźin gśegs pas ḥjam dpal la bskul źiṅ byin gyis brlabs nas ḥjam dpal gyis / khro bo rnam par rgyal baḥi rtogs pa gsaṅ baḥi rgyud ces bya ba gsuṅs te / de la ślo-ka stoṅ phrag bcu gñis pa gcig daṅ / de las bsdus pa ślo-ka stoṅ phrag gsum pa gcig daṅ gñis yod pa mi yul ni mi bźugs / de las bsdus pa ślo-ka stoṅ / leḥu ñi śu rtsa gcig yod pa las be con maṅ poḥi dkyil ḥkhor la sogs pa gśin rjeḥi gśed kyi dkyil ḥkhor drug / cho ga las tshogs du ma daṅ bcas pa ston pa daṅ /

---

caṇḍakilikilāya svāhā. After these, there is a new introduction, Namo ratnatrayāya ... tadyathā / Oṃ hara hara vajra, etc. down to the first hūṃ phaṭ. This entire subsection is called the *hṛdaya-mantra*, and the individual *mantras* contained in the subsection are also called *hṛdaya-mantras*. These are the *mantras* of the ten wrathful deities in the retinue of the central five deities, namely of Hūṃkāra, Vijaya, Nīladaṇḍa, Yamāntaka, Acala, Paramāśva, Aparājita, Amṛtakuṇḍalī, Trailokyavijaya, and Mahābala. Thus, *hara hara vajra* is the *hṛdaya-mantra* of Hūṃkāra. Now occurs a new introduction, Namaś caṇḍavajrakrodhāya, and this down to the hūṃ phaṭ is called the *upahṛdaya-mantra*, and the individual *mantras* contained in the subsection are also called *upahṛdaya-mantras*. Thus, *hulu hulu* is the prosperity *upahṛdaya* of Vajrakīla. The final hūṃ phaṭ is preceded by the *upahṛdaya-mantra*, amṛte, which is the *mantra* of the male and female messengers and servants.

[19] For Mgon po beṅ, one may refer to Réne de Nebesky-Wojkowitz, *Oracles and*

Only the fourteen "exemplars" (*dpe sna*) composed by *ācārya* Candragomin are authoritative. They include the *Sādhana* (Toh. 3083), the *Bsruṅ ḥkhor bri thabs* "Drawing of the protective circle" (Toh. 3086), the *Dhāraṇī-vidhi* (Toh. 3096), the *Balividhi* (Toh. 3084), and the *Ḥkhrul ḥkhor* (*yantra*) (Toh. 3087).

There are also the *Upadeśa* (Toh. 3110) by Vajrāsana, and the *Homavidhi* (Toh. 3105) by the *ācārya* *Tīkṣṇavajra. The two *maṇḍala* rites by *ācārya* Padmāṅkuśa (i.e. Toh. 3106) and by *ācārya* Varmavajra (i.e. Toh. 3108) are not "pure" because they discuss the vows, the *dhāraṇīs*, etc. of the five Families (*kula*). There is an explanation which ascribes to the authorship of Candragomin a *maṇḍala-vidhi* which accomplishes the four initiations, but this is a falsehood made by Tibetans.

As to the *Legs ldan* referred to in the (works of) Sitātapatrā, some Tibetans set forth that it is a designation of the *Legs ldan spun gsum*, but it is actually a reference to *Mgon po beṅ*.[19]

The *Gtsug-tor ḥbar-ba* (Toh. 600) is a selection from the first chapter of the *Mañjuśrī-mūla-tantra*. What is popularly known as the *Gtsug-tor nag-mo* is popularly said to be written by the non-humans of Tibet.

With regard to placing *dhāraṇīs* in icons, some Tibetans place the *dhāraṇīs* of the *Uṣṇīṣa* cycle within the Uṣṇīṣa, the *dhāraṇīs* of the *ūrṇā* gem by the *ūrṇā*, and so forth. However, our own school maintains that the *dhāraṇīs* of the successively higher Tantra divisions should be placed successively higher.

(e) **Male and Female Wrathful Deities of the Family**

In regard to the *dhāraṇīs* of the Male and Female Wrathful Deities of the Family, once when the Bhagavat dwelt in the palace of the Pure Abode, he exhorted Mañjuśrī and gave him blessing (*adhiṣṭhāna*). Thereupon, Mañjuśrī pronounced the *Krodhavijayakalpaguhya*, which has 12,000 *ślokas* in its full form and has 3,000 *ślokas* in its abridged form. Neither exists among men. The most abridged form has 1,000 *ślokas* in 21 chapters (Toh. 604). It sets forth the six *maṇḍalas* of Yamāntaka, among which is the *maṇḍala* of Be-coṅ maṅ-po (S. *mahā-daṇḍa*), as well as many rites (*vidhi*) together with the set of magical acts.[20]

Demons of Tibet (The Hague, Mouton & Co., 1956). On p. 17 we learn that this form of Mahākāla is characterised by his club, called the *beng*.

20 The expression *las tshogs*, translated here and afterwards as "set of magical acts" refers to the four kinds of magical acts, mentioned specifically later on and annotated in note 32. See F. D. Lessing, *Yung-Ho-Kung* (Stockholm, 1942), Vol. One, p. 151, for a summary table of their purposes; Sanskrit, Tibetan, and Chinese names; colors, and corresponding shape of altar.

/ skul byed maḥi gzuṅs daṅ / rgyal mtshan rtse moḥi dpuṅ rgyan la sogs pa rnams so /

/ rigs kyi pho ña pho moḥi rgyud ni / bu maṅ po ston paḥi gźuṅs daṅ / sgo bzaṅ poḥi gzuṅs daṅ / mi rgod rnam par ḥjoms paḥi gzuṅs la sogs pa rnams so /

/ mi gYo baḥi rtogs pa źes pa leḥu dgu pa gcig yod de sṅags btu nor ba sogs yod pas ma dag go /

/ de bźin gśegs paḥi rigs su gtogs paḥi byaṅ sems ni / dper na spyan ras gzigs padmaḥi rigs yin yaṅ / de bźin gśegs paḥi rigs kyi dkyil ḥkhor gyi naṅ du yod pa lta bu ste /

/ deḥi sde tshan gyi rgyud ni / ñe baḥi sras brgyad kyi mtshan brgya rtsa brgyad pa re re daṅ / yaṅ ḥjam dpal gyi mtshan brgyad pa daṅ / byams pas dam bcas paḥi gzuṅs la sogs pa rnams so /

/ de bźin gśegs paḥi rigs su gtogs paḥi lha daṅ / klu daṅ / gnod sbyin la sogs paḥi sde tshan gyi rgyud ni /

/ mdo sde sprin chen po la leḥu stoṅ phrag brgya yod paḥi leḥu gcig bod du ḥgyur pa las kluḥi dkyil ḥkhor daṅ cho ga maṅ po bśad pa daṅ / nor rgyun ma daṅ / gzaḥ rnams kyi yum źes bya ba daṅ /

/ bdud rtsi ḥbyuṅ baḥi gzuṅs źes bya ba chab gtor gyi rgyud de / bcom ldan ḥdas rgyal poḥi khab na bźugs paḥi tshe / khyim bdag bzaṅ skyoṅ źes bya bas spos chu la sman daṅ me tog sna tshogs btab pa źig khyer nas / bcom ldan ḥdas la ḥdi saṅs rgyas daṅ byaṅ chub sems dpaḥ thams cad daṅ / rigs drug la phul bas phan yon chen po ḥbyuṅ bar byin gyis brlab tu gsol źes źus pas / bcom ldan ḥdas kyis bdud rtsi ḥbyuṅ ba źes bya baḥi tiṅ ṅe ḥdzin la sñoms par źugs nas / sṅags drug / phyag rgya drug / tiṅ ṅe ḥdzin drug gsuṅs śiṅ byin gyis brlabs pa daṅ /

/ yi dvags kha nas me ḥbar ba la skyabs mdzad paḥi gzuṅs źes bya ba / bcom ldan ḥdas ser skyaḥi groṅ khyer gyi śiṅ nya-gro-dhaḥi kun

In addition, there are the *Cundīdevī-dhāraṇī* (Toh. 613), the *Dhvajāgrakeyūra-dhāraṇī* (Toh. 612), and others.

(f) **Male and Female Messengers of the Family**

In regard to the Tantras of the Male and Female Messengers of the Family, there are the *Bahuputrapratisaraṇa-nāma-dhāraṇī* (Toh. 615), the *Sumukha-nāma-dhāraṇī* (Toh. 614), the *Coravidhvaṃsana-nāma-dhāraṇī* (Toh. 629), and others.

The *Acalakalpa-tantra* (Toh. 631), in nine chapters, is not "pure" because of errors in the construction of *mantras* (T. *sṅags btu*).

(g) **The Bodhisattvas belonging to the Tathāgata Family**

For example, Avalokiteśvara is in the Padma Family, but he is also within the *maṇḍala* of the Tathāgata Family.

The Tantras of that classification are the 108 names (*aṣṭottaraśata-nāma*) of each of the eight close disciples ("near-by sons", *ñe baḥi sras*) (Toh. 634-641, inclusive), as well as the *Mañjuśrī-nāmāṣṭaśataka* (Toh. 642), the *Maitreyapratijñā-nāma-dhāraṇī* (Toh. 643), etc.

(h) **Denizens of the Pure Abode**

The Tantras in the division of *devas*, *nāgas*, *yakṣas*, etc. belonging to the Tathāgata Family, are as follows:

The *sūtra Mahāmegha* (Toh. 658) in 100,000 chapters is represented in Tibetan translation by only one chapter, which sets forth the *maṇḍala* of *nāgas*, and many rites. There are also the *Vasudhārā-nāma-dhāraṇī* (Toh. 662) and the *Grahamātṛkā-nāma-dhāraṇī* (Toh. 660).

The *Amṛtabhava-nāma-dhāraṇī* (Toh. 645) is a Tantra concerned with offerings to the *pretas*. When the Bhagavat sojourned in Rājagṛha, the householder *Bhadrapāla brought him perfumed water into which he had thrown medicine and flowers, and implored him, "May the Bhagavat bless this water, that it may give rise to great benefit when offered to all the Buddhas and Bodhisattvas and to the six Families." The Bhagavat thereupon equipoised himself in the *samādhi* called "Arising of the Ambrosia" (*amṛta-bhava*), and expressing the six *dhāraṇīs*, the six *mudrās*, and the six *samādhis*, he gave it his blessing.

Concerning the *Yi dvags kha nas me ḥbar ba la skyabs mdzad pa źes bya baḥi gzuṅs* (Toh. 646, "The *dhāraṇī* called 'Giving safeguard in the

dgaḥ ra ba na bźugs paḥi tshe / kun dgaḥ bos bas mthaḥ la brten pa na / nam smad cig yi dvags kha nas me ḥbar ba źig byuṅ nas khyod źag bdun nas ḥchiḥo / śi nas dmyal bar skyeḥo źes zer ro / bcom ldan ḥdas la źus pas / gtor maḥi gzuṅs cho ga daṅ bcas pa gsuṅs pa daṅ /

/ yaṅ sṅa ma ji lta ba bźin du yi dvags mo źig gis kyaṅ zer ba ston pa la źus pas / gzuṅs daṅ gtor maḥi cho ga gsuṅs pa kha ḥbar maḥi gzuṅs źes bya ba daṅ /

/ ye śes skar mdaḥi chab sbyin la sogs pa rnams so / kaṃ-ka-naḥi gzuṅs kyis bar do la chu sbyin byed pa gaṅ nas kyaṅ ma bśad do /

/ yaṅ tshogs bdag gi gzuṅs bya ba źig daṅ / tshogs bdag gi rgyud ces bya ba leḥu bcu gñis pa gcig yod de / de las tshogs bdag phyag gñis pa gcig daṅ phyag bźi pa la sogs paḥi rigs kha yar gyi sgrub thabs daṅ / tshogs bdag la brten nas nor sgrub thabs daṅ / dbaṅ sdud daṅ / drag poḥi las sbyor la sogs pa rnams ston te / de bźin gśegs paḥi rigs su gtogs par sṅa ma rnams bźed do /

/ dpal nag po chen poḥi rgyud ces bya ba leḥu brgyad pa gcig yod de / dpal ldan phyag drug paḥi sgos kyi rgyud yin la / rgyal po mig mi bzaṅ gyis źus śiṅ rta mgrin gyis gsuṅs paḥo / ḥdi kha cig gis de bźin gśegs paḥi rigs su gtogs par bźed la / kha cig gis rta mgrin gyis gsuṅs pa daṅ phyag drug pa ñid kyaṅ spyan ras gzigs yin paḥi phyir padmaḥi rigs su gtogs źes bźed do /

/ padmaḥi rigs kyi rgyud la / rigs kyi gtso bo / bdag po / yum / khro bo / khro mo / rigs kyi bkaḥ ñan pho moḥi rgyud de lṅaḥo /

/ rigs kyi gtso boḥi rgyud ni / bcom ldan ḥdas kyis mñan yod du ḥjam dpal la gsuṅs pa / steṅ phyogs kyi tshe dpag med kyi mtshan brgya rtsa brgyad pa yon tan bsṅags pa daṅ bcas pa ste / de la oṃ gsum ma gcig

case of the *preta* with fire streaming from his mouth'"), when the Bhagavat was sojourning in the city of Kapila (i.e. Kapilavastu) in the Nyagrodha grove, Ānanda stopped in an outlying district and in the second half of the night there appeared a *preta* with fire streaming from his mouth who told him, "You will die after seven days; upon dying, you will be born in the Avīci Hell." He applied to the Bhagavat, who expressed the *dhāraṇī* of the oblations (*bali*), together with the rite.

Again, when in like circumstances a female *preta* spoke, Ānanda applied to the Teacher, who expressed the *dhāraṇī* and rite of oblations (*bali-vidhi*), the *Kha ḥbar maḥi gzuṅs* (Toh. 647, "The 'Blazing mouth' *dhāraṇī*").

There is also the *Ye śes skar mdaḥi chab sbyin* (Toh. 649), among others. It is nowhere explained how one offers water to a dweller in the intermediate state (*antarābhava*) by means of the *Kaṅkana-dhāraṇī*.

There are also a *Gaṇapati-dhāraṇī* (Toh. 665), and a *Gaṇapati-tantra* (Toh. 666) in 12 chapters. The latter explains the *sādhanas* of the "partnership family" of the two-armed, the four-armed, etc. Gaṇapati, as well as the taking recourse to Gaṇapati for the means of gaining wealth, the performance of the magical acts of controlling (sentient beings) and of destroying (demons), etc. The former scholars maintained that they belonged to the Tathāgata Family.

There is a *Śrī Mahākāla-tantra* (Toh. 667), in eight chapters, which is, in fact, a *tantra* of Śrī Ṣaḍbhuja ("esteemed six-handed one"), and it was pronounced by Hayagrīva at the request of King Ugly-Eyes (*Virūpākṣa). Some maintain that this belongs to the Tathāgata Family, while others maintain that it belongs to the Padma Family because it was pronounced by Hayagrīva and because the Six-handed One himself is Avalokiteśvara.

(2) THE PADMA FAMILY

There are five sections to the Padma Family, namely: Lord of the Family, Master of the Family, Mother, Male and Female Wrathful Deities, and the Male and Female Servants.

(a) **Lord of the Family**

The Tantra of the Lord of the Family was pronounced by the Bhagavat in the city of Śravāstī to Mañjuśrī. It has the 108 names of Amitāyus of the upper quarter, accompanied with praises of his merits. One text

daṅ / oṃ gñis ma / oṃ puṇye puṇye źes paḥi sṅags tshan med pa gcig daṅ gñis yod do / de gñis las / gcig la bde ba can gyi tshe dpag med zer / gcig la ḥog min gyi tshe dpag med zer ba mi ḥthad de / gñis ka steṅ phyogs kyi tshe dpag med kyi gzuṅs su gsuṅs paḥi phyir / oṃ gñis ma la sṅags bar nas chad pas / mtshan brgya rtsa brgyad ma tshaṅ ba yin gyi / rgyud so so ba gñis ma yin no /

/ tshe dpag med ḥchi med rṅa sgraḥi gzuṅs bya ba bcom ldan ḥdas kyis dge sloṅ rnams la bde ba can gyi tshe dpag med kyi mtshan brgya rtsa brgyad pa yon tan bsṅags pa daṅ bcas pa gsuṅs pa ste / de la sogs pa rnams so /

/ rigs kyi bdag poḥi rgyud ni / spyan ras gzigs kyi rtsa rgyud chen po / thugs rje chen po padma dra baḥi rgyud ces bya ba / bcom ldan ḥdas kyis ri bo-ta-laḥi rtse mor gsuṅs pa leḥu bcu gñis pa / bcu gcig źal lha stoṅ ñis brgya bźi bcu rtsa bdun paḥi dkyil ḥkhor la sogs pa rtsa baḥi dkyil ḥkhor ñi śu rtsa bdun daṅ / de las ḥphros paḥi dkyil ḥkhor du ma ston pa źig /

/ don yod źags paḥi cho ga źib moḥi rgyud ces bya ba / bcom ldan ḥdas kyis ri bo-ta-laḥi rtse mor gsuṅs pa bsgyur ḥphrol lus pa bam po ñi śu rtsa bźi pa gcig yod de / gzuṅs daṅ cho ga źib mo las tshogs du ma daṅ bcas pa rgyas par ston no / yaṅ don yod źags paḥi gzuṅs chuṅ ba źig yod pa ni cho ga źib moḥi rgyud kyi stoṅ gzuṅs kyi skor zur du bkol ba yin gyi / rgyud logs pa min no / rgyud chen po bcom ldan ḥdas kyis bo-ta-lar gsuṅs pa bsgyur ḥphrol lus pa źig yod de / de las dkyil ḥkhor gcig bstan to /

/ spyan ras gzigs seṅ gi sgraḥi gzuṅs che chuṅ gñis yod de / chuṅ ba rdo rje gdan du gsuṅs la / che ba rgyal po dbaṅ phyug ḥod ces bya ba

[21] The *Ārya-Aparimitāyurjñāna-nāma-mahāyānasūtra.*

[22] The *Ārya-Aparimitāyurjñāna-nāma-mahāyānasūtra.*

[23] The *mantra* section which Toh. 674 lacks is: Oṃ puṇye puṇye mahāpuṇye aparimita-āyur-puṇya-jñāna-saṃbhāropacite.

[24] The *Tshe dpag med ḥchi med rṅa sgraḥi gzuṅs* is not found in the Derge edition of the Kanjur, but it is listed separately in the *Comparative Analytical Catalogue of the Kanjur Division* published in Kyoto, a catalogue based on the Peking edition of the Kanjur. This is presumably the *Ḥchi med rṅa sgraḥi gzuṅs* quoted in Tsoṅ-kha-pa's *Lam rim chen mo*, Tashilunpo ed., 91b-6:

/ saṅs rgyas bcom ldan bsam mi khyab /
/ dam paḥi chos kyaṅ bsam mi khyab /
/ ḥphags paḥi dge ḥdun bsam mi khyab /
/ bsam mi khyab la dad rnams kyi /
/ rnam par smin pa bsam mi khyab /
The Buddha Bhagavat is inconceivable;
The Illustrious Doctrine is also inconceivable;
The Noble Congregation is inconceivable;

(Toh. 674)[21] is "three-Oṃ'd" (*oṃ gsum ma*), and the second text (Toh. 675)[22] is "two-Oṃ'd" (*oṃ gñis ma*). One (i.e. Toh. 675) lacks the *mantra* section "*Oṃ puṇye puṇye...*" and the other (i.e. Toh. 674) has it.[23] Of those two, it is claimed that one represents the Amitāyus of Sukhāvatī and that the other represents the Amitāyus of Akaniṣṭha. That (claim) is not valid, because both have been uttered as the *dhāraṇī* of Amitāyus of the upper quarter (i.e. Akaniṣṭha). The "two-Oṃ'd" one has a *mantra* omission and so does not have the complete 108 names, but there are not two different Tantras.

The *dhāraṇī* called "Immortal drum-roll of Amitāyus" (*tshe dpag med ḥchi med rṅa sgraḥi gzuṅs*) was proclaimed by the Bhagavat to the *bhikṣus*, along with the 108 names of Amitāyus of Sukhāvatī and praises of his merits (apparently Toh. 676, the *Ārya Aparimitāyurjñānahṛdaya-nāma-dhāraṇī*).[24] And there are some other works.

(b) **Master of the Family**

In regard to the Tantras of the Master of the Family, the great fundamental Tantra (*mūla-tantra*) of Avalokiteśvara is called the *Padmajāla* (Toh. 681) of the great compassion. It was pronounced by the Bhagavat on the summit of Mt. Potala and has twelve chapters. It explains the 27 basic *maṇḍalas*, including the *maṇḍala* of the eleven-faced Avalokiteśvara with 1247 deities, and many *maṇḍalas* deriving from them.

The *Amoghapāśa-kalparājā* Tantra was (also) pronounced by the Bhagavat on the summit of Mt. Potala. A segment (Toh. 686) in 24 sections (*bam po*) was translated. It explains comprehensively the fine points of *dhāraṇīs* and rites together with many sets of magical acts. Moreover, there is a small *Amoghapāśa-dhāraṇī* (Toh. 687) which has been separately printed from the cycle of a thousand *dhāraṇīs* of the (original) *kalpa* Tantra, and so does not belong to a different Tantra. There was (another) segment (Toh. 689, the *Kalparājavidhi*) translated from the great Tantra pronounced by the Bhagavat on the Potala: it explains one *maṇḍala*.

There are two Avalokiteśvara Siṃhanāda *dhāraṇīs*, a larger (Toh. 703), and a smaller (Toh. 704). The Bhagavat pronounced the smaller on the

---

The maturation of those with faith in the inconceivable
Is inconceivable.

Toh. 676 contains the same in an alternate translation, preceded by the line / bde ba can gyi bsṅags pa brjod ("To speak the praise of Sukhāvatī:") and followed by the line / rnam dag źiṅ du skye bar ḥgyur ("They are born in the Pure Land").

mdze nad kyis zin pa gso baḥi don du ḥphags pa ḥjam dpal gyis źus na bcom ldan ḥdas kyis ri bo-ta-lar gsuṅs te / de la sogs paḥi spyan ras gzigs kyi skor maṅ du yod pa rnams so /

/ rigs kyi yum gyi rgyud ni / gtso che ba de bźin gśegs pa thams cad kyi yum sgrol ma las sna tshogs ḥbyuṅ baḥi rgyud ces bya ba leḥu sum cu rtsa lṅa pa gcig yod do / deḥi leḥu gsum par sgrol maḥi bstod pa phyag ḥtshol ñi śu rtsa gcig ma rgya skad sor bźad du yod do / kha cig gis de daṅ phyag ḥtshal ñi śu rtsa gcig ma zur du bkol ba gñis don mi gcig / zur du bsgyur ba de bla med kyi rgyud las yin te / slob dpon ñi ma sbas pas bla med du bkral bas so / źes zer yaṅ / ḥgrel byed kyis de ltar bkral na / de gñis don mi gcig mi dgos te / ḥjam dpal mtshan brjod slob dpon sgeg paḥi rdo rje daṅ / ṅag dbaṅ grags pas yo-gar bkral / dus ḥkhor ḥgrel chen gyis bla med du bkral / ḥphags pa lhas kyaṅ / a ni yig ḥbru kun gyi mchog / ces sogs draṅs nas rdzogs rim gyi don can du bśad pa bźin no /

/ sgrol maḥi mtshan brgya rtsa brgyad pa sems can rnams ḥjigs pa brgyad las skyob paḥi don tu phyag rdor gyis źus nas spyan ras gzigs kyis gsuṅs pa źig yod do / de la brten nas slob dpon tsa-ndra-gau-mis sgrub thabs brgya rtsa brgyad las tshogs daṅ bcas pa daṅ / phyag ḥtshal ñi śu rtsa gcig la brten paḥi sgrub thabs ñi śu rtsa gcig / las tshogs daṅ bcas pa mdzad do /

/ gźan yaṅ sgrol maḥi skor phran tshegs du ma daṅ bcas paḥo /

/ rigs kyi khro bo khro moḥi rgyud la / dpal rta mgrin gyi rtogs pa bdun cu pa la sogs paḥi rgyud chen po rnams bod du ma ḥgyur / ha-ya-grī-baḥi gzuṅs źes bya ba khol phyuṅ źig ḥgyur ro / ri khrod ma lo ma can gyi gzuṅs źes bya ba gzuṅs daṅ cho ga cuṅ zad ston pa źig daṅ / pa-rṇa-śa-ba-riḥi mdo źes kyaṅ bya / rtogs pa źes kyaṅ bya ba / sgrub thabs

[25] The *Mañjuśrī-nāma-saṃgīti* was edited by I. P. Minaeff in *St. Petersburg University, Historo-Philological Faculty*, Vol. 16 (1885), pp. 137, f. The quoted passage occurs in the verse on p. 140, lines 1-2:

/ tadyathā bhagavāṃ buddhaḥ saṃbuddho 'kārasaṃbhavaḥ /
/ akāraḥ sarvavarṇāgryo mahārthaḥ paramākṣaraḥ //

Vajrāsana, and he pronounced the larger on the summit of Mt. Potala at the request of Ārya Mañjuśrī in order to cure King *Īśvaraprabha of leprosy. Those and many others are in the cycle of Avalokiteśvara.

(c) Mother of the Family

The most important Tantra of the Mother of the Family is the *Sarva-tathāgata-mātṛtārā-viśvakarma-bhava-tantra-nāma* (Toh. 726) in thirty-five chapters. In its third chapter are praises of Tārā left in the original Sanskrit language, the "Twenty-one Salutations to Tārā" (*namastāre ekaviṃśati*). Some claim that these praises are not identical with the isolated text of twenty-one salutations (Toh. 438, the *Namastāre ekaviṃśatistotra-guṇahitasahita*) and that this separate translation is in the Anuttara Tantra because it has commentary in the Anuttara manner by the *ācārya* Sūryagupta (i.e. Toh. 1685-1689, inclusive). Now, when a commentator comments that way, there is no necessary implication that those two are not identical. [For example,] the *Mañjuśrī-nāma-saṃgīti* (Toh. 360) has been commented upon in the Yoga manner by the *ācāryas* Līlavajra (i.e. Toh. 2533) and *Mañjuśrīkīrti (i.e. Toh. 2534); but the great commentary on the Kālacakra (Toh. 845, the *Vimala-prabhā*) comments on it in the Anuttara manner, and Āryadeva explained it as having the meaning of the Steps of Completion [of the Anuttara Tantra] when he quoted the passage, "'A' is the foremost of all letters..." (*akāraḥ sarvavarṇāgryo...*).[25]

There is also the *Tārā-nāmāṣṭaśataka* (Toh. 727 and 728), which was pronounced by Avalokiteśvara at the request of Vajrapāṇi for the sake of protecting the sentient beings against the eight dangers. On the basis of that text, the *ācārya* Candragomin composed the *Aṣṭaśatasādhana* (Toh. 3665), including the set of magical acts; and on the basis of the *Namastāre ekaviṃśati*, he composed the *Ekaviṃśatisādhana*, including the set of magical acts (probably his works Toh. 3669-3670 are all meant).

Moreover, there are numerous minor texts in the cycle of Tārā.

(d) Male and Female Wrathful Deities of the Family

In regard to their Tantras, the great Tantras, such as the Śrī *Hayagrīva-saptati*, were not translated into Tibetan. A selection entitled *Hayagrīva-dhāraṇī* (Toh. 733) was translated. The *Parṇaśavarī-nāma-dhāraṇī* (Toh. 736) sets forth a sketch of the *dhāraṇī* and rite; and the *Parṇaśavarī-sūtra* (Toh. 735), also referred to as the (*Parṇaśavarī-*) *kalpa*, sets forth

daṅ cho ga daṅ las tshogs cuṅ zad ston pa źig yod de / de gsum khas med do /

/ rigs kyi bkaḥ ñan pho moḥi rgyud ni / phyir mi ldog pa stobs chen kyi mdo daṅ / dpal chen moḥi mdo la sogs pa rnams so /

/ rdo rjeḥi rigs la yaṅ rigs kyi gtso bo / bdag po / yum / khro bo / khro mo / pho ña / bkaḥ ñan pho moḥi rgyud rnams las /

/ rigs kyi gtso boḥi rgyud ni / ṅan soṅ thams cad yoṅs su sbyoṅ ba / mi ḥkhrugs paḥi gzuṅs źes bya ba źig yod de / bu ston rin po che la sogs pa sṅa ma rnams kyis rdo rjeḥi rigs kyi gtso bor mdzad gdaḥ źiṅ / de las gźan paḥi mtshan gźi ḥdzin rgyud yaṅ mi snaṅ ṅo /

/ rigs kyi bdag po ni phyag na rdo rje yin te / deḥi rgyud ni rdo rje sa ḥog gi rgyud la ḥgyur mi gcig pa gsum snaṅ ste / leḥu ñer lṅa pa sa paṅ gyis bsgyur ba daṅ / leḥu bcu gsum pa zaṅs dkar lo-tsā-ba ḥphags pa śes rab kyis bsgyur ba daṅ / leḥu bdun ma dge sloṅ byaḥi gdoṅ ba can gyis bsgyur ba rnams so / yaṅ ḥbyuṅ po ḥdul byed kyi rgyud daṅ / rdo rje gtum poḥi rgyud la rtsa rgyud gcig / deḥi rgyud phyi ma gcig / phyi maḥi yaṅ phyi ma gcig rnams yod do /

/ rdo rje rnam ḥjoms kyi gzuṅs la ślo-ka ñer lṅar lo-tsā-ba rnams kyis mdzad do / de rdo rje gdan du gsuṅs par kha cig smra ba la / slob dpon chen po saṅs rgyas gsaṅ bas / bsam gyis mi khyab paḥi mdo źes bya ba draṅs nas / rdo rje gdan ni mṅon par byaṅ chub paḥi gnas yin pas / de bdud ḥdul baḥi gnas yin gyi / sems can gźan ḥdul baḥi gnas ma yin pas

[26] The Gelugpa school obviously classifies the *Vajracaṇḍa-tantra* among the Kriyātantras, but the Tohoku Catalog numbers show that it was classified as Anuttara by the former lamas. In the Derge edition of the *Rgyud ḥbum*, the Anuttarayogatantra has numbers 360-478, Yogatantra numbers 479-493, Caryātantra numbers 494-501, and Kriyātantra numbers 502-827.

[27] This is the position of Sabari-pa's commentary called *Ratnamālā* (Toh. 2686).

a sketch of the *sādhana*, rite, and set of magical acts. Those three are the only ones extant.

(e) Male and Female Servants of the Family

The Tantras in this section are the *Balavatī-nāma-pratyaṅgirā* (Toh. 737), the *Mahālakṣmī-sūtra* (Toh. 740), and so on.

(3) THE VAJRA FAMILY

There are also five sections to the Vajra Family, namely: Lord of the Family, Master, Mother, Male and Female Wrathful Deities, and Male and Female Servants.

(a) Lord of the Family

Concerning the Lord of the Family, there is a *dhāraṇī* of Akṣobhya which purifies all the evil fates (Toh. 743, *Sarvakarmāvaraṇaviśodhanī*); but whether that belongs to the Tathāgata Family or to the Vajra Family needs to be investigated. Bu-ston rin-po-che and other former authorities take it as belonging to the Lord of the Vajra Family, and there is no other Tantra possessing the basic characteristics.

(b) Master of the Family

The Master of this Family is Vajrapāṇi. His Tantra is the *Vajra-pātāla-tantra*. There exist three translations, which (however) are not identical. The edition with 25 chapters was translated by the Sa-skya paṇḍita (i.e. Toh. 744, the edition of the Derge Kanjur); the edition with 13 chapters, by Ḥphags-pa śes-rab, the translator of Zaṅs-dkar; and the edition with 7 chapters, by *bhikṣu* Bya-gdoṅ-ba-can. Moreover, there is the *Bhūta-ḍāmara-tantra* (Toh. 747); and there is the *Vajracaṇḍa-tantra*, which has a Fundamental Tantra (Toh. 458), a Continuation Tantra (Toh. 459), and a Continuation of the Continuation (Toh. 460).[26]

The *Vajravidāraṇā-nāma-dhāraṇī* (Toh. 750) has been rendered into 25 *ślokas* by the translators. Some say it was recited on the Diamond Seat (*vajrāsana*).[27] However, the great instructor (*mahā-ācārya*) Buddha-guhya, quoting the *Acintya-sūtra* (possibly Toh. 47, the *Tathāgatācintya-guhyanirdeśa-sūtra*), objects saying that the Diamond Seat, being the place of Revelation-Enlightenments (*abhisaṃbodhi*), is the place

der ma gsuṅs so / źes bkag nas / rdo rje lhun poḥi ri rab kyi zom źes bya ba phyogs mtshams thams cad rdo rjes bltams pa źig ri bo mchog rab kyi śar lhoḥi phyogs na yod pa de na bcom ldan ḥdas bźugs paḥi tshe / rgyal po ma skyes dgraḥi miṅ gi rnam graṅs rgyal po log paḥi sñiṅ po źes bya bas yab rgyal po gzugs can sñiṅ po chos daṅ ldan pa bkroṅs / mi dge bcuḥi khrims bcaḥ bsogs kyis skye bo rnams mi dge ba byed du bcug pas ḥjig rten gyi ḥbyuṅ po dkar phyogs la dgaḥ ba rnams stobs ñams śiṅ / nag phyogs la dgaḥ ba rnams stobs rgyas te / nad la sogs pas skye bo rnams sdug bsṅal bar gyur pas / rgyal chen bźis bcom ldan ḥdas kyi druṅ du phyin nas / de dag las skyob paḥi thabs źus pas / bcom ldan ḥdas kyis phyag na rdo rje la de dag skyobs paḥi thabs la soms śig / ces bskul bas / phyag na rdo rjes saṅs rgyas kyi mthu daṅ / saṅs rgyas kyi byin gyis brlabs kyis rdo rje rnam ḥjoms kyi skur gyur nas smras par bśad ciṅ /

/ de la leḥu brgya rtsa brgyad yod paḥi naṅ nas bod du ḥgyur pa ḥdi leḥu daṅ po yin la / leḥu lhag ma rnams deḥi rgyud phyi ma yaṅ yin / bśad rgyud kyaṅ yin pas / rgyud do cog gi rtsa ba ste / źes bśad paḥi don leḥu daṅ po ḥdi leḥu lhag ma thams cad kyi rtsa rgyud du ston par zad kyi / ḥdi rgyud sde bźi po thams cad kyi rtsa bar bśad par ḥchad pa don min no / leḥu brgya rtsa brgyad du ma gtogs paḥi rnam ḥjoms kyi bśad rgyud rdo rje ri rab khaṅ bu brtsegs paḥi gzuṅs źes bya ba źig bod du ḥgyur te /

/ de dag rigs kyi bdag poḥi rgyud la gtso bo yin la / phran tshegs du ma daṅ bcas pa ḥgyur ro / sme brtsegs kyi gzuṅs ni sa paṇ sogs thugs gtsigs che bar mdzad ciṅ / bu ston rin po che sogs rgyud rnam dag yin min the tshom gyi gźir mdzad do /

/ rigs kyi yum gyi rgyud la / me lce ḥbar maḥi gzuṅs źes bya ba yod do /

where Māra (the evil principle) was overcome, but that no other beings were overcome there [while other beings are overcome by that *dhāraṇī*], for which reason it was not pronounced there. As a matter of fact, it was presented when the Bhagavat was residing on the South-east side of the noblest of mountains — the peak of Sumeru, the diamond heap, the edges of which consist of diamond (*vajra*). King Ajātaśatru, one of whose names is "King degenerate heart", had killed his father, the pious King Bimbisāra. By repeated imperial directives displaying the ten sinful deeds, men were installed in sinful conduct, so that of worldly creatures those who delighted in the righteous side found their power destroyed, while those who delighted in the wicked side found their power greatly enhanced, and men were suffering with illness and so on. For that reason, the Four Great Kings appeared before the Bhagavat and asked for a means of protection against those (delighting in the wicked side). The Bhagavat exhorted Vajrapāṇi, "Think of a means of protection against them!" Then, through the power of the Buddha and through the blessing of the Buddha, Vajrapāṇi assumed the *vajra-vidāraṇa* body (the body which shatters all impediments) and explained (the means) in speech.

That (original Tantra) had 108 chapters, but only the first one was translated into Tibetan. The remaining chapters not only constituted a Continuation Tantra, but also an Explanatory Tantra for that (first chapter). Thus, the statement (in the *Vajravidāraṇā-dhāraṇī*), "It is the fundamental one of all the Tantras", means that this first chapter is the Fundamental Tantra for the remaining chapters, and does not mean that this Tantra is fundamental to all the four Tantra divisions (i.e. the Kriyā, etc.). An Explanatory Tantra of the (*Vajra-*)*vidāraṇā* that was not among the 108 chapters, entitled *Vajrameruśikhara-kūṭāgara-dhāraṇī* (Toh. 751), has (also) been translated into Tibetan.

Those are the chief Tantras of the Master of the Family and have been translated together with a number of minor texts. The *Bhurkumkūṭa-dhāraṇī* (Toh. 756) was highly esteemed by the Sa-skya paṇḍita and others, but Bu-ston rin-po-che and others hesitated to declare it either a pure or an impure Tantra.

(c) Mother of the Family

In regard to her Tantra, there is the "*Dhāraṇī* of the Blazing Flames" (i.e. Toh. 752, the *Anala-pramohanī-dhāraṇī*).

/ rigs kyi khro bo khro moḥi rgyud la bdud rtsi thab sbyor źes bya ba yod do /

/ rigs kyi pho ña daṅ bkaḥ ñan pho moḥi rgyud la stobs po cheḥi gzuṅs daṅ / rdo rje lu gu rgyud daṅ / rdo rje mchu daṅ / rdo rje gnam lcags mchu la sogs pa rnams rnam dag yin źiṅ / stobs po cheḥi gzuṅs deḥi rigs kyi khro boḥi gzuṅs su ḥoṅ rgyu ḥdra ba źig snaṅ na ḥaṅ / sṅa ma rnams kyis rigs kyi pho ña daṅ / bkaḥ ñan pho moḥi skor du bgraṅs gdaḥ ḥo / rdo rje lcags mchu daṅ / lcags mchu nag po daṅ / khyuṅ gśog ḥbar ba sogs rdzun ma du ma snaṅ ṅo /

/ ḥjig rten paḥi rigs la gsum las / nor can gyi rigs la / nor bu bzaṅ poḥi gzuṅs daṅ / deḥi rtogs pa daṅ / gnod gnas dbaṅ po ḥbyuṅ baḥi rtog pa ste / ja-mbha-la ser poḥi rtogs pa gzuṅs daṅ dbaṅ bskur sogs ston pa daṅ / gar mkhan mchog gi rtog pa rnams te /

/ ḥdi la kha cig gis rnam sras gar mkhan mchog ces zer źiṅ / rnam sras drag por smra ba mi ḥthad de / bcom ldan ḥdas lcaṅ lo can gyi pho braṅ na bźugs paḥi tshe ḥkhor der ṅal bsos poḥi bu gar mkhan mchog ces bya ba źig kyaṅ ḥdug go / deḥi tshe rgyal po rnam thos sras kyis bcom ldan ḥdas la ḥkhor maṅ poḥi slad du rig sṅags gsuṅ bar gsol ba btab pas / bcom ldan ḥdas kyi sku las ḥod zer dpag tu med pa byuṅ / ḥjig rten gyi khams mthaḥ yas pa snaṅ bar byas / slar ḥdus nas ṅal bsos poḥi bu gar mkhan mchog gi spyi bor źugs pas gar mkhan mchog skad cig gis khro bo chen por gyur nas / bcom ldan ḥdas kyi spyan sṅar raṅ gi rig pa smras pas / bcom ldan ḥdas kyis de dag nus pa can du byin gyis brlabs śiṅ / de dag gi las tshogs rgyas par gsuṅs par bśad de / deḥi leḥu bcu pa yan gyis gar mkhan mchog ñid kyi rig sṅags daṅ las tshogs sogs ston ciṅ / leḥu bcu gcig par gnod sbyin gyi sde dpon chen po yaṅ dag śes kyis / bcom ldan ḥdas la / rnam thos sras la miṅ gi rnam graṅs du yod źus pas / bcom ldan

[28] According to Mkhas grub rje's explanation of this work, following immediately, the Tohoku Catalog is in error to assign two numbers, 766 and 767. What that catalog calls no. 767 is actually the eleventh chapter onwards of the same work.

(d) Male and Female Wrathful Deities of the Family

The Tantra here is the *Kuṇḍalyamṛta* (Toh. 755).

(e) Male and Female Servants of the Family

Concerning the Tantras belonging to the Male and Female Messengers and Servants of the Family, the *Mahābala-dhāraṇī* (Toh. 757), the *Vajraśṛṅkhala-tantra* (Toh. 758), the *Vajratuṇḍa* (Toh. 759), the *Vajra-lohatuṇḍa* (Toh. 760), and so on, are pure. The *Mahābala-dhāraṇī*, while showing some cause for being placed among the *dhāraṇīs* of the Wrathful Deities of the Family, was classified by the older authorities in the cycle of the Male and Female Messengers and Servants of the Family. There are also a number of counterfeit texts, such as the *Rdo rje lcags mchu* the *Lcags mchu nag po*, and the *Khyuṅ gśog ḥbar ba*.

(4) MUNDANE FAMILIES OF THE KRIYĀ TANTRA

(a) The Wealthy Family (maṇi-kula)

Here there are the *Maṇibhadra-dhāraṇī* (Toh. 764); its *Kalpa* (Toh. 765, the *Maṇibhadrayakṣasena-kalpa*); the *Jambhalajalendrayathālabdha-kalpa* (Toh. 770) which teaches how to imagine the Yellow Jambhala, the initiation, etc.; and the *Nartakapara-kalpa* (Toh. 766-767).[28]

In regard to the last-mentioned work, some claim that Vaiśravaṇa is the *nartakapara* ("unexcelled dancer"), but it is not valid to declare the latter Vaiśravaṇa, as has been done emphatically. Thus, (the Tantra says that) at the time when the Bhagavat was residing in his palace "Willow Leaves" (*aṭakāvatī*) there also lived at the same place among his retinue the son of Viśrama, called Nartakapara. At that time, King Vaiśravaṇa requested the Bhagavat to express the *vidyā-dhāraṇī* on behalf of the large retinue. Consequently, immeasurable rays of light, which illumined an infinity of world systems (*lokadhātu*), issued from the body of the Bhagavat. Then those rays returned and, converging, entered the crown of the head of Viśrama's son, Nartakapara; and Nartakapara instantly became a great wrathful deity (*mahākrodha*) and uttered in front of the Bhagavat his own *vidyās*. After the Bhagavat had made them efficacious by his blessing, he explained in detail the magical acts connected with those *vidyās*; and so all the chapters up to the tenth set forth the *vidyā-dhāraṇīs* and set of magical acts, etc. of

ḥdas kyis phyag na rdo rje byin gyis brlabs te / phyag na rdo rjes rnam thos sras kyi miṅ gi rnam graṅs śin tu maṅ po gsuṅs paḥi naṅ du ṅal bsos pɔ źes bya ba miṅ gi rnam graṅs gcig tu byuṅ bas / gar mkhan mchog rnam sras kyi bu yin gyi / rnam sras ñid ma yin no / leḥu bcu gsum pa daṅ bco lṅa bas rnam sras kyi cho ga daṅ las tshogs sogs ston / leḥu gźan gyis gźan ston no /

/ gźan phran tshegs du ma daṅ bcas pa bod du ḥgyur ro /

/ lṅas rtsen gyi rigs la / me-kha-laḥi gzuṅs źes bya ba yod de / bcom ldan ḥdas rgyal poḥi khab na bźugs paḥi tshe / sgra gcan zin bzaṅ po la srin po źig gis bsdigs pas ḥjigs skra gnas / bcom ldan ḥdas kyi druṅ du ṅu źiṅ mchis te / bcom ldan ḥdas la źus pas / bcom ldan ḥdas kyis me-kha-laḥi gzuṅs źes bya ba gsuṅs te / gnod sbyin źig gis phul baḥi rig sṅags śig go /

/ ḥjig rten paḥi rigs la rig sṅags kyi rgyal mo dbugs chen mo źes bya ba yod de / tho raṅs śig bcom ldan ḥdas kyi druṅ du ḥbyuṅ po thams cad kyi dbaṅ po ser skya źes bya ba mche ba gtsigs pa źig byuṅ nas / bcom ldan ḥdas bdag ni ḥbyuṅ po thams cad kyi dbaṅ po lags te / bdag bkres pa na dbugs btaṅ bas gaṅ la reg paḥi sems can de dag rims nad kyis btab par ḥgyur źiṅ / de dag gi srog bdag gi zas su zaḥo / gaṅ gis rig sṅags ḥdi śes pa de dag la dbugs btaṅ baḥi gnod pa ḥbyuṅ bar mi ḥgyur gyis gsan du gsol / źes rig sṅags smras te / phyin chad dbugs btaṅ baḥi gnod pa mi byed par dam bcas śiṅ dge bsñen byas par bśad do /

/ bya ba spyiḥi rgyud la / gsaṅ ba spyi rgyud / legs grub kyi rgyud / dpuṅ bzaṅ gis źus pa / bsam gtan phyi ma daṅ bźi yod de / de dag sṅa ma sṅa ma gźuṅ maṅ źiṅ phyi ma phyi ma ñuṅ ṅo /

/ de la gsaṅ ba spyiḥi rgyud kyis ma smin pa smin par byed paḥi thabs

[29] The *vidyā* contained in the text of this work has the expression Mahāśvāsa, which is of course the original for T. *dbugs chen po*. Hence the Sanskrit title can be reconstructed as *Ārya-Vidyārāja-Mahāśvāsa-nāma*.

[30] The name Piṅgala is transcribed in the *vidyā*, thus assuring the original Sanskrit.

Nartakapara. In the eleventh chapter, the great *yakṣa* general Saṃjñāya asks the Bhagavat for the various names of Vaiśravaṇa. Therefore, the Bhagavat blessed Vajrapāṇi, who thereupon recited a great number of Vaiśravaṇa's names, one of them being Viśrama. Hence Nartakapara is the son of Vaiśravaṇa and so cannot be identical with him. Chapters thirteen and fifteen describe the rite and the set of magical acts connected with Vaiśravaṇa. The other chapters deal with other matters.

In addition, many minor details have been translated into Tibetan.

(b) The Family of the Five (pañcaka-kula)

Here we have the *Mekhalā-dhāraṇī* (Toh. 772). When the Bhagavat was sojourning in the city of Rājagṛha, a cannibal demon (*rākṣasa*) threatened Rāhulabhadra, who accordingly was very frightened. He went weeping into the presence of the Bhagavat, and the Bhagavat, having been implored by him, uttered the *Mekhalā-dhāraṇī*, which is a *vidyā-dhāraṇī* offered by a *yakṣa*.

(c) The Family of the Worldlings (laukika-kula)

Here we have the *Rig sṅags kyi rgyal mo dbugs chen mo* (Toh. 773, but the catalog and the Kanjur text has °*rgyal po ... chen po*).[29] One day at dawn, the potentate of all the elementary spirits (*bhūta*), whose name was Piṅgala[30] and who had bared fangs, went into the presence of the Bhagavat and said, "Bhagavat, I am the potentate of all the elementary spirits. Whenever I am hungry, I breathe forth, and whatever living beings are contacted, they are smitten with plague and their vital air serves as my food. Pray listen to this *vidyā-dhāraṇī*, which will protect those who know it from being harmed when contacted by my breath", and he uttered the *vidyā-dhāraṇī*. Then he took a vow that he would thereafter not do harm by breathing, and he became a lay follower.

(5) GENERAL KRIYĀ TANTRA

In regard to the general Tantras of Kriyā, there are (now) the four: 1. *Sāmānyavidhīnām guhya-tantra* (Toh. 806), 2. *Susiddhi* (Toh. 807), 3. *Subāhuparipṛcchā* (Toh. 805), 4. *Dhyānottara* (Toh. 808). The further back in time we go, the more numerous were the texts (of this category); the later we go, the fewer they were.

Among them, the *Sāmānyavidhīnām guhya-tantra* teaches the initiation

dbaṅ bskur baḥi skor rnams ston te / de bźin gśegs paḥi rigs kyi dkyil ḥkhor sogs rigs gsum gyi dkyil ḥkhor stoṅ daṅ lṅa brgya ston ciṅ / de dag daṅ gźan yaṅ bya rgyud kyi dkyil ḥkhor yod do cog la thun moṅ du dgos śiṅ / rgyud sde gźan gsum la yaṅ thun moṅ du dgos paḥi sa chog daṅ / sta gon gyi cho gaḥi tshul rnams rgyas par ston te / de thams cad khrigs cags gcig tu bśad kyi / leḥur bcad pa med do /

/ legs grub ni khro bo legs grub ces bya bas bgegs bsruṅ ba sogs kyi las rnams sgrub ciṅ / khro bo de brjod byar ston pas legs grub kyi rgyud ces byaḥo / des rigs sṅags sgrub paḥi cho ga daṅ / las rab ḥbyams kyi dgos pa dṅos grub sgrub tshul daṅ / bya rgyud kyi bsruṅ ba daṅ / brten paḥi dam tshig rnams rgyas par ston no /

/ dpuṅ bzaṅ gis źus pa las ni / gsaṅ ba spyiḥi rgyud du ma bśad paḥi dbaṅ bskur gyi cho ga daṅ / legs grub tu ma bśad paḥi rig sṅags sgrub pahi tshul cuṅ zad daṅ / źi rgyas dbaṅ drag gi las rab ḥbyams la brten nas dṅos grub sgrub paḥi tshul rnams rgyas par ston no / dpuṅ bzaṅ ni phyag na rdo rjeḥi sras skye ba gcig gis thogs paḥi byaṅ chub sems dpaḥ yin par bśad do /

/ bsam gtan phyi ma ni rdo rje gtsug tor gyi rgyud ces bya baḥi bya rgyud kyi rgyud chen po źig gi dum bu yin la / deḥi rgyud phyi ma lta bu yin pa ḥbyed pa yaṅ yod do / des brjod bya rnam pa bcu ston te / gaṅ du bsgrub pa gnas kyi mtshan ñid / bdag gi de kho na ñid / rig sṅags kyi de kho na ñid / lhahi de kho na ñid / me la gnas paḥi bsam gtan / sgra la

[31] The name Susiddhikarin occurs in the *mantra* (Vol. Wa, 174a-5), *Oṃ susiddhikari svāhā.* It elsewhere (e.g. Wa, 169b-1) occurs in translation: *legs par grub byed ces bya ba.*

[32] The *Vajra-vidāraṇa-dhāraṇī* makes the four kinds of magical act more explicit in a statement immediately preceding the long *mantra* which is transcribed into the Tibetan. The statement runs: And by the power of the Buddha, Vajrapāṇi proclaimed this great mantra, which — [effectuates destructive magic, as follows:] 1. Threatens all sentient beings, 2. Expels all sentient beings, 3. Destroys all (opposing) *dhāraṇīs* of *vidyās* (i.e. *vidyā-dhāraṇī*), 4. Stays all (opposing) *dhāraṇīs* of *vidyās*, 5. Destroys all (evil) magical acts, 6. Nullifies all magical acts of others, 7. Decimates all the inimical spirits, 8. Frees from all (possession by) inimical spirits; [effectuates domineering magic, as follows:] 1. Summons all the elementary spirits (*bhūta*), 2. Overcomes all the elementary spirits, 3. Effectuates all the magical acts of the *dhāraṇīs* of *vidyās*; [effectuates all prosperity magic, as follows:] 1. Fulfills the previously unfulfilled, 2. Averts cessation of the previously fulfilled, 3. Yields everything desired; [effectuates all appeasing magic, as follows:] 1. Protects all the sentient beings; [in short,] it appeases (illness, etc.), makes prosper (life, etc.), or paralyzes and confuses all (evil) sentient beings. (Tibetan in Derge Kg. text of the *Vajravidāraṇā*, Vol. Waṃ, 42b-4, f.: / sems can thams cad skrag par byed pa / sems can thams cad ḥjil par byed pa / rig sṅags thams cad gcod par byed pa / rig sṅags thams cad gnon par byed pa / las thams cad ḥjoms par byed pa / gźan gyi las thams cad ḥjigs par byed pa / gdon thams cad rlag par byed pa / gdon thams cad las thar par byed pa / ḥbyuṅ po thams

(*abhiṣeka*) cycles which are the means of bringing those who are immature to maturation. It teaches 1500 *maṇḍalas* of the three families, i.e., *maṇḍalas* of the Tathāgata Family, etc. It teaches extensively the methods of soil rite (*sa chog*) and rite of preparation (*sta gon gyi cho ga*) which are the common requirement for those (1500 *maṇḍalas*) as well as for all the *maṇḍalas* of the Kriyā Tantra, and which are also the common requirement for the other three Tantra divisions (i.e., Caryā, Yoga, and Anuttara). All this is explained in one (continuous) piece of writing without subdivision into chapters.

Regarding the *Susiddhi*, a wrathful person named Susiddhi(karin)[31] performs the magical acts of protecting against obstructing demons; and because that wrathful person teaches the subject matter, it is called *Susiddhi-tantra.* It teaches in detail the rite of performing the *vidyā-dhāraṇī*, the method of accomplishing those *siddhis* which require a great number of magical acts, the protection according to the Kriyā Tantra, and the pledges (*samaya*) based (thereon).

The *Subāhuparipṛcchā* teaches in slight measure the initiation rites that are not explained in the *Sāmānyavidhīnām guhya-tantra* as well as the methods of performing the *vidyā-dhāraṇī* that are not explained in the *Susiddhi*; and it teaches in detail the methods of accomplishing *siddhis* by means of a great number of magical acts of appeasing, increasing prosperity, domineering, and destroying.[32] Subāhu is said to have been a son of Vajrapāṇi and a Bodhisattva bound to one more birth.

The *Dhyānottara* is a portion of the great Tantra of the Kriyā Tantra called the *Vajroṣṇīṣa-tantra.* It is also regarded as a kind of Continuation of that Tantra. It deals with ten kinds of subject matter: 1. The characteristics of the place where one practises; 2. The Self Reality; 3. The Reality of the *vidyā-dhāraṇī*; 4. The Reality of the God; 5. The meditation of dwelling in the fire; 6. The meditation of dwelling in the sound; 7. The meditation which grants liberation at the limit of the sound; 8. The rite of engaging in the practice of the *vidyā-dhāraṇī*; 9. The rite of

---

cad ḥgugs par byed pa / ḥbyuṅ po thams cad tshar gcod pa / rig sṅags kyi las thams cad byed du ḥjug pa / ma grub pa rnams grub par byed pa / grub pa rnams chud mi za bar byed pa / ḥdod pa thams cad rab tu sbyin pa / sems can thams cad sruṅ ba / źi ba / rgyas pa / sems can thams cad reṅs par byed pa / rmugs par byed paḥi gsaṅ sṅags kyi mthu chen po ḥdi saṅs rgyas kyi mthus lag na rdo rjes rab tu smras so.) It will be noticed that the *Vajra-vidāraṇā-dhāraṇī* emphasizes destructive or drastic magic (*abhicāra*), since it is the chief *dhāraṇī* of the Vajra Family. However, its list of magical acts is as complete as one could expect.

gnas paḥi bsam gtan / sgra mthar thar pa ster baḥi bsam gtan / rig sṅags bsgrub pa la ḥjug paḥi cho ga / sbyin sreg gi cho ga / dbaṅ bskur gyi cho ga rnams so / de la bdag gi de kho na ñid la sogs pa gsum gyis bya spyod gñis ka la gal che baḥi bzlas brjod yan lag bźi ston me gnas la sogs paḥi bsam gtan gsum ni bya spyod kyi las kyi dṅos gźi yin / rig sṅags bsgrub pa la ḥjug paḥi cho gas ni bsñen paḥi sṅon du ji ltar bya baḥi tshul daṅ / mjug tu ji ltar bya baḥi tshul rnams ston no /

/ bya rgyud kyi sgo nas ḥtshaṅ rgya baḥi lam gyi rim pa śes pa la rgyud bźi po deḥi don śes dgos pas / dgoṅs ḥgrel mkhan po ji lta buḥi rjes su ḥbraṅ bar bya źe na / tshad ldan gyi slob dpon chen po ca-ndra-go-mi daṅ / źi ba ḥtsho la sogs paḥi yig cha yod kyaṅ de dag gis cho ga phran tshegs las ma mdzad pas / bya spyod la mkhas paḥi slob dpon gñis / źes ḥphags yul na ñi zla ltar grags pa saṅs rgyas gsaṅ ba daṅ / byaṅ chub mchog gñis kyi rjes su ḥbraṅ bar bya ste / de las saṅs rgyas gsaṅ bas bsam gtan phyi maḥi ḥgrel pa daṅ / dpuṅ bzaṅ gis źus paḥi don bsdus kyi ḥgrel pa daṅ / tshig don gyi brjed byaṅ rnams mdzad ciṅ / byaṅ chub mchog gis legs grub kyi thabs ñe bar bsdus pa źes bya baḥi ḥgrel pa mdzad do /

the burnt offering; 10. The initiation rite. Of these, the three headed by "The Self Reality" show the four members of recitation that are of great importance in both the Kriyā and Caryā Tantras. The three kinds of meditation, starting with "dwelling in the fire", are the main part (*maula*) of the action of the Kriyā and Caryā Tantras. The rite of engaging in the practice of the *vidyā-dhāraṇī* shows how to perform the service (*sevā*) which precedes [that main part] and how to perform that which concludes [it].

If one is to understand the steps of the path of becoming a Buddha by way of the Kriyā Tantra, one must understand the meaning of those four Tantras (discussed above). Which commentators should be followed? The manuals of the great authoritative teachers Candragomin, Śāntarakṣita, and so on, treat only the minor matters of the rites. Therefore one must follow Buddhaguhya and *Varabodhi (T. *byaṅ chub mchog*), two learned teachers of the Kriyā and Caryā Tantras who are as honored in India as the sun and moon. Buddhaguhya wrote the *Dhyānottara-ṭīkā* (Toh. 2670), the *Subāhuparipṛcchā-piṇḍārtha* (Toh. 2671), and the *Tshig don gyi brjed byaṅ* (Toh. 2672). *Varabodhi wrote the commentary (on the *Susiddhi*) called *Legs grub kyi thabs ñe bar bsdus pa* (Toh. 3066, catalogued as *Legs par grub par byed paḥi sgrub paḥi thabs bsdus pa*).

/ gñis pa bya baḥi rgyud kyi dbaṅ bskur ba daṅ sdom pa gzuṅ baḥi rnam gźag ni / slob dpon a-bha-yā-ka-ras dkyil cho ga rdo rje phreṅ bar me tog phreṅ baḥi dbaṅ daṅ / chu chod phan gyi dbaṅ daṅ / rdo rje dril bu miṅ gi dbaṅ ste drug bskur bas / bya rgyud daṅ spyod rgyud kyi rgyud ñan pa daṅ ḥchad pa sogs thams cad la dbaṅ bar dṅos su bstan paḥi śugs kyis bya spyod gñis la dbaṅ drug po de las lhag pa med par bstan to /

/ ye śes thig leḥi rgyud las /

/ chu daṅ cod pan gyi ni dbaṅ /
/ bya baḥi rgyud la rab tu grags /
/ rdo rje dril bu miṅ gi dbaṅ /
/ spyod paḥi rgyud la rab tu grags /
/ phyir mi ldog pa yi ni dbaṅ /
/ rnal ḥbyor rgyud du gsal bar byas /

źes sogs gsuṅs pas / bya rgyud la me tog phreṅ baḥi dbaṅ daṅ / chu cod pan gyi dbaṅ tsam daṅ / spyod rgyud la deḥi steṅ du rdo rje dril bu miṅ gi dbaṅ gsum bsnan pa tsam daṅ / rnal ḥbyor rgyud la deḥi steṅ du phyir mi ldog pa rdo rje slob dpon gyi dbaṅ bsnan pa tsam las med par bstan ciṅ / bla med kyi rgyud la de dag gi steṅ du dbaṅ goṅ ma gsum daṅ bcas pa yod par bstan to /

/ ḥo na slob dpon sgra gcan ḥdzin dpal bśes gñen sogs kyis bya spyod la slob dpon gyi dbaṅ yod par gsuṅs pa ji ltar yin źe na / de ni luṅ bstan dbugs dbyuṅ rjes gnaṅ rnams la slob dpon gyi dbaṅ du bśad pa yin gyi /

[1] In this work, Derge Tg., *Rgyud ḥgrel*, Ṅi, 233a-3, the Hierophant's Initiation (*slob dpon gyi dbaṅ*) is called an Initiation of the Flask (*bum paḥi dbaṅ*), undoubtedly the basis for Mkhas grub rje's remark. The same work associates the Hierophant's Initiation with the Kriyā Tantra in a passage beginning Ṅi, 243b-7.

CHAPTER FOUR

b. *Fundamentals of Initiation and holding of vows in the Kriyā Tantra*

The *ācārya* Abhyākara teaches in the *Vajrāvali-nāma-maṇḍala-sādhana* (Toh. 3140) that when one is conferred the six Initiations (*abhiṣeka*), i.e. the flower garland, the water, the diadem, the thunderbolt, the bell, and the name, he is authorized for all such things as listening to and explaining the Tantras belonging to the Kriyā and Caryā Tantra classes and for concretely teaching the Initiation(s); and that consequently there are no other Initiations than those six in the Kriyā and Caryā Tantras.

It is said in the *Jñāna-tilaka-tantra* (Toh. 422),

> The water and the diadem Initiations
> Are celebrated in the Kriyā Tantra;
> The thunderbolt, bell, and name Initiations
> Are celebrated in the Caryā Tantra;
> The irreversible Initiation
> Is revealed in the Yoga Tantra;
> ......

The passage shows that only the flower garland, the water, and the diadem Initiations appear in the Kriyā Tantra; that to those the Caryā Tantra adds only the three Initiations [known as] thunderbolt, bell, and name; that the Yoga Tantra adds only the Initiation of the Hierophant (*vajra-ācārya*) [called] irreversible (*avaivartika*); and that there are no others [in those three Tantra divisions], while the Anuttara Tantra accompanies those with the three Higher Initiations.

Then how is it that an occurrence of the Hierophant's Initiation in the Kriyā and Caryā Tantras is stated, among others, by the *ācārya* Rāhula-śrī-kalyāṇamitra (in Toh. 1818, the *Yugalanaddhaprakāśa-nāma-sekaprākriyā*)?[1] He explains prophecy (*vyākaraṇa*), encouragement (*praśvāsa*), and permission (*anujñā*) to be the Hierophant's Initiation,

slob dpon gyi dbaṅ mtshan ñid tshaṅ ba min no / rdo rje slob dpon gyi dbaṅ mtshan ñid tshaṅ ba la ni sṅon du dam tshig gzuṅ ba daṅ / rig paḥi dbaṅ lṅa bskur ba tshul bźin byas nas / dam tshig gsum sbyin pa dgos so /

/ dam tshig gsum ni rdo rjeḥi dam tshig / dri buḥi dam tshig / phyag rgyaḥi dam tshig go / rdo rjeḥi dam tshig ni / rdo rje sems dpar sgom du bcug pa la rdo rjeḥi de kho na ñid bśad paḥi sgo nas lag tu rdo rje byin te ḥdzin tu ḥjug paḥo / dril buḥi dam tshig ni / dril buḥi de kho na ñid bśad de ḥdzin du ḥjug paḥo / phyag rgyaḥi dam tshig ni / rig ma byin te de daṅ ḥkhyud paḥi bde stoṅ sbyor du ḥjug paḥo /

/ yo-ga daṅ bla med gñis ka la rdo rje slob dpon kyi dbaṅ mtshan ñid tshaṅ ba yod kyaṅ / yo-gaḥi rdo rje daṅ dril buḥi dam tshig la / bla med daṅ mi ḥdra ba cher med mod kyi / phyag rgyaḥi dam tshig la khyad par śin tu che ste /

/ deḥi phyag rgyaḥi dam tshig ni lha sku phyag rgya chen po la byed pas / slob ma rdo rje sems dpaḥi skur sgom du ḥjug pa tsam yin la /

/ bla med kyi de ni lhaḥi sku phyag rgya chen po yaṅ yin mod kyi / der ma zad rig ma rdo rje dbyiṅs kyi dbaṅ phyug ma lta bur bskyed nas de daṅ ḥkhyud paḥi bde stoṅ sbyor ba rdo rje slob dpon gyi dbaṅ gi dṅos gźi yin te / brtag gñis las / śes rab bcu drug lon pa la / lag pa dag gis yaṅ dag ḥkhyud / rdo rje dril bu mñam sbyor ba / slob dpon gyi ni dbaṅ du ḥdod / ces gsuṅs pa ltar ro /

[2] The original Sanskrit is edited by D. L. Snellgrove, *The Hevajra Tantra*, Part II, p. 54 (verse II. iii. 13): pāṇibhyāṃ tu samāliṅgya prajñāṃ vai ṣoḍaśābdikāṃ / ghaṇṭāvajrasamāyogād ācāryasecanaṃ mataṃ. This verse is quoted in the *Āmnāya-mañjari* (Toh. 1198), Derge edition, 65a-6, 7; and it is also quoted in Rāhula-śrī-kalyāṇamitra's work (*op. cit.*, Ṅi, 242b-1, ff.) in this passage:

After that, he imagines himself with the form of the god of love (*kāmadeva* or *ṭakkirāja*) embraced by Vajradhātvīśvarī, the Great Seal (*mahāmudrā*) of the inner self, according to the verse:

The seal pledge (*mudrā-samaya*) is explained
as solidifying the 'body made of mind' (*manomayakāya*);
Because it solidifies all the body, it is called
a 'seal' (*mudrā*).

And it is said:
The initiation is the great thunderbolt;
The one saluted by the three realms
Should be conferred what arises from the places
Of the three secrets of all the Buddhas.

It is also said:
He embraces with his two hands
The sixteen year old Insight;
By the union of thunderbolt and bell
The Hierophant's Initiation is understood.

/ deḥi rjes su
/ yid kyi lus ni brtan byaḥi phyir /
/ phyag rgya dam tshig źes su bśad /
/ lus kun brtan par byed pas na /
/ de phyir phyag rgya źes su bsgrags /

but those are not the complete characteristics of the Hierophant's Initiation. For the complete characteristics of the Hierophant's Initiation, one must first take the pledges (*samaya*); according to the rules, he must be conferred the five Wisdom (*vidyā*) Initiations and then the three pledges.

The three pledges are (1) the thunderbolt pledge (*vajra-samaya*); (2) the bell pledge (*ghaṇṭā-samaya*); (3) the seal pledge (*mudrā-samaya*). The *thunderbolt pledge* consists [first] in making [the candidate] contemplate Vajrasattva; in order to convey the reality of the thunderbolt, the thunderbolt is laid in his hand and he is made to grasp it. The *bell pledge* consists in conveying the reality of the bell, and he is made to grasp it. The *seal pledge* consists in giving [the candidate] the *vidyā* and making him enter the union "bliss-void" (*sukha-śūnya*) by embracing that [*vidyā*].

Both the Yoga and the Anuttara Tantras have the complete characteristics of the Hierophant's Initiation; but although the thunderbolt pledge and the bell pledge in the Yoga and Anuttara Tantras are scarcely different, there is a great difference with regard to the seal pledge.

The seal pledge of the former (i.e. the Yoga Tantra) consists in making the Great Seal (*mahā-mudrā*), which is the body of the deity. Therefore, the disciple is only made to contemplate the body of Vajrasattva.

The one of the Anuttara Tantra also has the Great Seal, the body of the deity, but it is necessary in addition to produce a *vidyā* like Vajradhātvīśvarī. Then the union "bliss-void" by embracing that [vidyā] is the main part of the Hierophant's Initiation, just as is said in the *Hevajra-tantra*: "He embraces with his two hands the sixteen year old Insight (*prajñā*). By the union of thunderbolt and bell the Hierophant's Initiation is understood."[2]

źes bya ba ḥdis raṅ ḥdod paḥi lhaḥi gzugs naṅ gi bdag ñid kyi phyag rgya chen po rdo rje dbyiṅs kyi dbaṅ phyug mas ḥkhyud par bsams la /

/ dbaṅ bskur rdo rje chen po ste /
/ khams gsum pa yis phyag byas pa /
/ saṅs rgyas kun gyi gsaṅ gsum gyi /
/ gnas las byuṅ ba sbyin par bya / źes brjod do /

de skad du yaṅ / / śes rab bcu drug lon pa la /
/ lag la dag gis yaṅ dag ḥkhyud /
/ rdo rje dril bu mñam sbyar ba /
/ slob dpon dbaṅ du yaṅ dag ḥdod / ces gsuṅs so /

Kukuri-pa (Toh. 1630), Derge, Ya, 242b-2, defines the Hierophant's Initiation in terms of embracing the twelve year old Insight (*śes rab lo graṅs bcu gñis kun du ḥkhyud byas te*).

/ des na rgyud sde ḥog ma gsum la dṅos kyi rig ma lta smos kyaṅ ci ḥtshal / bsgoms paḥi lha mo yaṅ ḥkhyud pa daṅ sñoms par ḥjug paḥi dmigs pa byed pa yaṅ gaṅ nas kyaṅ ma bśad la /

/ bya rgyud kyi dbaṅ da lta dar cha che bde bźin gśegs paḥi rigs la gzuṅs grva lṅa daṅ / gdugs dkar daṅ / ḥod zer can daṅ / padmaḥi rigs la tshe dpag med je-tā-ri lha dgu ma daṅ / rdo rjeḥi rigs la phyag na rdo rje ḥbyuṅ po ḥdul byed daṅ / grub chen śa-va-ri-pas dkyil chog sogs mdzad pa nas brgyud paḥi rnam ḥjoms dkar po lha maṅ gi dbaṅ bskur sogs /

/ bya rgyud kyi dbaṅ bskur gaṅ byed kyaṅ / sṅon du sa chog daṅ sta gon tshul bźin byas la de nas me tog phreṅ baḥi dbaṅ daṅ / chu dbaṅ cod pan gyi dbaṅ gsum bskur / deḥi mthaḥ brten du luṅ bstan / dbugs dbyuṅ / rjes gnaṅ btags kyaṅ ruṅ / ma btags kyaṅ ḥgal ba med / de dag la dbaṅ bźi rdzogs par byed pa sogs ni raṅ bzo chos log tu śes par byaḥo /

/ gźan yaṅ dbaṅ bskur baḥi tshul la / yo-gaḥi rtsa rgyud de ñid bsdus pa las / rdo rje dbyiṅs kyi dkyil ḥkhor chen po ḥdir ḥjug pa la ni snod daṅ snod ma yin pa brtag mi ḥtshal lo / źes gsuṅs pa la ḥkhrul nas / snod du ruṅ mi ruṅ brgya phrag du ma la dus rer dbaṅ bskur byed pa snaṅ ste nor ba chen poḥo / de ñid bsdus pa las gsuṅs pa deḥi don ni / bśad rgyud rdo rje rtse mo las / snod du ruṅ mi ruṅ gñis las / snod ruṅ la dkyil ḥkhor du ḥjug pa daṅ dbaṅ bskur ba gñis gsuṅs te / snod du mi ruṅ ba la dkyil ḥkhor du ḥjug pa tsam byed kyi / dbaṅ gtan mi bskur bar bśad do / dkyil ḥkhor du ḥjug pa tsam byed ciṅ dbaṅ gtan mi bskur baḥi rigs de la / slob dpon kun dgaḥ sñiṅ pos mdzad paḥi dkyil chog rdo rje ḥbyuṅ ba las / de la deṅ khyod ces bya ba la sogs pa brjod par mi bya / źes dam gźag kyaṅ mi byed par bśad ciṅ /

/ snod du ruṅ mi ruṅ gi khyad par ni slob dpon a-bha-yas dkyil chog rdo rje phreṅ bar sdom pa ḥdzin par nus mi nus la bśad la / slob dpon chen po mar me mdzad bzaṅ pos mdzad paḥi gsaṅ ḥdus ḥjam rdor gyi

Hence, by no means do the three lower Tantra divisions seek for a concrete *vidyā* or explain at all the creation of a meditative object involving the embrace and equipoise with a contemplated goddess.

The Kriyā Tantra Initiations most widely disseminated nowadays are, (a) in the Tathāgata Family, the Initiations of the five *gzuṅs grva* (the *pañca-rakṣā*), Sitātapatrā, and Mārīci; (b) in the Padma Family, the Initiation of the Jetāri Amitāyus in a group of nine gods (i.e. Toh. 2700, the *Aparimitāyurjñānavidhi-nāma*); (c) in the Vajra Family, the Initiations of Vajrapāṇi Bhūtaḍāmara, moreover, of the white Vajravidāraṇa with many gods, as descended from the Mahāsiddha Śabari-pā's compositions, such as the *maṇḍala-vidhi* (i.e. Toh. 2932, the *Vajravidāraṇā-nāma-dhāraṇīmaṇḍalavidhiratnadyuti-nāma*).

Moreover, whatever be the Kriyā Tantra Initiation performed, first one makes according to the rules the soil rite (*sa chog*) and the preparation (*sta gon*). After those, the flower garland Initiation, the water Initiation, and the diadem Initiation are conferred. After the latter, prophecy, encouragement, and permission are valid when employed, and there is no violation when they are not employed. However, that those accomplish the four Initiations (i.e. the flask, and the three Higher ones), is tantamount to an arbitrary heretical innovation.

Furthermore, as regards the method of bestowing Initiation, it is said in the Fundamental Yoga Tantra, the *Tattvasaṃgraha* (Toh. 479), "For entry into this great *vajradhātu-maṇḍala*, one need not investigate whether somebody is a worthy or an unworthy receptacle." As a consequence of misunderstanding this statement, there has been the great blunder of bestowing Initiation each time upon hundreds of worthy and unworthy receptacles. The meaning of that citation from the *Tattvasaṃgraha* is explained in the Explanatory Tantra *Vajraśekhara* (Toh. 480) with the lines, "Of the worthy and the unworthy receptacles, the worthy receptacle may both enter the *maṇḍala* and be conferred Initiation"; thus the unworthy receptacle may only enter the *maṇḍala*, but meanwhile is not conferred Initiation. Concerning the principle of only entering the *maṇḍala* and meanwhile not being conferred Initiation, the *ācārya* Ānandagarbha's *maṇḍala-vidhi Vajrodaya* (Toh. 2516) says: "One should not say to that person, 'From now on, you, of such a name, ...'." This means that [the candidate] is not made to take the vow.

The *ācārya* Abhayākara explains in the *maṇḍala-vidhi Vajrāvali* (Toh. 3140) that the difference between a worthy and an unworthy receptacle is whether or not one is able to keep the vows (*saṃvara*). The very learned *ācārya* Śānti-pā, in his commentary (Toh. 1871, the *ṭīkā*) on

dkyil chog bźi brgya lṅa bcu paḥi ḥgrel pa slob dpon mkhas pa chen po śānti-pas mdzad pa las / sdom pa ḥdzin pa la yaṅ thun moṅ daṅ thun moṅ ma yin paḥi sdom pa ḥdzin pa gñis su byas nas / thun moṅ pa ni skyabs su ḥgro ba daṅ sems bskyed pa daṅ byaṅ chub sems dpaḥi sdom pa ḥdzin paḥo / źes bśad ciṅ / de la skyabs ḥgro phog / de nas smon sems phog / de nas ḥjug sdom phog / de nas rig paḥi dbaṅ lṅa tsam źig bskur bar bśad la / thun moṅ ma yin pa ni rigs lṅas bsdus pa rnams so / źes rigs lṅa spyi daṅ khyad paḥi gyi sdom pa ḥdzin par ḥdod ciṅ nus pa la bśad nas /

/ de la rig ḥdzin gyi sdom pa ḥdzin du bcug ste / rdo rje slob dpon gyi dbaṅ yan chad goṅ ma gsum daṅ bcas pa rdzogs par bskur bar bśad ciṅ / rdo rje slob dpon gyi dbaṅ mi bskur ba la rigs lṅaḥi sdom gzuṅ mi byed pa daṅ rigs lṅaḥi sdom gzuṅ byed pa la rdo rje slob dpon gyi dbaṅ bskur bar bśad do / des na bya spyod kyi rgyud kyi dbaṅ la rigs lṅaḥi sdom gzuṅ sogs śin tu mi ruṅ bas / paṇḍita padma lcags kyu daṅ / rdo rje go cha źes pa gñis kyis gdugs dkar gyi dkyil chog la rigs lṅaḥi sdom gzuṅ byas pa la yaṅ tshad mar mi gzuṅ ṅo / gsaṅ ba spyiḥi rgyud las kyaṅ skyabs su ḥgro ba daṅ / sems bskyed pa daṅ / byaṅ chub sems dpaḥi sdom pa ḥdzin pa tsam źig bśad do /

/ goṅ du rgyud sde goṅ ma gñis la bśad paḥi tshul de / bya spyod gñis la yaṅ slob dpon saṅs rgyas gsaṅ bas rnam snaṅ mṅon byaṅ gi ḥgrel bar / sdom pa ḥdzin mi nus pa la dkyil ḥkhor du ḥjug pa tsam daṅ / nus pa la thun moṅ gi sdom pa goṅ du bśad pa tsam ḥdzin du bcug nas miṅ dbaṅ man chad bskur bar bśad do /

/ mdor na thun moṅ daṅ thun moṅ ma yin paḥi sdom pa gaṅ yaṅ ḥdzin mi nus pa la dkyil ḥkhor du ḥjug pa tsam byed kyi / dbaṅ gaṅ yaṅ mi bskur bar yo-gaḥi rtsa rgyud de ñid bsdus pa daṅ bśad rgyud rdo rje rtse mo daṅ / dkyil chog rdo rje ḥbyuṅ ba gsum las bśad ciṅ / bla med kyi skabs kyi dkyil chog bźi brgya lṅa bcu baḥi ḥgrel par bśad la / tshul de

the great *ācārya* Dīpaṅkarabhadra's 450 verses of the Mañju-vajra *Guhyasamājamaṇḍala-vidhi* (Toh. 1865), explains that keeping the vows is of two kinds, keeping the common (*sādhāraṇa*) and the uncommon (*asādhāraṇa*) vows; that the vows held in common are (1) the taking of refuge [in the Three Jewels], (2) generating the Mind of Enlightenment, and (3) the Bodhisattva vow. For those, one [respectively] engages with the taking of refuge (*śaraṇa-gamana*), then the aspiration vow (*praṇidhāna-saṃvara*), and then the entrance vow (*praveśa-saṃvara*). He explains that then only the five *vidyā* Initiations are conferred. But the uncommon [vows] are those subsumed under the five Families; this refers to one who wishes and is able to keep the general and special vows of the five Families.

In regard to that, he (i.e. Śānti-pā) explains that when one is made to hold the *vidyādhara* vow, he is completely conferred the Hierophant's Initiation along with the three Higher ones. But when one is not conferred the Hierophant's Initiation, he is not made to hold the vows of the five Families; and when he is made to hold the vows of the five Families, he is conferred the Hierophant's Initiation. From this it follows that at the Initiations of the the Kriyā and Caryā Tantras it is most improper to take the vows of the five Families and so on. Hence, we do not accept as authoritative the *maṇḍala-vidhis* of Sitātapatrā by paṇḍita Padmāṅkuśa (i.e. Toh. 3106) and by Varmavajra (i.e. Toh. 3108), which introduce the taking of the vows of the five Families. The *Sāmānyavidhīnām guhya-tantra* (Toh. 806) also speaks merely of holding the vows of taking refuge, of generating the Mind [of Enlightenment], and of the Bodhisattva.

The above way of explaining (i.e. especially that by Śānti-pā) concerns the two higher Tantras (i.e. the Yoga and Anuttara Tantras). Furthermore, in both the Kriyā and Caryā according to Buddhaguhya's *Mahāvairocana-sūtra* commentary (Toh. 2663), the one who is unable to hold the vows may merely enter the *maṇḍala*, while if he is able, is made to hold only what have been explained above as the common vows and then is conferred the Initiations up to Name.

In short, whoever is unable to keep the common and the uncommon vows is permitted only to enter the *maṇḍala* without receiving any Initiation. This is the teaching of the Fundamental Yoga Tantra, the *Tattvasaṃgraha* (Toh. 479), its Explanatory Tantra, the *Vajraśekhara* (Toh. 480), and the [Yoga Tantra] *maṇḍala-vidhi*, the *Vajrodaya* (Toh. 2516). For the Anuttara phase, it is taught in the commentary (Toh. 1871) on the *maṇḍala-vidhi* in 450 stanzas (Toh. 1865). And Buddhaguhya ex-

bya spyod la yaṅ ḥdra bar slob dpon saṅs rgyas gsaṅ bas rnam snaṅ mṅon byaṅ gi ḥgrel par bśad do /

/ rig paḥi dbaṅ lṅa tsam bskur yaṅ rdo rje slob dpon gyi dbaṅ mi bskur ba la rigs lṅaḥi sgom gzuṅ mi byed ciṅ / rigs lṅaḥi sdom gzuṅ byed pa la rdo rje slob dpon gyi dbaṅ bskur dgos par slob dpon śānti-pa daṅ / grub chen lva-ba-pa daṅ / ratnarakṣita daṅ / slob dpon kun dgaḥ sñiṅ po daṅ / slob dpon a-bha-ya rnams kyis bśad do /

/ ḥo na dbaṅ gaṅ yaṅ mi bskur bar dkyil ḥkhor du ḥjug pa tsam byas pa la dgoṅs pa ci yod ce na / skyabs ḥgro blaṅs nas dad pas dkyil ḥkhor mthoṅ na / bskal pa du mar bsags paḥi sdig pa ḥdag ciṅ / ma ḥoṅs pa na sṅags kyi lam zab mo la ḥjug paḥi snod ruṅ du ḥgyur baḥi bag chags rgyud la bsgo baḥi dgo[ṅ]s pa yod do /

/ bya spyod kyi rig paḥi dbaṅ lṅa daṅ / yogaḥi rig paḥi dbaṅ lṅa gñis rig paḥi dbaṅ lṅa yin par mtshuṅs kyaṅ / don mi gcig ciṅ mchog dman gyi khyad par chen po yod do /

/ bya rgyud la rigs gsum yod paḥi de bźin gśegs paḥi rigs kyi dbaṅ bskur thob na rigs gźan gñis kyi dbaṅ ma thob kyaṅ rigs gsum gaḥi lha bsgom pa daṅ / sṅags bzla ba daṅ / rgyud ñan pa sogs la dbaṅ mod kyi / ḥo na kyaṅ lha de ñid kyi luṅ rjes gnaṅ thob dgos par legs grub las bśad do /

/ padmaḥi rigs kyi dbaṅ bskur thob ciṅ rigs gźan gyi dbaṅ ma thob na rigs gñis kyi sgo bzlas daṅ rgyud ñan pa sogs la dbaṅ gi / de bźin gśegs paḥi rigs la mi dbaṅ ṅo /

/ rdo rjeḥi rigs kyi dbaṅ bskur thob ciṅ rigs gźan gñis kyi dbaṅ ma thob na rdo rjeḥi rigs ñid kyi sgom bzlas daṅ / rgyud ñan pa sogs la dbaṅ gi rigs gźan gñis la mi dbaṅ ṅo /

/ bya spyod kyi dbaṅ bskur ba la ḥdzin du ḥjug paḥi thun moṅ gi sdom pa ḥdzin pa dẹ gaṅ.źe na / byaṅ sems kyi sdom pa ḥdzin pa yin te / ḥjug pa sems bskyed cho gas ḥdzin pa daṅ don gcig la / ḥjug sems bsgoms stobs kyis rgyud la skyes kyaṅ / cho gas ma bzuṅ na sdom par mi ḥgyur ro /

plains in his commentary (Toh. 2663) on the *Mahāvairocana* that the same principle governs both the Kriyā and the Caryā Tantras.

Moreover, if only the five *vidyā* Initiations are conferred, the Hierophant's Initiation is not conferred and one is not made to take the vows of the five Families. The *ācārya* Śānti-pā, the *mahāsiddha* Lva-ba-pa, Ratnarakṣita, the *ācārya* Ānandagarbha, and the *ācārya* Abhayākara all teach that whoever takes the vows of the five Families must be conferred the Hierophant's Initiation.

Now if someone were made only to enter the *maṇḍala* and not to be conferred Initiation, what would be the advantage? If one takes the refuge vow and beholds the *maṇḍala* with faith, there is the advantage that he becomes purified from sins accumulated for many aeons and plants in his stream of consciousness (*saṃtāna*) the disposition (*vāsana*) of becoming in future times a receptacle fit for entering the profound *mantra* path (i.e. the Vajra-yāna).

The five *vidyā* Initiations of the Kriyā and Caryā and the five *vidyā* Initiations of the Yoga are alike in being five *vidyā* Initiations; however, they do not have the same aim, there being the great distinction of high and low.

The *Susiddhi* (Toh. 807) explains that if, from among the three Families of the Kriyā Tantra, someone is conferred the Initiation of the Tathāgata Family, then even though he has not obtained Initiation in the other two Families (i.e. Padma and Vajra), he is authorized to contemplate the gods of the three Families, to mutter their *dhāraṇīs*, and to listen to their Tantras. However, he must obtain the prophecy and permission of such gods.

If someone has been conferred the Initiation of the Padma Family but not obtained Initiation in the other Families, he is authorized to contemplate, mutter, and listen to the Tantras in the two Families (i.e. Padma and Vajra); however, he has no authority in the Tathāgata Family.

If someone has obtained the Initiation of the Vajra Family but not obtained Initiation in the other two Families, he is authorized to contemplate, mutter, and listen to the Tantras in precisely that Vajra Family, but he has no authority in the other two Families.

What constitutes holding of the common vow which one is made to hold for Initiations of the Kriyā and Caryā? Holding the vow of the Mind of Enlightenment amounts to generating the Entrance Mind (*praveśa-citta*) and holding it ritually (with a *vidhi*). Even when the Entrance Mind is born in the stream of consciousness by the power of intense contemplation, if it is not held ritually, it does not become a vow (*saṃvara*; i.e. is not 'held together').

/ de la thun moṅ baḥi sdom ba zer baḥi rgyu mtshan ni pha rol tu phyin paḥi theg pa chen po daṅ / gsaṅ sṅags gñis gaṅ gi sgor ḥjug kyaṅ ḥdzin dgos śiṅ / sṅags kyi yaṅ rgyud sde bźi po gaṅ gi lam du ḥjug kyaṅ ḥdzin dgos la / bla med kyi yaṅ bskyed rdzogs gaṅ gi lam la slob kyaṅ ḥdzin dgos paḥi sdom pa yin pas thun moṅ gi sdom pa źes byaḥo /

/ skabs gaṅ du ḥdzin na slob ma sta gon gyi skabs daṅ dkyil ḥkhor du ḥjug paḥi skabs gñis kar ḥdzin paḥi tshul źig daṅ skabs sṅa mar ḥdzin la phyi mar mi ḥdzin paḥi tshul źig daṅ / phyi mar ḥdzin la sṅa mar mi ḥdzin paḥi tshul źig ste gsum tshad ldan gyi gźuṅ las bśad do /

/ tshig gaṅ gis ḥdzin na / dkon mchog gsum la bdag skyabs mchi / sdig pa thams cad so sor bśags / ḥgro baḥi dge la rjes yi raṅ / saṅs rgyas byaṅ chub yid kyis gzuṅ / saṅs rgyas chos daṅ tshogs mchog la / byaṅ chub bar du bdag skyabs mchi / raṅ gźan don ni rab bsgrub phyir / byaṅ chub sems ni bskyed par bgyi / byaṅ chub mchog gi sems ni bskyed bgyis nas / sems can thams cad bdag gis mgron du gñer / byaṅ chub spyod mchog yid ḥoṅ spyad par bgyi / ḥgro la phan phyir saṅs rgyas ḥgrub par śog / ces rdo rje gur gyi rgyud las gsuṅs pas so /

/ de la tshigs bcad daṅ po rkyaṅ pas ḥjug sdom ḥdzin paḥi tshul gsaṅ ḥdus kyi dkyil chog maṅ po daṅ / slob dpon a-bha-yā-karaḥi dkyil chog rdo rje phreṅ ba sogs maṅ por mdzad ciṅ / tshigs bcad rdzogs pas ḥdzin paḥi tshul yaṅ dkyil chog maṅ por mdzad do /

/ de la tshigs bcad daṅ po rkyaṅ bas byed na rkaṅ pa daṅ po gsum gyis ḥjug pa sems bskyed len paḥi sbyor ba ston źiṅ / saṅs rgyas byaṅ chub yid kyis gzuṅ / źes pa gcig pus smon sems cho gas ḥdzin pa daṅ / ḥjug sems cho gas ḥdzin pa gñis ka ston par brda ḥphrod dgos so / tshigs bcad rdzogs pas byed na / saṅs rgyas byaṅ chub yid kyis gzuṅ / źes pa mdor bstan pa yin la / saṅs rgyas chos daṅ tshogs mchog la / źes pa nas / sems can thams cad bdag gis mgron du gñer / źes paḥi bar gyis smon

[3] Later in this chapter, Mkhas grub rje refers to these two paths by the more standard expressions of 'Steps of Production' and 'Steps of Completion'.

The reason for calling the vow "common" (*sādhāraṇa*) is that it must be held whether one enters by way of the great Pāramitā vehicle or by way of the Mantra [vehicle]; and, moreover, if by way of the Mantra vehicle, that it must be held whichever one of the four Tantra divisions provides the path of entrance; and, moreover, if by way of the Anuttara [Tantra], that it must be held whether one is mastering the path of production (*utpatti*) or of completion (*niṣpanna*).[3] Consequently, one speaks of a "common vow".

As regards the occasions at which the disciple is to take it, the authoritative texts propound three views. According to one, he is to take it at the occasions both of the preparatory rite and of entering the *maṇḍala*; according to another, only at the first, not at the second occasion; according to still another, only at the second, not at the first occasion.

With what words does he take it? They are given in the *Vajrapañjarā-tantra* (Toh. 419):

(1) I take my refuge in the Three Jewels;
I confess every one of my sins;
I rejoice in the merits of the living beings;
I set my mind on the Enlightenment of the Buddha.

(2) I take my refuge, up to Enlightenment,
In the Buddha, his Law, and the supreme host;
For accomplishing my own and others' aim,
I generate the Mind of Enlightenment.

(3) After generating the Mind of Supreme Enlightenment,
I shall be host to all the sentient beings;
I shall practice zestfully the best practice of Enlightenment;
May I become a Buddha for the sake of the world!

Many *maṇḍala-vidhis* of the *Guhyasamāja* cycle, the *ācārya* Abhayākara's *maṇḍala-vidhi Vajrāvali* (Toh. 3140), and many other works, adopt the method of taking the entrance vow (*praveśa-saṃvara*) with only the first stanza. On the other hand, many *maṇḍala-vidhis* adopt the method of taking it with the full complement of stanzas.

If only the first stanza is used, it is necessary to interpret the first three lines as showing the receptive technique for generating the Entrance Mind, and the single line "I set my mind on the Enlightenment of the Buddha" as showing both the holding of Aspiration Mind ritually and and the holding of Entrance Mind ritually. If one does it with the full complement of stanzas, the line "I set my mind on the Enlightenment of the Buddha" is a synopsis; the section from "I take my refuge, up to Enlightenment", through "I shall be host to all the sentient beings"

sems cho gas ḥdzin pa ston źiṅ / byaṅ chub spyod mchog yid ḥoṅ spyad par bgyi źes pas ḥjug sems cho gas ḥdzin pa ston no /

/ de la smon sems cho gas ḥdzin paḥi tshe / bdag gis sems can thams cad kyi don du saṅs rgyas thob par byaḥo / sñam du dam bcas tsam kyis mi chog gi / de ltar dam bcas paḥi dam bcaḥ de saṅs rgyas ma thob kyi bar du mi gtaṅ ṅo / sñam du dam bcas paḥi tshul gyis ḥdzin dgos so /

/ de ltar smon sems cho gas ḥdzin tshul deḥi sgo nas bzuṅ na bslab bya la slob dgos śiṅ / bslab bya ni skyabs ḥgro daṅ sems bskyed kyi phan yon sems pa rnams ñin mtshan dus drug tu byed pa daṅ / nag poḥi chos bźi spaṅ źiṅ dkar poḥi chos bźi sgrub bsogs te / des na nag poḥi chos bźi ma spaṅs na / skye ba phyi ma rnams su sems bskyed mi skye baḥi rgyur ḥgyur ba yin gyi / tshe ḥdi la sems bskyed blaṅs zin gtoṅ ba min no / ḥo na sems bskyed gaṅ gis gtoṅ na sems can thams cad kyi don byed paḥi bsam pa btaṅ ba daṅ / saṅs rgyas thob ḥdod kyi bsam pa btaṅ na sems bskyed gtoṅ ṅo /

/ ḥjug sems cho gas bzuṅ nas byaṅ sems kyi sdom paḥi rtsa ltuṅ daṅ / yan lag gi ñes pa rnams legs par śes par byas la bsruṅ dgos so /

/ dbaṅ bskur gyi sṅa rol tu byaṅ sems kyi sdom pa ḥdzin pa la goṅ du bśad pa ltar gyi don dran paḥi sgo nas rjes zlos lan gsum byas paḥi tshig tha ma rdzogs pa na sdom pa rgyud la skyes pa yin pas / de ltar don dran paḥi sgo nas ma byas na byaṅ sems kyi sdom pa skye ba daṅ / ñams pa sos par mi ḥgyur źiṅ byaṅ sems kyi sdom pa ma skyes par gsaṅ sṅags kyi sdom pa skye ba mi srid do /

/ khrom chen po tshogs pa la sems bskyed de ḥbogs na / sṅon du yan lag bdun pa sogs daṅ / don daṅ phan yon bśad paḥi sgo nas legs par ṅes

[4] The six times may be deduced from later statements of this chapter to be dusk, dawn, morning, night, noon, and midnight.

[5] The four black natures and their antidotes called the four white natures are discussed in Tsoṅ-kha-pa's *Lam rim chen mo* (Bodhisattva section) on the basis of a passage from the *Kāśyapa-parivarta*, which is available in Sanskrit in the *Śikṣāsamuccaya* (reprint The Hague, Mouton & Co., 1957), p. 52, line 12, ff. The four white natures are incorrectly divided up by Cecil Bendall and W. H. D. Rouse, translators, *Śikshāsamuccaya* (London, 1922), p. 53. According to Tsoṅ-kha-pa's elaborate discussion, the four black natures in short are: 1. misleading the teacher, 2. lack of conscience toward others, 3. disparaging those who have set forth in the Great Vehicle (*mahāyāna*), 4. cheating another person; the four white natures in short are: 1. never speaking an untruth, 2. altruism toward others and no cheating, 3. regarding all Bodhisattvas as one's teacher, 4. inspiring sentient beings to the goal of Enlightenment. Of those, the first white nature is the antidote for the first black nature, the second white one for the fourth black one, the third white one for the third black one, and the fourth white one for the second black one.

[6] According to Tsoṅ-kha-pa's *Lam rim chen mo* (Bodhisattva section), Atīśa has explained the preliminary acts of generating the Mind of Enlightenment in terms of seven members in his *Gurukriyākrama* (Toh. 3977), and the seven members can be

shows the holding of Aspiration Mind ritually; and the line "I shall practice zestfully the best practice of Enlightenment" shows the holding of Entrance Mind ritually.

At the time of holding the Aspiration Mind ritually, it does not suffice to think the vow, "May I attain Buddhahood for the aim of all sentient beings", but one must hold it by the method which thinks in addition the vow, "Until I have attained Buddhahood I shall not give up that vow so vowed."

When one has thus ritually taken hold of the Aspiration Mind by way of that method of holding, one must learn certain things to be learned. What is to be learned is this: In the six times[4] of day and night he must give thought to the benefits of taking refuge and generating the Mind; and rejecting the four black natures (*kṛṣṇa-dharma*), he must accomplish and collect the four white natures (*śukla-dharma*).[5] Thus, if one does not reject the four black natures, they become a cause in his subsequent births for the non-birth of generation of the Mind, even though in the present life he take the generation of the Mind and not reject it. Now, the one who abandons the generation of the Mind abandons the hope of acting for the sake of all sentient beings; and the one who abandons the hope which is the desire of achieving Buddhahood, abandons the generation of the Mind.

When one has ritually taken hold of the Entrance Mind, he must well understand the basic transgressions and ancillary faults of the Bodhisattva vow and guard against them.

Before being conferred Initiation, one takes hold of the Bodhisattva vow. He repeats the words three times after his teacher while being mindful of the significance as explained above. When this repetition is finished, the vow is born in his stream of consciousness. If it is not performed with mindfulness of the significance in that way, there is neither the birth of the Bodhisattva vow nor mending of its violation. And when the Bodhisattva vow is not born, the Mantra vow cannot possibly be born.

When the generation of the Mind is administered to a large group of persons, they must first be made resolute by way of the seven-membered rite (*saptāṅgavidhi*)[6] and an explanation of the aim (*artha*) and benefit

followed with the materials either in the *Bhadracarī* (a portion of the *Avataṃsaka-sūtra*) or in the *Caryāvatāra* (of Śāntideva). According to the *Gurukriyākrama*, the seven members are in brief those stated subsequently by Mkhas-grub-rje in β. Generation of Deity in Front—IV'. Offering and praising, and V'. Confession of sins, etc. (in five parts), except that Atīśa omits "Refuge Formula", and counts "Exhortation and entreaty" as two items.

par byas te / dṅos gźiḥi skabs su sems can kyi don du rdzogs paḥi saṅs rgyas thob par byaḥo sñam pa gyis la rjes zlos gyis śig / ces brda sprad la rjes zlos byed du bcug na sems can thams cad kyi don du saṅs rgyas thob par byaḥo sñam paḥi blo bskyed pas bsod nams chen po ḥbyuṅ źiṅ / smon sems khyad par can cho gas gzuṅ ba ma byas pas bslab bya daṅ ḥgal baḥi ñes pa mi ḥbyuṅ ba yin no /

/ rgyud sde goṅ ma gñis kyi dbaṅ bskur ma thob par bya spyod gaṅ ruṅ gi dbaṅ tsam thob pa la / byaṅ sems kyi sdom pa las logs su gsaṅ sṅags kyi sdom pa bsruṅ rgyu med do / de yaṅ ma mthaḥ mi dge bcu spoṅ gi tshul khrims tsam daṅ / bslab pa lṅa bsruṅ ba dge bsñen gyi sdom pa tsam daṅ / ya mthaḥ bsñen rdzogs kyi so thar gyi sdom pa gaṅ ruṅ rgyud la med par byaṅ sems kyi sdom pa mi ḥchags pas / bya spyod gaṅ ruṅ gi dbaṅ bskur tsam thob pa yin na sdom pa gñis ldan du ṅes śiṅ / sdom pa gtoṅ baḥi rtsa ltuṅ yaṅ byaṅ sems kyi rtsa ltuṅ du zad do / ḥo na kyaṅ so thar daṅ byaṅ sems kyi bslab byar ma gtogs paḥi bya spyod kyi sgos kyi dam tshig bsruṅ rgyu du ma yod pa rnams ni legs grub las bśad do /

/ yo-ga daṅ bla med gñis kyi rdo rje slob dpon gyi dbaṅ man chad mtshan ñid tshaṅ ba thob nas sdom pa gsum ldan yin źiṅ rtsa ltuṅ ni byaṅ sems kyi sdom paḥi rtsa ltuṅ daṅ / sṅags kyi rtsa ltuṅ bcu bźi daṅ bcas pa thams cad do /

/ ḥo na bya spyod paḥi sdom pa la byaṅ sems kyi sdom paḥi rtsa ltuṅ las gźan paḥi rtsa ltuṅ med na / jo bos mdzad paḥi dam tshig bsdus pa las / kṛ-yaḥi rtsa ltuṅ sum cu sogs bśad pa daṅ ḥgal lo źe na / de las so thar gyi rtsa ltuṅ bźi / byaṅ sems kyi bcu gñis kṛ-yaḥi sum cu / spyod rgyud kyi bcu bźi / rnal ḥbyor rgyud kyi bcu bźi / rnal ḥbyor chen poḥi rgyud kyi bcu bźi / yaṅ bźi / yaṅ lṅa ste bdun cu tham paḥo / źes dgu bcu go bdun bgraṅ nas bdun cu tham paḥo / źes graṅs tsam la yaṅ ḥkhrul bar snaṅ baḥi phyir daṅ / bdag gi bla ma dam tshig rdo rjeḥi źal sṅa nas źes bya ba sogs snaṅ la / nag po dam tshig rdo rje jo boḥi bla ma ma yin paḥi phyir / de jo bos mdzad pa ma yin no /

(*hita*). In the phase of the main part [of the rite of taking the vow], they should be instructed, "Think, 'I shall attain complete Buddhahood for the aim of the sentient beings', and repeat it after me." When they have been drawn into repeating it after the instructor and have generated the cognition of thinking, "I shall attain Buddhahood for the aim of all the sentient beings", great merit arises. Also, when the Aspiration Mind is not taken with a special rite, there is no fault which violates the things to be learned.

When one is conferred Initiations of the Kriyā and Caryā and is not conferred Initiations belonging to the two higher Tantra divisions, there is no reason to protect a vow beyond the Bodhisattva one, that is, the Mantra vow. Moreover, when there is lacking in the stream of consciousness — at the lower end, merely the morality (*śīla*) of renouncing the ten unvirtuous deeds or merely the layman's vow to guard the five precepts; or at the upper end, the *prātimokṣa* vow of the ordained monk, then the Bodhisattva vow does not originate. Hence, if one is conferred merely an Initiation of either the Kriyā or Caryā, he certainly must have the two vows (i.e. *prātimokṣa* and Bodhisattva), and the basic transgression of abandoning the vow(s) amounts to a basic transgression of the Mind of Enlightenment. However, the *Susiddhi* (Toh. 807) gives many reasons for protecting special pledges (*samaya*) of the Kriyā and Caryā that are not included in the things to be learned of the *prātimokṣa* or the Bodhisattva [vows].

When one obtains the complete characteristics of the Hierophant's Initiation and below of the Yoga and Anuttara [Tantras], he possesses the three vows (i.e. *prātimokṣa*, Bodhisattva, and Mantra), and the basic transgressions are the basic transgressions of the Bodhisattva vow and all fourteen basic transgressions of the Mantra [vow].

Now, if for the vows of the Kriyā and Caryā there is no basic transgression other than that of the Bodhisattva vow, is this not in disagreement with the **Samaya-saṃgraha* composed by Jo bo [Atīśa], which mentions thirty basic transgressions of the Kriyā, and so on? That work says, "Four basic transgressions of the *prātimokṣa*, twelve of the Bodhisattva, thirty of the Kriyā, fourteen of the Caryā Tantra, fourteen of the Yoga Tantra, fourteen of the Mahā-yoga Tantra, an additional four, and still five more, make a total of seventy." Having enumerated ninety-seven, it gives a total of seventy; and the count alone is obviously a blunder. But there occurs the passage, "As my *guru* Samayavajra says..."; and since *Kṛṣṇasamayavajra was not the *guru* of Jo bo, that work is not composed by Jo bo.

/ gsum pa dbaṅ thob ciṅ sdom pa bzuṅ nas lam la slob paḥi rnam gźag ni / rgyud sde ḥog ma gsum la bskyed rim daṅ rdzogs rim gyi don daṅ tha sñad gaṅ yaṅ med de / bskyed rim mtshan ñid par ḥgro ba la ḥbras bu rdzogs paḥi saṅs rgyas kyi phun sum tshogs pa lṅa daṅ rnam pa mthun par da lta nas bsgom pa tsam yod pas mi chog gi / sbyaṅ gźi skye ḥchi bar do gsum daṅ rnam pa mthun par bsgom paḥi rnal ḥbyor dgos la / rgyud sde ḥog ma gsum la ḥbras buḥi skabs kyi phun sum tshogs pa lṅa daṅ rnam pa mthun par da lta nas bsgom pa yod kyaṅ / sbyaṅ gźi skye ḥchi bar do gsum daṅ rnam pa mthun par bsgom paḥi rnal ḥbyor med pas bskyed rim med do /

/ rdzogs rim mtshan ñid tshaṅ ba ni chos rnams kyi gnas lug stoṅ pa ñid bsgom pa daṅ / rluṅ gi rnal ḥbyor bsgom pa tsam gyis mi chog gi / ā-va-dhū-tīḥi naṅ du rluṅ źugs gnas thim gsum byas pa las byuṅ baḥi bde stoṅ gi ye śes daṅ / de las byuṅ baḥi lhaḥi sku daṅ / de gñis ḥdren paḥi thun moṅ ma yin paḥi thabs lus la gnad du bsnun paḥi rnal ḥbyor khyad par can gsum gaṅ ruṅ yin dgos la / rgyud sde ḥog ma gsum la gnas lugs kyi stoṅ ñid bsgom pa daṅ / rluṅ gi rnal ḥbyor bsgom pa yod kyaṅ / gźan rnams med pas rdzogs rim bsgom pa med do /

/ des na rgyud sde ḥog ma gsum la mtshan bcas daṅ mtshan med kyi rnal ḥbyor gñis gñis yod do /

[7] According to *Thob yig gsal baḥi me loṅ*, Vol. II, 72a-4, ff. the five perfections are: (1) perfection of body, *viz.*, possession of the seven members of the *saṃpuṭa*, decorated with the Characteristics and Minor Marks (sku phun sum tshogs pa mtshan dpes spras paḥi kha sbyor yan lag bdun daṅ ldan pa); (2) perfection of merit, *viz.*, gain of the ultimate merit, consisting in having eliminated [the imagination of both *nirvāṇa* and *saṃsāra*] and fully comprehended (yon tan phun sum tshogs pa spaṅs rtogs mthar phyin paḥi yon tan brñes pa); (3) perfection of retinue, *viz.*, comprised of one's own stream of consciousness (ḥkhor phun sum tshogs pa raṅ rgyud kyis bsdus pa); (4) perfection of place, *viz.*, the self-generated palace of divine knowledge (gnas phun sum tshogs pa ye śes raṅ snaṅ las grub paḥi gźal yas khaṅ); (5) perfection of affiliation, *viz.*, continuity of the affiliation of both body and mind (rigs ḥdra phun sum tshogs pa sku thugs gñis kyi rigs ḥdra rgyun mi ḥchad pa).

[8] In the Gelugpa sect, the three spheres of purification are related to the three bodies of the Buddha in this passage in Tsoṅ-kha-pa's *Ye rdor* (Gsuṅ ḥbum. Vol. Ca), 18a-1: "If one knows how to carry away the path of the Saṃbhogakāya of the Intermediate State, then he will know how to carry away the Dharmakāya of Death when generating the four Voids in the same way as in the sequence of Death; and if he knows those two, then he will also know how to carry away the Nirmāṇa-kāya of Birth" (bar do loṅs skuḥi lam ḥkhyer śes na ḥchi rim ji lta ba bźin stoṅ pa bźi bskyed nas ḥchi ba chos skur ḥkhyer śes par ḥgyur la / de gñis śes na skye ba sprul skur ḥkhyer ba yaṅ śes par ḥgyur ro).

c. *Fundamentals of studying the path after receiving Initiation and taken vows*

In the three lower Tantras (i.e., Kriyā, Caryā, and Yoga) there are neither the aims (*artha*) nor the terms (*vyavahāra*) of the Steps of Production (*utpatti-krama*) and the Steps of Completion (*niṣpanna-krama*). If one proceeds according to the characteristics of the Steps of Production, it is not sufficient to limit oneself to an intense contemplation (*bhāvanā*) in immediacy conforming to the five perfections[7] of the resultative complete Buddha, for it is also necessary to have the *yoga* of intense contemplation conforming to the three spheres of purification (*sbyaṅ gźi*), namely, birth, death, and the intermediate state.[8] In the three lower Tantras there is the intense contemplation in immediacy conforming to the five perfections of the resultative phase; however, as there is no *yoga* of intense contemplation conforming to the three spheres of purification, namely, birth, death, and the intermediate state, there are no Steps of Production.

For the complete characteristics of the Steps of Completion, it does not suffice to have merely the intense contemplation of voidness (*śūnyatā*) of the natural state (*gnas lugs*) of things (*dharma*) and the intense contemplation of the *yoga* of the winds (*vāyu*), but it is also necessary to have three special things, as the case may be: (1) the knowledge of bliss-void (*sukha-śūnya*) which occurs from making the wind(s) enter, stay, and rise for leaving in the central vein (*avadhūtī*);[9] (2) the divine body which occurs from that [knowledge]; and (3) the *yoga* of piercing the vital centers in the uncommon 'means' body (*upāya-deha*) attracted by those two (i.e. the knowledge and the divine body). In the three lower Tantras, there is the intense contemplation of the voidness of the natural state and there is the intense contemplation of the *yoga* of the winds; but as the others (i.e. the three special things) are lacking, there is no intense contemplation of the Steps of Completion.

Therefore, in each of the three lower Tantras, there are both the *yogas* called "with signs" (*sanimitta-yoga*) and "without signs" (*animitta-yoga*).

---

[9] The original Sanskrit for the three stages of the wind is found in the *Pañcakrama* (Yuganaddhakrama, verse 12) in comparison with its Tibetan translation. The three are *praveśa* (T. *ḥjug pa*), 'entrance'; *ālaya* (T. *gnas pa*), 'staying' or 'holding'; and *utthāna* (T. *ldaṅ ba*), 'rising for leaving'. Mkhas grub rje has the Tibetan word *thim* instead of *ldaṅ*. Among the meanings of *thim* are 'to creep away' and 'to evaporate', appropriate to the expiration of the breath.

/ de la bya rgyud kyi lam ñams su len tshul la gsum / bzlas brjod daṅ bcas paḥi bsam gtan / bzlas brjod la mi ltos paḥi bsam gtan / bsñen pa las su ruṅ nas dṅos grub bsgrub tshul lo /

/ daṅ po la gsum / bzlas brjod yan lag bźiḥi sṅon ḥgro daṅ / dṅos gźi daṅ / mjug tu ji ltar bya baḥo /

/ daṅ po ni / rigs spyiḥi sṅags rgya bcaḥ ba daṅ / phyogs bcuḥi saṅs rgyas daṅ byaṅ chub sems dpaḥ thams cad la phyag ḥtshal źiṅ bdag ñid ḥbul ba daṅ / skyabs su ḥgro źiṅ sems bskyed pa daṅ / sṅags daṅ phyag rgyas bsruṅ ba daṅ bźi byas nas / gnas khaṅ gi phyi rol tu phyin te / khrus la sogs pa byas nas naṅ du źugs te chas su źugs nas stan la ḥkhod de / mchod pa byin gyis brlab pa daṅ / bdag daṅ gnas bsruṅ ba la sogs pa rnams bya ste / de dag ni rgyud sde goṅ maḥi bsruṅ ḥkhor bsgom paḥi dod do /

/ gñis pa la gñis / bdag bskyed bsgoms nas bsñen pa bya ba daṅ / mdun bskyed bsgoms nas mchod pa ḥbul baḥi tshul lo /

/ daṅ po ni / gcig daṅ du bral la sogs pa dbu maḥi gtan tshigs la brten nas bdag gi sems raṅ bźin gyis grub pas stoṅ par legs par gtan la phab nas bsgom pa ni bdag gi de kho na ñid do / de nas gaṅ bsgom par bya baḥi lhaḥi de kho na ñid daṅ / bdag gi de kho na ñid dbyer med par raṅ bźin med par bsgom pa ni lhaḥi de kho na ñid de / de kho na ñid gñis

[10] The numbering in this paragraph is not in the Tibetan text, but is based upon the treatment in Tsoṅ-kha-pa's *Sṅags rim chen mo*, Peking ed., 53b-3 to 59a-4, which Mkhas grub rje severely condenses.

[11] Mkhas grub rje should have mentioned here — he makes it clear later on in the present chapter in the section "The Four Members, general" — that the Self Generation and the Generation in Front each constitute one member among the four members.

The Procedure of the Kriyā Tantra

There are three methods of procedure (*anuṣṭhāna*) in the Kriyā Tantra, namely, meditation (*dhyāna*) accompanied by muttering (*jāpa*), meditation independent of muttering, and accomplishment of *siddhi* after appropriate service (*sevā*).

(1) MEDITATION WITH MUTTERING

This has three sections, namely, the preliminary acts to the four members of muttering, the main part of the four members of muttering, and the terminating acts to the four members of muttering.

(a) **Preliminary acts to the four members of muttering**

This has four phases: 1. making the general *dhāraṇīs* and seals (*mudrā*) of the Families; 2. bowing to all the Buddhas and Bodhisattvas of the ten directions and offering up oneself to them; 3. taking refuge and generating the Mind [of Enlightenment]; 4. protecting through *dhāraṇīs* and seals (*mudrā*). [In the same phases one respectively,] 1. goes outside the dwelling; 2. goes through the bathing ritual and so on and then reenters the dwelling; 3. dresses in religious apparel and takes a seat; 4. performs such acts as blessing the offering and protecting oneself and the place. These acts are equivalent to the contemplation of the protective circle (*rakṣā-cakra*) of the higher Tantras.[10]

(b) **The main part of the four members of muttering**

Here there are two parts: the service to be done through contemplation of Self Generation; and the method of presenting offerings through the contemplation of Generation in Front.[11]

α. *Generation of Self into Deity*

The first god

The Self Reality (**ātma-tattva*) is the contemplation (*bhāvanā*) that (1) is free from such concepts as singleness and multiplicity by recourse to the reasoned formulations of the Mādhyamika; and (2) which decides that one's own mind is void because accomplished by intrinsic nature. After that, the God Reality (**devatā-tattva*) is the contemplation of the reality of the god to be contemplated and the Self Reality as inseparable and as devoid of intrinsic nature. The two realities constitute the Reality

po de lha drug gi naṅ nas de kho na ñid kyi lha ste / rgyud sde goṅ maḥi sva-bha-va daṅ śū-nya-tā sogs pa brjod nas stoṅ ñid bsgom paḥi dod do /

/ de nas stoṅ paḥi ṅaṅ las gaṅ bsgom par bya baḥi lha de ñid ṅo bo lha de ñid yin pa la / rnam pa gaṅ bzla bar bya baḥi sṅags kyi sgraḥi rnam par grag par bsams te / de la yid rtse gcig tu dmigs pa ni sgraḥi lhaḥo /

/ de nas raṅ gi sems nam mkhar zla baḥi dkyil ḥkhor gyi rnam par gyur paḥi steṅ du gaṅ bsgom par bya baḥi lha de ñid ṅo bo lha de ñid yin pa la rnam pa gaṅ bzla bar bya baḥi sṅags kyi yi ge gser źun maḥi mdog gi rnam par bsgom pa ni yi geḥi lhaḥo /

/ sgra daṅ yi geḥi lha de dag la gzuṅs riṅ daṅ / sñiṅ po / ñe sñiṅ gsum gaṅ ruṅ gis chog go /

/ de nas yig ḥbru de dag las ḥod zer dpag tu med pa ḥphros paḥi rtse mo las bsgom par bya baḥi lha de ñid kyi skuḥi rnam pa dpag tu med pa ḥphros pas / sems can thams cad kyi sdig sgrib daṅ sdug bsṅal thams cad sbyaṅs / saṅs rgyas sras bcas thams cad mchod pas mñes par byas te / ḥod zer lha daṅ bcas pa slar ḥdus / yig ḥbru la thim pas zla ba yi ge daṅ bcas pa yoṅs su gyur pa las / gaṅ bsgom par bya baḥi lhaḥi sku rdzogs par bskyed pa la dmigs pa ni gzugs kyi lha ste /

/ bdag bskyed bsgoms nas bsñen pa byed paḥi tshe gtso bo rkyaṅ pa bsgom pa ma gtogs ḥkhor daṅ gźal yas khaṅ sogs bsgom mi dgos so /

/ de nas śes na so soḥi sṅags daṅ phyag rgyas gtsug tor daṅ / mdzod spu daṅ / spyan daṅ / spuṅ ba gñis daṅ / mgrin pa daṅ / sñiṅ ga daṅ / lte ba rnams su reg ciṅ / de tsam mi śes na rigs gsum po gaṅ yin pa deḥi

[12] By the expressions '*svabhāva*' and '*śūnyatā*', the author presumably refers to the two *dhāraṇīs*: *Oṃ svabhāvaśuddhāḥ sarvadharmāḥ svabhāvaśuddho 'haṃ* and *Oṃ śūnyatājñānavajrasvabhāvātmako 'haṃ*. These occur in numerous *sādhanas*; e.g. B. Bhattacharyya, *Buddhist Iconography* (London, 1924), pp. 172-3. The first formula establishes the intrinsic purity of all the natures (*dharma*) and one's own intrinsic purity. The second equates oneself with the knowledge diamond of voidness (*śūnyatājñānavajra*). In Tsoṅ-kha-pa's *Sṅags rim chen mo*, 60a-6, ff., the first god is called the *don dam paḥi lha* (**paramārtha-deva*) and consists in the pride that oneself is one with the god (bdag daṅ lha gñis gcig par ṅa rgyal byas te), indissoluble like the mixture of water and milk (chu daṅ ḥo ma ḥdres pa bźin du dbyer mi phyed pa).

[13] The *Sṅags rim chen mo*, 60b-4, makes it clear that the Letter God is the inseparable union of oneself and the God Reality like the attachment of pure quicksilver to golden sand (śin tu dag paḥi dṅul chu gser gyi bye ma la źen pa ltar bdag daṅ lhaḥi de kho na ñid dbyer med paḥi rnam pa can).

[14] For these terms, see Chapter III, n. 18. When the deity contemplated is male, the *dhāraṇī* is of the *mantra* variety; when the deity is female, the *dhāraṇī* is a *vidyā*.

God (**tattva-devatā*) among the six gods. They are equivalent to the contemplation of voidness in the higher Tantra divisions that attends the muttering of such expressions as *svabhāva* and *śūnyatā*.[12]

The second god

Then one imagines that the god to be contemplated (i.e. created meditatively) out of the sphere of the Void is that very god in essence, and that his aspect (*ākāra*) is the intonation of the sounds of the *dhāraṇī* to be muttered. That [aspect] as the mind's sole meditative object (*ālambana*) is the Sound God (**śabda-devatā*).

The third god

Then one imagines that his own mind (*citta*) transforms itself in the sky into a moon disk (*candra-maṇḍala*) upon which the god to be contemplated is that very god in essence. The contemplation of its aspect as the aspect of the letters, the color of liquid gold, of the *dhāraṇī* to be muttered, is the Letter God (**akṣara-devatā*).[13]

For those Sound and Letter Gods, it is satisfactory to use either the long (*dīrgha*), the essence (*hṛdaya*), or the near-essence (*upahṛdaya*) *dhāraṇī*.[14]

The fourth god

Then one imagines that from those letters emanate innumerable rays of light, from the ends of which issue innumerable aspects of the body of that god to be intensely contemplated. They purify all sentient beings from their sins, obscurations, and sufferings, and they give joy to all the Buddhas and their sons [i.e. Bodhisattvas] by making offerings to them. Then the rays, together with the gods, are withdrawn, absorbed by the letters; and the moon, together with the letters, transforms itself into the perfected body of the god to be contemplated. This as the meditative object is the Form God (**rūpa-devatā*).

At the time of doing service through contemplation of Self Generation, one need only contemplate the Lord (**prabhu*) but not his retinue (*parivāra*), palace (*vimāna*), etc.

The fifth god

Then, if one knows [them] he touches with the various *dhāraṇīs* and seals (*mudrā*): 1. the crown of the head, 2. the space between the eyebrows (*ūrṇā-kośa*), 3. the eyes, 4. the shoulders, 5. the neck, 6. the heart, and 7. the navel. If one does not know [them] to that extent, he touches

rigs spyiḥi sṅags rgya gcig pus gnas de dag tu reg ciṅ byin gyis rlobs pa ni phyag rgyaḥi lha ste /

/ de ni rgyud sde goṅ maḥi skyed mched byin gyis rlob paḥi dod do /

/ de nas lhaḥi rnam pa gsal źiṅ ṅa rgyal brtan par byas te / de la yid kyis rtse gcig tu dmigs pa ni mtshan maḥi lhaḥo /

/ de rnams ni rgyud sde goṅ maḥi mṅon byaṅ lṅas bskyed kyi dod do /

/ bod kyi bla ma sṅa ma rnams bya baḥi rgyud la bdag ñid lhar bsgom pa med la / mdun du lha bsgom pa las dṅos grub len par byed pas lha rje bo lta bu las dṅos grub len pa źes bya ba daṅ / spyod paḥi rgyud la bdag bskyed bsgom pa yod kyaṅ de la ye śes pa bcug nas dbaṅ bskur ba daṅ / rigs bdag gi rgyas ḥdebs pa rnams med ciṅ / mdun du dam tshig pa mi

[15] *Sṅags rim chen mo*, 61b-2, 3, mentions that the *Dhyānottara-ṭīkā* (Toh. 2670) gives two other names of this God, 'God along with the aspect of conventional *samādhi*' and 'God along with discursive thought (*vikalpa*)' (bsam gtan phyi maḥi ḥgrel pa las / kun rdzob paḥi tiṅ ṅe ḥdzin rnam pa daṅ bcas pa źes pa daṅ / rnam par rtog pa daṅ bcas paḥi lha źes kyaṅ gsuṅs la). Nāgārjuna (Toh. 2736), Derge Tg., *Rgyud ḥgrel*, Ni, 117a-5, explains: "Thereupon, for the purpose of fortifying the ego, he recites, '*Oṃ*. I am intrinsically the whole soul of the natural realm of *yoga*'. Thereby he fortifies the ego" (de nas ṅa rgyal brtan par bya baḥi ched du / Oṁ yo-ga dha-rma dhā-tu sva-bhā-va sa-rva ā-tma-ko 'haṃ / źes brjod pas / ṅa rgyal brtan par byaḥo).

[16] The five Abhisaṃbodhis are presented in Chapter I. The correspondence between these and the first five of the six gods is made plain by key words in the respective descriptions: Abhi. no. 1, meditation on sixteen kinds of voidness, and God no. 1, contemplation of voidness; Abhi. no. 2, symbols of consonants, and God no. 2, sound god; Abhi. no. 3, sees directly the Samantabhadra, and God no. 3, the God seen on one's own mind; Abhi. no. 4, beams of light from all three realms enter thunderbolt of his heart, and God no. 4, the rays, together with the gods, withdrawn; Abhi. no. 5, transformation into body with Characteristics and Minor Marks, and God no. 5, blesses spots in his body. After the five Abhisaṃbodhis, the Buddha appears in the world of men; this phase is indicated by God no. 6, the yogin returning to the world while holding on to a divine consciousness.

[17] The 'symbolic being' (*samaya-sattva*) and the 'knowledge being' (*jñāna-sattva*) are among the most difficult and important ideas of the Buddhist Tantric literature. The *Sṅags rim chen mo*, 388a-5, explains the literal meaning of the *samaya* being as follows: "The explanation of the expression *dam tshig sems dpaḥ* is this: it is equivalent to *samaya-sattva* and means 'united' (*sameta*, T. *yaṅ dag par ḥgro ba*) and 'joined with' (*milat*, T. *ḥdu ba*)" (dam tshig sems dpaḥ źes zer baḥi sgra bśad ni ḥdiḥi skad dod sa-ma-ya-sa-tva la sa-me-ti yaṅ dag par ḥgro ba daṅ mi-la-ti ḥdu baḥo). This is consistent with the definitions in the *Tantrārthāvatāra-vyākhyāna* (Toh. 2502) when this work says (Derge Tg., *Rgyud ḥgrel*, Ḥi, 114b-2 ff.): "Furthermore, the beings (*sattva*) are of two kinds: (1) symbolic beings (*samaya-sattva*) and (2) knowledge beings (*jñāna-sattva*). The symbolic being is the one united with the image of deity through the force of fierce striving for union, resolute application, and *samādhi* on that sole object. There are two kind of knowledge being: (a) the being born from the perfections (*pāramitā*) and (b) the being born from knowledge (*jñāna*). The being born from the perfections is the one disposed to seek in ever higher steps by way of the stages (*bhūmi*) [usually ten in number] and perfections (*pāramitā*) [usually six in number]. The being born from knowledge is the corporeal manifestation of the Lord and retinue arisen from the higher comprehension (*adhigama*) of the pure Mind of Enlightenment"

those places with a single *dhāraṇī* and seal of that particular Family among the three Families. And having been [thus] blessed (*adhiṣṭhita*), they are the Seal God (**mudrā-devatā*).

That is equivalent to the blessing of the sense bases (*āyatana*) in the higher Tantra divisions.

The sixth god

Then, while the aspect of the god is bright, one fortifies the ego (*ahaṃkāra* or *garva*). That [aspect] taken as the mind's sole meditative object is the Sign God (**nimitta-devatā*).[15]

Those [gods] are equivalent to the generation by means of the five Abhisaṃbodhis in the higher Tantras.[16]

Discussion of Self Generation

The older *gurus* of Tibet maintained the following: In the Kriyā Tantra the contemplation of oneself as a god does not exist because the magical talent (*siddhi*) is obtained as a result of contemplating a god in front, for which reason they said, "One obtains *siddhi* from a god who is so to say a master (*lha rje bo lta bu*)." There is contemplation of Self Generation in the Caryā Tantra; nevertheless, after drawing in the *jñāna* beings, there is neither Initiation (*abhiṣeka*) nor the application of the seals (*mudrā-nyāsa*) of the Master of the Family; without generating the *samaya* beings in front, one invites the *jñāna* beings and,[17] after seating

---

(sems dpaḥi la yaṅ gñis te / dam tshig gi sems dpaḥ daṅ ye śes kyi sems dpaḥo / dam tshig gi sems dpaḥ ni sbyor baḥi brtson ḥgrus drag po daṅ / nan tan daṅ tiṅ ṅe ḥdzin rtse gcig paḥi stobs kyis lhaḥi gzugs brñan la sbyor baḥo / ye śes kyi sems dpaḥ la yaṅ gñis te / pha rol tu phyin pa las skyes pa daṅ / ye śes las skyes paḥi sems dpaḥo / pha rol tu phyin pa las skyes paḥi sems dpaḥ ni sa daṅ pha rol tu phyin paḥi sgo nas goṅ maḥi rim pa tshol baḥi phyir bkod paḥo / ye śes kyi sems dpaḥ las skyes pa [*sic*] ni byaṅ chub kyi sems rnam par dag pa de rtogs pa las byuṅ baḥi gtso bo daṅ ḥkhor gyi skur snaṅ baḥo). The typical sequence of generation is seen in this passage of the *Sṅags rim chen mo* (156b-7): "Having so contemplated one's *samaya* circle, one then invites the *jñāna* circle located in the sky there..." (raṅ gi dam tshig gi ḥkhor lo ji lta bar bsgoms nas der nam mkhaḥ la gnas paḥi ye śes kyi ḥkhor lo spyan draṅs nas...). In the same text (231a-6) the *jñāna* deities are invited from the *ākāśa*; and (230b-3), from the *ākāśa-dhātu* (the realm of space). The above explanations indicate that the *samaya-sattva* is the yogin who has identified himself with a deity he has evoked or imagined, while the *jñāna-sattva* is either a human Bodhisattva, or a celestial Bodhisattva or Buddha. However, when Mkhas grub rje writes "without generating the *samaya* beings in front..." he is stressing the 'God Reality' (**devatā-tattva*) rather than the Self Reality (**ātma-tattva*) among the two reality components of the first of the six gods. This usage of the term *samaya-sattva* is general in these texts and is consistent with the explanation in the *Sṅags rim chen mo* (388a-3, 4): "The *samaya-sattva* is the body of the deity graced with face and hands, actually the manifestation of one's

bskyed par ye śes spyan draṅs nas bźugs pa la mchod ciṅ dṅos grub len pas / lha grogs po lta bu las dṅos grub len pa źes bya ba daṅ / rnal ḥbyor rgyud la bdag ñid lhar bskyed pa la ye śes pa bcug / dbaṅ bskur / rigs bdag gi rgyas gi rgyas btab ste mthar gśegs gsol byed pa daṅ / bla med la bdag ñid lhar bskyed pa la ye śes pa bcug / dbaṅ bskur / rigs bdag gi rgyas btab ste mthar gśegs gsol mi byed paḥi tshul te / lhaḥi bskyed cho ga mi ḥdra ba bźiḥi sgo nas rgyud sde bźir ḥjog pa sogs kyi rnam gźag byed ciṅ / śes byed gsaṅ ba ḥdus paḥi bśad rgyud ye śes rdo rje kun las btus las / ye śes sems dpaḥi bde ba dam pa daṅ bral ba daṅ bdag ñid lhar bsñems pa daṅ bral bas bsgrub pa ni bya baḥi rgyud la rab tu gnas so /

/ bu ston rin po ches ni slob dpon saṅs rgyas gsaṅ bas bya baḥi rguyd la bdag bskyed yod par gsuṅs la / bya spyod mi ḥgal bar bźed pa la dgoṅs pa yin nam brtag par byaḥo / źes sogs gsuṅs te kha tshan ma bcad do /

/ raṅ lugs la bya rgyud la bdag ñid lhar bskyed pa daṅ / raṅ la ye śes pa bcug nas dbaṅ bskur ba daṅ / rigs bdag gi rgyas ḥdebs pa rnams thams cad yod par bźed pas / slob dpon saṅs rgyas gsaṅ bas rnam snaṅ mṅon byaṅ daṅ / phyag na rdo rje dbaṅ bskur baḥi rgyud draṅs pa ni / bya rgyud yin par mthun snaṅ du grub pa źig las bdag bskyed bśad pa źig ḥdren rgyu ma rñed nas draṅs pa ma yin te / bsam gtan phyi maḥi ḥgrel bar rdo rje gtsug tor gyi rgyud daṅ / rdo rje rnam ḥjoms kyi rgyud rgyas pa gñis las / lha drug bsgom paḥi tshul gsuṅs pa draṅs nas legs par bśad la / de gñis bya rgyud du mi ḥdod mkhan su yaṅ med ciṅ spyod bsdus las kyaṅ bya baḥi rgyud rdo rje gtsug tor las / źes gsuṅs paḥi phyir ro /

/ spyod rgyud la yaṅ bdag bskyed med par ḥdod pa ni gnas ma yin paḥi log rtog ste / rnam snaṅ mṅon byaṅ sogs daṅ dṅos su ḥgal baḥi phyir ro /

/ bya rgyud la bdag bskyed med na / rgyud rgyas pa rdo rje gtsug tor daṅ / bsdus pa bsam gtan phyi ma daṅ / rnam ḥjoms kyi rgyud rgyas pa daṅ / dpal rtog pa bsdus pa daṅ / ḥphags pa rab tu grub pa rnams las lha drug gi sgo nas bsgom paḥi tshul daṅ / bsñen sgrub yan lag bźis

---

own mind, a transfiguration of ordinary ego" (de la tha mal paḥi ṅa rgyal gsal ba raṅ gi sems kyi snaṅ baḥi ṅo bo źal phyag gis rnam par mdzes paḥi lhaḥi sku ni dam tshig sems dpaḥ). Again, by the term *jñāna-sattva* these contexts generally refer only to the celestial beings among the two kinds of *jñāna-sattva*. Material in subsequent chapters will shed further light on these terms.

them, makes offering and takes *siddhi*, for which reason(s) they said, "One takes *siddhi* from a god who is so to say a friend (*lha grogs po lta bu*)." In the Yoga Tantra one generates the self into a god, draws in the *jñāna* beings, is conferred Initiation, applies the seal of the Master of the Family, and finally asks the god to depart. In the Anuttara Tantra one generates the self into a god, draws in the *jñāna* beings, is conferred Initiation, applies the seal of the Master of the Family, and at the conclusion the gods are not asked to depart. The four Tantra divisions are determined according to the four different ways of generating the gods. This is made known in the Explanatory Tantra of the *Guhyasamāja*, the *Jñānavajrasamuccaya* (Toh. 447), which sets forth that the accomplishment free from the sublime joy of the *jñāna* beings and free from the pride of oneself as a god, is well established in the Kriyā Tantra.

Bu-ston Rin-po-che said, "The *ācārya* Buddhaguhya mentions that in the Kriyā Tantra there is Self Generation and he maintains that it is not in conflict with the Kriyā and Caryā, but the import here has to be investigated." Thus, he left the matter undecided.

Our own school maintains that in the Kriyā Tantra there are all those things: generation of self into a god, Initiation following the introduction of the *jñāna* being, and application of the seal of the Master of the Family. When the *ācārya* Buddhaguhya quotes the *Mahāvairocana* (Toh. 494) and the *Vajrapāṇy-abhiṣeka* (Toh. 496) Tantras, he does not derive a reason for asserting that the explanation of Self Generation is consistent with the Kriyā Tantra, because he has not quoted from that (class of) Tantra. But when in the *Dhyānottara-ṭīkā* (Toh. 2670) he quotes the **Vajroṣṇīṣa-tantra* and the **Vajravidāraṇā-vaipūlyatantra*, showing the method of contemplating the six gods, he well explains that [method to be Kriyā Tantra]; and the specialists who do not admit those two to be Kriyā Tantra are in turn without reason, because it is also said in the *Caryāmelāpaka* (Toh. 1803), "According to the Kriyā Tantra **Vajroṣṇīṣa*..."

Moreover, it is an unfounded, distorted view which holds that in the Caryā Tantra there is no Self Generation, because that view explicitly contradicts the *Mahāvairocana* (Toh. 494), etc.

Those who say there is no Self Generation in the Kriyā Tantra are in disagreement with the extensive Tantra (*vaipūlya-tantra*) **Vajroṣṇīṣa*, its concise form (*laghu-tantra*) *Dhyānottara* (Toh. 808), the **Vajravidāraṇā-vaipūlyatantra*, its eminent concise plan (*kalpa-laghu-tantra*) [the *Vajravidāraṇā-nāma-dhāraṇī*, Toh. 750], and the noble *Susiddhi* (Toh. 807), which clearly state the method of contemplation by way of the six

bsam gtan bsgom paḥi tshul gsal bar gsuṅs śiṅ / de dag mi gsal baḥi tshul gyis bya baḥi rgyud phal che ba las gsuṅs par slob dpon byaṅ chub mchog daṅ / saṅs rgyas gsaṅ ba gñis kas bśad pa daṅ ḥgal lo /

/ bsam gtan phyi mar bsñen sgrub yan lag bźi ston paḥi skabs su / sgra daṅ sems daṅ gźi la gźol / źes paḥi gźi ḥdi bdag ñid lhar bsgom pa la mi byed na rnam snaṅ mṅon byaṅ gi yaṅ de ston paḥi skabs kyi / gźi ḥdi raṅ gi lhar bźag pa / raṅ gi lus su rnam par brtag / ces paḥi gźi de yaṅ bdag ñid lhar bsgom pa la mi byed dgos par mtshuṅs śiṅ / de ltar na spyod rgyud la yaṅ bdag bskyed med par ḥgyur pas / yod par khyed raṅ ḥdod pa daṅ ḥgal lo /

/ gźan yaṅ slob dpon byaṅ chub mchog gis legs grub kyi mṅon rtogs su bdag ñid lhar bsgoms pas tha mal gyi ṅa rgyal ldog pa daṅ / chos thams cad kyi gnas lugs su gyur paḥi stoṅ ñid bsgom pa gñis med na / źi sogs kyi dṅos grub gaṅ yaṅ mi ḥgrub par bśad ciṅ / de ji lta bar phyag na rdo rje dbaṅ bskur baḥi rgyud las kyaṅ gsuṅs pas / bya rgyud la bdag bskyed med na bya rgyud la brten nas dṅos grub gaṅ yaṅ ḥgrub pa med par ḥgyur ro /

/ gźan yaṅ ḥphags pa klu sgrub kyis thugs rje chen po phyag stoṅ spyan stoṅ gi sgrub thabs su bdag bskyed daṅ ye śes pa gźug pa dbaṅ bskur rgyas gdab rnams bśad la / ḥphags pa thogs med kyis mdzad paḥi byams paḥi sgrub thabs gñis daṅ / dge sloṅ ma dpal mos mdzad paḥi bcu gcig gźal gyi sgrub thabs daṅ / slob dpon śānti-pa daṅ dze-ta-ri dgra las rnam par rgyal ba gñis kyis mdzad paḥi gzuṅs grva lṅaḥi sgrub thabs thams cad du bdag ñid lhar bsgom pa daṅ / de la ye śes pa ḥjug pa daṅ dbaṅ bskur ba daṅ rigs bdag gi rgyas gdab rnams bśad pa daṅ / gźan yaṅ sgrub thabs rgya mtsho / sgrub thabs brgya rtsa / sgrub thabs phyed ñis brgya ba rnams su bya rgyud kyi sgrub thabs bśad pa phal che bar bdag bskyed bśad pas de thams cad daṅ ḥgal lo /

/ gźan yaṅ bya rgyud kyi dbaṅ bskur baḥi tshe / ye śes ḥbebs su mi ruṅ bar ḥgyur te / slob ma la ye śes pa gźug tu mi ruṅ baḥi phyir ro / der

gods and the method of contemplation in the meditation by means of the four members of service; are in disagreement with the bulk of Kriyā Tantras, which state those [two methods] in an unclear way; and are in disagreement with the explanations by the two *ācāryas* *Varabodhi and Buddhaguhya.

The *Dhyānottara* (Toh. 808), when stating the four members of service, says: "Immerse yourself in the sound, the mind, and the ground." If the "ground" (*gźi*) of that passage does not mean the contemplation of oneself as a god, then when the *Mahāvairocana* (Toh. 494), teaching that, says: "This 'ground' is deposited in one's god, and it may be discerned in one's own body;" the "ground" of this passage would perforce also not mean the contemplation of oneself as a god. If that were the case, neither would there be Self Generation in the Caryā Tantra; consequently, if that were so, your own thesis [i.e. that of the older *gurus*] would be contradicted.

Moreover, the *ācārya* *Varabodhi explains in his lucid exposition (i.e. Toh. 3066) of the *Susiddhi* that if there were no revulsion from the ordinary pride by means of the contemplation of the self as a god, or if there were no contemplation of voidness in the sense of the natural state of all things, there would be no *siddhis*, such as 'appeasing', at all; and he points out that the *Vajrapāṇy-abhiṣeka-tantra* says the same. Therefore, if there were no Self Generation in the Kriyā Tantra, no *siddhis* whatsoever could be accomplished through the Kriyā Tantra.

Besides, that would disagree with all these works: Ārya Nāgārjuna's *Sahasrabhujāvalokiteśvarasādhana* (Toh. 2736), which explains Self Generation, the drawing in of the *jñāna* being, Initiation, and application of seal; Āryāsaṅga's *Maitreyasādhana* (Toh. 3648), the nun Dpal mo's *Ekādaśamukhāvalokiteśvarasādhana* (Toh. 2737), the *sādhanas* of the five Gzuṅs grva by the *ācāryas* Śānti-pā (his Toh. 3126) and Jetāri "he who has defeated the enemy" (probably Toh. 3119-3123 inclusive), all of which explain the contemplation of one's self as a god, and thereupon the entrance of the *jñāna* being, conferring of Initiation, and application of the seal of the Master of the Family; and moreover, the *Sgrub thabs rgya mtsho* (Toh. 3400-3644), the *Sgrub thabs brgya rtsa* (Toh. 3143-3304 and Toh. 3306-3399), and the *Sgrub thabs phyed ñis brgya ba* (Toh. 3645-3704), which generally set forth the Self Generation when presenting a *sādhana* of the Kriyā Tantra.

Furthermore, at the time of conferring the Initiation of the Kriyā Tantra, it would not be proper for the *jñāna* beings to descend, because it is not proper for the *jñāna* beings to enter the disciple. And that is

ma zad bya rgyud kyi dbaṅ bskur byar mi ruṅ bar ḥgyur te / slob dpon daṅ slob ma gaṅ yaṅ lhar bskyed du mi ruṅ baḥi phyir ro /

/ de lta na khyed raṅ gis gzuṅs grva lṅa sogs kyi dbaṅ cho ga tu slob dpon lhar bskyed pa daṅ / slob ma lhar bskyed pa daṅ / lus kyi gnas rnams su lha dgod pa sogs kyi rnam gźag byas pa daṅ khas blaṅs dṅos su ḥgal źiṅ / grub chen śa-va-ri-pas rnam ḥjoms dkar po lha maṅ gi dkyil chog tu bsñen paḥi tshe slob dpon lhar bskyed pa daṅ / dbaṅ bskur baḥi tshe slob ma lhar bskyed par bśad pa daṅ yaṅ ḥgal lo /

/ gźan yaṅ bya rgyud la pha rol tu phyin paḥi theg pa chen po las / gsaṅ sṅags kyi theg pa chen po khyad par du ḥphags par ḥjog paḥi ḥjog byed gzugs skuḥi rigs ḥdraḥi rgyu ma tshaṅ bar ḥgyur te / bdag ñid lhar bsgom pa ma tshaṅ baḥi phyir ro / bya rgyud la ḥbras bu lam byed ma tshaṅ bar ḥgyur te / ḥbras buḥi skabs kyi phun sum tshogs pa lṅa daṅ rnam pa mthun par da lta nas bsgom pa med paḥi phyir ro / yaṅ bya rgyud la chags pa lam byed ma tshaṅ bar ḥgyur te / brtag gñis daṅ saṃpu-ṭa gñis las ḥdod chags rigs bźi daṅ rgyud sde bźi sbyar nas gsuṅs paḥi skabs su lha pho mo phan tshun bltas paḥi chags pa lam byed bya rgyud la gsuṅs pa la / raṅ lhar bsgom du mi ruṅ na de byas med paḥi phyir ro /

/ ye śes rdo rje kun las btus kyi luṅ gi don ni / bya rgyud la bdag ñid lhar bsgom pa daṅ de la ye śes pa ḥjug pa med ces ston pa min gyi / bdag ñid lhar mi bsgom źiṅ ye śes pa raṅ la gźug pa mi byed par mdun

[18] The translation 'basis for the affiliation' has been suggested by a passage in Jñānavajra's commentary on the *Laṅkāvatāra-sūtra* called *Tathāgatahṛdayālaṃkāra* (Toh. 4019), Derge Tg., *Mdo-ḥgrel*, Pi, 75b-2, ff., where we find the expression (in the Tibetan translation) *rigs mthun paḥi rgyu* rather than *rigs ḥdraḥi rgyu*, but *mthun pa* and *ḥdra ba* are synonyms. Jñānavajra mentions here that there are three varieties of characteristic, the characteristic of evolution (*pravṛtti*), the characteristic of action (*karma*), and the characteristic of family (*kula*) (dbye na rnam pa gsum ste / ḥjug paḥi mtshan ñid daṅ las kyi mtshan ñid daṅ / rigs kyi mtshan ñid do). He proceeds to explain each of the three. When he comes to the third kind he says: "The third one is the *ālaya-vijñāna* (store consciousness) which is the abode of those two [i.e. the first two varieties]; it is called the 'characteristic of family' because it is their basis for affiliation" (gsum pa ni gñis po de rnams kyi gnas kuṅ gźi rnam par śes pa ste de rnams kyi rigs mthun paḥi rgyu yin pas rigs kyi mtshan ñid ces so). The translation "affiliation" has been used above, n. 7.

[19] The description of the four Tantras in terms of the four Passion Families is set forth in the *Sṅags rim chen mo*, 35a-3, ff. The mutual attraction of Insight (*prajñā*) and the Means (*upāya*) finds:

some deities laughing	—	Kriyā Tantra;
,, ,, gazing	—	Caryā Tantra;
,, ,, embracing	—	Yoga Tantra;
,, ,, in coition	—	Anuttara Tantra.

Tsoṅ-kha-pa emphasizes that this is not a description of the candidates of these Tan-

not all! It would not be proper to perform an Initiation of the Kriyā Tantra, because it is not proper for either the preceptor or disciple to generate [himself] into a god.

If what they claim is the case, their own position is in explicit disagreement with the fundamentals and assumptions of generating the preceptor into a god, generating the disciple into a god, and arranging of gods in locations of the body, as found in the Initiation rites of the five Gzuṅs grva, etc.; and also in disagreement with the explanation about generating the preceptor into a god at the time of service and generating the disciple into a god at the time of Initiation, as found in the *mahāsiddha* Śavari-pā's *Maṇḍala-vidhi* (Toh. 2932) of the many gods of the white *Vajravidāraṇā*.

Moreover, in the Kriyā Tantra there would not be a complete basis for the affiliation (*rigs ḥdraḥi rgyu*)[18] with the Formal Body (*rūpa-kāya*), which is what establishes the superiority of the *mantra-mahāyāna* over the *pāramitā-mahāyāna*, because the contemplation of oneself as a god is incomplete. There would not be a complete resultative path construction in the Kriyā Tantra, because there is no contemplation in immediacy conforming to the five perfections of the resultative phase. Also, in the Kriyā Tantra there would not be a complete construction of the path of passion (*anurāga*); both the *Hevajra-tantra* (Toh. 417-418) and the *Sampuṭa* (Toh. 381) relate the four Passion Families (*anurāga-kula*) to the four Tantra divisions and in the relevant sections say that the Kriyā Tantra prepares the path of passion consisting in the mutual gazing of the male and female gods,[19] so if it is not proper to contemplate oneself as a god, that [path] is not prepared.

In regard to the meaning of the scripture *Jñānavajrasamuccaya* (Toh. 447), it does not teach that in the Kriyā Tantra there is no generation of oneself into a god nor entrance of the *jñāna* beings into that person. Rather it teaches that there occurs in the Kriyā Tantra a method in

---

tra divisions; for the latter, see Mkhas grub rje, Chapter VI. Tsoṅ-kha-pa refers to the 23rd *mañjari* of the *Āmnāya-mañjari* (Toh. 1198) for illustration of the passion degrees as found among the 'passion deities' (*kāma-deva*) of the 'realm of desire' (*kāma-dhātu*). In that work (Derge ed., 216b-7, ff.) it is said that the joy of the laughing deities is illustrated by that of the Nirmāṇaratis; the joy of the gazing deities, by that of the Paranirmitavaśavartins; the joy of the embracing deities, by that of the Tuṣitas; and the joy of the deities in coitus, by that of the Trāyastriṃśas, the Caturmahārājakāyikas, and humans. These joys are also called the four joys (*dgaḥ ba* = S. *nanda* or *ānanda*). Non-tantric Buddhism relates the passion deities differently to the categories of 'laughing', etc.; see for example, Lin Li-kouang, *L'Aide-Mémoire de la Vraie Loi*, p. 55.

gyi lha la mchod ciṅ dṅos grub len paḥi tshul bya rgyud la yod par bstan pa yin te / bya rgyud kyi gdul bya phal pa raṅ ñid lhar bsgom pa blor mi śoṅ paḥi rigs can dbaṅ po rtul po la / bdag ñid lhar mi bsgom par mdun du lha bsgoms nas dṅos grub len tshul yaṅ bśad ciṅ / bya rgyud kyi ched du bya baḥi gdul bya yin na de la bdag bskyed bsgom pa bstan pas khyab par slob dpon saṅs rgyas gsaṅ bas bśad pa daṅ ḥdraḥo /

/ bya spyod gñis ka la ye śes pa raṅ la gźug du mi ruṅ bar ḥdod pa ni / phyag na rdo rje dbaṅ bskur baḥi rgyud las / lhaḥi sku gsuṅ thugs daṅ raṅ gi lus ṅag yid gsum dbyer mi phyed par mos pa goms pa brtan par gyur na lus kyi sgul bskyod thams cad phyag rgya bciṅs pa daṅ ḥdra ba daṅ / ṅag gi smra brjod thams cad sṅags bzlas pa daṅ ḥdra baḥi bsod nams ḥthob par bśad pa daṅ ḥgal te / raṅ la ye śes pa gźug tu mi ruṅ na ye śes paḥi sku gsuṅ thugs daṅ raṅ gi lus ṅag yid gsum dbyer med du mos su ruṅ ba ḥgal baḥi phyir ro /

/ ḥo na bya spyod gñis la ye śes pa raṅ la gźug pa daṅ de la dbaṅ bskur ba daṅ rigs bdag gi rgyas gdab pa rnams yod na / slob dpon saṅs rgyas gsaṅ ba daṅ byaṅ chub mchog gñis kyis ma bśad pa ji ltar yin źe na / de bya dgos par dṅos su ma bśad pa tsam yin gyi / mi bya bar bśad pa min pas byar mi ruṅ baḥi sgrub byed du mi ruṅ ṅo /

/ raṅ lugs la bya rgyud kyi gdul bya phal pa raṅ lhar mi bsgom par mdun du lha bsgoms nas dṅos grub len pa ni lam rdzogs par bsgom pa ma yin gyi lam la ḥjug paḥi sgo tsam mo / bya rgyud kyi gdul byaḥi gtso bo lam rdzogs par bsgom pa la ni / bdag ñid lhar bsgom pa med na lam gyi lus ma tshaṅ bar ḥgyur bas bdag bskyed med du mi ruṅ źiṅ / ye śes pa gźug pa dbaṅ bskur ba rigs bdag gi rgyas gdab pa rnams phun sum tshogs paḥi yan lag yin pas ma byas kyaṅ lam gyi lus chad paḥi ñes pa med par bźed do /

which, without contemplating oneself as a god and without introducing the *jñāna* beings into oneself, one makes offerings to the god in front and takes *siddhi*. It also explains that method as one in which ordinary candidates of the Kriyā Tantra with weak sense faculties and belonging to the class of people incapable of comprehending the contemplation of oneself as a god, take *siddhi* after contemplating the god in front. If one is a candidate for the high goal (*uddeśa*) of the Kriyā Tantra, he is taught the contemplation of the Self Generation, so the text is in agreement with the explanation of the teacher Buddhaguhya.

The thesis that in neither the Kriyā nor Caryā Tantras is it proper to introduce the *jñāna* beings into oneself, disagrees with the explanation by the *Vajrapāṇy-abhiṣeka-tantra* (Toh. 496) that if one becomes steadfastly habituated in the conviction that his own [ordinary] body, speech, and mind are inseparable from the [exalted] body, speech, and mind of a god, he acquires the merit of all his bodily movements being equivalent to the affixing of seals (*mudrā*) and all his vocal expressions being equivalent to the muttering of incantations (*dhāraṇī*); — thus, if it is not proper to draw the *jñāna* being into oneself, one must deny that it is proper to be convinced that one's [ordinary] body, speech, and mind are inseparable from the [exalted] body, speech, and mind of the *jñāna* being.

Now, if in both the Kriyā and Caryā Tantras the *jñāna* beings may enter the person and he may be conferred Initiation and may apply the seal of the Master of the Family, why is it that the two preceptors Buddhaguhya and *Varabodhi do not set those forth? They merely do not set forth in an explicit way the necessity of doing those things; but they do not say that they should not be done, and therefore one must not infer that they should not be done.

When in our school the ordinary candidate of the Kriyā Tantra takes *siddhi* after contemplation of the god in front and without the contemplation of himself as the god, that is just the gate of entrance to the path, not the contemplation which completes the path. In regard to the contemplation which completes the path for the leading candidates of the Kriyā Tantra, if there were no contemplation of oneself as a god the body of the path would be incomplete, for which reason it is improper to omit Self Generation. And since the entrance of the *jñāna* beings, conferring of Initiation, application of the seal of the Master of the Family, are 'limbs' (or 'ancillaries', *aṅga*) of perfection, then we maintain that even if they are not done, there is no fault which severs the body of the path.

/ srog rtsol bsgom pa źes pa rgyud sde ḥog ma gsum la yaṅ yod do / de daṅ gsaṅ ḥdus ḥphags lugs kyi skor nas bśad paḥi srog rtsol daṅ / dus ḥkhor sogs bla med kyi rgyud gźan nas bśad paḥi srog rtsol gsum gdon mi gcig go /

/ ḥo na rgyud sde ḥog ma gsum nas bśad paḥi srog rtsol de ji lta bu źe na / rnam snaṅ mṅon byaṅ gi rgyud daṅ deḥi ḥgrel pa slob dpon saṅs rgyas gsaṅ bas mdzad pa gñis las bśad de / dbaṅ poḥi sgo nas rgyu baḥi rluṅ ni srog go / rtog pa yul gźan la gyeṅ źiṅ ḥphro ba ni rtsol baḥo / rluṅ daṅ rtog pa gñis ka phyir ḥphror mi ḥjug par naṅ du ḥdzin pa ni / srog rtsol sdom pa ḥam ḥgog paḥi don no /

/ de skabs gaṅ du bsgom źe na / mtshan bcas kyi skabs su bsgom źiṅ / deḥi yaṅ skabs gaṅ du bsgom na / bya spyod kyi bsñen paḥi skabs su lha drug po bsgoms zin paḥi rjes daṅ / mdun bskyed bsgrubs zin paḥi rjes gaṅ ruṅ du bsgom mo /

/ dgos pa gaṅ gi don du bsgom na / tha mal gyi snaṅ źen ḥgog pa la lus lhar gsal ba la dmigs pa brtan po dgos / de brtan pa la rtog pa phyir ḥphro ba ḥgog dgos /

/ de ḥgog paḥi thabs gaṅ zab na / sems kyi rta rluṅ yin pas rluṅ naṅ du zin na / sems raṅ dbaṅ med par zin par ḥgyur bas / deḥi phyir du srog rtsol bsgom mo /

/ tshul ji ltar du bsgom na / lus gnad bcas te / steṅ gi rluṅ naṅ du lte baḥi bar du draṅs nas mnan / ḥog gi rluṅ yar la lte baḥi bar du draṅs nas bzuṅ ste yid lha la rtse gcig tu gtad de gnas źiṅ / de nas rluṅ ḥdzin ma thub na phyir btaṅ ste ṅal bzo źiṅ yid lha la rtse gcig tu gtad do / de nas yaṅ rluṅ naṅ du ḥdzin pa de lta buḥi tshul gyis bsgom mo /

[20] Kloṅ rdol bla ma, Ga, 4b-2, 3, says: "The Anuttara *prāṇāyāma* means the abolition of the coursing into the right and left channels; the present *prāṇāyāma* [i.e. of the Kriyā Tantra] means the abolition of the coming and going of the wind (*vāyu*) riding on discursive thought (*vikalpa*), as well as the inner containment [of the wind]" (bla med srog rtsol ro rkyaṅ rgyu ba bkag / ḥdi yi srog rtsol rnam rtog bźon paḥi rluṅ / ḥgro ḥoṅ bkag nas naṅ du sdom la don). The *Pradīpodyotana*, Derge Tg., *Rgyud ḥgrel*, Ha, 97a-1, when commenting on Chap. XII of the *Guhyasamāja-tantra*, says: "*Prāṇa* is life; *āyāma* is the dispersal to a distance; that is the explanation of *prāṇa-āyāma*" (srog ni ḥtsho baḥo / rtsol źin riṅ du spros pa gaṅ yin pa de ni / srog daṅ rtsol ba źes byar bśad).

[21] More fully, Buddhaguhya writes in his *Dhyānottara-ṭīkā* (Toh. 2670), Thu, 14b-2, 3: "*Prāṇa* is the vital air (*vāyu*) characterised as issuing from, and entering, the eyes, ears, nostrils, mouth, navel, male and female sex organs, the unclean orifice, the pores of head hair and body hair" (... srog ces bya ba ni mig daṅ / rna ba daṅ sna daṅ / kha daṅ / lte ba daṅ skyes pa daṅ / bud med kyi dbaṅ po daṅ / mi gtsaṅ baḥi khuṅ bu daṅ / skra and ba spuḥi bu ga nas ḥbyuṅ ba daṅ / ḥjug paḥi mtshan ñid kyi rluṅ ste).

Prāṇāyāma

There is also contemplation of *prāṇa-āyāma* in the three lower Tantras. However, *prāṇa-āyāma* as discussed in the circle of the Ārya school of the *Guhya-samāja*; *prāṇa-āyāma* as discussed in accordance with other Anuttara Tantras, such as the *Kālacakra*; and that [of the three lower Tantras] — are certainly three different things.[20]

Now, what is the *prāṇa-āyāma* discussed in the three lower Tantras? It is as the *Vairocana-tantra* (Toh. 494) and its commentary (Toh. 2663) by Buddhaguhya say: *prāṇa* is the vital air (*vāyu*) passing through the doors of the sense organs (*indriya*);[21] *āyāma* is the dispersal into other sensory domains (*viṣaya*) of the mental elements (**tarka*). Binding or abolishing the *prāṇa-āyāma* means preventing the vital air and the mental elements from escaping outside, and containing them inside.

On what occasion should that [particular *prāṇāyāma*] be contemplated? On the occasion of *yoga* with signs (*sanimitta-yoga*).[22] And on what occasion within that [*yoga* with signs] should it be contemplated? It is contemplated on the occasion of service (*sevā*) in the Kriyā and Caryā Tantras, either after completing contemplation of the six gods, or after accomplishing Generation in Front, as the case may be.

For the sake of what requirement is it contemplated? The requirement to solidify the meditative object involving the abolition of the craving for ordinary appearances and involving the transfiguration of one's body into that of a god. For solidifying that, the requirement to inhibit the escape of the mental elements.

What is the profound means of inhibiting that? The mind's steed is the vital air (*vāyu*); therefore, when the vital air is contained within, the mind is held with no freedom of its own. That is why one contemplates the *prāṇa-āyāma*.

What is the procedure in this contemplation? Controlling the vital centers of the body, one draws the upper vital air (*ūrdhva-vāyu*) inside to the navel, pressing it down; and draws the lower vital air (*adhas-vāyu*) up to the navel, holding it there. The mind is fixed solely upon the god. Thereupon, when one is no longer able to retain the vital air, it is emitted, and while one is relaxing, the mind is fixed solely upon the god. Then he again holds the vital air within and contemplates in the same manner.

---

[22] But Kloṅ rdo bla ma, Ga, 4b-3, is in disagreement with Mkhas grub rje: "In regard to the occasion, in the Anuttara [Tantra] it is contemplated only during the Steps of Completion (*niṣpanna-krama*); here it is contemplated in both the 'with signs' and 'without signs' phases" (dus ni bla med rdzogs rim kho nar sgom / ḥdir ni mtshan bcas mtshan med gñis kar sgom).

/ rgyud sde ḥog ma gsum gyi srog rtsol daṅ / bla med rnam bśad paḥi srog rtsol gñis bsgom paḥi skabs daṅ / dgos pa daṅ / sgom tshul gsum ga mi ḥdraḥo /

/ gñis pa mdun bskyed bsgrubs nas mchod pa sogs bya ba la drug / rten bskyed pa daṅ / brten pa lha spyan draṅs te bźugs su gsol ba daṅ / phyag rgya bstan pa daṅ / mchod bstod bya ba daṅ / bśad pa sogs bya ba daṅ / tshad med bźi bsgom paḥo /

/ daṅ po ni / raṅ gi mdun du bum bcaḥ ba sogs yod kyaṅ ruṅ / med kyaṅ ruṅ ste rin po che du ma las byas paḥi sa gźi gser gyi bye ma gdal ba bsams nas / oṃ tsa la bī hūṁ svā hā / źes pas byin gyis brlabs la /

/ deḥi steṅ du ḥo maḥi rgya mtsho chen po ña lcibs la sogs paḥi skyon daṅ bral ba / padma daṅ u-tpa-la la sogs paḥi me tog gis brgyan pa / rin po cheḥi byaḥi tshogs maṅ po ldiṅ pa bsams la / oṁ bi ma la dha ha hūṁ / źes pas byin gyis brlab /

/ deḥi dbus su ri rab gru bźi pa ṅos bźi nas gser daṅ dṅul daṅ i-ndra-nī-la daṅ sbur loṅ las byas paḥi them skas kyi phreṅ bas brgyan pa / mthaḥ thog thag dpag bsam gyi śiṅ legs par ḥkhruṅs pa la rnam par rgyal baḥi ba dan stoṅ ḥphur bas brgyan pa bsam / deḥi steṅ du padmaḥi sdoṅ bu rin po che du mas brgyan pa / rin po che sna tshogs kyi ḥdab ma can / gser gyi ze ba daṅ sbur loṅ gi zeḥu ḥbru daṅ ldan pa / sñiṅ poḥi thog la dṅul gyi ri mos bskor ba / dpag tshad du maḥi khyon can ri rab kyi dbus brtol nas byuṅ źiṅ / de las kyaṅ padmaḥi dra ba gźan brgya stoṅ khri bye ba sñeṅ byuṅ bar bsams la / phyag ḥtshal baḥi thal mo las phan tshun bsnol te / gYas paḥi mthe boṅ gis gYon paḥi mthe boṅ mnan la / na-maḥ sa-rba ta-thā-ga-ta-nāṁ sa-rba-thā u-dga-te spha-ra-ṇa hi-maṁ-ga ga-na-khaṁ svā-hā / źes lan brgya bzlas la byin gyis brlab /

/ steṅ du bla bre yaṅ skad cig gis bsam par byaḥo / deḥi steṅ du gźal yas khaṅ mtshan ñid tshaṅ ba bskyed la / deḥi naṅ du so soḥi gdan rnams bskyed ciṅ / rnam rgyal daṅ ḥod zer can sogs kyi mchod rten yaṅ gźal yas khaṅ gi naṅ du bskyed pas chog go /

[23] Mkhas grub rje bases this section on the *Sṅags rim chen mo*, 63b-5, ff.; and this section in the latter text borrows heavily from *Varabodhi's work (Toh. 3066).

The *prāṇa-āyāma* of the three lower Tantra divisions has different occasions, requirements, and methods of contemplation from the *prāṇa-āyāma* explained in the Anuttara [Tantra].

β. *Generation of Deity in Front*[23]

There are six things, offering and so on, to be done while accomplishing the Generation in Front: generation of the residence; invitation to the gods to be residents and offering of seats; exhibition of the seals; offering and praising; confession of sins; contemplation of the four boundless states.

I′. *Generation of the Residence* (**ādhārotpatti*)

If it is prescribed to have a flask and other things in front [of the officiant], that is proper; otherwise, their omission is proper. But he must imagine an earth surface (**bhūmitala*) made of many jewels and strewn with gold sand. He blesses it with the formula, *Oṃ calavī*[*ra*] *hūṃ svāhā.*

Upon it he imagines an ocean of milk, free from such a fault as fish-gills, adorned with such flowers as the red lotus (*padma*) and the blue lotus (*utpala*), and over which soar flocks of bejewelled birds. He blesses it with the formula, *Oṃ vimala-dhahā hūṃ.*

In the middle of this [ocean], he imagines a four-sided Sumeru mountain, adorned on all four sides with rows of stairs made [respectively] of gold, silver, sapphire (*indranīla*), and amber, all over which spring up wish-granting trees (*kalpa-vṛkṣa*) decorated with a thousand fluttering victory banners. He imagines rising above those to a height of many *yojanas* a lotus trunk which takes its origin from a shaft in the center of Mount Sumeru, is graced with many jewels, has leaves made of variegated jewels and [blossoms] whose filaments are of gold, anthers of amber, and tops of pistils ringed by lines of silver. In addition, there are other myriads of lotus nets outstretched. After joining the palms of his hands in salutation, he presses down his left thumb with the right and recites one hundred times, *Namaḥ sarva-tathāgatānāṃ sarvathā udgate spharaṇahimaṃgaganakhaṃ svāhā*, and so blesses [his vision].

Above it, he is to imagine a canopy (*vitāna*) [appearing] in an instant. On top of that [canopy], he generates the complete characteristics of an eaved palace (*kūṭāgāra*) and generates within it various seats; and he may also generate within the palace *stupas* of the varieties 'victorious' and 'radiant'.

/ gñis pa la / spyan ḥdren pa ni mchod yon gyis bya dgos pas thog mar mchod yon bsgrub par bya ste / deḥi snod ni gser dṅul la sogs pa daṅ / thams cad la thun moṅ du śis pa zaṅs kyi snod du / źi ba daṅ dṅos grub rab la nas daṅ ḥo ma / rgyas pa daṅ dṅos grub ḥbriṅ la til daṅ źo / drag śul daṅ dṅos grub tha mal paḥi gcin ḥbras ko na ba daṅ bcas pa ḥam / khrag gi mchod yon dbul / las thams cad la thun moṅ du śis pa ḥbras yos daṅ dri bzaṅ poḥi spos daṅ me tog dkar po daṅ ku śa daṅ til chu gtsaṅ daṅ sbyar ba bśams la / bdug spos kyis bdug ciṅ rig paḥi rgyal po daṅ rigs gsum spyiḥi sṅags daṅ / rigs so soḥi las thams cad paḥi sṅags rnams daṅ spyan draṅ paḥi sṅags rnams las gaṅ yaṅ ruṅ cig lan bdun bzlas la mchod yon byin gyis brlab bo /

/ de nas mdun gyi bris sku sogs gaṅ du yod paḥi phyogs su bltas te / phyag ḥtshal / pus mos la btsugs nas / sor mo rnams phan tshun bsnol te / thal mo bkan la / mdzub mo gñis gśibs te bsgreṅs śiṅ / mthe boṅ gñis gYab pa spyan draṅ baḥi phyag rgya bcas la /

/ dad pa daṅ ni dam tshig gis /
/ tshur gśegs tshur gśegs bcom ldan ḥdas /
/ bdag gi mchod yon ḥdi bźes nas /
/ mchod pas bdag la dgyes pa mdzod /

ces brjod de /

/ sṅags kyi mthar e-hye-hi btags la mchod yon gyi snod bzuṅ nas / de bźin gśegs paḥi rigs la mgo boḥi thad ka nas dbul źiṅ / gźan gñis la braṅ daṅ / lte baḥi thad ka nas phul bas / raṅ ḥdraḥi ye śes pa byon par bsam mo /

/ sṅags ni rig sṅags kyi rgyal poḥi sṅags kyis lha pho daṅ / rig sṅags kyi rgyal moḥi sṅags kyis lha mo spyan draṅ baḥam / yaṅ na so soḥi sṅags kyis bya baḥam / yaṅ na spyiḥi rigs kyi sñiṅ pos spyan draṅ ba mchog tu legs grub las gsuṅs te / rigs gsum la rim pa ltar / dzi-na-jik e-hye-hi / ā-ro-lik e-hye-hi / ba-dzra-dhrik e-hye-hi /

/ de yaṅ spyan draṅ rgyuḥi lha ḥgreṅ ba daṅ ḥdug pa daṅ / bzur ba la de ltar byas nas / mchod yon gyis spyan draṅ pa daṅ / mchod yon gsuṅs pa bźin ma ḥbyor na bzod par gsol nas / ci ḥbyor bas spyan

[24] The commentary on the *Subāhuparipṛcchā-tantra* called *Tshig gi don bśad paḥi brjed byaṅ* (Toh. 2672), Derge Tg., *Rgyud ḥgrel*, Thu. 90b-6, 7, says: "Seven Vidyārājas are mentioned in the *Vajrapāṇyabhiṣeka mahātantra*: Susiddhi, Mauli, Vajrakīlikīla, Ratnakīlikīla, Surūpa, Vajrabindu, and Vajralalita" (rig paḥi rgyal po bdun źes bya ba ni phyag na rdo rje dbaṅ bskur baḥi rgyud chen po las / rab tu grub pa daṅ / dbu rgyan rtse gsum daṅ / ba-dzra ki-li-ki-la daṅ / rin chen ki-li-ki-la daṅ / gzugs legs daṅ / rdo rje thigs pa daṅ / rdo rjeḥi rol paḥo). It seems that these Vidyārājas (and hence the Vidyārājñīs as well) are both magical formulas and deities.

II′. *Invitation to the gods to be residents* (*ādheya*) *and offering of seats*

The invitation must be done with an oblation (*arghya*), which therefore must be prepared beforehead. The vessel for that is of gold, silver, and so forth; and a copper vessel is auspicious for all [invitations] in common. For appeasing rites (*śāntika*) and their superior *siddhi*, barley and milk are required. For rites to increase prosperity (*pauṣṭika*) and their middling *siddhi*, sesamum and sour milk are needed. For terrible rites (*abhicāruka*) and their inferior *siddhi*, ordinary urine together with millet, or blood, is offered up. Parched rice, fragrant odors, white flowers, *kuśa* grass, and sesamum mixed in pure water, which are auspicious for all rites in common, are prepared and incensed with the odors of incense. One blesses the oblation by reciting seven times an appropriate one among the general *dhāraṇīs* of the Vidyārāja and of the three Families, among the *dhāraṇīs* of all the rites of the individual Families, or among the *dhāraṇīs* of Invitation.

Thereupon one looks in the direction of the painted image and so on in front, salutes it and kneels down, then executes the Seal of Invitation: he joins the fingers of his hands, allowing the palms of his hands to touch, stretches out both indexes, and beckons with his two thumbs. Then he recites:

> By reason of my faith and my pledge,
> Come hither, come hither, O Bhagavat;
> And after enjoying this oblation of mine,
> Because it was offered, make me joyful!

At the end of the *dhāraṇī* he adds "Come, come!" (*ehy ehi*). He grasps the vessel with the oblation and offers it to the Tathāgata Family, raising it level with his head. For the other two Families, he offers it on the level of his breast or navel, respectively. Then he imagines the arrival of *jñāna* beings who resemble himself.

Regarding the *dhāraṇīs*, the *Susiddhi* says that the male deities are best invited with the *dhāraṇī* of the Vidyārāja; the female deities with the *dhāraṇī* of the Vidyārājñī;[24] and that invitation is made either with the individual *dhāraṇīs* or with the general *hṛdayas* of the Families. [These last] are for the three Families, in order, "*Jinajik ehy ehi*!" "*Ārolik ehy ehi*!" and "*Vajradhṛk ehy ehi*!"

Moreover, the *Susiddhi* in its chapter on Invitation says that when the basic god to be invited is standing upright, or sitting, or is bent over, one should assume the same posture while inviting with the oblation; that if the prescribed oblation is not available, one should ask [the

draṅ bar legs grub kyi spyan draṅ paḥi rim par phye ba las gsuṅs so /

/ de nas padmaḥi ḥdug staṅs kyi phyag rgya sogs daṅ / oṁ ka-ma-la-ye svā-hā / źes sogs kyi sṅags kyis / lha rnams la ci rigs su gdan dbul źiṅ / bźugs su gsol / ye śes pa spyan draṅs nas / bźugs su gsol ba las / dam tshig pa bskyed pa slob dpon gñis kyis ma bśad pas bya mi dgos la / byar mi ruṅ ba ni ma yin no /

/ gsum pa ni / de nas / śaṁ-ka-re sa-ma-ye svā-hā / źes brjod ciṅ / lag pa gYas paḥi mthe boṅ gis mtheḥu chuṅ gi sen mo mnan la / sor mo lhag ma rnams rdo rje ltar byas pa dam tshig gi rdo rjeḥi phyag rgya bstan par byaḥo /

/ de nas rigs gsum gyi phyag rgya bstan nas / ji-na-jik la sogs paḥi sñiṅ po gsum brjod do / phyag rgya ni / lag pa gñis phan tshun du khu tshur bciṅs nas / mthe boṅ gñis bstan par byas pa daṅ / de ñid las gYon paḥi mthe boṅ naṅ du bcug ste / gYas paḥi mthe boṅ bstan pa daṅ / gYon paḥi mthe boṅ bstan pa gsum ni rim pa bźin du rigs gsum gyi phyag rgyaḥo /

/ de nas rigs rnams kyi dam tshig chen poḥi phyag rgya bciṅs te bskor bas / phyi ḥbraṅ gi bgegs la sogs pas ṅan du byas pa thams cad las bsruṅ ba chen por ḥgyur bar gsuṅs pas / de bźin du bya la / de ma grub na skabs kyi khro bo gaṅ yin paḥi sṅags yuṅs kar la bzlas pas / phyi ḥbraṅ gi bgegs bskrad par byaḥo /

/ bźi pa la gñis / mchod pa dbul ba daṅ / bstod pa bya baḥo /

/ daṅ po ni / mchod rdzas rnams kyi bgegs bsal ba daṅ / bsaṅ ba daṅ / gzi byin bskyed pa rnams byas nas dbul te / de la bya spyod daṅ yo-ga daṅ / bla med gsum gyi mchod pa ḥbul ba la graṅs daṅ / go rims daṅ / phyag rgya mi gcig pa maṅ du yod do / ho na bya spyod kyi mchod pa ḥbul baḥi graṅs daṅ / go rims daṅ / phyag rgya sogs ji ltar bya źe na /

/ mtheḥu chuṅ daṅ srin lag gñis naṅ du phan tshun bsnol nas / guṅ mo gñis gśibs te bsgreṅs paḥi tshigs gsum par mdzub mo bkug mthe boṅ

deity] for indulgence and do the invitation with whatever is available.

Thereupon, with seals such as the "lotus sitting posture" and with *dhāraṇīs* such as *Oṃ kāmalāya svāhā*, one offers seats to [other] deities according to circumstances, and bids them be seated. The two teachers (i.e. Buddhaguhya and *Varabodhi) do not refer to a generation of the *samaya* beings after the *jñāna* beings have been invited and asked to be seated. Therefore, it is not necessary to generate them, but neither is it improper to do so.

III′. *Exhibition of the Seals* (*mudrā-darśana*)

Then one recites *Śaṅkare samaye svāhā*, and displays the Symbolic Thunderbolt Seal (*samayavajra-mudrā*) by pressing the tip of his small finger with his right thumb, and suggesting the shape of a thunderbolt with the remaining [three] fingers.

Next, he exhibits the seals of the three Families and recites the three *hṛdayas*, *Jinajik*, and so on. In regard to the seals: both hands are joined so as to make a fist, showing both thumbs; within the same seal the left thumb is hidden inside [the fist], while the right thumb is showing; then the left thumb alone is shown. The three in the given order are the seals (*mudrā*) of the three Families.

Then one ties the Great Symbol (*mahāsamaya*) seals of the Families and gyrates them, which is said to provide a great protection against all injuries done by obstructive demons who pursue from without. When one proceeds that way and is not successful [in the protection], he should recite the *dhāraṇī* of whichever wrathful deity suits the occasion, while throwing white mustard seed, and the pursuing obstructive demons will be frightened away.

IV′. *Offering and Praising* (*pūjastutyādika*)

This will be treated in two parts, presentation of offerings and praising.

A′. *Presentation of offerings.* — The offering materials are offered after driving away their obstructive demons, purifying and glorifying them. There are many differences between the Kriyā-Caryā, the Yoga, and the Anuttara Tantras as regards the number of oblations, their sequence, and the [accompanying] seals. Then what are the number, sequence, and seals for the presentation of offerings in the Kriyā-Caryā?

(1) One executes the seal "Assigning [the offering]" by interlacing the two little fingers and two ring fingers, bringing the two middle fingers against one another, outstretched, drawing together the indexes at the

gñis ṅos la sbyar baḥi phyag rgya bcas la / bde bar gśegs so bcom ldan ḥdas / tshur gśegs ḥdir ni bźugs su gsol / bdag gi mchod yon bźes nas yaṅ / thugs kyis thugs dpag mdzad du gsol / bdag ni khyed la gus daṅ ldan źes daṅ / lhaḥi sṅags kyi mthar a-rghaṁ pra-tī-ccha svā-hā / źes pas mchod yon dbul /

/ gYas paḥi khu tshur gyi mdzub mo daṅ mthe boṅ skam pa ltar byas la / źabs bsil gyi snod nas me tog blaṅs te / sor mo rnams rim gyis dgrol baḥi phyag rgya daṅ / sṅar gyi tshigs bcad kyi mchod yon gyi gnas su źabs bsil bcug nas / oṁ pra-va-ra sad-ka-raṁ pā-dyaṁ pra-tī-ccha svā-hā / źes pas źabs bsil dbul /

/ de nas ḥbyor na me loṅ la gzugs brñan śar ba la dṅos su sku khrus gsol / ma ḥbyor ba ḥam / mchod gYog pa lta bus byed na / gźan rnams kyis thal mo bkan pa las mdzub mo daṅ mthe boṅ gi rtse mo gñis sbyar ba sku bsil baḥi phyag rgyas la / oṁ sa-rva de-va-tā a-ci-nti a-mṛ-ta svā-hā / źes pas khrus gsol /

/ de nas yid kyis na bzaḥ daṅ rgyan gsol te / rol mos mchod ciṅ yid kyis bstod paḥi glu dbyaṅs blaṅ bar byaḥo / de nas lag pa gYas skyabs sbyin byas paḥi ḥkhrig ma nas gYon pas bzuṅ pa driḥi phyag rgya byas la / gtsaṅ źiṅ gtsaṅ ma las byuṅ baḥi / lha rdzas bzaṅ poḥi dri ḥdi dag / bdag ni dad pas ḥbul lags kyis / bźes nas bdag la dgyes par mdzad / ā-ha-ra ā-ha-ra sa-rva vi-dya dha-ri pū-ji-te svā-hā / źes pas dri chab dbul lo / mar me ma gtogs pa gźan gsum la ḥaṅ mchod ḥbul gyi sṅags ḥdi bźin du byaḥo /

/ lag pa gñis sor mo phan tshun bsnol te lag paḥi naṅ du mdzub mo gñis rtse mo gcig tu byas la gdu buḥi tshul du byas nas / mthe boṅ glor bźag ste / padma ltar byas pa me tog gi phyag rgya daṅ / gtsaṅ źiṅ gtsaṅ

third joint, and joining the two thumbs on their edge; and recites:

O Bhagavat, who went to bliss,
Come hither and be seated.
Having enjoyed my oblation,
May your mind deepen my mind;
I am devoted to Thee!

At the end of the *dhāraṇī* of the deity, he presents the oblation while reciting, *Argham pratīccha svāhā* ("Accept the oblation, *svāhā*").

(2) With his right hand in a fist, he forms a pincers with his index and thumb and picks a flower from the vessel containing the water for the feet, then makes the seal of successively releasing the fingers. Substituting "feet-cooling water" for "oblation" in the stanza cited above, he offers the feet-cooling water, while reciting, *Oṃ pravaraṃ satkaraṃ pādyaṃ pratīccha svāhā* ("*Oṃ*! Accept this most excellent beneficent feet-cooling water, *svāhā*!").

(3) Thereupon he reflects the image in a mirror, if he can provide it, and gives an actual bath to the reflected image. If he cannot provide it, such persons as the assistant to the offering or other persons make the seal of "washing the body", that is, form a level surface with the backs of their hands, so that the tips of the thumbs and the index fingers touch each other. He offers a bath, while reciting, *Oṃ sarvadevatā-acintya-amṛta svāhā* ("*Oṃ*! The inconceivable ambrosia of all the gods, *svāhā*!").

(4) Next he mentally offers food and ornaments; and, while offering with music, he mentally performs melodies of praise. Then, with his right hand, he makes the seals of "taking refuge" and "making gifts". Seizing the wrist with the left hand, he makes the seal of "perfume", reciting:

These auspicious perfumes, divine substance,
Pure and born from purity, I present with devotion.
Having enjoyed them, make me joyful!

While reciting, *Āhara āhara sarvavidyādhari pūjite svāhā* ("Take it, take it, O Holder of all *vidyās*, while worshipped, *svāhā*"), he offers the perfumes. He uses this same *dhāraṇī* when he presents offerings in the other three cases, exclusive of the lamp [hence, in cases 5 to 7, below].

(5) He makes the "flower" seal after the model of the lotus: the fingers of both hands are interlaced; within the hands the tips of the index fingers come to a point making a bracelet, the thumbs touching the sides; and recites:

This auspicious flower, divine substance,

mar skyes pa yi / lha rdzas bzaṅ poḥi me tog ḥdi / rkaṅ pa phyi ma gñis goṅ daṅ ḥdras bas me tog daṅ /

/ lag pa gñis kyi mtheḥu chuṅ daṅ srin lag daṅ guṅ mo rnams kyi sor mo rnams phan tshun sbyar te / sṅa ma sṅa maḥi rgyab kyi sen moḥi druṅ du bkug nas mdzub mo gñis logs śig tu brkyaṅs te / mthe boṅ gñis glor bźag pa bdug spos kyi phyag rgya daṅ / nags tshal bcud ni yid du ḥoṅ / dri yis sbyar ba lha yi rdzas bdag ni dad pas ḥbul lags kyis / źes sogs kyis spos daṅ /

/ bzed paḥi thal mo las mdzub mo gñis cuṅ zad bkug pa lha bśos kyi phyag rgya daṅ / sman rnams bcud ni yid du ḥoṅ / sṅags kyi źal zas bśos ḥdi dag / bdag ni źes sogs kyis źal zas daṅ /

/ mthe boṅ daṅ guṅ mo gcig tu sbyar te bsgreṅs la / lag pa khu tshur gcig tu byas pa mar meḥi phyag rgya daṅ / gnod rnams ḥjoms śiṅ bkra śis pa / dge źiṅ mun pa rnam sel ḥdi / bdag ni dad pas ḥbul lags kyis / mar me ḥdi dag bźes su gsol / ā-lo-kā-ya ā-lo-kā-ya vidyā-dhāri pū-ji-te svā-hā / źes pas mar me dbul lo /

/ mchod yon man chad rnams dṅos su ma ḥbyor na sṅags rgya byas la / yid kyis dmigs pa gsal bar byas nas dbul bar gsuṅs so / dṅos su ḥbyor paḥi mchod pa la yaṅ kun gyi sṅon du yid ḥgro bas yid kyi mchod pa khyad che bar gsuṅs so /

/ gñis pa ni / de nas legs grub las / dkon mchog gsum daṅ rigs gsum gyi bdag po la bstod pa bya bar gsuṅs la ltar bya ste /

/ mgon po thugs rje che ldan pa /
/ thams cad mkhyen paḥi ston pa po /
/ bsod nams yon tan rgya mtshoḥi źiṅ /
/ de bźin gśegs la phyag ḥtshal lo /

Pure and born from purity, ...

with the other two lines as previously. (And offers a flower with the *dhāraṇī*).

(6) He makes the "perfumed incense" seal: the little, ring, and middle fingers of the two hands are brought against one another and the backs of the nails of each of these in that order are brought against each other; the two index fingers are stretched out at an angle, while the two thumbs are placed against their sides: and recites:

This divine substance composed with perfume,
The delightful elixir of forest glades,
I devoutly offer ...

(And offers incense with the *dhāraṇī*).

(7) He makes the seal of "food for the gods": the palms are cupped and the index fingers slightly drawn toward one another; and recites:

These repasts of *dhāraṇīs*,
The delightful elixir of medicines,
...

(And offers food with the *dhāraṇī*).

(8) He makes the seal of the "lamp": the thumb and middle finger are stretched upward, touching one another, the hand made into a fist; and recites:

Pray enjoy these lamps,
Auspicious and triumphant over harmful elements,
Virtuous and dispelling of darkness,
Which I offer with devotion.

While reciting, *Ālokaya ālokaya vidyādhari pūjite svāhā* ("Behold, behold! O Vidyādharin, while worshipped, *svāhā*"), he offers the lamps.

If the oblation and the succeeding offerings cannot be actually provided, it is taught that they may be offered mentally by visualizing them vividly. Indeed, it is taught that even when the offerings are actually provided, they are first to be passed mentally in review, for the mental offering is the chief thing.

B′. *Praising*. — Thereupon, one should proceed according to the *Susiddhi*, which says that the Three Jewels and the Masters of the three Families are to be praised.

I salute the Tathāgata, the Lord of great Compassion,
The omniscient Teacher, field of an ocean of merit and
noble qualities.
I salute the quiescent Law (*dharma*),

/ dag pas ḥdod chags bral bar gyur /
/ dge bas ṅan soṅ las grol ciṅ /
/ gcig tu don dam mchog gyur pa /
/ źi gyur chos la phyag ḥtshal lo /
/ grol nas grol baḥi lam yaṅ ston /
/ bslab pa dag la rab tu gnas /
/ źiṅ gi dam pa yon tan ldan /
/ dge ḥdun la yaṅ phyag ḥtshal lo /
/ gźon nuḥi cha lugs ḥchaṅ pa po /
/ śes rab sgron mes rab tu brgyan /
/ ḥjig rten gsum gyi mun sel ba /
/ ḥjam dpal la yaṅ phyag ḥtshal lo /
/ saṅs rgyas kun gyis rab tu bsṅags /
/ yon tan dam pa kun bsags pa /
/ spyan ras gzigs źes mtshan gsol ba /
/ rtag par brtse la phyag ḥtshal lo /
/ stobs po che la drag śul can /
/ rig sṅags rgyal po dge ba can /
/ gdul dkaḥ bo dag ḥdul ba po /
/ rdo rje ḥdzin la phyag ḥtshal lo /

źes pa daṅ /

/ gźan yaṅ skabs kyi lha gaṅ yiṅ gyi sgos kyi bstod pa yaṅ byas la / na-maḥ sa-rva bu-ddha bo-dhi-sa-tva-nāṁ / sa-rva-tra saṁ-ku-ru-mi ta a-bhi-jñā ra-śi-ni na-mo stu-te svā-hā / źes pa bstod pa ḥbyuṅ baḥi sṅags lan brgya bzlaḥo /

/ lṅa pa ni / sdig pa bśags pa daṅ / skyabs su ḥgro ba daṅ / rjes su yi raṅ ba daṅ / bskul źiṅ gsol ba ḥdebs pa daṅ / smon lam rnams bya baḥo /

/ drug pa ni / tshad med bźi bsgom pa daṅ / sems bskyed par bya baḥo / mchod bstod kyi rjes la bśags pa sogs daṅ / tshad med bźi bsgom pa daṅ / sems bskyed pa sogs byed paḥi don ni / rgyud sde goṅ mar yaṅ sgrub

[25] The four boundless states are compassion (*karuṇā*), friendship (*maitrī*), sympathetic joy (*muditā*), and indifference (*upekṣā*). These are explained in the *Sṅags rim chen mo*, 68b-3, ff. In the first state, one prays for tormented mankind to be freed from suffering; in the second, one prays for mankind to obtain complete happiness; in the third, one prays for mankind to have bliss as the Buddha has bliss; in the fourth, one prays for mankind to attain *nirvāṇa* as the Buddha has *nirvāṇa*.

Which, being pure, frees from craving,
Which, being virtuous, liberates from evil destiny,
Which, being solitary, is the ultimate goal.
I salute the Virtuous Host (*saṃgha*),
Which after liberation teaches the path of liberation,
Is well founded in the points of moral instruction,
Possesses the good qualities of the holy field.
I salute Mañjuśrī,
Who bears the aspect of a youth (*kumāra*)
And is adorned with the lamp of insight
That dispels the darkness of the three worlds.
I salute him, the ever-merciful one,
Called by the name Avalokita,
Who is praised by all the Buddhas
And has accumulated all holy merits.
I salute Vajrapāṇi,
Powerful, fiercesome, the virtuous *vidyārāja*
Who tames the obdurate.

Moreover, one makes praise by way of whatever be the deity of that occasion. and recites a hundred times the praising *dhāraṇī*, *Namaḥ sarvabuddhabodhisattvānāṃ sarvatra saṃkurumi ta abhijñā-rāśini namo stute svāhā* ("Homage to all the Buddhas and Bodhisattvas! Everywhere I fashion thy beams of supernormal faculties. *Namo stute svāhā*").

V′. *Confession of sins, etc.* (*pāpadeśanādika*)

Here follow:

A′. Confession of sins (*pāpa-deśanā*).

B′. Refuge formula (*śaraṇa-gamana*).

C′. Sympathetic delight (*anumodanā*) [with the merit (*puṇya*) and knowledge (*jñāna*) amassed by the Buddhas and Bodhisattvas].

D′. Exhortation and entreaty [to the Buddha to turn the Wheel of the Law and to not depart into *Nirvāṇa* as long as there be candidates].

E′. Fervent aspiration (*praṇidhāna*) [to alleviate the sufferings of humanity].

VI′. *Contemplation of the four boundless states* (*caturapramāṇa-bhāvanā*) *and Generation of the Mind* (*cittotpāda*)

The purpose of confession and so on, contemplation of the four boundless states,[25] and generation of the Mind [of Enlightenment] after offering and praising, is to purify the vow by fastening it with confession,

mchod kyi mchod ḥbul gyi rjes su rigs lṅaḥi sdom gzuṅ sogs byed pa bźin / bśags bsdams gyis sdom pa dag par byed pa la gnas paḥi mchod pas mchog sgrub paḥi mchod pa ñid mchod yul mñes par byed paḥi mchog yin paḥi don gyis yin la / ḥdir yaṅ de daṅ ḥdraḥo /

/ de dag gis bzlas brjod kyi yan lag soṅ nas / bzlas brjod dṅos la / bzlas brjod yan lag bźi tshaṅ ba dgos pas / bsam gtan phyi ma las / sgra daṅ sems daṅ gźi pa gźol /

/ źes gsuṅs paḥi gźiḥi yan lag ni / sṅags ḥkhor gaṅ gi thugs kar dgod paḥi gźi lhaḥi skuḥo / de la gñis las bdag ñid lhar gsal bar bsgom pa gźan gyi gźi ste / de gñis ni bzlas brjod yan lag bźiḥi naṅ nas yan lag re reḥo /

/ sems la gźol baḥi yan lag ni / mdun bskyed kyi thugs kar raṅ gi sems zla baḥi dkyil ḥkhor gyi rnam par gsal bar dmigs paḥo /

/ sgra la gźol baḥi yan lag ni / deḥi steṅ du gaṅ bzla bar bya baḥi sṅags kyi yig ḥbru gsal bar dmigs paḥo /

/ de nas bgraṅ phreṅ de bźin gśegs paḥi rigs la bo de tse / padmaḥi rigs la padmaḥi sñiṅ po / rdo rjeḥi rigs la ru-rakṣa mchog daṅ / ma ḥbyor na gźan yaṅ ruṅ la / graṅs stoṅ rtsa brgyad ṅam brgya rtsa brgyad dam / ṅa bźi ḥam / ñer gcig pa byin gyis brlabs la cho ga bźin du bzlas brjod byaḥo /

/ bzlas brjod bya baḥi tshul la gñis / yi geḥi gzugs la dmigs paḥi bzlas brjod daṅ / sgra la dmigs paḥi bzlas brjod do /

/ daṅ po la / mdun bskyed kyi thugs kaḥi yi geḥi gzugs la dmigs pa daṅ / raṅ gi sñiṅ gaḥi yi geḥi gzugs la dmigs paḥi bzlas paḥo /

/ daṅ po ni / sṅar bśad paḥi srog rtsol bsdams te bzlas brjod kyi yan lag bźi tshaṅ baḥi sgo nas / mdun gyi sku daṅ thugs kaḥi zla gdan deḥi

[26] This paragraph is rather obscure, but the *Sṅags rim chen mo* has helped solve the problem of translation. The expressions "completion and offering" doubtless refer to the *maṇḍala*. In that work, the section "completion and offering of the *maṇḍala*" (*dkyil ḥkhor bsgrub ciṅ mchod pa*) begins 229a-1, with "completion of the *maṇḍala*" (*dkyil ḥkhor bsgrub pa*) beginning 229a-2, and "*maṇḍala* offering" (*dkyil ḥkhor mchod pa*) beginning 236a-2. 'Locational offerings' are described in the same work, 237b-5, ff. under the heading, "The places for the offerings are as follows..." (*gnas gaṅ du ḥbul ba ni*).

[27] Buddhaguhya, when commenting upon that line of the *Dhyānottara* in his *ṭīkā* (Toh. 2670), Thu, 16a-5, ff., speaks of the latter 'ground' (*gźi*) as the 'Tathāgata ground' (*de bźin gśegs paḥi gźi*) in the phrase "in the heart of the Tathāgata ground meditated in front" (mdun du bsams paḥi de bźin gśegs paḥi gźiḥi thugs ka na).

which is comparable to taking the vows (*saṃvara*) of the five Families and so on in the higher Tantra divisions after presenting the offering [part] of [*maṇḍala*] completion and [*maṇḍala*] offering; the best procedural offering (*pratipatti-pūjā*) through locational offerings is for the purpose of the best delight of the offering domain. and this [offering] here is also similar to that [higher Tantra procedure].[26]

γ. *The Four Members, general*

Those two [i.e., the Generation of Self and the Generation in Front] constitute members of muttering (*jāpa-aṅga*). For the genuine muttering one must complete the four members of muttering. Consequently, the *Dhyānottara* says, "Immerse yourself in the sound, the mind, and the ground."

The "ground" member: The "ground" (T. *gźi*, S. **vastu*) is the body of the god in whose heart the *dhāraṇī* wheel is deposited. Of the two kinds, the "subjective ground" (*bdag gi gźi*) is the contemplation of oneself transfigured into a god; and the "objective ground" (*gźan gyi gźi*) is the contemplation of the god generated in front.[27] Those two are each a member among the four members of muttering.

The member of immersion in mind (**citta-nimna*): This has the vivid meditative object (*ālambana*) consisting in one's mind (*citta*) in the shape of a moon-*maṇḍala* in the heart of the deity generated in front.

The member of immersion in sound (**svara-nimna*): This has the vivid meditative object consisting in the letters of the *dhāraṇī* to be recited, located upon that [moon-*maṇḍala*].

The chaplet (*akṣa-mālā*) should be preferably made of [seeds of] the Bodhi tree for the Tathāgata Family, lotus pods for the Padma Family, and *rudrākṣa* (berries of Elaeocarpus Ganitrus) for the Vajra Family; but if those are not available, other materials will do. One blesses it by counting 1008, 108, 54, or 21 times, and recites according to the rite.

There are two methods for the muttering: muttering while dwelling on the shape of the syllables, and muttering while dwelling on their sound.

I′. *Muttering while dwelling on the shape of the syllables*

There are two kinds: muttering while dwelling on the shape of the syllables in the heart of the deity generated in front; muttering while dwelling on the shape of the syllables in one's heart.

The first kind: One binds the *prāṇa-āyāma* as previously described and mutters by way of the complete four members of muttering while

steṅ gi yi ge gsum ga la dus gcig tu dmigs te bzlas brjod bya źiṅ / dbugs gtoṅ ba na sṅags mi bzla bar raṅ lhar bsgoms paḥi sku la sems gtad nas ḥdug ciṅ / yaṅ sṅar bźin rluṅ bzuṅ nas bzlas pa byaḥo /

/ gñis pa ni / raṅ gi mdun du ha caṅ mi riṅ bar raṅ gi tshad las cuṅ zad mtho bar mdun bskyed kyi thugs kar zla baḥi steṅ du sṅags phreṅ bkod pa de rluṅ naṅ du ḥjug pa daṅ lhan cig tu tshur la raṅ gi sñiṅ gar spos la / de la dmigs nas dbugs ma btaṅ gi bar du bzlas brjod bya źiṅ / rluṅ gtoṅ ba na zla ba sṅags phreṅ daṅ bcas pa rluṅ daṅ mñam du phyir btaṅ nas mdun gyi lhaḥi thugs kar gnas par bsam źiṅ / yaṅ sṅar bźin raṅ gi sñiṅ gar spos la bzla bar byaḥo /

/ gñis pa ni / bzlas brjod kyi yan lag bźi thog mar gsal btab la / de nas sṅags kyi yi geḥi gzugs daṅ zla ba daṅ lhaḥi sku la mi dmigs par sṅags kyi sgraḥi gdaṅs la dmigs nas zlo ba ste / de yaṅ sṅags gźan gyis bton pa raṅ gis ñan pa lta bu min gyi / raṅ gis zlo baḥi tshe na sṅags deḥi sgra grag par dmigs nas byed paḥo /

/ sṅags kyi gdaṅs la dmigs pa ḥdi ñid kyi cho gas yid bzlas daṅ śub buḥi bzlas pa gñis ka bya ba daṅ / srog rtsol bsdoms pa na śub buḥi bzlas pa byed mi nus par ḥgrel pa las gsuṅs pas / thog mar śub buḥi bzlas pa bya źiṅ / de la sems gźan du mi gYeṅ ba na / de nas srog rtsol bsdoms nas yid bzlas bya ste / rags rim nas bya bar bśad do /

/ daṅ po la / lha daṅ zla ba daṅ sṅags phreṅ gsum la dmigs pa gsum daṅ / bar ba la zla ba daṅ sṅags phreṅ gñis tsam la dmigs pa gñis daṅ / tha ma la sgra tsam la dmigs pas dmigs pa gcig yin par ḥgrel bas bśad de / gaṅ zag gcig gis kyaṅ ḥdi gsum ga rim gyis byaḥo /

/ bzlas brjod kyi tshe ji ltar bya ba ni dpuṅ bzaṅ gi lṅa ba las / bzlas brjod byed tshe mi myur mi dal źiṅ / sgra cher mi bya ha caṅ chuṅ ba

simultaneously dwelling on the body of the deity generated in front and on the three syllables which are on the moon seat in the heart [of the deity's body]. When exhaling, one should not mutter *dhāraṇīs*, but hold the mind fixed on one's own body contemplated as the deity. Then, again holding the breath, one should mutter as before.

The second kind: The garland of *dhāraṇīs* is at a modest distance in front of himself, slightly higher than himself, upon the moon in the heart of the deity generated in front. While inhaling, he attracts that [moon and garland] into himself and transfers it into his own heart. He dwells on it while muttering, as long as he does not release his breath; but when he exhales the wind, he is to imagine that the moon, along with the garland of *dhāraṇīs*, is emitted together with the wind and then is stationed in the heart of the god in front. Again in the same manner as before he transfers it into his own heart.

II′. *Muttering while dwelling on the sound of the syllables*

First one distinctly recalls the four members of muttering. Then, without dwelling on the shape of the syllables of the *dhāraṇī*, the moon, or the body of the god, one dwells on the tone of the sounds of the *dhāraṇī* while he recites. Moreover, it is not as though the *dhāraṇī* were being uttered by another person and being heard by oneself, but rather one dwells on the tone of the sounds of that *dhāraṇī* at the time oneself is reciting it.

This rite of dwelling on the tone of the *dhāraṇī* involves both mental recitation and whispered recitation. The commentary (Toh. 2670) [on the *Dhyānottara*] states that one cannot employ whispered recitation while restraining the *prāṇa-āyāma*; [the work] explains the sequence in outline this way: first one performs the whispered recitation; when, during that [recitation], the mind is not distracted, then one restrains the *prāṇa-āyāma*, performing the mental recitation.

According to the commentary, in the first case (I′, the first kind), there are three meditative objects: the god, the moon, and the *dhāraṇī*-garland; in the second case (I′, the second kind), there are two meditative objects: the moon and the *dhāraṇī*-garland; in the third case (II′), there is only one meditative object: the sound [of the *dhāraṇī*]. A single person must proceed by these three steps.

The fifth chapter of the *Subāhu* (Toh. 805) tells what should be done at the time of muttering:

> While muttering, one should be neither hurried nor slow,
> Neither too loud nor too low,

min / smra źiṅ ma yin gźan du gYeṅ bźin min / gug skyed klad kor tsheg rnams ñams pa min / źes daṅ / le lo ḥdod chags mi dger ldan paḥi sems / gaṅ daṅ gaṅ du gYeṅ źiṅ rgyu ba dag / de daṅ de nas myur du bzlog nas ni / gsaṅ sṅags yi ge mchog la legs par sbyar / źes daṅ / legs grub las / bzlas paḥi tshe lha la sogs paḥi skabs kyi dmigs pa las gźan paḥi dmigs pa mchog rnams kyaṅ yid la mi bya bar gsuṅs so /

/ źi rgyas la dal bu daṅ / drag po la gźan gyis thos par bzlaḥo / bzlas paḥi yun ni sṅa dro mel tshe thun gcig daṅ / srod daṅ tho raṅs thun phyed phyed daṅ / ñin guṅ thun phyed dam sum cha ḥam bźi cha ḥam yaṅ na cuṅ zad bzlaḥo / bzlas paḥi rjes su sbyin sreg byed pa mchog go /

/ bzlas paḥi graṅs ni legs grub las / bco lṅa man chad graṅs rnams la / spyir na yi ge du yod pa / de sñed ḥbum phrag bzlas brjod bya / yi ge sum cu rtsa gñis la / bzlas brjod sum ḥbum bya bar bśad / de bas yi ge maṅ po la / sṅon du bsñen pa khri byaḥo / źes gsuṅs te / gtso bo rkyaṅ pa min pa la bzlas pa bya mi dgos so /

/ bzlas paḥi ḥphro la gñid bro ba ḥam glal lam sprid pa ḥam lud paḥam ḥog rluṅ ṅam bśaṅ gci sogs byuṅ na de ma thag phreṅ ba bźag ste / bcag pa sogs byas nas ñe reg byas te / graṅs kyi thog ma nas brtsam par gsuṅs te / de yan chad bzlas paḥi graṅs su mi gźug go / gźan yaṅ bag med pas lha gźan gyi bzlas pa byas na ḥaṅ / yid kyis gsol ba btab nas / bzlas brjod bskyar ba daṅ / bgegs kyis brlams pa daṅ / nad kyis gzer ba daṅ / lhod pa daṅ / bag med pa daṅ / lus daṅ sems skyo ba daṅ / cho ga ji skad bśad paḥi dus las ḥdas par byas pa daṅ / ma bsdams pa daṅ / mi gtsaṅ bas bzlas brjod byas pa daṅ / mtshan mo rmi lam ṅan pa byuṅ bas ñin mo rigs kyi bdag po gaṅ yin gyi sṅags brgya ma bzlas par / bzlas brjod byas pa rnams bzlas paḥi graṅs su mi gźug par legs grub las gsuṅs so /

[28] Bracketed interpolations in the citation are drawn from oral explanations by the Mongolian Lama Dilowa Hutukhtu.

Neither speaking nor distracted,
Nor disregarding the upper and lower vowel signs,
the *anusvāra*, or the *visarga*.

And also:

The one whose mind is slothful, lascivious, and unvirtuous,
Whenever and wherever it may wander, distracted,
Then and therefrom he must quickly turn it back
And apply it to the excellent syllables of the *mantra-dhāraṇī*.

Furthermore, the *Susiddhi* (Toh. 807) says that at the time of muttering, when one is in the phase of dwelling upon a god, and so forth, although there be other excellent objects upon which to dwell, one should pay no attention to them.

In rites of appeasing and increasing prosperity, one recites leisurely; and in terrible rites, audible to others. The periods of recitation are as follows: a full watch in the morning and at night; a half watch at dusk and at dawn; at noon, either a half, a third, a fourth part of a watch, or even a brief recitation. It is preferable to follow the recitation with a burnt offering (*homa*).

Regarding the number of recitations, the *Susiddhi* says:

In general, if there be of syllables
The numbers of fifteen or fewer,
One must mutter [each syllable] 100,000 times;
Up to thirty-two syllables, it is said
The muttering [of the entire formula] must be done 300,000 times;
When the syllables are more than that,
Do the preliminary service [of the entire formula] 10,000 times.[28]

It is not necessary to do the recitation for any other [deity] besides the Lord.

When during the recitation one becomes drowsy, yawns, sneezes, coughs aloud, breaks wind, or feels an urge to ease nature, etc., he immediately sets aside his chaplet, interrupts [the service], makes ablutions, and starts again from the beginning of the count. What has been recited before does not count. Moreover, the *Susiddhi* teaches that if through inadvertence one makes the recitation of another deity and has appealed to him mentally, he recommences his muttering; also, that if one is oppressed by inimical spirits or plagued by disease, slothful, careless, fatigued in body and mind; if he has transgressed the times set for the ritual, is uncontrolled, mutters with an impure mind, has had an evil dream the night before but not recited a hundred times on the following day the *dhāraṇī* of the Master of the Family, his mutterings do not count

yaṅ der gnas gcig tu phyed bzlas gźan du phyed bzlas pas / bzlas pa thams cad rdzogs kyaṅ / de dag thams cad don med du gsuṅs so /

/ thun gyi dus ni / ñi maḥi dkyil ḥkhor phyed śar ba nas / skyes bu gcig gi grib maḥi bar ṅaṅ / ñin guṅ la chu tshod brgyad dam dguḥi dus daṅ / phyi dro skyes bu gcig gi grib ma lus pa nas / ñi maḥi dkyil la bor phyed nub paḥi bar gyi dus daṅ / ñi maḥi dkyil ḥkhor phyed nub pa nas / srod phyed kyi bar ni srod la brtsam paḥi dus daṅ / tho raṅs kyi phyed nas / ñi maḥi dkyil ḥkhor phyed śar baḥi bar ni dus ḥtshams gñis paḥo /

/ nam phyed nas ni / drag śul gyi las daṅ / mi snaṅ ba la sogs pa daṅ / dur khrod kyi las rnams bya la / de las bzlog paḥi skabs su źi ba sogs bya bar bśad ciṅ / thun kyi dus de dag las gźan du bzlas pa byas pa rnams graṅs su mi gźug par bśad do /

/ mṅon rtogs las / zlos pas bzlas brjod zin pa daṅ / rigs kyi yum daṅ bdag po la / ñi śu rtsa gcig bzlas brjod ni / byas pas rtag tu bsruṅ bar bya / źes draṅs pa ltar bya ste / rigs gsum gyi rigs kyi yum ni spyan daṅ / gos dkar mo daṅ / mā-ma-kīḥo /

/ gsum pa bzlas brjod yan lag bźiḥi mjug tu ji ltar bya ba ni / bum paḥi phyag rgyas lha la dṅos grub kyi rgyur dge rtsa dbul lo /

/ phyag rgya des ḥphreṅ ba ḥbul ba yin źes pa ni ma brtags paḥo / ḥo na kyaṅ bzlas pa ḥjog pa na ḥphreṅ ba lhaḥi druṅ du bźag nas gtsaṅ sbra la gnas pas bzlas pa byed dus ma gtogs lus la mi bcaṅ ṅo / de nas bzod gsol daṅ / gśegs gsol sogs byed /

/ thun gyi dṅos gźi la bzlas pa byas nas / thun ḥtshams su gtoṅ baḥi rim pa ni / lha drug bsgom paḥi go rims las lugs bzlog tu gtoṅ ba ste /

/ bzlas paḥi sṅags kyi sgra la dmigs pa ni / sṅags kyi yig ḥbru la dmigs

[29] That is to say, Locanā is the Mother of the Tathāgata Family, Pāṇḍarā of the Padma or Lotus Family, and Māmakī of the Vajra or Thunderbolt Family. These names are not obviously consistent with the descriptions of the Families given in Chapter III. In fact, the names represent a development of Tantric tradition later than the materials of that Chapter. In particular, with the great expansion of the Tārā cult, numerous varieties of this goddess were worshipped. A variety of Tārā often called Samayatārā is associated with the Family of Amoghasiddhi. In differentiation, the Mother of the Padma Family was renamed Pāṇḍarā, "the white lady", actually the white-dressed Tārā.

[30] This *mudrā* is described in the *Sṅags rim chen mo*, 74a-2, 3.

in the recitation. Furthermore, the same work states that if one recites half in one location and half somewhere else, though he completes the whole recitation, it is all to no purpose.

The times of the watches are as follows: The morning interval is from the moment when half of the sun disk emerges until it casts a man sized shadow. Noon is the eighth or ninth *chu tshod* [approx. 45 minute period, ¼ of a watch]. The afternoon interval is from the moment when there remains a man sized shadow until half of the sun disk is submerged. The initial interval of night is from the moment when half of the sun disk is submerged through half the night. The period from this half-way point to dawn when half the sun disk has emerged is called the second interval [of night].

Midnight onwards is the time for terrible rites, such [*siddhis*] as invisibility, and the cemetary rites; while in other periods one performs the appeasing rites, etc., as is explained [by *Varabodhi]. He explains that recitations made at other times than the established watches do not count.

One should do just as quoted in the "Lucid Exposition" (*abhisamaya*) [i.e., the commentary (Toh. 3066) by *Varabodhi on the *Susiddhi*]:

> One must complete the muttering with recitation;
> Then permanently protect it by doing
> The muttering twenty-one times
> To the Mother and Master of the Family.

The Mothers of the three Families are Locanā, Pāṇḍarā, and Māmakī.[29]

(c) Terminating acts to the four members of muttering

The way in which one concludes the four members of muttering is to offer his roots of merit (*kuśala-mūla*) as a cause (*hetu*) for *siddhi* to the deity by means of the seal of the flask (*kalaśa-mudrā*).[30]

Those who say that with this seal the chaplet is offered, have not studied [sufficiently]. However, after finishing the recitation, the chaplet is deposited in front of the deity, for it should not be borne on the body apart from the time of doing recitation while abiding in religious purity. Then one asks indulgence [for possible omissions and other imperfections of the service], escorts the deity away, and so forth.

Having recited for the main part of the watch, the steps of release at the limit of the watch are this: One releases in reverse order to the sequence in which the six gods were contemplated.

The meditative object in the sound of the *dhāraṇī* being recited is released by dwelling on the letters of the *dhāraṇī*; those, in turn, by

pas gtoṅ ṅo / de yaṅ zla ba tsam la dmigs pas so / zla ba ni lhaḥi sku ḥbaḥ źig la dmigs pas so / mdun gyi sku de yaṅ raṅ gi lhaḥi sku ḥbaḥ źig tu sems pas so /

/ bdag bskyed kyi lhaḥi sku de yaṅ deḥi thugs kaḥi yig ḥbru ḥbaḥ źig tu sems pas so / de yaṅ sgra la dmigs pas so / sgra yaṅ lhaḥi ye śes kyi sku la dmigs pas so / de yaṅ chos kyi sku la dmigs pas so / de yaṅ mi dmigs par bdag gi de kho na ñid la dmigs par byaḥo / de yaṅ sgyu ma daṅ smig rgyu la sogs par snaṅ ba rnam smin gyi lus la sems pas te /

/ dmigs pa rnams rim gyis bsdus nas mthar stoṅ pa ñid la mñam par ḥjog ciṅ / de nas sgyu ma lta bur ldaṅ ba yin pas thun btaṅ baḥi skabs su yaṅ lhaḥi ṅa rgyal mi ḥdzin pa min no / de ltar byed pa de bla med kyi skabs su ñer bsdu byed paḥi dod do /

/ de nas śer phyin gyi glegs bam bklag pa daṅ / mchod rten gdab pa sogs byaḥo / ñin gcig bźin du ḥaṅ mchod paḥi snod rnams bkru ba daṅ / me tog phul ba rnams dus gsum du phyag pa daṅ / bla gos la sogs paḥi gos rnams dus gsum du bsṅags śiṅ bkru ba ḥam / bdug pa ḥam bsaṅ gtor byaḥo /

/ bzlas brjod daṅ / sbyin sreg daṅ / mchod pa sogs la / ñal ba daṅ ḥphres pa ma gtogs par rtag tu bla gos bgo la / ñal ba daṅ khrus byed pa ma gtogs par mthaṅ gos mi spaṅ źiṅ rdul gyis ma gos par byaḥo /

/ bu mos bkal baḥi skud pa dmar po le brgan rtsi ḥam / gur kum gyis btsos pa la mdud pa bor te / Oṁ ā-ha-ra ā-ha-ra ba-nddā-ni śu-kra dha-ra-ṇi si-ddha-rthe svā-hā / źes pa stoṅ bzlas la srod kyi dus su-rked pa la bciṅs nas ḥdzag pa bsruṅ ṅo /

/ gñis pa bzlas brjod la mi ltos paḥi bsam gtan la gsum / me la gnas paḥi bsam gtan bśad pa / sgra la gnas paḥi bsam gtan bśad pa / sgra mthar thar pa ster baḥi bsam gtan bśad paḥo /

/ daṅ po ni / gaṅ zag ji lta bu źig gis bsgom na lha drug bsgoms pa mthar phyin pa źig gis bsgom mo /

[31] In the Anuttara Tantra, the equivalent phase is apparently the unification of body and mind as discussed by Mkhas grub rje near the end of his book and as already alluded to as the 'Perfection of Affiliation' among the five perfections in note 7, above.

[32] In the *Mañjuśrī-mūla-tantra*, Sanskrit text p. 427, Tibetan text (Toh. 543), Derge Kg., *Rgyud ḥbum*, Na, 286b-1, the *dhāraṇī* is given with *hara hara* instead of *āhara āhara*.

dwelling on only the moon. The moon is released by dwelling on just the body of the deity; that body in front, by thinking only of one's own divine body.

That divine body of Self Generation is released by thinking only of the syllables in its heart; that, in turn, by dwelling on the sound; the sound, in turn, by dwelling on the Knowledge Body of the god; that, in turn, by dwelling on the Dharma-kāya. In turn, unsupported by that, one should dwell on the Self Reality (**ātma-tattva*). That, in turn, is released by thinking of the Maturation Body (*vipāka-kāya*) which appears as an illusion, mirage, and so forth.

Having summarized by steps those meditative objects, finally he is equipoised in voidness (*śūnyatā*). Thereupon, because he emerges in the fashion of an illusion, even at the time of giving up the watch, he should not release his hold on divine egoity. This procedure is equivalent to the unification in the phase of the Anuttara [Tantra].[31]

Thereupon one reads a Prajñāpāramitā book, establishes a *stūpa*, and so on. Moreover, everyday the offering vessels are washed, flower offerings three times swept away, upper and other robes three times praised and washed, or censed, or sprinkled [with holy water].

When muttering, making the burnt offering, making the offerings [for *siddhi*], etc., he must always wear the upper robe, except for the time of sleeping and reclining; and must not remove his lower robe nor allow it to be soiled with dust, except for the time of sleeping and washing.

He must tie a knot in a thread spun by a virgin (*kanyā*) and dyed with the red juice of the Safflower, or with saffron. He recites a thousand times, *Oṃ āhara āhara bandhane śukradhāraṇī siddhārthe svāhā*[32] ("Oṃ. May the retainer of semen withhold, withhold, while the fettering is efficacious! *Svāhā*"), and binds [the thread] on his loins at night. This protects against seminal emission.

(2) MEDITATION WITHOUT MUTTERING

This has three sections, namely, exposition of the meditation (*dhyāna*) of dwelling in the flame, exposition of the meditation of dwelling in the sound, and exposition of the meditation granting freedom at the limit of the sound.

a) Meditation of dwelling in the flame

What type of person has this contemplation? The one who has come to the limit of the contemplation of the six gods has this contemplation.

/ tshul ji ltar bsgom na raṅ lha bsgoms paḥi thugs kar gsal źiṅ ḥbar ba mar me lta buḥi me lce bsgoms paḥi naṅ du bdag gi de kho na ñid rtogs paḥi raṅ gi sems kyi de ñid rnam pa gaṅ bzla bar bya baḥi sṅags kyi sgraḥi rnam par grag par bsgom mo /

/ mthar phyin paḥi tshad ni phyi rol tu bzaḥ btuṅ la loṅs ma spyad kyaṅ / bkres skom gyi gnod pa mi ḥbyuṅ ba daṅ / naṅ du bde drod la brten paḥi tiṅ ṅe ḥdzin skye baḥo /

/ gñis pa ni / raṅ lhar bsgoms paḥi thugs kar zla baḥi dkyil ḥkhor gyi naṅ du raṅ ḥdraḥi lhaḥi sku phra mo źig bsgoms paḥi thugs kar gsal źiṅ ḥbar ba mar me lta bu bsam źiṅ / deḥi naṅ du sṅags kyi sgra grags par bsgom mo / ḥdi ni bzlas brjod daṅ bcas paḥi skabs kyi yi geḥi sgra la dmigs pa daṅ mi ḥdra ste / de śub bu daṅ yid bzlas gaṅ yin ruṅ raṅ gis bzlas paḥi sgra la dmigs pa yin la / ḥdi ni raṅ gis bzlas pa ma yin mar meḥi naṅ du sṅags kyi sgra grag pa la logs nas ñan pa lta bur dmigs pa ste/ me gnas kyi skabs su yaṅ ḥdi daṅ ḥdraḥo /

/ ḥdi yaṅ rnam pa sṅags kyi sgraḥi rnam par grag pa la ṅo bo raṅ gi sems kyi ṅo bor bsgom mo /

/ ḥdi la daṅ po lhaḥi sku la sogs pa rim gyis gsal btab ste / de nas lhaḥi sku la sogs pa gźan rnams yid la mi byed par sgra ḥbaḥ źig la sems ḥdzin pa yin la / me gnas kyi tshe me daṅ sgra gñis la sems ḥdzin pa yin no /

/ mthar phyin paḥi tshad ni / dper na lha bsgoms pa mthar phyin pa na / lha gtso ḥkhor thams cad sku mdog phyag mtshan sogs ma ḥdres par mig gis mṅon sum du mthoṅ ba las kyaṅ gsal ba cig car du ḥchar ba ltar / ḥdi yaṅ mthar phyin pa na sṅags kyi yi geḥi sgra sṅa phyi rim can du ḥchar ba ma yin par rna bas mṅon sum du thos pa las kyaṅ gsal baḥi rnam pa cig car du yid ṅor ḥchar baḥo /

/ de thams cad ni mtshan ma daṅ bcas paḥi rnal ḥbyor ro /

What is the method of contemplation? One contemplates himself as the deity; in his heart he contemplates a tongue of flame, like a bright and blazing butter lamp, and in it he discerns the Self Reality; and he contemplates the aspect of his mind's reality as the tone of the sound of whatever *dhāraṇī* is to be uttered.

The standard for having come to the limit is as follows: When one does not feel the pangs of hunger and thirst, although not partaking of external food or drink, and when one depends on internal warmth and beatitude, the *samādhi* is produced.

(b) Meditation of dwelling in the sound

One contemplates himself as the deity; in his heart, inside the moon-*maṇḍala*, he contemplates a tiny body of the deity, similar to himself. In its heart, he imagines [a flame] like that of a burning butter lamp, and within [the flame], he contemplates the tone of the sounds of the *dhāraṇī*. This is not the same as the dwelling on the sounds of the syllables in the phase attended with muttering. In that case, it was a dwelling on the sounds recited by oneself, whether the recitation be whispered or mental. In the present case, there is no recitation by oneself: one dwells on the tone of the sounds of the *dhāraṇī* within the flame, heard as a bystander. The situation in the phase of dwelling in the flame is also like the present case.

And again the present case, one contemplates its aspect as the tone of the sounds of the *dhāraṇī* and its essence as the essence of one's own mind.

In the present case, one vividly imagines the body of the god, and so on, in sequence. Thereupon, one hold the mind solely on the sound, paying no attention to other objects, such as the body of the god. On the other hand, at the time of dwelling in the flame, one holds the mind on both fire and sound.

The standard for having come to the limit is as follows: For example, when one goes to the limit of the contemplation of a god, the bodies, colors, hand symbols, and so on, of the chief god and of all his retinue become simultaneously more clearly visible than ever when seen without loss of definition before the [ordinary] eye. Likewise in the present case, when one reaches the limit, the sounds of the syllables of the *dhāraṇī* do not appear one after another, but arise in the mind simultaneously, more clearly and distinctly than when heard by the ear as audible sound.

All those [i.e., (1) Meditation with muttering, and (a) and (b) of (2) Meditation without muttering] are *yoga* with signs (*sanimitta-yoga*).

/ gsum pa ni / spyir źi lhag zuṅ ḥbrel gyi tiṅ ṅe ḥdzin pha rol tu phyin paḥi theg pa daṅ / sṅags kyi theg pa gñis kaḥi lam gyi gźuṅ śiṅ lta bu yin la / de la pha rol tu phyin paḥi theg par źi gnas sṅon du bsgrubs nas / mtshan ñid tshaṅ ba grub pa na de la brten nas lhag mthoṅ bsgrubs te / de mtshan ñid tshaṅ ba grub pa na źi lhag zuṅ ḥbrel du ḥgro ba yin la / sṅags kyi rgyud sde bźi po gaṅ las kyaṅ / źi gnas logs su sgrub tshul bśad kyaṅ ma bśad / dgos kyaṅ mi dgos te / lhaḥi rnal ḥbyor bsgoms pa ñid kyis źi gnas mtshan ñid tshaṅ ba ḥgrub pa yin pas /

/ rgyud sde goṅ ma gñis su rags pa daṅ / phra baḥi lhaḥi rnal ḥbyor gñis mthar phyin pa na źi gnas mtshan ñid tshaṅ ba ḥgrub ciṅ / bya spyod gñis su deḥi dod lha drug bsgom pa daṅ / me gnas daṅ sgra gnas kyi bsam gtan mthar phyin pa na ḥgrub ste /

/ sgra nas kyi bsam gtan bsgoms paḥi raṅ stobs kyis lus sems śin tu sbyaṅs pa dṅos su ḥdren thub pa na źi gnas mtshan ñid tshaṅ ba grub pa yin no /

/ bya spyod la sku phyag rgya chen po bsgom pa / gsuṅ sṅags bsgom pa / thugs de kho na ñid bsgom pa gsum las /

/ daṅ po ni / lha drug bsgom paḥo /

/ gñis pa ni / bzlas pa daṅ bcas paḥi bsam gtan gyi skabs kyi sṅags kyi yi geḥi sgra la dmigs pa daṅ / yi geḥi gzugs la dmigs pa rnams kyaṅ yin mod kyi / dṅos gźi ni me daṅ sgra la dmigs paḥi bsam gtan gñis kyi skabs kyi sṅags kyi sgra la dmigs paḥo /

/ gsum pa ni / thugs de kho na ñid la dmigs pa daṅ / mtshan ma med paḥi rnal ḥbyor daṅ / sgra gnas kyi bsam gtan gyi mthaḥ ste / rjes su chos skuḥi rigs ḥdraḥi rgyu stoṅ ñid bsgoms pas / chos skuḥi thar pa ster bas sgra mthar thar pa ster baḥi bsam gtan te de gsum don gcig go /

[33] In the Anuttara Tantra, the two *yogas* are covered in the 'Steps of Production (*utpatti-krama*). 'Rough' then means the rough visualization of the limbs of the deity (lhaḥi yan lag rags par snaṅ ba tsam mṅon sum, *Sṅags rim chen mo*, 350a-3); or "Here, the 'rough' form is the god(s) arranged in the *maṇḍala*; and the 'fine' form is the deity arranged in their eye and other [bodily locations]" (ḥdir rags pa ni dkyil ḥkhor la bkod paḥi lha yin la phra ba ni de dag gi mig la sogs pa bkod paḥi lhaḥo, *Sṅags rim chen mo*, 350b-2, 3).

[34] Buddhaguhya (Toh. 2670), Thu, 26b-7, describes the meditation this way: "The expression 'granting freedom at the limit of the sound' should be considered. The previously mentioned 'limit of the sound' is silence (**niḥśabda*); when one dwells solely on the sound of the *mantra* and then releases it, there is the limit of the sound. The meditation is the mindfulness that the *mantra* at the limit of the sound has granted the freedom abiding in the intrinsic nature of the Dharmakāya" (sgra mthar thar pa ster ba ñid / ces gsuṅs pa de brtag par byaḥo / de la goṅ du smos paḥi sgraḥi mthaḥ ni sgra med pa ste / gsaṅ sṅags kyi sgra tsam la gnas pa yoṅs su btaṅ ba ni sgraḥi mthaḥ / sgraḥi mthaḥ der gsaṅ sṅags kyi chos kyi skuḥi raṅ bźin du gnas pa rnam par thar pa ster ba dran pa ni bsams paḥo).

(c) Meditation granting freedom at the limit of the sound

In general, the *samādhi* in which Calming (*śamatha*) and Higher Vision (*vipaśyanā*) are combined together (*yuganaddha*) is the backbone, so to say, of the path of both the Pāramitā-yāna and Mantra-yāna. Of those, in the Pāramitā-yāna, having first developed Calming and having attained in full measure its characteristics, one develops, on the basis of that, Higher Vision. Having attained in full measure the characteristics of the latter, one proceeds to Calming and Higher Vision combined together. However, in none of the four Tantra divisions is the method of accomplishing explained in terms of Calming, nor is that necessary, because by the contemplation itself of the *yoga* of the deity, one develops the complete characteristics of Calming.

Thus, in the two higher Tantras [i.e., the Yoga and Anuttara] one accomplishes the complete characteristics of Calming when reaching the limit of the two *yogas* of the deity, the rough and the fine.[33] The equivalent to that in the Kriyā-Caryā is the accomplishment [of those complete characteristics] when contemplating the six gods and when reaching the limit of the meditations of dwelling in the flame and dwelling in the sound.

If, through one's own power of contemplation in the meditation of dwelling in the sound, one is able to attract in actuality the physical and mental cathartic (*kāya-praśrabdhi* and *citta-praśrabdhi*), one accomplishes the complete characteristics of Calming.

In the Kriyā-Caryā one contemplates the body as the Great Seal (*mahāmudrā*), speech as Incantation (*dhāraṇī*), and mind as Reality (*tattva*).

Body as the Great Seal: This is the contemplation of the six gods.

Speech as Incantation: This is the meditative object in the sounds of the syllables of the Incantation, and the meditative object in the form of the syllables, in the phase of meditation attended with muttering. However, the main part is the meditative object in the sounds of the Incantation in the phases of meditation of dwelling in the flame and meditation of dwelling in the sound.

Mind as Reality: This is [the three things, *viz.*] the meditative object in the Reality of the mind, the *yoga* without signs, and the limit of the meditation of dwelling in the sound. Because it constitutes the contemplation of voidness which is the basis of the affiliation with the Dharmakāya at a subsequent time, it grants the freedom of the Dharmakāya, and thus is the meditation which grants freedom at the limit of the sound.[34] That being so, those three are identical.

/ de la mtshan ma daṅ bcas paḥi bsam gtan mthar phyin kyaṅ / de dag la ḥkhor baḥi rtsa ba bcod paḥi dṅos gñen med pas / ḥkhor baḥi rtsa ba gcod pa la mtshan ma med paḥi rnal ḥbyor dgos so / de bsgom pa na lhaḥi sku la sogs pa kun rdzob paḥi rnam pa gaṅ yaṅ mi bsgom par stoṅ pa ñid kyi dpyad sgom daṅ ḥjog sgom la mkhas par byas nas man ṅag bźin du bsgom mo / de bsgoms paḥi raṅ stobs kyis lus sems śin sbyaṅs dṅos su ḥdren thub pa na / lhag mthoṅ mtshan ñid tshaṅ ba grub pa yin no /

/ gsum pa bsñen pa las su ruṅ nas dṅos grub sgrub paḥi tshul ni / śes rab daṅ / tshe ḥphel ba la sogs pa źi rgyas daṅ / drag poḥi las sgrub paḥi sṅon du bsñen pa btaṅ ste / de nas las la sbyar dgos te / ḥdi ni rgyud sde bźi gaḥi lugs so /

/ de la tshe bskal chen maṅ po thub pa la sogs paḥi dṅos grub chen po rnams sgrub pa la ni / mtshan bcas daṅ / mtshan med kyi rnal ḥbyor gñis ka mthar phyin pa dgos kyi / nad źi ba daṅ gdon źi ba sogs kyi dṅos grub sgrub pa la ni de tsam mi dgos so /

/ źi ba daṅ rgyas pa daṅ / drag poḥi las ni rim pa bźin du / de bźin gśegs paḥi rigs daṅ / padmaḥi rigs daṅ / rdo rjeḥi rigs kyis bsgrub ste / dṅos grub mchog daṅ / ḥbriṅ daṅ / tha ma yaṅ de ltar bsgrub bo / rigs gsum po re re la yaṅ dṅos grub rab ḥbriṅ tha ma gsum gsum daṅ / źi rgyas daṅ drag po gsum gsum yod pas / raṅ raṅ gi rigs kyi bdag po daṅ / rigs kyi yum daṅ / rigs kyi khro bos źi sogs gsum byaḥo /

/ dṅos grub gsum du ḥbyed lugs la sgo maṅ ste / ṅo boḥi sgo nas ni rig ḥdzin daṅ / mṅon śes daṅ / bstan bcos kun śes pa sogs ni rab bo / mi snaṅ ba daṅ bcud len daṅ / rkaṅ mgyogs sogs ni ḥbriṅ ṅo / gźan dbaṅ du ḥdu ba daṅ bsad bskrad sogs ni tha maḥo /

[35] The two Tibetan terms are employed by Tsoṅ-kha-pa in his *Lam rim chen mo*, especially in the *śamatha* section. The first (*dpyad sgom*) is deliberative insight, and the second (*ḥjog sgom*) is the stoppage of the mind on a sole object or single area of thought.

[36] By service, Mkhas grub rje has already indicated that he means the four members of muttering. When he states below that one must also accomplish the *yoga* without signs for the great magical talents (*siddhi*), it might be inferred that meditation without muttering can be considered a type of service. In the Anuttara Tantra there are two kinds of service according to the *Guhyasamāja-tantra*. In the last chapter of the Sanskrit text, which is called the *Uttaratantra* and published as a separate work in the Tibetan translation (Toh. 443; the *Mūlatantra* is Toh. 442), there is this verse (p. 162, lines 18-19): / sāmānyottamabhedena sevā tu dvividhā bhavet / vajracatuṣkeṇa sāmānyam uttamaṃ jñānāmṛtena ca /. However, as the verse is quoted in Tibetan translation in the *Sṅags rim chen mo* (129b-4), with concluding line *mchog ni yan lag drug gis so*, it appears that *jñānāmṛtena* is a corruption for *ṣaḍaṅgena*; and the verse is translated accordingly: "By the varieties of common and superior, service is of two kinds — common by the diamond quaternion, superior by the six members." The

Even when one reaches the limit of the meditations with signs he is still without the basic antidote that eradicates the root of the 'cycle of transmigration' (*saṃsāra*). For eradicating the root of *saṃsāra*, one must have the *yoga* without signs (*animitta-yoga*). In the latter contemplation, one does not contemplate any conventional aspect, such as the body of a god, but contemplates according to the precepts through becoming skilled in the analyzing contemplation (*dpyad sgom*) and the stoppage contemplation (*hjog sgom*) of voidness.[35] If, through one's own power of contemplation in that manner, one is able to attract in actuality the physical and mental cathartic, one accomplishes the complete characteristics of Higher Vision.

(3) ACCOMPLISHMENT OF SIDDHI AFTER APPROPRIATE SERVICE

It is the method in all four Tantra divisions that before one accomplishes the rites [called] Appeasing, Prosperity, and Terrible, with [their attendant *siddhi*, of the varieties] 'insight', 'prolongation of life', and so on, one must first enact the service (*sevā*)[36] and then attend to the rites.

Thus, for accomplishing the great *siddhis*, such as prolonging life through many great aeons (*mahākalpa*), one must reach the limit of both the *yoga* with signs and the *yoga* without signs; but for accomplishing the *siddhis* of allaying illness and allaying demons, etc., that much is not necessary.

Appeasing, Prosperity, and Terrible rites (*karma*) are accomplished in that order by, respectively, the Tathāgata Family, the Padma Family, and the Vajra Family. In the same order, one accomplishes superior, middling, and lower *siddhis*. Moreover, as in each of the three Families there are all three of the *siddhis* called superior, middling and lower, as well as all three of the rites called Appeasing, Prosperity, and Terrible, one performs the three rites of Appeasing, etc. by means of the Master of the Family, Mother of the Family, and Wrathful One of the Family, respectively, in each of the Families.

There are many ways of distributing the *siddhis* among the three classes. Classified according to their nature, 'wisdom holding' (*vidyādhara*), supernormal faculties (*abhijñā*), and perfect comprehension of the *śāstras* (technical treatises), are superior. Invisibility, vigour, and swiftness of foot, are middling. Subjecting others to one's will, killing, and frightening, are lower.

---

two kinds of service are prevalent respectively on the Steps of Production and the Steps of Completion.

/ rtags kyi sgo nas ni rdzas ḥbar ba daṅ / du ba ḥthul ba daṅ dro ba las gsum mo /

/ gźi las ni / lus kyi daṅ rdzas kyi daṅ loṅs spyod kyi dṅos grub bo /

/ gsuṅ ba poḥi sgo nas ni ḥphags pa daṅ / lha daṅ / sa bla baḥi sṅags so /

/ dṅos grub ster ba po mchog yin yaṅ sgrub pa pos legs par ma ḥbad paḥi bsñen pa las dṅos grub tha ma stsol ba yaṅ yod la / legs par bsñen na ni tha mas kyaṅ gźan la bslaṅs nas dṅos grub mchog ster ba yaṅ yod do /

/ rmi lam cho ga bźin brtags pa na / rmi lam du dkon mchog gsum daṅ / raṅ gi lha daṅ / byaṅ sems daṅ ḥkhor rnam bźi daṅ / ri daṅ glaṅ po daṅ / ḥbab chu daṅ nor daṅ / gos rñed pa sogs dgaḥ baḥi rmi lam rmis na sgrub pa brtsam par byaḥo /

/ lhaḥi rnal ḥbyor gyi skabs su bkres pa chuṅ ba daṅ nad las thar pa daṅ / śes pa khyad par can ḥbyuṅ ba daṅ / lhag par gzi mdaṅs che źiṅ brtan pa daṅ / rmi lam bzaṅ źiṅ bden pa rmi ba daṅ / bzlas brjod la dgaḥ ru soṅ ba daṅ / ṅal ba chuṅ źiṅ dri źim po bro ba daṅ / yon tan lhur len pa daṅ / lha la gus pa cher soṅ na bzlas sgom gnad du soṅ baḥi rtags su legs grub las bśad la /

/ bsam gtan phyi ma las / ma dad pa daṅ sñoms las daṅ / bkres skom gyi zil gyis non pa daṅ rgod pa daṅ yid kyi gduṅ ba che ba daṅ / las la the tshom za ba daṅ bzlas brjod daṅ / bsam gtan la mi źen pa daṅ / cal col gyi gtan la dgaḥ ba daṅ / bya ba min pa la ḥjug pa daṅ / gdon gyis brlams pa daṅ / rmi lam ṅan pa rmi ba sogs ni lha gźan du phyogs paḥi rgyu daṅ / chags sdaṅ daṅ / rgyags pa daṅ / sgyu la sogs pa źi ba daṅ / bzlas brjod la yid rgyun ldan du gnas pa ni lha mṅon du phyogs paḥi rgyur gsuṅs so /

[37] These omens are mentioned in the *Mañjuśrī-mūla-tantra* (S. 291.20 = T. 225a-4; S. 318.25 ff. = T. 244b-1 ff.), with the Sanskrit terms respectively, *jvalita*, *dhūma*, and *uṣma*.

[38] The translation 'earth-bound' is consistent with the pronouncer of the lowest type of incantation aiming at an occult power; it is also consistent with one of the Sino-Japanese equivalents for *bhauma* given in Shūki Yoshimura, *Chibetto-go Jiteṇ. Sōkō-han* (Kyoto, 1955-56), p. 1005.

Classified by their omens, the three types occur after blazing substance, rising smoke, and warmth.[37]

Classified by their bases, there are the *siddhis* of [one's own] body, of [ritual] substances, and of possessions (*bhoga*).

Classified by their pronouncers, there are the Incantations (*dhāraṇī*) of the nobility (*ārya*), of the gods (*deva*), and of the earth-bound (*bhauma*).[38]

Although the bestower of *siddhi* be of highest rank, he may even grant lower *siddhi* because the one who accomplishes did not serve with the proper exertion. If one serves well, then even a low ranking deity, having petitioned other [higher ranking ones], may grant superior *siddhi*.

How is a dream interpreted ritually? When in a dream one has a joyful dream of the Three Jewels [i.e., the Buddha, Dharma, and Saṅgha], one's own deity (*svadevatā*), the Bodhisattvas and the fourfold congregation (*catuḥpariṣad*) [i.e., lay Buddhists, novices, postulants, and monks (and nuns)]; mountains, elephants, cascades, the obtaining of riches and clothing, and so on, he should exert himself toward the accomplishment.

The *Susiddhi* explains that when one is in the phase of *yoga* of the deity, these are the omens that his muttering and contemplation are succeeding: trifling hunger, freedom from illness, outstanding awareness, great and strong nimbus (*tejas*), good dreams and prophetic dreams, rapture during the muttering, negligible fatigue, emission of fragrant odors, earnest application to acquiring merit, deep reverance toward the deity.

The *Dhyānottara* explains the causes for departure of the deity to be these: lack of faith, slothfulness, discomfiture by hunger and thirst, distraction, downheartedness, doubts concerning the rite, disinclination toward the muttering and meditation, delight in idle talk, prohibited pursuits, demonic obsession, the dreaming of bad dreams, and so on; and explains the causes for approach of the deity to be these: the allaying of craving, hatred, pride, deceit, and so on, and the continuous dwelling of the mind in the muttering.

/ gñis pa spyod paḥi rgyud kyi rnam gźag la gñis / rgyud kyi dbye ba bstan pa daṅ / lam gyi rim pa la slob paḥi tshul lo /

/ daṅ po ni / spyod rgyud kyi rgyud thams cad kyi gtso bo ni rnam par snaṅ mdzad mṅon par byaṅ chub paḥi rgyud yin la / de gsuṅ pa po gaṅ gis gnas gaṅ du gsuṅs na / rgyal ba śā-kya thub pa ḥdiḥi loṅs spyod rdzogs paḥi sku rnam par snaṅ mdzad gaṅ chen mtshos gźi daṅ sñiṅ po me tog gis brgyan paḥi ḥjig rten gyi khams kyi ḥog min stug po bkod paḥi gnas su gsuṅs te / de la gźi daṅ sñiṅ po me tog gis brgyan paḥi ḥjig rten gyi khams kyi bkod pa phyag na rdo rje dbaṅ bskur baḥi rgyud las rags rim gsuṅs śiṅ / saṅs rgyas phal po che las rgyas par gsuṅs te /

/ de la gliṅ bźi baḥi ḥjig rten gyi khams bye ba phrag brgya bsdoms pa la stoṅ gsum gyi stoṅ chen poḥi ḥjig rten gyi khams gcig go / de bye ba phrag brgya bsdoms pa la gźi daṅ sñiṅ po me tog gis brgyan paḥi ḥjig rten gyi khams kyi rgyud gcig go / de bye ba phrag brgya bsdoms pa la deḥi rgyud bar ma gcig go / de bye ba phrag brgya bsdoms pa la deḥi rgyud rab ḥbyams gcig go / de bye ba phrag bsdoms pa la gźi daṅ sñiṅ po me tog gis brgyan paḥi ḥjig rten gyi khams kyi bkod pa ste / de yoṅs su rdzogs paḥo /

[1] Buddhaguhya's extended commentary on the *Mahāvairocana-tantra* (Toh. 2663, the *Ḥgrel bśad*) states in the commentary on the first chapter that of the four bodies of the Buddha, two do not teach, namely, the Dharma-kāya and the body residing in the *bodhicitta*. By the blessing (*adhiṣṭhāna*) of those, the other two bodies, the Saṃbhoga-kāya and Nirmāṇa-kāya, teach the Dharma. The first two bodies are beyond speech, the other two, expressive. To use the terminology of Junjiro Takakusu, *The Essentials of Buddhist Philosophy*, 2d ed. (Honolulu, 1949), p. 149, the first two are the Buddha's *static* aspect, the other two his *dynamic* aspect. The Diamond Realm (*vajra-dhātu*) and Nature Realm (*dharma-dhātu*) correspond, respectively, to these two aspects. These two realms are represented symbolically by the two chief *maṇḍalas* of the Japanese Shingon Sect. Buddhaguhya explains in the same place that *dharma* is of two kinds: *dharma* of full comprehension and *dharma* of scripture (*rtogs paḥi chos daṅ luṅ gi chos*). The *dharma* of full comprehension is, in turn, of two kinds: supreme (*paramārtha*) and conventional (*saṃvṛti*). The supreme kind has the characteristic of thusness, the void intrinsic nature. The conventional *dharma* is the per-

CHAPTER FIVE

2. FUNDAMENTALS OF THE CARYĀ TANTRA

There are two parts: the varieties of the Tantra, and method of studying the steps of the path.

a. *The varieties of the Tantra*

The chief of all Tantras of the Caryā Tantra class is the *Mahāvairocana-abhisaṃbodhi-tantra* (Toh. 494). By whom was it preached, and where? It was preached by Vairocana, the Body of Complete Enjoyment (*saṃbhoga-kāya*)[1] of the Victor Śākyamuni, by the lake of the snowy range in the Akaniṣṭha Ghanavyūha of the worldly realms (*lokadhātu*) called Kusumatalagarbhālaṃkāra ("Adornment with flowery floors and inner chambers").[2] The general features of a wordly realm Kusumatalagarbhālaṃkāra are stated in the *Vajrapāṇy-abhiṣeka-tantra* (Toh. 496); an extensive description is found in the *Buddhāvataṃsaka* (Toh. 44, chapter eight).

There, 1000^3 of worldly realms of the four continents constitute a 1000^3 system called *Trisāhasramahāsāhasra* worldly realms. 1000^3 of those taken together are a single series of the worldly realm Kusumatalagarbhālaṃkāra. 1000^3 of those taken together are a single medium series. 1000^3 of those taken together are a single wide-spread series. 1000^3 of those taken together are an array (*vyūha*) of worldly realms Kusumatalagarbhālaṃkāra. That takes in everything.

---

vasion of the three realms (desire, form, and formless) by the Tathāgata's Body Speech, and Mind. It is basic to the Tantras that men *affiliate* with those three mysteries of the Buddha by means of finger gestures (*mudrā*), incantations (*dhāraṇī*), and profound concentration (*samādhi*). The object is to merge one's stream of consciousness (*citta-saṃtati*) with that of a Bodhisattva of the tenth stage in the retinue of the Saṃbhoga-kāya (cf. Chapter I, p. 21, above) and thus to receive the teaching of the Saṃbhoga-kāya.

[2] The Sanskrit expression Kusumatalagarbhālaṃkāra is drawn from the *Gaṇḍavyūha*, p. 396.21, Kusumatalagarbhavyūhālaṃkāra, translated into Tibetan, Derge Kg., Phal Chen, Vol. A, 229a-2, gźi daṅ sñiṅ po me tog gi rgyan gyis brgyan pa.

/ rgyud ḥdi de bźin gśegs paḥi rigs kyi rgyud yin te ḥdi las rnam par snaṅ mdzad kyi dkyil ḥkhor gźal yas khaṅ sum rim / gtso boḥi źal nub sgo la gzigs pa gcig gis thog draṅs paḥi dkyil ḥkhor gsum ston no / deḥi rgyud phyi ma źig kyaṅ yod de / de las kyaṅ dkyil ḥkhor gñis tsam ston no /

/ spyod rgyud kyi padmaḥi rigs kyi rgyud bod du ma ḥgyur ro /

/ rdo rjeḥi rigs la phyag na rdo rje mṅon par dbaṅ bskur baḥi rgyud ni rtsod med do / phyag na rdo rje gos sṅon can gyi rgyud daṅ / rdo rje sa ḥog gi rgyud la sogs pa la bu ston rin po che la sogs pas the tshom gyi gnas su mdzad do /

/ gñis pa la bźi / lam bsgom paḥi snod du ruṅ bar bya baḥi phyir dbaṅ bskur ba daṅ / snod du gyur nas dam tshig daṅ sdom pa dag par bya ba daṅ / dam tshig la gnas nas sṅon du bsñen pa ji ltar bya ba daṅ / bsñen pa las su ruṅ nas dṅos grub ji ltar bsgrub paḥo / daṅ po gñis ni bya rgyud daṅ thun moṅ pa yin pas bśad zin to /

/ gsum la gñis / mtshan ma daṅ bcas paḥi rnal ḥbyor daṅ / mtshan ma med paḥi rnal ḥbyor ro / deḥi daṅ po ni stoṅ ñid kyis ma zin paḥi lhaḥi rnal ḥbyor yin źiṅ / gñis pa ni stoṅ ñid kyis zin paḥi lhaḥi rnal ḥbyor la byaḥi / stoṅ ñid rkyaṅ ba bsgom pa la mi bya ste / stoṅ ñid rkyaṅ pa bsgoms pas ḥtshaṅ mi rgya źiṅ / mtshan ma med paḥi rnal ḥbyor gyis dṅos grub gñis ka mi ḥgrub par gsuṅs pas so / mtshan bcas kyi rnal ḥbyor bsgom paḥi sṅon du stoṅ ñid bsgom pa btaṅ yaṅ de tsam gyis mtshan med kyi rnal ḥbyor du mi ḥgroḥo /

/ mtshan ma daṅ bcas paḥi rnal ḥbyor la gñis / phyiḥi yan lag bźiḥi bzlas brjod daṅ / naṅ gi yan lag bźiḥi bzlas brjod do /

/ daṅ po ni / raṅ gi sems raṅ bźin gyis grub pas stoṅ par gtan la phab

[3] The three tiers are presumably the Body, Speech, and Mind of the Tathāgata. Accordingly, the eaved and storied palace represents the Nature Realm (*dharma-dhātu*), as in note 1, above.

[4] Kloṅ rdol Bla ma states (Dza, 10a-7) that the Continuation Tantra is Chapter Seven in the edition of the Basic Tantra: deḥi rgyud phyi ma rim par phye ba ḥam leḥu bdun pa.

[5] Discussed in Chap. IV, above, pp. 141-55.

[6] The two kinds are explained in Tsoṅ-kha-pa's *Sṅags rim chen mo*, Peking ed., 86a-4, by a quotation from the *Mahāvairocana-tantra*: "O Master of the secret folk (*guhyakādhipati*), there are two kinds of divine form (or: form of the gods): pure and impure. The pure one has the nature of full comprehension and is free from all image. The impure one is the form attended with image; it has color and shape. By means of the two kinds of divine form, two kinds of requirements are fulfilled. By the one attended with image, the magical talent (*siddhi*) attended with image arises; by the one free from image, the magical talent free from image." The two kinds of yoga are of course involved respectively with the two kinds of divine form.

[7] By "both *siddhis*" Mkhas grub rje has in mind the ones attended with image and the ones free from image, as per the preceding note.

This [Mahāvairocana] Tantra is a Tantra of the Tathāgata Family. It describes three *maṇḍalas*, beginning with the one in which the face of the Lord is turned toward the West gate — (the three) constituting three tiers of the storied-palace (*kūṭāgāra*) in the *maṇḍala* of Vairocana.[3] There is also a Tantra Continuation, which, however, describes only two *maṇḍalas*.[4]

No Tantras of the Padma Family in the Caryā Tantra class have been translated into Tibetan.

In the Vajra Family, there is no controversy concerning the *Vajrapāṇy-abhiṣeka-tantra* (Toh. 496). But such works as the *Nīlāmbaradhara-vajrapāṇi-tantra* (Toh. 498) and the *Vajrapātāla-tantra* (Toh. 499) were viewed with suspicion by Bu ston Rin po che and others.

b. *Method of studying the steps of the path*

There are four parts: initiation (*abhiṣeka*) given for the sake of making one a fit receptacle for intense contemplation of the path; purification of the vows (*saṃvara*) and pledges (*samaya*); procedure of preliminary service (*pūrva-sevā*) after being committed to the pledges; manner of accomplishing *siddhis* after aptitude in the service. The first two parts because shared with the Kriyā Tantra, have already been discussed.[5]

(1) PROCEDURE OF PRELIMINARY SERVICE AFTER BEING COMMITTED TO THE PLEDGES

There are two phases: Yoga with images; Yoga without images. The first of these is the yoga of the deity not governed by voidness; the second, the yoga of the deity governed by voidness.[6] However, one should not contemplate only voidness, because one does not become a Buddha by merely contemplating voidness: it is explained that one does not accomplish both *siddhis* by means of the Yoga without images.[7] Moreover, if someone enacts the contemplation of voidness prior to the contemplation of Yoga with images, with that alone he does not pass into Yoga without images.

(a) **Yoga with images (sanimitta-yoga)**

This has two sections: Muttering, consisting of four external members; Muttering, consisting of four internal members.

Muttering, consisting of four external members

One contemplates the inseparability of the 'Self Reality' (*ātma-tattva)*

paḥi bdag gi de kho na ñid daṅ / lhaḥi gnas lugs raṅ bźin gyis grub pas stoṅ paḥi lhaḥi de kho na ñid gñis dbyer mi phyed par bsgoms paḥi stoṅ paḥi ṅaṅ las raṅ gi sems zlą baḥi dkyil ḥkhor gyi rnam par bsgom mo / deḥi steṅ du oṃ yig gser gyi mdog can bsam / de las ḥod kyi spro bsdu byas ḥdus yoṅ su gyur pa las / raṅ ñid rnam par snaṅ mdzad chen po źal gcig phyag gñis mñam gźag gi phyag rgya mdzad pa / sku gser gyi mdog can ḥbar baḥi phreṅ bas ḥkhrigs pa / padma dkar po daṅ zla baḥi gdan la bźugs pa / dbu rgyan daṅ thor tshugs can / dar laḥi stod gYogs daṅ / smad gYogs bsnams par bskyed pa ni bdag gi gźiḥo / skad cig gis dkroṅ skyed byed paḥaṅ bśad do /

/ de nas raṅ gi mdun du raṅ ḥdraḥi de bźin gśegs pa bsgom ste gźan gyi gźiḥo /

/ deḥi thugs kar raṅ gi sems zla baḥi dkyil ḥkhor gyi rnam par bsgom pa ni sems la gźol baḥi gźiḥo /

/ deḥi steṅ du bzlas byaḥi sṅags kyi yi ge dgod pa ni sgra la gźol baḥo / de la dmigs nas śub bu daṅ yid kyi bzlas pa bya źiṅ lha la sems ḥdzin pa daṅ / yid bzlas kyi tshe srog rtsol bsdams nas bya ba ni bya rgyud kyi skabs daṅ ḥdra la / de la bzlas paḥi graṅs ni ḥbum mo /

/ gñis pa ni stoṅ paḥi ṅaṅ las / A Ā Aṃ Aḥ / bźi gaṅ ruṅ las sṅar ltar bskyed paḥam / yaṅ na rgyal ba śā-kya thub par bskyed de / bdag gi gźiḥo / deḥi thugs kar zla baḥi dkyil ḥkhor yoṅs su dag pa me loṅ ṅos gñis pa lta bu bsam ste / de la brtan pa thob pa raṅ gi lus lhaḥi lus su mthoṅ gi bar du bsgom par gsuṅs so /

/ zla baḥi naṅ du sṅar bśad pa lta buḥi rnam snaṅ bsgom ste gźan gyi gźiḥo /

/ deḥi thugs kar bdag gi sems zla baḥi dkyil ḥkhor gyi rnam par bsam ste sems la gźol baḥo /

/ deḥi steṅ du sṅags kyi yi ge bsam ste sgra la gźol baḥo / de la yaṅ bzlas brjod gñis bya ba daṅ srog rtsol bsdam pa sṅar bźin bya ste / bzlas brjod ḥbum phrag gcig go /

[8] Cf. the *Mahāvastu* in the selection of Franklin Edgerton, *Buddhist Hybrid Sanskrit Reader* (New Haven, Conn., 1953), p. 31: "risen like a pillar of jewels" and "rising like a second sun" (ratanayūpam iva abhyudgato ... dvitīyaṃ ādityam iva udayantam).

[9] See above, pp. 173-4.

— wherein one concludes that one's own mind is void of intrinsic nature (*svabhāva-siddhi*), from the 'Deity Reality' (*devatā-tattva*) — wherein one [concludes that] the ultimate state of the deity is void of intrinsic nature. And one contemplates one's own mind under the aspect of the moon-disk in the realm of the void. On the moon-disk he imagines the syllable *Oṃ* in golden color, emitting beams of light. He gathers them together and from their metamorphosis is himself generated into Vairocana with one face and two hands, making the seal of equipoise (*samāpatti-mudrā*), his gold-colored body wrapt by a blazing garland and seated on a cushion of a white lotus and a moon. He has head ornaments and chignon and is attired in upper and lower monk's garb of silk. This is the 'Subjective Ground' (*bdag gi gźi*). It is also called the 'momentary reproduction risen (**abhyudita*)'.[8]

Thereupon he contemplates the Tathāgata, like himself, in front of himself. This is the 'Objective Ground' (*gźan gyi gźi*).

The intense contemplation of his own mind in the shape of a moon-disk within the [Tathāgata's] heart is the 'Ground Immersed in the Heart' (*sems la gźol baḥi gźi*).

The arrangement on that [moon-disk] of the syllables of the *dhāraṇī* to be recited is the 'Immersion in Sound' (*sgra la gźol ba*). Dwelling on that, he makes the whispered and mental recitation while holding his mind on the deity. While reciting mentally he must bind the *prāṇa* and *āyāma* as in the case of the Kriyā Tantra.[9] The recitation is to be made 100,000 times.

Muttering, consisting of four internal members

From the sphere of the void, one generates as before [a deity] or the Victor Śākyamuni from any of the four letters A, Ā, Aṃ, Aḥ. This is the 'Subjective Ground'. It is taught that in the heart of that [deity] he imagines an unblemished moon-disk like a mirror with two surfaces. He fixes [his attention] on it, contemplating his own body until he sees it as the body of the deity.

He intensely contemplates Vairocana on the moon, as described before. This is the 'Objective Ground'.

In the heart [of Vairocana] he imagines his own mind in the shape of a moon-disk. This is the 'Immersion in the heart'.

On it he imagines the syllables of the *dhāraṇī*. This is the 'Immersion in Sound'. Here, too, the two kinds of recitation and the binding of the *prāṇa* and *āyāma* are the same as before. Recitation is to be performed 100,000 times.

/ gñis pa mtshan ma med paḥi rnal ḥbyor ni / chos thams cad raṅ bźin gyis grub pas stoṅ par gcig tu bral sogs kyi rigs pas ṅes par byas paḥi ṅes śes kyi rgyun goms par byed pa yin la /

/ de bsgom paḥi lag rjes la / mtshan bcas kyi rnal ḥbyor mthar phyin pa las lhaḥi sku mṅon sum bźin du yid ṅor gsal ba de ñid / blo kha phyogs pa tsam gyis rtsol med du snaṅ stoṅ tshogs pa sgyu ma lta buḥi lhaḥi skur ḥchar baḥi lhag mthoṅ mtshan ñid tshaṅ ba ḥdren thub kyi bar du bsgom mo /

/ de ltar mtshan med kyi rnal ḥbyor bsgom paḥi tshul rgyas par rnam snaṅ mṅon byaṅ daṅ / deḥi ḥgrel pa slob dpon saṅs rgyas gsaṅ bas mdzad paḥi bsdus ḥgrel las gsuṅs te / dbu ma sgom rim daṅ yaṅ mthun no /

/ gsum pa bsñen pa las su ruṅ nas / dṅos grub bsgrub paḥi tshul ni / ral gri la sogs pa phyi rdzas la brten nas / ral griḥi rig pa ḥdzin pa sogs bsgrub pa daṅ / naṅ gi lus kyi gnas rnams su sa chu mi rluṅ gi dkyil ḥkhor bsgoms nas / źi rgyas la sogs paḥi las bsgrub pa daṅ / ḥjam dpal la sogs paḥi sgrub pa byas nas / byaṅ sems de dag gis mgo la ñug paḥam /

[10] For *manas*-face and *buddhi*-side, consider the previous remark about "a mirror with two surfaces". This terminology seems to be consistent with Kashmir Śaivism's description of *buddhi* as a two-sided mirror: cf. K. C. Pandey, *Abhinavagupta; an Historical and Philosophical Study* (Benares, 1935), p. 252. In the latter system, one side of the *buddhi*-mirror reflects external objects, such as a jar seen by the eyes, at the time of perception. The other side of the *buddhi*-mirror reflects the revived residual traces (*saṃskāra*), as in remembrance and the dream state. In the present Buddhist nomenclature, the first side of the *buddhi* is called the *manas*-face; the reverse side of the *buddhi*, the *buddhi*-side. Hence, the limit of Yoga with images is still involved with the first side of the "mirror" but with eidetic or "realistic" imagery. Thereafter, Yoga without images is involved with the reverse, or inward-directed, side, on which one cognizes things as arising dream-like or as void — to use Mahāyāna Buddhist language. The first kind of Yoga is thus equivalent to the non-tantric Buddhist terminology of *śamatha*, "calming", or *samādhi* with a single area of thought. This *samādhi* leaves an impression or "signature", which becomes the motivating impression, a *samādhi-saṃskāra*, for the second kind of Yoga, which cognizes the illusion and is thus equivalent to the non-tantric Buddhist terminology of *vipaśyanā*, "higher vision".

[11] The implications of the foregoing note and Mkhas grub rje's present statement is that success in Yoga with images and in Yoga without images attracts, respectively, the complete characteristics of calming (*śamatha*) and of higher vision (*vipaśyanā*). Hence, these two Yogas attain the aims of non-tantric Buddhist meditation while not employing the specific procedures of orthodox Buddhism. It is not obvious if Mkhas-grub-rje has in mind a particular definition when he refers to the "complete characteristics of higher vision". However, in consideration of Tsoṅ-kha-pa's *Lam rim chen mo*, especially the meditative section (*śamatha*), the complete characteristics of calming would certainly include the cathartic of body and of mind (*kāyacittapraśrabdhi*). The complete characteristics of higher vision would require the complete characteristics of calming as a base (hence the *samādhi-saṃskāra* alluded to in the foregoing note) and would include the full comprehension of both the supreme and the conventional (as alluded to in note 1, above).

(b) **Yoga without images (animitta-yoga)**

This is the habituation in the decisive knowledge that concludes through higher cognition that all things (*sarvadharmāḥ*) are void and not isolated, as regards accomplishment by intrinsic nature.

The "signature" (*lag rjes*) of that intense contemplation is the transfiguration of the body of the deity on the *manas*-face (*yid ṅo*) as though before the eyes, after reaching the limit of Yoga with images. And when he contemplates in the manner by which that brightness appears only on the *buddhi*-side (*blo kha phyogs pa*)[10] without leaving it, and the body of the deity appears to be like the illusion of a void accumulation, he is able to attract the complete characteristics of higher vision (*vipaśyanā*).[11]

The method of intense contemplation in Yoga without images is explained intensively in the above way by the *Vairocana* (Toh. 494) as well as in the concise commentary (the *Piṇḍārtha*, Toh. 2662) by Buddhaguhya. Moreover, it is consistent with the Mādhyamika *Bhāvanā-krama*.[12]

(2) MANNER OF ACCOMPLISHING SIDDHIS AFTER APTITUDE IN THE SERVICE

In this Tantra it is set forth that by taking recourse to external materials such as the sword (*khaḍga*), one accomplishes the [*siddhi*] *khaḍga-vidyādhara*,[13] and so forth; that by contemplating intensely the earth, water, fire, and wind *maṇḍalas* at their positions within the body,[14] one accomplishes the rites of Appeasing, Increasing, and so forth; that by

---

[12] By *Bhāvanā-krama*, Mkhas grub presumably refers to all three works of that title by Kamalaśīla (Toh. 3915-3917). Tibetan tradition holds that Kamalaśīla was following the Mādhyamika position. In the Caryā Tantra section of Tsoṅ-kha-pa's *Sṅags rim chen mo*, only the last of the three works (*sgom rim tha ma*) is cited. This is a passage including a quotation from the *Ārya-Ratnamegha-sūtra*, and Tsoṅ-kha-pa's comments (92a-1): "This states that the analysis by discriminative insight (*pratyavekṣaṇa-prajñā*) is the engagement in Yoga without images, and states accordingly that if one gives up the discriminative insight, he does not engage in Yoga without images." Tsoṅ-kha-pa regularly exchanges the terminology of "discriminative insight" (T. *so sor rtog paḥi śes rab*) with "higher vision" (*lhag mthoṅ*): hence Mkhas grub's remark that the *Bhāvanā-krama* is consistent with those Tantric works in this respect.

[13] Cf. *Sādhanamālā*, Vol. I, p. 156: "When there is *siddhi*, he gains mastery of the *khaḍga-vidyādhara*" (*siddhe sati khaḍgavidyādharādhipatir bhavati*).

[14] The usual location of these "disks" (*maṇḍala*) is water disk in heart, earth disk in privities, fire disk in throat, and wind disk in navel.

legs źes bya ba byuṅ byuṅ du bzlas brjod byas paḥi mthar de dag byuṅ ba na / byaṅ chub kyi sems mi brjed paḥi tiṅ ṅe ḥdzin ḥthob par rgyud ḥdi las gsuṅs te / de la sogs paḥi dṅos grub bsgrub tshul du ma źig gsuṅs so /

evoking Mañjuśrī and so forth, those Bodhisattvas touch one's head, or say, "Excellent! (*sādhu*!)"; and that if they appear at the conclusion of reciting "Appear, appear!" one obtains the *samādhi* 'The unforgotten Mind of Enlightenment'. And the Tantra explains many methods of accomplishing such *siddhis* as those.

/ gsum pa rnal ḥbyor rgyud kyi rnam gźag la gñis / yo gaḥi chos ḥkhor bskor tshul daṅ / lam gyi rim pa la slob tshul lo /

/ daṅ po ni / yo gaḥi lugs kyi mṅon par rdzogs par ḥtshaṅ rgya baḥi tshul bśad zin la / yo gaḥi sgos kyi chos kyi ḥkhor lo bskor tshul ni /

/ ḥog min na bźugs paḥi rnam par snaṅ mdzad de ṅes pa lṅa ldan gyi loṅs spyod rdzogs paḥi sku yin pas ḥog min las gźan du nas yaṅ mi gśegs śiṅ / des rnam par snaṅ mdzad sprul sku źal bźi pa cig sprul pa des ri rab kyi rtse mor byon nas rdo rje rin po cheḥi khaṅ bu brtsegs paḥi gźal med khaṅ du bźugs te / srid pa tha ma paḥi byaṅ chub sems dpaḥ seṅ geḥi gzugs su sprul paḥi seṅ geḥi khri la bźugs śiṅ / mi bskyod pa la sogs paḥi de bźin gśegs pa gźan bźi yaṅ / srid pa tha ma paḥi byaṅ chub sems dpaḥ glaṅ po che la sogs paḥi gzugs su sprul paḥi glaṅ po che la sogs paḥi khri la bźugs nas /

/ chos kyi ḥkhor lo bskor baḥi yo-gaḥi rgyud thams cad rtsa rgyud daṅ / bśad rgyud daṅ / cha mthun gyi rgyud gsum du ḥdus so /

/ de la rnal ḥbyor rgyud thams cad kyi rtsa ba ni de ñid bsdus pa yin la / der daṅ por gleṅ gis don gñis phun sum tshogs paḥi rnam snaṅ bstan

[1] *Supra*, Chapter I.

[2] The title *Tattvasaṃgraha* means "collection of categories". According to Padmavajra's *Tantrārthāvatāravyākhyāna* (Toh. 2502), which we cite in abbreviation as *Avatāra-vyākh*, there are thirty-seven categories (*tattva*), which we give in Sanskrit reconstruction: (1) hṛdaya, (2) mudrā, (3) mantra, (4) vidyā, (5) adhiṣṭhāna, (6) abhiṣeka, (7) samādhi, (8) pūjā, (9) ātmatattva, (10) devatattva, (11) maṇḍala, (12) prajñā, (13) upāya, (14) hetu, (15) phala, (16) yoga, (17) atiyoga, (18) mahāyoga, (19) guhyayoga, (20) sarvayoga, (21) jāpa, (22) homa, (23) vrata, (24) siddhi, (25) sādhana, (26) dhyāna, (27) bodhicitta, (28) śūnyatā-jñāna, (29) ādarśa-jñāna, (30) samatā-jñāna, (31) pratyavekṣaṇa-jñāna, (32) kṛtyānuṣṭhāna-jñāna, (33) viśuddhadharmadhātu-jñāna, (34) ākarṣaṇa, (35) praveṣaṇa, (36) bandhana, (37) vaśīkāra.

[3] According to Śākyamitra's commentary on the *Tattvasaṃgraha* called *Kosalālaṃkāra* (Toh. 2503), 2b-1, the initial summary of the merits (*guṇa*) of Vairocana begins with the words, "*vajra-adhiṣṭhāna* of all the Tathāgatas". Hence, the two goals are "surpassing possession of both the diamond blessing (*vajra-adhiṣṭhāna*) of all the

CHAPTER SIX

3. FUNDAMENTALS OF THE YOGA TANTRA

There are two parts: the method by which the Yoga Wheel of the Law was set in motion; the method of studying the steps of the path.

a. *Method by which the Yoga Wheel of the Law was set in motion*

Since the method of becoming a Manifest Complete Buddha (*abhisaṃbuddha*) according to the Yoga school has already been explained,[1] we now take up the method by which the special Wheel of the Law of Yoga was set in motion.

Vairocana, dwelling in the Akaniṣṭha Heaven, does not proceed elsewhere because he is the Sambhoga-kāya possessing the five certainties. But with the magical apparition (*nirmita*) of a Vairocana Nirmāṇa-kāya having four heads, he proceeded to the summit of Mt. Sumeru and took his place in the eaved palace (*kūṭāgāra*) of precious thunderbolts. There he took his place on a lion's throne (*siṃhāsana*) formed of the Bodhisattvas in their last life who had been transformed into the appearance of lions. Then he took his place on a throne consisting of elephants and the like, formed by the remaining four Tathāgatas who are Akṣobhya and so forth and by the Bodhisattvas in their last life who had been transformed into the appearance of elephants and the like.

Thereupon, he set in motion the Wheel of the Law of the Yoga Tantra, including the Fundamental Tantra of all the Tantras of the Yoga class, the Explanatory Tantras, and the Tantras which conform to [respective] sections (*cha mthun*) [of the Fundamental Tantra].

Among them, the fundamental one of all the Yoga Tantras is the *Tattvasaṃgraha* (Toh. 479).[2] In that work the initial summary (*nidāna*) shows Vairocana as having the perfection of the two goals (*artha*).[3]

Tathāgatas and the manifold knowledge of the pledge (*samaya*)" (de bźin gśegs pa thams cad kyi rdo rjeḥi byin gyis brlabs daṅ / dam tshig gi ye śes rnam pa sna tshogs

pas de la thob ḥdod bskyed do / de skyes pa na thob bya de mṅon du byed paḥi thabs ni de man chad kyi rgyud thams cad kyis ston la / ḥjig rten las ḥdas ma ḥdas kyi dṅos grub bsgrub paḥi thabs thun moṅ pa ni rtsa baḥi rgyud kyis ston ciṅ / de la yaṅ dum bu bźi ste / rdor dbyiṅs daṅ ḥjig rten gsum rgyal lam khams gsum rnam rgyal daṅ / ḥgro ḥdul daṅ / don grub gyi dum buḥo /

/ de la de bźin gśegs pa daṅ deḥi rigs gñis las / de bźin gśegs paḥi sgra ni de bźin gśegs paḥi rigs lṅa ka la ḥjug la / de bźin gśegs paḥi rigs kyi sgra ni rnam snaṅ gi rigs kyi byaṅ sems sogs la ḥjug gi / rigs bźiḥi byaṅ sems sogs la mi ḥjug go /

/ de la dum bu daṅ pos ni de bźin gśegs pa daṅ / de bźin gśegs paḥi rigs kyi dbaṅ du byas paḥi lam rnams ston no / gñis pas ni rdo rjeḥi rigs te mi bskyod paḥi rigs daṅ / gsum pas ni padmaḥi rigs te ḥod dpag med kyi rigs daṅ / bźi pas ni sems can gyi ḥdod pa rdzogs par byed paḥi rin po cheḥi rigs te rin ḥbyuṅ gi rigs kyi dbaṅ du byas paḥi lam rnams ston no /

/ rigs lṅa yod pa las rtsa rgyud la bźi las ma bśad pa ni sems can gyi bsam pa rdzogs par byed paḥi byed pa poḥi sgo nas rin po cheḥi rigs yin la / las su bya baḥi sgo nas las kyi rigs yin pas las daṅ byed pa po gcig tu bsdus pa yin par saṅs rgyas gsaṅ bas bśad do /

/ de la rgyud phyi ma źig daṅ phyi maḥi phyi ma źig daṅ gñis yod de /

/ rgyud phyi ma ni naṅ gi tiṅ ṅe ḥdzin gyi rnal ḥbyor la dgaḥ baḥi gdul bya mchog gi don du gsuṅs pa ste / dum bu bźi ga las gsuṅs paḥi

---

kyi khyad par daṅ ldan pa). We observe that the two goals are respectively noumenal and phenomenal. In non-Tantric Mahāyāna Buddhism, the two goals of the Bodhisattva are (1) for himself, Complete Enlightenment, and (2) for others, helping them to Nirvāṇa.

[4] *Avatāra-vyākh.*, Derge ed., 98a-1: "'Magical success' (*siddhi, dṅos grub*) means the complete attainment of what was aspired" (kun gyis smon par bya baḥi gnas te). *Ibid.*, 98a-1, 2: "Accomplishment of *siddhi*' (*siddhi-sādhana, dṅos grub bsgrub pa*) is the means (*upāya*) of attaining it. Contemplating the deity and performing rosary muttering, while taking recourse to such substances as malachite (*lig-bu-mig*) and (?) lamp-black [or antimony] (*srod-añjana*), one attains whatever he desires."

[5] The Vajradhātu section is probably the most important one. It is the basis of the *Vajradhātu Maṇḍala*, for which see B. Bhattacharyya, ed., *Niṣpannayogāvalī of Mahāpaṇḍita Abhayākaragupta* (Baroda, 1949), pp. 54, ff. This *maṇḍala* was elaborated in China and became one of the two chief *maṇḍalas* of the Shingon Sect of Japanese Buddhism. The other *maṇḍala* of the latter sect is elaborated from a **Dharmadhātu Maṇḍala*, presumably drawn from the *Mahāvairocana-tantra* (Toh. 494) which is the chief Caryā Tantra in the Indo-Tibetan classification.

[6] In the Derge edition of the *Tattvasaṃgraha*, which runs in the *Rgyud ḥbum*, Vol. Ña from folio 1 to 142a, the Tantra Continuation begins at 106a-6. Presumably the Continuation of the Continuation is the last part of the *Tattvasaṃgraha* text as found in the Kanjur. Ānandagarbha's *Tattvāloka* (Toh. 2510) discusses the Tantra Con-

Therefore, it generates the desire to attain them. Assuming that [the desire] has been generated, all of the subsequent Tantra teaches the means of realizing those goals to be attained, and the Fundamental Tantra teaches the common means of accomplishing mundane and supramundane *siddhis*.[4] Furthermore, that work has four sections, namely,

(1) Diamond (or Thunderbolt) Realm (*vajra-dhātu*);[5]
(2) Victory over the Three Worlds (*trilokyavijaya*);
(3) Training the Living Beings (*jagad-vinaya*);
(4) Achieving the Objective (*siddhārtha*).

The text contains the expressions "Tathāgata" and "Tathāgata Family" (*tathāgata-kula*). "Tathāgata" stands for the five Tathāgata Progenitors. "Tathāgata Family" stands for the Bodhisattvas and so forth of Vairocana's Family, and does not stand for the Bodhisattvas and so forth of the other four Families.

The first section [of the four sections] shows the ways of subduing the Tathāgata (i.e., Vairocana) and the Tathāgata Family. Again, the second, third, and fourth sections, respectively, show the ways of subduing the Vajra Family, which is Akṣobhya's Family; the Padma Family, which is Amitābha's Family; the Ratna Family fulfilling the desires of the living beings, which is Ratnasambhava's Family.

The fact that the Fundamental Tantra only describes four, although there are five Families, is explained by Buddhaguhya as a merger of action (*karma*) and agent (*kāraka*) since it has the Ratna Family in the sense of the agent that accomplishes the wishes of the living beings and has the Karma Family in the sense of the action that does so.

That Tantra has a Tantra Continuation (*uttaratantra*) and a Continuation of the Continuation (*uttarottara*).[6]

The Tantra Continuation was expressed for sake of the highest candidate who delights in the *yoga*[7] of inner *samādhi*.[8] It explains exten-

---

tinuation in the first chapter, ending Li, 24b-7; thereafter, Ānandagarbha discusses the Continuation of the Continuation in the manner now to be set forth by Mkhas grub rje. Śākyamitra's *Kosalāṃkāra* commentary (Toh. 2503) on the *Tattvasaṃgraha* finishes its commentary on the Tantra Continuation at Derge Vol. Ri, 165b-5, and its commentary on the Continuation of the Continuation at Ri, 187b-3.

[7] *Avatāra-vyākh.*, 97a-4: "'Union' (*yoga*, *rnal ḥbyor*) means union (*sbyor ba*) with the *dharmadhātu* [the interior objects of the mind (*manas*), according to Buddhist Abhidharma theory; the 'source of natures' (*dharmodaya*) and the Absolute 'Object' (*paramārtha*) in Buddhist Tantra] by means of Knowledge (*jñāna*)..."

[8] *Avatāra-vyākh.*, 96a-2, 3: "'Profound Concentration' (*samādhi*, *tiṅ ṅe ḥdzin*) is the mental orientation that is the gateway of personal liberation through suppressing other wanderings of discursive thought and through fixing the mind one-pointedly on the meditative object. Furthermore, it has two varieties: Intrinsic Profound Con-

mchog gi dṅos grub bsgrub paḥi thabs rnams rgyas par bśad pa daṅ / ma tshaṅ ba kha bskaṅ ba sogs kyi sgo nas bśad do /

/ rgyud phyi maḥi phyi ma ni naṅ gi tiṅ ṅe ḥdzin gyi rnal ḥbyor gyis ḥjigs skrag la / bzlas pa daṅ mchod pa sogs kyi phyiḥi bya ba la dgaḥ baḥi gdul bya phal paḥi dbaṅ du byas nas gsuṅs te / dum bu bźi ga nas gsuṅs paḥi ḥjig rten paḥi dṅos grub bsgrub paḥi thabs rnams rgyas par bśad pa daṅ kha bskaṅ ba sogs kyi sgo nas bśad do /

/ ḥo na rgyud sde bźir ḥjog tshul gñis las / gcig la phyiḥi bya ba khrus daṅ gtsaṅ sbra sogs daṅ / naṅ gi rnal ḥbyor gñis las phyiḥi bya ba la dgaḥ baḥi gdul byaḥi dbaṅ du byas nas gsuṅs pa bya rgyud daṅ / phyiḥi bya ba daṅ naṅ gi rnal ḥbyor gñis cha mñam du spyod pa la dgaḥ baḥi gdul byaḥi dbaṅ du byas na gsuṅs pa spyod rgyud daṅ / de gñis las naṅ gi tiṅ ṅe ḥdzin gyi rnal ḥbyor la dgaḥ baḥi gdul byaḥi dbaṅ du byas nas gsuṅs pa rnal ḥbyor rgyud daṅ / naṅ gi rnal ḥbyor la dgaḥ baḥi gdul byaḥi dbaṅ du byas nas gsuṅs śiṅ rnal ḥbyor de las rnal ḥbyor gźan goṅ na med paḥi rgyud la rnal ḥbyor bla med kyi rgyud du bźag pa daṅ /

/ rnal ḥbyor rgyud kyi rgyud phyi maḥi phyi ma phyiḥi bya ba la dgaḥ baḥi gdul byaḥi ched du bśad pa gñis ḥgal lo sñam na / dper na gsaṅ ba ḥdus paḥi gdul bya la bskyed rim mthar phyin nas kyaṅ thun moṅ gi dṅos grub don du mi gñer bar / rdzogs rim ñams su blaṅs nas chod la mchog gi dṅos grub thob pa don du gñer baḥi gdul bya mchog rin po

centration and Conforming Profound Concentration. Intrinsic Profound Concentration is the liberation of the Tathāgata and of the *mahāsattvas* [i.e. the Great Bodhisattvas, perhaps those on the last three Stages]. Conforming Profound Concentration means that the *yogin* who is practising *dhāraṇīs* accomplishes in conformity with that [liberation of the Tathāgata and of the *mahāsattvas*]" (tiṅ ṅe ḥdzin ni rnam par rtog paḥi rgyu ba gźan bkag nas dmigs paḥi don la sems rtse gcig par gnas nas raṅ gi rnam par thar paḥi sgo yid la byed paḥo / de la yaṅ gñis te / raṅ bźin gyi tiṅ ṅe ḥdzin daṅ / rjes su mthun paḥi tiṅ ṅe ḥdzin to / raṅ bźin gyi tiṅ ṅe ḥdzin ni de bźin gśegs pa daṅ sems dpaḥ chen po rnams kyi rnam par thar paḥo / rjes su mthun pa ni sṅags spyod paḥi rnal ḥbyor pa ñid de daṅ rjes su mthun par bsgrub pa ste)...

9 *Avatāra-vyākh.*, 97b-5: "'Muttering' (*jāpa*, *bzlas pa*) is the means of pleasing the deity by way of muttering incantations and of uttering the [deity's] "heart" (**hṛdaya*) (*sñiṅ po brjod pa*) ..."

10 *Avatāra-vyākh.*, 96a-5, 6: "'Offering' (*pūjā*, *mchod pa*) is the method of pleasing oneself and others with necessary items that are excellent (phun sum tshogs par ldan paḥi yo byad kyis bdag gźan mñes par bya baḥi thabs). Furthermore, it has two varieties, external offering and internal offering..."

11 *Thob yig* II, 71b-1, ff., gives the information as presented in the *Pradīpodyotana* (Toh. 1785). The five types are called "jewel-like person" (*rin po che lta buḥi gaṅ zag*), "red-lotus-like person" (*pad-ma lta buḥi gaṅ zag*), "white-lotus-like person" (*pad dkar lta buḥi gaṅ zag*), "sandlewood-like person" (*ca-nda-na lta buḥi gaṅ zag*), and "blue-lotus-like person" (*ut-pa-la lta buḥi gaṅ zag*). A verse is expressed for each; the one for the "jewel-like person" running as follows: "The person called jewel-like has pure

sively the means of accomplishing the highest *siddhis* that are mentioned in the four sections; and it explains in a way that supplements points not adequately covered [in the Fundamental Tantra].

The Continuation of the Continuation was expressed for subduing the ordinary candidates who, fearing the danger attendant on the *yoga* of inner *samādhi*, have delight in such outer actions as muttering (*jāpa*)[9] and offering (*pūjā*).[10] It explains extensively the means of perfecting the mundane (*laukika*) *siddhis* that are mentioned in the four sections; and it explains in a way that supplements points [not adequately covered in the Tantra and its Continuation].

Now, there are two methods laid down in the four Tantra divisions, namely, *outer action* (*bāhya-kriyā), such as bathing, cleaning, etc.; and *inner yoga* (*adhyātma-yoga). The Kriyā Tantra was expressed for subduing the candidates (*vineya*) who delight in *outer action*, while the Caryā Tantra was expressed for subduing the candidates who delight in practicing *outer action* and *inner yoga* in equal measure. The Yoga Tantra was expressed for subduing the candidates who delight in the *yoga of inner samādhi*, while the Anuttara Yoga Tantra is the incomparable Tantra for subduing the candidates who delight in *inner-yoga*.

Is this contradiction to the second exposition — that of the Continuation of the Continuation of the Yoga Tantra — expounded for the sake of the candidates who delight in *outer action*? To answer the question, we note that among the candidates of the *Guhyasamāja*[11] there is the highest candidate, called the "jewel-like person", who, having arrived at the limit of the Steps of Production (*utpatti-krama*), does not aim at the common (*sādhāraṇa*) *siddhis*, but taking the Steps of Completion

---

morality, is accomplished in learning, possesses insight (*prajñā*), is one in mental series (**ekasaṃtāna, *ekatantra*) [with the Saṃbhoga-kāya], and teaches well what he has learned" (tshul khrims dag ciṅ mkhas la sgrin / śes rab ldan ciṅ rgyud gcig pa / thos nas legs par ston pa ni / rin chen źes byaḥi gaṅ zag go). Bhavyakīrti writes in his *Pradīpodyotana-vyākhyāṭīkā* (Toh. 1793), Derge, f. 3a-3: "The 'sandlewood-like' is in the family of fools (*blun poḥi rigs can*); the 'blue-lotus-like' has inferior faculty (*indriya*) (*dbaṅ po dman pa*); the 'white-lotus-like' has intermediate faculty (*dbaṅ po bar pa*); the 'red-lotus-like' has keen faculty (*dbaṅ po rno ba*); the 'jewel-like' has the most excellent of faculties (*dbaṅ po rab kyi rab po*)." *Thob yig* II, 72a-5, ff., on the basis of the *Pradīpodyotana*, shows a difference of instruction to these candidates in terms of alternatives (*ṣaṭkoṭi, mthaḥ drug*), which are: evident meaning (*nītārtha, ṅes don*), hinted meaning (*neyartha, draṅ don*), standard terminology (*yathāruta, sgra ji bźin pa*), coined terminology (*na-yathāruta, sgra ji bźin pa ma yin*), twilight language (*saṃdhi-bhāṣā, dgoṅs pa can*), non-twilight language (*na-saṃdhi-bhāṣā, dgons pa can ma yin pa*). The evident meaning, standard terminology, and twilight language are expressed to the 'jewel-like person'. The other three alternatives are expressed to the other four types of persons.

che lta buḥi gaṅ zag daṅ / bskyed rim mthar phyin par byas nas thun moṅ gi dṅos grub grub pa chen po brgyad la sogs pa don du gñer baḥi gdul bya phal pa padma dkar po lta bu la sogs paḥi gaṅ zag rigs bźi ste / ched du bya baḥi gdul bya rigs gñis yod pa ltar / rnal ḥbyor rgyud kyi ched du bya baḥi gdul bya la yaṅ gtso bo daṅ phal pa gñis yod paḥi naṅ nas ched du bya baḥi gdul byaḥi gtso boḥi dbaṅ du byas nas bśad pa yin gyi / phal paḥi dbaṅ du byas pa min pas ñes pa med do /

/ ḥo na dum bu bźiḥi lam ḥdi gaṅ zag tha dad pa bźi ḥam / ḥo na te gaṅ zag gcig rim gyis ḥkhrid paḥi gnas skabs mi ḥdra ba bźi yin sñam na / ḥdi la dpal mchog ḥgrel chen las / de bźin gśegs pa lṅaḥi zlos pa po ste sgrub pa po ni raṅ bźin bzaṅ ba / dug gsum cha mñam la spyod pa daṅ / de bźin gśegs paḥi rigs kyi sgrub pa po ni ḥdod chags śas che ba daṅ / dum bu gñis paḥi gdul bya ni źe sdaṅ śas che ba daṅ / gsum paḥi gdul bya ni gti mug can nam log lta can daṅ / bźi paḥi gdul bya ni ser sna śas che bar gsuṅs pas / gaṅ zag rgyud tha dad pa bźi yin no /

---

[12] According to *Pradīpodyotana*, Derge, Ha, 154a-5, ff., the accomplishment of supramundane *siddhi* through the Steps of Completion is indicated by this verse of the *Guhyasamāja* (Chap. XV, p. 108): "Having the pledge of *yoga* and stationed in the diamond of meditation, he sees the Body associated with the *dharmacakra*, surrounded by all the Buddhas" (dharmacakragataṃ kāyaṃ sarvabuddhaiḥ parivṛtam / paśyate yogasamayo dhyānavajrapratiṣṭhitaḥ /). Supramundane *siddhi* is accomplished by this seeing.

[13] The number of *mahāsiddhis* is also eight in the Hindu Yoga; see Alain Danielou, *Yoga, The Method of Re-Integration* (London, 1949), pp. 137 ff. A list of eight in the Buddhist Tantras is found in *Sādhana-mālā*, Vol. II, No. 172, p. 350, Abhayākaragupta's *Kurukullāsādhana*. Using the Tibetan translation (Toh. 3209) for the equivalent Tibetan terms, we have 1. khaḍga, ral gri; 2. añjana, mig rtsi; 3. pādalepa, rkaṅ paḥi byug pa; 4. antardhāna, mi snaṅ bar ḥgyur ba; 5. rasarasāyana, bcud kyis len; 6. khecara, mkhaḥ spyod; 7. bhūcara, źiṅ skyoṅ [sic. for źiṅ spyod]; 8. pātālasiddhi, sa ḥog grub pa. Tsoṅ-kha-pa discusses the list in several of his works, e.g. his *Rgyud bśad thabs kyi man ṅag gsal bar bstan pa* (Toh. 5286), f. 49a; and his *Srog rtsol gyi de kho na ñid gsal ba* (Toh. 5285), f. 39a. Tsoṅ-kha-pa's lists have *ri-lu* (**piṇḍarūpa*) in place of 7. bhūcara; and assuming an equivalence here, the eight may be explained (with the aid of Tsoṅ-kha-pa's works) as follows:

1. "To be invincible with the sword (i.e. in battle)."
2. "To remove blindness"; an ointment for the eyes, which when applied, enables one to see all the *devas* and *nāgas*.
3. "To be swift of foot"; or the foot ointment enabling one to be so.
4. "To be invisible".
5. "To have the elixir of youth."
6. "To walk in the sky."
7. "To shape into a ball" (assuming *ri-lu* stands for the *bhūcara* item); this means to shape any of the nine kinds of flesh, namely that of man, elephant, horse, cow, dog, ass, camel, buffalo, and wolf, into the size of a thumb; and to shape any of the "ambrosias" (*amṛta*), such as ordure, urine, blood, and semen, into the size of a barley grain.

(*niṣpanna-krama*) to heart, prudently aims at obtaining the highest *siddhis*.[12] There are also the ordinary candidates, the four classes of persons called "white lotus-like" and so forth, who, having arrived at the limit of the Steps of Production, seek the common *siddhis*, such as the eight *mahāsiddhis*.[13] Hence there are two kinds of candidates for the high goal (*uddeśa*) [of that Tantra]. In the same way, there are also the chief and the ordinary among the candidates for the high goal of the Yoga Tantra. When the topic is the subduing of the chief among the candidates for the high goal, there is no [discussion of] subduing the ordinary ones. Hence there is no discrepancy.

Does this path of four sections refer to four different persons, or to four different phases in the sequential guidance of a single person? The great commentary on the *Śrī-Paramādya* (i.e. the *Śrī-Paramādiṭīkā*, Toh. 2512, by Ānandagarbha) states that the reciter and evoker of the five Tathāgatas has a good nature and acts with the three poisons in equal parts;[14] the evoker of the Tathāgata Family has a preponderance of lust (*rāga*); the candidate of the second section has a preponderance of hatred (*dveṣa*); the candidate of the third one, delusion (*moha*) or wayward views (*mithyā-dṛṣṭi*); the candidate of the fourth, avarice (*mātsarya*). For this reason, there are four different mental series (*saṃtāna*) of persons.[15]

---

8. "To have dominion over the entities of the underworld."

The word *añjana* of No. 2 presumably refers to the same substance as the *srod-añjana* of the Tibetan text in note 4, above.

[14] The three poisons are lust (*rāga*), hatred (*dveṣa*) and delusion (*moha*). The meaning of acting with the three poisons in equal parts is found in non-Tantric Buddhism, e.g. Asaṅga's *Śrāvakabhūmi*; cf. his definition of the *samaprāptaḥ pudgalaḥ* (Sanskrit from Bihar manuscript of *Śrāvakabhūmi*; Tibetan, Derge ed., *Sems tsam*, Vol. Dzi, 68a-5, f.) — he means a person who has previously not developed a penchant toward some particular fault (lust, etc.), and hence when those faults (the three poisons) do arise, they arise equally. The idea is that none of the three poisons is sufficiently strong to appear in a dominant role, and this is consistent with saying the candidate has "a good nature".

[15] The correspondences between the sections, Tantric Families, and persons can be tabulated as follows:

	Section of Fundamental Tantra	Family	Lord	Person's Consciousness
1.	Diamond Realm	Tathāgata	Vairocana	lust
2.	Victory over the Three Worlds	Vajra	Akṣobhya	hatred
3.	Training the Living Beings	Padma	Amitābha	delusion
4.	Achieving the Objective	(Ratna (Karma	Ratnasambhava) Amoghasiddhi)	avarice

/ dum bu bźi paḥi gdul bya ser sna can du gsuṅs paḥi tshig zur gyis slob dpon ḥdiḥi dgoṅs pa yaṅ sṅar slob dpon saṅs rgyas gsaṅ bas bśad pa daṅ mthun par mṅon no /

/ yaṅ ḥgrel pa de las / ṅo bo ñid daṅ / rnam par smin pa daṅ / loṅs spyod rdzogs pa daṅ / sprul paḥi sku daṅ bźi dum bu bźiḥi rigs daṅ rim pa bźin sbyar ba daṅ / de bźin du me loṅ lta bu daṅ / mñam pa ñid daṅ / so sor rtog pa daṅ / bya ba grub paḥi ye śes bźi daṅ rim pa bźin sbyar ba daṅ / byaṅ chub kyi sems daṅ / sbyin paḥi phar phyin daṅ / śes rab kyi phar phyin daṅ / brtson ḥgrus kyi phar phyin daṅ rim pa bźin du sbyar nas / bśad pa ni thob byaḥi ḥbras buḥi sgo nas bśad ste /

/ de ltar byas na gdul bya re reḥi thob bya la yaṅ rigs bźi ga tshaṅ ba dgos pas / cha mñam la spyod pa sogs kyi gdul bya rigs bźi po re re yaṅ dum bu bźi gaḥi gdul byar ḥoṅ ṅo /

/ rnam snaṅ gi go ḥphaṅ mṅon du byed pa ni / dum bu bźi po re re las rgyas pa daṅ / ḥbriṅ daṅ / bsdus pa la dgaḥ baḥi gdul bya gsum gyis / daṅ poḥi sbyor ba daṅ / dkyil ḥkhor rgyal mchog daṅ / las rgyal mchog gi tiṅ ṅe ḥdzin gsum bsgom tshul rgyas ḥbriṅ bsdus pa gsum gsuṅs so /

16 For the priority of Buddhaguhya to Ānandagarbha, see Chapter I, note 13, *supra.* The *Avatāra-vyākh.*, which is a commentary on Buddhaguhya's *Avatāra* (2501), clarifies Mkhas grub rje's point here, because in a passage beginning 113b-7 it explains that "since the living beings to be trained are of four kinds according as they possess lust, hatred, delusion, or pride (*māna*), his [the Bhagavat's] teachings are of four kinds as antidotes. ... As the antidote for the sentient beings who are high in wealth, proud, etc., he taught the perfections of enjoyment in the Ratna Family..." The expression "pride" for the candidate of the fourth section is consistent with Asaṅga's *Śrāvaka-bhūmi*; but in Asaṅga's non-Tantric Buddhism, this candidate is given the meditative object of "analysis of the elements" (*dhātuprabheda*). The explanation "sentient beings who are high in wealth, proud, etc." shows that the expression "avarice" is sufficiently close to the connotation here of "pride" to justify speaking of indirect consistency.

17 *Avatāra-vyākh.*, 98a-4, 5: "'Mirror-like Knowledge' is the higher cognition that appearances are devoid of intrinsic nature" (me loṅ lta buḥi ye śes ni snaṅ la raṅ bźin med par rtogs paḥo). "'Equality Knowledge' is the higher cognition that makes no distinction between oneself and another" (mñam pa ñid kyi ye śes ni bdag gźan du mi ḥbyed par rtogs paḥo). "'Discriminative Knowledge' is the higher cognition that universal characteristics (*sāmānya-lakṣaṇa*) and individual characteristics (*sva-lakṣaṇa*) are devoid of intrinsic nature" (so sor rtog paḥi ye śes ni spyi daṅ raṅ gi mtshan ñid raṅ bźin med par rtogs paḥo). "'Knowledge of the procedure of duty' is what works for goals without distinguishing oneself and another" (bya ba grub paḥi ye śes ni bdag gźan du mi ḥbyed par don mdzad paḥo). *Avatāra-vyākh.*, 98a-5, ff. also explains the fifth *jñāna* — the 'Knowledge of the pure Natural Realm' (*viśuddhadharmadhātu-jñāna*). It is the location of the realm of the other four [i.e. where they are] as well as their object (*viṣaya*) [i.e. what they 'know'] (de dag gi ṅaṅ du yaṅ gnas pa ste / de dag gi yul du gyur pa). The text explains the four Knowledges in terms of the 'Knowledge of the pure Natural Realm', and concludes its treatment by identifying the fifth *jñāna* with the great Nirvāṇa.

18 *Avatāra-vyākh.*, 98a-3: "'Mind of Enlightenment' (*bodhicitta*) is the resolve of enlightenment attended with voidness and compassion. Besides, there are two kinds:

When this teacher (i.e. Ānandagarbha) uses the expression "avarice" for the candidate of the fourth section, his purport appears indirectly (*zur gyis*) to be consistent with the earlier explanation by the teacher Buddhaguhya.[16]

The same commentary matches correspondentially the four Bodies (*kāya*), the *svabhāva-*, *vipāka-*, *saṃbhoga-*, and *nirmāṇa-kāyas*, with the Families of the four sections in the given order. It likewise sets in correspondence the four knowledges (*jñāna*) — the 'mirror-like' (*ādarśa*), the 'equality' (*samatā*), the 'discriminative' (*pratyavekṣaṇa*), and the 'procedure of duty' (*kṛtyānuṣṭhāna*) in the given order;[17] and sets in correspondence Mind of Enlightenment (*bodhicitta*),[18] Perfection of Giving (*dāna-pāramitā*), Perfection of Insight (*prajñā-pāramitā*), and Perfection of Striving (*vīrya-pāramitā*) in the given order. This exposition is made from the standpoint of the fruit to be obtained.

According to this procedure, all four Families are required for the attainments of the individual candidates [each in one Family]. Therefore, the candidate who acts in equal parts must be a candidate of the four sections under the four Families.

For realizing the rank of Vairocana, one considers that in each of the four sections there are three types of candidates, namely, those who delight in the extended, in the average, or in the concise. Consequently, the three *samādhis* called initial training triumphant *maṇḍala*, and triumphant ritual act,[19] each have three modes of development, namely, extended, average, and concise.

---

absolute (*paramārtha*) and relative (*saṃvṛtti*). Some persons assert a third one, a non-dual Mind of Enlightenment" (byaṅ chub sems ni stoṅ pa ñid daṅ sñiṅ rjer ldan pa ni byaṅ chub kyi sems te / de la yaṅ gñis te / don dam pa daṅ / kun rdzob bo / kha cig na re gñis su med paḥi byaṅ chub kyi sems daṅ gsum mo źes kyaṅ zer to).

19 These are summarized at the outset of Ānandagarbha's *Vajrodaya* (Toh. 2516): 1. Prathama-prayoga-nāma-samādhi, daṅ poḥi sbyor ba źes bya baḥi tiṅ ṅe ḥdzin (Derge, *Rgyud ḥgrel*, Khu, 1-16b); 2. Vijaya-maṇḍala-nāma-samādhi, dkyil ḥkhor rgyal mchog gi tiṅ ṅe ḥdzin brtan pa (16b-19b); 3. Karma-vijaya-nāma-samādhi, las kyi rgyal mchog ces bya baḥi tiṅ ṅe ḥdzin (19b-20a). The same expressions are employed in the Anuttara-yoga-tantra; and while there are differences of usage, they indicate some of the subject matter that is common to the Yoga-tantra and the Anuttara-yoga-tantra, as alluded to earlier in Chapter IV (p. 157, *supra*) and later in Chapter VII. In Anuttara-yoga-tantra terminology, the three *samādhis* constitute the Steps of Production (*utpatti-krama*). This is the position of Bhavyakīrti in his *Pradīpodyotana-vyākhyāṭīkā* (3a-6) and of Tsoṅ-kha-pa in his *Sṅags rim*, Peking edition, 366b-5. In both texts the first *samādhi* consists of four successive *yogas* called *yoga*, *anuyoga*, *atiyoga*, and *mahāyoga*. According to the *Sṅags rim*, *ibid.*, the first *samādhi* covers the first two parts of the *ṣaḍaṅga-yoga*, i.e. generation of the palace and attraction of the residents; cf. Chapter I, note 24, *supra*. The Yoga-tantra also speaks of various types of yoga: cf. nos. 16-20 among the thirty-seven categories listed in note 2,

/ de la rgyas paḥi tiṅ ṅe ḥdzin sum tshan bźi po re re la dum bu so so nas dkyil ḥkhor chen po daṅ / gzuṅs dkyil daṅ / chos dkyil daṅ / las dkyil gyi skabs kyi daṅ po sbyor ba sogs kyi tiṅ ṅe ḥdzin gsum gsum gsuṅs pas ḥdi la dum bu re re las kyaṅ tiṅ ṅe ḥdzin gsum bsgom tshul tshan pa bźi bźi gsuṅs so /

/ ḥbriṅ gi tiṅ ṅe ḥdzin sum tshan bźi ni dum bu raṅ raṅ gi phyag rgya bźiḥi dkyil ḥkhor gyi skabs nas gsuṅs paḥi tiṅ ṅe ḥdzin gsum mo /

/ bsdus paḥi tiṅ ṅe ḥdzin sum tshan bźi ni dum bu raṅ raṅ gi phyag rgya gcig paḥi dkyil ḥkhor gyi skabs nas gsuṅs paḥi tiṅ ṅe ḥdzin gsum mo /

/ de ñid snaṅ ba las / dum bu bźiḥi rigs bźi daṅ / phyag rgya bźi sbyar ba ni sku phyag rgya chen po / thugs dam tshig gi phyag rgya / gsuṅ chos kyi phyag rgya / ḥphrin las las kyi phyag rgya yin pas / dum bu bźi daṅ phyag rgya bźi rim pa bźin du sbyar ro /

/ yaṅ dkyil ḥkhor bźi daṅ phyag rgya bźi rim pa bźin du sbyar te / dkyil ḥkhor chen po la sogs paḥi dkyil ḥkhor bźi sku gsuṅ thugs phrin las bźi rim bźin gtso che baḥi phyir ro / de dag ni rnam snaṅ daṅ / mi bskyod pa daṅ / ḥod dpag med daṅ / rigs gźan gñis kyi rigs la sku daṅ gsuṅ daṅ thugs daṅ ḥphrin las su byas pa yin no /

/ rdo rje dbyiṅs kyi dum buḥi dkyil ḥkhor lta bu la yaṅ raṅ gi rigs kyi sku phyag rgya chen po gtso che mod kyaṅ thugs dam tshig gi phyag rgya sogs med pa min pas / phyag rgya bźiḥi rgyas btab par gsuṅs te gźan rnams la yaṅ de bźin du śes par byaḥo /

---

above. However, more study is necessary to determine the extent to which these *yogas* correspond to those of the Anuttara-yoga-tantra.

[20] The four *maṇḍalas* are explained in Buddhaguhya's *Avatāra*, 12a-4, ff. (immediately after this passage the author makes the remarks cited by Mkhas grub rje, p. 333, *infra*): "In the case of the *mahā-maṇḍalas*, because the array of deities is an arrangement in the Body of Form (*rūpa-kāya*), one understands them (the *mahā-maṇḍalas*) as comprising the magical manifestation of shapes (*vikurvāṇa*) from the treasury of inexhaustible Body" (dkyil ḥkhor chen po rnams su ni lha rnams dgod pa gzugs kyi skur bkod paḥi phyir / sku mi zad paḥi mdzod rnam par sprul pa bsdus pa yin par bltaḥo). "The *samaya-maṇḍala* is characterized by an arrangement of thunderbolt (*vajra*), iron hook (*aṅkuśa*), arrow (*śara*), (?) *mgu ba*, and so on, which are symbolizing agents for the way in which emancipation is comprehended; hence, comprises the magical manifestation of shapes from the arranged treasury of inexhaustible Mind" (dam tshig gi dkyil ḥkhor ni ji ltar rtogs paḥi rnam par grol baḥi sgo mtshon par byed pa rdo rje daṅ lcags kyu daṅ / mdaḥ daṅ mgu ba la sogs pa rnam par bkod pa ñe baḥi mtshan ñid ni thugs mi zad pa rnam par bkod paḥi mdzod rnam par sprul pa bsdus paḥo). "The *dharma-cakra* arranges and disposes the deities who stand for the practice which is the means of teaching how the Doctrine (*dharma*) is comprehended; hence, is the blessing (*adhiṣṭhāna*) for the magical manifestation of shapes from the arranged treasury of inexhaustible Speech of all the Tathāgatas"

Again, the three extended *samādhis* each have four classes agreeing with the various sections [of the Fundamental Yoga Tantra], that is, each of the three *samādhis*, beginning with that of initial training, have the phases of *mahā-maṇḍala*, *dhāraṇī-maṅḍala*, *dharma-maṇḍala*, and *karma-maṇḍala*.[20] In other words, each of the four sections has its classes of the mode of development of the three *samādhis*.

The three average *samādhis* each have four classes according to the sections, each with its own seal (*mudrā*), at the phase of each of the four *maṇḍalas*.

The three concise *samādhis* each have four classes according to the sections, each with its own seal (*mudrā*), at the phase of a single *maṇḍala*.

According to the *Tattvāloka* (Toh. 2510, by Ānandagarbha), the correspondences between the four Families of the four sections and the four seals are as follows: Body (*kāya*) and the Great Seal (*mahā-mudrā*), Mind (*citta*) and the Symbolic Seal (*samaya-mudrā*), Speech (*vāg*) and the Law Seal (*dharma-mudrā*), and Marvellous Action (*karma*) and the Action Seal (*karma-mudrā*). Thus, the four sections and the four seals are made to correspond in the given order.

Moreover, the four *maṇḍalas* and the four seals (*mudrā*) correspond in the given order, because the four *maṇḍalas* beginning with the *mahā-maṇḍala* lay stress on Body, Mind, Speech, and Marvellous Action in the given order. Those mean the Body, Mind, Speech, and Marvellous Action in the Families of Vairocana, Akṣobhya, Amitābha, and in the other two Families.

Although the *maṇḍala* in the Diamond Realm section, for instance, stresses the Great Seal of Body of its own Family, it is not the case that the Symbolic Seal of Mind, and the others, are lacking, so one speaks of applying seals of the four Seals. One must understand the other [*maṇḍalas*] in the same way.

(chos kyi ḥkhor'lo ni ji ltar rtogs paḥi chos bstan paḥi thabs spyod pa mñam par gźag pa rnam par bkod ciṅ gnas paḥi lha rnams te / de bźin gśegs pa thams cad kyi gsuṅ mi zad pa rnam par bkod paḥi mdzod rnam par sprul par byin gyis brlabs paḥo). "Accordingly, in the case of the *karma-maṇḍala*, it arrays the deities who are the offering and other rites; hence one should understand it as displaying in concise form the practice of all Tathāgatas for the aim of sentient beings" (de bźin du las kyi dkyil ḥkhor la yaṅ mchod pa la sogs paḥi las kyi lha rnams bkod pas de bźin gśegs pa thams cad kyi sems can gyi don spyod pa la sogs pa bsdus pa bstan par bltaḥo). It will be noted that Mkhas grub rje uses the expression **dhāraṇī-maṇḍala* (*gzuṅs dkyil*) in place of Buddhaguhya's **samaya-maṇḍala* (*dam tshig gi dkyil ḥkhor*). In this case, the word *dhāraṇī* probably means "memory", retention by the Mind.

/ de yaṅ rnam snaṅ sku gtso che yaṅ gsuṅ thugs ḥphrin las gsum med pa min pas / phyag rgya bźiḥi rgyas ḥdebs pa daṅ / mi bskyod pa thugs gtso che yaṅ sku gsuṅ ḥphrin las gsum yaṅ yod pa daṅ / ḥod dpag med gsuṅ yin yaṅ sku thugs ḥphrin las gsum yaṅ yod pa daṅ / rigs gźan gñis gtso bor ḥphrin las yin yaṅ sku gsuṅ thugs yod pas phyag rgya bźiḥi rgyas ḥdebs te /

/ a-va-tā-ra las / rim pa ḥdis ni sku la sogs pa rnam pa bźi gtso bor gyur baḥi phyir / dkyil ḥkhor bźir gsuṅs mod kyi / ḥo na kyaṅ phal cher lus med paḥi sems mi srid la / sems daṅ lus med paḥi ṅag kyaṅ mi srid de / de bas na dkyil ḥkhor so so las kyaṅ sku la sogs pa bźi char dgos par bltaḥo / de bas na rigs kyi dkyil ḥkhor thams cad du yaṅ sku la sogs paḥi mtshan mar gyur pa go rim bźin du phyag rgya chen po daṅ / dam tshig daṅ / chos daṅ / las kyi phyag rgya daṅ rnam pa bźi ḥdir bśad do / źes gsuṅs so /

/ de dag gi rnam dbye źib par śes na / dpal mchog ḥgrel chen las dum bu bźiḥi lam re ḥgaḥ gaṅ zag gcig ḥtshaṅ rgya baḥi cha rkyen du dril nas bśad ciṅ / re ḥgaḥ gaṅ zag rgyud so so baḥi lam du bśad pa rnams mi ḥgal bar śes par ḥgyur ro /

/ rnal ḥbyor rgyud la sbyaṅ gźi srid pa skye baḥi rim pa kun nas ñon moṅs kyi phyogs daṅ bstun nas bsgom pa med ciṅ ḥbras buḥi gnas skabs daṅ mthun par bsgom pa yod do / de la mṅon byaṅ lṅa rdzogs paḥi mthar rnam par snaṅ mdzad du saṅs rgyas par bsgom pa la sṅon byuṅ gi rnam thar re re daṅ re re sbyar nas bśad pa slob dpon rnam pa gsum gas mdzad pa mi snaṅ źiṅ / mṅon byaṅ lṅa rdzogs paḥi mthar rnam par snaṅ mdzad du saṅs rgyas paḥi bar gyi rim pa rnams sa bcu paḥi byaṅ sems kyi mdzad pa daṅ / de phyin cad kyi mdzad pa saṅs rgyas zin gyi mdzad par byed pa slob dpon kun sñiṅ gi de ñid snaṅ baḥi dgoṅs paḥo /

/ saṅs rgyas zin gyi mdzad pa daṅ mthun par lha bsgom pa la phyag rgya bźiḥi rgyas ḥdebs med na lam gyi rkaṅ ba stor ba lta bu yin pas cuṅ zad bśad par byaḥo /

Moreover, the Body of Vairocana is emphasized; but his Speech, Mind, and Marvellous Action are not lacking, so one applies seals of the four Seals. Again, the Mind of Akṣobhya is emphasized, but his Body, Speech, and Marvellous Action are also present. In the same way, it is the Speech of Amitābha, but there are also his Body, Mind, and Marvellous Action. In the other two Families, the main thing is Marvellous Action, but as Body, Speech, and Mind are also there, one applies the seals of the four Seals.

The *Avatāra* (Toh. 2501, the *Tantrārthāvatāra* by Buddhaguhya) says: "This sequence emphasizes four types beginning with Body; for this reason one speaks of four *maṇḍalas*. Nevertheless, it is not possible in general to have a mind without a body, nor a voice without body and mind. Consequently, even in the various *maṇḍalas* one must have the four portions, beginning with Body. Therefore, all the *maṇḍalas* of the Families are here explained as having the signs of Body and so forth, and, in their proper order, the four Seals, the Great Seal and the Symbolic, Law, and Action Seals."

If one comprehends their varieties down to the minute details, one understands that there is no contradiction between the two explanations when the *Śrī-Paramādiṭīkā* (of Ānandagarbha) sometimes explains the path of four sections by partitioning it into partial conditions for a single person to become a Buddha and sometimes explains it in the sense of the path of the various mental series of persons.

In the Yoga Tantra there is no contemplation of the sphere of purification — [in this case] the steps of birth state (**utpatti-bhava-krama*) — conforming to the category of corruption (*saṃkleśa*) [as in the case of the Anuttara Tantra], but there is a contemplation conforming to the resultative phase. The three *ācāryas* (i.e., Ānandagarbha, Buddhaguhya, and Śākyamitra) have not discussed the contemplation of Buddhahood as Vairocana at the end of completing the five Revelation-Enlightenments (*abhisaṃbodhi*) nor correlated each [of those five] with preceding biographical elements. However, the purport of the *Tattvāloka* (Toh. 2510) of Ānandagarbha is that the steps between the end of completing the five Revelation-Enlightenments and Buddhahood as Vairocana are the acts of a Bodhisattva of the Tenth Stage, and that the subsequent acts are the acts in the province of a Buddha.

If one intensely contemplates a god in conformity to the acts in the province of a Buddha but does not apply the seals of the four Seals, then links of the path are missing. Consequently, these must be briefly discussed.

/ gñis pa la lṅa / phyag rgya bźiḥi sgra don / dbye ba / go rims / rgyas btab paḥi dgos pa daṅ phan yon / ji ltar rgyas ḥdebs tshul lo /

/ daṅ po ni / phyag rgyas btab paḥi don ni ḥdar mi ruṅ ba yin pas / lha sgom paḥi tshul la phyag rgya bźiḥi rgyas btab pa ni tshul de las ḥdar mi ruṅ baḥo /

/ gñis pa ni phyag chen / dam rgya / chos rgya / las rgya ste bźi daṅ / sbyaṅ gźiḥi phyag rgya / sbyoṅ byed lam gyi phyag rgya / sbyaṅs pa ḥbras buḥi phyag rgya ste gsum mo /

[21] *Avatāra-vyākh.*, 94a-6, ff.: "'Seal' (*mudrā*) signifies the ability to arouse gladness or to make an impression, so there is the term *mudrā* ('*joyous seal*'). It is 'joyous' by reason of its ability to please the noble ones (*ārya*); it is a 'seal' by reason of the incision as a seal impression, since it cannot be effaced by others and speedily secures the desired thing" (phyag rgya ni mgu bar byed paḥam / ḥdegs (*sic.* for ḥdebs) par byed nus paḥi don daṅ ldan pas phyag rgya źes bya ste / ḥphags pa rnams mñes par byed nus pas na mgu ba źes byaḥo / gźan gyis gźig par mi nus śiṅ ḥdod paḥi dṅos po myur du ḥgrub paḥi phyir rgyas ḥdebs par ḥbyed pas na phyag rgya źes byaḥo). The text continues with an explanation of synonyms. It is also called **nimitta* (*mtshan ma*), 'attribute'; **lakṣman* (*rtags*), 'sign'; and **upalakṣana* (*ñe baḥi mtshan ñid*), 'referent'. All the synonyms are explained in terms of Knowledge (*jñāna*), from which the *mudrā* issues and to which it refers.

[22] *Avatāra-vyākh.*, 94b-5, f.: "Among them, the Great Seal (*mahā-mudrā*) shows the nature of deities by images of their bodies; and since it is the preeminent basis for vividly contemplating the nature of deity by way of body, it is called 'Great Seal'. There are two kinds: (1) the Consummated Body, and (2) the Sealed Body [i.e. Body created by the seal of the Family Progenitor]. (1) The Consummated Body means the Family, Family Lord, and so on, with full complement of the four seals, and appearing beautifully with their attire and ornaments. (2) The Sealed Body means the Form Goddess and so on, whom the candidate should resort to for the purpose of training, as they dwell on *stūpas* and thrones, having adopted the secret form of one's own attire. Each of those two has the varieties external and internal. The created images (*pratibimba*), such as those painted or drawn, are external. The ones imagined by oneself are internal. Their seals are called 'great'" (de la phyag rgya chen po ni lhaḥi skuḥi gzugs brñan pas lha rnams kyi tshul bstan pa ste / lus kyi sgo nas lhaḥi tshul gsal bar bsgom paḥi rgyur che bas na phyag rgya chen po źes byaḥo / de la yaṅ gñis te / yoṅs su rdzogs paḥi sku daṅ / phyag rgyaḥi skuḥo / de la yoṅs su rdzogs paḥi sku ni rigs daṅ rigs kyi gtso bo la sogs pa rnams te phyag rgya bźi rdzogs śiṅ cha lugs daṅ rgyan gyis mdzes par snaṅ baḥo / phyag rgyaḥi sku ni gzugs kyi lha mo la sogs pa dag gdul bya ji lta bu de ḥdul baḥi don du raṅ gi cha lugs su gyur paḥi gzugs sbas nas mchod rten khri la bźugs pa la sogs par bsten par byaḥo / de dag la yaṅ phyi naṅ gi bye brag gis rnam pa gñis su śes par bya ste / bris pa daṅ brtsams pa la sogs paḥi gzugs brñan byas pa rnams ni phyiḥo / ñid kyis bsam pa pa ni naṅ gi ste / de dag gi phyag rgya chen po źes byaḥo).

[23] *Avatāra-vyākh.*, 95a-1, f.: "The Symbolic Seal (*samaya-mudrā*) shows the nature of the mind of deities. Through its blessing of the Symbolic Seal the Knowledge possessed of perfect merit is displayed, and displayed as the seal which liberates the mind. Thus, by reason of not transgressing those deities, it is called 'Symbolic Seal'" (dam tshig gi phyag rgya ni lha rnams kyi sems kyi tshul bstan pa ste / yon tan phun sum tshogs pa daṅ ldan paḥi ye śes de ñid dam tshig gi phyag rgya byin gyis brlabs nas bstan

b. *Method of studying the steps of the path*

This has five parts: meaning of the expression 'four seals'; varieties; sequence; requirement and benefit of applying seals; and method of applying seals.

(1) MEANING OF THE EXPRESSION 'FOUR SEALS'

One should not overlook the meaning of impressing with seals:[21] it is the method of intense contemplation of a god. The impression with the seals of the four seals must not transgress that method.

(2) VARIETIES

Here there are the four seals, (a) Great Seal,[22] (b) Symbolic Seal,[23] (c) Law Seal,[24] (d) Action Seal.[25] Moreover, there are the three seals, (e) Seal of the sphere of purification, (f) Seal of the path of purification, (g) Seal of the fruit of purification.

---

pa ste / sems kyi rnam par thar paḥi phyag rgyar bstan pas lha rnams de las mi ḥdaḥ bas na dam tshig gi phyag rgya byaḥo). The passage continues with mention of some other views held in certain quarters. It should be observed that since the word *samaya* is also used with the meaning of 'pledge' in this literature, the term *samaya-mudrā* may also be translated as 'seal of the pledge'.

[24] *Avatāra-vyākh.*, 95a-4, 5: "The Law Seal (*dharma-mudrā*) shows the nature of the speech of deities. It has the characteristic of such syllables of the Law as *vajrajñāna* and *samayas tvaṃ*, which are attributes or signs of the pure intrinsic nature of speech; and it teaches all the sublime doctrines constituting the meaning of the language of deities" (chos kyi phyag rgya ni lha rnams kyi tshig gi tshul du bstan pa ste / gsuṅ rnam par dag paḥi raṅ bźin gyi mtshan maḥam rtags su gyur paḥi chos kyi yi ge vajra-jñāna daṅ / samaya-stvaṃ źes bya ba la sogs paḥi mtshan ñid de / lha rnams kyi tshig gi don dam paḥi chos thams cad ston par byed paḥo).

[25] *Avatāra-vyākh.*, 95a-6, 7: "The Action Seal (*karma-mudrā*) shows the nature of the conduct of deities. There are two kinds: (a) bound, and (b) imagined. Among them, (a) the bound one is when the seal is separated into two thunderbolt fists, and it has the characteristic of such seals as that of highest enlightenment (*paramabodhi*). (b) the imagined one is the four-mouthed thunderbolt imagined in one's own heart, whose shape teaches that at the time of evoking any particular deity all the latter's marvellous actions pervade intrinsic nature" (las kyi phyag rgya ni lha rnams kyi spyod paḥi tshul bstan pa ste / de la yaṅ gñis te / ḥchiṅ ba daṅ / bsam paḥo / de la ḥchiṅ ba ni phyag rgya rdo rje khu tshur gñis su phral ba daṅ / byaṅ chub mchog gi phyag rgya la sogs paḥi mtshan ñid do / bsam pa ni lha gaṅ yaṅ ruṅ ba dag bsgrub paḥi tshe phrin las thams cad ni raṅ bźin kun las khyab par bstan paḥi ṅo bo rdo rje kha bźi pa raṅ gi sñiṅ gar bsam mo).

/ sbyaṅ bya gźiḥi phyag rgya la tha mal gyi lus yid ṅag de dag gi bya ba bźi rim pa ltar phyag chen / dam rgya / chos rgya / las rgya daṅ bźiḥi sbyaṅ gźiḥi gtso bo yin no /

/ yaṅ ḥdod chags źe sdaṅ gti mug ser sna bźi rim pa ltar phyag chen sogs bźiḥi sbyaṅ gźir sbyor te / deḥi rgyu mtshan ni / goṅ du ḥdod chags śas che ba sogs kyi gdul bya rigs bźi dum bu bźiḥi gdul byar rim pa ltar sbyar źiṅ / dum bu bźi daṅ phyag rgya bźi rim pa bźin du sbyar nas bśad paḥi don gyis so /

/ yaṅ sa chu me rluṅ gi khams bźiḥi sbyaṅ gźir rim pa bźin sbyor te / deḥi rgyu mtshan ni / phyag rgya bźi dum bu bźiḥi rigs daṅ sbyor źiṅ / rigs bźi po sa khams rnam par dag pa rnam snaṅ / chu khams rnam par dag pa mi bskyod pa / me khams rnam par dag pa ḥod dpag med / rluṅ khams rnam par dag pa don grub yin paḥi don gyis so /

/ sbyoṅ byed lam gyi phyag rgya la dum bu bźi daṅ phyag rgya bźi sbyor te / dum bu daṅ po nas bstan paḥi lam rnams sku phyag rgya chen poḥi lam gtso che / gñis pa nas bstan paḥi lam rnams thugs dam tshig gi phyag rgyaḥi lam gtso che / gsum pa nas bstan paḥi lam rnams gsuṅ chos kyi phyag rgyahi lam gtso che / bźi pa nas bstan paḥi lam rnams ḥphrin las las kyi phyag rgyaḥi lam gtso che baḥi don gyis so /

/ yaṅ dum bu re reḥi dkyil ḥkhor chen po nas bstan paḥi tiṅ ṅe ḥdzin gsum la sogs paḥi lam rnams sku phyag rgya chen poḥi lam gtso che źiṅ / de bźin du gzuṅs dkyil daṅ / chos dkyil daṅ / las dkyil gsum gyi skabs nas bstan paḥi lam rnams rim pa ltar thugs dam rgya daṅ gsuṅ chos rgya daṅ ḥphrin las las kyi phyag rgya gsum re reḥi lam gtso che baḥi phyir rim pa bźin sbyar ro /

[26] The correspondences here can be tabulated as follows:

	Seal	Path of action	Person's Consciousness	Elements
1.	Great Seal	body	lust	earth
2.	Symbolic Seal	mind	hatred	water
3.	Law Seal	voice	delusion	fire
4.	Action Seal	conduct of body, mind, and voice	avarice	wind

[27] The correspondences here can be tabulated as follows:

	Maṇḍala	Seal	Object Symbolized	External Symbolizer	Internal Symbolizer
1.	Great (*mahā*)	Great Seal of Body	Form of deity's Body	Hand gesture	Identification of oneself and deity
2.	Memory (*dhāraṇī*)	Symbolic Seal of Mind	Knowledge of Deity's Mind	Hand symbol	Identification with Deity and with his Knowledge
3.	Law (*dharma*)	Law Seal of Speech	Voice Elegancies of	Syllables imagined in	Identification with deity,

The sphere of purification[26]

In regard to the Seal of the sphere of purification, the ordinary body, mind, voice, and their conduct are, in that order, the chief spheres of purification for the Great Seal, Symbolic Seal, Law Seal, and Action Seal.

Moreover, lust, hatred, delusion, and avarice are, in that order, correlated with the spheres of purification for the four Seals, beginning with the Great Seal. The reason for that is as follows: previously the candidates with preponderance of lust, etc., were correlated in sequence as candidates of the four sections of the four Families, and the four sections and the four seals were set in correspondence in the proper order.

Again, the four elements, earth, water, fire, and wind, are correlated in that order with the spheres of purification. The reason for that is as follows: the four Seals have been placed in correspondence with the Families of the four sections; and in those four Families, Vairocana is the perfect purity of earth, Akṣobhya the perfect purity of water, Amitābha the perfect purity of fire, and Amoghasiddhi the perfect purity of wind.

The path of purification[27]

In regard to the Seal of the path of purification, the four sections are correlated to the four seals: among the paths taught in the first section, the chief is the path of the Great Seal of Body; among the paths taught in the second section, the chief is the path of Symbolic Seal of Mind; among the paths taught in the third section, the chief is the path of the Law Seal of Speech; among the path taught in the fourth section, the chief is the path of the Action Seal of Marvellous Action.

Furthermore, among the paths beginning with the three *samādhis* shown in the *mahā-maṇḍala* of each section, the chief is the path of the Great Seal of Body. In the same way, among the paths showing [those *samādhis*] in the phases of the *dhāraṇī-maṇḍala*, the *dharma-maṇḍala*, and the *karma-maṇḍala*, the chief paths, respectively, are those of the Symbolic Seal of Mind, the Law Seal of Speech, and the Action Seal of Marvellous Action. Therefore, those [Seals] are correlated in the given order.

			Deity	Deity's body	and array of interior syllables
4.	Action (*karma*)	Action Seal of Wondrous Action	(not stated)	(not stated)	(not stated)

/ dkyil ḥkhor bźi po re reḥi rnam snaṅ la sogs paḥi lha re re la yaṅ phyag rgya bźiḥi rgyas ḥdebs paḥi phyag rgya re re la yaṅ mtshon byaḥi don daṅ / mtshon byed kyi phyag rgya gñis gñis / mtshon byed kyi phyag rgya la yaṅ phyiḥi mtshon byed kyi phyag rgya daṅ / naṅ gi mtshon byed kyi phyag rgya gñis su phye bas gsum gsum yod de /

/ de la phyag rgya chen po la rnam snaṅ la sogs pa lha de daṅ / deḥi skuḥi gzugs kyi rnam pa ni mtshon byaḥi don no / sku deḥi raṅ bźin du bźugs paḥi rnam pa daṅ mthun par bcas paḥi lag paḥi ḥdu byed ni mtshon byed phyiḥi phyag rgyaḥo / de daṅ dus mñam du bdag ñid lha de daṅ deḥi skur gsal bar dmigs pa ni mtshon byed naṅ gi phyag rgyaḥo /

/ dam tshig gi phyag rgya la lha de daṅ deḥi thugs rnam par mi rtog paḥi ye śes phyag mtshan gyi rnam par śar bar bsam pa ni mtshon byaḥi don no / de daṅ rnam pa mthun par bcas paḥi lag paḥi ḥdu byed ni mtshon byed phyiḥi phyag rgyaḥo / de daṅ dus mñam du raṅ ñid lha de daṅ der bsgoms paḥi rnam par mi rtog paḥi ye śes phyag mtshan gyi rnam par śar bar bsam pa ni mtshon byed naṅ gi phyag rgyaḥo /

/ chos kyi phyag rgya la lha de daṅ deḥi chos phuṅ brgyan khri bźi stoṅ ston paḥi gsuṅ dbyaṅs yan lag drug cu ni mtshon byaḥi don no / lha de daṅ der bsgoms paḥi lce daṅ lkog ma la sogs paḥi gnas rnams su yi ge dgod pa ni mtshon byed phyiḥi phyag rgyaḥo / raṅ lha de daṅ der gsal baḥi gsuṅ yig ḥbruḥi rnam par śar bar bsam pa ni mtshon byed naṅ gi phyag rgyaḥo /

/ sbyaṅs pa ḥbras buḥi phyag rgya la hbras buḥi skabs kyi sku daṅ thugs daṅ gsuṅ daṅ ḥphrin las te bźi daṅ / phyag chen sogs bźi rim pa bźin sbyor ba daṅ / yaṅ ye śes bźi daṅ phyag rgya bźi rim pa bźin sbyor te / deḥi rgyu mtshan ye śes bźi daṅ dum bu bźi sbyar źiṅ dum bu bźi daṅ phyag rgya bźi sbyar baḥi don gyis so / yaṅ sku bźi daṅ phyag rgya bźi rim pa bźin sbyor te / deḥi rgyu mtshan yaṅ sku bźi daṅ dum bu bźi sbyar źiṅ dum bu bźi daṅ phyag rgya bźi sbyar baḥi don gyis so /

[28] The correspondences here can be tabulated as follows:

	Blessing and Seal	Body	Knowledge	Bodhisattva activity
1.	Body and Great Seal	Svabhāva	Mirror-like	bodhicitta
2.	Mind and Symbolic Seal	Vipāka	Equality	dāna-pāramitā
3.	Speech and Law Seal	Saṃbhoga	Discriminative	prajña-pāramitā
4.	Wondrous Action and the Action Seal	Nirmāṇa	Procedure of Duty	vīrya-pāramitā

Again, for each deity, beginning with Vairocana, of each of the four *maṇḍalas*, one executes the seals of the four Seals; and for each seal there are the symbolized object and the seal of the symbolizing agent. The seal of the symbolizing agent is, in turn, divided into the seal of the external symbolizing agent and the seal of the internal symbolizing agent. Hence, there are three for each [namely, the symbolized object and the seals of the external and internal symbolizing agent].

In the case of the Great Seal, the symbolized object is the deity, Vairocana and so on, and the aspect of his bodily form. The seal of the external symbolizing agent is the hand gesture (**saṃskāra*) executed in conformity with the aspect in which his body abides naturally. The seal of the internal symbolizing agent, simultaneous with that [seal of the external symbolizing agent], is the vivid visualization of oneself as that deity and as his body.

In the case of the Symbolic Seal, the symbolized object is the deity and the non-discursive knowledge of his Mind, imagined to arise as hand symbols (*hasta-cihna*) [as, e.g., thunderbolt (*vajra*), noose (*pāśa*), etc.]. The seal of the external symbolizing agent is the hand gesture executed in conformity with that [hand symbol]. The seal of the internal symbolizing agent, simultaneous with that, is the contemplation of oneself as the deity and the non-discursive knowledge in him, imagined to arise as hand symbols.

In the case of the Law Seal, the symbolized object is the deity and his sixty elegancies of voice which express the 84,000 doctrines (*dharma*)). The seal of the external symbolizing agent is the deity and the arrangement of syllables contemplated in him in such places as the tongue and throat. The seal of the internal symbolizing agent is imagining oneself as the deity and (imagining) the arising in him of vivid phonemes.

The fruit of purification[28]

In regard to the Seal of the fruit of purification, one correlates the Body, Mind, Speech, and Marvellous Action of the fruitional phase in regular order with the four Seals beginning with the Great Seal. Moreover, one correlates the four Knowledges (*jñāna*) with the four Seals in regular order, for the reason that the four Knowledges are correlated with the four sections and the four sections are correlated with the four Seals. Furthermore, the four Bodies and the four Seals are correlated in regular order, for the reason that the four Bodies are correlated with the four sections and the four sections are correlated with the four Seals.

/ gsum pa ni / dam tshig pa bskyed pa la ye śes pa bcug nas de la phyag rgya bźiḥi rgyas ḥdebs pa yin gyi / dam tshig pa rkyaṅ pa daṅ / ye śes pa rkyaṅ pa gaṅ ruṅ re re la ma yin te / phyag rgya bźiḥi rgyas btab paḥi don ni ye śes paḥi sku gsuṅ thugs mdzad pa bźi daṅ dam tshig paḥi sku gsuṅ thugs mdzad pa bźi bsres nas dbyer mi phyed par byed pa yin pa la / gaṅ ruṅ re re pa la bsre rgyu med paḥi phyir te / bdag bskyed mdun bskyed gñis ka la ḥdraḥo /

/ de ltar yin par dpal mchog las / gaṅ la gaṅ gi rgyas btab pa / de ni de yi raṅ bźin ñid / ces pa daṅ / rtse mo las / kun gyi goṅ maḥam ḥog ma yi / ñi tshe ba de spaṅ bar bya / źes kun gyi goṅ ma ye śes pa daṅ / ḥog ma dam tshig pa ñi tshe ba ste phyogs re la rgyas ḥdebs pa spaṅ bar gsuṅs so /

/ de la slob dpon kun dgaḥ sñiṅ poḥi lugs la / dam rgya / chos rgya las rgya / phyag chen gyi rim pas bya bar bźed do / slob dpon saṅs rgyas gsaṅ ba daṅ śā-kya gñen gyis kyi lugs la / phyag chen dam rgya las rgya chos rgyaḥi rim pas bya bar bźed kyi / slob dpon de gñis kyi bźed pa sṅa rabs pa maṅ pos brjod pa ni de gñis kyi bźed pa ma go bar snaṅ ṅo /

/ kha cig na re / slob dpon de gñis kyi bźed pa mi ḥthad de / stod ḥgrel las / dam tshig gi phyag rgyas bsgrubs / chos kyi phyag rgyas bkod / las kyi phyag rgyas ḥphrin las la sbyar / phyag rgya chen pos rab tu gnas paḥi tshul gyis bźad par bya bar gsuṅs paḥi phyir / źes pa daṅ / lha re re

[29] This half-verse was translated with the help of Ānandagarbha's voluminous commentary, Toh. 2512, *Śrī-Paramādiṭīkā*, in which the exact citation was once located (probably in Derge Tanjur, *Rgyud*, Vol. I) but folio reference later lost. Our notes do show a similar verse of the *Śrī-Paramādya* (Toh. 488) at Derge *Rgyud ḥbum*, Vol. Ta, 241a-7: / lhag paḥi lha ni gaṅ gaṅ gis / phyag rgya gaṅ daṅ gaṅ ḥchiṅ ba / de daṅ de yi rnal ḥbyor gyis / phyag rgya de daṅ de sbyor bya /. This is commented upon by Ānandagarbha in Vol. I, 90b-2, ff., where *lhag paḥi lha* is expanded to *raṅ gi lhag paḥi lha* ("one's own presiding deity") and identified with the *jñānasattva* (*ye śes sems dpaḥ*). It appears that *adhideva* (*lhag paḥi lha*) was the principal word in the *āgama* literature of these Tantras to become glossed later on as *jñānasattva*.

[30] Here the 'latter' is the *yogin* identified with the Symbolic Being. The *yogin* has no 'own-being' or 'self-existence' (*svabhāva*): it belongs to the *adhideva* or Knowledge Being. We find a similar idea in the Anuttara-yoga-tantra when the five Buddhas are equated with the five personality aggregates (*skandha*) as their 'intrinsic nature' (*svabhāva*), while Buddhism declares that the five personality aggregates are devoid of intrinsic nature (*niḥsvabhāvatā*). Buddhaguhya differentiates the Knowledge Being and the Symbolic Being as follows in his *Avatāra*, 7b-1, ff.: "Furthermore, all those are of two kinds: (a) the self-existent (*svabhāvin*) discerned as deity, (b) those discerned by persons pledged (**samayin*) [to them]. Among those, (a) the ones discerned as deity are any ones discerned as having attributes (*nimitta*) manifested by the deities, or as having the shape of a deity, or as fashioned congruently with the latter's parts. (b) The ones discerned by persons pledged [to them] are any ones imagined as arising from the body of a deity and as having the shape of a deity which the pledged person has generated in conformity with that [body of a deity], or imagined congruently with

(3) SEQUENCE

One generates the Symbolic Being (*samaya-sattva*) and draws in the Knowledge Being (*jñāna-sattva*), then applies the seals of the four Seals, but not if there is only the Symbolic Being or only the Knowledge Being. The purpose of executing the seals of the four Seals is to merge and unify the Body, Speech, Mind, and Acts of the Knowledge Being with the body, speech, mind, and acts of the Symbolic Being. There would be no foundation for merger if either were present by itself. This is comparable to having both Self Generation and Generation in Front [in the Kriyā and Caryā Tantras].

That situation is referred to by the *Paramādya* (Toh. 488) when it says:[29]

> Whichever [*adhideva* = *iṣṭadevatā* 'over-lord'] is impressed by someone's seal,
> The former is the latter's Self-existence;[30]

and by the *Vajraśekhara* (Toh. 480) when it says:

> One should avoid the extreme of
> Either 'the uppermost' or 'the lower'.

Here 'the uppermost' is the Knowledge Being; 'the lower' is the Symbolic Being. One should avoid applying the seal to an extreme, i.e., to a single side.

The school of Ānandagarbha maintains that they are to be made in the sequence, Symbolic Seal, Law Seal, Action Seal, and Great Seal. The school of the two *ācāryas* Buddhaguhya and Śākyamitra maintans that they are to be made in the sequence, Great Seal, Symbolic Seal, Action Seal, and Law Seal. The thesis of the latter two *ācāryas* has been discussed by many past teachers, but the thesis was not understood.

Some assert that what is maintained by the two *ācāryas* [i.e. Buddhaguhya and Śākyamitra] is untenable, because the "Super-commentary" (T. *stod ḥgrel*, Toh. 2510, Ānandagarbha's *Vyākhyā* on the *Tattvasaṃgraha*) sets forth that one accomplishes with the Symbolic Seal, arranges with the Law Seal, attends to marvellous action with the Action Seal, and stabilizes in the manner of consecration (*pratiṣṭhā*) with the Great

---

the latter's parts" (de dag thams cad kyaṅ rnam pa gñis te / lhar brtag paḥi raṅ bźin daṅ / dam tshig can kyi skye bos brtags paḥo / de la lha rnams kyis sprul paḥi mtshan mar gyur pa gaṅ yin pa ḥam gaṅ lhaḥi ṅo bo ñid dam / deḥi cha śas su bye brag med par byas te brtag pa de ni lhar brtags paḥo / gaṅ yaṅ lhaḥi lus las / de daṅ rjes su mthun par dam tshig can gyis bskyed paḥi lhaḥi ṅo bo ñid dam / deḥi cha śas su bye brag med par mos pa de ni dam tshig can gyi skye bos brtags par grags so). The idea seems to be that the Knowledge Being is a veritable manifestation of the self-existent Buddhas, or of tenth stage Bodhisattvas such as Mañjuśrī, while the Symbolic Being is the imaginary deity which the yogin generates himself into.

yaṅ phyag rgya bźi daṅ / dgug gźug bciṅ dbaṅ du bya ba ste bźi daṅ / dbaṅ bskur daṅ / byin brlab gñis / tiṅ ṅe ḥdzin daṅ mchod pa gñis / phyag rgya daṅ sñiṅ po gñis / sṅags daṅ rig pa gñis te / sgo bcu drug bcu drug gi sgo nas bskyed dgos pa la / slob dpon de gñis kyi lugs de la sgo bcu drug ma tshaṅ baḥi phyir / źes zer ro /

/ de ni mi ḥthad de / dam tshig gi phyag rgyas bsgrubs / źes sogs kyi don ḥdi yin pas go rim pa ḥdi ltar ṅes dgos paḥi rgyu mtshan ḥdi yin / źes bśad pa mi snaṅ bas / slob dpon de gñis kyi lugs mi ḥthad de / kun dgaḥ sñiṅ po daṅ mi mthun paḥi phyir / źes par soṅ nas snaṅ bas / ḥo na kun dgaḥ sñiṅ poḥi lugs de yaṅ mi ḥthad de / saṅs rgyas gsaṅ ba daṅ mi mthun paḥi phyir / źes smras na ci zer / slob dpon de gñis kyi lugs ltar

[31] The sixteen ancillaries are listed by Ānandagarbha in his "Supercommentary", *Derge Tanjur Rgyud*, Vol. Li, 117a-1, 2, 3.

[32] A concise Sanskrit version of the fourfold process is found in the *Sādhana-mālā*, No. 110, p. 230, last line to 231.1: Oṃ vajrāṅkuśī ākarṣaya Jaḥ, Oṃ vajrapāśī praveṣaya Hūṃ, Oṃ vajrasphoṭa bandhaya Vaṃ, Oṃ vajrāveśe vaśīkuru Hoḥ. "Oṃ, May the diamond hook attract, Jaḥ!" "Oṃ, May the diamond noose draw in, Hūṃ!" "Oṃ, May the diamond chain tie, Vaṃ!" "Oṃ, May the diamond bell subdue, Hoḥ!"

[33] *Avatāra-vyākh.*, 98b-1, 2: "Attracting is the invitation by offerings. There are two kinds: invitation from the Dharmadhātu Palace of Akaniṣṭha, and attraction from the worldly realms of the ten quarters" (dgug pa ni mchod ciṅ spyan draṅs pa ste / de la yaṅ gñis te ḥog min gyi gnas chos kyi dbyiṅs kyi pho braṅ nas spyan draṅ ba daṅ / phyogs bcuḥi ḥjig rten gyi khams nas dgug paḥo).

[34] *Avatāra-vyākh.*, 98b-2, 3: "Drawing in is of three kinds: (1) the merging of the two *maṇḍalas* [of residence and residents] by drawing into the image *maṇḍala* and drawing into the retinue; (2) the merging of the two *sattvas* [the yogin and pledged deity] by drawing into the Symbolic Being; (3) the descent of the Knowledge Being by drawing into the disciple who is a fitting vessel" (gźug pa la yaṅ gsum ste gzugs brñan gyi dkyil ḥkhor du gźug pa la / ḥkhor du gźug pa dkyil ḥkhor rnam pa gñis gcig tu bya ba daṅ / dam tshig sems dpaḥ la bcug nas sems dpaḥ rnam gñis gcig tu bya ba daṅ / snod du gyur paḥi slob ma la bcug nas ye śes dbab par bya baḥo).

[35] *Avatāra-vyākh.*, 98b-3: "Tying means binding so there is no distinction between the evoker and the thing evoked" (bciṅ ba ni sgrub pa daṅ bsgrub bya ba gñis tha mi dad par bciṅ baḥo).

[36] *Avatāra-vyākh.*, 98b-3: "Subduing means making (them) rejoice, pleasing (them)" (dbaṅ du bya ba ni dgyes pa bsgrub pa ste mñes pa bya baḥo).

[37] *Avatāra-vyākh.*, 95b-5, ff.: "Initiation is the means of attaining power over all nature. There are two kinds: (1) Initiation (just) for the sake of conferring; (2) initiation for the purpose of generating the power. Among those, (1) means the Buddhas Bhagavats, who have exhausted the Knowable (*jñeya*) and attained the ultimate of merit (*guṇa*); in order that they may be honored by other [Buddhas] they are initiated with the flower garland, the jewel garland, and so on. (2) means the Bodhisattvas, who as yet have not exhausted the Knowable and attained the ultimate of merit; in order that they may exhaust the Knowable and attain the ultimate of merit, they are initiated by the five Families with the diadem and other [initiations] representing the five knowledges..." (dbaṅ bskur ba ni thams cad kyi bdag ñid la dbaṅ thob par bya baḥi thabs su gyur pa ste / de yaṅ gñis te / bskur baḥi don du dbaṅ bskur ba daṅ / mthu bskyed paḥi phyir dbaṅ bskur baḥo / de la saṅs rgyas bcom ldan ḥdas rnams ni śes

Seal; and that, moreover, each deity must be evoked by way of all sixteen ways:[31] the four Seals; the fourhold process[32] of 'attracting' (*ākarṣaṇa*),[33] 'drawing in' (*praveṣaṇa*),[34] 'tying' (*bandhana*),[35] and 'subduing' (*vaśīkāra*);[36] both Initiation (*abhiṣeka*)[37] and Blessing (*adhiṣṭhāna*);[38] both 'profound concentration' (*samādhi*) and 'offering' (*pūjā*); both 'seal' (*mudrā*) and 'heart' (*hṛdaya*);[39] and both 'incantation' (*mantra*) and 'wisdom' (*vidyā*). Then they assert that the position of the two *ācāryas* is untenable because the sixteen ways are not complete [in their system].

Those assertions [themselves] are untenable. When the remarks, "one accomplishes with the Symbolic Seal", and so forth, were made, they were not attended with explanations of the type, "This is the meaning of those statements", or, "This is the reason why there must necessarily be such a sequence." Hence, if it is reasonable to say that the position of the two *ācāryas* is untenable because it is inconsistent with that of Ānandagarbha, we may as well say that the position of Ānandagarbha is untenable because it is inconsistent with that of the two *ācā-*

---

bya rdzogs śiṅ yon tan mthar phyin pa yin pas de dag la ni gźan gyis mchod paḥi phyir me tog gi phreṅ ba daṅ / rin po cheḥi phreṅ ba la sogs pas dbaṅ bskur baḥo / byaṅ chub sems dpaḥ rnams ni da duṅ du śes bya ma rdzogs śiṅ yon tan gyi rnam pa mthar ma phyin pas de dag ni śes bya daṅ yon tan rdzogs śiṅ mthar phyin par bya baḥi phyir / rigs lṅas ye śes lṅaḥi dbu rgyan la sogs pa dbaṅ bskur baḥam / ...).

[38] *Avatāra-vyākh.*, 95b-2, 3: "Blessing is the means of fulfilling all wishes accordingly. There are two kinds: blessing of intrinsic nature and blessing with power [in the latter case, e.g. when one is empowered by the Buddha for a supernormal function]. As to the rite for gaining blessing-whatever the deity one wishes to contemplate, or with conviction toward which one has contemplated, one vividly contemplates the latter's body as the Great Seal, and by descent of the Knowledge Being, and so on, stations the deity..." (byin gyis brlabs pa ni gaṅ ltar ḥdod pa de bźin bya baḥi thabs te / de la yaṅ gñis te / raṅ bźin byin gyis brlabs pa daṅ / mthus byin gyis brlabs paḥo / byin gyis brlab par bya baḥi cho ga ni bdag lha gaṅ bsgom par ḥdod paḥam / gaṅ la mos śiṅ goms par gyur pa deḥi sku phyag rgya chen por gsal bar bsgoms nas ye śes dbab pa la sogs pa lha gnas par byas nas...). The passage continues with quotation of a verse from the Continuation Tantra involving the seal of Vajradhātvīśvara and blessing at the heart, *ūrṇākośa* (between the eyebrows), neck, and crown of head; blessing at those four places is also discussed in Ānandagarbha's "Super-commentary" (Toh. 2510), Vol. Śi, 197a.

[39] *Avatāra-vyākh.*, 93b-7, f.: "Heart is of two kinds: with attributes and without attributes (*sanimitta* and *animitta*). The one without attributes means the Dharmakāya; it is also referred to as the highly secret nature, with meaning of the universal essence. The one with attributes is said to be the eleven 'heart [incantations]' of the various Families, and so on, as the case may be..." (de la sñiṅ po źes bya ba ni rnam pa gñis te / mtshan ma yod pa daṅ / mtshan ma med paḥo / de la mtshan ma med pa ni chos kyi sku la bya ste / de ni thams cad kyi sñiṅ poḥi don śin tu gsaṅ bar gyur paḥi ṅo bo de la yaṅ de skad brjod do / mtshan ma yod pa ni rigs so soḥi sñiṅ po bcu gcig pa la sogs par gsuṅs pa gaṅ yaṅ ruṅ ba dag go / ...).

byas na sgo bcu drug ma tshaṅ baḥi rgyu mtshan yaṅ smra dgos so /

/ ḥo na khyed raṅ gi lugs la slob dpon de gñis kyi bźed pa ji ltar yin źe na / dbu ma la ḥjug pa las / sems ḥgags pas de sku yis mṅon sum mdzod / ces gsuṅs paḥi don daṅ mthun par / chos kyi sku de loṅs spyod rdzogs paḥi skuḥi rten la mṅon du mdzad dgos pas sku phyag rgya chen poḥi rgyas ḥdebs daṅ por byed / chos sku mṅon du ma mdzad par ḥphrin las ḥbad med lhun grub mi ḥbyuṅ bas / dam rgya dus gñis par byed / chos sku mṅon du mdzad nas ḥphrin las ḥbad med lhun grub ḥbyuṅ bas / dam rgyaḥi rjes su las rgya byed / gsuṅ dbyaṅs yan lag drug cus chos ston pa ñid ḥphrin las kyi gtso bo yin pas las rgyaḥi rjes la chos rgyaḥi ḥdebs byed pa yin no /

/ yaṅ ḥo na khyed kyi lugs la slob dpon kun dgaḥ sñiṅ poḥi bźed pa ji ltar źe na / dam tshig gi phyag rgyas raṅ daṅ lha gñis su med par sṅar ma grub pa gsar du bsgrubs nas de kho na ñid kyi don la mñam par ḥjog pa yin pas / dam rgya daṅ por byed / de kho na ñid kyi don la rtse gcig tu mñam par ḥjog pa daṅ / ṅag nus pa mthu can du gyur pa med par ḥjig rten las ḥdas paḥi lha ḥphrin las la bskul mi nus pas / chos rgya dus gñis par byed / thugs de kho na ñid la mñam par gźag ciṅ ṅag nus pa mthu can grub nas ḥphrin las la sbyor bas / las rgya dus gsum par byed / phyag rgya chen po nas raṅ daṅ lha gñis su med par grub zin gyi don la rab tu gnas paḥi tshul gyis mñam par gźag par bya ba yin pa la sṅon du gñis su med par ma grub par gñis su med paḥi don la mñam par ḥjog pa mi ḥoṅ bas phyag rgya chen poḥi rgyas ḥdebs rjes la byed par bstan pa yin no /

/ ḥo na raṅ lugs de gñis gaṅ byed zer na / gaṅ byas kyaṅ chog go / ḥo na kyaṅ dkyil chog rdo rje ḥbyuṅ ba la brten nas byed na / slob dpon kun sñiṅ gi lugs ñid byed dgos so /

ryas. Furthermore, we should give as a reason that if one does it according to the position of those two *ācāryas*, the sixteen ways are *not* complete.

[Suppose it be asked:] "Then, what is the position in your own school regarding the thesis of those two *ācāryas*?" It is consistent with the remark in the *Madhyamakāvatāra* [of Candrakīrti], "The one whose mind is thwarted must do it in immediacy with the body." Thus, the Dharma-kāya must be realized in immediacy on the foundation of the Saṃbhoga-kāya. For this reason, one performs first the seal execution of the Great Seal of Body. When the Dharma-kāya is not realized in immediacy, there is no effortless and spontaneous origination of Marvellous Action. For this reason, one performs second the Symbolic Seal. When the Dharma-kāya is realized in immediacy, there is effortless and spontaneous origination of Marvellous Action. For this reason, after the Symbolic Seal one performs the Action Seal. The teaching of the Law by means of the sixty elegancies of voice is the chief of Marvellous Actions. For this reason, after the Action Seal one performs the seal execution of the Law Seal.

[Suppose it be asked:] "This being so, what is the position in your school regarding the thesis of Ānandagarbha?" When one newly accomplishes what has not been previously accomplished — namely, non-duality between oneself and the god by means of the Symbolic Seal, he is equipoised one-pointedly on the meaning of reality. For this reason, one performs first the Symbolic Seal. If one is equipoised one-pointedly on the meaning of reality, but cannot lend power to his voice, he is unable to exhort the supra-mundane deity to Marvellous Action. For this reason, one performs second the Law Seal. When one's mind is equipoised on reality and one is able to lend power to his voice, he [the deity] attends to Marvellous Action. For this reason, one performs third the Action Seal. When one has consummated non-duality of oneself and the god by way of the Great Seal, he is equipoised by means of staying in the meaning; but when one has not completed first the non-duality, he is not equipoised in the meaning of non-duality. For this reason, it is taught that one performs next the seal execution of the Great Seal.

[Suppose it be asked:] "Well now, in your own school which of the two is followed?" Either of them. However, if one takes recourse to the *Maṇḍalavidhisarvavajrodaya* (Toh. 2516, by Ānandagarbha), he must perform according to the position of *ācārya* Ānandagarbha.

/ bźi pa ni / dgos paḥi gtso bo ni tha mal paḥi lus ṅag yid gsum bya ba daṅ bcas pa bźi / rgyal baḥi sku gsuṅ thugs ḥphrin las daṅ bcas pa bźir bsgyur baḥo /

/ lṅa pa ni / de la phyag rgya ḥbyuṅ baḥi rgyu / phyag rgya raṅ gi ṅo bo ḥchaḥ baḥi cho ga / ḥgrub paḥi rgyu / grub pa dbaṅ du ḥgyur baḥi rgyu daṅ bźi las /

/ ḥbyuṅ baḥi rgyu ni dam rgyaḥi phyag rgya thams cad rdo rje bsdams pa las ḥbyuṅ bar rgyud las bśad pa la / kha cig gis a-va-tā-ra daṅ ko-sa-laḥi rgyan gñis las / rdo rje bsdams pa phyag rgya thams cad kyi rgyu yin par bśad ciṅ / de brgyud rgyu la dgoṅs / slob dpon kun sñiṅ gis rgyu yin pas ma khyab par bśad de / dṅos rgyu la dgoṅs pa yin zer nas / daṅ por rdo rje bsdams pa bcas te / de las rnam snaṅ gi dam rgya ḥchaḥ / deḥi rdo rje bsdams pa daṅ po bcas pa de ma bkrol bar rnam snaṅ gi dam rgya las lha gźan gyi dam rgya ḥchaḥ / de las yaṅ gźan gyi rim pa ltar ḥchaḥ bar byed pa mi ḥthad de / rgyud daṅ rdo rje ḥbyuṅ ba gñis ka las / dam tshig gi phyag rgya thams cad ni / rdo rje bsdams pa las ḥbyuṅ bas na / źes gsuṅs pa daṅ / rdo rje bsdams pa daṅ bcas nas / źes pa dam rgya thams cad kyi mgor sbyar rgyu yin paḥi phyir ro /

/ kha cig va-jra-sa-tva / źes pas rdo rje bsdams pa bcas la / des mig byin gyis brlabs te / źes zer ba mi ḥthad de / va-jra-sa-tva źes pa mig byin gyis rlob paḥi sṅags ma yin gyi / rdo rje bsdams pa bcaḥ baḥi sṅags yin paḥi phyir ro / rdo rje ḥbyuṅ ba las / ba-dzra-dri-ḍha-tiṣṭa źes pa mig byin gyis rlob paḥi sṅags su gsuṅs pa yin no / des na dam rgya thams cad la re reḥi sṅon du rdo rje bsdams pa re re bcaḥ mi dgos na ba-dzra-sa-tva źes paḥi sṅags kyaṅ re re la re re brjod mi dgos par ḥgyur ro / deḥi phyir ba-dzra-sa-tva źes pas rdo rje bsdams pa bcas la / ba-dzra-dṛ-ḍha-

[40] It is with some reluctance that the four Aristotelian causes are employed to translate the four Tibetan expressions; still literal translations from the Tibetan would have conveyed little sense in these contexts. It is an open problem as to why the four causes so well known from Greek philosophy should have served so aptly in translating these expressions.

[41] The *dhāraṇī* as found in Mkhas grub rje's text is obviously a corruption. The correction *vajradṛṣṭi* is based upon this passage of Ānandagarbha's *Vajrasattvodaya* (Toh. 2517), Ku, 56a-6, f.: "Then he disposes [the *dhāraṇī*] *vajradṛṣṭi* (O, diamond sight!) in the two eyes; and having tied the Symbolic Seal of the Bhagavat, he mutters '*vajrasattvadṛśya*' and sees that Knowledge Being. Then, to contemplate [that Being] within one's own body, muttering Jaḥ, Hūṃ, Vaṃ, Hoḥ, he manages [respectively] to attract, draw in, tie, and subdue [the Knowledge Being]" (de nas vajradṛṣṭi źes bya ba mig gñis su bkod la / bcom ldan ḥdas kyi dam tshig gi phyag rgya bciṅs nas / vajrasatvadṛśya źes brjod de / ye śes sems dpaḥ de mthoṅ nas / raṅ gi lus la rab tu bsgoms / jaḥ hūṃ baṃ hoḥ bkug ciṅ bcug la bciṅ ba daṅ / dbaṅ du byas la bsgrub par bya).

(4) REQUIREMENT AND BENEFIT OF SEAL EXECUTION

The chief requirement is that the vulgar body, speech, and mind, together with their conduct, be transmuted into the Buddha's Body, Speech, and Mind, together with their Marvellous Action.

(5) METHOD OF SEAL EXECUTION

[For each seal] there are four [causes]: the 'efficient cause' of the seal, the 'formal cause' (*svarūpa*) of the seal and the rite of executing it, the 'material cause', and the 'final cause'.[40]

Symbolic Seal

The Tantras teach that the thunderbolt tie (*vajrabaṇdha*) is the 'efficient cause' of all Symbolic Seals. Some persons assert that when the *Avatāra* (Toh. 2501 by Buddhaguhya) and the *Kosalālaṃkāra* (Toh. 2503 by Śākyamitra) explain the cause of all the seals to be the thunderbolt tie, their purport is the 'remote (or ancestral) cause' (*brgyud rgyu*), disagreeing with the cause as given by Ānandagarbha, whose purport is the 'near (or actual) cause' (*dṅos rgyu*). [Those persons conclude:] Hence, first one executes the thunderbolt tie, then executes the Symbolic Seal of Vairocana; and, without untying the original thunderbolt tie, enacts after the Symbolic Seal of Vairocana the Symbolic Seals of the other deities. It is improper to execute [the seals] in any other sequence, because both the Tantras and the *Vajrodaya* (Toh. 2516) say, "All the Symbolic Seals arise from the thunderbolt tie", and say, "Having executed the thunderbolt tie", thus [positing it] as the cause added at the inception of all Symbolic Seals.

Some persons, while muttering "*Vajrasattva*" execute the thunderbolt tie, and claim that thereby the eyes are blessed (*adhiṣṭhita*). That is not valid, because "*Vajrasattva*" is not a *dhāraṇī* for blessing the eyes, but the *dhāraṇī* for executing the thunderbolt tie. According to the *Vajrodaya*, "*Vajradṛṣṭi*" is the *dhāraṇī* for blessing the eyes.[41] Thus, if it were not necessary to execute a thunderbolt tie before each Symbolic Seal, it would likewise be not necessary to utter each time the *dhāraṇī* "*Vajrasattva*" [but it is necessary]. Therefore, one enacts the thunderbolt tie while muttering "*Vajrasattva*"; and, gazing with the eye of divine knowledge (*jñāna-cakṣus*) which is the eye blessed (or empowered) by muttering "*Vajradṛṣṭi*" one sees with direct perception the Knowledge Being (*jñāna-cattva*) Vairocana dwelling in front. Thereupon, while muttering "*Oṃ*

ti-ṣṭha źes pas mig byin gyis brlabs paḥi ye śes kyi mig gis bltas pas rnam par snaṅ mdzad ye śes pa mdun na bźugs pa mṅon sum du mthoṅ bar bas na / de nas Oṃ ba-dzra-dha-tvi-śva-rī źes pas rnam snaṅ gi dam rgya bcas la / dzaḥ hūṃ baṃ hoḥ źes pa bźis rim pa ltar dgug gźug bciṅ dbaṅ du byas nas raṅ daṅ ye śes pa gñis su med par bya / de nas ba-dzra-sa-tva źes pas rnam snaṅ gi rgyab tu ñi maḥi rgyab yol bsam / ba-dzra-sa-tva sa-ma-ya-stvaṃ ā-haṃ / źes pas raṅ ñid ye śes pa daṅ gñis su med paḥi bdag ñid du ṅa rgyal bya /

/ de rnams kyi rgyas btab nas / kha cig lha thams cad kyi rgyas btab zin paḥi rjes la lha thams cad kyi thugs kar zla baḥi dkyil ḥkhor gyi steṅ du daṅ poḥi rdo rje rtse lṅa ba re re źes zer bar byed do / bsgom don la ni de tsam gyis mi chog ste / rgyas btab zin paḥi rjes thogs ñid du rnam par snaṅ mdzad kyi thugs rnam par mi rtog paḥi ye śes de ñid zla baḥi steṅ du rdo rje dkar po rtse lṅa baḥi rnam par bsgoms te / de la sems rtse gcig ñid du dmigs nas spyiḥi sṅags gsum gsum daṅ / raṅ raṅ gi gsum gsum bzlas te / de la yun riṅ du dmigs pa ni phyag rgya ḥgrub paḥi rgyuḥo /

/ de nas raṅ gi phuṅ po sogs stoṅ pa ñid du rigs pas bśig nas sgom pa ni dbaṅ du byed paḥi rgyuḥo /

/ chos kyi phyag rgya ḥbyuṅ baḥi rgyu ni brjod pa sgraḥi ḥdu byed do /

/ rgyas ḥdebs paḥi tshul ni lha de daṅ deḥi lkog mar hrīḥ las padma dmar po ḥdab ma brgyad pa lceḥi phyogs kyi ḥdab ma gcig lcer gyur paḥi steṅ du rdo rje dkar po rtse lṅa pa mchur ñal pa źig bsam / Oṃ ba-dzra-dzi-hva źes pas byin gyis brlabs la ba-dzra-dzā-na la sogs paḥi raṅ raṅ gi chos kyi yi ge rnams rdo rjeḥi lte ba la dkris paḥi tshul du bkod la / chos kyi yi ge dag tu brjod pa rnams rgyas ḥdebs paḥi tshul lo /

/ de la lus kyi phyag rgya phyag chen ḥchaḥ ba bu ston rin po che daṅ / ri bo dge ldan pa gñis kaḥi phyag len la mdzad pa la / kha cig na re / chos rgya la lus kyi phyag rgya bcaḥ ba gaṅ nas kyaṅ bśad pa med zer ro / de ni śin tu mi ḥthad de / dpal mchog las / laṅs paḥam ni ḥdug paḥam /

[42] The *dhāraṇī* as found in Mkhas grub rje's text is obviously a corruption. He himself pointed out in an earlier chapter that only in the Anuttara-yoga-tantra would Vajradhātvīśvarī (the Queen of the Diamond Realm) be invoked in such a context. Again, Vairocana is certainly the Vajradhātvīśvara.

Vajradhātvīśvara" ('Oṃ, the Lord of the Diamond Realm'),[42] one executes the Symbolic Seal of Vairocana; and muttering "Jaḥ", "Hūṃ", "Vaṃ", "Hoḥ" in that order, one respectively attracts, draws in, ties, and subdues [the Knowledge Being], bringing about non-duality between oneself and the Knowledge Being. Then, muttering "*Vajrasattva*", one imagines in back of Vairocana a sun halo; and muttering "*Vajrasattva samayas tvam ahaṃ*" ('O Vajrasattva, you the symbol am I'), one brings about the 'pride' (*garva*) in oneself that oneself and the Knowledge Being are non-dual.

Some persons who have executed those seals assert that when one has finished executing the seals of all the deities, subsequently, on the moon in the heart of each of the deities there appears a five-pronged 'primordial thunderbolt' (*ādi-vajra*). But that alone does not suffice for the aim of the contemplation. After finishing execution of the seals, one first contemplates on the moon a white five-pronged thunderbolt, representing the non-discursive knowledge which is Vairocana's heart. Dwelling upon it as the sole area of thought, one mutters thrice each general *dhāraṇī* and mutters thrice each special *dhāraṇī*. Dwelling on that for an extended period constitutes the 'material cause' of the seal.

Thereupon, the contemplation which destroys one's personality aggregates (*skandha*) and so forth, by understanding them to be voidness (*śūnyatā*), constitutes the 'final cause'.

Law Seal

The 'efficient cause' of the Law Seal is the instigation (*saṃskāra* as the *preraṇa*) of the sounds of the recitation.

The method of casting the seal is as follows: One imagines the deity and in that deity's throat the syllable "Hrīḥ", from which arises an eight-petalled red lotus. The single petal in the direction of the tongue changes into a tongue, and upon that there appears a white five-pronged thunderbolt resting on the lip. [The tongue] is blessed by muttering, "*Oṃ vajra-jihvā*" ('Oṃ, the diamond tongue'). The various individual syllables of the Law (*dharma*), such as "*Vajrajñāna*" ('Diamond Knowledge'), are arranged in a circle on the nave of the thunderbolt. The recitations [of those] as syllables of the Law constitute the method of casting the seal.

Therein lies the procedure of both Bu-ston Rin-po-che and Ri-bo Dge-ldan-pa for executing the Great Seal, which is the Seal of Body. Some [objecting] assert that nowhere is the Law Seal explained as executing the Seal of Body. That [objection] is exceedingly invalid. It is said in the *Paramādya* (Toh. 488):

gaṅ dag der ni gnas paḥam / thams cad rjes chags sbyor ba yis / dṅos grub thams cad thob par ḥgyur / źes gsuṅs śiṅ / deḥi ḥgrel par dpal mchog ḥgrel chen las / de ñid brjod pas raṅ gi lhaḥi gzugs brñan laṅs paḥam ḥdug pa bsgom par byaḥo / thams cad rjes chags rnal ḥbyor gyis / źes bya ba ni ḥdir raṅ bźin gyis rnam par dag paḥi ṅo bo ñid do / de ltar byas pas ci źig ḥgrub ce na / dṅos grub thams cad thob par ḥgyur / źes bya ba la / rigs thams cad kyi lha rnams kyi chos kyi phyag rgya ni dṅos grub thams cad de de ḥgrub par ḥgyur ro / źes gsuṅs te / de ñid brjod pas / źes pa chos kyi yi ge ṅag tu brjod pa daṅ / raṅ gi lha ste / gaṅ la phyag rgyas gdab par bya baḥi lha laṅs paḥam ḥdug pa la sogs paḥi rnam pa daṅ mthun paḥi lus kyi rnam ḥgyur gyi phyag rgya bcaḥ ba daṅ / sems de kho na ñid kyi don la mñam par bźag pa gsum dus gcig tu tshogs par byed pa ni phyag rgya ḥbyuṅ baḥi rgyu yin pa la / phyag chen bcaḥ ba med na ḥgrub paḥi rgyu ma tshaṅ bar ḥgyur bas / ḥdir phyag chen ḥchaḥ ba ḥgog pa śin tu mi rigs so /

/ chos rgya dbaṅ du ḥgyur baḥi rgyu ni lus lha gaṅ yin pa deḥi rnam par gsal ba daṅ / thugs de kho na ñid rtogs paḥi don la rtse gcig tu dmigs paḥi zab gsal gñis med kyi ṅaṅ las rdo rje daṅ bcas paḥi lce yar rkan la sbyar nas / de nas rdo rje phra mo nas ḥbru tsam ḥphros pa snaḥi rtse mor bsgoms te / de la reg mthoṅ gi mtshan ma byuṅ byuṅ du bsgoms pas chos rgya la brten nas dṅos grub śin tu chen po rnams ḥgrub pa ni chos rgya dbaṅ du gyur baḥi tshad do /

/ las rgya ḥbyuṅ baḥi rgyu ni rdo rje khu tshur ro /

/ rgyas ḥdebs paḥi tshul ni gYon paḥi rdo rje khu tshur gyi steṅ du gYas paḥi rdo rje khu tshur bźag la pad skor sṅon du ḥgro bas lha de daṅ deḥi phyag mtshan med paḥi phyag chen ḥchaḥ ba yin te / raṅ raṅ gi

[43] "Material cause" would be more consistent with the context, esp. the next sentence, as well as with the fact that the "efficient cause" was already explained only in terms of the sounds of the recitation. Hence we assume a text corruption of *ḥgrub* into *ḥbyuṅ*.

[44] From the discussion in the *Sṅags rim*, 103a, it is plain that "tip of nose" does not mean end of nose but root of nose, or point between the eyes, because the tiny thunderbolt is meditatively lifted from the nostril to stand at the tip of the nose (*de nas bteg ste sna khuṅ nas sna rtser ḥgreṅ ste...*). At the same place Tsoṅ-kha-pa mentions the view of Buddhaguhya that contemplation of the tiny thunderbolt is attended with *prāṇāyāma*.

[45] *Avatāra-vyākh.*, 195a-3: "Regarding the 'thunderbolt fist', what teaches the Tathāgatas' merits of Body, Speech, and Mind assembled together is the thunderbolt fist" (rdo rje khu tshur źes pa ni / de bźin gśegs pa rnams kyi sku gsuṅ thugs kyi yon tan gcig tu ḥdus par bstan pa ni rdo rje khu tshur te). This explanation is suggestive of the fact that the Action Seal represents the wondrous action of Body, Speech, and Mind.

> By the *yoga* of complete attraction towards (*anurāga*)
> [the deity],
> Be he standing, or sitting, or just abiding there,
> One obtains all *siddhis*.

On this the *Paramādiṭīkā* (Toh. 2512) comments:

> While reciting Thatness, one must contemplate the image of one's deity, whether standing or sitting. "By the *yoga* of complete attraction towards" means here the 'formal cause', intrinsically pure. What is 'materialized' by proceeding that way? "One obtains all *siddhis*"; and the Law Seal of the deities of all the Families 'materializes' all those *siddhis*.

The expression "while reciting Thatness" means vocalizing the syllables of the Law. One executes a seal consisting in an attitude of body conforming to the aspect of the god on whom the seal is to be cast, whether he be standing, sitting, or so on. One equipoises his mind in the meaning of Thatness. The synchronisation of the three is the 'efficient cause' [?][43] of the seal. If the Great Seal were not executed, there would be an incomplete 'material cause'. Consequently, it is most improper to oppose the execution of the Great Seal at this point.

The 'final cause' of the Law Seal is as follows: the body is transfigured into the aspect of the particular god, and the mind is focussed on the sole area of comprehending reality. One contemplates that from the realm of non-duality of the Profound [the mental component] and the Bright [the physical component] the tongue with the thunderbolt touches the upper palate; that thereupon a tiny thunderbolt (*sūkṣma-vajra*) no bigger than a barley grain stays on the tip of his nose,[44] which [tiny thunderbolt] one contemplates until he can feel and see it. Thus, by taking recourse to the Law Seal very great *siddhis* are 'materialized', which is the standard for the 'final cause'.

Action Seal

The 'efficient cause' of the Action Seal is the thunderbolt fist (*vajra-muṣṭi*).[45]

The method of casting the seal is as follows: one places the right thunderbolt fist on top of the left thunderbolt fist; and, preceding with the 'lotus whirling', executes the Great Seal of the deity and without his hand symbols. One recites [the deity's] own *dhāraṇī*, releases the

sṅags brjod la phyag rgya ḥgrol ba na se gol gtog ciṅ ḥphrin las mdzad par mos paḥo /

/ ḥgrub paḥi rgyu ni phyag rgya ḥchaḥ baḥi dus su lha de daṅ deḥi thugs kar sna tshogs rdo rje re re sgom źiṅ de ñid bya ba sgrub paḥi ye śes kyi ṅo bor mos paḥo /

/ dbaṅ du ḥgyur baḥi rgyu ni lus kyi spyod lam thams cad gar la sogs pas lhas lha mchod pa daṅ / ṅag gi smra brjod thams cad glu la sogs paḥi sgo nas lhas lha mchod pa daṅ / bzaḥ btuṅ la sogs pa thams cad kyaṅ ṅo bo lha daṅ stoṅ pa ñid dbyer med pa las rnam pa gzugs sgra la sogs par śar bar mos nas lhas lha mchod par mos pa rgyun ldan du dran śes na re bsten nas bsgom pa ste / de ltar bsgoms pas goms pa brtan pa na lus ṅag gi spyod lam thams cad kyis lhaḥi ḥphrin las ḥgrub pa na dbaṅ du gyur paḥo /

/ phyag chen ḥbyuṅ baḥi rgyu ni gtso cher rdo rje khu tshur ro /

/ rgyas ḥdebs paḥi tshul ni raṅ bźin du bźugs paḥi phyag rgya chen po bcaḥ ba ste / byaṅ chub mchog gi phyag rgya la sogs paḥo /

/ ḥgrub paḥi rgyu ni lha de daṅ deḥi thugs kar daṅ poḥi rdo rje rtse lṅa pa re re sgom paḥo /

/ dbaṅ du ḥgyur baḥi rgyu ni zab gsal gñis su med paḥi lhaḥi rnal ḥbyor la brtan pa thob thob tu sgom pa yin te / ḥdi go sla ba la dgoṅs nas dṅos su ma bśad do /

/ de la rnam snaṅ gi rgyas ḥdebs zin nas mi bskyod paḥi rgyas ḥdebs byed na / raṅ ñid rnam par snaṅ mdzad kyi rnam par bsgoms pa ñid kyis byed dam mi bskyod paḥi rnam par bsgyur nas byed / daṅ po ltar na rnam snaṅ la rgyas btab par ḥgyur gyi mi bskyod pa la rgyas btab par mi ḥgyur ro / gñis pa ltar na śar gyi mi bskyod pa tshur ḥphos te śar kyi reḥu mig stoṅ par sgom mam / mi bskyod pa gñis sgom pa gaṅ byed ce na /

seal; and, snapping his fingers, imagines with conviction that he performs the Marvellous Action.

The 'material cause' is as follows: At the time of executing the seal, one contemplates the deity and a crossed thunderbolt (*viśva-vajra* or *karma-vajra*) in the deity's heart, and imagines with conviction that [the crossed thunderbolt] is the essence of the Knowledge of the Procedure of Duty (*kṛtyānuṣṭhāna-jñāna*).

The 'final cause' is as follows: one contemplates with conviction that the gods make offering to the gods by means of all sorts of bodily postures (*īryāpatha*), such as dancing; that the gods make offering to the gods by way of all sorts of vocal expressions (*abhilāpana*), such as singing; that even the food, drink, and so forth, are all in essence the indissoluble union of the deities and voidness; and that the various types of action (*karma*) appear in shapes and sounds. And one contemplates with reliance on continual mindfulness and awareness of the conviction that the gods make offering to the gods. When one is firmly habituated in contemplating that way, and when one 'materializes' the Marvellous Action of the gods by means of all the attitudes of body and voice, there is the 'final cause'.

Great Seal

The 'efficient cause' of the Great Seal is chiefly the thunderbolt fist.

The method of casting the seal is to enact the Great Seal which abides in self-existence (*svabhāva*). This is such a seal as the one of highest enlightenment (*paramabodhi*).

The 'material cause' is the contemplation of those gods and of a five-pronged 'primordial thunderbolt' in each of their hearts.

The 'final cause' consists in attaining firmness in the deity yoga (*devatā-yoga*) of non-duality of the Profound and the Bright, until contemplating it as attained. As this is easy to comprehend, its purport need not be explicitly explained.

[*A Remark on the Procedure*]

"After executing the seal of Vairocana, when one is executing the seal of Akṣobhya, does one do that by contemplating oneself in the aspect of Vairocana, or does he do that after transforming himself into Akṣobhya? In the former case, would not the seal be executed on Vairocana and the seal not executed on Akṣobhya? In the latter case, is it that one contemplates Akṣobhya of the East shifting hither, leaving the Eastern Square (*koṣṭhaka*) empty, or does one contemplate two Akṣobhyas?"

/ raṅ ñid rnam snaṅ gi rnam pa las ma gYos par śar gyi mi bskyod pa ñid kyi phyag rgya ḥchaḥ ba daṅ / mi bskyod paḥi ye śes pa mdun bźugs pa la lta ba daṅ / raṅ la dgug gźug bciṅ dbaṅ du bya ba rnams byed par sgom pa yin no / de ltar yaṅ mi bskyod pa de ye śes pa daṅ dbyer med du ḥdres pas raṅ daṅ ye śes pa dbyer med du ḥdres par yaṅ ḥgyur te / raṅ daṅ mi bskyod pa rgyud gcig tu sgom pa yin paḥi phyir ro /

/ des rtsa baḥi lha gźan rnams la yaṅ śes par byaḥo /

Without oneself changing from the aspect of Vairocana, one executes the seal of Akṣobhya of the East, sees the Knowledge Being (*jñāna-sattva*) of Akṣobhya dwelling in front [of himself], and contemplates the deeds of 'attracting', 'drawing in', 'tying', and 'subduing' [of that Knowledge Being] in himself. In that way, not only is that Akṣobhya [of the East] indissolubly combined with the Knowledge Being, but also oneself is indissolubly combined with the Knowledge Being, because there is the contemplation that oneself and Akṣobhya have a single 'mental series (or stream of consciousness)' (**ekasaṃtāna*, **ekatantra*).

This has to be understood as applying to all the other basic deities as well.

/ ḥdir rnal ḥbyor bla med kyi rnam gźag la / rgyud gñis su dbye ba daṅ / phye ba so soḥi don daṅ / brjod byaḥi don ñams su len tshul lo /

/ daṅ po ni sdom ḥbyuṅ daṅ / gur daṅ / saṅs rgyas thod pa sogs nas bla med kyi rgyud dbye gźir byas pa la / rnal ḥbyor gyi rgyud daṅ / rnal ḥbyor maḥi rgyud ces pa daṅ / dus ḥkhor sogs las / bla med kyi rgyud dbye gźir byas pa la / thabs rgyud daṅ / śes rab kyi rgyud ces pa daṅ / rdo rje sñiṅ po rgyan gyi rgyud sogs nas / mkhaḥ ḥgro phaḥi rgyud daṅ / mkhaḥ ḥgro maḥi rgyud /

/ ces ḥbyuṅ ba rnams kyi rnal ḥbyor gyi rgyud daṅ / thabs rgyud daṅ / mkhaḥ ḥgro phaḥi rgyud ces pa rnams / don gcig la miṅ ḥdogs mi ḥdra baḥo / yaṅ rnal ḥbyor maḥi rgyud daṅ / śes rab kyi rgyud daṅ / mkhaḥ ḥgro maḥi rgyud rnams kyaṅ / don gcig miṅ gi rnam graṅs yin no /

/ des na bla med daṅ yo-ga gñis so sor ma phye bar thun moṅ du rnal ḥbyor gyi rgyud ces pa daṅ / bla med kyi rgyud tsam la rnal ḥbyor chen poḥi rgyud ces ḥbyuṅ ba daṅ / bla med kyi rgyud dbye gźir byas nas phye baḥi ya gyal la rnal ḥbyor rgyud / ces ḥbyuṅ ba rnams miṅ gi tha sñad ḥdra baḥi don mi ḥdra baḥi khyad par legs par phyed dgos so /

/ gñis pa phye ba so soḥi don la / gźan lugs dgag pa daṅ raṅ lugs bźag pa gñis /

/ daṅ po ni / kha cig na re / bla med kyi rgyud dbye gźir byas nas /

[1] These two parts, constituting the present chapter, are based on Tsoṅ-kha-pa's discussion in his *Mthaḥ gcod* (Toh. 5284, Ca, 15b-5, ff.).

[2] For the bracketted *mahā* in [*mahā*] *yoga-tantra*, cf. Chap. III, note 1, *supra*.

CHAPTER SEVEN

4. FUNDAMENTALS OF THE ANUTTARA-YOGA TANTRA

There are three parts: division into two Tantras; meaning of the several divisions;[1] procedure in the meaning of the subject matter.

a. *Division into two Tantras*

The *Sambarodaya* (Toh. 373), the *Vajrapañjarā* (Toh. 419), the *Buddhakapāla* (Toh. 424), and other [Anuttara-yoga] Tantras, make a basic division of the Anuttara-yoga Tantra into [*mahā*] *yoga-tantra*[2] and *yoginī-tantra*. The *Kāla-cakra* (Toh. 362) and others make a basic division of the Anuttara-yoga Tantra into *upāya-tantra* and *prajñā-tantra*. The *Vajrahṛdayālaṃkāra* (Toh. 451) and others speak of the *ḍāka-tantra* and the *ḍākinī-tantra*.

Among those expressions, [*mahā*] *yoga-tantra*, *upāya-tantra*, and *ḍāka-tantra* are different terms with the same meaning. Moreover, *yoginī-tantra*, *prajñā-tantra*, and *ḍākinī-tantra* are also synonymous terms.

Now, that which is held in common between the two Tantras, Yoga and Anuttarayoga, is called the *yoga-tantra*. Peculiar to the Anuttara-yoga is the *mahāyoga-tantra*; and when one makes the basic division in the Anuttara-yoga Tantra, *yoga-tantra* pertains to a single one of the [two] divisions. These expressions present similarities as terms but have different meanings; hence they must be well distinguished.

b. *Meaning of the several divisions*

There are two sections: refutation of other schools; establishment of our own school.

(1) REFUTATION OF OTHER SCHOOLS

Some persons, when making the basic division in the Anuttara-yoga

pha rgyud ma rgyud gñis med kyi rgyud gsum du ḥbyed ciṅ / de gsum naṅ phan tshun gcig yin na gcig śes ma yin par ḥgal bar ḥdod do / de la yaṅ rjod byed sgraḥi khyad pa gyis rgyud gsum so sor ḥbyed pa daṅ / brjod bya don gyi khyad par gyis rgyud gsum so sor ḥbyed pa daṅ / źu ba poḥi khyad par gyis rgyud gsum so sor ḥbyed par byed do /

/ de yaṅ bla med kyi rgyud kyi dbaṅ du byas nas / gleṅ gźiḥi skabs su ḥdi skad bdag thos kyi mgo draṅs paḥi rgyud yin na pha rgyud yin pas khyab ste / dper na gsaṅ ba ḥdus paḥi rgyud lta buḥo / gleṅ gźi ḥchad pa na / gsaṅ ba mchog gis dgyes pa na / źes pas thog draṅs paḥi rgyud yin na / ma rgyud yin pas khyab ste / dper na bde mchog gi rgyud lta buḥo / des na rtsa rgyud brtag pa gñis pa las / ḥdi skad bdag thos daṅ / deḥi thun moṅ ma yin paḥi bśad rgyud gur las / gsaṅ ba mchog gis dgyes pa na / źes daṅ / thun moṅ paḥi bśad rgyud saṃ-pu-ṭa las / ḥdi skad daṅ / gsaṅ ba mchog gi dgyes pa gñis ka byuṅ bas gñis med kyi rgyud yin no / źes zer źiṅ / deḥi śes byed ni grub chen nag po spyod pas bśad pa ltar ro / źes zer ro /

/ de ni śin tu ḥaṅ mi ḥthad de / des na bde mchog gi rgyud kyaṅ gñis med kyi rgyud du thal / rtsa rgyud las / gsaṅ ba mchog gis dgyes pa na / źes ḥbyuṅ źiṅ / thun moṅ ma yin paḥi bśad rgyud mṅon brjod bla ma las / ḥdi skad bdag thos daṅ / thun moṅ paḥi bśad rgyud saṃ-pu-ṭa las / de gñis ka ḥbyuṅ bas so / ḥdod mi rigs te / de ma rgyud du khas blaṅs pa daṅ / ma rgyud daṅ gñis med kyi rgyud ḥgal bar khas blaṅs pas so / gźan yaṅ / kye rdo rje pha rgyud du thal ba sogs gnod byed du ma źig yod do /

/ brjod bya don gyi khyad par gyis rgyud gsum so sor ḥbyed pa ni /

Tantra, divide it into three: Father (*pitṛ*) Tantra, Mother (*mātṛ*) Tantra, and Non-dual (*advaita*) Tantra, and maintain that the three are mutually exclusive in the sense that if a Tantra belongs to one division, it cannot belong to any of the others. Furthermore [to justify that division], there is a division into three [kinds of] Tantra by the distinctions of the enunciation of the promulgation (**vācakāna, rjod byed*); another tripartition by distinctions of the meaning of the subject matter (**vācya, brjod bya*); another tripartition by distinctions of the petitioner.

(a) **Tripartition by enunciation of the promulgation**

Now, when the Anuttara Tantra is taken into account, such Tantras as are introduced by the phrase, "Thus I have heard" (*evaṃ mayā śrutam*), are reckoned as Father Tantras, e.g. the *Guhyasamāja-tantra* (Toh. 442); and those introduced by such phrases as "[I] delight in the Highest of Secrets" (**rahasya paramaṃ rame*) belong to the group of Mother Tantras, e.g., the *Saṃvara-tantra* (Toh. 368). Again, in the Fundamental Tantra of *Hevajra* (Toh. 417 and 418) there is "Thus I have heard"; and in its unshared [with other Tantras] Explanatory Tantra, the *Pañjarā* (Toh. 419), there is "[I] delight in the Highest of Secrets"; while in the shared Explanatory Tantra, the *Saṃpuṭa* (Toh. 381), there are both "Thus I have heard", and "[I] delight in the Highest of Secrets"; consequently it is a Non-dual Tantra. That is what is claimed; the authority for it is said to be the explanation by the great magus Nag-po-spyod-pa.

The position is completely untenable; it leads to the absurdity that the *Saṃvara-tantra* would in such a case also be a Non-dual Tantra. The Fundamental Tantra (Toh. 368) has "[I] delight in the Highest of Secrets"; the unshared Explanatory Tantra, the *Abhidhānottara* (Toh. 369) has "Thus I have heard", and the shared Explanatory Tantra, the *Saṃpuṭa* (Toh. 381) has both [phrases]. The position is untenable, because this [i.e., the *Saṃvara-tantra*] was held to be a Mother Tantra and it was held that the Mother Tantras and Non-dual Tantras exclude one another. Moreover, there would be the absurdity that the *Hevajra-tantra* would also be a Father Tantra [because it begins with "Thus I have heard"] which would lead to many serious difficulties.

(b) **Tripartition by meaning of the subject matter**

There is a division into three Tantras by the distinctions of the Steps of Production (*utpatti-krama*), the distinctions of the Steps of Com-

bskyed rim gyi khyad par daṅ / rdzogs rim gyi khyad par daṅ / rjes spyod rnam dag gi khyad par gyis rgyud gsum so sor ḥbyed paḥo /

/ daṅ po ni / bla med gyi rgyud dbye gźir byas la / dkyil ḥkhor gaṅ du de bźin gśegs pa lṅa lha moḥi rnam par ston źiṅ / gtso bo lha mos byed paḥam ḥkhor lha moḥi tshogs śas che ba ma rgyud daṅ / dkyil ḥkhor gaṅ du de bźin gśegs pa rigs lṅa lha phoḥi rnam par ston źiṅ / lha phos gtso bo byed paḥam / ḥkhor lha phoḥi tshogs śas che ba pha rgyud du ḥjog par byed do / deḥi śes byed ni / gur las / saṅs rgyas rnams ni thams cad kyi / mkhaḥ ḥgro ma yi dam paḥi tshogs / mkhaḥ ḥgro lṅa po rab bsgrub phyir / mkhaḥ ḥgro ma yi rgyud bśad do / źes gsuṅs pa ltar / saṅs rgyas rnams ni rigs lṅa yin la / mkhaḥ ḥgro ma yi dam paḥi tshogs / źes pas lha mo śas che ba bstan ciṅ / mkhaḥ ḥgro lṅa po rab bsgrub phyir / źes pas / de bźin gśegs pa lṅa lha moḥi rnam par bskyed pa ston la / de ltar sgrub paḥi mkhaḥ ḥgro maḥi rgyud bśad / ces paḥi don no / de la pha rgyud la dṅos su ma gsuṅs kyaṅ / ma rgyud la dṅos su gsuṅs paḥi śugs las pha rgyud la ḥaṅ bstan ces ḥdod do /

/ luṅ de deḥi rgyu mtshan du ḥdren pa ḥbrel med yin te / luṅ de ñid ni / gur rigs bsdus kyi dkyil ḥkhor gyi gtso bo lṅa bsgrub ba ste bskyed pa ston paḥi phyir du gsuṅs pa yin źiṅ / mkhaḥ ḥgro źes ḥbyuṅ ba lha mo kho na la byed mi dgos so /

/ rdzogs rim kyi khyad par gyi rgyud gsum so sor ḥjog pa ni / dkyil ḥkhor ḥkhor loḥi rdzogs rim brjod byaḥi gtso bor ston paḥi rgyud yin na ma rgyud daṅ / thig le daṅ phra moḥi rnal ḥbyor gyi rdzogs rim brjod byaḥi gtse bor ston paḥi rgyud yin na pha rgyud daṅ / de gñis ka brjod byaḥi gtso bor byas nas ston paḥi rgyud yin na gñis med kyi rgyud du ḥdod ciṅ / mtshan gźi ni sṅar ltar la / naṅ phan tshun yaṅ ḥgal bar ḥdod do /

/ de la dkyil ḥkhor ḥkhor loḥi rdzogs rim ni / phyiḥi phyag rgya la brten paḥi rdzogs rim bsgom tshul la ḥdod pas / des na bde mchog gi rgyud kyaṅ gñis med kyi rgyud du thal / phyiḥi phyag rgya la brten paḥi

[3] Presumably Mkhas grub rje, following Tsoṅ-kha-pa, means that the term *mkhaḥ ḥgro* is frequently used as an abbreviation for *mkhaḥ ḥgro ma* (*ḍākinī*), but as it stands, regarded as unabbreviated, refers to a male deity, the *ḍāka*. The *Āmnāya-mañjari* (Toh. 1198), says in the ninth *mañjari*, Derge edition, 93b-7: "'Sky walker (*ḍāka*)' means the Bhagavat; 'sky walker (*ḍākinī*)' means the goddesses" (mkhaḥ ḥgro ni bcom ldan ḥdas so / mkhaḥ ḥgro ma ni lha mo rnams so).

[4] An "external *mudrā*" in such a context suggests a concrete goddess or phenomenal woman.

pletion (*nispanna-krama*), and the distinctions of the purification of attendants (**anucāra-viśuddhi*).

Tripartition by Steps of Production

One assumes the basic division of the Anuttara Tantra. Then, in whatever *maṇḍala* the five Tathāgatas manifest themselves as goddesses (*devī*), a goddess is the Lord, or the goddesses constitute the majority in the retinue, one has a Mother Tantra. In whatever *maṇḍala* the five Tathāgatas manifest themselves as male deities, a male deity is the Lord, or the male deities constitute the majority in the retinue, one has a Father Tantra. The authority for that is given as this passage in the *Pañjarā* (Toh. 419): "Because it portrays the illustrious host of Ḍākinī and the five Ḍākinī of all the Buddhas, it is explained as *Ḍākinī-tantra*." "All the Buddhas" means the five Progenitors. "Illustrious host of Ḍākinī" refers to the preponderance of goddesses. "Because it portrays the five Ḍākinī" shows the generation of the five Tathāgatas under the aspect of goddesses. Finally, it means that one explains as *Ḍākinī-tantra* one that portrays in that manner. Furthermore, they maintain that although a Father Tantra is not explicit in that passage, it implies likewise for Father Tantras because the Mother Tantra is explicit.

There is no cogency in introducing that scripture as proof. That scripture was expounded to show the generation which portrays the five lords of the *maṇḍala* of the 'concise *pañjarā* family' (*gur rigs bsdus*). It is not necessarily the case that the expression 'Sky walker' (*mkhaḥ ḥgro*) refers only to a goddess (*devī*).[3]

Tripartition by Steps of Completion

When the Tantra shows chiefly the subject matter of the Steps of Completion (*niṣpanna-krama*) [concerned with] the circle of the *maṇḍala*, it is a Mother Tantra. When the Tantra shows chiefly the subject matter of the Steps of Completion [concerned with] the drop (*bindu*) and subtle yoga (*sūkṣma-yoga*), it is a Father Tantra. When the Tantra shows chiefly the subject matter of both, it is a Non-dual Tantra. That is what is maintained. The source [given as authority] is the same as before. We maintain that it is internally contradictory.

Now, in regard to the Steps of Completion [concerned with] the circle of the *maṇḍala*, they maintain a method of contemplation of the Steps of Completion based on an external seal (*mudrā*).[4] Consequently, it reduces to the absurdity that the Saṃvara-Tantra is also a Non-dual Tantra, because in the method of contemplating the Steps of Completion

rdzogs rim bsgom tshul bde dgyes gñis khyad par med ciṅ / thig le daṅ phra moḥi rnal ḥbyor gyi rdzogs rim bde mchog śin tu rgyas paḥi phyir ro / ḥdod na / naṅ phan tshun ḥgal bar khas blaṅs pa daṅ ḥgal lo /

/ rjes spyod rnam dag gi khyad par gyis rgyud gsum so sor ḥjog pa ni / bla med kyi rgyud gaṅ źig / phuṅ khams skye mched kyi rnam dag gtso bor ston paḥi rgyud yin na pha rgyud / rtsaḥi rnam dag gtso bor ston pa ma rgyud / de gñis kaḥi rnam dag gtso bor ston pa gñis med kyi rgyud de / mtshan gźi ni sṅar ltar ro źes zer ro /

/ de la bde mchog daṅ kye rdor la pha rgyud ma rgyud gaṅ yaṅ min paḥi gñis med kyi rgyud du ḥjog mi ḥjog gi khyad par mi ḥthad de / bde mchog las rtsaḥi rnam dag ston par khas blaṅs śiṅ / kye rdor las bdag med lha mo bco lṅa phuṅ sogs kyi ṅo bor bsgom paḥi rnam dag ston la / bde mchog las kyaṅ gzugs kyi phuṅ po sogs bcu bdun lha bcu bdun gyi ṅo bor bsgom paḥi phuṅ sogs kyi rnam dag ston źiṅ / de las lhag paḥi rnam dag kye rdor las ma gsuṅs paḥi phyir / ḥdod pa la sṅar ltar ro /

/ des na khyad par des ḥjog mi nus so /

/ gsum pa źu ba poḥi khyad par gyis rgyud gsum so sor ḥjog pa ni / źu ba po lha phos źus pa gsaṅ ba ḥdus pa lta bu pha rgyud daṅ / źu ba po lha mo rdo rje phag mos źus pa bde mchog lta bu ma rgyud daṅ / brtag pa daṅ po rdo rje sñiṅ pos źus pas lha phos źus śiṅ / brtag pa gñis pa bdag med mas źus pas lha mos źus la / lha pho mo gñis kas źus pas gñis med kyi rgyud yin zer źiṅ /

/ phan tshun ḥgal bar yaṅ ḥdod do / ḥo na gsaṅ ḥdus kyaṅ gñis med kyi rgyud du ḥgyur te / rtsa rgyud lha phos źus śiṅ / bśad rgyud lha mo bźis źus pa lha mos źus pas so / ḥdod na sṅar ltar ro / brtag gñis kyaṅ brtag pa daṅ po pha rgyud daṅ gñis pa ma rgyud du thal lo /

[5] Snellgrove, *The Hevajra Tantra*, Part I, pp. 126-7, displays in diagrams III and IV the correspondences between the fifteen *yoginīs* and the respective spheres of purification.

[6] With reference to the *Sambara Maṇḍala* in B. Bhattacharyya, *Niṣpannayogāvalī of Mahāpaṇḍita Abhayākaragupta* (Baroda, 1949), one can assume that the number of seventeen gods is arrived at by arbitrarily taking two groups of eight from among the three groups of eight male deities assigned respectively to the *Citta*, *Vāk*, and *Kāya* Circles, and taking the seventeenth as the central deity Sambara. In Lui-pa's *Śrī-Bhagavadabhisamaya-nāma* (Toh. 1427), the female deities of this *maṇḍala* are made to correspond to the thirty-seven *bodhipakṣyā dharmāḥ*.

[7] In Snellgrove (*op.cit.*), Part II (presumably the second assembly of the *Hevajra*), is requested by several different deities. Besides Vajragarbha, the *yoginīs* become interlocutors in II, iii; and Nairātmyā begins her questions in II, iv.

based on an external seal, there is no distinction between the *Saṃvara* and the *Hevajra*, and because the Steps of Completion [concerned with] the drop and subtle yoga are discussed elaborately in the *Saṃvara-tantra*. If this is admitted, [so] is the internal contradiction, and the thesis is refuted.

Tripartition by purification of attendants

Whatever Anuttara Tantra is a Tantra showing chiefly the purification of the personality aggregates (*skandha*), realms (*dhātu*), and sense bases (*āyatana*), is a Father Tantra. Whatever one shows chiefly the purification of the 'veins' (*nāḍī*) is a Mother Tantra. Whatever one shows chiefly both is a Non-dual Tantra. Their authority is the same as before.

In that case, it is illogical to either classify or not classify the *Saṃvara* and the *Hevajra* among the Non-dual Tantras as being neither Mother nor Father Tantras. The reason is as follows: It is agreed that the *Saṃvara* teaches the purification of the 'veins'. The *Hevajra* teaches the purification by contemplating the fifteen goddesses beginning with Nairātmyā as the nature of the personality aggregates and so on.[5] The *Saṃvara* also teaches the purification of the personality aggregates and so on by contemplating the seventeen elements beginning with *rūpa-skandha* as having their nature in the seventeen gods.[6] The *Hevajra* teaches no purification beyond this. Our conclusions are as stated above.

Therefore, those distinctions cannot be used for classification.

(c) Tripartition by the petitioner

If the petitioner is a male deity, as in the case of the *Guhyasamāja*, it is a Father Tantra. If the petitioner is a female deity, as in the case of the *Saṃvara*, which is requested by Vajravārāhī, it is a Mother Tantra. The first assembly [of the *Hevajra* Tantra] is requested by Vajragarbha, hence requested by a male deity; the second assembly is requested by Nairātmyā, hence requested by a female deity;[7] and for the reason that both male and female deities make request, it is a Non-dual Tantra. That is what they claim.

Again we maintain that this involves an internal contradiction. If their thesis were granted, the *Guhyasamāja* would also be a Non-dual Tantra, for its Fundamental Tantra (Toh. 442) was requested by a male deity, and the Explanatory Tantra *Caturdevī-paripṛcchā* (Toh. 446) was requested by goddesses. Our conclusions are as stated above. Moreover, it reduces to the absurdity that of the two assemblies, the first is a Father Tantra and the second is a Mother Tantra.

/ yaṅ rjod byed sgraḥi khyad par gyis rgyud gsum so sor ḥjog pa grub chen nag po spyod paḥi bźed par ḥdod pa yaṅ mi ḥthad de / deḥi bźed pa ni / rgyud kyi thog mar ḥdi skad bdag thos ḥbyuṅ ba daṅ / gsaṅ ba mchog gis dgyes pa na / źes sogs ḥbyuṅ ba rnams tshig mi ḥdra yaṅ / gleṅ gźiḥi tshig rnams kyis bde stoṅ dbyer med brjod byar ston pas / raṅ bźin rnam dag la khyad par med par ston paḥi phyir du / raṅ bźin dbye ba yod min źes / thugs kyi rdo rjes de skad gsuṅs / źes gsuṅs kyi / luṅ de ñid gleṅ gźis rgyud gsum so sor ḥjog paḥi rgyu mtshan du ḥdod pa la ḥbrel cuṅ zad kyaṅ med do /

/ yaṅ kha cig dus ḥkhor rgyud ḥgrel gyi rjes su ḥbraṅs nas / deḥi lugs su rloms te / bla med kyi rgyud la pha rgyud ma rgyud gñis su ḥbyed pa sgra ji bźin par gzuṅ du mi ruṅ baḥi draṅ don daṅ / bla med kyi rgyud yin na gñis med kyi rgyud yin pas khyab pa sgra ji bźin paḥi ṅas don du ḥdod la / de ltar ḥdod bźin du ḥaṅ / bla med kyi rgyud la pha rgyud ma rgyud gñis med kyi rgyud gsum du ḥbyed ciṅ / de rnams kyi ḥjog byed du dkyil ḥkhor gaṅ du ñin mtshan mñam pa dag pas lha gtso ḥkhor thams cad źal phyag mñam pa ston paḥi bla med kyi rgyud ni pha rgyud de gsaṅ ḥdus lta bu daṅ / dkyil ḥkhor gaṅ du sṅa phyiḥi thun ḥtshams dag pas / lha gtso ḥkhor źal phyag mi mñam pa śas cher ston paḥi bla med kyi rgyud ni ma rgyud de bde mchog lta bu daṅ / deḥi śugs kyis dkyil ḥkhor gaṅ du lha gtso bo yab yum źal phyag mi mñam źiṅ / ḥkhor yab yum źal phyag mñam par ston paḥi bla med kyi rgyud ni gñis med kyi rgyud de dus ḥkhor lta buḥo / zer źiṅ / de rnams ni dus ḥkhor gyis bstan par ḥdod do /

/ de ni mi ḥthad de / des na ḥdus pa yaṅ gñis med kyi rgyud du ḥgyur te / bla med kyi rgyud yin na gñis med kyi rgyud yin pas khyab pa sgra ji bźin paḥi ṅes don yin pas so / ḥdod na / lha gtso bo yab yum źal phyag mi mñam źiṅ / ḥkhor yab yum źal phyag mñam par thal / ḥdod paḥi

Further observations

Furthermore, it is not valid to divide into three kinds of Tantra by the distinctions of enunciation of the promulgation, claiming the great magus Nag-po-spyod-pa as authority. What he maintains is that such expressions as "Thus I have heard" and "[I] delight in the highest of secrets", occurring at the beginning of the Tantras, differ in words and that, nevertheless, the introductory words teach the subject matter of the inseparability of Beatitude and Void (*sukha-śūnya*) in order to show that there is no distinction in what is intrinsically pure (*svabhāva-viśuddhi*). It is said, "The thunderbolt of mind (*citta-vajra*) has this proclaimed: 'There are no *varieties* of intrinsic nature (*svabhāva*)'." Hence, there is no cogency at all in holding the introduction of that scripture as the reason for establishing a tripartition of the Tantras.

Others, following the *Kālacakra-tantra* Commentary (Toh. 845), become conceited in that school and maintain that when an Anuttara Tantra is distinguished as Father Tantra or Mother Tantra, it has hinted meaning (*neyārtha*), which is not appropriate for grasping the standard term (*yathāruta*); and that when an Anuttara Tantra is agreed to be a Non-dual Tantra, it has evident meaning (*nītārtha*), which [grasps] the standard term. Moreover, according to that thesis, the Anuttara Tantra is divided into three Tantras as Father Tantra, Mother Tantra, and Non-dual Tantra. Their standard of classification is as follows: In whatever *maṇḍala* day and night are equally pure, so the Anuttara Tantra shows equality of heads and arms for the lord and his retinue, it is a Father Tantra, e.g. the *Guhyasamāja*. In whatever *maṇḍala* the intervals of the earlier and later watches are pure, so the Anuttara Tantra teaches, for the most part, inequality of heads and arms for the lord and his retinue, it is a Mother Tantra, e.g. the *Saṃvara*. As a consequence, in whatever *maṇḍala* the lord as Father-Mother (*yab-yum*) has inequality of heads and arms, while the retinue as Father-Mother has equality of heads and arms, the Anuttara Tantra portraying that is a Non-dual Tantra, e.g. the *Kālacakra*. That is what they claim, and they maintain it is taught by the *Kālacakra*.

That is not valid. In such a case, the *Guhyasamāja* would also be a Non-dual Tantra, because when there is an Anuttara Tantra it is always a Non-dual Tantra, this being the evident meaning' of the term ['without superior', *anuttara*] itself. Concede that, and you must concede the utter absurdity of [introducing as criterion] the inequality of heads and arms of the lord in Father-Mother and the equality of heads and

phyir / des na dus ḥkhor las / bla med kyi rgyud la pha rgyud / ma rgyud gñis su phye ba sgra ji bźin pa min paḥi draṅ don du bstan pa ma yin gyi / de ñid las pha rgyud ma rgyud du ḥbyed tshul khyad par pa bla med kyi dkyil ḥkhor gaṅ du ye śes pa dgug gźug byed pa na / lha pho yaṅ dag par rgyu źiṅ / rnal ḥbyor ma mi gYo bar gnas par ston pa pha rgyud daṅ / dkyil ḥkhor gaṅ du ye śes pa dgug gźug byed pa na / rnal ḥbyor ma rnams yaṅ dag par rgyu źiṅ / lha pho mi gYo bar gnas par ston paḥi bla med kyi rgyud rnams ma rgyud du ston paḥi rnam gźag mdzad pa ni / tshul des ḥdul baḥi gdul bya draṅ baḥi phyir du re gźan ṅor mdzad paḥi rnam gźag yin pas / de ḥdra ba sgra ji bźin pa ma yin paḥi draṅ don du gsuṅs pa yin no /

/ ñin mtshan mñam pa dag pas lha thams cad źal phyag mñam pa daṅ / sṅa phyiḥi thun ḥtshams dag pas lha thams cad źal phyag mi mñam par ston paḥi dkyil ḥkhor dus ḥkhor las gsuṅs pa pha rgyud daṅ ma rgyud kyi ḥjog byed du byed pa ni ḥbrel med yin te / deḥi don ni de ñid las gsuṅs paḥi ḥdus paḥi dkyil ḥkhor daṅ / sgyu ḥphrul dra baḥi dkyil ḥkhor gyi lha gtso ḥkhor thams cad źal phyag mñam par ston pa de ñid dus kyi dag pa sbyor baḥi tshe na / ñin mtshan mñam pa dag pas źal phyag mñam pa / źes sbyor ba daṅ / de las bstan paḥi bde mchog sdom pa che chuṅ gi dkyil ḥkhor lha źal phyag mi mñam par ston pa rnams dus kyi dag pa sbyor baḥi tshe na / sṅa phyiḥi thun ḥtshams dag pas źal phyag mi mñam paḥo / źes dkyil ḥkhor gyi dag pa sbyor ba ston pa yin no /

/ gñis pa raṅ lugs ni /

/ bla med kyi rgyud la / thabs śes gñis med kyi rgyud du byas paḥi ya gyal gyi thabs daṅ / pha rgyud la thabs su byas paḥi thabs gñis miṅ ḥdra yaṅ don mi ḥdra / deḥi ya gyal gyi śes rab daṅ / ma rgyud la śes rab tu byas paḥi śes rab gñis miṅ ḥdra yaṅ don mi ḥdraḥo / deḥi ya gyal gyi thabs śes ji lta bu źe na / deḥi thabs ni bde chen lhan cig skyes paḥi ye śes yin la / śes rab ni chos thams cad raṅ bźin med par rtogs paḥi ye

arms of the retinue in Father-Mother. Thus, the *Kālacakra* does not teach the varieties of Father Tantra and Mother Tantra in the Anuttara Tantra except in the hinted meaning of a standard term. That work [i.e., the *Kālacakra*] does indeed set forth the distinction in the method of dividing into Father Tantra and Mother Tantra: if one attracts the Knowledge Being (*jñāna-sattva*) and draws it into any Anuttara *maṇḍala*, and the male deity moves correctly while the *yoginī* remains immobile, one has Father Tantra; if one attracts the Knowledge Being and draws it into any [Anuttara] *maṇḍala*, and the *yoginīs* move correctly while the male deities remain immobile, one has a Mother Tantra. That method of formulation is a formulation for the sake of drawing (*neya*) the candidate (*vineya*) for training (*vinaya*), installing him temporarily in another viewpoint. Hence it is expressed in the 'drawing meaning' (*neya-artha*) [or 'hinted meaning'] of 'coined terminology' (*na-yathāruta*) of such sort [as 'Father Tantra', 'Mother Tantra'].

Moreover, there is no cogency in positing a Father Tantra and a Mother Tantra on the grounds that the *Kālacakra* speaks of a *maṇḍala* in which all the gods have equality of heads and arms due to the purity of equal day and night, or in which all the gods have inequality of heads and arms due to the purity of earlier and later intervals of watches. The meaning of that is as follows: the lords and the retinues of the *Samāja-maṇḍala* and the *Māyājāla-maṇḍala* mentioned in that work show equality of heads and arms; when one coordinates the purity of that precise time, the coordination is, "equality of heads and arms due to the purity of equal day and night". The deities in the larger and smaller *maṇḍalas* of *Saṃvara* taught in that work show inequality of heads and arms; when one coordinates the purity of that time, the coordination of purity of the *maṇḍala* is, "inequality of heads and arms due to the purity of earlier and later intervals of watches".

(2) ESTABLISHMENT OF OUR SCHOOL

In the Anuttara Tantra, the term 'means' (*upāya*) taken by itself as it occurs in the Tantras which have non-duality of means (*upāya*) and insight (*prajñā*) has a different meaning from the term 'Means' (*upāya*) standing for the Father Tantra; and the term 'insight' taken by itself has a different meaning from the term 'Insight' standing for the Mother Tantra. Then what are 'means' and 'insight' taken by themselves? That 'means' is the Knowledge born together with (*sahaja*) Great Beatitude (*mahāsukha*). That 'insight' is the knowledge which fully comprehends that all natures (*sarvadharmāḥ*) are devoid of intrinsic reality (*niḥsvab-*

śes yin pas / bla med kyi rgyud yin na de ḥdra baḥi thabs śes dbyer med brjod byar ston pas khyab ste /

/ ḥdus paḥi rgyud phyi mar ston pa la ḥkhor gyi byaṅ chub sems dpaḥ rnams kyis / rnal ḥbyor bla med kyi rgyud kyi rnal ḥbyor gyi don ji lta bu lags / źes źus paḥi lan du / ston pas / thabs daṅ śes rab sñoms ḥjug pa / rnal ḥbyor źes ni bya bar bśad / ces sogs gsuṅs so / des na de ḥdra baḥi thabs śes kyi sgo nas pha rgyud ma rgyud so sor ḥjog mi nus te / de lta na ḥdus pa pha rgyud min pa daṅ / kye rdor ma rgyud min par thal / de gñis kas gñis med brjod byar ston pa la khyad par med paḥi phyir / źes dus ḥkhor rgyud hgrel daṅ / rdo rje sñiṅ ḥgrel las gsuṅs paḥi phyir ro /

/ des na sṅar bśad pa de ḥdra baḥi thabs śes gñis med kyi rgyud dbye baḥi ya gyal du mi bgraṅ bar / de ñid dbye gźir byas nas pha rgyud daṅ ma rgyud gñis su ḥbyed par byed pa yin no / pha rgyud daṅ thabs rgyud don gcig tu byas paḥi thabs de gaṅ / ma rgyud daṅ śes rab kyi rgyud don gcig tu byas paḥi śes rab de gaṅ yin sñam na /

/ thog mar śes rab ṅos gzuṅ bar bya ste / gur gyi leḥu bcu pa las / ḥkhor rnams kyis ston pa la / bcom ldan ḥdas ji ltar na rnal ḥbyor maḥi rgyud kyi mtshan rab tu ḥjug pa lags / rdo rje ḥdzin gyis bkaḥ stsal pa / śes rab pha rol phyin paḥi thabs / ḥdi ni rnal ḥbyor mar brjod do / phyag rgya chen po rab sbyor bas / gaṅ phyir de ñid la ḥjug pa / rnal ḥbyor ma yi rgyud ces bya / źes gsuṅs paḥi don bśad na / phyag rgya chen po ni ḥdir bde chen lhan skyes kyi ye śes yin la / de gaṅ du sbyor na / de kho na ñid du ḥjug paḥi sgo nas rab tu sbyor bas na de ḥdra bahi bde stoṅ dbyer med du sbyar ba ḥdi ni rnal ḥbyor źes brjod de / de la ma ni sku gñis kyi naṅ nas chos skuḥi thun moṅ ma yin paḥi rigs ḥdraḥi rgyu yin źiṅ / snaṅ phyogs thabs kyi cha daṅ / stoṅ phyogs śes rab kyi cha gñis kyi naṅ nas / stoṅ phyogs śes rab kyi cha yin paḥi phyir ma ste / de ḥdra baḥi stoṅ phyogs śes rab kyi char gyur paḥi bde stoṅ dbyer mi phyed paḥi ye śes brjod byaḥi gtso bor rtsal du bton nas ḥchad ciṅ / snaṅ phyogs thabs

[8] In the published text of the *Guhyasamāja*, Chap. XVIII is the Continuation Tantra of the Tibetan Kanjur. The question occurs in the text, 150.5, the answer (as quoted) 153.4.

[9] The latter, quoted in *Sṅags rim* at 339b-6, is Vajragarbha's commentary on the *Hevajra-tantra* called *Piṇḍārtha-ṭīkā*.

[10] Of course, the feminine noun *yoginī* is formed by adding *ī* to *yogin*.

hāva). If one has an Anuttara Tantra, it necessarily teaches the subject matter of the inseparability of 'means' and 'insight' in those senses.

In the Continuation (Toh. 443) of the *Guhyasamāja-tantra* (Toh. 442), the Bodhisattvas of the retinue ask the Teacher the meaning of the term *yoga* of the Anuttara-yoga-tantra. In reply to that question, the Teacher says, "The equal entrance (*samāpatti*) into means and insight is explained as *yoga*", and so on.[8] Hence, one cannot classify Father Tantras and Mother Tantras by way of 'means' and 'insight' in those senses. If one did, it would lead to the absurdity that the *Guhyasamāja* would not be a Father Tantra, nor the *Hevajra* a Mother Tantra. But both alike teach the subject matter of the non-dualty [of means and insight], for this is stated in the *Kālacakra-tantra* Commentary (Toh. 845, as well as in the Vajragarbha Commentary (probably Toh. 1180).[9]

Hence, the means and the insight in the senses described above do not serve to differentiate the varieties of Non-dual Tantra. But when one assumes the varieties at the outset, they ['Means' and 'Insight'] separate them into Father Tantra and Mother Tantra. What is the meaning of 'Means' (*upāya*) when Father Tantra and *upāya-tantra* are taken as identical? What is the meaning of 'Insight' (*prajñā*) when Mother Tantra and *prajñā-tantra* are taken as identical?

First we must establish 'Insight'. The tenth [sic. for thirteenth] chapter of the *Pañjarā* (Toh. 419) states as follows:

> The members of the retinue asked the Teacher, "Bhagavat, how did the name *Yoginī-tantra* arise?" Vajradhara spoke: "The 'means' of *Prajñā-pāramitā* is proclaimed to be *yoginī*. The one who adds the Great Seal (*mahā-mudrā*) enters Reality (*tattva*) [*or*: enters that very *yoginī*]; hence the name *Yoginī-tantra*."

How is that passage explained? 'Great Seal' means the Knowledge born together with Great Beatitude. Where is that added? It is added by way of entering Reality (*tattva*), for which reason, such an indissoluble combination of Beatitude and Void (*sukha-śūnya*) is called *yoga*. With the feminine suffix (*-inī, ma*)[10] it means the cause (*hetu*) of the uncommon (*asādhāraṇa*) affiliation with the Dharma-kāya among the two Bodies: i.e., from among the part of the 'Means' on the phenomenal side and the part of the 'Insight' on the void side, it is the 'Insight' on the void side, hence the feminine suffix. Thus, a *Yoginī-tantra* is explained as one which explicitly emphasizes the subject matter of the Knowledge of indissoluble Beatitude and Void in the part of 'Insight' on the Void

kyi char gyur paḥi gzugs skuḥi thun moṅ ma yin paḥi rigs ḥdraḥi rgyu maḥi sku daṅ / deḥi sgrub tshul rtsal du bton nas mi ḥchad pas rnal ḥbyor maḥi rgyud ces bya bar bśad do / de ltar na ma rgyud kyi ḥjog byed ni stoṅ phyogs śes rab kyi cha bde stoṅ dbyer med kyi ye śes brjod byaḥi gtso bor byas na ḥchad ciṅ / snaṅ phyogs thabs kyi cha sgyu maḥi sku sgrub tshul sogs rtsal du bton nas mi ḥchad paḥi rgyud dṅos sam / deḥi sder gtogs kyi bla med kyi rgyud gaṅ ruṅ yin paḥo /

/ pha rgyud daṅ thabs rgyud don gcig tu byas paḥi thabs de gaṅ źe na /mkhaḥ ḥgro rgya mtsho las / rnal ḥbyor rnams la rgyud rgyal du / de daṅ de yi cho ga dbye śes / ḥod gsal sgyu ma bdag gis ni / sgyu ma ḥjig rten la bśad do / źes gsuṅs pas bstan te / deḥi don bśad na / bśad ces draṅ ṅo / gaṅ gis na rdo rje ḥchaṅ bdag gis so / gaṅ na sgyu maḥi sku sgrub paḥi thabs so / gaṅ la na / gdul byaḥi ḥjig rten rnams laḥo / gaṅ du na / bla med kyi rgyud la rnal ḥbyor gyi rgyud daṅ / rnal ḥbyor maḥi rgyud gñis su phye baḥi ya gyal rnal ḥbyor gyi rgyud kyi rgyal po rnams suḥo / tshul ji ltar na / snaṅ mched thob gsum ḥod gsal daṅ bcas pa lugs ḥbyuṅ du bskyed ciṅ / de las lugs ldog tu ldaṅ baḥi tshe / stoṅ pa bźiḥi bźon paḥi rluṅ ḥod zer lṅa ba las sgyu maḥi sku sgrub tshul rtsal du bton pa sogs / de daṅ deḥi cho gaḥi dbye ba ji lta ba bźin du śes paḥi sgo nas / ḥod gsal las sgyu lus su ldaṅ tshul lo /

/ don bsdus na / stoṅ phyogs bde stoṅ dbyer med kyi ye śes kyaṅ brjod byar rgyas par ston paḥi rgyud gaṅ źig / snaṅ phyogs thabs kyi char gyur paḥi stoṅ pa bźiḥi bźon paḥi rluṅ ḥod zer lṅa ba las sgyu maḥi sku sgrub tshul rtsal du bton nas rgyas par ḥchad paḥi bla med kyi rgyud dṅos sam / deḥi sder gtogs kyi rgyud gaṅ ruṅ yin pa źes paḥo / de rnams kyi mtshan gźi cuṅ zad cig ṅos gzuṅ na / ḥdus pa lta bu pha rgyud dṅos

[11] As suggested in note 1, above, Tsoṅ-kha-pa's words are being liberally adopted here; and what he means by "coming forth with skill" is clear from his *Ye rdor* (Toh. 5286, Vol. Ca, 17b-4, ff.): "Those lacking skill in the means turn the wheel of phenomenal existence [i.e. are reborn in the ordinary way] upon fulfilling the Intermediate State through the winds and mind-only at the conclusion of the four Voids; the one holding the precepts of skill in the means knows how to carry away the Intermediate State's Saṃbhoga-kāya, generated as the Illusory Body accomplished from the winds and mind-only at the conclusion of the Voids" (... thabs mkhas pa daṅ bral ba rnams la stoṅ pa bźiḥi mthar rluṅ sems tsam las bar do grub nas srid paḥi ḥkhor lo bskor ba de ñid / thabs mkhas kyi man ṅag daṅ ldan pas stoṅ pa rnams kyi mthar rluṅ sems tsam las grub paḥi sgyu maḥi skur bskyed paḥi bar do loṅs skur ḥkhyer śes pa yin te / ...). (The passage continues as cited in Chap. IV, note 8, *supra*.)

[12] The five winds as discussed in Tsoṅ-kha-pa's *Srog rtsol gyi de kho na ñid gsal ba* (Toh. 5285, Vol. Ca) are Amoghasiddhi's *samāna*, the yellowish-green wind-wind; Amitābha's *udāna*, the red fire-wind; Akṣobhya's *prāṇa*, the white water-wind; Ratnasambhava's *apāna*, the yellow earth-wind; and Vairocana's *vyāna*, the pervasive (? colorless) wind.

side in that way, while not explaining the Illusory Body which is the uncommon affiliation with the Formal Body (*rūpa-kāya*) in the part of 'Means' on the phenomenal side or the coming forth with skill[11] in the method of accomplishing that [Illusory Body]. That being the case, a Mother Tantra is established as follows: It is any Tantra which emphasizes the subject matter of the Knowledge of the indissolubility of Beatitude and Void in the part of 'Insight' on the Void side, while not especially emphasizing such things as the method of accomplishing the Illusory Body in the part of 'Means' on the phenomenal side, or any Anuttara Tantra belonging to its category.

What is that 'Means' when Father Tantra and *upāya-tantra* are identified? It is taught by the *Ḍākārṇava* (Toh. 372) in these words:

> In the king of Tantras among the '*yogas*' —
> Knowing them and the varieties of their rites,
> I have explained the Illusion of the Clear Light
> To the illusory world.

How is that passage explained? The explanation is suggestive (*neya*). By whom [is it explained]? By Vajradhara himself. What [does he explain]? The 'Means' of producing the Illusory Body. To whom [does he explain]? To the world of candidates (*vineya*). Where? Dividing the Anuttara Tantra into [*mahā*] *yoga-tantra* and *yoginī-tantra* — in the 'kings' of the [*mahā*] *yoga-tantras* taken by themselves. By what method is it done? One generates in the forward direction the three [called] Light (*āloka*), Spread-of-Light (*ālokābhāsa*), and Culmination-of-Light (*ālokopalabdhi*), together with the Clear Light (*prabhāsvara*); and at the time of emerging from the latter, in the reverse direction one accomplishes the Illusory Body from the five rays of wind (*vāyu*)[12] riding on the four Voids. The method consists in emerging in the Illusory Body from the Clear Light by way of knowing in exactitude such things as the coming forth with skill and the varieties of their rites.

In short, the basic classification of the Anuttara Tantras is into those which teach elaborately the subject matter of the Knowledge of the indissolubility of Beatitude and Void on the side of the Void, and into those which teach elaborately the coming forth with skill in the method of accomplishing the Illusory Body from the five rays of wind riding on the four Voids in the part of the 'Means' — or any Tantras belonging to the [respective] categories. To mention a few examples with their [respective] character — the *Guhyasamāja* (Toh. 442), for instance, is a basic Father Tantra; and the Tantras of the red and black Yamāri (Toh. 467-470; 473-475; 478), the Vairocana *Māyājāla* (Toh. 466) which

daṅ gśin rjeḥi gśed dmar nag gi rgyud / rnam snaṅ sgyu ḥphrul dra ba ste / bla med sgyu dra / rdo rje sñiṅ po rgyan gyi rgyud rnams pha rgyud kyi sder gtogs paḥi rgyud yin / bde mchog / kye rdor / dus ḥkhor / sgyu thod gdan gsum / phyag chen thig le / saṅs rgyas mñam sbyor sogs ma rgyud yin no /

/ des na pha rgyud kyi gtso bo ḥdus pa yin źiṅ / ma rgyud kyi gtso bo bde mchog yin te / ḥdus pa nas ston paḥi bskyed rdzogs daṅ / las tshogs rgyas pa ḥdra ba pha rgyud gźan gaṅ nas kyaṅ mi ḥbyuṅ źiṅ / bde mchog gis ston paḥi bskyed rdzogs daṅ las tshogs rgyas pa ḥdra ba ma rgyud gźan gaṅ nas kyaṅ mi ḥbyuṅ baḥi phyir ro /

/ de ltar pha rgyud ma rgyud gñis su phye baḥi bla med kyi rgyud la rnam pa gñis su ḥgyur te / rjod byed sgraḥi rgyud daṅ / brjod bya don gyi rgyud do / de la rjod byed sgraḥi rgyud ni / rdo rje ḥchaṅ gis gsuṅs paḥi bla med kyi rgyud gźuṅ mthaḥ dag go / brjod bya don gyi rgyud ni rnam pa gsum ste / rgyuḥi rgyud / thabs kyi rgyud / ḥbras buḥi rgyud rnams so / de ltar na rgyuḥi rgyud daṅ / gźiḥi rgyud don gcig / thabs rgyud daṅ / lam gyi rgyud don gcig /

/ gźiḥi rgyud ni / nā-ro-pas bla med kyi ched du bya baḥi gdul byaḥi gtso bo rin po che lta buḥi gaṅ zag la bźed / śā-nti-pa daṅ / a-bha-yas blo bur dri bcas kyi sems kyi chos ñid raṅ bźin rnam dag la bźed do /

/ ḥbras buḥi rgyud ni / thob bya mthar thug rdo rje ḥchaṅ gi go ḥphaṅ dam / mi slob paḥi zuṅ ḥjug gam / kha sbyor yan lag bdun ldan gyi go ḥphaṅ rnams don gcig tu byas pa deḥo /

[13] The meaning here is that if one takes into consideration the basic Tantra, the Continuation and Explanatory Tantras, the commentarial and oral traditions, then the *Guhyasamāja*, on the one hand, and the *Saṃvara*, on the other hand, represent the most ample treatment of the three topics mentioned. (The last topic, "the set of ritual acts", of course refers to the rites for accomplishing *siddhis*). Therefore, Tsoṅ-kha-pa wrote his great Tantric commentaries principally on the *Guhyasamāja* and the *Saṃvara*.

[14] *Guhyasamāja*, Chap. XVIII, 153.6-7 says: "'Tantra' is explained as 'continuous series' (*prabandha*). That continuous series is threefold through the division — *ādhāra*, *prakṛti*, and *asaṃhārya*." The succeeding verse explains that *prakṛti* is the *hetu*, *asaṃhārya* is the *phala*, and *ādhāra* is the *upāya*. The Tibetan translation of these verses is slightly inconsistent with the present context, because *ādhāra* was translated by T. *gźi*, and *prakṛti* by T. *raṅ bźin*. Now, however, *gźi* should be expressing the word *prakṛti*, because Tantra of Cause (*hetu*) and Tantra of Ground (**prakṛti*, T. *gźi*) are identified.

[15] This explanation involves a sense of the word *tantra* virtually equivalent to the old Buddhist term *saṃtāna* 'stream of consciousness'.

[16] Cf. Chap. IV, note 7, where the seven members of the *sampuṭa* are identified with "perfection of body". The Tibetan author Dbyaṅs-can Dgaḥ-baḥi-blo-gros writes in his *Dpal gsaṅ ba ḥdus pa ḥphags lugs daṅ mthun paḥi sṅags kyis lam rnam gźag legs bśad skal bzaṅ ḥjug ṅogs*, 15a-5, ff.: "Subsequent to the affiliation of pair combined with learning (*śaikṣa-yuganaddha*), there arose the Body of pair combined beyond

is the Anuttara *Māyājāla*, and the *Vajrahṛdayālaṃkāra* (Toh. 451) are Tantras belonging to the category of the Father Tantra. The *Saṃvara* (Toh. 368), *Hevajra* (Toh. 417-418), *Kālacakra* (Toh. 362), *Mahāmudrā-tilaka* (Toh. 420), the upper *māyā* in three residences (Toh. 425, the *Mahāmāyā* in three chapters), and the *Buddhasamāyoga* (Toh. 366, 367) are Mother Tantras.

Then of the Father Tantras, the *Guhyasamāja* is the chief; and of the Mother Tantras, the *Saṃvara* is the chief. The reason is that the other Father Tantras cannot compare with the *Guhyasamāja* in regard to extensive treatment of the Steps of Production (*utpatti-krama*), Steps of Completion (*niṣpanna-krama*), and set of ritual acts (*las tshogs*). And similarly, the other Mother Tantras cannot compare with the *Saṃvara* in regard to extensive treatment of the Steps of Production, Steps of Completion, and set of ritual acts.[13]

The Anuttara Tantras, so divided into Father Tantra and Mother Tantra, are further divided into Tantra of the sound which promulgates and Tantra of the meaning in the subject matter. The Tantra of the sound which promulgates comprises all the passages of the Anuttara Tantra that are proclaimed by Vajradhara. The Tantra of the meaning in the subject matter is of three kinds, Tantra of Cause (*hetu-tantra*), Tantra of Means (*upāya-tantra*), and Tantra of Effect (*phala-tantra*). Then, Tantra of Cause and Tantra of Ground (**prakṛti-tantra*) are identical, while Tantra of Means and Tantra of Path (*mārga-tantra*) are identical.[14]

Tantra of Ground. Naro-pā maintains that this is the "jewel-like person", who is the chief among the candidates for the high goal of the Anuttara [Tantra]. Śānti-pā and Abhayākara maintain that it is the True Nature of Mind (*citta-dharmatā*) intrinsically pure but possessed of adventitious defilements.[15]

Tantra of Effect. This is the rank of Vajradhara, which is the supreme attainment. The terminology 'pair combined beyond learning' (*aśaikṣa-yuganaddha*) and 'rank possessing the seven members of the *saṃpuṭa*' has the same meaning.[16]

---

learning (*aśaikṣa-yuganaddha*) and the rank of the seven members of the *saṃpuṭa* appeared directly; as long as *saṃsāra* is not emptied [of its suffering denizens] That abides immovable. The seven members of the *saṃpuṭa* are as stated by the *ācārya Vāgīśvarakīrti* [presumably in his *Saptāṅga*, Toh. 1888, Derge Tanjur *Rgyud*]: '(1) Saṃbhoga [-kāya], (2) *saṃpuṭa*, (3) Great Beatitude (*mahāsukha*), (4) no intrinsic nature (*niḥsvabhāva*), (5) state of being filled with compassion, (6) non-interruption, and (7) no cessation'" (slob paḥi zuṅ ḥjug gi rigs ḥdra phyi ma mi slob paḥi zuṅ ḥjug gi skur gyur nas kha sbyor yan lag bdun ldan gyi go ḥphaṅ mṅon du mdzad de / ḥkhor

/ thabs sam lam gyi rgyud ni / thob bya mthar thug de thob par byed paḥi thabs lam rim pa gñis yan lag daṅ bcas paḥo /

/ mdor na rgyuḥi rgyud dam / gźiḥi rgyud rin po che lta buḥi gaṅ zag des / thob bya mthar thug mi slob paḥi zuṅ ḥjug gi go ḥphaṅ de thob paḥi phyir du lam ñams su len paḥi thabs sam lam gyi rgyud mthaḥ dag bsdu na rnam pa bźir ḥdu ste / thog mar rgyud ma smin pa smin par byed pa dbaṅ gi rgyud / smin pa mi ñams par bsruṅ ba dam tshig daṅ sdom paḥi rgyud / ñams su blaṅ byaḥi ṅo bo bskyed rdzogs kyi rgyud / ñe rgyu spyod paḥi rgyud daṅ bźir ḥduḥo /

---

ba ji srid ma stoṅs kyi bar mi gYo bar bźugs pa yin no / kha sbyor yan lag bdun ni / slob dpon ṅag dbaṅ grags pas / loṅs spyod rdzogs daṅ kha bde chen raṅ bźin med sñiṅ rjes yoṅs gaṅ rgyun mi chad daṅ ḥgog pa med / ces gsuṅs pa ltar ro). The Kloṅ-rdol-bla-ma writes in Section Ga (Toh. 6534), 18b-3: "The seven members of the *saṃpuṭa* are as follows: (1) the Formal Body (*rūpa-kāya*) adorned with the [thirty-two) Characteristics (*lakṣaṇa*), (2) *saṃpuṭa* with one's own manifested *vidyā*, (3) mind dwelling with Great Beatitude, (4) comprehension, with that Beatitude, of the lack of intrinsic nature, (5) rejection, with compassion, of the quiescence extreme, (6) no interruption in affiliation with the Body, (7) no cessation of wondrous action" (kha sbyor yan lag bdun po ni / gzugs sku mtshan spras daṅ po daṅ / raṅ snaṅ rig mar kha sbyor gñis / thugs ni bde chen daṅ gnas gsum / bde des raṅ bźin med rtogs bźi / sñiṅ rjes źi mthaḥ spaṅs pa lṅa / sku yi rigs ḥdra chad med drug / ḥphrin las ḥgog med bdun paḥo). Those explanations are consistent with the exposition in *Sṅags rim*, 292a-4, ff.

17 The term *ñe rgyu* (**upacāra*), "convergence", is clarified by several passages in *Sṅags rim*, e.g. 411a-1, 2; 416b-1, 2; 417a-5, ff. It means the portion of the Steps of Completion that constitutes portents that one is close to the final attainment of Complete Buddhahood. For example, the forms of the void (*stoṅ gzugs rnams*), i.e. the mystic signs beginning with "smoke" are called "convergence". This convergence is variously expressed as the "non-duality of the profound and the bright" (*zab gsal gñis med*) or the "non-duality of Beatitude and the Void" (*bde stoṅ gñis med*).

Tantra of Means or of Path. This comprises the two *kramas* (*utpatti-krama* and *niṣpanna-krama*], along with their members (*aṅga*), of the path which is the means of attaining that supreme attainment.

In short, if one compiles all the Tantras of Means or of the Path, constituting the procedure of the path by which that "jewel-like person" who is the Tantra of Cause or Tantra of Ground may attain that rank of 'pair combined beyond learning' which is the supreme attainment, they fall in four classes:

(1) At the outset the Tantras of Initiation which mature that Tantra [of Ground] that is not yet mature;

(2) The Tantras of Pledges (*samaya*) and Vows (*saṃvara*) which protect the maturation from deterioration;

(3) The Tantras for Production (*utpatti*) and Completion (*niṣpanna*) of that essence which is to be taken to heart;

(4) The Tantras of Convergence [upon the supreme attainment].[17]

/ smin byed dbaṅ gi lam źes pa ni /

/ rdo rje theg paḥi thun moṅ min paḥi lam gyi thog mar ṅes par dbaṅ bskur ḥgro dgos pas lam gyi thog ma yin no / de la gsum / gaṅ du dbaṅ bskur ba dkyil ḥkhor gyi mtshan ñid / gaṅ gis dbaṅ bskur ba rdo rje slob dpon gyi mtshan ñid / des dkyil ḥkhor gaṅ du slob ma la ji ltar dbaṅ bskur baḥi tshul lo /

/ daṅ po ni / thog mar slob ma dkyil ḥkhor du bcug nas / deḥi rjes su dbaṅ bskur baḥi phyir du gźug par bya baḥi dkyil ḥkhor ni / slob dpon rdo rje dril bu pas / dbaṅ bskur dkyil ḥkhor sṅon ḥgro bar / źes sogs gsuṅs pa ltar / dkyil ḥkhor la / rdul tshon / ras bris / bsam gtan / lus dkyil daṅ rnam pa bźir ṅes la /

/ de la bsam gtan gyi dkyil ḥkhor ni / slob dpon daṅ slob ma gaṅ yaṅ ruṅ baḥi dbaṅ du byas pa ma yin gyi / de ni slob dpon tiṅ ṅe ḥdzin śin

[1] Saraha writes in his *Śrī-Buddhakapālatantrapañjika-jñānavatī* (Toh. 1652), Derge Ra, 105a-5: "'*Maṇḍa*' means essence (*or* pith, **sāra*, **hṛdaya*); '*-la*' means seizing that — thus, 'seizing the essence' (*maṇḍala*)" (dkyil ni sñiṅ poḥo / ḥkhor ni de len pa ste sñiṅ po len źes paḥo). *Avatāra-vyākh.* 96b-3, ff.: "'*Maṇḍala* means an 'enclosing of essence' (*maṇḍa-la*) because of having the 'essence' in the sense of 'enclosing' it. That is to say, the *maṇḍala* of perfectly pure shape is a *maṇḍala* because encompassed by the circle of wisdom-knowledge (*vidyā-jñāna-cakra*); or, the *maṇḍala* with the Lord in the middle is a *maṇḍala* because the Lord of the Family is surrounded by his retinue. For these purposes one may have, as appropriate, numerous and few aspects, shapes, and colors. There are two kinds of *maṇḍalas*: absolute (*paramārtha*) and relative (*saṃvṛti*). The absolute one is the wisdom-knowledge possessing (*-la*) the higher cognition of the Mind of Enlightenment (*bodhicitta*). ... There are two kinds of relative *maṇḍala*, categorized as 'intrinsic-nature *maṇḍala*' and 'reflected-image *maṇḍala*'" (dkyil ḥkhor ni dkyil ḥkhor du ldan pas dkyil ḥkhor te / dbyibs rnam par dag paḥi dkyil ḥkhor la / rig paḥi ye śes kyi ḥkhor gyis bskor baḥi phyir na dkyil ḥkhor źehaṃ / dbus kyi gtso bo dkyil ḥkhor la rigs kyi gtso bo la sogs paḥi ḥkhor gyis bskor baḥi phyir na dkyil ḥkhor te / maṅ ñuṅ gi rnam pa daṅ / dbyibs daṅ / kha dog ji lta bu dag na yaṅ ruṅ ste / de la yaṅ rnam pa gñis te / don dam pa daṅ kun rzdob bo / don dam pa ni byaṅ chub sems rtogs par gyur pa daṅ ldan paḥi rig paḥi ye śes kyi ṅo bo ste / ... / kun rdzob kyi dkyil ḥkhor la yaṅ gñis te / raṅ bźin gyi dkyil ḥkhor daṅ / gzugs brñan gyi dkyil ḥkhor gyis bsdus paḥo).

CHAPTER EIGHT

[c. *Procedure in the meaning of the subject matter*]

(1) THE PATH OF INITIATION WHICH PRODUCES MATURATION

Since it is certainly necessary to be conferred Initiation (*abhiṣeka*) at the beginning of the uncommon path (*asādhāraṇa-mārga*) of Vajrayāna, this is the inception of the path. There are three [observances] for it: the characteristics of the *maṇḍala* in which Initiation is conferred; the characteristics of the hierophant who confers Initiation; the method by which the hierophant initiates the disciple in whatever *maṇḍala*.

(a) Characteristics of the maṇḍala in which Initiation is conferred

At the outset the disciple is introduced into the *maṇḍala*,[1] and then he is conferred Initiation. Regarding the *maṇḍala* to be entered for that purpose, it is just as stated by the *ācārya* Vajraghaṇṭa, "The preliminaries of the *maṇḍala* for the Initiation..." As he points out, the *maṇḍalas* are certainly of four types, those made of powdered colors, those painted on textiles, those formed by meditation, and the body as a *maṇḍala*.[2]

As to the meditation *maṇḍala*, it is not that *any* hierophant or disciple is fit for conferring or receiving the Initiation. Rather, it is stated as

---

[2] The *Sṅags rim*, 225b-6, quotes the third chapter of the *Abhidhāna* (Toh. 369) for a further classification: "The *maṇḍala* of syllables (*akṣara*) is the first; the second is the *maṇḍala* of attributes (*nimitta*); that of hand gestures is the third; that of useful images is the fourth; the one having a display of flowers is the fifth; the sixth is the *maṇḍala* of the [deity] host" (mṅon brjod kyi gsum pa las / yi geḥi dkyil ḥkhor daṅ po ste / gñis pa mtshan maḥi dkyil ḥkhor yin / lag paḥi phyag rgya gsum pa ste / gzugs brñan dgos pa bźi paḥo / me tog dgram pa lṅa pa ste / drug pa tshogs kyi dkyil ḥkhor ro / źes gsuṅs so).

tu brtan pa daṅ / slob ma dbaṅ po śin tu rno źiṅ mos pa brtan pa sogs mtshan ñid khyad par can daṅ ldan pa la dmigs bsal du gsuṅs pa yin no /

/lus dkyil du dbaṅ bskur ba la / thog mar bla med kyi rdul tshon daṅ ras bris kyi dkyil ḥkhor gaṅ yaṅ ruṅ bar dbaṅ bskur mtshan ñid tshaṅ ba thob ste / de nas lus dkyil du dbaṅ bskur ba yin gyi / thog mar phyi dkyil du dbaṅ ma thob par lus dkyil du dbaṅ bskur du mi ruṅ ṅo /

/ thog mar rgyud ma smin pa smin par byed paḥi thabs dbaṅ bskur mtshan ñid tshaṅ ba rdul tshon daṅ ras bris gaṅ du thob kyaṅ dbaṅ gi go chod kyi / ḥo na kyaṅ slob ma tshogs gsog pa daṅ sgrib pa sbyoṅ baḥi sgo maṅ źiṅ / sṅags kyi lam gyi snod khyad par can du ḥgyur baḥi dgos pa che bas / deḥi phyir rgyud daṅ grub chen gyi gźuṅ tshad ldan phal che ba las / rdul tshon gyi dkyil ḥkhor mchog tu gsuṅs so /

/ gñis pa ni / brtan źiṅ dul la blo gros ldan / źes sogs bla ma lṅa bcu pa nas gsuṅs pa ltar gyi phyi naṅ gi de ñid bcu daṅ / mdo sṅags kyi bstan bcos daṅ / rgyud la mkhas pa sogs kyi mtshan ñid tshaṅ ba / khyad par

[3] For this work, cf. Sylvain Lévi, "Autour d'Aśvaghoṣa", *Journal Asiatique*, CCXV (Oct.-Dec. 1929), p. 260, lines 11-14: "Steadfast [in body], controlled [in speech], intelligent, forbearing, just, and without deceit; skilled in the praxis of *mantra* and *tantra*, compassionate, and learned in the expository texts; experienced in the ten categories, expert in drawing the *maṇḍala*; who can explain the *mantras*, is devoted and ruler of his senses, so should be the Hierophant (*ācārya*)."

/ dhīro vinīto matimān kṣamāvān ārjavo 'śaṭhaḥ /
/ mantratantraprayogajñaḥ kṛpāluḥ śāstrakovidaḥ // 8 //
/ daśatattvaparijñātā maṇḍalālekhyakarmavit /
/ mantravyākhyākṛd ācāryaḥ prasannaḥ syāj jitendriyaḥ // 9 //

[4] These are set forth and explained by Tsoṅ-kha-pa in his commentary on the *Gurupañcāśikā* called *Slob maḥi re ba kun sloṅ* (Toh. 5269), 7b-3, ff. He quotes two groups of ten from the *Vajrahṛdayālaṃkāra* (Toh. 451), as follows (with incorporation of some of his commentary): — These are the secret [or "inner"] ten categories:

1, 2. The rites of the two "reversals" (*phyir zlog pa*) [reversal through contemplation of the ten wrathful deities (*krodha*), for example; and reversal by means of tying, etc. after the drawing (of the Knowledge Being)];

3, 4. The [Initiations of] Secret (*guhya*) and Insight-Knowledge (*prajñā-jñāna*) [which imply the Flask (*kalaśa*) and the Fourth (*caturtha*), Initiations].

5. The rite of "tearing apart" (*ḥbyed*) the *saṃpuṭa* (*kha sbyor*) [i.e. having forced away the enemy guardians (*dgra bo sruṅ ma*), to practice *abhicāra* ("destructive magic")].

6. Devoted food offering (*bali*) [e.g. the 15-fold *bali* for the protectors of the quarters (*dik-pāla*)].

7. Diamond muttering (*vajrajāpa*) [of mind and voice].

8. The rite of accomplishing the fierce act (*drag śul*) [i.e. tying down the gods with the magic nail (*kīla*)].

9. Consecration (*pratiṣṭhāna*).

10. Accomplishing the *maṇḍala* [of the deities generated in front; extending them offerings and praises; entering the *maṇḍala* and then receiving Initiation and being favored with permission (*anujñā*)].

the exception in the possession of distinguished characteristics that the hierophant is firm in *samādhi*, the disciple keen in sense organs and firm in conviction.

In regard to Initiation in the body *maṇḍala*, one must first obtain the complete characteristics of Initiation in the Anuttara *maṇḍala* of powdered colors, or painted on textile, as the case may be, and then be conferred Initiation in the body *maṇḍala*. Without having first obtained Initiation in an external *maṇḍala*, one should not be conferred Initiation in the body *maṇḍala*.

The Initiation conferred in either the powdered-colors or painted [*maṇḍala*] is serviceable when it has the complete characteristics of Initiation constituting the means of maturing the initially unmatured stream of consciousness (*saṃtāna*). However, there are many approaches by which the disciple acquires the equipment (*saṃbhāra*) and eliminates the obscuration; and the chief requirement is that he become an outstanding vessel for the *mantra* path. Hence, the majority of the Tantras and authoritative texts of the *mahāsiddhas* have declared the *maṇḍala* of powdered colors to be the better [of the two].

(b) Characteristics of the hierophant who confers Initiation

They are just as said in the *Fifty Stanzas in Praise of the Guru* (*Gurupañcāśikā* of Aśvaghoṣa, Toh. 3721), "Steadfast, self-controlled, intelligent..."[3] That is to say, he has the complete characteristics of the internal and external ten categories (*daśatattva*),[4] of erudition in the expository

---

These are the outer ten categories:

1. The *maṇḍala* [of form and formless].
2. Intense concentration (*samādhi*) [i.e. *devatā-yoga*, and of the (three) kinds beginning with "initial training" (*prathama-prayoga*)].
3. Seal (*mudrā*) [e.g. the seals which apply seals to the gods].
4. [Male] stance [the (five) kinds beginning with "left leg bent and right foot forward" (*ālīḍhastha*)].
5. Seated position [the (two) kinds beginning with "feet crossed in the diamond manner" (*vajra-paryaṅkạ*)].
6. Muttering, 7. Burnt offering, 8. Worship;
9. Preliminary ritual (*las la sbyor ba*) [protecting, invitation, etc.].
10. Concluding acts (*slar sdud*) [having finished the offering, praising, etc., to pray that the gods depart].

Tsoṅ-kha-pa explains (*ibid.*, 8b-1, 2) that the latter ten (i.e. the ten outer ones) characterise the Hierophant (*vajra-ācārya*) of the (three) lower Tantras; and that the former ten (i.e. the inner ones) characterise the Hierophant of the Anuttara (Tantra).

du / rtsa baḥi ltuṅ ba rab ḥjoms byed / ces gsuṅs pa ltar rtsa ltuṅ gis daṅ por ma gos paḥam brgyal gos kyaṅ bdag ḥjug sogs kyi sdom pa sor chud par byas te / slob ma la dbaṅ bskur baḥi tshe na sṅags sdom daṅ ldan par byas nas dbaṅ bskur dgos kyi / de ltar ma byas par dbaṅ bskur na / slob mas dbaṅ thob paḥi go mi chod pas deḥi rgyud la sṅags kyi lam gyi gźi med par son baḥi phyir raṅ gźan gñis ka bslus par ḥgyur ro /

/ gźan yaṅ / bsñen sogs dag par ma byas par / dkyil ḥkhor las la ḥjug pa daṅ / źes gsuṅs paḥi dkyil ḥkhor gyi las daṅ / bsñen sogs kyi tshad ji lta bu źe na / de la dkyil ḥkhor gyi las ni / raṅ ñid bdag ḥjug len pa daṅ / gźan la dbaṅ bskur ba daṅ / rab gnas daṅ / sbyin sreg sogs yin la / las de rnams la ḥjug pa na / gaṅ la brten paḥi lhaḥi rnal ḥbyor bsñen pa kha skoṅ daṅ bcas pa sṅon du btaṅ nas byed dgos kyi / de lta min na / sñiṅ po mdor bsags las / raṅ ñid sun ḥbyin pa daṅ ñams par byed ciṅ / gnod pa byed par gsuṅs pas so /

/ bsñen paḥi tshad ni / brtag gñis las / dkyil ḥkhor bdag poḥi bzlas pa ḥbum / dkyil ḥkhor pa yi khri yin te / źes gsuṅs pa ltar bla med kyi dkyil ḥkhor phal che ba las / gtso boḥi bzlas pa ḥbum / ḥkhor rnams la khri phrag re re bya dgos par gsuṅs kyaṅ / bde mchog las / rgyas pa de ltar byed ciṅ / ḥbriṅ daṅ bsdus paḥi rnam gźag gsuṅs la / dus ḥkhor la yaṅ gtso bo la ḥbum daṅ / ḥkhor gyi bsñen pa thugs dkyil gyi lha rnams la khri phrag re re bzlas pas chog par gsuṅs so / bzaṅ po yoṅs gzuṅ daṅ / dkyil chog rdo rje ḥphreṅ ba las / me tog phog paḥi lha la ḥbum bzla dgos par gsuṅs kyaṅ / ḥdir de ltar ṅes par byed dgos par mi bźed do / sṅags rim las ye śes ḥbebs paḥi sṅags la bsñen pa khri phrag gcig daṅ / deḥi bcu chaḥi sbyin sreg byed dgos pa ni / dus ḥkhor gyi dbaṅ du byas pa yin par gsuṅs śiṅ / gźan la ṅes par dgos par ma gsuṅs la / bzlas paḥi kha skoṅ gi sbyin sreg bya mi dgos par gsuṅs śiṅ / ḥdus paḥi dkyil cho ga las / ye śes ḥbebs paḥi bzlas pa ḥbum daṅ / bgegs mthar byed kyi ḥphreṅ

[5] There are fourteen basic transgressions, for which see Chapter IX. The citation is from the *Vajrapañjarā*, Chap. 8, according to *Sṅags rim*, 125b-2.

[6] There is a quotation from this work, along the lines indicated by Mkhas grub rje, in *Sṅags rim*, 130a-2, but with no clue as to a more standard form of the title by which it can be identified in the Tohoku Catalog.

[7] Possibly Toh. 5287, by Tsoṅ-kha-pa.

texts (*śāstra*) of the *sūtras* and *mantras* as well as in the Tantras, and so forth. Above all, they are just as said, "He is victorious over the basic transgressions."[5] That is to say, either he is not defiled by the basic transgressions in the first place, or if inadvertently defiled by them, restores his vow (*saṃvara*) by personally entering [the *maṇḍala*] and so forth. At the time he confers Initiation upon the disciple, it is necessary that he confer Initiation while governed by the *mantra* vow; for should he confer Initiation while not so governed, the disciple has no advantage in obtaining the Initiation for the reason that the ground (**prakṛti*, T. *gźi*) of the *mantra* path is not installed in his stream of consciousness and with the consequence that both parties are deceived.

Furthermore, what are the *maṇḍala* acts and measure of service meant when it is said, "If one engages upon the *maṇḍala* acts without having performed in pure manner the service, ..."? The *maṇḍala* acts are the [hierophant's] own entrance into the *maṇḍala*, conferring of Initiation upon another, consecration (*pratiṣṭhā*), burnt offering (*homa*), and so on. And when one engages upon those acts, he must first perform the service, along with supplementary observances, consisting in *yoga* of the deity on whom one relies. Otherwise, he would stun, damage, and harm himself, as pointed out in the *Sñiṅ po mdor bsags*.[6]

The measure of service (*sevā*) is just as said in the *Hevajra* (I, x, 25a-b): "One should recite 100,000 times for the *maṇḍala* Lord (*cakreśa*); 10,000 times for the *maṇḍala* retinue (*māṇḍaleya*)"; and the greater number of Anuttara *maṇḍalas* require the recitation of the Lord to be done 100,000 times, that of the members of the retinue 10,000 times for each one. Moreover, the *Samvara* states that the elaborate service is done that way, and that there are medium and brief services. Also, the *Kālacakra* mentions that it suffices to recite 100,000 times for the Lord and, in the service of the retinue, 10,000 times for each deity in the Mind *maṇḍala* (*citta-maṇḍala*). The *Suparigraha* (Toh. 1240) and the *Vajrāvali* (Toh. 3140) *maṇḍala-sādhanas* state that one must recite 100,000 times for the deity on whom the flower falls; however, we do not necessarily require that. The *Sṅags rim* (Toh. 5281, by Tsoṅ-kha-pa) states that it is a feature of the *Kālacakra* to require a recitation 10,000 times of the *dhāraṇī* which causes the Knowledge Being to descend, and to do the burnt offering in ten parts for that. That work (the *Sṅags rim*) does not specify such a requirement for other [Tantras]; and it specifies that there is no necessity to perform the burnt offering which supplements the recitation. In "The *Guhya-samāja maṇḍala-vidhi*",[7] it is said that one recites 100,000 times to make the Knowledge Being descend and recites 10,000 times

sṅags khri bzla bar gsuṅs la / bsñen paḥi kha skoṅ gi sbyin sreg byed mi byed gñis ka ma gsuṅs kyaṅ / gźin rjeḥi gśed dmar nag gi dkyil chog las / bsñen paḥi kha skoṅ gi sbyin sreg ṅes par byed dgos par gsuṅs pas / sṅa rtiṅ rnams guṅ bsgrigs nas śes par byaḥo /

/ bsñen paḥi sṅags la rtsa sṅags ṅes par mi dgos pas / sñiṅ po rnams la bsñen pa soṅ na / des bdag ḥjug sogs kyi las la ni go chod par gsuṅs so /

/ kha cig na re / gtso boḥi bzlas pa ḥbum / ḥkhor rnams la khri bzla bar gsuṅs pa spyir yin gyi / da lta rtsod dus su bźi ḥgyur bzla bar sdom ḥbyuṅ las gsuṅs so / źes ser ba mi ḥthad de / sdom ḥbyuṅ las gsuṅs pa ni / las tshogs kyi dṅos grub sgrub paḥi las bsñen gyi dbaṅ du byas nas gsuṅs pa yin gyi / dkyil ḥkhor gyi las la ḥjug paḥi sṅon rol gyi bsñen pa la de ltar dgos par sdom ḥbyuṅ las ma gsuṅs śiṅ gźan tshad ldan gaṅ gis kyaṅ ma gsuṅs paḥi phyir ro /

/ kha cig na re / kye rdor lta buḥi dkyil gcig gi gtso ḥkhor gyi bsñen tshad soṅ na / dkyil ḥkhor gźan la sgos kyi bsñen pa bya mi dgos par dbaṅ bskur sogs kyi dkyil ḥkhor gyi las la źugs pas chog ste / lha thams cad ṅo bo gcig yin paḥi phyir / źes zer la / de la raṅ bźin rnam dag tu ṅo bo gcig yin paḥi phyir źes zer ba daṅ / rgyud gcig ciṅ bde stoṅ du ṅo bo gcig yin paḥi phyir źes pa gaṅ zer yaṅ ḥdra bas / bya rgyud kyi je-tā-riḥi tshe dpag med lha dgu lta bu źig gi dbaṅ thob na bla med sogs kyi dkyil ḥkhor thams cad kyi dbaṅ thob par ḥgyur te / lha thams cad ṅo bo gcig yin pas so /

/ kha cig na re / bskyed rim thun bźir bsgom nas bsñen paḥi tshad rdzogs par byas su zin kyaṅ / slob mas dbaṅ bskur bar gsol ba btab ciṅ / slob dpon gyis źal gyis bźes paḥi skabs su bum pa la brten paḥi bsñen pa gso ba / dkyil ḥkhor spyi daṅ / khyad par du bde mchog nag po la bya dgos so / źes zer ba mi ḥthad de / de ni bod kyi rtog bzo ḥbaḥ źig yin gyi / tshad ldan gyi gźuṅ gaṅ nas kyaṅ de dag gsuṅs pa med paḥi phyir ro /

/ des na bskyed rim thun bźir bsgoms nas bsñen tshad tshul bźin du

[8] Possibly Toh. 5339, by Tsoṅ-kha-pa.

[9] Cf. Chapter III, note 18, where the distinction is shown in terms of *mantras*.

[10] Presumably based on Toh. 2700, Jetāri's *Aparimitāyurjñānavidhi-nāma*.

[11] For the four watches, *Sṅags rim*, 400a-2, mentions in a quotation from Jalandhari-pa, "... dawn, noon, late afternoon, night..." (... tho raṅs daṅ ñi ma guṅ daṅ phyi dro daṅ mtshan mo...). These are evidently the watches of dawn, noon, evening twilight, and midnight.

the *dhāraṇī*-garland that puts an end to hindrances, but there is no mention there of whether or not one performs the burnt offering that supplements the recitation. It is said in "The *maṇḍala-vidhis* of the red and black Yamāris"[8] that one must certainly perform the burnt offering which supplements the recitation. Hence, one may understand [what to do] through [this] compilation of former and latter passages.

Regarding the *dhāraṇī* to be used in the service, it is not necessary to use the *mūla-dhāraṇī*, because he [presumably Tsoṅ-kha-pa] says that if one uses the *hṛdaya* ones for the service, they are serviceable for the acts of own entrance [into the *maṇḍala*], etc.[9]

According to some persons, the statement that one recites 100,000 times for the Lord, and recites 10,000 times for the members of the retinue, is the general rule, but that now in this age of strife (*kali-yuga*) it should be done four times as often, and they cite the *Saṃvarodaya* (Toh. 373). Their position is not valid. The *Saṃvarodaya* refers to the service consisting in the acts which accomplish the *siddhis* of the ritual acts; but the *Saṃvarodaya* does not set forth such a requirement in regard to the preliminary service of entering into the *maṇḍala* acts, and no other authoritative text asserts such a thing.

According to some persons, when one has gone through the service for the Lord and the retinue of a single *maṇḍala*, say that of Hevajra, one is not required to perform any special service in other *maṇḍalas* and may enter into their *maṇḍala* acts, such as Initiation, because all the deities are of one essence. That would amount to asserting that it is because they are of one essence in their intrinsic purity or because they are of one essence in the sense of a single stream of consciousness and of Bliss-Void (*sukha-śūnya*). As a consequence, if one were to receive the Initiation of, say, the Jetāri Amitāyus in a group of nine gods of the Kriyā Tantra,[10] one would [automatically] receive Initiation in all *maṇḍalas*, Anuttara and so forth, because [using their argument] all deities are of one essence.

According to some persons, after the disciple has finished the measure of service through contemplating the Steps of Production in four watches (*catuḥsandhyā*)[11] and he petitions for the conferring of Initiation, when the Hierophant deigns to grant it, he (the disciple) must reinstitute service based on the Flask in the case of general *maṇḍalas* and especially that of the black Saṃvara. That assertion is not valid. It is merely a Tibetan phantasy, because it is not said by any authoritative text.

Indeed, when one contemplates the Steps of Production in four watches he must complete in correct manner the measure of service; and when

rdzogs par byas pa daṅ / bskyed rim bsgoms pa la brten nas raṅ gi sems dag paḥi mtshan ma byuṅ ba daṅ / lhas dbaṅ bskur ba ma bkag pa tsam gyi mtshan ma ni / dbaṅ bskur ba sogs dkyil ḥkhor gyi las la ḥjug pa la ma mthaḥ yaṅ tshaṅ dgos so / yaṅ lhaḥi gnaṅ ba byuṅ na ni / bsñen paḥi graṅs ma rdzogs kyaṅ dbaṅ bskur ba sogs dkyil ḥkhor gyi las la źugs pas chog ste / de ñid kyis bsñen tshad kyi dod thub ciṅ / de ñid mchog yin pas so /

/ gsum pa la gsum / rdul tshon daṅ / ras bris daṅ / lus dkyil du dbaṅ bskur baḥi tshul lo /

/ daṅ po la gsum / dkyil ḥkhor bri baḥi tshul daṅ / dkyil ḥkhor sgrub paḥi tshul daṅ / bsgrubs nas dbaṅ bskur baḥi tshul lo /

/ daṅ po la gsum / saḥi cho ga daṅ / sta gon gyi cho ga daṅ / dkyil ḥkhor bri baḥi cho ga dṅos bstan paḥo /

/ daṅ po la lṅa / sa brtag pa / sa bslaṅ ba / sa sbyaṅ ba / sa gzuṅ ba / sa bsruṅ źiṅ byin gyis brlab paḥo /

/ daṅ po ni / saḥi phyogs de dkyil ḥkhor bri baḥi mtshan ñid daṅ ldan mi ldan brtag paḥo /

/ sa bslaṅ ba la gñis / mṅon pa las bslaṅ ba daṅ / mi mṅon pa las bslaṅ baḥo /

/ daṅ po ni / de ltar brtag nas ruṅ baḥi mtshan ñid daṅ ldan par śes na / tshur mthoṅ la snaṅ du ruṅ baḥi sa deḥi bdag po rgyal po daṅ / groṅ dpon sogs la sa phyogs der dkyil ḥkhor bri baḥi gnaṅ bźu baḥo /

/ gñis pa ni / tshul mthoṅ la snaṅ du mi ruṅ baḥi źiṅ skyoṅ ste / mi mṅon paḥi sa deḥi bdag po la gnaṅ ba gsol nas / gnaṅ ba gyur baḥi mos

[12] These signs are ordinary determined by dreams. Thus, *Sṅags rim*, 133b-3, says: "However, the one who has already done the service consisting in contemplation and muttering, must for the performance of Initiation examine his dreams [and decide that] permission has been granted and that it is not opposed; as [the *gurus*] have said that, one must act accordingly" (ḥon kyaṅ bsgom bzlas kyi bsñen pa sṅon du soṅ bas dbaṅ byed pa laḥaṅ rmi lam brtags nas gnaṅ ba thob pa daṅ ma bkag pa gaṅ ruṅ dgos par gsuṅs pas de bźin du byaḥo).

[13] This paragraph appears to be a reply to all three previous paragraphs each beginning, "According to some persons..." The author has preferred not to reply specifically to the second of those three positions. To use the terminology of the two Truths, it is a matter of Absolute Truth (*paramārtha-satya*) that all the deities are of one essence, but the manifestation of those deities is a matter of Conventional Truth (*saṃvṛti-satya*).

he is based in cultivation of the Steps of Production, the sign of his mental purity must arise; and there must be the sign that the Initiation is not opposed by the deity:[12] these are the minimum requirements for engaging in the *maṇḍala* acts, such as Initiation. Furthermore, if the permission (*anujñā*) of the gods has been received, one may enter into Initiation and the other acts of the *maṇḍala* even if the [prescribed] amount of service is not completed. That very [permission] substitutes for the measure of service, because that [permission] is paramount.[13]

(c) Method by which the hierophant initiates the disciple in whatever maṇḍala

There are three divisions: the method of Initiation in the *maṇḍala* of powdered colors, that in the *maṇḍala* painted on cloth, and that in the body as *maṇḍala*.

α. *Method of Initiation in the maṇḍala of powdered colors* (*rajomaṇḍala*)

There are three parts: the method of drawing the *maṇḍala*, the method of accomplishing the *maṇḍala*, and the method of initiation after accomplishing it.

I′. *Method of drawing the maṇḍala*

There are three sections: the ritual of the site, the ritual of the preparatory acts, and the ritual of drawing the *maṇḍala*.

A′. *Ritual of the site.* — This has five divisions: investigating the site, begging for the site, clearing the site, seizing the site, protecting and blessing the site.

1′. *Investigating the site.* — This means investigating a site with reference to whether or not it has the characteristics for drawing a *maṇḍala*.

2′. *Begging for the site.* — There are two parts to this: begging from a manifest being, and begging from a non-manifest being.

a′. *Begging from a manifest being.* — Having examined the site and satisfied himself that it has the required characteristics, one begs permission to draw a *maṇḍala* at that site from the master of the site, the king, or the head of a village, who is visible to him.

b′. *Begging from a non-manifest being.* — When it is not feasible for a 'field protector' (*kṣetrapāla*) to appear to the vision, one begs permission from the invisible master of that site. Without exception, it is man-

pa byed pa sogs tsam ni dkyil ḥkhor thams cad kyi cho ga la dgos par khyad par med do /

/ yaṅ bde mchog daṅ / dus ḥkhor sogs la ni / saḥi lha mo la gnaṅ bźu ba daṅ / bde mchog la khyad par bde gśegs sa bslaṅ źes pa / ḥjig rten las ḥdas pa la gnaṅ ba gsol ba yod ciṅ / dus ḥkhor la yaṅ de daṅ rnam pa mthun pa tsam źig gsuṅs pa rnams ni / de rnams kyi cho gaḥi khyad par yin gyi / ḥdus pa sogs la de ltar ma gsuṅs kyaṅ / cho ga chad paḥi skyon du mi ḥgyur te / lugs so so ba yin pas so /

/ gsum pa sa sbyaṅ ba la gñis / brkos pas sbyaṅ ba daṅ / rko mi dgos paḥi sbyoṅ tshul lo /

/ daṅ po ni / dkyil ḥkhor gyi khaṅ pa thog mar bzos nas der dkyil ḥkhor bri ba lta bu daṅ / rgyal poḥi pho braṅ gi phyi rol daṅ / groṅ khyer sogs kyi phyi rol dbye thaṅ kha lta bur dkyil ḥkhor bri ba la ni / sa brkos nas rdo ba daṅ / tsher ma daṅ / gyo mo la sogs paḥi zug rṅu ḥbyin pas sbyaṅ dgos la / de ltar ma byas na mi ruṅ bas /

/ de la thog mar sa gaṅ nas brko baḥi lto ḥphyeḥi mchan khuṅ thigs par bya baḥi phyir du / lto ḥphye brtag paḥi thig btab ste / deḥi mchan khuṅ thigs par byas nas / thog mar de nas ḥbyor kham gñis gsum źig brko bar bya ste / de nas phyogs gaṅ nas brkos kyaṅ sa bdag daṅ mi thug paḥi dgos pa yod do /

/ gñis pa ni / gtsug lag khaṅ daṅ / lha khaṅ daṅ / khaṅ khyim la sogs par bri ba na / sa brkos pas sbyaṅ mi dgos śiṅ / rdzas sṅags tiṅ ṅe ḥdzin gsum gyis sbyaṅs pas cho ga la / de la rdzas ni chu thal ba / yuṅs kar la sogs pa daṅ / sṅags ni / oṃ bhū khaṃ la sogs paḥo / tiṅ ṅe ḥdzin ni/

[14] In the extensive treatment by the *Sṅags rim*, the investigation of the "breast goer" is done in accordance with Vibhūti's *maṇḍala-vidhi* (possibly Toh. 1832, Vibhūticandra's *Piṇḍīkṛtasādhanapañjikā*), cited a number of times beginning *Sṅags rim*, 139b-4. The "breast goer" (S. *uraga*, T. *lto ḥphye*) is ordinarily understood as a serpent, but it is hard to believe that this meaning is intended in the present context. The eight serpent kings (*nāga-rāja*) are disposed along the "breast goer": Kulika at the tip of the tail, Karkoṭaka the sacral place, Mahāpadma the shoulders, Vāsuki the heart, Śaṅkhapāla the navel, Takṣaka the neck, Padma the ears, and Ananta at the head. The treatment suggests that the *uraga* is a substitution for *kūrma* ("tortoise"). The site is taken as a square, and each side, representing the four cardinal directions of East and so on, is divided into three parts representing three months, and each part divided into thirty for the days of a month, so each side is divided into 90 spaces (which, to use zodiacal terminology, would be called "degrees"). On the first day of autumn, the "breast goer" has its head at the N.E. point, its tail at the S.W. point and faces the South direction. It slowly revolves, each day making a clockwise transit into another space, until at the end of six months [during which the sun, starting at the N.W. point, proceeds counter-clockwise in its six months of Southern declination] its head arrives at the S.W. point, its tail at the N.E. point. Then it proceeds clockwise for six months, facing North [while the sun proceeds counter-clockwise through

datory in the ritual of all *maṇḍalas* to have conviction that permission has been granted.

Moreover, in the *Saṃvara*, *Kālacakra*, etc., one asks the Earth Goddess (*pṛthivī*) for permission. In particular, in the *Saṃvara* one says, "O Sugata, [I] beg the site", which amounts to asking permission of a supra-mundane being; and in the *Kālacakra* there is something consistent with that. These remarks concern special features of their rites. However, in the *Guhyasamāja*, among others, it is not set forth that way; and this is no fault of omission, because there are various [proper] schools.

3′. *Clearing the site.* — There are two parts to this: method of clearing with digging; method of clearing with digging not required.

a′. *Method of clearing with digging.* — For drawing the *maṇḍala*, whether it be a case of first building a *maṇḍala* house and drawing the *maṇḍala* therein, or a case of a picture at a spot outside the royal palace, outside the city, and so forth, it is necessary to dig up the site and remove stones, thorns, broken bricks, sherds, and similar pains of the earth, thus clearing the site. If that is not done, it is not proper [to draw the *maṇḍala*].

In order to "line" the "armpit" (*kakṣa*) of the "breast goer" (*uraga*) at the place where one commences to dig, one strikes a line (**sūtra-nyāsa*) to determine the "breast goer".[14] When one has "lined" its "armpit", he thereupon digs out first two or three shovelfuls, after which he may proceed with digging wherever he wishes without risking offence to the 'field protector' (or, *genius loci*, S. *kṣitipati*).

b′. *Method of clearing with digging not required.* — If one draws [the *maṇḍala*] in such places as a monastery (*vihāra*), temple (*devakula*), and residence (*layana*), it is not necessary to purify by digging the soil, but one has a purificatory ritual with substances, incantations, and intense concentration. In this case, the substances are water, ashes, white mustard seed, etc. The incantations are *Oṃ*, *bhū*, *khaṃ*, etc. The intense

---

its six months of Northern declination]. For the place of initial digging, Tsoṅ-kha-pa cites that work of Vibhūti as follows: "From [head in] East, disregard 27 spaces [toward West, and take] the next nine spaces. From Northern [latitude of head] disregard 13-1/2 spaces [toward South, and take] the next 4-1/2 spaces. One begins to dig in the center of this [rectangular] sign [a 9 × 4½ space rectangle]" (śar nas cha ni ñi śū rtsa bdun dor / byaṅ nas phyed daṅ bcu bźiḥi cha dor bar / śar nub cha dgu lho byaṅ phyed daṅ lṅa / ḥdi ni mtshan gyi mdun du thog mar brko). Presumably, when the head is in a different direction from East, one modifies the instructions accordingly. Apparently, the 9 × 4½ spaced rectangle is the "armpit" (*kakṣa*) of the "breast goer".

stoṅ pa ñid bsgoms nas sbyaṅ baḥo / ḥdi ni brkos nas sbyaṅ ba la ḥaṅ dgos so /

/ bźi pas gzuṅ ba ni / de ltar legs par sbyaṅs paḥi sa deḥi dbus su raṅ ñid dkyil ḥkhor gyi śar sgo gaṅ du ḥoṅ ba deḥi phyogs su kha bltas la ḥdug ste / sgrub thabs rdzogs par bsgoms nas / sa der yaṅ ji ltar bsgoms pa de ḥdra baḥi dkyil ḥkhor bri bar byaḥo sñam du blos dam bcaḥ ba ni sa gzuṅ baḥo /

/ lṅa pa ni / de nas phyogs kyi slob dpon bźis sgo bźi nas ma-ṇḍa-la sṅon du ḥgro baḥi mchod pa phul la / dkyil ḥkhor bri bar gsol ba gdab pa ni / bdag bskyed kyi dkyil ḥkhor ñer bsdu mi byed par ḥdegs paḥi phyag rgya daṅ / sṅags kyis nam mkhar bteg la bya / de nas raṅ ñid gtso bo las mar me gcig las gñis chad kyi tshul gyis skabs gaṅ yin gyis khro boḥi dbaṅ por bsgyur bar bya źiṅ / de la khro bo gaṅ du bsgyur na / bde dgyes lta bu la khams gsum rnam rgyal daṅ / dus ḥkhor lo rdo rje śugs daṅ / ḥdus pa la źe sdaṅ rdo rje lta buḥo / de ltar raṅ raṅ gi khro bo de ñid kyi ṅa rgyal bzuṅ ste / slob dpon dbaṅ ldan du soṅ nas / bgegs la bkaḥ bsgo byas te / de nas slob dpon thams cad kyis phyogs bźi la sogs par / rkaṅ stabs kha sbyor sogs rgyas bsdus ci rigs par byas la / bgegs lhag ma rnams la phur gdab bya ba daṅ / bsruṅ ḥkhor bsgoms nas bgegs bsruṅ źiṅ sṅags daṅ phyag rgyas dkyil ḥkhor gyi sa gźi rdo rjeḥi raṅ bźin du byin gyis rlob paḥo /

/ sa cho ga gi rim pa ḥdi ni / bla med kyi dkyil ḥkhor phal che baḥi lugs yin la / dus ḥkhor lta bu la cuṅ źig mi mthun pa yod do /

/ gñis pa sta gon la bźi / saḥi lha mo sta gon daṅ / dkyil ḥkhor gyi lha

[15] The "*maṇḍala* of self-generation" seems to be the *maṇḍala* as contemplated according to the foregoing sub-section "Seizing the site".

[16] The stances meant are five according to Tsoṅ-kha-pa's *Sṅags rim*, 150a-2, ff., and according to Ānandagarbha's *Tattvāloka* (Toh. 2510), Derge Li, 254b-4, 5. They are five of the six (omitting *vaiṣṇava*) in Manomohan Ghosh, transl., *The Nāṭyaśāstra ascribed to Bharata-muni* (Calcutta, 1951), 201-3. In the order given below, with descriptions as cited by Tsoṅ-kha-pa, *ibid.*, they are performed, respectively, in the four direction, 1. East, 2. South, 3. West, 4. North, and finally in 5. the center.

1. *ālīḍha* (*gYas brkyaṅ*). The calf of the left leg is drawn back and the right leg, five spans (*tāla*) away, is stretched out straight.
2. *pratyālīḍha* (*gYon brkyaṅ*). The reverse of *ālīḍha*.
3. *vaiśākha* (*sa ga*). The two legs are placed 26 *aṅgulis* apart; and showing the sides of the toes of the feet, the shanks of the legs are held straight.
4. *maṇḍala* (*zlum po*). The two legs are placed a pair (*do pa*) of *hastas* apart, mimicking a wing of the Haṃsa bird.
5. *samapāda* (*mñam pa*). The toes of both feet are placed in mutual conjunction, with the big toe and the heel of each foot against one another.

Furthermore, *Kuladatta's *Kriyāsaṃgraha* (Toh. 2531), Derge Ku, 286b-287a, describes seven stances (*rkaṅ stabs bdun*), showing eleven varieties, or methods, of

concentration is the purification through contemplation of Voidness. The latter is also required when purifying through digging.

4′. *Seizing the site.* — When the site has been well cleared in that way, one seats himself in its center, facing what is to be the east gate of the *maṇḍala*. Having passed completely in review the 'procedure of evocation' (*sādhana*), he thinks, "I shall draw a *maṇḍala* on this site and just as I have contemplated it." This vow with his cognition is what is called "seizing the site".

5′. *Protecting and blessing the site.* — Then the four hierophants in the [cardinal] directions make preliminary *maṇḍala* offering at the four gates and petition for drawing of the *maṇḍala* as follows: without contracting the *maṇḍala* of self-generation,[15] they lift it to the sky with the gesture of uplifting and with incantations. Then they create by transformation from their own Lords, in the manner in which a second flame separates from the first, the power of Wrath appropriate to the occasion. In to what wrathful deities do they transform? In the case of *Saṃvara* and *Hevajra*, into such a one as Trailokya-vijaya ("victorious over the three worlds"); in the case of the *Kālacakra*, into such a one as Vajravega ("the thunderbolt gust"), and of the *Guhyasamāja*, into such a one as Dveṣavajra ("the diamond of hate"). In that way, each one seizes the egotism (*ahaṃkāra*) of precisely his own wrathful deity; and the hierophants, having gone to the north-east corner, issue commands to the obstructing demons [to depart]. Next, all the hierophants perform, beginning in the four cardinal directions, extensively or summarily as indicated, the stances,[16] the *saṃpuṭa*[17] and so on, and nail the rest of the obstructing demons with the magic nail (*kīla*). By contemplating the 'protective circle' (*rakṣā-cakra*) they guard against [further] obstructive demons; and by means of incantations and gestures, they bless (i.e. energize) the site of the *maṇḍala* into the intrinsic nature of diamond (*vajra*).

Those steps in the ritual of the site are the most general procedure for the Anuttara *maṇḍala*; they differ only triflingly for, say, the *Kālacakra*.

B′. *Ritual of the preparatory acts.* — This has four divisions: preparation of the earth goddess, preparation of the *maṇḍala* deities, preparation of

gYas brkyaṅ, ten of *gYon brkyaṅ*, six of *sa gaḥi rkaṅ stabs*, seven of *zlum poḥi rkaṅ stabs*, five of *mñam poḥi rkaṅ stabs*, one of *rus sbal gyi rkaṅ stabs* (**kūrmastha*), and two of *rkaṅ gcig gi rkaṅ stabs* (**ekapādastha*).

17 The word *saṃpuṭa* probably means here the placement of the hand palms together.

sta gon daṅ / bum pa sta gon daṅ / slob ma sta gon no / de la sta gon daṅ lhag gnas don gcig ciṅ / dbaṅ bskur baḥi skabs ma yin paḥi sgrub mchod daṅ / bdag ḥjug sogs kyi dus su slob ma lhag gnas bya mi dgos so /

/ saḥi lha mo lhag gnas bya baḥi tshul ni / dkyil ḥkhor gaṅ du bri baḥi sa deḥi dbus su saḥi lha moḥi tshom bu bkod la / der dam tshig pa bskyed / de la ye śes pa bcug mchod pa phul nas dkyil ḥkhor bri bar gnaṅ ba gsol źiṅ / dbaṅ po ḥtshol baḥo / skabs der gtor ma ḥbul mi ḥbul gyi lugs gñis yod do /

/ gñis pa lha sta gon ni / dgos pa gaṅ gi phyir daṅ / tshul ji ltar źe na / dgos pa ni sa la rdul tshon gyi dkyil ḥkhor ḥbri bar ḥgyur pa byin gyis rlob paḥi don du lha la gsol ba btab nas sñan gsan ḥbebs paḥo /

/ bya tshul ni gaṅ du ḥbri baḥi sa der driḥi thig le daṅ / me tog gi tshom bu bkod nas bya ba yin la / de yaṅ driḥi thig le sogs gaṅ du byas pa de ñid du rdul tshon gyi lha mtshan gyi gnas mi ḥphyug par bya baḥi phyir du thog mar thig ḥdebs dgos kyi / thig ma btab paḥi sṅa rol tu lhag gnas byed paḥi lag len ni legs par ma mthoṅ la / des na thig ḥdebs pa la yaṅ las thig daṅ ye thig gñis yod paḥi thog mar las thig btab ste de nas ye thig ḥdebs pa yin gyi / thog mar ye thig btab ste / de nas las thig ḥdebs pa mi ḥthad de / ye thig ni las thig byin gyis rlob byed ma yin par ḥgyur ba daṅ / lha bskyed paḥi tshe na ḥaṅ daṅ por ye śes pa bskyed nas / de la dam tshig pa gźug dgos pa sogs gnod byed du ma źig ḥoṅ baḥi phyir ro /

/ de na bla ma sṅa ma rnams kyi phyag len la / las thams cad par bskyed paḥi lugs med kyaṅ / raṅ lugs la las thig dkyil ḥkhor gaṅ yin pa deḥi las thams cad par bskyed nas byin gyis brlabs te / thig ḥdebs par byed dgos so / dper na / las thams cad paḥi lha gaṅ du bskyed paḥi bum pa la las bum zer ba bźin no / de ltar bskyed dgos par pa-ṇḍi-ta don yod rdo rje la sogs paḥi mkhas pa du mas gsuṅs so /

/ de la las thig ḥdebs byed kyi thig skud ni srad bu dkar po kha dog

[18] As one gathers from the *Sṅags rim*, 160b-4, ff., the 'knowledge line' is pitched upon the 'action line'; hence both are necessary for the basic structural lines of the *maṇḍala*. For a sketch of the first structural lines to be drawn in the *maṇḍala*, see F. D. Lessing, "The Eighteen Worthies Crossing the Sea", *Reports from the scientific expedition to the North-Western provinces of China under the leadership of Dr. Sven Hedin* (= *The Sino-Swedish Expedition Publication* 38) (Stockholm, 1954), p. 126. According to *Sṅags rim*, 165b-6, ff., of the eight chief lines (*thig chen brgyad*, the *brahmā* lines (*tshaṅs thig*) are pitched first. These are the North to South line and the East to West line, of which the former is first in the *yoginī-tantra* and the latter is first in the (*mahā-*) *yoga-tantra*. Next come the basic lines (*rtsa thig*), the sides of the square, namely the 1. East, 2. West, 3. North, 4. South lines; and here we assume that the order depends on whether it is a *yoginī-tantra* or a (*mahā-*) *yoga-tantra*. Finally, there are the Fire to Wind (S.E. to N.W.) diagonal (*zur thig*) and the second diagonal.

the flask, preparation of the disciple. Here the term 'preparation' (*sta gon*, S. **sāmantaka*) is synonymous with 'foundation' (*lhag gnas*, S. **adhiṣṭhāna*). It is not necessary to prepare the disciple at the time of *sādhana* offering, [the hierophant's] own entrance [into the *maṇḍala*], or other such acts, when it is not the phase of Initiation.

1′. *Preparation of the earth goddess.* — In the middle of the site upon which the *maṇḍala* will be drawn, one arranges a small heap of the earth goddess (*pṛthivī*). There he generates the Symbolic Being (*samaya-sattva*). Having presented offerings to the Knowledge Being (*jñāna-sattva*) so it will enter that [heap], he asks permission to draw the *maṇḍala*, and seeks the testimony [of earth]. There are two schools of thought as to whether or not one offers a *bali* on that occasion.

2′. *Preparation of the maṇḍala deities.* — Why the requirement, and what the method? The requirement is for blessing the *maṇḍala* of powdered colors drawn on the site. The gods are beseeched to lend a gracious ear.

The method of doing it is as follows: On the site where one is going to draw [the *maṇḍala*] one places a drop of perfume and a small heap of flowers. Moreover, in that very place where one has applied the drop of perfume and the other, one must pitch a line at the outset so there will be no mistake regarding the placing of the divine marks of powdered color. In contrast, the procedure of making preparation without first pitching the line is not well regarded. Now, for pitching the line, there are both the 'action line' (*karma-sūtra*) and the 'knowledge line' (*jñāna-sūtra*); and of these, one first pitches the 'action line' and after that, pitches the 'knowledge line'.[18] In contrast, to first pitch the 'knowledge line' and after that the 'action line' is not valid, because [in such a case] the 'knowledge line' would not bless (i.e. energize) the 'action line', and because, moreover, at the time of generating the gods, that would require first generating the Knowledge Being and then drawing the Symbolic Being into that, and so forth, thus resulting in much harm.

In the procedure of the former *gurus* there is no manner of generating all the acts. However, in our school, whatever be the *maṇḍala*, the 'action line' generates all the acts and blesses them. So it is necessary to pitch that line. It is analogous to the case of that flask, in which is generated the deity of all the acts, being called the 'action flask'. Many knowledgable men, such as the *paṇḍita* Amoghavajra, have expressed the necessity to generate in that manner.

The string for pitching the line is made of uniformly white thread, the color being produced by 'moistening' by means of rubbing the line

gcig pa rdo rgyus sogs kyi thig chal gyis gśer par byas nas rlon thig btab la / ye thig ma btab paḥi bar der driḥi thig le sogs byas te /

/ sta gon gyi lha dam tshig pa bskyed nas ye śes pa ḥjug paḥi tshe / sṅar sa cho ga gi skabs su nam mkhar brteg paḥi dkyil ḥkhor de ñid mar phab nas bstim pa ma gtogs / ye śes pa ḥjug tshul gźan bya mi dgos pas / de bstims nas mchod bstod bdud rtsi myaṅ ba sogs byas te sñan gsan ḥbebs pa yin no /

/ de nas ye thig ḥdebs pa ni / ḥdebs byed kyi thig skud ni rigs lṅaḥi ṅo bor bskyed paḥi srad bu kha dog lṅa pa / de re re la ḥaṅ raṅ daṅ mthun pa lṅa lṅa byas la / lṅa lṅa ñi śu rtsa lṅa po de rnams phyogs gcig tu bsgril nas skam thig byed do /

/ gsum pa bum pa sta gon ni / sta gon gyi dkyil ḥkhor nam mkhar btegs nas / ye thig ma btab paḥi goṅ du byed pa daṅ / yaṅ thog mar bum pa sta gon byas la / de nas sta gon gyi dkyil ḥkhor bteg ste / ye thig ḥdebs paḥi lugs gñis yod pa ni raṅ raṅ gi skabs su bśad pa ltar byaḥo /

/ de nas raṅ raṅ gi sgrub paḥi tshul legs par śes pas dgod ciṅ / de la rgyas par byed na bum pa lha graṅs daṅ mñam pa daṅ / ma grub na bum pa lṅa byas la / gtso bo yab yum la gcig daṅ / śar la sogs paḥi phyogs bźiḥi lha rnams bskyed paḥi bum pa bźi daṅ bcas pa rnams bśams te / de rnams kyaṅ phyogs rnams su tshul ji ltar dgod pa daṅ / bum paḥi naṅ du lha rnams bskyed tshul śes dgos so /

/ de yaṅ ma grub na bum pa gñis la brten nas / gcig rnam rgyal daṅ / gcig las bum du byaḥo / bum pa bsgrub paḥi dgos pa rnam rgyal bum pa ni / dbaṅ bskur ba daṅ bdag ḥjug sogs kyi tshe / chu dbaṅ maṅ du bskur ba daṅ / las bum ni dkyil ḥkhor daṅ / mchod rdzas daṅ / bdag daṅ / gnas daṅ / slob ma la bsaṅ gtor bya baḥi phyir yin no /

/ bum pa sgrub paḥi tshul la / kha cig / rnam rgyal bum par lha thams cad bskyed / de nas deḥi steṅ du bźag paḥi duṅ chos daṅ / thog pa sogs su yaṅ lha rdzogs par bskyed paḥi lugs gcig daṅ / yaṅ duṅ chos ṣu lha

[19] As Tsoṅ-kha-pa writes in his *Dbaṅ don* (Toh. 5287), Vol. Ca, 22a-1: "One contemplates the nature of Akṣobhya [represented by] a black thread and [generated] from *Hūṃ*; Vairocana, a white one and from *Oṃ*; Ratnasaṃbhava, a yellow one and from *Svā*; Amitābha, a red one and from *Āḥ*; and Amoghasiddhi, a green one and from *Hā*" (thig skud nag po Hūṃ las mi bskyod pa / dkar po Oṃ las rnam snaṅ / ser po Svā las rin ḥbyuṅ / dmar po Āḥ las ḥod dpag med / ljaṅ khu Hā las don grub kyi ṅo bor bsgoms la). The standard order of reciting the "heart" *mantras* is: *Oṃ Āḥ Hūṃ Svā-hā*.

[20] Mkhas grub rje may be referring to the *Sṅags rim*; for example, material in the extended treatment of the thread rite, ending 191a-4.

with chalk, and so on. Then one pitches the 'wet line'. And as long as the 'knowledge line' has not yet been pitched, one applies there the drop of perfume, and so on.

After generating the preparatory-deity Symbolic Being, when the Knowledge Being enters, that *maṇḍala* which previously in the phase of ritual of the site had been raised to the sky, is now caused to descend; and, except absorbing it, one need not do anything else for drawing in the Knowledge Being. After absorbing it, one makes offering and praises, enjoys the ambrosia (*amṛta*), and so forth, and beseeches [the gods] to lend a gracious ear.

Next, one pitches the 'knowledge line': The string for pitching it is made of thread in five colors generated into the essence of the five Families. Each [Family] is represented by five of its own [-colored threads];[19] thus, with five of each [color], there are 25 in all, and those twisted together make the 'dry line'.

3'. *Preparation of the flask.* — One may lift the *maṇḍala* of preparation to the sky before the 'knowledge line' is pitched; or may first prepare the flask and then lift the *maṇḍala* of preparation. These two modes of pitching the 'knowledge line' are performed as explained in their individual sections.[20]

Then, with good understanding of the individual evocation method [namely, of the particular mode of pitching to be employed], one arranges [the flasks]. In the most elaborate form, the number of flasks is equal to that of the deities. If that cannot be realized, one works with five flasks, preparing one for the Lord in Father-Mother union, and four flasks starting with the East for generating the deities of the four cardinal directions. Here one must also keep in mind the manner of arranging the flasks in the four directions and the procedure of evoking the deities within the flasks.

Again, if one cannot realize that (i.e. as much as five), he relies on two flasks: one, the victorious flask (*vijaya-kalaśa*), the other, the action flask (*karma-kalaśa*). As to the purposes of the flasks, the victorious flask is used at the time of Initiation and the [hierophant's] own entrance [into the *maṇḍala*] as well as for conferring the numerous water initiations. The action flask is used for sprinkling the *maṇḍala*, the offering materials, himself (i.e. the hierophant), the place, and the disciples.

As to the method of "accomplishing" the flasks, one school holds that all the deities should be generated in the victorious flask, and that thereupon one should fully generate the deities also in the conch (*śankha*), in the skull bowl (*kapāla*), etc. which are placed on top of that [victorious

dṅos su mi bskyed par rnam rgyal du bskyed paḥi lha de rnams duṅ chos su me loṅ naṅ du gzugs brñan śar ba lta bur bsgom paḥi lugs gcig daṅ / yaṅ rnam rgyal du bskyed pa ḥdra ba la duṇ chos su gtso bo yab yum tsam bskyed paḥi lugs te / de ltar lugs gsum byuṅ ba ni mi ḥthad de / tshad ldan sus kyaṅ ma bśad paḥi phyir ro / de rnams kyi ḥkhrul gźi ni / grub chen mtsho skyes kyis / baṃ las byuṅ baḥi bum pa ni / rin chen bum paḥi steṅ gźag bya / der ni lha rnams bskyed par bya / źes gsuṅs paḥi / der ni źes pa rnam rgyal la ma go bar / duṅ chos la bzuṅ bas nor ba yin no / gźan yaṅ dus ḥkhor las / rgyal ba daṅ / rnam par rgyal ba daṅ / rnam rgyal chen po gsum gsuṅs paḥi rgyal ba daṅ rnam rgyal ni bum pa bcu gsuṅs paḥi steṅ ḥog gi bum pa gñis yin la / rnam rgyal chen po ni duṅ chos la byas nas / der lha thams cad bskyed par gsuṅs kyaṅ / rnam rgyal sogs bum pa gźan rnams su lha re re las bskyed par ma gsuṅs pas śes du mi ḥgroḥo /

/ raṅ lugs la rnam rgyal bum par dkyil ḥkhor gaṅ yin pa deḥi lha thams cad bskyed dgos par khyad par med kyaṅ / gźal yas khaṅ bskyed pa daṅ / mi bskyed paḥi lugs gñis yod do /

/ rnam rgyal bum paḥi steṅ du bźag paḥi duṅ chos sogs dri bzaṅ kyi chus bkaṅ ba de ñid ni / u-da-ka daṅ / yi ge gsum bzlas pas / rdo rje bdud rtsiḥi chur thog mar bsgrubs nas rnam rgyal du bskyed paḥi lha la mchod yon dbul baḥi phyir du yin / de ltar yin par grub chen lva-ba-pa daṅ / saṅs rgyas thod paḥi dkyil chog la sogs pa tshad ldan du mas gsuṅs so / de nas duṅ chos kyi chus mchod yon phul / me tog daṅ gtor ma phul la / mchod bstod byas nas / yo ga man chad la bźu baḥi lugs med kyaṅ / bla med kyi skabs su / lha rnams bum chu daṅ ṅe bo gcig tu bźu bar byed la/ de yaṅ gtso bo yab yum sñoms par źugs nas / chags pa chen poḥi mes źu ste bum chu daṅ dbyer med du gyur par sems pa yin no / ḥo na ḥkhor rnams yab yum du med pas ji ltar bya sñam na / skyon med de / dkyil ḥkhor deḥi gtso ḥkhor thams cad rgyud gcig yin pas / gtso bo yab yum

[21] This citation is part of a longer quotation in the *Sṅags rim*, 197b-5, ff. from Mtsho skyes' commentary on the *Hevajra-tantra*, the *Pañjikā-padmin* (Toh. 1181).

[22] Cf. Mario E. Carelli, ed., *Sekoddeśaṭīkā of Naḍapāda* (*Nāropā*) (Baroda, 1941), text, 19.7-8 (Tibetan, Toh. 1351, Derge Vol. Na, 234a-6, 7): *pūrvāparajayavijaya-ghaṭa = śar daṅ nub kyi rgyal ba daṅ rnam par rgyal baḥi bum pa*; *vijayaśaṃkha = rnam par rgyal ba duṅ*. In three-dimensional representation, the ten flasks are placed in the ten directions, eight in the plane, one at the zenith and one at the nadir. For obvious physical reasons, in two-dimensional representation the latter two —*jaya* and *vijaya*, are placed in the East and in the West.

[23] *Sṅags rim*, 196b-3, also mentions "three syllables" (*yi ge gsum*) without making them explicit, but the standard meaning can be assumed: *Oṃ, Āḥ. Hūṃ*; and the discussion, *ibid.*, folio 215b makes this clear.

flask]. Another school holds that one should not generate the deities concretely in the conch, but that those deities generated in the victorious flask should be contemplated as arising in the conch like a reflection in a mirror. Still another school maintains the same thing as concerns generating in the victorious flask, but holds that only the Lord in Father-Mother union is generated in the conch. The three schools having those positions are not valid, because no authority has explained it accordingly. The source of their error is found in a saying of the *mahāsiddha* Mtsho-skyes: "The flask arising from the [syllable] *Baṃ* should be placed upon the precious flask(s). There (*der*) one should generate the deities."[21] The mistake lay in not understanding the word "there" to refer to the victorious flask but (mistakenly) to the conch. Moreover, the *Kālacakra* mentions three flasks — *jaya*, *vijaya*, and *mahāvijaya*. Of these, the *jaya* and *vijaya* are the two flasks above and below among the ten flasks mentioned [in that Tantra]. The *mahāvijaya* flask is taken as the conch.[22] Thus, while the passage spoke of generating all the deities "there", it did not say one should generate any of the deities in flasks other than the *vijaya* and so on. Hence, it could not serve as an authority.

According to our own school, without exception one must generate all the deities of the *maṇḍala* in question in the victorious flask (*vijaya-kalaśa*). However, there are two ways of doing it, according to whether or not one generates a palace (*vimāna*).

When filling with scented water the conch and so on that are placed on top of the victorious flask, one recites "*udaka*" ('water') and the three syllables.[23] This is done so as to first succeed in rendering it into 'diamond ambrosia' (*vajrāmṛta*) water, and then in presenting it as a sacrifice (*argha*) to the deities generated in the victorious flask. That is stated as the case by many authorities, among which are the *mahāsiddha* Lva-ba-pa and the *Buddhakapālamaṇḍalavidhi* (presumably Toh. 1657, by Saraha). Thereupon, one presents the sacrifice with the water of the conch, presents flowers and food, making offerings and praises. As to what is done next, the Tantra divisions of Yoga and below have no rules about the fusing [of the deities with the water], but in the Anuttara phase the deities and the water of the flask are fused into a single essence. The idea is that the Lord has entered the sameness of Father-Mother union, who fuse together by the fire of great passion (*mahārāga*) and become indivisible from the water of the flask. Suppose one would ask how this would happen in the case of the retinue members who are not in Father-Mother union. The Lord and all his retinue of that *maṇḍala* have a single stream of consciousness. Therefore, when the divine

bde bas źu nas dgyes paḥi stobs kyis ḥkhor rnams kyaṅ źu ba yin la / raṅ lugs la mtshan maḥi lha rnams kyaṅ bźu bar byed pa yin no /

/ kha cig rdo rje bdud rtsiḥi chu źes pa / rdo rjeḥi mgo la chu blugs nas de la byed par snaṅ ste / de ḥdra ba de ni śes pas bltas na bźad gad kyi gnas yin no /

/ bźi pa ni / slob ma sta gon byas paḥi dgos pa gaṅ yin sñam na / sṅags kyi snod ruṅ du byas nas rgyud sbyoṅ ba daṅ / sta gon gyi skabs su bla mas naṅ dbaṅ bskur de rdo rje theg par rigs ṅes par byas nas dbaṅ bskur ba dgos kyi / de ltar ma byas par dbaṅ bskur du mi ruṅ ste / dper na ḥkhor los bsgyur baḥi rigs su skyes paḥi gźon nu deḥi rgyal srid du dbaṅ bskur du ruṅ gi / dmaṅs rigs la sogs pa deḥi rgyal srid du dbaṅ bskur du mi ruṅ ba bźin no /

/ gsum pa ni / ye thig btab nas / deḥi ḥog tu rdul tshon gyi dkyil ḥkhor bri la / de ltar bris zin nas brten paḥi dkyil ḥkhor gyi skabs su phyag rgya gsum gaṅ ruṅ dgod par bya ste / de la phyag rgya gsum ni / thugs dam tshig gi phyag rgya / de mtshon par bya baḥi phyir du raṅ raṅ gi lha gnas su raṅ raṅ gi phyag mtshan dgos pa ḥam / gsuṅ chos kyi phyag rgya / de mtshon par bya baḥi phyir du lha gnas rnams su raṅ raṅ gi sa bon dgod pa ḥam / sku phyag rgya chen po / de mtshon par bya baḥi phyir du lha gnas rnams su rdul tshon gyi lhaḥi sku gzugs rdzogs par bri ba ḥam / lha gnas rnams su de daṅ deḥi lhaḥi sku lugs ma ḥjog pa gaṅ ruṅ byas pas chog go /

/ de ltar rten daṅ brten par bcas paḥi dkyil ḥkhor bris zin nas / gdugs daṅ / rgyal mtshan daṅ / mchod paḥi yo byad rnams kyis dkyil ḥkhor brgyan par byaḥo /

/ gñis pa ni / de ltar rten daṅ brten paḥi dkyil ḥkhor bris źiṅ brgyan pa sogs byas zin nas sgrub dgos pas / de la bdag mdun tha dad du byed

[24] "Attribute deities" means deities distinguished by visible symbols, especially by hand symbols (*hasta-cihna*).

couple fuses through bliss, by the force of their joy the members of the retinue also fuse. According to our own school, the attribute deities (*nimitta-devatā*)[24] also are made to fuse [with the water].

There are even some who while reciting "diamond ambrosia water" pour water on the head of the *vajra*. When such a thing is seen by knowledgable persons, it is an occasion for mirth (*or* simply ridiculous).

4′. *Preparation of the disciple.* — What is the requisite in the preparation of the disciple? The requisite is to purify his stream of consciousness upon making him a fit receptacle for the *mantra* [-path, i.e. Vajrayāna]; and in the phase of this preparation the requisite is his guru's conferring the inner initiation, i.e. to initiate [the disciple] upon determining his Family in the Vajrayāna. If that [determination] is not made, it is not proper to confer initiation. This is analogous to the case of a prince born in the family of a world emperor (*cakravartin*): it is proper to confer upon him the consecration (*abhiṣeka*) of kingdom, but it is not proper to confer the consecration of kingdom upon a *śūdra*, and so on.

C′. *The ritual of drawing the maṇḍala.* — Having pitched the 'knowledge line', one next proceeds to draw the *maṇḍala* of powdered colors. This done, one must arrange, in the phase of the *maṇḍala* of the residents (*ādheya*), one or other of the three seals, as indicated. Here, the three seals (*mudrā*) are as follows:

1. The pledge seal (*samaya-mudrā*) of mind. In order to symbolize that, one arranges the hand symbol (*hasta-cihna*) of each deity in that deity's position [in the *maṇḍala*].

2. The law seal (*dharma-mudrā*) of speech. In order to symbolize that, one arranges the seed [syllable] (*bīja-akṣara*) of each deity in that deity's position.

3. The great seal (*mahā-mudrā*) of body. In order to symbolize that, one draws in powdered colors the complete form of the body of each deity in that deity's position. It is also acceptable to place in their positions a cast image of the deity.

When the drawing of the *maṇḍala* of residence (*ādhāra*) and of residents (*ādheya*) is finished, the *maṇḍala* is decorated with parasols, banners, and offering utensils.

II′. *Method of "accomplishing" the maṇḍala*

After finishing the drawing and adorning in that way of the *maṇḍala* of residence and residents, one must "accomplish" it. There are two schools, according to whether 'self generation' and 'generation in front'

pa daṅ / tha mi dad du byas paḥi lugs gñis las / grub chen dā-ri-ka-pas bde mchog la bdag mdun tha dad du mdzad pa daṅ / dus ḥkhor la tha dad byed pa yod kyi / gźan ḥphags yul gyi chen po dag gi bźed pa la bdag mdun tha mi dad du mdzad pa śin tu maṅ ṅo /

/ tha dad du byed paḥi lugs ni / sṅon du bdag bskyed rdzogs par bsgoms nas mdun bskyed sgrub pa la ḥjug pa na / raṅ ñid mdun bskyed kyi dkyil ḥkhor gyi dbus su phyin paḥi dmigs pa yaṅ mi byed / mdun bskyed kyi gtso boḥi ṅa rgyal yaṅ mi byed par mdun bskyed sgrub par byed pa yin no /

/ tha mi dad du byed pa la / bod kyi bla ma sṅa ma rnams kyi lugs daṅ / ḥphags yul gyi chen po dag gi bźed pa gñis su yod ciṅ /

/ de la bod kyi bla ma kha cig ni / daṅ por bdag bskyed ye śes pa ḥjug pa mchod bstod bdud rtsi myaṅ ba yaṅ rdzogs par byas te / ñer bsdu mi byed par mdun bskyed sgrub par byed la / deḥi bdag bskyed mdun bskyed kyi gtso boḥi ṅa rgyal yaṅ mi byed par / mdun bskyed rdzogs par bskyed nas / de tshaṅ ba daṅ bdag bskyed kyi gźal yas khaṅ mdun bskyed kyi gźal yas khaṅ daṅ bsre / bdag bskyed kyi gtso bo sogs lha thams cad mdun bskyed kyi lha rnams daṅ bsre bar byed la / de la bdag mdun bsre ba źes kyaṅ zer ro /

/ de nas raṅ bźin gyi gnas nas ye śes pa spyan draṅs / rdo rje gsor źin rtsa sṅags brjod nas / phyi ḥbraṅ gi bgegs bskrad / dmigs pas bsruṅ ḥkhor pa phye nas ye śes pa ḥjug / źugs pa daṅ ra-kṣa sogs brjod nas / rdo rje bsdams paḥi phyag rgyas bsruṅ ḥkhor pa sdom par byed /

/ de nas sgrub mchod źag bdun tsam sbrel nas byed na / sta gon gyi dkyil ḥkhor nam mkhar bteg pa de las mar me gcig las gñis chad kyi tshul du źag re bźin dkyil ḥkhor re re rdul tshon gyi dkyil ḥkhor la stim par byed ciṅ / yaṅ gśegs gsol byed paḥi do nub sta gon gyi dkyil ḥkhor nam

[25] In *Sṅags rim*, 231a-6, the Knowledge Beings are invited from the sky (*ākāśa, nam mkhaḥ*), and *ibid.* 230b-3, this is the "realm of space" (*ākāśadhātu*).

are different or identical. Of these two schools, the *mahāsiddha* Dārikapa makes a difference between 'self generation' and 'generation in front' in the *Saṃvara*, and makes a difference between them in the *Kālacakra*. However, many other great men of India took 'self generation' and 'generation in front' as identical.

A′. *The school which makes them different.* — First one fully contemplates the 'self generation', and then enters upon the accomplishment of 'generation in front'. At the time of the latter, one neither imagines himself proceeding to the center of the *maṇḍala* generated in front of himself, nor holds to the 'pride' of the Lord generated in front, but accomplishes [only] the 'generation in front'.

B′. *The school which makes them identical.* — Here there are the school of the former Tibetan *gurus* and what is maintained by the great men of India.

1′. *Tibetan gurus.* — Certain Tibetan *gurus* have held that first one completes 'self generation', drawing in of the Knowledge Being(s)(*jñāna-sattva*), offerings, praises, and enjoyment of the ambrosia; and without contracting [the 'self generation'] accomplishes the 'generation in front'. Without feeling the 'pride' of the Lord of his 'self generation' and 'generation in front', he fully generates the 'generation in front'. When that is completed, he merges the 'self generation' palace and the 'generation in front' palace; and he merges all the deities, starting with the Lord, of the 'self generation', with the deities of the 'generation in front'. That is what they called "merger of self and in-front".

[Stating the process more fully,] one invites the Knowledge Beings from their natural abode (**svābhāvika-sthāna*).[25] Brandishing the thunderbolt and muttering the basic *dhāraṇī*, he imagines that he scares away the obstructive demons pursuing from without. Hence, the protective circle expands outward and the Knowledge Beings enter. As they enter, he mutters '*rakṣa*' ("Protect!") etc. and binds the protective circle with the seal called "Thunderbolt tie" (*vajrabandha*).

Then for seven consecutive days he makes the offerings going with the accomplishment. During that time, in the manner in which a second flame separates from the first, each day he separates a *maṇḍala* from the preparatory *maṇḍala* lifted to the sky and makes each one of those [secondary] *maṇḍalas* merge with the *maṇḍala* of powdered colors. On the evening of "dismissing the deities" [i.e., last day of the ritual], without leaving the preparatory *maṇḍala* in the sky, he makes it merge [with the

mkhar mi ḥjog par stim par byed de / de la dkyil ḥkhor bdun bsres paḥi tha sñad byed do / sṅar sa cho ga gi skabs kyi dkyil ḥkhor de la / dam tshig pa daṅ ye śes pa gñis bsres pa daṅ / de gñis sta gon gyi dkyil ḥkhor daṅ bsres pas sum bsres su soṅ / bdag bskyed kyi dam tshig pa daṅ ye śes pa gñis daṅ / mdun bskyed kyi de gñis bsres pas bźi bsres / deḥi steṅ du sṅar gyi gsum bsres pas bdun bsres su soṅ la / deḥi tshul ni bla maḥi man ṅag yin pas zab par ḥdod do /

/ bdag mdun tha mi dad ḥdod paḥi rgya gar baḥi lugs la rnam pa gñis yod paḥi daṅ po ni /

/ bdag bskyed sṅon du zur du mi sgom par mdun bskyed bsgrub paḥi rdul tshon nam ras bris kyi dbus su raṅ ñid phyin paḥi mos pa byas nas / de ñid du chos ḥbyuṅ daṅ ḥbyuṅ ba rim brtsegs pa skyed pa daṅ / sa bon las phyag mtshan daṅ / de nas lha bskyed paḥi cho ga sum bskyed dus mñam du byas la sku gsuṅ thugs byin brlab / ye śes pa dgug gźug / rigs bdag gi rgyas gdab rnams zin pa daṅ / raṅ ñid gtso bo las mar me gcig las gñis chad kyi tshul du śar sgo logs su phye nas mchod pa ḥbul źiṅ bdag ḥjug len pa sogs byed / de phyin chad bla ma daṅ / gtso bo tha mi dad du byas pa las dbaṅ len pa sogs byed pa yin no / ḥdi ḥdra baḥi tshul ni grub chen rnams kyis mdzad pa la med kyaṅ / pa-ndi-ta mkhas pa du mas bźed par snaṅ bas / gśin rjeḥi gśed dmar nag la ḥdi ltar byas pas chog gi /

/ ḥdus pa sogs la ḥdi ltar byas na ni skye ḥchi bar doḥi sbyaṅ gźi daṅ chos mthun paḥi mṅon rtogs sgom paḥi tshul med pas / de ḥdra ba byar mi ruṅ la / klu byaṅ sogs grub chen gyis mdzad pa ltar rje ñid kyis dkyil chog daṅ / sgron gsal gyi mchan du bkod pa ltar bya dgos te / de la thog mar bdag bskyed dkyil ḥkhor rgyal mchog yan chad rdzogs par bsgom / mchod bstod bdud rtsi myaṅ ba sogs tshar ba daṅ / bdag bskyed ñer

[26] In *Sṅags rim*, 378b-1, the "matrix of natures" is the "realm of space"; cf. foregoing note.

[27] The application of these statements is made explicit in *Sādhana-mālā*, No. 251, text pp. 490-91. The data can be tabulated as follows:

	Germ syllable	*Emblem*	*Body of deity*
1.	*Yaṃ*	Semi-circle	blue wind
2.	*Raṃ*	Triangle	red fire
3.	*Laṃ*	Circle	white water
4.	*Vaṃ*	Square	yellow earth

This passage also makes clear that "ascending steps" means each next one upon the preceding one, starting with the corresponding states in row No. 1.

[28] The reference is to the three *samādhis*, which in the Anuttara terminology mean a division of the Steps of Production (*utpatti-krama*); see Chap. VI, note 19.

maṇḍala of powdered colors]. This is referred to as "the sevenfold merger of *maṇḍalas*". [In term of residents,] there is [given] the former *maṇḍala* in the phase of the ritual of the site. Therein the Symbolic Beings and Knowledge Beings have the twofold merger. The merger of those two with the *maṇḍala* of preparation is the threefold merger. The merger of the Symbolic Beings and Knowledge Beings of 'self generation' with those two of 'generation in front', is the fourfold merger. The merger of the latter [fourfold group] with the former threefold one is the sevenfold merger. As this method is a precept of *gurus*, it is held to be profound.

2′. *Indian teachers.* — There were two Indian schools maintaining the identity of 'self generation' and 'generation in front'.

a′. *The first Indian school.* — The first of these held that without first separately contemplating 'self generation' one convinces himself that he is transported to the center of the *maṇḍala* of powdered colors, or of the painted one, that is "accomplished" in the 'generation in front'. Right there he generates the "matrix of natures" (*dharmodaya*)[26] and the ascending steps of the (four) "factors of becoming" (i.e., wind, fire, water, earth). Simultaneously, he generates in a three-part rite, (a) the seed [syllables], (b) from these the hand symbols, and (c) next the generation of the deities [in their bodily aspects].[27] [The deities] bless his body, speech, and mind. He attracts and draws in the Knowledge Beings. He executes the seal of the Master of the Family. When that is finished, he separates himself from the Lord through the East Gate in the manner of separating a second flame from the first one. Then he presents offerings, takes personal entrance [into the *maṇḍala*], etc. Thereupon, he regards his *guru* and the Lord as identical and takes Initiation from him, etc. The *mahāsiddhas* have not set forth a method of that sort, but it is maintained by many learned paṇḍits. In fact, it is feasible, because it is done that way in "[The *maṇḍala-vidhis* of] the red and black Yamāris."

b′. *The second Indian school.* — However, if one were to do it that way in the case of the *Guhyasamāja* among others, there would be no method of contemplating the "Spheres of Purification", namely, birth, death, and the intermediate state, or of contemplating with direct comprehension their concordant natures. Consequently, it is not right to do it that way [in cases such as the *Guhyasamāja*]. One must proceed according to the works of Nāgabodhi and other *mahāsiddhas*, who give the formulation adopted by Tsoṅ-kha-pa in his *Maṇḍala-vidhi* (Toh. 5287) and in his *Prādīpodyotana Ṭippanī* (Toh. 5282). There one first fully contemplates the 'self generation', triumphant *maṇḍala*, and onwards.[28]

bsdu byas nas / bdag ñid gtso bo rkyaṅ paḥi rnam par gnas par byas la / des rdul tshon nam ras bris kyi dkyil ḥkhor gyi dbus su phyin paḥi mos pa byas nas / las bum gyi chus dkyil ḥkhor la mi gnod par gtor la bsaṅ / de nas dkyil ḥkhor ḥod gsal du bcug ste / dkyil ḥkhor gyi rnam pa sogs spros pa bsdu ba yin gyi / caṅ med du gtoṅ ba ma yin paḥi khyad par phyed par byas nas / chos ḥbyuṅ daṅ ḥbyuṅ ba bźi bskyed pa daṅ / de nas gźal yas khaṅ bskyed pa daṅ / gźal yas khaṅ bskyed zin nas thun moṅ daṅ / thun moṅ ma yin paḥi gdan rnams bskyed de / de rnams kyi steṅ du sa bon de las sku yoṅs su rdzogs par bskyed nas / raṅ ñid gtso boḥi bskyed cho ga gis bskyed de / deḥi ṅa rgyal gnas pas sku gsuṅ thugs byin gyis rlob paḥi sems dpaḥ sum brtsegs daṅ / ye śes pa dgug gźug / rig bdag gi rgyas ḥdebs rnams tshaṅ nas / raṅ ñid gtso bo las mar me gcig las gñis chad gyi tshul gyis dkyil ḥkhor gyi śar sgor ḥdug ste / mchod ciṅ dbaṅ len pa sogs ni sṅar daṅ ḥdraḥo /

/ ye śes pa ḥjug pa ni sṅon du raṅ bźin gyi gnas nas spyan draṅs paḥi ye śes pa bcug ste / deḥi ḥog tu sṅar nam mkhar bteg paḥi sta gon gyi

[29] Dharmakīrti's *pañjikā* commentary on the *Hevajra* called "The Eye Opener" (*spyan ḥbyed*), Toh. 1191, says, 255a-1, 2: "For doing that, one contemplates the three stories of *sattvas* (*de la sems dpaḥ sum brtsegs bsgom*), and attracts and draws in the Circle of Knowledge [Beings] (*jñāna-cakra*) (*ye śes ḥkhor lo dgug gźug bya*). Meanwhile he obtains the blessing of sensory bases, the blessing of body, speech, and mind; initiation; makes offerings and praises, and enjoys the ambrosia (*skye mched byin gyis brlab pa daṅ sku gsuṅ thugs kyi byin gyis brlab pa daṅ / dbaṅ bskur ba daṅ mchod pa daṅ bstod pa daṅ bdud rtsi myaṅ baḥi bar du byaḥo*)." Also, *ibid.*, 242a-7 to 242b-1: "In regard to that, one should know that the *vajra-sattva* is Voidness (*śūnyatā*) or Insight (*prajñā*); the *mahā-sattva* is Means (*upāya*) or many lights (*āloka*); and the *samaya-sattva* is the indissoluble union of those lights and Voidness. The *hṛdaya-hevajra* (the "Heart Hevajra") is the *mahātmaka* arising from that indissoluble union". The passage continues with extensive treatment of the three stories of *sattvas* and *hṛdaya-hevajra*. In particular (*ibid.*, 242b-3, 4), "The fruitional (*ḥbras buḥi*) *vajra-sattva* is the Dharmakāya; *mahā-sattva*, Saṃbhogakāya; *samaya-sattva*, Nirmāṇakāya; and *hṛdaya-hevajra*, Mahāsukhakāya." Outside of these "fruitional" Bodies (*kāya*), Dharmakīrti is referring to procedures of the Steps of Production; the Bodies, namely Dharmakāya and so on, constitute achievements of the Steps of Completion. The *Guhyasamāja*, 45.1, 2, refers to the three *sattvas* with this verse: "One should complete the great thunderbolt of five colors, which is the constructive imagination of 'symbolic', 'knowledge', and '*vāksamaya*', by contemplations of the supreme Lord of the World." On this, the *Pradīpodyotana* (commentary on Chap. XI) comments (Derge ed., 79b-5): "'Symbolic' means the Symbolic Being (*samaya-sattva*); 'knowledge', the Knowledge Being (*jñāna-sattva*), '*vāksamaya*', the Samādhi Being (*samādhi-sattva*). 'One should complete' means contemplation through unification of those three *sattvas*" (dam tshig ni dam tshig sems dpaḥo / ye śes ni ye śes sems dpaḥo / tshig gi dam tshig ni tiṅ ṅe ḥdzin gyi sems dpaḥ ste / rdzogs par bya ba ni sems dpaḥ gsum po de dag gcig tu byas nas bsgom paḥo). The two groups of *sattva* terminology can be equated by this passage in Padmavajra's commentary on the *Śrī-Ḍākārnava* called *Vāhikaṭīkā* (Toh. 1419), Derge Dza, 152b-2: "The Dharmakāya of the *yogins* is the Samādhi Being; the Saṃbhogakāya, the Knowledge Being; the Nirmāṇakāya, the

He completes the offerings, praises, enjoyment of ambrosia; and having contracted the 'self generation' he abides as the Lord alone. [To state this more fully: —] He convinces himself that he proceeds to the center of the *maṇḍala* made of powdered colors or painted on canvas; and he sprinkles the *maṇḍala* in a way not to harm it, with water of the action flask. Then he inserts the *maṇḍala* in the "Clear Light", thus contracting the imaginative and other aspects of the *maṇḍala*; but takes care to not be abandoned in "Nothingness" (*akiñcanya*). Then he generates the "matrix of natures" and the four "factors of becoming" and thereupon generates the palace. Upon finishing the generation of the palace, he generates [therein] the common and the uncommon seats. Upon them he generates the seed [syllables] and from those, in a perfect manner, the bodies [of the deities themselves]. He generates himself into the Lord by the appropriate rite and dwells in his (i.e. the Lord's) egotism. Meanwhile he "piles up" the three Beings (*sattva*)[29] who bless his (i.e. the officiant's) body, speech, and mind; he attracts and draws in the Knowledge Being and executes the seal of the Master of the Family. Having completed those [steps], in the same manner as before he separates himself from the Lord in the manner of a second flame separating from the first, and sits at the East Gate of the *maṇḍala*, worshipping, receiving Initiation, and so on.

Regarding the entry of the Knowledge Beings, the Knowledge Beings who have been previously invited from their natural abode are caused to enter. Next, the *maṇḍala* which previously had been lifted to the sky

---

Symbolic Being, because one creates [those Beings] in direct vision in this world by means of those Bodies that way" (rnal ḥbyor pa rnams kyi chos kyi sku tiṅ ṅe ḥdzin sems dpaḥo / loṅs spyod rdzogs paḥi sku ye śes sems dpaḥo / sprul paḥi sku dam tshig sems dpaḥ źes bya ba ste / mṅon sum du ḥdir de ltar sku ḥdis byed paḥi phyir ro). Hence, the *vajrasattva* is the Samādhi Being; the *mahāsattva* the Knowledge Being; the *samayasattva* the Symbolic Being; and unification of those three, the *hṛdaya-hevajra*. Regarding the "piling up" of the *sattvas*, this procedure is indicated by a verse in the *Guhyasamāja*, Chap. XII, p. 56: / sarvākāravaropetaṃ kāyavākcitta-vajriṇam / hṛdaye jñānasamayaṃ mukuṭe vajrāgradhāriṇam //. The commentary in *Pradīpodyotana*, Ha, 92a-4, shows that the *yogin* "piles up" these Beings by imagining them in his heart within each other somewhat like Chinese boxes. Thus, he says, "... the 'knowledge' and 'symbolic' (*jñānasamaya*) are on the moon disk located in the lotus of the heart (*hṛdaye*); having contemplated the Knowledge Being, one imagines in the latter's heart the Samādhi Being, and on the latter's head, i.e. located on the crown of his head, the *vajrin* (who unites body, speech, and mind--*kāyavākcitta*), i.e. Vajradhāra..." (deḥi ḥog tu sñiṅ gaḥi padma la gnas paḥi zla baḥi dkyil ḥkhor la ye śes dam tshig ste / ye śes sems dpaḥ bsgoms nas / deḥi yaṅ thugs kar tiṅ ṅe ḥdzin sems dpaḥ bsam źiṅ dbu rgyan te / spyi gtsug gi gnas su rdo rje ḥdzin pa źes bya ba rdo rje ḥchaṅ chen po...).

dkyil ḥkhor rdzogs par phab nas nub sṅa ma la ḥjug pa yin gyi / de nas yaṅ nub phyi ma la ḥbebs rgyu med do /

/ de la lṅa bsres kyi tha sñad rgya gar mkhas paḥi gźuṅ gis ma bśad la / sṅags rim las gcig nas drug gi bar źes gsuṅs kyi / de las lhag paḥi bsre tshul gyi tha sñad rgya gar pa la gcig kyaṅ med ciṅ / bźi bsres daṅ gsum bsres kyi tha sñad yod do / de la lṅa bsres kyi tshul ni / sṅar sa cho ga gi skabs kyi dam tshig pa daṅ / ye śes pa gñis / de gñis sta gon gyi dkyil ḥkhor daṅ bsres pas sum bsres / de ḥdir mdun bskyed kyi dam tshig pa daṅ / ye śes pa gñis daṅ bsres pas lṅa bsres su soṅ ba yin gyi / bdag bskyed ni ñer bsdu tshar bas bsre rgyu med la / spyir bdag mdun tha mi dad paḥi tha sñad rgya gar pa la yod kyaṅ / bdag mdun bsres paḥi tha sñad med do / bdag mdun tha mi dad paḥi don ni / mdun bskyed kyi rdul tshon gyi dkyil ḥkhor de ñid gźal yas khaṅ dṅos daṅ / raṅ ñid deḥi dbus kyi gtso bo dṅos kyi ṅa rgyal ḥjog pa yin no /

/ yaṅ dkyil hkhor sgrub tshul la / bla ma kha cig gi phyag len la / sgrub mchod źag sbrel nas byed paḥi tshe / ñi ma sṅa ma la dkyil ḥkhor bsgrubs / ye śes pa bcug nas yod pa la / ñi ma phyi ma la sgrub paḥi tshe śū-nya-tā la sogs pas sbyaṅ baḥi sṅon du rdul tshon daṅ ras bris gaṅ yin yaṅ sṅar gyi ye śes pa nam mkhar bteg nas sbyaṅs te / bsgrubs tshar ba daṅ yaṅ ḥbebs par byed do / de ni legs pa ma yin te / gnod pa du maḥi gnas su gyur paḥi phyir / ḥdi ltar ras bris yin na / brtan bźugs byas paḥi rab gnas ñams par ḥgyur pa daṅ / rdul tshon la ḥaṅ / sṅar rdul tshon ñid rigs lṅaḥi ṅo bor bskyed nas de la ye śes pa gcug pa de ñid kyaṅ ḥdegs dgos pa daṅ / thig la yaṅ ye thig rigs lṅaḥi ṅo bor bskyed nas de la ye śes pa bcug ste / las thig gi steṅ du ḥdebs pa la / las thig byin gyis brlabs nas las thig la ye śes pa thim paḥi mos pa byas pa de yaṅ ḥdegs dgos pa daṅ / chu dbaṅ gi skabs su slob ma mi bskyod par bskyed pa la ye śes pa bcug nas yod pa la / cod pan gyi dbaṅ bskur baḥi sṅon du

[30] *Sṅags rim*, 231b-1, has a quotation from the writer Saraha. Tsoṅ-kha-pa comments on this that it refers to "four fold merger" (*bźi bsres*), but this term does not occur in Saraha's passage itself. Evidently, Mkhas grub rje means that Indian texts set forth these procedures, whether or not they employ those specific terms.

is brought entirely down. As [the Knowledge Beings] have entered on the previous evening, there is no reason [for them] to be brought down on the subsequent evening.

Here the terminology "fivefold merger" is not set forth by the texts of the Indian scholars. The *Sṅags rim* mentions "from one to six" and has in addition the terminology "method of mutliple merger" which does not occur even once in the Indian texts, which do, however, speak of "fourfold merger" and "threefold merger".[30] The method of "fivefold merger" is as follows: The Symbolic Beings and Knowledge Beings of the preceding phase of ritual of the site make two. The merger of those two with the *maṇḍala* of preparation is the threefold merger. When this is merged with the Symbolic Beings and Knowledge Beings of the 'generation in front' there is the fivefold merger. However, when one finishes the contraction of 'self generation' there is no basis for merger; and in general the Indian teachers have the expression "identity of self and in-front" but lack the expression "merger of self and in-front". The idea of the "identity of self and in-front" is to posit the pride that the *maṇḍala* of powdered colors generated in front is a concrete palace and that oneself is the concrete Lord in its center.

Again, as regards the method of accomplishing the *maṇḍala*, the technique of certain *gurus* when performing the offerings going with the accomplishment for consecutive days, is to accomplish the *maṇḍala* on the first day and have the Knowledge Beings enter and remain. Then, when accomplishing it on subsequent days, before one purifies the *maṇḍala*, be it of powdered colors or painted on cloth, one lifts the foregoing Knowledge Beings to the sky, proceeds to purify it by [muttering] "*śūnyatā*" ("voidness"), etc., and having accomplished it, makes them redescend. This is not a good thing, because it offers many opportunities for harm. Doing it that way, if it be a *maṇḍala* painted on cloth, one would destroy the "consecration" which affords the condition for steadiness [of the mental picture]. If it be one made of powdered colors, it would be necessary after first generating the powdered colors into the essence of the five Families, to make the Knowledge Beings enter that, and again lift (them). In the case of the line, it would be necessary to generate the 'knowledge line' into the essence of the five Families and make the Knowledge Beings enter that, lifting (them) over the 'action line'; and when it (i.e. the 'knowledge line') blesses the 'action line', it would be necessary to convince oneself that the Knowledge Beings are absorbed in the 'action line', and again to lift them. In the phase of the water initiation, one generates the disciple into Akṣobhya, makes the

slob ma bsaṅ sbyaṅ byed dgos pas / deḥi sṅon du mi bskyod pa de ñid bteg nas byed dgos pa sogs gnod byed mthaḥ yas pa yod do / de ltar byed paḥi rgyu gaṅ la thug na / stoṅ par sbyaṅs paḥi don caṅ med du bzuṅ pas lan no /

/ de la sbyoṅ tshul ni de kho na ñid kyi ḥod gsal gyi ṅaṅ du sku la sogs paḥi rnam pa bsdus pa la byed pa yin no /

/ des na ras bris daṅ rdul tshon gyi cho gaḥi khyad par ji lta bu źe na / de la gsum ste / sa cho ga gi khyad par daṅ / sta gon gyi khyad par daṅ / dṅos gźiḥi khyad par ro /

/ daṅ po ni / sṅar sa chog lan maṅ po byas paḥi ḥphro na re ba yin na ni / ras bris daṅ rdul tshon gñis ka la sa chog mi dgos par khyad par med ciṅ / ras bris la sa chog gaṅ du byed kyaṅ brkos nas sbyaṅ ba mi dgos par / rdzas sṅags tiṅ ṅe ḥdzin gsum gyis sbyaṅs pa sa chog la / brtag pa daṅ / bslaṅ ba yaṅ mi dgos so / gzuṅ ba daṅ / bsruṅ źiṅ byin gyis rlab paḥi cho ga rdul tshon daṅ ḥdra bar byed dgos te / sa phyogs byin gyis rlab pa daṅ / bgegs bsruṅ ba sogs kyi dgos pa gñis ka la khyad par med paḥi phyir ro / rdzas sṅags sogs kyis sbyaṅ ba yaṅ ṅes gzuṅ du dgos pa min pas / byas kyaṅ phun sum tshogs pa yin la / ma byas kyaṅ chog chad paḥi ñes pa med do /

/ gñis pa sta gon gyi khyad par ni / sgra gcan ḥdzin dpal bśes gñen gyis mdzad paḥi ras bris rkyaṅ ba la brten paḥi ḥdus paḥi dkyil chog zuṅ ḥjug gsal ba daṅ / gźan yaṅ ṅag dbaṅ grags pa daṅ / rtag paḥi rdo rjes mdzad paḥi ras bris rkyaṅ baḥi dkyil chog rnams las ras bris la sta gon dgos mi dgos gñis ka ma bśad kyaṅ /

[31] For material in a Western language on this topic, see Marcelle Lalou, *Iconographie des étoffes peintes* (= *Buddhica*, Tome VI) (Paris, 1930).

[32] This author is probably the Suvāgīśvarakīrti, responsible for several Tantric commentaries. His name is preserved in Sanskrit in certain Tanjur colophons.

Knowledge Being enter him and remain; and because it is necessary to sprinkle the disciple before conferring the diadem initiation, before doing the latter one would have to raise that same Akṣobhya. There is no limit to these harmful aspects. Whatever be the reason for doing it that way, his goal of purification in the void "responds" by holding him in "Nothingness".

Here, the method of purification consists in consolidating the corporeal and other aspects in the realm of the Reality "Clear Light".

[β. *Method of initiation in the maṇḍala painted on cloth*]

Now, what is the difference between the ritual of the *maṇḍala* painted on cloth (*paṭa*)[31] and of that consisting of powdered colors (*rajas*)? There are three [possible] differences: difference in the ritual of the site, difference in the preparation, and difference in the body of the rite.

Difference in the ritual of the site

When one has performed the ritual of the site many times previously, and has good reason to believe that there is a remainder, it is not necessary to have a ritual of the site in the case of either a *maṇḍala* painted on cloth or one made of powdered colors, and hence there is no difference [on this score]. Wherever ones performs the ritual of the site for the case of a painted *maṇḍala*, it is not necessary to purify through digging: one may purify by means of substances, incantations, and intense concentration. The inspection of, and begging for, the site are likewise dispensable. However, it is necessary to perform the ritual of seizing as well as the ritual of protecting and [obtaining] blessing in the same manner as for the *maṇḍala* of powdered colors, because there is no difference between the two in the requirement to bless the "area" and to perform such acts as protecting against obstructive demons. Also, it is not mandatory to adhere to the purification by means of substances, incantations, and intense concentration: if these are employed, there is the optimum situation; but if not employed, there is no definite ritual default.

Difference in the preparation

We find no discussion of whether or not there is a requirement of preparation in the case of a *maṇḍala* painted on cloth, in these works: the *Yugalanaddhaprakāśa* (Toh. 1818) composed by *Rāhula-śrī-mitra and which is a *maṇḍala-vidhi* of the *Guhyasamāja* concerned with only the painted *maṇḍala*; the *maṇḍala-vidhis* concerned with only the painted *maṇḍala* composed by **Vāgīśvarakīrti*[32] and by *Śāśvatavajra.

/ raṅ lugs la sṅags rim las ras bris kyi sta gon gyi khyad par bstan paḥi skabs su / bum pa sta gon daṅ / slob ma la dbaṅ bskur ba yin na / slob ma sta gon gñis ras bris la byed dgos par gsuṅs śiṅ / gsuṅs pa ltar byed kyaṅ dgos la / sa lha sta gon daṅ / lḥa sta gon gñis byed par yaṅ ma gsuṅs la / byed kyaṅ mi dgos te /

/ saḥi lha mo sta gon gyi dgos pa ni / sa phyogs der dkyil ḥkhor bri baḥi gnaṅ ba gsol baḥi phyir du yin pas / dkyil ḥkhor mi ḥbri na de mi dgos paḥi phyir daṅ / lha sta gon gyi dus su driḥi thig le daṅ me tog gi tshom bu ḥgod pa ni ḥbri ba yin na lha mtshan mi ḥphyug paḥi phyir du yin la / sta gon gyi sgrub ciṅ mchod nas gsol ba ḥdebs pa ni / saṅ ḥbri baḥi dkyil ḥkhor byin gyis rlob paḥi don du sñan gsan ḥbebs paḥi phyir yin pas / mi ḥbri na de ltar byed mi dgos paḥi phyir ro / ci ste lha sta gon byed na ras bris kyi dkyil ḥkhor de ñid kyi steṅ du las thig daṅ ye thig gñis ka rdzogs par ḥdebs dgos par gyur ro /

/ dṅos gźiḥi chog ni rdul tshon daṅ khyad par med do /

/ gsum pa lus dkyil sgrub tshul la / bod kyi bla ma kha cig ni / bsam gtan gyi dkyil ḥkhor sgrub pa ltar du / bsgrub gźiḥi dkyil ḥkhor mdun gyi nam mkhar bskyed de / deḥi gtso bo daṅ raṅ gi bla ma gñis tha mi dad du mos paḥi lus la lus dkyil gyi lha rnams bkod nas sgrub par byed do / de ni mi ḥthad de / de ḥdra ba de ni bsam gtan gyi dkyil ḥkhor sgrub tshul du soṅ gi / lus dkyil sgrub tshul gyi don med de / lus dkyil bsgrub gźiḥi gnas gźal yas khaṅ ma bcos pa dgos pa las / de la ni dṅos gnas la grub paḥi lus kyi cha gaṅ yaṅ bsgrub gźir ma soṅ bar rtog pas btags paḥi bsgrub gźi ḥbaḥ źig tu soṅ baḥi phyir ro / de ḥdra bas slob ma la dbaṅ

[33] *Sṅags rim*, 234a-6, cites the Tantra *Vajramālā* (Toh. 445): "The body becomes a palace, the hallowed fane of all the Buddhas" (*lus ni gźal yas khaṅ du gyur / saṅs rgyas kun gyi yaṅ dag rten*), and comments, "a palace through metamorphosis (*parāvṛtti*) of the body" (*lus yoṅs su gyur pa las gźal yas khaṅ*).

In our school, it is set forth in the *Sṅags rim* in the section treating the difference of preparation for the painted *maṇḍala* that since there is a preparation of the flask and a conferring of initiation upon the disciple, it is necessary in the case of the painted *maṇḍala* [to so treat] both the disciple and the preparation; and hence we do it that way. But as the *Sṅags rim* [at that point] does not mention doing the preparation of the earth goddess or preparation of the *maṇḍala* deities, these two preparations are not required [in the case of the painted *maṇḍala*].

The purpose of the preparation of the earth goddess is to obtain her permission for drawing a *maṇḍala* on that spot. Hence, when one does not draw a *maṇḍala*, that [preparation] is not required. Also, the placing of the fragrant drop and the heap of flowers at the time of preparation of the deities is done so that while one is drawing there will be no confusion in the marks of the deities. The worship and prayers during the accomplishment of the preparation are so that the deities will lend a gracious ear for the sake of blessing the *maṇḍala* to be drawn the following day; consequently, if one does not draw it, one need not go through this preparation. And what if one did? When doing the preparation of the deities, it would be necessary to fully pitch both the 'action line' and the 'knowledge line' upon that *maṇḍala* painted on cloth!

Difference in the body of the rite

There is no difference from that of powdered colors in the body (*maulī*) of the rite.

[γ. *Method of initiation in the body maṇḍala*]

As to the method of accomplishing the body *maṇḍala* (*deha-maṇḍala*), some Tibetan *gurus* hold that the *maṇḍala* to be accomplished is generated in the sky in front in the same way as the accomplishment of the meditation *maṇḍala*. One convinces himself that his *guru* is identical with the Lord of that [*maṇḍala*] and arranges the deities of the body *maṇḍala* in the body [of his *guru*], thus managing the accomplishment. That is not valid. Such a procedure applies in the method of accomplishing the meditation *maṇḍala*, but it is useless for the method of accomplishing the body *maṇḍala*. As against the unfabricated palace (*vimāna*) which the body *maṇḍala* requires as the realization basis,[33] that [invalid procedure] would not realize any bodily parts produced in a concrete status, because there would be merely a realization in terms of imaginative figments. Hence, when one would confer inititiation upon

bskur kyaṅ lus dkyil du dbaṅ bskur bar mi ḥgyur te / gaṅ du dkyil ḥkhor bsgrubs pa der dbaṅ ma bskur / bla mas ma bsgrubs paḥi lus la slob ma dbaṅ len du bcug paḥi phyir / ḥbrel med du ḥgyur la / dkyil ḥkhor bsgrubs pa de ñid du dbaṅ bskur ba yin na ni / lus dkyil du dban bskur bar ma soṅ bsam gtan kyi dkyil ḥkhor du dbaṅ bskur baḥi tshul du soṅ ba yin no /

/ sa skya paḥi rje btsun goṅ ma rnams ni / lus kyi dkyil ḥkhor zur du mi bsgrub par / bla mas lus dkyil gyi mṅon rtogs bsgom pa de ñid / lus dkyil bsgrub par bźed pa ltar legs pas / raṅ lugs kyaṅ de ltar byaḥo / de la lus dkyil du bdag ḥjug len paḥi tshul ni / mṅon byaṅ lṅa las gźiḥi he-ru-ka bskyed pa la raṅ ñid ṅa rgyal ḥjog ciṅ / de nas sñiṅ poḥi rnal ḥbyor ma bźi la sogs paḥi lha drug cu rtsa gñis po thams cad la yaṅ ṅa rgyal bźag nas / khyad par du gźiḥi he-ru-kaḥi thug kar dpyid thig las naṅ gi he-ru-ka yab yum bskyed pa la / ṅaḥo sñam paḥi ṅa rgyal śugs drag bskyed par byaḥo / deḥi tshe na haṅ gźiḥi he-ru-ka daṅ / naṅ gi he-ru-ka gñis ṅo bo gcig la rnam pa tha dad du snaṅ baḥi mos pa brtan poḥi ṅaṅ nas bum pa bsgrubs la / de nas raṅ ñid gtso boḥi ṅa rgyal bzuṅ ba de ñid gtso bo mar me gcig las gñis chad kyi tshul du phye nas śar sgo logs su gnas par byas la / de man chad naṅ gi he-ru-ka yab yum daṅ raṅ gi rtsa baḥi bla ma dbyer med du mos par byas nas / de las dbaṅ len pa daṅ / bdag ñid ḥjug pa sogs byas te /

/ slob ma la dbaṅ bskur baḥi dus su / raṅ ñid gźi daṅ naṅ gi he-ru-ka gñis daṅ ḥdres par mos te lha rnams gsal btab la / de nas slob ma dkyil

[34] For the Sa-skya school, see Giuseppe Tucci, *Tibetan Painted Scrolls* (Roma, 1949), esp. pp. 7-17 and 100, ff. Tsoṅ-kha-pa's biography shows that during a period of study at the Sa-skya monastery for a year in his 20's Tsoṅ-kha-pa listened to the lama Rdo-rje-rin-chen's explanations of the Sa-skya interpretation (*sa lugs*) of the *Hevajra-tantra*. However, the method which Mkhas grub rje now sets forth is based on the *Cakrasaṃvara-tantra*.

[35] The sixty-two deities meant are those in the *Śrīcakrasaṃvara* or *Sambara maṇḍala*, namely, Sambara and Vajravārāhī (2); *yoginī* of the heart (4); male and female deities in mind circle, *cittacakra* (16); in speech circle, *vākcakra* (16); in body circle, *kāya-cakra* (16); gatekeepers (8). For an outline of this *maṇḍala*, see B. Bhattacharyya, *Niṣpannayogāvalī of Mahāpaṇḍita Abhayākaragupta* (Baroda, 1949), pp. 44-6. For the body *maṇḍala* in terms of these deities, see Giuseppe Tucci, *Indo-Tibetica*, Vol. III, Pt. II, pp. 38, ff.

[36] The expression "four *yoginī* of the heart" (*sñiṅ poḥi rnal ḥbyor ma bźi*) is employed in Tsoṅ-kha-pa's *Ḥdod pa ḥjo* (Toh. 5320), Vol. Ta, e.g. 120a-6 in that work. They are Ḍākinī, Lāmā, Khaṇḍarohā, and Rūpiṇī.

[37] In the work just cited (*Ḥdod pa ḥjo*), the union of Sambara and Vajravārāhī constitutes Śrī-Heruka *Yab-yum* ("Father-Mother" union). At 128a-1, *ibid.*, Tsoṅ-kha-pa cites the *Vasanta-tilaka* (Toh. 1448): "The mouth of the mare is fiery; the sow (*vārāhī*) is called *tilaka*" (rgod maḥi kha ni me yi gzugs / phag mo ti-la-ka źes brjod). Tsoṅ-kha-pa goes on to explain that this *tilaka* is generated from the red part [of the *bindu*] at the navel (*lte baḥi dmar cha*). In the same work (citation mislaid), there is a quota-

a disciple, the latter would not be conferred initiation in the body *maṇḍala*. Wherever one would accomplish the *maṇḍala*, there no initiation would be conferred, because the disciple would be induced to receive initiation in a body not accomplished by the *guru*, and there would be dissociation. If one is conferred initiation in that [so] realized *maṇḍala*, he is not conferred initiation in the body *maṇḍala*, but it is the method of conferring initiation in the meditation *maṇḍala*.

The early venerables of the Sa-skya school[34] maintained that one does not accomplish the body *maṇḍala* separately, but that the contemplation in which the *guru* visualizes the body *maṇḍala* accomplishes the body *maṇḍala*. As their position is excellent, our school follows suit. Here the method of taking personal entrance into the body *maṇḍala* is as follows: One generates the "ground" (*gźi*) Heruka from the five Revelation-Enlightenments (*abhisaṃbodhi*) and deposits one's egotism therein. Then he deposits his egotism also in all the sixty-two deities,[35] starting with the four *yoginī* of the heart.[36] Preeminently, he generates the "Father-Mother" union of the personal ("inner") Heruka from the "drop of springtime" (*vasanta-tilaka*)[37] in the heart of the "ground" Heruka and generates the powerful force of egotism, thinking "I am [he]." At that time he also accomplishes the flask through the state of steadfast conviction that the different aspects of the "ground" Heruka and the personal Heruka are of a single essence. Next, while himself holding on to the egotism of the Lord, he separates from the Lord in the manner of a second flame separating from the first and comes to a stop at the Eastern gate. Subsequent to that, he convinces himself that the personal Heruka in "Father-Mother" union and his own basic *guru* are indissoluble; then takes initiation from him, and himself does the entering [into the body *maṇḍala*], and so forth.

At the time of conferring initiation upon the disciple, one must be convinced that he himself coalesces with the "ground" and personal Herukas, while he vividly imagines the deities. After that, at the time

---

tion to the effect that *vasanta* is Sambara and *tilaka* is Vajravārāhī; hence these are respectively the white and red parts of the *bindu*. This use of the term *vasanta-tilaka* agrees with the explanation of the verse meter called Vasanta-tilaka, e.g. from translation by Dr. Sūryakānta of Kṣemendra's *Suvṛttatilaka* in *The Poona Orientalist*, XVII, 1-4 (1952), p. 205: "A Vasantatilaka shines in rendering the mingling up of the dreadful and the heroic sentiments." Here the dreadful element is represented by Vajravārāhī and the heroic element by Sambara. The two elements are evidently what is referred to by the term "two parts of Heruka" (*he-ru-ka cha gñis pa*) in *Sṅags rim*, 233b-4.

ḥkhor du gźug paḥi tshe na ḥaṅ rdul tshon gyi dkyil ḥkhor la ḥjug pa ltar ma yin gyi / bla maḥi skuḥi cha de daṅ de gźal yas khaṅ du bskyed pa der gźug ciṅ / me tog ḥthor du ḥjug pa na ḥaṅ / bla maḥi thugs kaḥi naṅ gi he-ru-kaḥi thugs kar gtor baḥi mos pa byed du ḥjug la / bum paḥi dbaṅ sogs kyaṅ bla maḥi sku las len du ḥjug pa yin gyi / dkyil ḥkhor sgrub pa daṅ dbaṅ bskur ba gñis ḥbrel med mi byaḥo / lus dkyil du dbaṅ bskur baḥi tshul ḥdi yaṅ dril bu pa lta buḥi dbaṅ du byas gyi / gsaṅ ḥdus la lus dkyil yod kyaṅ der dbaṅ bskur ba med do /

of introducing the disciple into the *maṇḍala*, it is unlike the entrance into the *maṇḍala* of powdered colors. Rather, he is introduced into the part(s) of the *guru*'s body and into that generated into a palace; and when he is directed to throw the flower, he is directed to have conviction that he casts it into the heart of the personal Heruka of the *guru*'s heart. Moreover, he is made to take the initiations, beginning with that of the flask, from the *guru*'s body, but one should not dissociate initiation from accomplishment of the *maṇḍala*. This method of conferring initiation in the body *maṇḍala* is also followed in the initiations set forth by Ghaṇṭapā, for example; but while there is a body *maṇḍala* in the *Guhyasamāja* there is no initiation therein.

/ ji ltar dbaṅ bskur baḥi tshul la gñis / rgyud smin par byed pa slob ma la dbaṅ bskur baḥi chog daṅ / lha la dbaṅ bskur ba rab gnas kyi cho ga bstan paḥo /

/ daṅ po la gñis / dkyil ḥkhor du ḥjug pa daṅ / źugs pa la dbaṅ bskur baḥo /

/ daṅ po ni / ḥjug paḥi dus su dam tshig daṅ sdom pa bzuṅ nas ḥjug dgos pas / de la rigs lṅaḥi sdom gzuṅ byas nas thun moṅ ma yin paḥi sṅags kyi sdom pa sṅar med gsar du skye ba daṅ / ñams pa sor chud pa la / ma mthaḥ rdo rje slob dpon gyi dbaṅ bskur ba man chad daṅ ḥbrel baḥi sgo nas rigs lṅaḥi sdom gzuṅ lan gsum byas pa dgos kyi / de ma yin paḥi mṅon rtogs tsam bsgom pa daṅ / rjes gnaṅ tsam gyi skabs su rigs lṅaḥi sdom pa gzuṅ ba lan gsum byas kyaṅ sdom pa gsar du skye ba daṅ / sdom pa sor chud par mi ḥgyur mod / ḥo na kyaṅ de ltar byas pa la dgos pa chen po yod de / sṅar yod brtan źiṅ goṅ nas goṅ du khyad par du ḥgyur baḥi phan yon chen po yod pas so /

/ de ltar sdom gzuṅ byed paḥi dus la ni / śiṅ rta chen po dag gi bźed pa mi ḥdra ba gsum byuṅ ste / slob ma sta gon gyi dus su byed la / gźan du mi byed pa daṅ / yaṅ dkyil ḥkhor du ḥjug paḥi tshe byed ciṅ gźan du mi byed pa daṅ / gñis kaḥi dus su byed paḥi lugs mi ḥdra ba gsum byuṅ ba de rnams gaṅ gi rjes su ḥbraṅs kyaṅ yan lag gźan rnams tshaṅ na sdom pa skye ba la khyad par med pas raṅ raṅ gi lugs ma ḥchol bar byaḥo /

CHAPTER NINE

δ. *Manner of conferring initiation*

There are two methods: the ritual of conferring initiation on the disciple for maturing his stream of consciousness, and the consecration ritual conferring initiation on a deity.

I′. *Ritual of conferring initiation on the disciple*

This has two phases: entering the *maṇḍala*, and initiation of the one who has entered.

A′. *Entering the maṇḍala.* — At the time of entering, it is necessary to take the pledges (*samaya*) and vows (*saṃvara*). In this regard, one must take the vows of the five Families. As to the uncommon (*asādhāraṇa*) *mantra* vows, one must newly produce those not previously held and mend those violated. For the initiations of Hierophant and below, it necessary, at the very least, to take the vows of the five Families, reciting each thrice. Otherwise, if one contemplates the visualization (*abhisamaya*) alone, or takes the vows of the five Families, reciting them thrice, at the phase of the permission (*anujñā*) alone, the vows are neither produced newly nor mended. Now, even though the carrying out of that procedure constitutes an imposing requirement, one should first become steadfast [in those vows] because the benefit to be derived is imposing and will be outstanding in an ever loftier way.

In regard to the time when one so takes the vows, the great "Chariots" (who lay down the path) have three different theses: (1) doing it at the time of preparation of the disciple, and not at any other time; (2) doing it at the time of entering the *maṇḍala* and at no other time; and (3) doing it at both those times. No matter which of those different ways one may follow, if he satisfies the other requirements, the vow will be born; and since there is no difference in this respect among them, one need not be wrong in [following] any of these ways.

/ de yaṅ dbaṅ daṅ bdag ḥjug gi skabs su sdom gzuṅ byed paḥi sṅon du slob dpon gyis brda sprad pa sogs kyi sgo nas blaṅ dor gyi gnas rnams rags pa phal che ba ma mthaḥ yaṅ ṅes par byas nas len ḥdod daṅ bsruṅ sems kyi ḥdun pa śugs drag gis len pa dgos kyi / gźan du dbaṅ gral du ḥdug pa tsam gyis dbaṅ thob par ḥgro ba dkaḥo /

/ sdom gzuṅ gi skabs su yaṅ slob dpon daṅ mñam du ḥam / sṅon du bzlas pas byaṅ sems kyi sdom pa mi skye bar ḥphags pa thogs med sogs tshad ldan rnams kyis gsuṅs pas / slob dpon gyis bzlas paḥi rjes su bzla ba daṅ /

/ bdag ḥjug gi tshe na ḥaṅ dkyil ḥkhor gyi gtso bo daṅ bla ma tha mi dad du mos pa des sdom gzuṅ gi tshig rnams brjod pa deḥi rjes su raṅ gis bzlas paḥi mos pa byas nas brjod pa ṅes par dgos la /

/ ḥdi rnams la rtsal du bton nas dmigs phyed pa śin tu gal che ste / sṅags kyi lam gyi gźi rtsar gyur pas so / des na sṅags sdom skye ba ṅes par dbaṅ bskur ba la ltos dgos kyaṅ / dbaṅ bskur ba rdzogs pa la ltos mi dgos te / dper na dge sloṅ gi sdom pa skye ba gsol bźiḥi las la ltos dgos kyaṅ / cho gaḥi gtso bo rnams tshaṅ nas brjod pa gsum paḥi don gyi sum gñis yan chad rdzogs paḥi dus su skye ba bźin no /

/ dbaṅ bskur ba la / bla med kyi bskur rgyuḥi dbaṅ la bźir ṅes te / bum pa / gsaṅ ba / śes rab ye śes / dbaṅ bźi pa rnams so /

/ bum dbaṅ la bźi ste / dkyil ḥkhor gaṅ du ḥthob pa daṅ / graṅs ji tsam źig yin pa daṅ ṅo bo gaṅ yin pa daṅ / byed las ji ḥdra ba źig yin paḥo /

/ daṅ po ni / rdul tshon nam ras bris gaṅ ruṅ du bum dbaṅ bskur ba na / bsgrubs paḥi dkyil ḥkhor ba rnams kyis bum pa bzuṅ nas dbaṅ bskur baḥi bya ba dṅos su mdzad pa yaṅ ma yin la / de ltar bsgom pa yaṅ ma yin źiṅ / dbaṅ lha zur nas spyan draṅs pa rnams kyi naṅ nas / spyan ma la

[1] The idea here is that the point about reciting after the Master in taking these Tantric vows is followed after the model of taking the Bodhisattva vow. Asaṅga is an authority on the Bodhisattva path, not on the Tantras.

Moreover, prior to making [the disciples] take the vows in the phases of initiation or personal entrance [by the Hierophant into the *maṇḍala*], the Hierophant must at the very least confirm them, by means of instructions, in the simplest and most elementary topics of what to take and what to reject [i.e. a delineation of the good and the bad], wherefor they may desire to take [the vows] and will take [them] with keen enthusiastic craving of the mind to protect [them]. Whereas, if [the candidates] are merely seated for initiation in rows, it is difficult [for them] to proceed to the attainment of initiation.

Furthermore, according to Āryāsaṅga and other authorities, in the phase of making [the disciples] take the vows, if [the disciples] recite the vow "Mind of Enlightenment" in unison with, or prior to, the Master (*ācārya*), it is not "born" [in their stream of consciousness], so they should recite after the Master's recitation.[1]

Again, at the time of [the Hierophant's] personal entrance [into the *maṇḍala*], it is certainly necessary that [the disciples] be convinced that the Lord of the *maṇḍala* and the *guru* are not separate, and when they recite after the *guru* the words of taking the vow, they must recite with that conviction.

[The Hierophant] should bear these things in mind as being of greatest importance, for these are the foundation and root of the *mantra* path. Thus, the birth of the *mantra* vow certainly requires dependence on initiation, but does not require dependence on completion of initiation. For example, it is like the case of the *bhikṣu* vow being born with the requirement of dependence on the *jñāpti-caturtha-karma* (three proposals followed by one decision), but one who has fulfilled the chief elements of that rite and [that *bhikṣu* vow] is born at the time one completes the first two-thirds of the aimed-at three proposals.

B′. *Conferring initiation after entrance.* — There are certainly four basic initiations conferred in the Anuttara [Tantras]. These are 1′. that of the flask (*kalaśa*), 2′. the secret one (*guhya*), 3′. the insight-knowledge (*prajñā-jñāna*), and 4′. the fourth initiation (*caturtha* or *turīya-abhiṣeka*).

1′. *Initiation of the flask.* — This has four topics: the *maṇḍala* in which it is attained; the number of kinds; its essential nature; and its efficacy.

a′. *Maṇḍala in which it is attained.* — When initiation of the flask is conferred, whether by means of a *maṇḍala* of powdered colors or one painted on cloth, neither do the accomplished *maṇḍala* inhabitants hold the flask and actually do the deeds of conferring initiation, nor does one contemplate in that way. One should be convinced that among the

sogs pa rnams kyis bum pa bzuṅ nas dṅos su dbaṅ bskur baḥi mos pa phyed kyaṅ / bum pa ḥjog mkhan slob dpon kyis byed ciṅ / dbaṅ bskur mkhan ni dbaṅ lha rnams kyis byed kyaṅ / bsgrubs paḥi dkyil ḥkhor ba rnams la slob dpon gyis mchod ciṅ / slob ma la dbaṅ bskur ba la dgoṅs pa gton paḥi gsol ba ḥdebs pa yin la / gsol ba btab pa ltar du dkyil ḥkhor pa rnams kyis kyaṅ / de la dgoṅs pa gtaṅ nas dbaṅ bskur baḥi bya ba mdzad par mos pa byed dgos pas / rdul tshon nam ras bris kyi dkyil ḥkhor du bum dbaṅ thob ces bya ba yin no /

/ graṅs ni gźan rnams la mi mthun pa du ma yod kyaṅ / ḥdus paḥi lugs ltar byas na / bum dbaṅ bcu gcig daṅ / dbaṅ goṅ ma rnams daṅ bcas pas bcu bźir ḥgyur te / bśad rgyud rdo rje phreṅ ba las / dbaṅ bskur re re sa reḥo / źes gsuṅs pa ltar / de las sa bcu bźir bśad pa daṅ bstun paḥo /

/ bum dbaṅ la thun moṅ pa rdo rje slob maḥi dbaṅ daṅ / thun moṅ ma yin pa rdo rje slob dpon gyi dbaṅ ṅo /

/ de yaṅ mi bskyod pa chuḥi dbaṅ / rin chen ḥbyuṅ ldan cod pan gyi dbaṅ / ḥod dpag med rdo rjeḥi dbaṅ / don yod grub pa dril buḥi dbaṅ / rnam par snaṅ mdzad miṅ gi dbaṅ daṅ lṅa ste / de rnams la rig paḥi dbaṅ źes paḥi tha sñad ḥdogs pa ni / spyan ma la sogs paḥi rig pa rnams kyis

[2] *Sṅags rim*, 317a-5, ff., explains on the basis of the *Mahāmudrātilaka* (Toh. 420) that the number fourteen comes from making the initiations of the flask total eleven, and that then the three higher initiations bring the total to fourteen. Mkhas grub rje in his commentary on the *Hevajra-tantra*, the *Brtag ḥgrel* (Toh. 5483), Vol. Ja, 121a-2, quotes the *Jñānatilaka-tantra* (Toh. 422): "Dharmameghā is the stage of a Buddha; Samantaprabhā is the stage of a Samyaksaṃbuddha; *Samantālokābhāsaprabhā is the stage of a Nirmāṇakāya [fashioned] by Srī-vajrasattva Bhagavat; *Samantālokopalabdhiprabhā is the stage of the Sambhogakāya; *Anabhilāpyāpramāṇā is the stage of Mahāsukha" (chos kyi sprin ni saṅs rgyas kyi sa / kun tu ḥod ni yaṅ dag par rdzogs paḥi saṅs rgyas kyi sa / kun tu snaṅ ba mched paḥi ḥod ni dpal rdo rje sems dpaḥ bcom ldan ḥdas kyis sprul paḥi skuḥi sa / kun tu snaṅ ba thob paḥi ḥod ni loṅs spyod rdzogs paḥi skuḥi sa / brjod du med pa tshad med pa ni bde ba chen poḥi sa ste). Of course, Dharmameghā is the tenth stage (cf. Chap. I, note 8, above), and the rest follow in order. However, immediately thereafter, Mkhas grub rje quotes the same Tantra to the effect that the eleventh stage is associated with the Nirmāṇakāya, the twelfth with the Sambhoga-kaya, the thirteen with the Dharmakāya, the fourteenth with Mahāsukha; that a fifteen stage would be called *Jñānavatī, and that there is no information (*btags pa min*) about a sixteenth. This last group of correspondences is consistent with the ordering of Buddha bodies to initiations, as done in the present chapter. Moreover, Dbyaṅs-can-dgaḥ-baḥi-blo-gros, following the Ārya school of the *Guhyasamāja*, writes in his *Dpal gsaṅ ba ḥdus pa ḥphags lugs daṅ mthun paḥi sṅags kyis lam rnam gźag legs bśad skal bzaṅ ḥjug ṅogs*, folio 20b-1, f.: "The one who has arrived at the limit of the subtle and the coarse of the Steps of Production which conclude the maturation of the stream of consciousness, is associated with attainment of the eighth stage. Both the arcane body and arcane speech of the Steps of Completion are associated with the latter part of the eighth stage as well as with the ninth stage. Both the arcane mind and the illusory body are associated with the first part of the tenth stage. Both the Clear Light and the coupling in the realm of learning are associated with the latter part of the tenth stage. The coupling beyond learning is

initiatory deities invited from the "corners" (*zur*), Locanā and the others hold the flask and actually confer initiation; however, the lifting of the flask is done by the "preceptor" (*upādhyāya*) and the Hierophant (*ācārya*). The initiatory deities perform the initiation itself; however, the Hierophant makes the offering to the accomplished *maṇḍala* residents, and the disciple implores the initiators to consider him favorably. He convinces himself that according as he implores, the initiators in turn consider him favorably and do the acts of conferring initiation. Whether the *maṇḍala* be of powdered colors or one painted on cloth, that is the "attaining of the flask initiation".

b′. *The number of kinds.* — Although there are many inconsistences in other schools, if one takes it in accordance with the *Guhyasamāja* school, there are eleven types of flask initiation, which together with the higher initiations, make fourteen. Their Explanatory Tantra *Vajramālā* (Toh. 445) says, "Each initiation pertains to a stage (*bhūmi*)." That is consistent with the presentation in that work that there are fourteen stages.[2]

Among the initiations of the flask, there is the common one (*sādhāraṇa*), which is the Neophyte's Initiation (*vajraśiṣya-abhiṣeka*), and the uncommon one (*asādhāraṇa*), which is the Hierophant's Initiation (*vajrācārya-abhiṣeka*).

Furthermore, they have a five-fold classification as follows:[3]

1. The water initiation (*toyaseka*) of Akṣobhya;
2. The diadem initiation (*mauliseka*) of Ratnasambhava;
3. The diamond initiation (*vajraseka*) of Amitābha;
4. The bell initiation (*ghaṇṭaseka*) of Amoghasiddhi;
5. The name initiation (*nāmaseka*) of Vairocana.

For these initiations there exists also the term "wisdom initiation" (*vidyāseka*). This expression is used because Locanā and the other "wis-

---

posited on the eleventh stage, Samantaprabhā. That is the purport of the *Caryāmelāpaka* (Toh. 1803)" (rgyud smin zin paḥi bskyed rim phra rags mthar phyin pa sa brgyad pa thob pa daṅ sbyar / rdzogs rim gyi lus dben daṅ / ṅag dben gñis sa brgyad paḥi smad daṅ sa dgu pa gñis daṅ sbyar / sems dben daṅ sgyu lus gñis sa bcu paḥi stod daṅ sbyar / ḥod gsal daṅ slob paḥi zuṅ ḥjub gñis sa bcu paḥi smad daṅ sbyar / mi slob paḥi zuṅ ḥjug sa bcu gcig pa kun tu ḥod la ḥjog pa ni spyod bsdus kyi dgoṅs pa yin no), This explanation fits in well with the standard explanation of the ten stages, which divides them into the first seven and the last three. The career of the Bodhisattva ends at the tenth stage, when he becomes tantamount to a Buddha but not to a complete Buddha or Tathāgata, for whom the eleventh stage, or Samantaprabhā, is reserved; cf. Har Dayal, *The Bodhisattva Doctrine* (London, 1932), p. 291.

[3] The Sanskrit terms derive from *Sekoddeśaṭikā*, text 27.22, ff.; for alternate terminology, *udakābhiṣeka*, and so on, cf. *Advayavajra-saṃgraha*, p. 36.

bum pa ḥdzin mkhan byas nas bskur baḥi dbaṅ yin pas na de skad daṅ yaṅ ma rig paḥi gñen por rig pa ye śes bskyed paḥi nus pa ḥjog byed yin pas de skad ces byaḥo /

/ a-bha-yas gsuṅs paḥi dbaṅ daṅ po me tog ḥphreṅ baḥi dbaṅ źes pa bum dbaṅ bcu gcig la mi the yaṅ ṅes par bya dgos te / deḥi dgos pa ni gaṅ la me tog phog paḥi lha de la bla mas slob ma gtad pa la brten nas de bźin gśegs pa deḥi rigs su mṅon par ḥtshaṅ rgya bar ḥgyur bar śes śiṅ deḥi nus pa ḥjog tshul ston paḥo /

/ chu dbaṅ gis ni de la brten paḥi lam bsgom pa na / rigs der ḥtshaṅ rgya ba la gegs byed kyi dri ma ḥkhrud paḥi nus pa daṅ /

/ cod pan gyi dbaṅ gis ni de bsgoms pa las rigs der saṅs rgyas paḥi tshe mtshan so gñis kyi naṅ nas dbuḥı gtsug tor bltar mi mṅon paḥi nus daṅ / rigs bdag gaṅ gis byed paḥi nus pa ḥjog la /

/ rdo rje dbaṅ gis ni rigs der saṅs rgyas paḥi thugs rnam par mi rtog paḥi ye śes ḥgrub paḥi nus pa daṅ /

/ dril buḥi dbaṅ gis ni rigs der saṅs rgyas paḥi tshe na / gdul bya la chos kyi sgo brgyad khri bźi stoṅ gis ston paḥi gsuṅ ḥgrub paḥi nus pa daṅ /

/ miṅ gi dbaṅ gis ni rigs der saṅs rgyas pa na de bźin gśegs pa mtshan ḥdi źes bya bar ḥgyur ro / źes pa de ḥdra baḥi mtshan gyi nus pa ḥjog go /

/ de rnams ni rigs so soḥi dbaṅ du byas pa yin gyi / rdo rje slob dpon gyi dbaṅ gis ni / sku gsuṅ thugs kyi rdo rje gsum dbyer mi phyed paḥi rdo rje ḥchaṅ ḥthob pa daṅ / spyir bla na med paḥi byaṅ chub las phyir mi ldog ciṅ / khyad par lam ḥdi las rdzogs paḥi byaṅ chub ḥthob pa las phyir mi ldog paḥi nus pa daṅ / sa bcu pa la źugs paḥi sems dpaḥ chen po rnams la saṅs rgyas kyis khams gsum chos kyi rgyal por dbaṅ bskur ba daṅ tshul mtshuṅs pas / khams gsum chos kyi rgyal poḥi rgyal srid du

This is the explanation by Lwa-ba-pa in his *Ratnapradīpoddyota* on the *Cakrasambaramaṇḍalavidhi* (Toh. 1444), Wa, 265b: "Those five initiations which have the nature of the five Tathāgatas are also referred to by the expression '*vidyābhiṣeka*', because they accomplish the five *vidyājñāna* which are the transmutation of the five *avidyā* and because in each case the initiation is conferred by the *vidyā-devī*, namely Buddhalocanā and so on. They represent the sequence of the five initiations" (de bźin gśegs pa lṅaḥi ṅo bo dbaṅ bskur ba lṅa po de dag la rig paḥi dbaṅ bskur baḥi sgras kyaṅ brjod par bya yin te / ma rig pa lṅa yoṅs su gyur paḥi ṅo bo / rig paḥi ye śes lṅa po rnams sgrub par byed paḥi phyir daṅ thams cad du saṅs rgyas spyan la sogs pa rig paḥi lha mos dbaṅ bskur bar byed paḥi phyir ro / de dag ni dbaṅ bskur ba lṅaḥi rim paḥo). The *Sṅags rim*, 265a-6, refers to this passage, and 265a-5, to

doms" (*vidyā*) hold the flask and confer initiation, and also because the initiation establishes the capacity of producing "wisdom-knowledge" (*vidyā-jñāna*) as the antidote for unwisdom (*avidyā*).[4]

The first initiation as reported by Abhayākara is "Initiation of the Flower Wreath"; and, while it is not included among the eleven flask initiations, it certainly must be performed. It is required for the following reason: The *guru* makes the disciple understand that by relying in the direction of the deity on whom the [thrown] flower falls, he will reach Complete Enlightenment in the Family of that Tathāgata. Hence it shows the method of establishing the capacity of that [attainment].

Through the water initiation, by contemplating the path based on it, one is able to wash off the defilement that obstructs the attainment of Complete Enlightenment in that Family [i.e. which is pointed to by means of the thrown flower].

Through the diadem initiation, by contemplating that, one establishes, for the time of becoming a Buddha in that particular Family, the capacity of the invisible *uṣṇīṣa-śiraskatā* among the thirty-two characteristics (*lakṣaṇa*), and the capacity for doing whatever is the function of that Family Master.

Through the diamond initiation, one has the capacity for accomplishing the non-discursive knowledge (*nirvikalpa-jñāna*) of the mind of Buddhahood in that Family.

Through the bell initiation, one is able to accomplish the speech which, in the time of Buddhahood in that Family, teaches the Doctrine (*dharma*) to the candidates by means of the 84,000 "doors" of the *dharma*.

Through the name initiation, one establishes the capacity of the name indicated by the prophecy, "You will be a Tathāgata of such a name when becoming a Buddha in that Family."

Those [five initiations] are under the control of the various Families. Then, by means of the Hierophant's Initiation (*vajrācārya-abhiṣeka*), one achieves [the rank of] Vajradhara, which is the inseparability of the three thunderbolts (*vajra*) of Body, Speech, and Mind; in general has the capacity to not regress from the Incomparable Enlightenment and in particular the capacity through this path to not regress from attaining the Complete Enlightenment. Moreover, it is comparable to the method of initiation as "King of the Law of the Three Worlds" (*traidhātuka-dharmarāja*) which the Buddhas confer upon the Bodhisattvas who have entered upon the Tenth Stage, and so it is the initiation into the kingdom

---

Abhayākara's *Vajrāvali* (Toh. 3140); in the latter text it is said that the initiations accomplish the "antidotes for *avidyā*" (*avidyā-pratipakṣa, ma rig paḥi gñen po*).

dbaṅ bskur ba yin pas gźan la rgyud ḥchad pa daṅ dbaṅ bskur ba sogs / rdo rje slob dpon gyi las thams cad la dbaṅ baḥi nus pa khyad par can bźag paḥi sgo nas de la dbaṅ pa yin no /

/ bum dbaṅ rnams kyi ṅo bo ni / chu daṅ çod pan sogs kyi raṅ raṅ gi cho gas dbaṅ bskur baḥi tshe dbaṅ po rnon po la bde ba dṅos su skye ba ḥoṅ bas / de daṅ stoṅ ñid kyi lta ba phu thag chod pa gñis sbyaṙ baḥi bde stoṅ gi ye śes ñid la byed ciṅ / de min na ḥaṅ deḥi tshe bde ba skyes paḥi mos pa byas pa daṅ / lta ba dran paḥi bde stoṅ mos pa yid byed kyis dran pa daṅ / rdo rje slob dpon gyi dbaṅ gi ṅo bo yaṅ dṅos daṅ bsgoms paḥi rig ma gaṅ ruṅ daṅ raṅ ñid rdo rje ḥchaṅ du gsal ba gñis ḥkhyud pa las byuṅ baḥi bde ba daṅ lta ba dran nas bde stoṅ gi ye śes skyes paḥi mos pa byed pa ma mthaḥ yaṅ dgos kyi / de lta bu ma yin na dbaṅ de rnams thob par gźag mi nus so /

/ sgra bśad pa ni thams cad la bum paḥi chuḥi bya ba rjes su ḥgro bas de skad ces byaḥo /

/ byed las ni / dkyil ḥkhor gyi lhaḥi gsal baḥi dbye ba mthaḥ yas pa yod kyaṅ / de thams cad rigs so so pa lṅa daṅ / sku gsuṅ thugs kyi rdo rje gsum daṅ / de gsum dbyer med pa rigs thams cad kyi bdag po drug pa rdo rje ḥchaṅ du ma ḥdus pa cuṅ zad kyaṅ med pas / bum paḥi dbaṅ gis kyaṅ / skabs ḥdir de dag la brten paḥi bskyed rim yan lag daṅ / bcas pa mthaḥ dag bsgom pa la dbaṅ źiṅ deḥi snod ruṅ du byed pa daṅ / ḥbras bu sku bźiḥi naṅ nas sprul paḥi sku ḥgrub paḥi nus pa ḥjog pa yin no /

/ gñis pa gsaṅ baḥi dbaṅ ni / dkyil ḥkhor gaṅ du ḥthob pa la ḥgaḥ źig

[5] As Dayal (*op.cit.*), p. 275, reports from the *Mahāvastu*, "the ninth and tenth *bhūmis* are named *Yauvarāja* (Installation as Crown-Prince) and *Abhiṣeka* (Coronation) respectively. But no details are given." Sthiramati in his *Sūtrālaṃkāravṛttibhāṣya* (Toh. 4034), Derge Tanjur, *Sems-tsam*, Vol. Tshi, 251a-b, compares the initiation of the tenth stage to the initiation of a king. He may well have derived material for his remarks from Vasubandhu's commentary on the *Daśabhūmi* (Toh. 3993), Derge Tanjur, *Mdo-ḥgrel*, Vol. Ṅi, 248b-5, ff. Of course, Mkhas grub rje's description shows that this attainment of the rank of Vajradhara is not equivalent to the status of a complete Buddha; the name Vajradhara here means, as so often in this literature, the seed Vajradhara, or Vajrasattva (as contrasted with the fruitional Vajradhara, or Heruka). For example, in Chapter Eight, above, in the section on protecting and blessing the site, the hierophants are said to transform themselves into wrathful deities. Tsoṅ-kha-pa sets forth in the *Sṅags rim*, 151a-5, ff., the meditative procedure, prefaced with the remark that the hierophant generates his mind for the goal of disposing it at the rank of Vajradhara, thinking, "I shall frighten the obstructing demons" (rdo rje ḥchaṅ gi go ḥphaṅ la dgod paḥi don du bgegs bskrad par byaḥo sñam du sems bskyed). The meditative sequence involves first attaining the realm of the Void. There follows the evocation of the surroundings. Then the text states, "In the center of that, one instantly becomes the Wrathful Deity Trailokyavijaya ("Victorious over the three worlds") whose other name is Hūṃkāra, the transformation of Vajrasattva's nature..." (deḥi dbus su skad cig gis raṅ ñid rdor sems kyi ṅo bo yoṅs su gyur paḥi khro bo ḥjig rten gsum rgyal miṅ gźan hūṃ mdzad ces pa...).

of the King of the Law of the Three Worlds.[5] Thus, he has been empowered in the sense of having been bestowed an especial capability of faculty in all the acts of the Hierophant, such as teaching the Tantras to others and conferring initiation.[6]

c′. *The essential nature of the flask initiations.* — When the one with keen faculties (*tīkṣṇendriya*) is conferred initiation with the individual rites of water, diadem, and so on, Bliss (*sukha*) is born in him in actuality. Resolutely combining that with the visualization of Voidness (*śūnyatā*), he operates in the knowledge of Bliss-Void (*sukha-śūnya*). Even if such [faculties] are lacking, at that time it is necessary at the very least that one arouse the conviction that Bliss has been born and be mindful of the visualization [of the Void], thus being mindful through a mental orientation of conviction that there is Bliss-Void. And for the essential nature as well as concrete fact of the Hierophant's Initiation, it is necessary at the very least that one arouse the conviction that the knowledge of Bliss-Void has been born through (a) the Bliss arising from the vivid embrace of whatever the *vidyā* contemplated and oneself as Vajradhara; and (b) mindfulness of the visualization [of the Void]. But if even that [minimum] is not present, it cannot be maintained that initiations have been attained.

Lexicons explain that all these [initiations] are preceded by use of the water of the flask; hence their name.

d′. *Their efficacy.* — Although there is no limit to the differentiation of the *maṇḍala* deities, there are practically none of them that are not comprised in the various five Families; in the three thunderbolts of Body, Speech, and Mind; or in the inseparability of those three, namely Vajradhara, master of all the Families. Hence in the present phase, even with the initiations of the flask one contemplates all the Steps of Production, and their ancillaries, that are based on those [deities]; is initiated while being a good vessel for it; and establishes the capacity for accomplishing the Nirmāṇakāya among the four Bodies in the fruitional stage.

2′. *The secret initiation.* — Some persons hold the view that the *maṇ-*

---

[6] The *Sṅags rim*, 265b-1, ff. points out that the hierophant is empowered to teach the lower Tantras as well the Steps of Production of the Anuttara Tantra; this we assume is a position taken by adoption of the fourteen stages classification, for in the latter classification the hierophant has not yet been conferred the three higher initiations belonging to stages twelve through fourteen and so cannot teach them to others. Of course, one would be forced to a different position by adoption of the eleven-stage system referred to in note 2, above.

bha-gaḥi dkyil ḥkhor du ḥthob zer ba ni mi ḥthad de / bha-gar ḥthob par tshad ldan sus kyaṅ ma bśad ciṅ / dus ḥkhor las bha-gaḥi dkyil ḥkhor du dbaṅ bskur bar gsuṅs pa ni de ñid kyi sgos kyi khyad par yin la / slob ma la bha-ga bstan paḥi sgo nas dbaṅ bskur bar gsuṅs śiṅ / de ḥdra gźan gaṅ la yaṅ ma gsuṅs so /

/ de yaṅ rgyud sde daṅ tshad ldan gyi gźuṅ las dṅos kyi rig ma las rgya la brten nas dbaṅ bskur bar bśad pa ni bla med kyi ched du bya baḥi gdul bya rin po che lta buḥi dbaṅ du mdzad pa yin pas / de la ni bla ma las rgya brten paḥi mtshan ñid tshaṅ bas dkyil ḥkhor paḥi lha thams cad dmigs pas spyan draṅs pa raṅ gi lus la bcug nas rig ma daṅ sñoms pa bźugs pas chags pa chen poḥi mes źu ba thig leḥi ṅo bor gyur pa yum gyi padmar phab pa daṅ yum gyi khams dmar po gñis ḥdres pa la kun rdzob byaṅ chub sems kyi dkyil ḥkhor źes tha sñad byas pa der ḥthob bo /

/ bskur tshul ni / yab yum gyi khams dkar dmar yum gyi pa-dma nas yab yum gyi mtheb srin gyis blaṅs te / raṅ gi lce thog tu bźag pas so /

/ ṅo bo ni khams de mgrin par sleb pa na / bla ma yab yum gyis bde stoṅ sbyar baḥi rten yin pa daṅ / lha thams cad bźu baḥi ṅo bo yin pas bde ba khyad par can dṅos su skyed nus śiṅ deḥi tshe lta baḥi rgyas btab paḥi bde stoṅ gi ye śes yin la /

/ da ltaḥi dus su ḥaṅ bla ma daṅ ye rgya sñoms ḥjug byas par mos paḥi sgo nas khams dkar dmar gyi ṅo bor bskyed paḥi bdud rtsi lce la bźag paḥi tshe na dbaṅ po rno ba la bde ba dṅos su skye ba srid ciṅ de

[7] *Sṅags rim*, 118b-5, 6, says: "When one speaks of initiation in the three *maṇḍalas*, which are the two *bodhicitta-maṇḍalas* — because *bodhicitta* is both absolute (*paramārtha*) and relative (*saṃvṛti*) — plus the *bhaga-maṇḍala*, that means the phases of the three higher initiations" (byaṅ chub sems la don dam daṅ kun rdzob byaṅ chub sems kyi dkyil ḥkhor gñis daṅ / bha-gaḥi dkyil ḥkhor gsum du dbaṅ bskur ba gsuṅs pa ni dbaṅ goṅ ma gsum gyi skabs yin gyi). Since Mkhas grub rje now says that the secret initiation is not held in the *bhaga-maṇḍala* and subsequently says that the insight-knowledge initiation is attained in the *bhaga-maṇḍala*, it follows that the secret initiation is attained in the relative *bodhicitta-maṇḍala* and the fourth initiation in the absolute *bodhicitta-maṇḍala*. The former of these conclusions is borne out by Mkhas grub rje's discussion of the secret initiation. Tsoṅ-kha-pa writes in his *Don gsal* (Toh. 5290), Vol. Cha, 52a: "Besides, the *maṇḍala* of that *bhaga* and the *maṇḍala* of *bodhicitta* both are of the varieties 'relative' and 'absolute'" (yaṅ na bha-ga ñid deḥi dkyil ḥkhor daṅ byaṅ chub kyi sems kyi dkyil ḥkhor la kun rdzob daṅ don dam pa gñis su byaḥo). Since the *bhaga* is also of two kinds, one may wonder which *bhaga* is meant in the case of the three higher initiations, in particular the insight-knowledge initiation. Tsoṅ-kha-pa writes in his *Bźis źus* (Toh. 5285), Vol. Ca, 42b-5, f.: "Furthermore, of the two kinds of *bhaga-maṇḍala* — the *bhaga-maṇḍala* in which the third initiation is attained is just the *bhaga* of the *vidyā*, and the *bhaga-maṇḍala* different from that is the *maṇḍala* of residence and residents generated in the *bhaga* of the 'Mother'. The *dharmodaya* ("source of natures") is explained by the commentary to be the *maṇḍala* generated within the *bhaga* shape [i.e. triangle] and is a *bhaga-maṇḍala*" (de lta naḥaṅ

ḍala in which the initiation is obtained is a *bhaga-maṇḍala.*[7] This is untenable, for the authoritative writers do not explain it as obtained in the *bhaga*. It is true that according to the *Kālacakra*, initiation is obtained in a *bhaga-maṇḍala*, but this is a special feature of that [Tantra], which sets forth the initiation of the disciple by way of displaying to him the *bhaga*, and such a thing is not set forth in other [Tantras].

Although it is stated in the Tantras and authoritative texts that there is an initiation based on the Action Seal (*karma-mudrā*) of a concrete "wisdom" (*vidyā*), this means the initiation of the "jewel-like" individual among the candidates for the high goal of the Anuttara[-tantra]. Here, the *guru*, with complete characteristics for recourse to the Action Seal, with visualization of all the gods of the *maṇḍala*, invites them and draws them into his own body. Then he unites with the *vidyā*; and when the substance of the drop [?semen] (*bindurūpabhūta*), molten by the fire of great passion, falls into the "lotus" (*padma*) of the "Mother" (*yum*) and mixes with the red element (*dhātu*) of the "Mother", he achieves there what is referred to as "relative *bodhicitta-maṇḍala*".

The procedure of conferring the initiation is as follows: the red-and-white element of the "Father-Mother" union are taken from the "lotus" of the Mother with the ring fingers of the "Father-Mother" and placed on the tip of their own tongue(s).

As to the essential nature [of the initiation], when that element reaches the throat, the *guru*, by reason of being the basis for the combination of Bliss and the Void by way of "Father-Mother" union, and by reason of being the molten nature of all the deities, is able to produce concretely a special Bliss and at that time executes the seal of the visualization [of the Void], so he has the knowledge of Bliss-Void.

Nowadays, a person with keen faculties has Bliss produced concretely through a conviction that the *guru* and the "Knowledge Seal" (*jñāna-mudrā*) have united at the time of placing on the tongue the "ambrosia" (*amṛta*) generated into the essential nature of the red-and-white element. And even if a person does not have such faculties, he certainly must

---

bha-gaḥi dkyil ḥkhor la gñis las / dbaṅ gsum pa gaṅ du thob paḥi bha-gaḥi dkyil ḥkhor ni rig maḥi bha-ga ñid la / de las gźan paḥi bha-gaḥi dkyil ḥkhor ni yum gyi bha-gar bskyed paḥi rten daṅ brten paḥi dkyil ḥkhor ro / chos ḥbyuṅ bha-gaḥi rnam pa can gyi dbus su bskyed paḥi dkyil ḥkhor la / bha-gaḥi dkyil ḥkhor ro źes ḥgrel pas bśad do). For this second kind of *bhaga*, the absolute kind, see D. L. Snellgrove, *The Hevajra Tantra*, Part I (London, 1959), p. 73. The first kind of *bhaga*, the relative kind, means the *bhagas* belonging to the *vidyās*, who are Locanā and so on; hence, the *cakras* in the body.

lta min na ḥaṅ bde ba skyes paḥi mos pa byas pa dan lta ba sbyar ba ṅes par dgos so /

/ gaṅ daṅ sñoms par ḥjug paḥi las rgya daṅ ye rgyaḥi sgra bśad na skye ba sṅa maḥi las kyis bud med kyi lus su ḥphaṅs śiṅ der grub pas las rgya źes daṅ / yan lag gis phan tshun ḥkhyud pa sogs kyi las rnams raṅ gis bsgoms pa la ltos mi dgos par phyag rgya de ñid kyis nus pas na las rgya źes byaḥo / da lta spyi la yoṅs su grags paḥi ye rgyaḥi sgra bśad ni / dṅos gnas la bud med du grub pa med kyaṅ / ye śes ni raṅ gi tiṅ ṅe ḥdzin yin pa / de rgyas śiṅ bskyed paḥi phyag rgya yin pas na ye rgya źes byaḥo /

/ byed las ni / bla ma yab yum gyi byaṅ sems dṅos sam / der mos pa byas paḥi bdud rtsi de ñid myaṅs pas raṅ gi rtsaḥi gnas rnams su sleb pa na / de na gnas paḥi khams skar dmar daṅ / ṅag gi rtsa ba rluṅ byin gyis brlabs śiṅ las ruṅ du byas pa la brten nas rdzogs rim kyi lus dben daṅ ṅag dben sems dben kun rdzob sgyu maḥi rdzogs rim rnams bsgom pa la dbaṅ bar byas śiṅ / deḥi snod ruṅ du bya baḥi sgo nas lus la gnad du bsnun nas bsgoms pas / lam dus su dhū-tīḥi naṅ du rluṅ źugs gnas thim gsum byas pa las stoṅ pa bźi skye ba daṅ / deḥi stobs kyis rluṅ sems tsam las grub paḥi sgyu maḥi lus grub nas mthar ḥbras bu ṅag gi rtsa ba rluṅ dag paḥi loṅs spyod rdzogs paḥi sku ḥgrub paḥi nus pa ḥjog pa yin no /

/ sgra bśad pa ni / rdzas gsaṅ ba myaṅs pa las ḥthob paḥi dbaṅ yin pas na de skad ces byaḥo /

/ gsum pa śes rab ye śes kyi dbaṅ la / dkyil ḥkhor gaṅ du ḥthob pa ni bla ma daṅ / slob ma daṅ / rig ma rgyud sde nas gsuṅs pa ltar gyi thun moṅ baḥi lam la myoṅ ba thon ciṅ sṅags kyis rgyud byin gyis brlabs pa / ḥdod paḥi sgyu rtsal drug cu la mkhas pa la sogs pa / mtshan ñid rnams tshaṅ baḥi slob dpon sogs kyi dbaṅ du byas na / bla mas gsaṅ dbaṅ gi dus su sñoms ḥjug byas paḥi rig ma de ḥam de daṅ ḥdra ba gaṅ yaṅ ruṅ ba slob ma la gnaṅ źiṅ / slob dpon gyis brda legs par sprad nas dri ba dri lan

[8] The *ṣaḍaṅga-yoga* of the Steps of Completion are these six: *pratyāhāra*, *dhyāna*, *prāṇāyāma*, *dhāraṇā*, *anusmṛti*, and *samādhi*. Tsoṅ-kha-pa's *Mthaḥ gcod* (Toh. 5284), Vol. Ca, 116a-4, ff., gives the views of his own school (*raṅ gi lugs*). Here we find that the arcane state of body is prevalent in both *pratyāhāra* and *dhyāna*, the arcane state of speech in *prāṇāyāma*, the arcane state of mind in *dhāraṇā*. (So much for the efficacy of the secret initiation: the arcane state of mind means the four voids in the forward direction). Furthermore, the reverse order of the four voids takes place in *anusmṛti* (which concerns the insight-knowledge initiation); and the "coupling" (*yuganaddha*) occurs in the last *aṅga-samādhi* (treated in the discussion of the fourth initiation).

[9] For the sixty-four *kalā* of the *Kāma-sūtra*, see Louis Renou and Jean Filliozat, *L'Inde Classique* (Paris, 1953), II, appendix 11 (pp. 755-6). However, Kloṅ rdol bla

arouse the conviction that Bliss has been born and combine that with visualization [of the Void].

In explanation of the "Action Seal" and the "Knowledge Seal" with which one enters union — by reason of acts (*karma*) of former lives, one flings himself on the body of a woman and there realizes, hence "the Action Seal"; and such actions as the mutual embrace with limbs do not require any contemplation by oneself — only the seal itself (*or* herself) is necessary, hence "the Action Seal". Nowadays, the general explanation of the expression 'renowned Knowledge Seal' is as follows: one does not realize in a concrete place, i.e. the woman. However, Knowledge is one's own *samādhi.* Being the seal which expands and generates that, it is called "Knowledge Seal".

As to the efficacy, — by reason of the *guru*'s tasting that "ambrosia" (*amṛta*) — either the actual *bodhicitta* of the "Father-Mother" union, or in conviction that it is there — it reaches the locations of his 'veins' (*nāḍī*) and blesses (i.e. empowers) the red-and-white element and the wind of the speech 'vein' located there. Taking recourse to the serviceability, he contemplates and controls the *saṃvṛti-māyā* Steps of Comp[etion, which are the arcane state of body, of speech, and of mind [phases] of the Steps of Completion.[8] Also, through the "gate" of being a fit vessel for that, he contemplates in piercing the "centers" [i.e. lotus or *cakra* centers] of the body. Thus, in the time of the path, he makes the wind enter, dwell, and dissolve in the "middle vein" (*avadhūtī*); from that the four Voids are produced; and through their power he accomplishes the "illusory body" (*māyā-deha*) that is accomplished from the Winds and Mind-only. Thereby he establishes the capacity of accomplishing ultimately the fruit, which is the Saṃbhogakāya of the pure wind of the speech "vein".

Lexicons say it is called "secret" (*guhya*) because it is the initiation obtained from tasting the secret substance.

3′. *The insight-knowledge initiation. — Maṇḍala in which it is obtained.* The *guru*, disciple, and *vidyā*, having emerged from experiencing the common path (*sādhāraṇa-mārga*) as set forth in the Tantras, bless (i.e. energize) their stream of consciousness (**saṃtāna*, *tantra*) with incantations. They are governed by such hierophants as have in full measure the characteristics of skill in the sixty arts of *kāma*.[9] The *guru* offers to the disciple that *vidyā* with whom he had entered in union at the time of the secret initiation, or a similar *vidyā* as appropriate. The hierophant

---

ma, Section Ma, 3b-2, makes a distinction between the sixty-four *kalā* and the sixty-four *kāma-kalā*. The latter he discusses, *ibid.*, 4b-4, ff.

sogs ji lta ba bźin byas te sñoms par źugs paḥi tshe dgaḥ bźi skyes pa las ḥthob pas na bha-gaḥi dkyil ḥkhor du ḥthob pa yin no /

/ ṅo bo ni sñoms par źugs pa las dhūtīr rluṅ źugs pa la brten nas khams dkar po źu ba spyi bo nas mgrin par sleb pa na dgaḥ ba daṅ / de nas sñiṅ kar sleb pa na mchog dgaḥ daṅ / de nas lte bar sleb pa na khyad par gyi dgaḥ ba daṅ / de nas rdo rjeḥi nor buḥi rtser sleb pa na phyir mi ḥpho baḥi man ṅag gis bzuṅ nas deḥi tshe lhan cig skyes dgaḥi ye śes skyes pa na de daṅ stoṅ pa ñid sbyar baḥi bde stoṅ gi ye śes dbaṅ po rnon po la dbaṅ dus su skyes pa ḥoṅ yaṅ / de ni rim gñis kyi naṅ nas skabs gaṅ du ḥjog na rdzogs rim du gźag dgos so / de yaṅ dhū-tīḥi naṅ nas babs paḥi khams yin na lhan skyes ma mtshon par phyir ḥpho ba mi srid ciṅ skabs ḥdiḥi dgaḥ bźi la ni yas babs min pa mas brtan mi ḥoṅ ṅo / deḥi skabs kyi dgaḥ bźi daṅ stoṅ ñid sbyor ba ni dṅos so /

/ da lta de ḥdra baḥi dpon slob rig ma daṅ bcas pa bśad pa bźin gyi mtshan ñid tshaṅ ba mi ḥoṅ bas / bla mas gnaṅ bar mos paḥi ye rgya daṅ / dri ba sogs byed tshul brda ḥphrod par byas la / raṅ daṅ rig ma gñis kyi lus ḥdod lha yab yum du yid ṅor gsal bźin paḥi ṅaṅ nas sñoms ḥjug byas par bsams pas dbaṅ po rnon po la bde ba dṅos su skyes pa ḥoṅ la / dṅos su ma skyes na ḥaṅ deḥi tshe goṅ ltar dgaḥ bźi skyes paḥi mos pa brtan po daṅ lta ba dran paḥi stoṅ ñid sbyar baḥi sgo nas / bde stoṅ skyes so sñam paḥi mos pa yid byed brtan po ma mthaḥ yaṅ dgos kyi / de tsam yaṅ ma byuṅ na śes rab ye śes kyi dbaṅ thob par ḥjog mi nus so /

/ byed las ni / snaṅ ba thams cad bde stoṅ gi ṅo bor ḥchar baḥi gegs kyi dri ma sbyaṅs nas / de ḥchar baḥi nus pa daṅ / rim pa bźi paḥi ḥod

10 *Sṅags rim*, 436b-5, when listing the *cakras* along the central channel of the body, having 'petals' or 'veins' in the numbers of 4 (crown of head), 32 (middle of forehead), 16 (neck), 8 (heart), 64 (navel), 32 (sacral place), and 8 (tip of the gem), refers to these centers as 'lotus-like', 'bhaga-like', and '*cakra*-like' (pad-ma ñid daṅ bha-ga ñid daṅ ḥkhor lo ñid). However, the initiation concerns only the four centers at the neck, heart, navel, and base of spine — the locations of the four *vidyās* or goddesses — and the combination of the four joys with the four voids.

offers explanations and exact replies to questions, after which [the disciple] attains [the initiation] through generation of the four joys. Hence he attains it in the *bhaga-maṇḍala*.[10]

Intrinsic nature of the initiation. After [the candidate's] entering into union, when he takes recourse to drawing the wind into the "middle vein," the melted white element reaches the neck from the middle of the forehead, at which time there is "joy" (*ānanda*). After that, it reaches the heart, at which time there is "super joy" (*parama-ānanda*). After that, it reaches the navel, at which time there is "extraordinary joy" (*virama-ānanda*). After that, it reaches the tip of the thunderbolt gem, and by his abiding by the precept to not allow it to be emitted, at that time there is produced the knowledge of "together-born joy" (*sahaja-ānanda*). The knowledge of Bliss-Void which combines that [joy] with Voidness is born in the one with keen faculties at the time of the initiation. Again, in which phase of the two series of Steps (*krama*) is it laid down? It must be laid down in the Steps of Completion. Does the element descend from within the "central vein"? When the "together-born [joy]" does not manifest, there is no possibility of emission; and in the four joys of this phase, there is no descent from above and no retention from below. The main thing is the combination of the four joys of that phase with the Voidness.

Nowadays, we do not find such hierophants, neophytes, along with a *vidyā*, that possess the complete characteristics as have been set forth. Hence, the *guru* conveys the method of constructing the "Knowledge Seal" which [the disciple] is convinced he grants, method of the questions, and so on. [The disciple] imagines he has been made to enter into union on account of the vividness in his mind that the body of himself and the *vidyā* is the desire god (*kāma-deva*) in the sense of the "Father-Mother" union. Thereby, in the one with keen faculties, bliss is produced concretely. Even if it is not produced concretely, at that time he must at the very least be steadfast in orienting the mind to the conviction that Bliss-Void has been produced, by way of combining a steadfastness of conviction that the four joys, as previously set forth, have arisen, with the Voidness remembered as the visualization [of the Void]. If not even that is obtained, one has no capacity to establish the attainment of the Insight-knowledge initiation.

The efficacy. It purifies all the appearances constituting defilements that hinder the awakening to the essential nature of Bliss-Void; it has the capacity for that awakening; it makes one a fit vessel for contemplating the Clear Light of the fourth step (*krama*); and it deposits an

gsal bsgom paḥi snod ruṅ du byas / ḥbras bu źu ba de lhan skyes chos sku ḥgrub paḥi lag rjes ḥjog pa yin no /

/ bźi pa tshig dbaṅ ni / dṅos su da lta skye ba med kyaṅ / snod ruṅ gis dbaṅ bźi bar ḥgyur ba ni / dbaṅ bźi rdzogs par bskur baḥi skabs su / gsum pa mos pa tshun chad kyis ṅes paḥi tshe na de ñid dper byas te des mtshon paḥi zuṅ ḥjug gi go ba slob ma la brda sprad nas de la go ba chags pa la tshig dbaṅ thob par ḥjog la /

/ deḥi tshul ni / bźi pa de yaṅ de bźin te / źes pas dbaṅ gsum paḥi dus su raṅ daṅ rig ma gñis kyi lus ḥdod lha yab yum du dṅos gnas la grub pa med kyaṅ / yid ṅor gsal bźin paḥi ṅaṅ nas sems bde stoṅ dpeḥi ḥod gsal dus mñam du ḥbyuṅ ba bźin du / lam dus su lus la gnad du bsnun nas bsgoms pa la brten nas rim pa bźi paḥi mthar lus śin tu phra baḥi rluṅ sems tsam las grub paḥi ḥjaḥ lus rdo rjeḥi skur dṅos su soṅ ba daṅ / sems stoṅ ñid mṅon sum du rtogs paḥi don gyi ḥod gsal du soṅ ba gñis dus mñam du gyur pa nas de ḥdra baḥi sku daṅ thugs ṅo bo gcig paḥi zuṅ ḥjug thob pa ni slob paḥi zuṅ ḥug ces pa daṅ / deḥi rigs ḥdraḥi rgyun goms pa las ḥbras bu de daṅ rnam pa mthun paḥi mi slob paḥi zuṅ ḥjug kha sbyor yan lag bdun ldan gyi go ḥphaṅ sgrub tshul la ṅo sprod pa yin no /

/ des na de ltar dbaṅ bźi bskur ba las sku bźiḥi sa bon thebs paḥi bskur tshul daṅ ḥthob tshul śin tu gal cheḥo /

/ dbaṅ don lam gyi rim par bsgrigs nas ñams su blaṅs paḥi bla med kyi lam ni bskyed rdzogs gñis su ṅes la / de la thog mar bskyed rim bsgoms

[11] *Guhyasamāja-tantra*, 160.11-13, including: *caturthaṃ tat punas tathā.*

imprint that accomplishes, in the fruitional fusing, the "together-born" Dharmakāya.

4′. *The initiation of the syllable* (*akṣara-abhiṣeka*). — Although nowadays it is not produced concretely, for the fit vessel, the occurrence of the fourth initiation is as follows: In the phase of completely conferring the fourth initiation, when one is certified by not less than conviction of the third one, that very [third one] is made the example, as [the *guru*] imparts to the disciple an understanding of the "coupling" (*yuganaddha*) symbolized thereby. When understanding has been aroused in him, it establishes the attainment of the initiation of the syllable.

As to its method, it is said, "The fourth is just the same."[11] In illustration: at the time of the third initiation, even when there was no realization in a concrete place that the body of oneself and the *vidya* was the desire god in the sense of the "Father-Mother" union, still, on account of the vividness in the mind, the mind experienced bliss-void and simultaneously the symbolic Clear-Light. [Analogically,] at the limit of the fourth step, after one has taken recourse to the contemplation in the time of the path involved with piercing the "centers" in the body — his body proceeds concretely as a diamond body which is a rainbow body produced from the very subtle wind and mind-only, and simultaneously his mind proceeds in the Clear Light of the [Absolute] Object, which comprehends Voidness in immediacy. The attainment in that way of the consubstantial "coupling" of body and mind is called "coupling in the realm of learning" (*śaikṣa-yuganaddha*). The fruit, or equivalent, resulting from the continous contemplation of the affiliation of that ["coupling"] is explained as the "coupling beyond learning" (*aśaikṣa-yuganaddha*) or the means of accomplishing the rank of 'having the seven members of the *saṃpuṭa*'.

[II′. *Consecration ritual conferring initiation on a deity*]
(Not discussed.)

[(2) THE RELATION BETWEEN STEPS AND INITIATIONS ALONG THE PATH]

Now, of utmost importance are the methods of initiating that way and the methods of obtaining the four Bodies, the seeds of which are cast by the four initiations.

When we correlate the meaning of initiation to steps of the path, certainly the incomparable path we must take to heart is [both the] Steps of Production (*utpatti-krama*) and Steps of Completion (*niṣpanna-*

nas / des rgyud smin par byas te rdzogs rim bsgom dgos kyi / de lta min par rim pa gñis pa bsgoms kyaṅ bśad pa ltar mi skye bas thog mar bskyed rim dgos śiṅ deḥi snod ruṅ du bya baḥi phyir du daṅ por bum dbaṅ bskur dgos pa yin la /

/ de ltar rim pa daṅ pos rgyud smin par byas te de nas rim pa gñis pa bsgom dgos pas / de la thog mar lus dben daṅ ṅag dben sogs kyis ro rkyaṅ gi rluṅ rnams dhū-tīr źugs gnas thim gsum byas paḥi lag rjes la snaṅ mched thob gsum dpeḥi ḥod gsal daṅ bcas paḥi sems dben ḥdren la / de las mthar rluṅ sems tsam las grub paḥi ma dag paḥi sgyu lus ḥgrub ste de rnams rim can du skye bas las de rnams bsgom paḥi snod ruṅ du bya baḥi phyir du deḥi rjes su gsaṅ dbaṅ bskur ba yin no /

/ de nas ma dag paḥi sgyu lus de ñid ril ḥdzin daṅ rjes gźig gi bsam gtan gñis kyis ḥod gsal du bcug nas dag par byas pa las stoṅ ñid mṅon sum du rtogs paḥi don gyi ḥod gsal mtshan ñid pa skye bar ḥgyur bas / deḥi snod ruṅ du byed paḥi dbaṅ gsum pa gsaṅ gi rjes su bskur ba yin no /

/ don gyi ḥod gsal de las lugs ldog tu ldaṅ ba na sku dag paḥi sgyu maḥi sku daṅ thugs don gyi ḥod gsal gñis ṅo bo gcig paḥi slob paḥi zuṅ ḥjug ḥthob la / deḥi rgyun goms pa las mi slob maḥi zuṅ ḥjug kha sbyor yan lag bdun ldan gyi go ḥphaṅ mṅon du byed pas deḥi snod ruṅ du byed paḥi dbaṅ bźi pa gsum paḥi rjes su bskur ba yin no / des na thob bya de las mthar thug pa med pas dbaṅ bźi pa las goṅ na dbaṅ gźan med do /

/ dbaṅ gi graṅs daṅ go rims der ṅes pa bźin du lam gyi graṅs daṅ go rims kyaṅ ji ltar bśad pa de ltar ṅes pas / dbaṅ bskur byed pa daṅ / raṅ ñid bdag ḥjug sogs byed nahaṅ lam de lta buḥi ched du byed dgos kyi / go ba dmigs phyed pa gal cheḥo /

[12] These four lights are elsewhere referred to as the four voids.

[13] Tsoṅ-kha-pa, *Mthaḥ gcod* (*op. cit.*), 59a-3, f., explains these two *dhyānas* on the basis of Nāgārjuna's *Pañcakrama*. "Contraction" means drawing all the winds from the head downwards and from the feet upwards into the heart; and "expansion" means that the *yogin* then enters the Clear Light.

krama or *saṃpanna-krama*). Among those, one first contemplates the Steps of Production. Having thereby matured the stream of consciousness, one must contemplate the Steps of Completion. If one did otherwise, even though he contemplate the Steps of Completion there would be no origination as explained. Therefore, the Steps of Production are required first; and in order to be a fit vessel for that, first the Initiation of the Flask must be conferred.

Having in that way matured the stream of consciousness with the first Steps, one must contemplate the second ones. For the latter, there must be produced in sequence, (a) first, the imprint, by means of the arcane body (*kāya-viveka*) and arcane speech (*vāg-viveka*), of making the winds of the right "vein" (*rasanā*) and left "vein" (*lalanā*) enter, dwell, and dissolve in the central "vein" (*avadhūtī*); (b) guidance of the arcane mind (*citta-viveka*) through light (*āloka*), spread of light (*ālokābhāsa*), and culmination of light (*ālokopalabdhi*), together with the symbolic Clear Light;[12] (c) at their limit, accomplishment of the impure illusory body produced from the winds and mind-only. In order to render one a fit vessel for contemplating those acts, after that [flask initiation] the secret initiation is conferred.

Thereupon, by means of the two *dhyānas*, "contraction" (*piṇḍagrāha*) and "expansion" (*anubheda*),[13] that impure illusory body is purified by being made to enter the Clear Light, and there arises the characteristic of the Clear Light of the [Absolute] Object, which comprehends Voidness in immediacy. The third initiation which renders one a fit vessel for that is conferred subsequently to the secret initiation.

On proceeding in the "backward" (*pratiloma*) order from that Clear Light of the [Absolute] Object, one achieves the "coupling in the realm of learning" which consubstantiates the body — the purified illusory body, and the mind — the Clear Light of the [Absolute] Object. From continuous contemplation of that ["coupling"], one brings about directly the "coupling beyond learning", which is the rank where one has the seven members of the *saṃpuṭa*. Hence the fourth initiation, which renders one a fit vessel for that, is conferred subsequently to the third. As that goal (i.e. the coupling beyond learning) cannot be surpassed, neither is there another initiation beyond the fourth initiation.

As the number and succession of initiations is determined *supra*, so the number and succession of paths is determined as explained. Therefore, when bestowing initiation or when personally entering [the *maṇḍala*], it is necessary to conform to those paths. It is very important to understand this and bear it in mind.

/ dam tshig daṅ sdom paḥi rnam gźag ni śin tu yaṅ gal che bas /

/ dbaṅ mtshan ñid pa thob ma thag nas rtsa ltuṅ bcu bźi daṅ sbom po brgyad la sogs paḥi rtsa ba daṅ yan lag gi ltuṅ ba rnams legs par ṅes par byas te / dran śes rgyun ldan du bsten nas rtsa ltuṅ la srog bsdos byed ciṅ sbom po sogs yan lag gi ltuṅ ba rnams kyis gos naḥaṅ raṅ raṅ gi phyir bcos kyis legs par bcos nas źag tu mi ḥgrogs par byaḥo /

/ gaṅ dag bum dbaṅ ma bskur bar dbaṅ goṅ ma bskur bar byed pa ni mi ḥthad de / dkyil ḥkhor du ma bcug pa daṅ lha ṅo ma bstan par dbaṅ gaṅ ma bskur bas ni dbaṅ gaṅ yaṅ thob paḥi go mi chod paḥi phyir ro / de ltar ma byas par gsaṅ dbaṅ bskur ba na slob dpon gyi rgyud la sṅags sdom yod na rtsa ltuṅ ḥbyuṅ źiṅ sdom pa gtoṅ bas de ḥdra baḥi dbaṅ bskur baḥi slob dpon gyis sṅags kyi lam bsgoms nas dṅos grub thob kyaṅ dmyal bar skye bar gsuṅs pas / gnas ḥdi la gzab par byaḥo /

/ yaṅ gcig dus ḥkhor gyi lugs la ḥaṅ dbaṅ bdun med par mchog dbaṅ tsam bskur nas ḥkhrid ḥbogs pa yod do / de ni goṅ du bśad pa ltar / ri bo dag kyaṅ ma smin mi la gsaṅ ba sbyin las so / źes gsuṅs pa ltar gyi rtsa ltuṅ ḥbyuṅ bas / raṅ gźan thams cad phuṅ bar ḥgyur źiṅ saṅs rgyas kyi bstan pa la de las gnod pa med do / dus ḥkhor lo ni ṅes par rdul tshon gyi dkyil ḥkhor du dbaṅ bskur dgos te / dkyil ḥkhor bźeṅs nas

[14] The following list of the fourteen is based on Aśvaghoṣa's *Mūlāpattisaṃgraha* (Toh. 2478), and Sanskrit for major part as edited by Sylvain Lévi and translated, *Journal Asiatique*, Oct.-Dec., 1929, pp. 266-7; using also Tsoṅ-kha-pa's *Gsaṅ sṅags kyi tshul khrims kyi rnam bśad, Dṅos grub kyi sñe ma* (Toh. 5270), in Vol. Ka of his Collected Works.

1. To disparage one's master (*ācārya*).
2. To transgress the directives (*ājñā*) [i.e. the three vows of the Sugata].
3. To express anger toward 'diamond brothers' (*vajrajñātṛ*) [i.e. fellow initiates of a single master].
4. To abandon love (*maitrī*) of the sentient beings.
5. To abandon the Mind of Enlightenment (*bodhicitta*).
6. To disparage the Doctrine (*dharma*) of one's own [i.e. *mantra*] or of another's [i.e. *prajñā-pāramitā*] tenets (*siddhānta*).
7. To tell the secrets (*guhya*) to immature [i.e. uninitiated] persons.
8. To abuse the five *skandhas* for their nature belongs to the five Buddhas [such abuse including all injury, mortification, and suppression].
9. To have reservations concerning the natures (*dharma*) intrinsically pure.
10. To have love (*maitrī*) for the wicked (*duṣṭa*) [especially those who damage and destroy the Doctrine; but one should have compassion (*karuṇā*) for them].
11. To apply discursive thought (*kalpana*) to the wordless natures.
12. To have belittling thoughts (*cittadūṣaṇa*) toward the believers (*śrāddhasattva*).
13. To not adhere to the pledges (*samaya*) in the way they were taken.
14. To disparage women, who are the source of insight (*prajñā-svabhāva*) ['insight' here sometimes meaning the knowledge of great bliss (*mahāsukha*)].

[15] For the eight gross or grave transgressions, see Lévi (*op. cit.*), pp. 267-8; the Tibetan blockprint *Byaṅ sems daṅ rig pa ḥdzin paḥi phyir bcos / sdom pa ñi śu pa / byaṅ sems kyi rtsa ltuṅ bsdus paḥi tshigs su bcad pa / rtsa ltuṅ bcu bźi pa / sbom po*

[(3) VOWS AND PLEDGES]

An exposition of pledges (*samaya*) and vows (*saṃvara*) is also of utmost importance.

Immediately after one obtains the characteristic of initiation, [that initiate] must be made certain [in his mind] about the fundamental and ancillary transgressions, namely, the fourteen fundamental transgressions (*mūlāpatti*),[14] the eight gross transgressions (*sthūlāpatti*),[15] and so on. Taking his stand on constant mindfulness and awareness [of the pledges and vows], he jeopardizes his life against the fundamental transgressions, and should he be defiled by any of the ancillary transgressions, such as the gross ones, he will make amends by expiating each single one, and not associate with them for a day.

It is not right to confer the [three] higher initiations upon one who has not been conferred the initiation of the flask; and the one who has not been introduced into the *maṇḍala* and has not faced the deities should not be conferred any initiation, because the attainment of any initiation would be indecisive [in his case]. Otherwise, [the scriptures] say, even though the hierophant who confers the secret initiation has the *mantra* vow in his stream of consciousness, a fundamental transgression occurs and he throws away the vow, so that even though a hierophant who so initiates were to contemplate the *mantra*-path and obtain *siddhi*, he would be reborn in hell. Hence, one must be careful in this matter.

Again there are some who teach that in the *Kālacakra* school one is conferred only the highest initiation and not the seven [lower] initiations. As is explained above, that is a fundamental transgression, the one called 'mountains', namely, "To divulge the secret(s) to an immature person."[16] Indeed, it is a calamity for themselves and others; there is no greater injury to the teaching of the Buddha than that. The *Kālacakra* certainly requires an initiation in the *maṇḍala* of powdered colors: its

---

brgyad pa daṅ bcas paḥi bslab bya mdor bsdus, has this list of eight: 1. to procure (goods) by the power of insight; 2. to procure by his power of 'ambrosia' (*amṛta*); 3. to not maintain secrecy toward the unfit vessel; 4. to dispute in an assembly; 5. to teach heterodox doctrines to the faithful; 6. to stay seven days among the *śrāvakas*; 7. to falsely pride himself on *yoga*; 8. to teach the Doctrine to a non-believer.

16 Certain texts assign symbolical words to represent numbers; this procedure is useful in forming *ślokas*, for example, in works on astrology. The word 'mountains' is used for the seventh of the fundamental transgressions because there are seven mountains in traditional Indian mythology. Similarly, the word 'Manu' is used for the fourteenth one, because there are fourteen Manus.

sbyin par bya / źes paḥi ḥbrel par / rdul tshon gyi dkyil ḥkhor du dbaṅ bskur bar bya yi / ras bris sogs su ni ma yin no / źes gsuṅs so /

/ de ltar dbaṅ mtshan ñid tshaṅ ba thob nas dam tshig daṅ sdom pa tshul bźin du bsruṅ dgos la / de yaṅ sbom po sogs kyi ñes pa chuṅ ṅus gos na de ma thag bśags par bya źiṅ / rtsa ltuṅ byuṅ na bdag ḥjug sogs kyi sgo nas slar sor chud par byaḥo / gtso bor rtsa ltuṅ gis gtan nas ma gos par bya dgos te / ḥdul baḥi pham pa bźi cig car byuṅ ba las kyaṅ sṅags kyi rtsa ltuṅ byuṅ ba rnam smin cheḥo / de ltar bsgrims nas rtsa ltuṅ gis gtan nas ma gos na tshe ḥdir lam ma bsgoms kyaṅ skye ba phyi ma rnams su bśes gñen dam pas rjes su bzuṅ ste lam ñams su len du ḥoṅ bas khyab pa rten ḥbrel gyi chos ñid yin pas skye ba bdun nas bcu drug tshun la ḥtshaṅ rgya bas khyab bo /

/ de ltar dam tshig daṅ sdom pa tshul bźin du bsruṅ baḥi gaṅ zag gis ñams su blaṅ baḥi lam la bskyed rdzogs gñis su ṅes paḥi rgyu mtshan gyis / bskyed rim yan lag daṅ bcas pa bsgoms pas smin byed kyi lam cha tshaṅ bar ḥgyur la / de nas rdzogs rim yan lag daṅ bcas pa bsgoms pas grol byed kyi lam cha tshaṅ bar ḥgyur źiṅ / theg chen gyi slob paḥi lam thams cad smin byed kyi lam daṅ grol byed kyi lam gñis su ḥdus paḥi phyir / bskyed rim mtshan ñid pa bsgom pa sṅon du btaṅ nas rdzogs rim bsgom par byed dgos pas na go rim yaṅ de ltar ṅes te / bskyed rim gyis rgyud smin par ma byas na rdzogs rim gyis rgyud grol bar mi ḥgyur baḥi phyir /

/ kha cig bskyed rim gyis skye ba sbyoṅ źiṅ rdzogs rim gyis ḥchi ba sbyoṅ bas bskyed rdzogs gñis sbyaṅ gźi mi gcig par smra ba daṅ / yaṅ bskyed rim gyis sgo ṅa skyes sogṣ skye gnas bźi sbyoṅ baḥi phyir / lhaḥi bskyed chog mi ḥdra ba bźi yod zer ba sogs ni bla med kyi lam bsgoms

[17] The standard Buddhist list is: (1) birth from the womb (*jarāyu-jā*), (2) birth from eggs (*aṇḍa-jā*), (3) production by warmth and moisture (*saṃsveda-jā*), and (4) spontaneous birth (*upapādukā*).

commentary on the line, "Having 'erected' a *maṇḍala*, one shall confer", states, "One shall confer the initiation in the *maṇḍala* of powdered colors, but not in those of painted cloth, and so on."

Having in that way obtained the complete characteristic of initiation, one must guard the pledges and vows according to the rules. Moreover, if one is defiled by minor faults, such as the gross ones, he must confess them immediately; and should a fundamental transgression occur, he must restore himself to purity by way of such acts as personally entering [the *maṇḍala*]. The principle thing is that one must systematically act so as not to be defiled by the fundamental transgressions. An occurrence of a fundamental transgression of the *mantra* [-path] entails greater consequence than a simultaneous occurrence of the four "defeats" of the Vinaya [vow]. Controlling oneself in that way, if one is regularly undefiled by the fundamental transgressions, even if he does not contemplate the path in this life, in subsequent lives he will be taken in hand by illustrious guides, and full of the procedures of the path he will be the true nature (*dharmatā*) of Dependent Origination (*pratītya-samutpāda*), expanding to the state of Buddhahood in from seven to sixteen lives.

[(4) STEPS OF PRODUCTION AND STEPS OF COMPLETION]

The person who in that way guards his pledges and vows according to the rules, must be certain regarding both the Steps of Production and the Steps of Completion in the path to be taken to heart. That is to say, by contemplating the Steps of Production with its ancillaries, he fulfills the portion "path of maturation" (**vipāka-mārga*); and by contemplating the Steps of Completion with its ancillaries, he fulfills the portion "path of liberation" (**vimukti-mārga*), because all paths of learning belonging to the Mahāyāna can be grouped into "path of maturation" and "path of liberation". Again, the requirement to first contemplate the characteristic of the Steps of Production, and then to contemplate the Steps of Completion, gives the definite sequence, because if the stream of consciousness is not matured by the Steps of Production, the stream of consciousness cannot be liberated by the Steps of Completion.

Some say that the Steps of Production purify birth, while the Steps of Completion purify death, so the two have a different "sphere of purification". And furthermore they assert that because the Steps of Production purify the four modes of birth,[17] which are 'birth from an egg', and so on, there are four different ways of generating deities. Such assertions are not valid: they evince complete misunderstanding of the

nas tshe gcig la saṅs rgyas ḥgrub tshul la go ba ma chags par soṅ ḥdug pas mi ḥthad ciṅ /

/ raṅ lugs la ni / bskyed rdzogs gñis kas skye ḥchi bar do gsum sbyaṅ gźir byas nas lam bgrod par byed dgos la / de yaṅ ḥjam bu gliṅ paḥi mi mṅal skyes khams drug ldan gyi dbaṅ du byas pa yin par rgya gar mkhas paḥi gźuṅ las byuṅ źiṅ / rigs pas kyaṅ bsgrub par bźed pa legs so /

/ bskyed rim źes paḥi sgra bśad ni / rtog pas btags paḥam / blos bcos śiṅ bskyed paḥi sgo nas bsgom par bya baḥi rim pa yin pas de skad ces gsuṅs śiṅ /

/ rdzogs rim ni / blos btags pa la ma ltos par raṅ grub tsam nas yod paḥi lus kyi rtsa rluṅ thig le la dmigs nas dhū-tīḥi naṅ du rluṅ źugs gnas thim gsum bya baḥi phyir bsgom par bya baḥi rim pa yin pas na rdzogs rim źes bya ba daṅ / gdod ma nas raṅ bźin gyis grub pas stoṅ paḥi stoṅ pa ñid daṅ / lus la gnad du bsnun pa las skyes paḥi bde chen gyi ye śes gñis dbyer mi phyed par bsgom par bya baḥi rim pa yin pas na / de skad ces byaḥo /

/ de la bskyed paḥi rim pa ni zur du bśad pa las śes par bya źiṅ / rdzogs rim la thog mar E Vaṃ gyi don bśad na / spyir bla med kyi rgyud sde thams cad kyi brjod byaḥi gtso bo bde stoṅ dbyer med ni E Vaṃ gyi yi ge gñis kyi mtshon don yin pas / brjod byaḥi gtso bo ni yi ge gñis kyi mtshon don du ḥdus so / de la thob bya ḥbras buḥi E Vaṃ thob byed lam gyi E Vaṃ / ḥdren byed rtags kyi E Vaṃ daṅ gsum gyi daṅ po ni /

/ E gru gsum gyis mtshon paḥi chos ḥbyuṅ gru gsum gyi naṅ du yaṅ dag par rdzogs paḥi saṅs rgyas kyi ye śes raṅ snaṅ las grub paḥi gźal yas khaṅ gdan daṅ bcas pa daṅ / Vaṃ yig gis mtshon paḥi gtso bo rdo rje ḥchaṅ ḥkhor gyi lha daṅ bcas pa ste / mdor na sṅon byuṅ gi rgyud gsuṅ paḥi dus kyi rten daṅ brten paḥi dkyil ḥkhor mtshon par byed do /

[18] In Tsoṅ-kha-pa's school, for example, as set forth in his *Don gsal* (*op. cit.*), folio 25a-b, birth is associated with the Nirmāṇakāya, death with the Dharmakāya, and the intermediate state with the Saṃbhogakāya. Hence, the Tantric procedures are set up for affiliation (*rigs ḥdra*) with the Buddha Bodies.

[19] According to *Sekoddeśaṭīkā*, 7.19-20, the six *dhātu* are earth (*pṛthivī*), water (*toya*), fire (*tejas*), wind (*vāyu*), space (*ākāśa*), and knowledge (*jñāna*).

method for accomplishing Buddhahood in one life through contemplation of the Anuttara path.

Our school teaches to walk the path, making birth, death, and the intermediate state,[18] three "spheres of purification" for both the Steps of Production and the Steps of Completion. Furthermore, according to the texts of the Indian sages, the men of Jambudvīpa who are born from a womb are put in control by having the six elements (*dhātu*),[19] so what we maintain is certified by reason.

The explanation of the expression 'Steps of Production' is as follows: It is called that because it is the steps in the contemplation to be performed through the production of figments by ideation, or constructs by the cognition (*buddhi*).

That of 'Steps of Completion' is as follows: One takes as meditative object the winds (*vāyu*) and drop (*bindu*) in the "veins" of the body (*deha*) that is only self-produced and independent of figments by the cognition. Then one contemplates so as to make the wind enter, dwell, and dissolve in the central channel (*avadhūtī*). When those are the steps, they are called 'Steps of Completion'. Furthermore, they are the steps to be contemplated for the inseparability of the Voidness of the Void (*śūnya-śūnyatā*) — because primordially accomplished by intrinsic nature, and the knowledge of great bliss born from piercing the "centers" in that body; hence they are called that.

Among them, the Steps of Production should be understood from the specialized explanations. As to the Steps of Completion, first, what is the explanation of the meaning of *E-vaṃ*? In general, the principal subject matter of all the Anuttara Tantra divisions is the inseparability of Bliss and Void (*sukha-śūnya*); this is the symbolic meaning of the two syllables *E* [Void] and *Vaṃ* [Bliss]. Consequently, the principal subject matter is comprised in the symbolic meaning of the two syllables. Now, there are three *E-vaṃ* (1) the *E-vaṃ* of the fruit to be attained; (2) the *E-vaṃ* of the path of attainment; (3) the *E-vaṃ* as signs guiding that [path].

E-vaṃ of the fruit

The first kind is the palace and its thrones sprung from the self-luminous knowledge of the Samyaksaṃbuddha within the triangle of the Dharmodaya ("source of natures"), symbolized by the triangular E; and the Lord Vajradhara, with his god retinue, symbolized by the syllable *Vaṃ*. In brief, they symbolize the *maṇḍala* of residence and of residents of our previous discussion of the Tantras.

/ lam gyi E Vaṃ la stoṅ pa bśad pa / bde ba bśad pa / bde stoṅ dbyer med du sbyor tshul bśad pa daṅ gsum gyi daṅ po ni /

/ gsaṅ ḥdus rtsa rgyud leḥu gñis par rnam snaṅ gis byaṅ chub kyi sems kyi tshigs bcad gsuṅs pa de bśad gźir byas nas / de ḥchad byed kyi ḥgrel pa byaṅ chub sems ḥgrel źes pa mgon po klu sgrub kyis mdzad pa deḥi naṅ nas sṅags la spyod paḥi byaṅ chub sems dpaḥ chen pos / don dam paḥi byaṅ chub kyi sems bsgoms paḥi sgo nas bskyed par byaḥo / źes paḥi don sems tsam pas gzuṅ ḥdzin gñis stoṅ gi de kho na ñid la ḥdod pa phyin chad rigs pas bkag nas chos thams cad bden par grub pas stoṅ paḥi stoṅ ñid rigs tshogs nas ji ltar gtan la phab pa ltar sṅags la ḥaṅ lta ba de kho na ltar yin gyi / de las lhag paḥi lta ba sṅags la med ces paḥi don du gsuṅs so /

/ de bas na gaṅ zag raṅ skye thub paḥi rdzas yod kyis stoṅ paḥi stoṅ ñid daṅ bde ba chen po sbyor bar bśad pa med la / ḥo na kyaṅ sems tsam paḥi lta ba daṅ sbyor ba śā-nti-pas bśad ciṅ / raṅ rgyud paḥi lta ba daṅ sbyor ba bha-va-bha-dra daṅ / a-bhya-ka-ra sogs kyis gsuṅs kyaṅ /

/ bla med kyi ched du bya baḥi gdul byaḥi gtso bo yin na / phar phyin theg paḥi gdul bya dbaṅ po rno śos las kyaṅ ches dbaṅ po śin tu rno bas khyab pas / de la thal ḥgyur baḥi lta ba dṅos su ston paḥi snod du ruṅ baḥi phyir / ched du bya baḥi gdul bya la dgoṅs nas raṅ rgyud pa phyin chad kyi lta baḥi rnam gźag gsuṅs pa med gsuṅ ṅo /

[20] *Guhyasamāja-tantra*, p. 12: "My *citta* is free from all substance; avoids the personality aggregates, realms, and sense bases, as well as subject and object; is primordially unborn, the intrinsic nature of voidness, — through the sameness of *dharmanairātmya*" (sarvabhāvavigataṃ skandhadhātvāyatanagrāhyagrāhakavarjitaṃ / dharmanairātmyasamatayā svacittam ādyanutpannaṃ śūnyatābhāvam /).

[21] This passage is quoted in the *Sṅags rim* at 448b-2: "The Bodhisattvas who engage in practice by way of the Mantra [-yāna] should first generate in the relative (*saṃvṛti*) way the *bodhicitta* which has the intrinsic nature of aspiration, and then should generate by the power of meditation the absolute (*paramārtha*) *bodhicitta*. Therefore, one must refer to its intrinsic nature (*svabhāva*)" (byaṅ chub sems dpaḥ gsaṅ sṅags kyi sgoḥi spyad pa spyod pa rnams kyis de ltar kun rdzob kyi rnam pas byaṅ chub kyi sems smon paḥi raṅ bźin can bskyed nas don dam paḥi byaṅ chub kyi sems bsgoms paḥi stobs kyis bskyed par bya ba yin te deḥi phyir deḥi raṅ bźin brjod par byaḥo).

[22] This position of the Cittamātra school is especially set forth in the *Madhyāntavibhaṅga* (Toh. 4021) and Vasubandhu's commentary (*bhāṣya*) thereon (Toh. 4027): see

E-vaṃ of the path

For this *E-vaṃ*, there are (a) the exposition of the Void, (b) the exposition of Bliss, and (c) the exposition of combining Bliss and Void in an indissoluble manner.

(a) *Exposition of the Void.* — We take as the basis of the exposition the verse concerning *bodhicitta* expressed by Vairocana in the second chapter of the Fundamental Tantra *Guhyasamāja.*[20] In the commentary explaining that verse, namely, the *Bodhicittavivaraṇa* (Toh. 1800, 1801) composed by *nātha* Nāgārjuna, it is stated that the great *bodhisattva* practising in the *mantra*[-path] should generate the supreme (*paramārtha*) *bodhicitta* by way of contemplation (*bhāvanā*).[21] As to the meaning of that, he subsequently refuted by valid reasons the thesis of the Cittamātra school positing the Reality of the Void [subjacent to] perceiver and thing perceived;[22] and stated as the meaning that just as the [thesis] 'voidness which is void of real production of all dharmas' is established in the Set of Principles [i.e. the basic Mādhyamika works of Nāgārjuna], so also there must be such a view in the *mantra*[-*yāna*], and that, indeed, there is no higher view in the *mantra*[-*yāna*].

(b), (c). Therefore, he does not set forth the combination of bliss and voidness that is void of personality (*pudgala*) which is a self-reproductive substance.[23] However, the combination is set forth by Śānti-pa with the Cittamātra viewpoint; and the combination is stated by Bhavabhadra, Abhayākara, and others, with the Svātantrika viewpoint.

If it is the case of the chief among the candidates for the high goal of the Anuttara[-Tantra], his faculties are surely keener than the keenest faculties of candidates of the Pāramitā-yāna, so he is a fit vessel for teaching concretely the Prāsaṅgika viewpoint; and bearing in mind that he is a candidate for the high goal, [we] assert that there is no statement of exposition [for his case] in the lower viewpoint of the Svātantrika.

---

for example, Th. Stcherbatsky, *Madhyānta-Vibhanga*, Discourse on Discrimination between Middle and Extremes, ascribed to Bodhisattva Maitreya, and commented by Vasubandhu and Sthiramati, translated from the Sanskrit (= *Bibliotheca Buddhica*, XXX) (Leningrad, 1936) [only the first chapter, with commentary and sub-commentary has been translated therein].

23 The meaning seems to be that the *bodhisattva* who has generated the *paramārtha-bodhicitta* corresponds in the phase of the path to the lord Vajradhara in the phase of the fruit, while the viewpoint 'voidness which is void of real production of all dharmas' corresponds in the phase of the path to the Dharmodaya triangle in the phase of the fruit. Voidness is on the side of dharma, while bliss is on the side of person. Since the combination bliss-void requires a person, the Vajrayāna stresses *dharma-nairātmya* but not *pudgala-nairātmya*.

/ des na rdzogs rim gyi rnam gźag rgyas par gźan du śes par bya źiṅ / goṅ gi bśad pa de rnams kyi rigs paḥi śes byed mthaḥ chod par śes par ḥdod na / sṅags rim chen mo las śes par byaḥo /

/ de ltar na rgyud sde spyiḥi rnam par gźag pa rgyas par brjod zin te / mkhas grub thams cad mkhyen pa dge legs dpal bzaṅ pos mdzad paḥo /

[24] There follow some verses which we do not translate, as they are not essential to the work and have probably been added in later editions of the text.

Of course, the exposition of the Steps of Completion is to be known elsewhere in its full extent. If one wishes to know decisively the authoritative presentation for the principles set forth above, he must turn to the *Sṅags rim chen mo* [of Tsoṅ-kha-pa].

[The author does not treat (3) *E-vaṃ* as the signs guiding].

Thus ends the extensive Fundamentals of the Buddhist Tantras, composed by Mkhas-grub-thams-cad-mkhyen-pa Dge-legs-dpal-bzaṅ-po.[24]

INDEX OF WORKS CITED

I. SANSKRIT AND TIBETAN WORKS[1]

Abhidhāna. See *Abhidhānottara.*

Abhidhānaśāstraviśvalocana-ityaparābhidhānamuktāvalī-nāma by Dpal ḥdzin sde (Toh. 4453), 36.

Abhidhānottara (= *Abhidhāna-uttaratantra-nāma*) (Toh. 369), 253, 271.

Abhidharmakośa-kārikā by Vasubandhu (Toh. 4089) (ed. by V. V. Gokhale, "The Text of the Abhidharmakośa-kārikā of Vasubandhu", *JBBRAS*, Vol. 22, 1946), 18, 81, 83.

Abhidharmakośabhāṣya by Vasubandhu (Toh. 4090) (*L'Abhidharmakośa de Vasubandhu*, 1° and 2° chapitres, by de la Vallée Poussin, Paris, 1923; 4° chapitre, Paris, 1924), 18.

Abhidharmakośasāstrakārikābhāṣya by Saṃghabhadra (Toh. 4091), 83.

Abhidharmakośaṭīkā (the 'Vyākhyā') by Prince Yaśomitra (Toh. 4092), 83.

Abhidharmakośaṭīkālakṣaṇānusāriṇī-nāma by Pūrṇavardhana (Toh. 4093), 83.

Abhidharmasamuccaya by Āryāsaṅga (Toh 4049), 57, 95, 99.

Abhisamaya (*Tib. mṅon rtogs* = *Legs par grub par byed paḥi sgrub paḥi thabs bsdus pa,* q.v.), 193.

Abhisamayālaṃkāra (*-nāma-prajñāpāramitopadeśaśāstrakārikā*) by Maitreya (Toh. 3786), 46, 84, 95, 97, 99.

Abhisamayālaṃkāra Sphuṭārthā (= *Abhisamayālaṃkāra-nāma-prajñāpāramitopadeśasāstravṛtti*) by Haribhadra (Toh. 3793), 91.

Acalakalpa-tantra (= *Ārya-Acala-nāma-dhāraṇī*) (Toh. 631), 121.

Acintya-sūtra (possibly Toh. 47, *the Tathāgatācintyaguhyanirdeśa-sūtra*), 129.

Advayavajra-saṃgraha by Advayavajra (ed. by H. P. Śāstri, in GOS, Vol. 40, Baroda, 1927), 34, 313.

[1] Indexed in order of the English alphabet. There is no attempt to provide Western bibliography for any of these works. When Western translations or other studies on any works have been utilized in the foregoing translation and notes, bibliography for those cases alone will be included with the particular item. This includes all works positively available in extant Sanskrit or Tibetan. In the latter case they are identified by the label 'Toh.' among their numbers (1-4569) of the canonical works (Kanjur, with no named author; and Tanjur, with named authors) ordinarily by the original Sanskrit book title as found in *A Complete Catalogue of The Tibetan Buddhist Canons*, ed. by Prof. Hakuji Ui, *et al* (Sendai, Japan, 1934); and among their numbers (5001-7083) of the extra-canonical works, with their Tibetan titles, as found in *A Catalogue of the Tohoku University Collection of Tibetan Works on Buddhism*, ed. by Prof. Yensho Kanakura, *et al* (Sendai, Japan, 1953), or cited as a blockprint in some collection. Any other works, such as those not translated into Tibetan or those unidentified, will be cited only in the Index of Names and Subjects.

Ajātaśatrukaukṛtyavinodana-sūtra (Toh. 216), 55.
Amarakoṣa by Amarasiṃha (Toh. 4299), 79.
Āmnāya-mañjarī (= *Śrīsaṃpuṭatantrarājaṭīkāmnāyamañjarī-nāma*) by Abhayākaraputra (Toh. 1198), 142, 169.
Amoghapāśa-kalparāja-tantra (Toh. 686), 125.
Amṛtabhava-nāma-dhāraṇī (Toh. 645), 121.
Anala-pramohanī-dhāraṇī (= *Ārya-Vajrājitānalapramohanī-nāma-dhāraṇī*) (Toh. 752), 131.
Anantamukhanirhāra-dhāraṇī-ṭīkā by Jñānagarbha (Toh. 2696), 104.
Anantamukhanirhāra-dhāraṇī-vyākhyānakārikā by Jñānagarbha (Toh. 2695), 104.
Anantamukhasādhaka-nāma-dhāraṇī (Toh. 525), 105.
Aparimitāyurjñānavidhi-nāma by Jetāri (Toh. 2700), 145, 276.
Ārya-Agrapradīpadhāraṇīvidyārāja (Toh. 528), 12.
Ārya-Aṅgulimālīya-nāma-mahāyānasūtra (Toh. 213), 49, 97.
Ārya-Aparimitāyurjñānahṛdaya-nāma-dhāraṇī (Toh. 676), 125.
Ārya-Aparimitāyurjñāna-nāma-mahāyāna-sūtra (Toh. 674), 125.
Ārya-Aparimitāyurjñāna-nāma-mahāyāna-sūtra (Toh. 675), 125.
Ārya-Daśabhūmivyākhyāna by Vasubandhu (Toh. 3993), 97, 316.
Ārya-Lalitavistara-nāma-mahāyāna-sūtra (LV) (Toh. 95), 43-4-5.
Ārya-Mañjuśrīnāmasaṅgītiṭīkā by Mañjuśrīkīrti (Toh. 2534), 127.
Ārya-Ratnameghasūtra (Toh. 231), 211.
Ārya-Sahasrabhujāvalokiteśvarasādhana by Nāgārjuna (Toh. 2736), 162.
Āryasañcaya. See *Sañcayagāthā*.
Ārya-Sitātapatrāparājitābalividhi-nāma by Candragomin (Toh. 3084), 119.
Ārya-Sitātapatrāparājitā-nāma-sādhana by Candragomin (Toh. 3083), 119.
Ārya-Subāhuparipṛcchā-nāmatantra-piṇḍārthavṛtti possibly by Padmavajra (Toh. 2673), 102.
Ārya-Tathāgatoṣṇīṣasitātapatrā-nāma-dhāraṇīvidhi-nāma by Candragomin (Toh. 3096), 119.
Ārya-Tathāgatoṣṇīṣasitātapatrāparājitā-nāma-maṇḍalavidhi-nāma by Padmāṅkuśa (Toh 3106), 119, 147.
Ārya-Tathāgatoṣṇīṣasitātapatrā-aparājitadhāraṇī (Toh. 593), 116.
Ārya-Tathāgatoṣṇīṣasitātapatre aparājita-nāma-dhāraṇī (Toh. 592), 116.
Ārya-Tathāgatoṣṇīṣasitātapatrāparājita-mahāpratyaṅgirāparamasiddha-nāma-dhāraṇī (Toh. 591), 116-7.
Ārya-Tathāgatoṣṇīṣasitātapatrāparājita-nāma-upadeśa by Vajrāsana (Toh. 3110), 119.
Ārya-Aṣṭadaśasāhasrikā-prajñāpāramitā-nāma-mahāyānasūtra (Toh. 10), 47.
Ārya-Aṣṭasāhasrikā-prajñāpāramitā (Toh. 12), 47.
Ārya-Aṣṭasāhasrikāprajñāpāramitāvyākhyābhisamayālaṃkārāloka-nāma (*the* '*Āloka*') by Haribhadra (Toh. 3791), 91.
Ārya-Prajñāpāramitāsaṃgrahakārikā (*the* '*Aṣṭasāhasrikā-piṇḍārtha*') by Diṅnāga (Toh. 3809), 99.
Ārya-Vidyārāja-mahāśvāsa-nāma (Toh. 773), 134.
Aṣṭasāhasrikāprajñāpāramitā-pañjikāsārottamā-nāma by Śānti-pā (Ratnākaraśānti) (Toh. 3803), 53.
Aṣṭāṅgahṛdayasaṃhitā-nāma by Vāgbhaṭa (Toh. 4310), 78-9.
Aṣṭaśatasādhana by Candragomin (Toh. 3665), 127.
Avadānaśataka (= *Pūrṇapramukhāvadānaśataka*) (Toh. 343), 79.
Avadānakalpalatā (= *Bodhisattvāvadānakalpalatā*) (Toh. 4155), 77, 79.
Avalokiteśvarasiṃhanāda-nāma-dhāraṇī (Toh. 703, the larger of two), 125.
Avalokiteśvarasiṃhanāda-nāma-dhāraṇī (Toh. 704, the smaller of two), 125.
Avataṃsaka-sūtra (= *Buddha-Avataṃsaka-nāma-mahāvaipūlya-sūtra*) (Toh. 44), 47, 49, 55, 153, 205.

Avatāra (= *Tantrārthāvatāra*) by Buddhaguhya (Toh. 2501), 25, 222, 224, 227, 234, 241.
Avatāra-vyākhyāna (= *Tantrārthāvatāravyākhyāna*) by Padmavajra (Toh. 2502), 25, 116, 162, 214, 216-7, 222, 228-9, 236-7, 244, 270.
Avikalpapraveśa-dhāraṇī (Toh. 142), 49.
Bahubhūmika. See *Yogācārabhūmi*.
Bahuputrapratisaraṇa-nāma-dhāraṇī (Toh. 615), 121.
Bde bar gśegs paḥi bstan paḥi gsal byed, Chos kyi ḥbyuṅ gnas gsuṅ rab rin po cheḥi mdzod ces bya ba, by Bu-ston (Toh. 5197) (tr. by E. Obermiller, *History of Buddhism*, Parts I and II, Heidelberg, 1931), 16, 44, 46, 66, 68, 72.
Bhadracarī (= *Ārya-Bhadracaryāpraṇidhānarāja*) (Toh. 1095) (also: last chapter of *Avataṃsaka-sūtra*), 153.
Bhagavadratnaguṇasañcayagāthā-nāma-pañjikā (*the* '*Pañjikā*') by Haribhadra (Toh. 3792), 91.
Bhagavato Bhaiṣajyaguruvaiḍūryaprabhasya pūrvapraṇidhānaviśeṣavistāra-nāma mahāyānasūtra (Toh. 504), 109.
Bhāvanākrama by Kamalaśīla (Toh. 3915-3917, three different works), 211.
Bhoṭasvāmidāsagurulekha by Buddhaguhya (Toh. 4194), 25.
Bhūmivastu. See *Yogācārabhūmi*.
Bhurkumkūṭa-dhāraṇī (= *Krodhabhurkumkūṭarāja-stotramantra*) (Toh. 756), 131.
Bhūtaḍāmara-mahātantrarāja-nāma (Toh. 747), 129.
Bkaḥ gdams pa daṅ dge lugs bla ma rag rim gyi gsuṅ ḥbum mtshan tho, by Kloṅ-rdol-bla-ma (Toh. 6555), 11.
Bodhicittavivaraṇa by Nāgārjuna (Toh. 1800, 1801), 335.
Bodhimaṇḍalalakṣālaṃkāra-nāma-dhāraṇī (Toh. 508), 107.
Bodhimārgapradīpapañjikā-nāma by Atīśa (Dīpaṃkaraśrījñāna) (Toh. 3948), 100.
Bodhisattvabhūmi by Āryāsaṅga (Toh. 4037), 95, 99.
Bodhisattvacaryāvatāra by Śāntideva (Toh. 3871), 93, 153.
Brtag ḥgrel (= *Dpal brtag pa gñis paḥi rnam par bśad pa, Rdo rje mkhaḥ ḥgro ma rnams kyi gsaṅ baḥi mdzod ces bya ba*) by Mkhas-grub-rje (Toh. 5483), 12, 312.
Bsruṅ ḥkhor bri thabs (Sanskrit title lacking) by Candragomin (Toh. 3086), 119.
Bstan rtsis (= *Thub paḥi dbaṅ poḥi bstan rtsis dge ldan raṅ lugs bźin gsal bar brjod pa mkhas pa dgyes paḥi mchod sprin*) *by Blo bzaṅ tshul khrims rgya mtsho* (also called: *Mi pham tshaṅs sras dgyes paḥi rdo rje*) (blockprint in East Asiatic Library, University of California), 11.
Buddhakapāla (= *Śrī-Buddhakapāla-nāma-yoginītantrarāja*) (Toh. 424), 251.
Buddhakapālamaṇḍalavidhi (= *Śrī-Buddhakapālamaṇḍalavidhikrama-pradyotana-nāma*) by Saraha (Toh. 1657), 289.
Buddhānusmṛtivṛtti by Vasubandhu (Toh. 3982; catalog says by Asaṅga), 97.
Buddhapālita-vṛtti (= *Buddhapālitamūlamadhyamakavṛtti*) by Buddhapālita (Toh. 3842), 87.
Buddhasamāyoga (= *Śrī-Sarvabuddhasamāyogaḍākinījāla-sambara-nāma-uttaratantra*) (Toh. 366) and (= *Sarvakalpasamuccaya-nāma-sarvabuddhasamāyogaḍākinījāla-sambara-uttarottaratantra*) (Toh. 367), 267.
Buddhāvataṃsaka. See *Avataṃsaka-sūtra*.
Byaṅ sems daṅ rig pa ḥdzin paḥi phyir bcos / sdom pa ñi śu pa / byaṅ sems kyi rtsa ltuṅ bsdus paḥi tshigs su bcad pa / rtsa ltuṅ bcu bźi pa / sbom po brgyad pa daṅ bcas paḥi bslab bya mdor bsdus, author unknown (blockprint in library of Alex Wayman), 329.
Bźis źus. See *Srog rtsol gyi de kho na ñid gsal ba*.
Bzo daṅ gso ba, skar rtsis rnams las byuṅ baḥi miṅ gi graṅs, by Kloṅ-rdol-bla-ma (Toh. 6547), 321.
Cakrasambaramaṇḍalavidhi (= *Śrī-Cakrasambaramaṇḍalavidhiratnapradīpoddyota-nāma*) by Lwa-ba-pa (Toh. 1444), 29, 314.

Cakrasaṃvara-tantra (= *Tantrarājaśrīlaghusambara-nāma*). See *Saṃvara-tantra.*
Candravyākaraṇasūtra by Candragomin (Toh. 4269), 77.
Caryāmelāpakapradīpa by Āryadeva (Toh. 1803), 35, 165, 313.
Catuḥśaıaka-śāstrakārikā-nāma by Āryadeva (Toh. 3846), 89.
Caturdevīparipṛcchā (Toh. 446), 257.
Chandoratnākara by Ratnākaraśānti (Toh. 4303, 4304), 79.
Cittavajrastava by Māgārjuna (Toh. 1121), 93.
Cundīdevī-dhāraṇī (Toh. 613), 121.
Daśabhūmika-sūtra (a large section of the *Avataṃsaka-sūtra*) (ed. by J. Rahder, *Daśabhūmikasūtra et Bodhisattvabhūmi*, Paris, 1926), 19.
Daśasāhasrikā (= *Ārya-Daśasāhasrikā-prajñāpāramitā-nāma-mahāyānasūtra*) (Toh. 11), 47.
De bźin gśegs pa bdun gyi sṅon gyi smon lam gyi khyad par rgyas paḥi gzuṅs bklag paḥi cho ga mdo sde las btus pa (Sanskrit title lacking) by Śāntarakṣita (Toh. 3133), 109.
Dhāraṇīśvara-rāja-paripṛcchā. See *Tathāgata-mahākaruṇānirdeśa-sūtra.*
Dharmacakra-sūtra (Toh. 337), 45.
Dharmadharmatāvibhaṅgavṛtti by Vasubandhu (Toh. 4028), 95.
Dharmadhātustava by Nāgārjuna (Toh. 1118), 93.
Dharmadharmatāvibhaṅga-kārikā by Maitreya (Toh. 4022), 95, 97.
Dharmānusmṛtivṛtti by Vasubandhu (Toh. 3983; catalog says by Asaṅga), 97.
Dharmasaṃgīti-sūtra (= *Ārya-Dharmasaṃgīti-nāma-mahāyānasūtra*) (Toh. 238), 55
Dhvajāgrakeyūra-dhāraṇī (Toh. 612), 121.
Dhyānottara-paṭalakrama (Toh. 808), 135, 137, 165, 167.
Dhyānottara-paṭala-ṭīkā by Buddhaguhya (Toh. 2670), 139, 162, 165, 172, 186-7, 189, 198, 203.
Don gsal (= *Rnam gźag rim paḥi rnam bśad, Dpal gsaṅ ba ḥdus paḥi gnad kyi don gsal ba*) by Tsoṅ-kha-pa (Toh. 5290), 318, 332.
Dpal gsaṅ ba ḥdus pa ḥphags lugs daṅ mthun paḥi sṅags kyis lam rnam gźag legs bśad skal bzaṅ ḥjug ṅogs, by Dbyaṅs-can Dgaḥ-baḥi-blo-gros (blockprint in East Asiatic Library, University of California), 266, 312.
Dpal gsaṅ ba ḥdus pa mi bskyod rdo rjeḥi dkyil ḥkhor gyi cho ga, Dbaṅ gi don gyi de ñid rab tu gsal ba źes bya ba (also '*Dbaṅ don*') by Tsoṅ-kha-pa (Toh. 5287), 275, 286, 295.
Dpal gźin rje gśed lha bcu gsum ma rnams kyi dkyil ḥkhor du dbaṅ bskur ba sgrub paḥi thabs kyi cho ga, Rin po cheḥi phreṅ ba, by Tsoṅ-kha-pa (Toh. 5339), 276.
Ekādaśamukhāvalokiteśvarasādhana by Dpal mo (Toh. 2737), 167.
Ekākṣarīmātā-nāma-sarvatathāgata-prajñāpāramitā (Toh. 23), 47.
Ekaviṃśatisādhana by Candragomin (probably his *Ārya-Tārādevīstotrapuṣpamālā-nāma*, Toh. 3670, with 'las tshogs' in *Ārya-Tārāstotrakarmasādhana-nāma*, Toh. 3669), 127.
Ekottarakarmaśataka by Guṇaprabha (Toh. 4118), 83.
Gaṇapati-dharaṇī (= *Ārya-Gaṇapati-hṛdaya*) (Toh. 665), 123.
Gaṇapati-tantra (= *Mahāgaṇapati-tantra-nāma*) (Toh. 666), 123.
Ghanavyūha-sūtra (= *Ārya-Ghanavyūha-nāma-mahāyānasūtra*) (Toh. 110), 21-2-3, 205.
Gnod ḥjoms (= *Ārya-Śatasāhasrikāpañcaviṃśatisāhasrikāṣṭādaśasāhasrikāprajñāpāramitābṛhaṭṭīkā*) by Daṃṣṭrasena (Toh. 3808), 99.
Grahamātṛkā-nāma-dhāraṇī (Toh. 660), 121.
Gsaṅ sṅags kyi tshul khrims kyi rnam bśad, Dṅos grub kyi sñe ma, by Tsoṅ-kha-pa (Toh. 5270), 328.
Gsaṅ sṅags rig pa ḥdzin paḥi sde snod las byuṅ baḥi miṅ gi graṅs, by Kloṅ-rdol-bla-ma (Toh. 6534), 268.
Gser ḥphreṅ (= *Śes rab kyi pha rol tu phyin paḥi man ṅag gi bstan bcos mṅon par rtogs*

paḥi rgyan ḥgrel pa daṅ bcas paḥi rgya cher bśad pa, Legs bśad gser gyi phreṅ ba) by Tsoṅ-kha-pa (Toh. 5412), 96.

Gtsug tor ḥbar ba źes bya baḥi gzuṅs (Sanskrit title lacking) (Toh. 600), 119.

Guhyasamājatantra (= *Sarvatathāgatakāyavākcittarahasyaguhyasamāja-nāma-mahākalparāja*) (Toh. 442, mūla-tantra = first 17 chapters of Sanskrit text; Toh. 443, uttara-tantra = 18th chapter of Sanskrit) (edited B. Bhaṭṭacharyya, GOS, Baroda, 1934), 28, 35, 68-9, 102, 172-3, 200, 219-220, 253, 257, 259, 262-267, 283, 295-297, 301, 307, 312-3, 323, 334-5.

Guhyasamājamaṇḍala-vidhi by Dīpaṃkarabhadra (Toh. 1856), 147.

Guhyasamājamaṇḍalavidhi-ṭīkā by Ratnākaraśānti (Toh. 1871), 145, 147.

Gurukriyākrama by Atīśa (Dīpaṃkarajñāna) (Toh. 3977), 152-3.

Gurupañcāśikā by Aśvaghoṣa (Toh. 3721), 272.

Gzaḥ dguḥi mchod paḥi cho ga (Sanskrit title lacking) (no author mentioned) (Toh. 3129), 114-5.

Hayagrīvadhāraṇī (= *Ārya-Avalokiteśvarahayagrīva-dhāraṇī* (Toh. 733), 127.

Ḥchi med rṅa sgraḥi gzuṅs. See *Tshe dpag med ḥchi med rṅa sgraḥi gzuṅs*.

Ḥdod pa ḥjo (= *Rnal ḥbyor gyi dbaṅ phyug lū-i-pas mdzad paḥi bcom ldan ḥdas ḥkhor lo bde mchod gi mṅon.par rtogs paḥi rgya cher bśad pa, Ḥdod pa ḥjo ba*) by Tsoṅ-kha-pa (Toh. 5320), 304.

Hetubindu-nāma-prakaraṇa by Dharmakīrti (Toh. 4213), 83.

Hevajrapiṇḍārtha-ṭīkā by Vajragarbha (Toh. 1180), 262-3.

Hevajratantra (= *Hevajra-tantrarāja-nāma*) (Toh. 417-418) ed. and tr. by D. L. Snellgrove, *Hevajra Tantra*, Parts I and II, Oxford University Press, London, 1959), 12, 18, 28, 34-5, 142-3, 169, 253, 256-7, 262-3, 275, 277, 283, 288, 296, 304, 312, 319.

Hevajratantra, the vajrapañjikā called "The Eye Opener" (spyan ḥbyed) (= *Rgyud kyi rgyal po chen po dpal dgyes pa rdo rjeḥi dkaḥ ḥgrel spyan ḥbyed ces bya ba*, Sanskrit title lacking) by Dharmakīrti (Toh. 1191), 296.

Hevajratantrapañjikāpadmin-nāma by Mtsho skyes (Toh. 1181), 288.

Ḥgrel chen (= *Dpal dus kyi ḥkhor lo ḥgrel chen*) by Mkhas-grub-rje (Toh. 5463), 12.

Ḥkhrul ḥkhor (Sanskrit title lacking; would be *Yantra*) by Candragomin (Toh. 3087), 119.

Ḥphags pa mtshan yaṅ dag par brjod paḥi rgya cher ḥgrel pa mtshan gsaṅ sṅags kyi don du rnam par lta ba (Sanskrit title lacking) by Līlavajra (Toh. 2533), 127.

Jambhalajalendrayathālabdhakalpa (Toh. 770), 133.

Jantupoṣaṇabindu (= *Nītiśāstrajantupoṣaṇabindu-nāma*) by Nāgārjuna (Toh. 4330), 95.

Jīvasūtra by Nāgārjuna (Toh. 4307), 95.

Jñānālokālaṃkāra-sūtra (= *Ārya-Sarvabuddhaviṣayāvatārajñānālokālaṃkāra-nāma-mahāyānasūtra*) (Toh. 100), 49, 97.

Jñānatilaka-tantra (= *Śrī-Jñānatilakayoginītantrarājaparamamahādbhuta-nāma*) (Toh. 422), 312.

Jñānavajrasamuccaya (= *Vajrajñānasamuccaya-nāma-tantra*) (Toh. 447), 165, 169.

Kālacakra-tantra (= *Paramādibuddhoddhṛtaśrīkālacakra-nāma-tantrarāja*) (Toh. 362), 12, 35, 173, 259, 261, 275, 281, 283, 289, 293, 319, 329.

Kālacakra-tantra Commentary. See *Vimalaprabhā*. See *Ḥgrel chen*.

Kalāpasūtra by Śarvavarman and Vararuci (Toh. 4282; catalog says by Rgyal poḥi lha), 77.

Kalāpasūtravṛtti-nāma by Durgasiṃha (Toh. 4283), 77.

Kalparājavidhi (= *Ārya-Amoghapāśa-kalparājavidhi-nāma*) (Toh. 689), 125.

Kāma-sūtra by Śrī Vātsyāyana Muni, with *Jayamangala* Commentary of Yashodhar, ed. by Śrī Gosvamī Dāmodar Shastri (Benares City, 1929), 320.

Kāraṇa-prajñapti by Mahāmaudgalyāyana (Toh. 4087), 83.

Karma-prajñapti by Mahāmaudgalyāyana (Toh. 4088), 83.

Karmaśataka (Toh. 340), 45.

Karmasiddhiprakaraṇa by Vasubandhu (Toh. 4062), 95.
Kāśyapa-parivarta (= *Ārya-Kāśyapaparivarta-nāma-mahāyānasūtra*) (Toh. 87), 152.
Kauśika (= *Ārya-Kauśika-prajñāpāramitā-nāma*) (Toh. 19), 47.
Kāvyādarśa by Daṇḍin (Toh. 4301), 77, 79.
Kha ḥbar baḥi gzuṅs (= *Yi dvags mo kha ḥbar ma dbugs dbyuṅ baḥi gtor maḥi cho ga*; Sanskrit title lacking) (Toh. 647), 123.
Kloṅ-rdol-bla-ma, Collected Works (Toh. 6532-6561), 11, 36, 172-3, 206, 268, 320.
Kosalālaṃkāra (= *Kosalālaṃkāratattvasaṃgrahaṭīkā*) by Śākyamitra (Toh. 2503), 22, 24, 30, 214, 217, 241.
Kriyāsaṃgraha by Kuladatta (Toh. 2531), 282.
Kuṇḍalyamṛta (= *Ārya-Kuṇḍalyamṛtahṛdayacaturtha-nāma-dhāraṇī*) (Toh. 755), 133.
Kurukullāsādhana by Abhayākaragupta (Toh. 3209), 220.
Lam rim chen mo by Tsoṅ-kha-pa (Toh. 5392), 11, 78, 124, 152, 200, 210-1.
Laṅkāvatāra-sūtra (Toh. 107), 22, 47, 49, 168.
Laṅkāvatāra-sūtra-vṛtti-Tathāgatahṛdayālaṃkāra by Jñānavajra (Toh. 4019), 168.
Ldan-dkar-ma (= *Pho braṅ stod thaṅ ldan dkar gyi chos ḥgyur ro cog ti dkar chag*) by Dpal-brtsegs, Nam-mkhaḥi-sñiṅ-po, etc. (Toh. 4364), 85.
Legs par grub par byed paḥi sgrub paḥi thabs bsdus pa (Sanskrit title lacking) by Byaṅ chub mchog (*Varabodhi) (Toh. 3066), 139, 167, 174, 193.
Lokānandanāṭaka by Candragomin (Toh. 4153), 79.
Loka-prajñapti by Mahāmaudgalyāyana (Toh. 4086), 83.
Lokātītastava by Nāgārjuna (Toh. 1120), 93.
Madhyamakahṛdaya-kārikā by Bhavya (Bhāvaviveka) (Toh. 3855), 89.
Madhyamakālaṃkāra-kārikā by Śāntarakṣita (Toh. 3884), 91.
Madhyamakālaṃkāra-vṛtti by Śāntarakṣita (Toh. 3885), 91.
Madhyamakāloka by Kamalaśīla (Toh. 3887), 91.
Madhyamakapañcaskandha (Presumably = *Pañcaskandhaprakaraṇa*) by Candrakīrti (Toh. 3866), 95.
Madhyamaka-ratnapradīpa by Bhavya (Bhāvaviveka) (Toh. 3854), 94.
Madhyamakāvatāra by Candrakīrti (Toh. 3861), 89.
Madhyamakāvatāra-bhāṣya by Candrakīrti (Toh. 3862), 89.
Madhyāntavibhaṅga-kārikā by Maitreya (Toh. 4021), 95, 334.
Madhyāntavibhaṅga-bhāṣya by Vasubandhu (Toh. 4027), 95, 334.
Madhyāntavibhaṅga-ṭīkā by Sthiramati (Toh. 4032) tr. in part by Th. Stcherbatsky, *Madhyānta-Vibhanga*, Bibliotheca Buddhica, Leningrad, 1936), 335.
Mahābala-dhāraṇī (= *Ārya-Mahābala-nāma-mahāyānasūtra*) (Toh. 757), 133.
Mahābhāṣya (= *Vyākaraṇa-Mahābhāṣya*) by Patañjali (ed. Kielhorn, 1906, ff.), 75, 77.
Mahābherīhāraka-sūtra (= *Ārya-Mahābherīhārakaparivarta-nāma-mahāyānasūtra*) (Toh. 222), 49.
Mahāmantrānudhārisūtra (Toh. 563), 113.
Mahāmāyā (= *Śrī-Mahāmāyā-tantrarāja-nāma*) (Toh. 425), 267.
Mahāmāyāsādhanamaṇḍalavidhi by Kukuri-pā (Toh. 1630), 143.
Mahāmayūri-vidyārājñī (Toh. 559), 113.
Mahāmegha (= *Ārya-Mahāmeghavātamaṇḍalasarvanāgahṛdaya-nāma-mahāyānasūtra*) (Toh. 658), 121.
Mahāmudrātilaka (= *Śrī-Mahāmudrātilaka-nāma-mahāyoginī-tantrarājādhipati*) (Toh. 420), 267, 312.
Mahāparinirvāṇa-sūtra (Toh. 120), 49.
Mahāpratisarācakralekhanavidhi possibly by Jetāri (Toh. 3127), 113.
Mahāratnakūṭa (= *Ārya-Mahāratnakūṭadharmaparyāya-śatasāhasrikagranthe trisaṃvara-nirdeśaparivarta-nāma-mahāyānasūtra* (Toh. 45), 47.
Mahāsahasrapramardana-nāma-sūtra (Toh. 558), 113.
Mahāśītavanasūtra (Toh. 562), 113.

Mahāvairocana-abhisaṃbodhi-tantra. See *Mahāvairocana-tantra*.
Mahāvairocana-tantra (also: *Mahāvairocana-abhisaṃbodhi-tantra* = *Mahāvairocanābhisaṃbodhivikurvitādhiṣṭhānavaipulyasūtrendrarāja-nāma-dharmaparyāya*) (Toh. 494), 147, 165, 167, 173, 205-6-7, 211, 216.
Mahāvairocana(-abhisambodhi)tantrapiṇḍārtha by Buddhaguhya (Toh. 2662), 211.
Mahāvairocana(-abhisambodhi)tantraṭīkā by Buddhaguhya (Toh. 2663), 147, 149, 173.
Mahāvastu, in the selection of Franklin Edgerton, *Buddhist Hybrid Sanskrit Reader* (New Haven, 1953), 208; as reported in Har Dayal, *The Bodhisattva Doctrine* (London, 1932), 19, 313.
Mahāyānasaṃgraha by Āryāsaṅga (Toh. 4048), 95, 99.
Mahāyānasaṃgraha-bhāṣya by Vasubandhu (Toh. 4050), 97.
Mahāyānottaratantra-śāstra by Maitreya (Toh. 4024), 24-5, 48, 41-2, 95, 97.
Mahāyānottaratantraśāstravyākhyā by Āryāsaṅga (Toh. 4025); tr. from Tibetan by E. Obermiller, "The Sublime Science of the Great Vehicle to Salvation," *Acta Orientalia*, Vol. IX (1931); ed. in Sanskrit by E. H. Johnston as *Ratnagotravibhāga Mahāyānottaratantraśāstra*, appendix to *JBRS*, Patna, 1950; 24, 50-1, 97.
Maitreyapratijñā-nāma-dhāraṇī (Toh. 643), 121.
Maitreyasādhana by Āryāsaṅga (Toh. 3648), 167.
Maṇḍala-vidhi in 450 stanzas (alias for *Guhyasamājamaṇḍalavidhi-nāma*) by Dīpaṃkarabhadra.
Maṇibhadra-nāma-dhāraṇī (Toh. 764), 133.
Maṇibhadrayakṣasena-kalpa (Toh. 765), 133.
Mañjuśrī-Mukhāgama (the larger, *Dvikramatattvabhāvanā-nāma-mukhāgama*, Toh. 1853) (the smaller, *Mukhāgama*, Toh. 1854) both by Buddhaśrījñāna, 35.
Mañjuśrī-mūla-tantra (Toh. 543); (ed. by T. Gaṇapati Śāstri, *Ārya-mañjuśrī-mūlakalpa*, Trivandrum Sanskrit Series, Vol. 70, 1920; Vol. 76, 1922; Vol. 84, 1925), 75, 103, 106, 111, 119, 194, 202.
Mañjuśrī-nāma-saṃgīti (= *Mañjuśrījñānasattvasya paramārthanāma-saṃgīti*) (Toh. 360) (ed. by I. P. Minaeff, St. Petersburg University, Historo-Philological Faculty, Vol. 16, 1885), 127.
Mañjuśrī-nāmāṣṭaśataka (Toh. 642), 121.
Mañjuśrī-siddhaikavīra-tantra (= *Siddhikavīra-mahātantrarāja-nāma*) (Toh. 544), 111.
Manusmṛti (Nārāyan Rām Āchārya, ed., *Manusmṛti with the Commentary Manvarthamuktāvali of Kullūka*, Bombay, 1946), 74.
Mārīci-kalpa (= *Mayāmārīcijātatantrād uddhṛtakalparāja-nāma*) (Toh. 565), 113.
Mārīci-nāma-dhāraṇī (Toh. 564), 113.
Māyājāla (= *Māyājāla-mahātantrarāja-nāma*) (Toh. 466), 100, 261, 265, 267.
Māyāmārīci-saptaśata-nāma (= *Ārya-Mārīcimaṇḍalavidhimārīcijātadvādaśasahasrād uddhṛtakalpahṛdayasaptaśata-nāma*) (Toh. 566), 113.
Mekhalā-dhāraṇī (Toh. 772), 135.
Mthaḥ dpyod (= *Phar phyin gyi mchan ḥgrel bźad paḥi dgoṅs rgyan*) by Ḥjam dbyaṅs bźad paḥi rdo rje (blockprint in East Asiatic Library, University of California), 84.
Mthaḥ gcod. See *Rin po cheḥi myu gu*.
Mukhāgama. See *Mañjuśrī-Mukhāgama*.
Muktitilaka by Buddhaśrījñāna (Toh. 1859), 37.
Mūla-Madhyamaka-kārikā (= *Prajñā-nāma-mūlamadhyamakakārikā*) by Nāgārjuna (Toh. 3824), 85, 87, 89, 94.
Mūlamadhyamakavṛtty-akutobhaya ascribed to Nāgārjuna (Toh. 3829), 89.
Mūlāpattisaṃgraha (= *Vajrayānamūlāpattisaṃgraha*) by Aśvaghoṣa (Toh. 2478) (ed. and tr. by Sylvain Lévi in *Journal Asiatique*, Oct.-Dec., 1929, pp. 266-7), 328.
Nāgānanda-nāma-nāṭaka by Harṣadeva (Toh. 4154), 79.
Namastāre ekaviṃśati-stotra-guṇahitasahita (Toh. 438), 127.
Nartakaparakalpa (= *Mahāyakṣasenapatinartakapara-kalpa*) (Toh. 766-767), 132-3.

Naya-śatapañcaśatikā (= *Ārya-Prajñāpāramitā-naya-śatapañcaśatikā*) (Toh. 17), 47.
Ñi-khri snaṅ ba. See *Pañcaviṃśati ... vṛtti* by Vimuktasena.
Nilāmbaradharavajrapāṇi-tantra-nāma (Toh. 498), 207.
Nirvikalpastava (= ? *Nirupamastava*, Toh. 1119) by Nāgārjuna, 93.
Niṣpannayogāvalī by Abhayākaragupta (Toh. 3141) (ed. by B. Bhattacharyya, *Niṣpannayogāvalī of Mahāpaṇḍita Abhayākaragupta*, Baroda, 1949), 216, 256, 304.
Nyāyabindu-nāma-prakaraṇa by Dharmakīrti (Toh. 4212), 73.
Padārthacandrikāprabhāsa-nāma-aṣṭāṅgahṛdayavivṛti by Candranandana (Toh. 4312), 81.
Padmajāla (= *Ārya-Avalokiteśvarapadmajāla-mūlatantrarāja-nāma*) (Toh. 681), 125.
Pañcakrama by Nāgārjuna (Toh. 1802), 157, 326.
Pañcarakṣārcanavidhi possibly by Jetāri (Toh. 3128), 113.
Pañcarakṣāvidhi by Śānti-pā (Ratnākaraśānti) (Toh. 3126), 113, 167.
Pañcaśatikā-prajñāpāramitā (Toh. 15), 47.
Pañcaskandhaprakaraṇa by Vasubandhu (Toh. 4059), 95.
Pañcaviṃśati-prajñāpāramitā-mukha (Toh. 20), 47.
Pañcaviṃśatisāhasrikā-prajñāpāramitā (Toh. 9), 47, 96.
Pañcaviṃśatisāhasrikā-prajñāpāramitā by Haribhadra (Toh. 3790), 91.
Pañcaviṃśatisāhasrikāprajñāpāramitopadeśaśāstrābhisamayālaṃkāravṛtti (also: the '*Ñi khri snaṅ ba*') by Vimuktasena (Toh. 3787), 91.
Pāṇinīya-vyākaraṇa (presumably = *Pāṇinivyākaraṇasūtra*, Toh. 4420) by Pāṇini, 75.
Pañjarā. See *Vajrapañjarā-tantra.*
Paramādiṭīkā. See *Śrī-Paramādiṭīkā.*
Paramādya. See *Śrī-paramādya.*
Parṇaśavarī-nāma-dhāraṇī (Toh. 736), 127.
Parṇaśavarīsūtra (Toh. 735), 127.
Paryāyasaṃgrahaṇī by Āryāsaṅga (Toh. 4041), 95.
Piṇḍīkṛtasādhanapañjikā by Vibhūticandra (Toh. 1832), 280.
Pradīpodyotana-nāma-ṭīkā by Candrakīrti (Toh. 1785), 22, 70-1-2, 218, 296-7.
Pradīpodyotana-ṭippaṇī (in Tibetan: the '*Mchan ḥgrel*' = *Rgyud thams cad kyi rgyal po dpal gsaṅ ba ḥdus paḥi rgya cher bśad pa sgron ma gsal baḥi tshig don ji bźin ḥbyed paḥi mchan gyi yaṅ ḥgrel*) by Tsoṅ-kha-pa (Toh. 5282), 295.
Pradīpodyotana-vyākhyāṭīkā(= *Pradīpodyotanābhisaṃdhiprakāśikā-nāma-vyākhyāṭīkā*) by Bhavyakīrti (more likely by Āryadeva) (Toh. 1793), 219, 220, 223.
Prajñāhṛdaya (= *Bhagavatī-prajñāpāramitā-hṛdaya*) (Toh. 21), 47, 55, 109.
Prajñā-mūla. See *Mūla-madhyamaka-kārikā.*
Prajñā-nāma-mūlamadhyamaka. See *Mūla-madhyamaka-kārikā.*
Prajñāpāramitā-hṛdaya. See *Prajñāhṛdaya.*
Prajñāpāramitāhṛdayasādhana ascribed to Ārya Nāgārjuna (Toh. 2640), 109.
Prajñāpāramitāhṛdayasādhana-nāma by Dārika-pā (Toh. 2641), 109.
Prajñāpāramitā-pañcaśatikā (= *Ārya-Bhagavatī-prajñāpāramitā-pañcaśatikā*) (Toh. 18), 47.
Prajñāpāramitāsaṃgrahakārikā by Diṅnāga. See under *Ārya*°.
Prajñāpradīpa (= *Prajñāpradīpamūlamadhyamakavṛtti*) by Bhāvaviveka (Toh. 3853), 87, 89.
Prajñāpradīpaṭīkā (the '*Avalokitavrata*') by Avalokitavrata (Toh. 3859), 89.
Prajñāśataka-nāma-prakaraṇa by Nāgārjuna (Toh. 4328), 95.
Pramāṇa-sūtra (= *Pramāṇasamuccaya-nāma-prakaraṇa*) by Diṅnāga (Toh. 4203), 73.
Pramāṇavārttika by Dharmakīrti (Toh. 4210), 73.
Pramāṇaviniścaya by Dharmakīrti (Toh. 4211), 73.
Prasannapadā (= *Mūlamadhyamakavṛttiprasannapadā-nāma*) by Candrakīrti (To 3860), 87, 94.
Pratimokṣasūtraṭīkā-vinayasamuccaya by Dri-med-bśes-gñen (Toh. 4106), 83.

Pratisarāvidyārājñī (Toh. 561), 113.
Pratisarāvidyāvidhi possibly by Śānti-pā (Toh. 3125), 113.
Pratītyasamutpādādivibhaṅgabhāṣya by Vasubandhu (Toh. 3995), 97.
Pratītyasamutpāda-hṛdaya-dhāraṇī (Toh. 519), 107.
Rasāyanaśāstroddhṛti by Nāgārjuna (Toh. 4314), 95.
Raśmivimalaviśuddhaprabhā-dhāraṇī (Toh. 510), 107.
Ratnamālā (= *Vajravidāraṇā-nāma-dhāraṇīvṛttiratnamālā-nāma*) by Sabari-pā (Toh. 2686), 128.
Ratnapradīpoddyota. See *Cakrasambaramaṇḍalavidhi* by Lwa-ba-pa.
Ratnāvalī (= *Rājaparikathāratnamālā*) by Nāgārjuna (Toh. 4158), 86-7.
Rgyud bśad thabs kyi man ṅag gsal bar bstan pa (= *Dpal gsaṅ ba ḥdus paḥi bśad paḥi rgyud ye śes rdo rje kun las btus paḥi rgya cher bśad pa, Rgyud bśad ... bstan pa*) by Tsoṅ-kha-pa (Toh. 5286), 156, 220, 264.
Rgyud sde spyi rnam (= *Rgyud sde spyiḥi rnam par bźag pa rgyas par bśad pa*) by Mkhas-grub-rje (Toh. 5489), the work herein transcribed, translated, and annotated; also, 12-13, 85.
Rgyud sde spyiḥi rnam par gźag pa, Rgyud sde rin po cheḥi gter sgo ḥbyed paḥi lde mig, by Bu-ston (Toh. 5167), 12.
Rgyud sde spyiḥi rnam par gźag pa, Rgyud sde thams cad kyi gsaṅ ba gsal bar byed pa, by Bu-ston (Toh. 5168), 12.
Rgyud sde spyiḥi rnam par gźag pa, Rgyud sde rin po cheḥi mdzes rgyan, by Bu-ston (Toh. 5169), 12.
Rig sṅags kyi rgyal mo dbugs chen mo (Toh. 773; catalog has ... rgyal po ... chen po; Sanskrit title lacking), 135.
Rin po cheḥi myu gu (*the 'Mthaḥ gcod'* = *Rgyud kyi rgyal po dpal gsaṅ ba ḥdus paḥi rgya cher bśad pa, Sgron ma gsal baḥi dkaḥ baḥi gnas kyi mthaḥ gcod, Rin po cheḥi myu gu*) by Tsoṅ-kha-pa (Toh. 5284), 250, 320.
Rten ḥbrel rtsom ḥphro sogs ljags rtsom ḥphro can gyi skor, by Dkon mchog ḥjigs med dbaṅ po (blockprint in East Asiatic Library, University of California), 86, 96.
Sāccha lṅa gdab paḥi cho ga (no Sanskrit title or author name) (Toh. 3080), 116, 117.
Saddharmasmṛtyupasthāna-sūtra (Toh. 287), 45.
Sādhanamālā (*approximately* = *Sgrub thabs brgya rtsa*, q.v.; ed. by B. Bhattacharyya, Vols. I,II, GOS, Vols. 26, 41), 211, 220, 236, 294.
Śālistambaka-mahāyānasūtraṭīkā by Vasubandhu (Toh. 3986; catalog gives Nāgārjuna as author), 97.
Samādhirāja-sūtra (= *Ārya-Sarvadharmasvabhāvasamatāvipañcita-samādhirāja-nāma-mahāyānasūtra*) (Toh. 127), 47, 49.
Samāja. See *Guhyasamājatantra*.
Sāmānyavidhīnāṃ guhya-tantra (= *Sarvamaṇḍala-*°) (Toh. 806), 135, 137, 147.
Samayabhedoparacanacakre nikāyabhedopadeśanasaṃgraha-nāma by Vinītadeva (Toh. 4140), 67.
Sambandhaparīkṣā-prakaraṇa by Dharmakīrti (Toh. 4214), 73.
Sambarodaya (= *Śrī-Mahāsambarodaya-tantrarāja-nāma*) (Toh. 373), 251, 277.
Sambuddhabhāṣitapratibimbalakṣaṇavivaraṇa-nāma, presumably by Ārya Śāriputra (Toh. 4315), 81.
Saṃdhinirmocana-nāma-mahāyānasūtra (Toh. 106), 47, 49, 51.
Sampuṭa (= *Saṃpuṭa-nāma-mahātantra*) (Toh. 381), 169, 253.
Sampuṭikā (= *Sampuṭa*), 36.
Saṃtānāntarasiddhi-nāma-prakaraṇa by Dharmakīrti (Toh. 4219), 73.
Samuccaya. See *Pramāṇa-sūtra*.
Saṃghānusmṛtivyākhyā by Vasubandhu (Toh. 3984; catalog gives Asaṅga as author), 97.

Saṃvara-tantra (= *Tantrarājaśrīlaghusambara-nāma*) (Toh. 368), 35-6, 253, 255, 257, 259, 261, 266-7, 275, 281, 283, 293, 304.
Sañcayagāthā (= *Ārya-Prajñāpāramitā-sañcayagāthā*) (Toh. 13), 55, 91.
Sañcayagāthāpañjikā by Buddhaśrījñāna (Buddhajñānapāda) (Toh. 3798), 91.
Sandhivyākaraṇa-nāma-tantra (Toh. 444), 71.
Saptāṅga by Vāgīśvarakīrti (Toh. 1888), 267.
Saptaśatikā (= *Ārya-Saptaśatikā-nāma-prajñāpāramitā-mahāyānasūtra*) (Toh. 24), 47.
Saptatathāgata-pūrvapraṇidhānaviśeṣavistāra-sūtra (Toh. 503), 109.
Sarvadhāraṇīmaṇḍala-vidhi by Ratnakīrti (Toh. 3136), 109.
Sarvadurgatipariśodhanī-uṣṇīṣavijaya-nāma-dhāraṇī (Toh. 597), 115.
Sarvatathāgatādhiṣṭhānahṛdayaguhyadhātukaraṇḍa-nāma-dhāraṇīmahāyānasūtra (Toh. 507), 107.
Sarvatathāgata-mātṛtārā ... See *Tārā-bhava-tantra*.
Sarvatathāgatoṣṇīṣa-sitātapatrā-nāma-aparājitapratyaṅgirāmahā(vidyārājñī) (Toh. 590), 117.
Sarvatathāgatoṣṇīṣavijaya-nāma-dhāraṇī-kalpasahita (Toh. 594), 115.
Sarvatathāgatoṣṇīṣavijaya-nāma-dhāraṇī-kalpasahita (Toh. 595), 115-6.
Sarvatathāgatoṣṇīṣodbhūtasitātapatrā-nāma-vṛtti by Śuraṃgamavarma (Toh. 2689), 117.
Śatapañcāśatka-nāma-stotra by Mātṛceṭa (Toh. 1147) (ed. and tr. by D. R. Shackleton Bailey, *Śatapañcāśatka of Mātṛceṭa* (Cambridge, 1951), 79.
Śatasāhasrikā-prajñāpāramitā (Toh. 8), 47.
Śatasāhasrikāprajñāpāramitābṛhaṭṭīkā ascribed to King Khri sroṅ lde btsan (Toh. 3807), 96, 97.
Satyadvaya-vibhaṅgakārikā by Jñānagarbha (Toh. 3881), 91.
Satyadvaya-vibhaṅgavṛtti by Jñānagarbha (Toh. 3882), 91.
Sarvakarmāvaraṇaviśodhanī-nāma-dhāraṇī (Toh. 743), 129.
Sbas don (= *Bde mchog bsdus paḥi rgyud kyi rgya cher bśad pa, Sbas paḥi don kun gsal ba*) by Tsoṅ-kha-pa (Toh. 5316), 100.
Sdom pa gsum (= *Sdom gsum gyi rnam par bźag pa mdor bsdus te gtan la dbab paḥi rab tu byed pa, Thub bstan rin po cheḥi byi dor*) by Mkhas-grub-rje (Toh. 5488), 12, 22.
Sekoddeśaṭīkā by Nāro-pā (Toh. 1353) (ed. by Mario E. Carelli, Baroda, 1941), 288, 313, 332.
Sgrub thabs brgya rtsa (sādhana collection, Toh. 3143-3304 and Toh. 3306-3399), 167.
Sgrub thabs phyed ñis brgya ba (sādhana collection, Toh. 3645-3704), 167.
Sgrub thabs rgya mtsho (sādhana collection, Toh. 3400-3644), 167.
Śikṣāsamuccaya-kārikā by Śāntideva (Toh. 3939), 152.
Śikṣāsamuccaya by Śāntideva (Toh. 3940) (ed. by Cecil Bendall, reprint Mouton & Co., 1957; tr. by Cecil Bendall and W. H. D. Rouse, London, 1922), 152.
Śiṣyahitā vyākaraṇakalāpasūtravṛtti by Ugrabhūti (Toh. 4286), 77.
Slob maḥi re ba kun sloṅ (= *Bla ma lṅa bcu paḥi rnam bśad, Slob maḥi* ...) by Tsoṅ-kha pa (Toh. 5269; commentary on *Gurupañcāśikā*), 272.
Sman a-baḥi cho ga (*Sanskrit title doubtful*) by Nāgārjuna (Toh. 4308), 95.
Smṛtisaṃdarśanāloka (= *Śrīsaṃpuṭatilaka-nāma-yoginītantrarājaṭīkāsmṛtisaṃdarśanāloka-nāma*) by Indrabhūti (Toh. 1197), 102.
Sṅags rim chen mo (*usual reference for the work, Rgyal ba khyab bdag rdo rje ḥchaṅ chen poḥi lam gyi rim pa, gsaṅ ba kun gyi gnad rnam par phye ba*) by Tsoṅ-kha-pa (Toh. 5281), 12, 30, 36-7, 158-163, 168, 174, 184, 186, 192, 198, 200, 206, 211, 223, 244, 262, 268, 271, 273-284, 288, 292, 298-9, 302-305, 312-318, 322, 334, 337.
So sor ḥbraṅ maḥi ḥkhor lo bri baḥi thabs (Sanskrit title lacking) by Ratnākaraśānti (Toh. 3118), 113.
Śramaṇerakārikā (= *Āryamūlasarvāstivādiśrāmaṇerakārikā*) by Śākyaprabha (Toh. 4124), 85.

Śramaṇerakārikā-vṛttiprabhāvatī by Śakyaprabha (Toh. 4125), 85.
Śramaṇerakārikā (= *Triśatakārikāvyākhyāna*) by Vinītadeva (Toh. 4126), 83.
Śramaṇeravarṣāgrapṛcchā by Padmasambhava (Toh. 4132), 67.
Śrāvakabhūmi by Āryāsaṅga (Toh. 4036), 95, 221-2.
Śrī-Bhagavadabhisamaya-nāma by Lūi-pā (Toh. 1427), 256.
Śrī-Buddhakapālatantrapañjikā-jñānavatī by Saraha (Toh. 1652), 270.
Śrī-Mahākāla-tantra (Toh. 667), 123.
Śrī-Mālādevīsiṃhanāda-sūtra (Toh. 92), 49, 97.
Śrī-Paramādiṭikā (also: *Paramādiṭikā*) by Ānandagarbha (Toh. 2512), 221, 227, 234, 245.
Śrī-Paramādya (also: *Paramādya*) (Toh. 487: *Śrī-Paramādya-nāma-mahāyānakalparāja*; Toh. 488: *Śrī-Paramādyamantrakalpakhaṇḍa-nāma*), 221, 234-5.
Śrī-Vajracaṇḍacittaguhya-tantra (Toh. 458), 128-9.
Śrī-Vajracaṇḍacittaguhya-tantrottara (Toh. 459), 129.
Śrī-Vajracaṇḍacittaguhya-tantrottarottara (Toh. 460), 129.
Srog rtsol gyi de kho na ñid gsal ba (also: *Bźis źus = Dpal thams cad gsaṅ baḥi mchog gsaṅ chen źes bya baḥi rgyud kyi dum bu, dpal gsaṅ ba ḥdus paḥi bśad paḥi rgyud lha mo bźis yoṅs su źus paḥi rgya cher bśad pa, srog rtsol gyi de kho na ñid gsal ba*) by Tsoṅ-kha-pa (Toh. 5285), 220, 264, 318.
Stoṅ thun chen mo (= *Zab mo stoṅ pa ñid kyi de kha na ñid rab tu gsal bar byed paḥi bstan bcos, Skal bzaṅ mig ḥbyed*) by Mkhas-grub-rje (Toh. 5459), 12.
Subāhuparipṛcchā (also: the '*Subāhu*') (Toh. 805: *Ārya-Subāhuparipṛcchā-nāma-tantra*), 135, 137, 176, 189.
Subāhuparipṛcchā-sūtra (Toh. 70: *Ārya-Subāhuparipṛcchā-nāma-mahāyāna-sūtra*), 47.
Subāhuparipṛcchā-piṇḍārtha by Buddhaguhya (Toh. 2671), 139.
Suhṛllekha by Nāgārjuna (Toh. 4182), 93.
Śūnyatāsaptati by Nāgārjuna (Toh. 3827), 87.
Śūnyatāsaptati-vṛtti by Nāgārjuna (Toh. 3831), 89.
Suparigraha (= *Suparigraha-nāma-maṇḍalavidhisādhana*) by Thub dkaḥ zla ba (Toh. 1240), 275.
Surūpa-nāma-dhāraṇī (Toh. 540), 109.
Susiddhi (= *Susiddhikaramahātantrasādhanopāyikapaṭala*) (Toh. 807), 137, 139, 149, 155, 167, 177, 183, 191, 193, 203.
Sūtrālaṃkāra (= *Mahāyānasūtrālaṃkāra-nāma-kārikā*) by Maitreya (Toh. 4020), 95, 97.
Sūtrālaṃkāravyākhyā by Vasubandhu (Toh. 4026), 95.
Sūtrālaṃkāravṛttibhāṣya by Sthiramati (Toh. 4034), 316.
Sūtrasamuccaya by Nāgārjuna (Toh. 3934), 93.
Suvarṇa-prabhāsa-sūtra (Toh. 555: **Suvarṇaprabhāsottamavijayasūtra*; Toh. 556 and Toh. 557: *Suvarṇaprabhāsottamasūtrendrarāja*) (ed. in Sanskrit by Johannes Nobel: *Suvarṇabhāsottamasūtra. Das Goldglanz-Sūtra, Ein Sanskrit-Text des Mahāyāna-Buddhismus*... Leipzig, 1937), 109-111.
Svalpākṣaraprajñāpāramitā (Toh. 22), 47, 109.
Tantrārthāvatāra. See *Avatāra*.
Tantrārthāvatāravyākhyāna. See *Avatāra-vyākhyāna*.
Tārā-bhava-tantra (= *Sarvatathāgatamātṛtārāviśvakarmabhava-tantra-nāma*) (Toh. 726), 100, 127.
Tārādevīstotraikaviṃśatikasādhana-nāma by Sūryagupta (Toh. 1685); this is followed by other works by Sūryagupta on the *Ekaviṃśatisādhana*, namely, Toh. 1686, the *karmāṅga*; Toh. 1687, the *upadeśakrama*; Toh. 1688, the *sādhana*; Toh. 1689, the *cūḍāmaṇi*, 127.
Tārā-nāmāṣṭaśataka (Toh. 727, 728), 127.

Tarkajvāla (= *Madhyamakahṛdayavṛttitarkajvālā*) by Bhavya (Bhāvaviveka) (Toh. 3856), 67, 89, 94.
Tathāgatagarbha-sūtra (Toh. 258), 49, 97.
Tathāgatamahākaruṇānirdeśa-sūtra (also the '*Dhāraṇīśvararājaparipṛcchā*') (Toh. 147), 49, 97.
Tattvāloka (= *Sarvatathāgatatattvasaṃgrahamahāyānābhisamaya-nāma-tantratattvālokakarī-nāma-vyākhyā*) by Ānandagarbha (Toh. 2510), 24, 126, 225, 227, 235-6-7, 282.
Tattvasaṃgraha (= *Sarvatathāgatatattvasaṃgraha-nāma-mahāyānasūtra*) (Toh. 479), 24-5, 35, 145, 147, 214-5-6-7, 235.
Thob yig (= *Thob yig gsal baḥi me loṅ*) by Blo-bzaṅ-ḥphrin-las (blockprint in East Asiatic Library, University of California), 11, 26, 112, 156, 218-9.
Triṃśikā-kārikā by Vasubandhu (Toh. 4055), 95.
Trisamayavyūharāja-nāma-tantra (Toh. 502), 100, 105.
Triśaraṇasaptati by Candrakīrti (Toh. 3971), 93.
Tshe dpag med ḥchi med rṅa sgraḥi gzuṅs (entered in the *Comparative Analytical Catalogue of the Kanjur*, Otani University, Kyoto), 125.
Tshig don gyi brjed byaṅ (= *Tshig gi don bśad paḥi brjed byaṅ*) (no Sanskrit title) by Buddhaguhya (Toh. 2672), 139, 176.
Uṣṇīṣasitātapatrāhomavidhi by Tīkṣṇavajra (Toh. 3104), 119.
Uṣṇīṣavijaya-dhāraṇī (= *Sarvatathāgatoṣṇīṣavijaya-nāma-dhāraṇī-kalpasahita*) (Toh. 596), 115.
Uṣṇīṣavijaya-nāma-dhāraṇī-kalpa (= *Sarvatathāgatoṣṇīṣavijaya-nāma-*°) (Toh. 598), 28, 115.
Uṣṇīṣodbhūtasitātapatrāvidhi-nāma by Śūraṃgamavarmavajra (Toh. 3108), 119, 147.
Vacanamukhyāyudhopama by Smṛtijñānakīrti (Toh. 4295), 77.
Vādanyāya-nāma-prakaraṇa by Dharmakīrti (Toh. 4218), 73.
Vāhikaṭīkā (= *Śrī-Ḍākārṇavamahāyoginītantrarājavāhikaṭīkā-nāma*) by Padmavajra (Toh. 1419), 101, 296.
Vaidalya-sūtra-nāma by Nāgārjuna (Toh. 3826), 87.
Vaidalya-nāma-prakaraṇa by Nagārjuna (Toh. 3830), 89.
Vairocana-tantra. See *Mahāvairocana-tantra.*
Vajracchedikā (= *Ārya-Vajracchedikā-nāma-prajñāpāramitā-mahāyānasūtra*) (Toh. 16), 47.
Vajrahṛdayālaṃkāra-tantra-nāma (Toh. 451), 251, 267, 272.
Vajralohatuṇḍa-nāma-dhāraṇī (Toh. 760), 133.
Vajramālā (= *Śrī-Vajramālābhidhānamahāyogatantra-sarvatantrahṛdayarahasyavibhaṅga-nāma*) (Toh. 445), 70-1, 302, 313.
Vajrameruśikhara-kūṭāgāra-dhāraṇī (Toh. 751), 131.
Vajrapañjarā-tantra (= *Ārya-Ḍākinīvajrapañjarā-mahātantrarājakalpa-nāma*), (Toh. 419), 37, 151, 251, 253, 255, 263, 274.
Vajrapāṇyabhiṣeka-mahātantra (Toh. 496), 165, 167, 171, 176, 205.
Vajrapātāla-tantra (= *Ārya-Vajrapāṇinīlāmbaradharavajrapātāla-nāma-tantra*) (Toh. 499), 207.
Vajrapātāla-tantra (= *Ārya-Vajrapātāla-nāma-tantrarāja*) (Toh. 744), 129.
Vajrasattvodaya-nāma-sādhana by Ānandagarbha (Toh. 2517), 240.
Vajraśekhara (= *Vajraśekhara-mahāguhyayogatantra*) (Toh. 480), 25, 145, 235.
Vajraśṛṅkhalatantrakalpa (Toh. 758), 133.
Vajratuṇḍa-nāma-nāgasamaya (Toh. 759), 133.
Vajrāvali (= *Vajrāvali-nāma-maṇḍala-sādhana*) by Abhyākaragupta (Toh. 3140), 141, 145, 151, 275.
Vajravidāraṇā-nāma-dhāraṇī (Toh. 750), 116, 129, 131, 136, 165.

Vajravidāraṇā-nāma-dhāraṇī-maṇḍalavidhiratnadyuti-nāma by Sabari-pā (Toh. 2932), 145, 169.
Vajrodaya (= *Vajradhātumahāmaṇḍalavidhisarvavajrodaya-nāma*) by Ānandagarbha (Toh. 2516), 145, 147, 223, 239, 241
Vasudhārā-nāma-dhāraṇī (Toh. 662), 121.
Vastusaṃgrahaṇī by Āryāsaṅga (Toh. 4039-4040), 95.
Vigrahavyāvartanī-kārikā-nāma by Nāgārjuna (Toh. 3828), 87.
Vigrahavyāvartanī-vṛtti by Nāgārjuna (Toh. 3832), 89.
Vimala-prabhā (= *Vimalaprabhā-nāma-mūlatantrānusāriṇī-dvādaśasāhasrikālaghukālacakra-tantrarāja-ṭīkā*) by Somanātha (Toh. 845), 121, 259, 263.
Vimaloṣṇīṣa-dhāraṇī (= *Samantamukhapraveśaraśmivimaloṣṇīṣaprabhāsasarvatathāgatahṛdayasamayavilokita-nāma-dhāraṇī*) (Toh. 599), 115.
Vimaloṣṇīṣa-dhāraṇī-vṛtti (= *Samantamukhapraveśaraśmivimaloṣṇīṣaprabhāsasarvatathāgatahṛdayasamayavilokita-nāma-dhāraṇīvṛtti*) by Sahajalalita (Toh. 2688), 117.
Vimaloṣṇīṣa-dhāraṇī ... **stūpa-vidhi* (= Toh. 3068, *Ḥphags pa kun nas sgor ḥjug paḥi ḥod zer gtsug tor dri ma med paḥi gzuṅs bklag ciṅ mchod rten brgya rtsa brgyad dam mchod rten lṅa gdab paḥi cho ga mdo sde las btus pa*; or Toh. 3069, *Ḥphags pa kun nas sgor ḥjug paḥi ḥod zer gtsug tor dri ma med par snaṅ baḥi gzuṅs bklag ciṅ mchod rten brgya rtsa brgyad dam mchod rten lṅa gdab paḥi cho ga mdo sde las bsdus pa*; neither Sanskrit title available) by Śāntarakṣita, 117.
Viṃśatikā-kārikā by Vasubandhu (Toh. 4056.) 95.
Vinayakārikā (= *Vinaya-puṣpamālā-nāma*) by Viśākhadeva (Toh. 4123), 85.
Vinayasūtra by Guṇaprabha (Toh. 4117), 83.
Vinayasūtraṭīkā by Dharmamitra (Toh. 4120), 83.
Vinayasūtravṛtti-svavyākhyāna by Guṇaprabha (Toh. 4119), 83.
Vinayavastu (Toh. 1), 45.
Vinayavibhaṅga-padavyākhyāna by Vinītadeva (Toh. 4114), 83.
Viniścaya-saṃgrahaṇī by Āryāsaṅga (Toh. 4038), 95.
Vivaraṇa-saṃgrahaṇī by Āryāsaṅga (Toh. 4042), 95.
Vyākhyāyukti by Vasubandhu (Toh. 4061), 95.
Yamāri, Tantras of the Red (*rakta*) and the Black (*kṛṣna*) (especially: Toh. 468, *Śrī-Vajramahābhairava-nāma-tantra*; and Toh. 470, *Śrī-Vajrabhairavakalpa-tantrarāja*), 265.
Ye rdor. See *Rgyud bśad thabs kyi man ṅag gsal bar bstan pa.*
Yi dvags kha nas me ḥbar ba la skyabs mdzad pa źes bya baḥi gzuṅs (no Sanskrit title) (Toh. 646), 121.
Yogācārabhūmi (= *Bahubhūmika*) by Asaṅga (Toh. 4035); *Bhūmi-vastu* by Asaṅga includes the *Bahubhūmika* (Toh. 4035), *Śrāvakabhūmi* (Toh. 4036), and *Bodhisattvabhūmi* (Toh. 4037), 71, 95.
Yogaratnamālā-nāma-hevajrapañjikā by Kṛṣṇa Pandit (Toh. 1183) (ed. by D. L. Snellgrove in his *Hevajra Tantra* Vol. II; see *Hevajratantra*), 28.
Yugalanaddhaprakāśa-nāma-sekaprākriyā by Rāhula-śrī-mitra (Toh. 1818), 141-2, 301.
Yuktiṣaṣṭhikā-kārikā-nāma by Nāgārjuna (Toh. 3825), 87, 89.
Yuktiṣaṣṭhikā-vṛtti by Candrakīrti (Toh. 3864), 89.

II. WESTERN WORKS[2]

Danielou, Alain. Yoga, *The Method of Re-Integration* (London, 1949), 220.
Dasgupta, Shashibhusan. *Obscure Religious Cults* (Calcutta: Firma K. L. Mukhopadhyay, 1962), 36.

Fa-tsun. Mi Tsung Tao Tz'u Ti Lun (translation into Chinese of Mkhas-grub-rje's *Rgyud sde spyi rnam*, in 26th year of the Republic = 1937), 13.
Ghosh, Manomohan, tr. *Nāṭyaśāstra ascribed to Bharata-muni*, Vol. I (Calcutta, 1951), 282.
Lalou, Marcelle. *Iconographie des étoffes peintes*, Buddhica, Tome VI (Paris, 1930), 300.
Lamotte, Étienne. *Histoire du bouddhism indien* (Louvain, 1958), 66.
——, *Le traité de la grande vertu de sagesse*, Tome I (Louvain, 1944), 16.
Lessing, Ferdinand D. "The Eighteen Worthies Crossing the Sea", in *The Sino-Swedish Expedition Publication* 38 (Stockholm, 1954), 284.
——, *Mongolian-English Dictionary*, compiled by Mattai Haltod and others (University of California Press, Berkeley, 1960), 14.
——, *Yung-Ho-Kung*; *an iconography of the Lamaist cathedral in Peking* (Stockholm, 1942), 119.
Lin Li-Kouang. *L'Aide-Memoire de la Vraie Loi* (Paris, 1949), 169.
Nebesky-Wojkowitz, René de. *Oracles and Demons of Tibet* (The Hague, Mouton & Co., 1956), 18, 118.
Obermiller, Eugene. "The Doctrine of Prajñā-pāramitā as exposed in the Abhisamayālaṃkāra of Maitreya", *Acta Orientalia*, XI (1932), 17.
Pandey, K. C. *Abhinavagupta*; *an Historical and Philosophical Study* (Benares, 1935), 210.
Renou, Louis and Filliozat, Jean. *L'Inde classique*, Tome II (Paris, 1953), 320.
Sūryakānta, Dr., tr. "Kṣemendra's Suvṛttatilaka", *Poona Orientalist*, XVII, 1-4 (1952), 305.
Takakusu, Junjiro. *The Essentials of Buddhist Philosophy*, 2nd ed. (Honolulu, 1949), 204.
Tucci, Giuseppe. *Indo-Tibetica*, Vol. III, Pt. II (Roma, 1936), 304.
——, *Tibetan Painted Scrolls* (Roma, 1949), 11, 304.
Wayman, Alex. "Notes on the Sanskrit term Jñāna", *Journal of the American Oriental Society*, 75:4 (Oct.-Dec., 1955), 37.
Yoshimura, Shūki. *Chibetto-go Jiten, Sōkōhan* (Kyoto, 1955-56), 202.

[2] Indexed by author or translator. Works already included in the preceding list are omitted. However, all authors mentioned in the basic translation of Mkhas-grub-rje's work and its annotation are to be found in the Index of Names and Subjects.

INDEX OF NAMES AND SUBJECTS[1]

abhāva (non-concrete), 53; *-śūnyatā* (Voidness of non-substantiality), and *-svabhāva-śūnyatā* (Voidness of both non-substantiality and intrinsic nature), 28.

Abhaya (= Abhayākara), 97

Abhayākara, 105, 141, 145, 149, 151, 267, 335

abhicāra (= *abhicāruka*), see under Action (= Acts)

Abhidharma, 57, 81-85, 217

abhidhāna (Lexicography), 77

abhijñā (Faculty, supernormal), 201

abhilāpana (Vocal expression), 247

abhisamaya, the eight, 46-7, 109; as Visualization, 309

abhisaṃbodhi (Revelation-Enlightenment), 27-37, 129, 162-3, 227, 305

abhiṣeka (Initiation, q.v.)

abhyudita, 209

Ablutions, 191

Absolute (= Absolute Object, Supreme Goal; *paramārtha*), 91; — Mind of Enlightenment (*bodhicitta*), 334; Clear Light of the Absolute Object, 37, 39, 217, 325, 327; — *maṇḍala*, 270; — *bhaga* and *bodhicitta maṇḍala*, 318; — Production, 91; Voidness of the Supreme Goal (*paramārtha-śūnyatā*), 28; — Truth (*paramārtha-satya*), 278.

Acala, 118

ācārya, 43, 227, 235-239; Hierophant, q.v.

Action (= Acts, *karma*), 21, 217, 230-232, 235, 247, 267, 277, 285, 321; — of Buddha, 29, 35-39; Marvellous — (= Wondrous —), 26, 225-235, 239, 241, 247; Magical — in connection with Service (*sevā*) and Burnt Offering (*homa*), 119, 123, 127, 129, 135-137, 267, and of three kinds, Appeasing (*śāntika*), Prosperity (*pauṣṭika*), and Terrible or Drastic (*abhicāruka*) (with the third divided into Domineering and Destroying to make four), 117, 136-7, 177, 191, 193, 201, 211, 272; of *maṇḍala*, q.v., 275-279

adbhutadharma, 55

Adamantine *samādhi* (*vajropama-samādhi*), 37

ādarśa (Mirror), 223

ādarśa-jñāna (a kind of Knowledge, q.v.)

ādhāra (Residence), 266, 291; *ādhārotpatti* (Generation of Residence), 175

ādheya (Residents), 177, 291

adhideva, 234-5

adhigama (Higher Cognition or Comprehension), 91, 162

adhimukticaryā, 105

adhiprajñā, 57

adhisamādhi, 57

adhiśīla, 57

adhiṣṭhāna (see Blessing); also used once in meaning of 'Foundation', 285

adhiṣṭhita (Blessed, or Empowered), 163, 241

adhyātma-vidyā (Science, inner), 73

[1] As far as possible, the main collection of page numbers for an equivalent pair of Sanskrit and English terms, each of which are indexed separately in their proper alphabetical order, will be given under the English term. However, in some cases, e.g. *maṇḍala*, the total set of page references will be under the Sanskrit term. In a few cases, e.g. *vajra* (Diamond, Thunderbolt), it will be necessary to consult both the Sanskrit and the English equivalents.

ādi-vajra (First or Primordial Thunderbolt), 31, 33, 243
Aeon, incalculable (*asaṃkhyeya-kalpa*), 17; Great — (*mahā-kalpa*), 201
Affiliation (T. *rigs ḥdra*), 156, 168-9, 194, 199, 205, 263, 265-6, 268, 325, 332
āgama (Scripture), 91, 234
Age of Strife (*kaliyuga*), 79
Agent (*kāraka*), 217
Aggregates (= Personality Aggregates; *skandha*), 57
ahaṃkāra (Ego, Egotism), 163, 283
Aim (*artha*), 153, 157
Air, vital (see under Wind)
Ajātaśatru, the King, 59, 61, 131
ājñā (Directive, Promulgation), 328; of variety, Specialized and General, 112
Ājñātakauṇḍinya, 41
Akaniṣṭha, 21-27, 35, 39, 125, 215, 236;— Ghanavyūha, 21, 205
ākāra, 161
ākarṣaṇa (Attracting), 214, 237
ākāśa (Space or Sky), 287, 292
akiñcanya (Nothingness), 297
akṣa-mālā (Chaplet), 187
Akṣapāda, 73
akṣara (Syllable, q.v.), 271; *-abhiṣeka* (Initiation of the Syllable), 325; *-devatā* (Latter Deity), 161
Akṣobhya, 29, 34, 37, 100-103, 107, 129, 215, 217, 221, 225, 227, 231, 247, 249, 264, 286, 299, 301, 313
alala, 65
ālambana (Object, meditative), 161, 187
alaṃkāra (Embellishments of poetry), 77, 79, 95
ālaya (Holding, as of the breath), 157; *-vijñāna* (Store Consciousness), 51, 168; *-vijñāna-āśraya* (Store consciousness basis), 29
ālīḍha, 282; *-stha*, 273
āloka (a Light, q.v.); *ālokābhāsa* (Spread-of-Light); *ālokopalabdhi* (Culmination-of-Light)
Alternatives (*koṭi*), six (*ṣaṭkoṭi*), 219
Amarasiṃha, 79
Amber, 175
Ambrosia (*amṛta*), 37, 42, 121, 181, 220, 287-293, 296-7, 319, 321, 329
Amitābha, 31, 34, 37, 100-1, 217, 221, 225, 227, 231, 264, 286, 313
Amitāyus, 115, 123, 125, 145; the Jetāri-, 277
Amoghasiddhi, 34, 37, 100-1, 192, 221, 231, 264, 286, 313
Amoghavajra, 285
amṛta (see Ambrosia)
Amṛtakuṇḍalī, 118
amṛte (a *mantra*), 118
Anabhilāpyāpramāṇā, 312
anadhyāya (Academic holidays), 74
Ānanda, 23, 59-65, 109, 123
ānanda (see Joy)
Ānandagarbha, 24-27, 145, 149, 216-7, 221-227, 234-241, 282
ānantarya, 21
Ancillaries (*aṅga*), 171, 269, 320; of Steps of Production, 317, 331; sixteen (from among thirty-seven Categories, q.v.), 236-239
aṇḍa-jā (Birth from eggs), 330
aṅga (Ancillaries, q.v.)
Anger, 328
Āniñjyo-nāma-samādhi (Unstirring *samādhi*), 27
anitya (Impermanent), 85
añjana (Ointment, lampblack or antimony), 221
aṅkuśa (Iron hook), 224
antarābhava (Intermediate State), 123
Antidotes, 222, 315
Antimony (*añjana* or *srod-añjana*), 216
anubheda (Expansion, mystical), 327
anucāra-viśuddhi (Purification of Attendants), 255
anujñā (Permission or Authorization), 55, 141, 272, 309
anumodana (Sympathetic delight), 185
Anūnatvāpūrṇatvanirdeśa-parivarta, 48-9
anurāga (Passion), 169, 245
anusmṛti (one of the *ṣaḍaṅga*), 320
anuṣṭhāna (Procedure), 28-9, 159
anusvāra, 191
Anuttarayoga-tantra. See under Tantra
anuvyañjana (Marks, the eighty minor), 19, 30, 35
Apabhraṃśa, 69
apāna (a Wind), 264
Aparājita, 118
Aphorisms, 53
Apparition, 22-3, 35
Aramoniga, 107
Arapacana-Mañjughoṣa, 111
argha (Sacrifice), 289
arghya (Oblation), 177

Arhat, 59, 63-67, 81, 83, 105; Arhatship, 42, 61, 63
Aristotelian causes, 240
Armpit (*kakṣa*), 281
Arms, 259, 261
Array (*vyūha*), 205
Arrow (*śara*), 224
artha (Meaning, Entity, Aim, or Goal), 79, 93, 153, 157, 215; *-prabhāsvara* (Clear Light of the [Absolute] Object), 37, and see under Absolute
Arts, 73, 81, 95
ārya (Noble, Nobility, Noble One), 203, 228
Āryadeva, 35, 127
Āryāsaṅga (= Asaṅga), 95-99, 167, 221-2, 310-1
āryasatya (Noble Truth), see under Truth
Āryaśūra, 78
Ārya Vimuktasena, 85, 91, 97
asādhāraṇa (Uncommon, Unshared), 147, 263, 309, 313; *-mārga* (Uncommon Path), see under Path
aśaikṣa-mārga (Path beyond Training), see under Path
aśaikṣa-yuganaddha (Pair combined beyond Learning), see under Union
asaṃhārya, 266
asaṃkhyeya-kalpa (Aeons, incalculable), 17
asaṃskṛta (Unconditioned), 49, 53; *-śūnyatā* (Voidness of the Unconditioned), 28
Asaṅga. See Āryāsaṅga
Ascetic virtue (*dhūta-guṇa*, twelve or thirteen), 69
Ashes, 281
Aśoka, 67-8
Aspects (*ākāra*), 270
Aspiration, fervent (*praṇidhāna*), 185
Āspharaṇaka-samādhi (Space-filling *samādhi*), 27
Assemblies (of the *Hevajra*), 257
aṣṭāṅga (the eight topics, of medical treatise), 79
aṣṭau vimokṣāḥ (Eight Releases), 63
aṣṭottaraśata-nāma (One-hundred and eight Names), 121
Astrology, 329
asura, 103
Aśvaghoṣa, 78, 273, 328
Aśvajit, 41
Aṭakāvatī (name of the Lord's Palace), 133
Atīśa (= Dīpamkaraśrījñāna), 97, 100, 105, 125-155
atiśūnya, 71
ātmagraha (Adherence to the view of 'Self') 93
ātmatattva (Self Reality), 195, 214
Attracting (of Deity; *ākarṣaṇa*), 237, 240, 243, 249, 295-297
Attributes (*nimitta*), 228, 234, 271
aupapāduka-jñāna (the Knowledge spontaneously generated), 43
Auspicious days, the four, 75
Authorization (*anujñā*), 55
Avadāna (Parables), 55
avaivartika (Irreversible), 141
Avalokita (= Avalokiteśvara), 185
Avalokiteśvara, 22, 51, 89, 102, 107, 113, 115, 121-127
āvaraṇa (Obscuration), 53
Avarice (*mātsarya*), 221-223, 230-1
Avīci (a Hell), 107, 115, 117, 123
avidyā (Nescience), 37, 314; *-pratipakṣa* (Antidote for Nescience), 315
Awakened (the Buddha), see under Buddha
āyāma (of compound *prāṇāyāma*), 209
āyatana (Sensory base), 57, 163, 257
āyuṣmat ('Long Living,' one in the spiritual life), 41, 43

B

Ba-so-chos-kyi-rgyal-mtshan, 11, 78
Backward (*pratiloma*), 327
bāhya-kriyā (Action, outer), 219; *bahirdhā-śūnyatā* (Voidness of the External), 28
Bailey, D.R. Shackleton, 78
bāla (Infants), 79
bali (Food Offering), see under Offering; *-vidhi* (Rite of Oblations), 123
Ball (*piṇḍarūpa*), 220
bandhana (Tying), 214, 237
Banners, 175, 291
Barley, 177; — grain, 220, 245
Base of spine (see Center), 322
Bath, 159, 181, 219
bden par grub pa (Tib. for 'real production', 'really existent'), 53
Bdud bzlog byed tshul (a certain forged text), 109
Be-coṅ maṅ-po (*mahādaṇḍa*), 119

Beatitude (= Bliss, q.v.)
Bees, 48
Begging, 279; — bowls (*pātra*), 43
Beings (*sattva*), 162, 297; also: manifest and non-manifest, 279; living (= sentient), 217, 221-2, 328; intent on Enlightenment (Bodhisattva, q.v.), 16; Symbolic Being (*samaya-sattva*), 162-3, 179, 235-6, 285, 287, 295-299; Samādhi Being, 296-7; Knowledge Being (*jñāna-sattva*), 37, 162-167, 171, 177, 179, 234-237, 240-243, 249, 261, 272, 275, 285, 293-301
Believers (*śrāddhasattva*), 328
Bell, 34, 141, 313
Bendall, Cecil, 152
Benefit (*hita*), 155
Bhadanta Vimuktasena, 97
Bhadra, 66-7
Bhadrayānīya, 85
Bhadrika, 41
bhaga, 318-9, 322
Bhagavat, 17, 27, 35, 39-45, 55-63, 105, 107, 111, 115-125, 131-135, 177, 181, 236, 240, 254, 263, 312
Bhattacharyya, B., 68, 216, 256, 304
bhauma (Earth-bound), 203
Bhavabhadra, 335
bhāvanā (Contemplation, q.v.)
Bhāvaviveka, 67, 87-94
bhāveya (to be Contemplated, or to be Cultivated), 45
Bhavya (= Bhāvaviveka, q.v.)
Bhavyakīrti, 219, 223
bhikṣu (Monk), 61-67, 105
Bhikṣuṇīprātimokṣasūtra, 83
Bhikṣuprātimokṣasūtra, 83
bhūmi (Stage, q.v.); in meaning of 'our world', 79; *-tala* (Earth surface), 175
Bhūmi (referring to *Yogācārabhūmi*), 95, 99
bhūta (Elementary Spirits), 135-6
Bhūtaḍāmara, 145
Bihar Society, 70
bīja-akṣara (Syllable, germ or seed, q.v.), 291
bimba, 107
Bimbisāra (the King), 131
bindu (Drop; = Vasanta-tilaka, the Drop of Springtime), 71, 255, 304-5, 333; *-rūpabhūta* (Substance of drop; possibly semen), 319
Birth, 157, 295, 330-333; four kinds of —, 330; bound to one more birth (*ekajāti-pratibaddha*), 35
Bkra-śis-dpal-bzaṅ (the father of Mkhas-grub-rje), 11
Bla-ma-rje (presumably = Red-mdaḥ-pa) 86-7, 97, 99
Blessing (*adhiṣṭhāna*), 26, 55, 119, 163, 204, 214, 224, 228, 232, 241, 283, 296
Bliss (= Beatitude; *sukha*), 184, 268, 291, 317-323, 333, 335; Great — (*mahā-sukha*), 261, 263, 267-8, 328; Bliss-Void (= Beatitude and Void; *sukha-śūnya*), 143, 157, 259, 263, 265, 268, 277, 317, 319, 323, 325, 333, 335
Blo-bzaṅ-ḥphrin-las, 11
Blo-bzaṅ-tshul-khrims-rgya-mtsho, 11
blo kha phyogs pa (*buddhi*-side), 211
Blood, 177, 220
Bodhi-tree, 39, 41, 187
bodhicitta (Mind of Enlightenment), 147-152, 155, 159, 162, 185, 204, 213-4, 222-3, 270, 309, 315, 321, 324, 328, 334; of varieties, Absolute (*paramārtha-bodhicitta*), 318, 334, 335, and Relative (*saṃvṛti-bodhicitta*), 318, 334; *bodhicit-totpādika* (Generating the Mind of Enlightenment), 17, 153, 185, which includes Aspiration Mind (*praṇidhi-citta*), 151-155, and Entrance (or Progressing) Mind (*prasthāna-citta*), 149-153
bodhipakṣyā dharmāḥ (the Natures bordering on Enlightenment), 256
Bodhisattva (a Being intent on Enlightenment), 12, 16, 19, 21, 27, 36-7, 45, 47, 55, 69-70, 89, 103, 105, 121, 137, 161, 187, 203, 205, 213-216, 227, 235-6, 263, 310, 313, 315, 334-5; from Eight Stage onward called 'non-regressing' or 'irreversible' (*avaivartika*), 19; celestial and human —, 163; belonging to Tathāgata Family, 121; as former lives of Buddha (Jātaka), 55; his Path, 70; his Vows, 153; the eight Great Bodhisattvas called 'close disciples', each with one-hundred and eight names, 121
Body (*deha, kāya*), 21, 33, 39, 41, 55, 109, 142-3, 156-7, 161-2, 167-173, 187-191, 194-206, 209, 211, 220, 223-245, 263, 266, 268, 272, 291, 294-297, 302, 305, 307, 312, 317-322, 325, 327, 333; of Buddha, 156, 312, 332, which are usually three, Dharma-kāya, 21, 25, 53,

107, 156, 195, 198-9, 204, 220, 237, 239, 263, 296, 312, 325, 332, Saṃbhoga-kāya (Body of Complete Enjoyment), 19-23, 27, 29, 33, 35, 39, 49, 51, 70, 156, 205, 232, Nirmāṇa-kāya (Creative Body), 21, 25, 35, 39, 106, 156, 204, 215, 223, 232, 296, 312, 315, 332, and the latter two usually called Formal or Material Body (*rūpa-kāya*), 21, 27, 41, 169, 224, 265, 268; other Bodies of Buddha, possibly identifiable with one or other of the preceding, Svabhāva-kāya (Intrinsic-nature or Self-existent Body), 49-53, 223, 232; Vipāka-kāya (Maturation Body), 27, 195, 232; also: Arcane — (*kāya-viveka*), 312, 320-1, 327; Consummated, 228; Divine, 157, 195; Diamond, 325; Fruitional, 317, 325; Illusory — (*māyā-deha*), Knowledge — (*jñānamaya-kāya* or *jñāna-kāya*), 26, 37, 195; 'Means' — (*upāya-deha*), 157; Mental — (*manomaya. kāya*), 26-7, 142; Pure , 37; Rainbow)-—, 325; Vajra-vidāraṇa —, 131; of Deity, 197, 231, 234, 294, 297; of Guru, 307; of the Path, 171; of Tathāgata, 21, 109, 205-6; of the Victorious One, 48. Body, in the sense of 'main part' (*maula, maulī*), 139, 303; in the sense of therapeutic investigation, 79

Border countries (*pratyanta-janapada*), 69

Boundless states (*apramāṇa*), 184 (listed), 185

Brahmā, 18, 43, 109

Brahmadatta, 41

Brahman, 74

Brahmin, 69, 75, 105, 107

brda (Symbolic meaning), 71

Breast goer (*uraga*), 280-1

Breath, 189

brgyud rgyu (Remote or Ancestral cause), 241

Bṛhaspati, 73

Bright (the physical component), 245, 247, 268

Bsam yas, 84

Bu-ḥdren-rgyal-mo (the mother of Mkhas-grub-rje), 11

Buddha, 11-2, 21-45, 48, 51-57, 63, 67-71 85, 91, 105-6, 131, 139, 142, 151, 156-7, 161-163, 184-5, 203-207, 220, 227, 234-237, 241, 255, 302, 312-316, 328-9; Buddhahood, 35, 39, 41, 53, 153, 155, 227, 268, 315, 331, 333; Awakened-not-Expanded (*buddha*, but *avibuddha*), 31, 51; Awakened-Expanded (*buddha* and *vibuddha*), 33, 51, = Complete Buddha, 49, 313, 316, = Manifest Complete Buddha (*abhisaṃbuddha*), 17, 19, 43, 215; also: Buddhas of the past, 43; of ten directions, 27; tile Buddha, 116-7; Buddha-field (*buddhakṣetra*), 23, 107

Buddhaguhya, 25, 27, 129, 139, 147, 165, 167, 172-3, 179, 186, 198, 204, 211, 217, 222-227, 234-5, 241, 244

Buddhajñāna (= Buddhajñānapāda), 37, 91, 97

Buddhalocanā, 314

Buddhapālita, 87-91

buddhi, 210, 333; *buddhi*-side, 210-1

Bya-gdoṅ-ba-can (the *bhikṣu*), 129

C

caitta, 37, 71

cakra (Wheel; Center in body), 36, 69, 113, 319-322; sometimes = *maṇḍala*, as *cittacakra*, *kāya*-, and *vāk*-, 304, and *cakreśa* (Lord of *maṇḍala*), 275; see also Wheel, Center, Circle

Calming (*śamatha*), 57, 199, 210

caṇḍā-yoga (Yoga of Heat), 36

Caṇḍālī, 36

Candidates (*vineya*), 17, 29, 31, 35, 37, 47, 57, 143, 171, 217, 219-223, 231, 261, 265, 267, 311, 315, 319, 323, 335

Candragomin, 77, 79, 119, 127, 139

Candrakīrti, 87, 89, 91, 94, 239

Candranandana, 79

Canopy (*vitāna*), 176

caramabhavika (Last Life), 21, 35, 105

Carelli, Mario E., 288

caryā-bhaga (Practical part), 81

Category, ten (External or Inner), 272-3; thirty-seven, 214; of Corruption, 227

Cathartic (*praśrabdhi*), mental or physical, 199, 201, 210

catuḥpariṣad (Fourfold Congregation), 203

catuḥsandhyā (Watches, four), 277

caturmahārāja (Great Kings, the four), 111; *-kāyika* (belonging to the Four-Great-King realm), 169

caturtha (the Fourth), 272, 311

Cause (*hetu*), 51, 53, 105, 193, 214, 263, 266; Actual —, 241; Ancestral —, 241; Buddhahood —, 53; Efficient —, 241-

247; Final —, 241-247; Formal 241, 245; Material, 241-247; Near ,— 241; Remote, 241; Tathāgata —, 53
Cave, 59, 115
Center, 282, 297, 299, 321-2, 325, 333; *bhaga*-like, *cakra*-like, and lotus-like, 322
Central vein (= Central channel; *avadhūtī*), 157, 333
Certainty (the five of the Saṃbhogakāya), 21; Wheel of Absolute —, 37
Cessation (*nirodha*), 45; Cessation-Equipoise (*nirodha-samāpatti*), 65
Ceylon (Siṅgala), 89
Chalk, 287
chandas (Prosody), 77
Chaplet, 187, 191, 193
Characteristic (*lakṣaṇa*), 18-21, 30, 35, 49, 57, 61, 168, 222, 268, 271, 273, 315, 323, 329, 331; two kinds, Individual (*svalakṣaṇa*) and Universal (*sāmānya-lakṣaṇa*), 57, 222; Voidness of Individual Characteristics (*svalakṣaṇa-śūnyatā*), 28; three kinds (*pravṛtti*, *karma*, and *kula*), 168; three kinds (*parinispanna*, *paratantra*, and *parikalpita*), 49; — of the place, 137
Chicken-foot Mountain (Kukkuṭapāda), 59
Chignon, 209
Chariot, 309
chos rje (*dharmasvāmin*), 11
chos sde ñi śu (the twenty treatises by Maitreya, Asaṅga, and Vasubandhu), 95
chu tshod (forty-five minute period), 193
Cintāmaṇi-dhāraṇī, 111
Circle (*cakra*), 294; of Body (*kāyacakra*), of Speech (*vākcakra*), of Mind (*cittacakra*), 256, 304; of Wisdom-Knowledge, 270; of nine Male Yakṣas, 113; of *jñāna*, 163, 296; of *samaya*, 163; Protective —, 113, 119, 283
citta (Mind, Thought, or Consciousness), 53, 71, 93, 161, 187, 225, 256; *-cakra*, 256, 304; *-dharmatā* (Supreme state of Thought), 29, 31, 53, 267; *-dūṣaṇa* (Belittling Thoughts), 328; *-mātra* (Mind Only), 53, 97; *-nimna* (Immersion in Mind), 187; *-saṃtati* (Stream of Consciousness), 205; *-vajra* (Thunderbolt of Mind, 259; see also *bodhicitta*
cittotpāda (= *bodhicittotpādika*) 185,
Cloth (*paṭa*), 301
Cognition (*buddhi*), 111, 333; Higher Cognition (*adhigama*), 91
Collection of parts (Kalāpa), 77
Colors, unspecified, 42, 197, 206, 270, and for Powdered —, see under *maṇḍala*; black and white *dharmas*, 153; black and white Threads, 285-6; white Thunderbolt, 31, 33, 243; white Cloth, 67; white-dressed Tārā, 192; white Vajravidaraṇa, 145, 169; white and saffron-colored Arapacana-Mañjughoṣa, 111; white Water-Wind, 264; white Water, 294; white Mustard Seed, 281; white and red parts of *bindu* (= red and white Element), 304-5, 319, 321; white, red, and blue Lotuses, 69, 175, 219-221; red Thread, 286; red Fire-Wind, 264; red Fire, 294; red and black Yamāri-s, 265, 277, 295; yellow Jambhala, 133; golden Sand, 160; color of liquid Gold, 161; yellow Earth-Wind, 264; yellow Earth, 294; yellow Thread, 286; blue Wind, 294; green Thread, 286; yellowish-green Wind-Wind, 264; Rainbow Body, 325; Colorless Wind, 264
Compassion (*karuṇā*), 55, 71, 125, 184, 222, 267-8, 328
Complete Buddha (*abhisaṃbuddha*); see Buddha
Comprehension, Higher, 162
Concentration, profound (*samādhi*, q.v.), 26, 205, 217; has varieties Intrinsic and Conforming, 217-8, 273
Conch (*śankha*), 287, 289; -shell, 69
Conduct, 230-1, 241
Confession, of sins (*pāpa-deśanā*), 153, 175, 185
Congregation, fourfold (*catuḥpariṣad*), 203
Consecration, 235, 272, 275, 291, 299, 325
Consonants, 20-1, 162
Contemplation (*bhāvanā*; also *samādhi*), 27, 29, 39, 99, 157, 159, 162-3, 167, 169, 173, 175, 186-7, 195-203, 207-211, 229, 243-4, 247, 249, 255, 272-3, 278, 281, 283, 295-6, 301, 304, 311, 321, 325, 333, 335; Analyzing — (*dpyad sgom*) and Stoppage — (*ḥjog sgom*), 201; — of four Boundless States (*caturapramāṇa-bhāvanā*), 185; see also Concentration, profound

Continents, four, 205
Continuous series (*prabandha*), 266
Contraction (*piṇḍagrāha*), 327
Conventional (*saṃvṛti-*), 204, 278; also see under Term
Convergence (*upacāra*), 268
Copper, 177
Coronation (*abhiṣeka*), 316
Corruption (*kleśa*), 21, 48-9, 53, 57, 227; 84,000 —, 57
Council, First, 59; Second, 63; Third, 67
Courtesans, celestial (*divya-veśyā*), the thirteen, 36
Crown, 161, 237
Cycle, initiation, 137; of life or transmigration (*saṃsāra*), 23, 49, 200; of Tantras, 105; the *uṣṇīṣa* cycle, 119

D

ḍāka (Sky Walker, male), 254
ḍākinī (Sky Walker, female), 100, 254, 265, 304
daṃṣṭrā (Teeth), 79
Daṃṣṭrasena, 97
Dancer, 133
Daṇḍin, 78
Dangers, eight, 127
Danielou, Alain, 220
Dārika-pā, 109, 293
darśana (Doctrinal viewpoint), 93; *-bhaga* (Doctrinal part), 81; *-mārga* (Path of Vision), 16, 45
Dasgupta, S.B., 36
Dawn, 19, 37, 39, 43, 135, 152, 191, 193, 276
Dayal, Har, 19, 313, 316
Dbyaṅs-can Dgaḥ-baḥi-blo-gros, 266, 312
de Jong, J. W., 14, 70
Death, 157, 295, 331-333
Declination, Northern, 281; Southern, 280
Deer Park, 41
Defeats, four (*pārājika*, involving expulsion from the monk order), 331
Defilement (see also Corruption), 48, 53, 223, 267
deha (Body, q.v.)
Deity (see also God), 160, 163, 169, 176-7, 193, 197-8, 203, 207, 216, 224-5, 228-237, 241-249, 255-6, 271-2, 277, 279, 287-295, 303-305, 309, 313, 319, 325, 329, 331; Attribute — (*nimitta-devatā*), 163, 291; Female —, 116, 160, 177, 256-7; Male —, 116, 160, 177, 254-257, 261; *maṇḍala* —, 283, 285, 303, 317; Passion — (Gazing, Laughing, Embracing, or in Coition), 168-9; Pledged —, 236; Preparatory —, 287; Wrathful —, 119, 123, 127, 129, 133, 179, 283, 316, and (ten in no.) 118, 272 (listed, 118)
Delusion (*moha*), 57, 221-2, 230-1
Demons, 123, 179, 201, 283, 293, 316; Demonic possession, 79
Dependent Origination (*pratītya-samutpāda*), 331
deva (a God, q.v.), 41, 55, 59, 61, 65, 103, 121, 203, 220; *-kula* (Temple), 281; *-putra* (Sons of the Gods), 43, 89, 115, 117; *-tattva* (= *devatā-tattva*), 159, 163, 214
Devaputramāra, 18
Devaśarman, 81, 87, 89
devatā (Deity, q.v.)
Devendra Śatakratu (= Indra), 23
devī (Goddess, q.v.)
Devī Pratibhānavatī, 111
Dge-legs-dpal-bzaṅ-po, 11
dgra bo sruṅ ma (Enemy guardians), 272
Dhanika, 63
dhāraṇā, 320
dhāraṇī, 105-109, 113-127, 131, 135, 149, 159-163, 171, 177-183, 189, 193-4, 197, 199, 203, 205, 209, 218,; 40, 241-245, 275, 293; four kinds, 217 of Tantric Families, 119, 137, 177; *mūla-*, 277; *vidyā-*, 133-139; *dhāraṇī*-garland, 189, 277; "Blazing Mouth" *dhāraṇī*, 123; "Dhāraṇi of the Blazing Flames," 131; illustrations of *dhāraṇī* at 175, 177, 179, 181, 183, 185, 195, 286
dharma (Doctrine, the Law, Natures), 45, 55, 57, 67, 183, 203-205, 224, 233, 243, 315, 328, 335, with varieties of Full Comprehension (*adhigama*) and of Scripture (*āgama*), 204; Absolute (*paramārtha-*) and Relative (*saṃvṛti-*), 204-5; Universal Characteristic of (*-sāmānyalakṣaṇa*) and Individual Characteristic of (*-svalakṣaṇa*), 57; Good, or White (*śukla-*) and Evil, or Black (*kṛṣṇa-*), 153; also: *-cakra* (Wheel of Doctrine), 224; *-dhātu* (Realm of Natures), 24, 204, 206, 217, 236; *-dhātu-jñāna* (Knowledge of the Nature Realm),

34-5; *-dhātuskandha*, 101; *-megha* (name of the Tenth Stage), 19; *-mudrā* (Seal of the Doctrine), 71; *-nairātmya* (Selflessness of Natures), 87, 334-5), *-rāja* (King of the Law), 67, 91, 115; -skandha (Aggregate of Doctrines, 84,000 in no.), 57
Dharmadāsa, 77
Dharmaguptika, 85
Dharmakīrti, 73, 87, 296
Dharmamitra, 83
Dharmasaṅgīti Cave, 115
Dharmaskandha (a class of Abhidharma literature), 81
dharmasvāmin (T. *chos rje*), a religious title, 11
dharmatā (True Nature), 331
dharmodaya (Source of Natures), 217, 295, 318, 333, 335
dhātu (Element, Realm, Relic). 50, 107, 257, 319, 332-3; *ākāśa-* (Realm of Space), 292; *kāma-* (Realm of Desire), 169; *loka-* (Worldly Realm), 205; *vajra-* (Diamond Realm), 204, 217; *-prabheda* (Analysis of the Elements), 222; also see under *dharma*
Dhātukāya (Set of Elements), 83
Dhītika, 63
dhūma (Smoke, an Omen), 202
dhūta-guṇa (Ascetic virtue), 69
dhyāna (Meditation), 27, 159, 195, 214, 320, 326, 327
Diadem, 34, 141, 236, 313, 317
Diamond (*vajra*), 34, 102, 283; also: — Ambrosia (*vajrāmṛta*), 289, 291; — Bell, 236; — Blessing, 214; — Brothers (*vajrajñātṛ*), 328; — Chain, 236; — Feet-cross (*vajraparyaṅka*), 273; — Heap, 131; — Hook, 236; — Knowledge (*vajrajñāna*), 243; — of Meditation, 220; — Muttering (*vajrajāpa*), 272; — Realm (Lord of and Queen of), 243; — Seat (*vajrāsana*), 89, 129; — Sight, 240; — Sow (Vajravārāhī), 36; — Tongue (*vajrajihva*), 243; — Vehicle, see Vajrayāna and Vehicle
Dice, 103
Digging, 281, 283
dikpāla (Protector of a Direction), 272
Dilowa Gegen Hutukhtu, 14, 190
Diṅnāga, 73, 83, 75, 97
Dīpaṃkara, 19
Dīpaṃkarabhadra, 30, 147
Direction(s), 105, 282, 283, 287, 289, 328; specific —, 280-288, in addition West, 207
Diagonal, 284
Directive (*ājña*), 328
dīrgha (Long), 161; *-mantra*, 117
Disciple (*śrāvaka*), 16, 143, 151, 169, 236, 273ff., 299ff., 315, 319, 321; the eight close disciples, 121
Discrimination (*pratyavekṣaṇā*), 29, 34, 223
Discursive thought (*vikalpa*), 162, 172
Disk (of Earth, Water, Fire, Wind), 211
Dismissing the Deities, 293
Divine Consciousness, 162; — Form (two kinds), 206
divya-veśyā (Celestial Courtesan), 36
Dkon-mchog-ḥjigs-med-dbaṅ-po, 86
Dkon-mchog-bstan-paḥi-sgron-me, 84
dṅos rgyu (Actual cause), 241
Doctrine (*dharma*), 55, 93, 224, 233, 328, 329
doṣa (Faults, of poetry), 77, 79
Dpal-ḥdzin-sde, 36
Dpal-ldan Ma-Khol, 78
Dpal-mo, 167
dpe sna (Exemplar), 119
dpyad sgom (Analyzing Contemplation), 201
drag śul (Fierce act), 272
Drama (*nāṭya*), 77, 79
Drawing (*neya*), 261; see *neyārtha*
Drawing in (*praveṣaṇa*), 237, 240, 243, 249, 287, 295, 296, 297
Drawing (of the *maṇḍala*), 279-283, 291, 303
dṛdha-vajra (Firm Thunderbolt), 31
Dream, 63, 107, 111, 191, 203, 210, 278
Drop (*bindu*), 69, 255, 257, 285, 303, 319, 333; Best of Drops (Tilottama), 36; Drop of Springtime (Vasanta-tilaka), 305; Substance of the Drop (*bindurūpabhūta*), 319
duḥkha (Suffering), 21, 45, 85
Durgasiṃha, 77
Dusk, 18, 19, 152, 191
duṣkṛtam (Evil action), 65
duṣṭa (Wicked), 328
dveṣa (Hatred), 57, 221
dveṣavajra (Dimond of Hate), 283

E

Ear, 172, 285, 287
Earth (*pṛthivī*), 175, 211, 230, 231, 285, 295, 332
Earth-bound (*bhauma*), 202, 203
East, 249, 281, 282, 284, 287, 288
Eastern Square (*koṣṭhaka*), 247
Eaved building (*kūṭāgāra*), 105
Edgerton, Franklin, 208
Egg-born (*aṇḍa-jā*), 330
Ego (*ahaṃkāra, garva*), 163, 164; Egotism, 283, 297, 305
ekajātipratibaddha (Bound to one more Birth), 35
ekasaṃtāna (One in mental series), 219
ekatantra (= *ekasaṃtāna*), 219
Elder (*sthavira*), 59, 67
Element, 50, 222, 230, 231, 319, 333; red —, 319; white —, 323; of Fire (*tejodhātu*), 41; of the Tathāgata (Tathāgatadhātu), 51; six — (*dhātu*), 322
Elephant, 215, 220
Embellishment, poetical, 77, 79
Emblem (Circle, Semi-circle, Square, Triangle), 294
Embryo of the Tathāgata (Tathāgatagarbha), 49-53
Enclosing (*-la*) of Essence (*maṇḍa-*), 270
Encouragement (*praśvāsa*), 141
Enemy Guardians, 272
Enlightenment, 151, 152, 185, 227; Complete —, 12; Highest —, 31, 229, 247; Incomparable —, 315; see also *bodhicitta* (Mind of Enlightenment)
Entity (*artha*), 49, 93
Entrance, 151, 285, 287, 295, 305, 307, 311; — into *maṇḍala*, 151, 309, 331; Equal — (*samāpatti*), 263
Equality (*samatā*), 34, 223; — with all the Tathāgatas (*sarvatathāgatasamatā*), 35
Equipment (*saṃbhāra*), 17, 19, 273
Equipoise (= Equal Entrance; *samāpatti*), 19, 29, 31, 145
Essence (*hṛdaya*), 161
E-vaṃ, 71, 333-337
Evaṃ mayā śrutam, 253; — *ekasmin samaye*, 55, 69
Evil action (*duṣkṛtam*), 65
Evocation (*sādhana*), 101, 287
Exemplar (*dpe sna*), 119
External, 228, 230, 233
Expanded, fully (*vibuddha*), 51
Expansion (*anubheda*), 327
Explanation (*upadeśa*), 55, 57
Explanatory Tantra (see Tantra), 131
Extreme, 335
Eye, 17, 161, 172, 220, 241, 244

F

Fa-tsun, 13
Faculty (*indriya*), inferior, etc., 219;; keen (*tīkṣṇendriya*), 317-323, 335; —, supernormal (*abhijñā*), 185, 201
Factors of becoming (= Elements; *mahābhūta*), 295, 297
Faith (*adhimukti*), 105, 177, 203
Family, good son (*kulaputra*), 43
Family, Tantric (*kula*), 101-2, 177, 221, 225, 228, 231; three Families, 179; five —, 119, 147, 149, 187, 217, 236, 287, 299, 309, 317; sixfold and sevenfold, 100-1; also: Arapacana —, 113; Concise Pañjarā —, 255; of the Five, 103, 135; Karma —, 217; Mundane —, 133; Padma —, 102-3, 121, 123, 145, 149, 187, 201, 205, 217; Passion — (*anurāga-kula*), 168-9; Prosperity —, 103; Ratna —, 217, 222; Tathāgata —, 102-3, 107-111, 121, 123, 129, 137, 145, 149, 177, 187, 201, 207; Vajra —, 102-3, 129, 145, 149, 187, 201, 207, 217; Wealthy —, 102-3, 133; of the Worldlings, 103; also: Lord of the —, 103, 105, 123, 129, 228, 270; Master of the —, 103, 105, 111, 123, 129, 131, 163, 165, 171, 183, 191, 193, 201, 295, 297; Messengers, male and female, of the —, 103, 118, 121, 133; Mother of the —, 103, 113, 123-131, 167, 193, 201, 310; Servants, male and female, of the —, 118, 123, 129, 133; Wrathful one of the —, 201
Father Tantra (see Tantra), 100
Father-Mother (*yab-yum*), see under Union
Feet, 326; in the diamond-cross (*vajraparyaṅka*), 273
Fertility, 114-5
Field protector (*kṣetrapāla* or *kṣitipati*), 279, 281
Filliozat, Jean, 320
Finger, 247; Gestures of — (*mudrā*), 205
Fire (= Flame), 123, 137, 139, 195, 211, 230-1, 283-4, 295, 297, 305, 319, 332
Fish-gills, 175

Flame (= Fire, q.v.)
Forehead, middle of, 322, 323
Flask, 39, 73, 140, 175, 193, 199, 272, 277, 285, 287, 288, 311, 312, 313, 319, 329; Action —, 285, 287, 297; — Initiation, 34; Precious —, 289; Preparation of the —, 287; three (*jaya, vijaya, mahāvijaya*), 289; Victorious — (*vijaya-kalaśa*), 287
Flesh, 9 kinds, 220
Flowers, 45, 121, 141, 181, 183, 195, 236, 271, 275, 285, 289, 303, 315
Flux (*sāsrava*), 85
Food, 39, 181, 247, 289
Foot, 220
Form (*rūpa*), 93, 206, 230
Formula, 175; Magical — (= Incantation), 176
Foundation (*adhiṣṭhāna*), 285
Fourth (*caturtha*), 272
Friendship (*maitrī*), 184
Fruit, 229, 233, 333, 335; of the Path, 19; Ultimate —, 53; Superior —, 55

G

gadya (Prose), 77
Galdan Monastery, 11
Gaṇapati, 123
gaṇḍi (Gong), 65
Ganges, 17, 41, 61, 63
Garland (of *dhāraṇīs*), 189, 209, 236
garva (Ego, Pride), 163, 243
Gate, 283, 321; East —, 283, 295, 297, 305
gāthā (Verse), 53, 69
Gauḍa style, 79
Gautama, *ṛṣi* (Tib. *glaṅ skyes*), 73
Gelugpa, 11, 12, 128, 156
Gem, tip of, 322; *ūrṇā* Gem, 119
Generation (= Production, *utpatti*), 165; of two kinds: Self-generation, 158, 159, 161, 163, 165, 167, 171, 187, 195, 235, 282, 283, 291, 293, 295, 297, 299; and Generation-in-Front, 153, 159, 173, 175, 187, 189, 235, 291, 293, 295; also: Generation of the Residence and the Residents, 175; — of four Joys, 323. See *bodhicittotpādika* and Steps of Production (*utpatti-krama*)
Gesture, 230, 283
geya (Prose and Verse mingled), 53
Ghaṇṭa-pā, 307
ghaṇṭaseka (Bell Initiation), 313
Ghosh, Manomahan, 282
Gleṅ gźi ma, 109
Gnod ḥjoms, 97
Goal (*artha*), 215, 216; High —, (*uddeśa*), 45, 47, 221
God (see also: Deity), 23, 45, 107, 113-117, 145, 149, 160-199, 203, 227, 229, 239, 245, 247, 256, 257, 261, 272, 273, 277, 279, 285, 319; Desire or Love — (*kāmadeva, ṭakkirāja*), 142, 323, 325; Pure — (*śuddhāvāsa*), 23; Tuṣita —, 115; six Gods (Reality, Sound, Letter, Form, Seal, and Sign), 117, 160-163; — (*deva*, q.v.)
Goddess, 28, 79, 109, 113-115, 145, 255, 257, 322; Earth — (*pṛthivī*), 281-285, 303; Form —, 228
Gold, 161, 175, 177
Goods, 329
Gong (*gaṇḍi*), 65
gotra (Species), 50
graha (Possession by a spirit), 79
Grain of rice, 39
Grammar (*śabda-vidyā*), 73, 75, 79
Grammarian, 73, 75
Grand Scripture (*vaipulya*), 55
Grass, *kuśa*, 177
Great: — Bliss (*mahāsukha*), 328; — Kings (*mahārāja*), 109, 111, 131; — Passion (*mahārāga*), 289; — Seal (*mahāmudrā*), 143; — Vehicle (*mahāyāna*), 57, 95; — Wrathful Deity (*mahākrodha*), 133
Gṛdhrakūṭa, 45
Ground (Tib. *gźi*; S. *prakṛti, vastu*), 167, 186, 187, 209, 275, 305; Objective — (*gźan gyi gźi*), 187, 209; Subjective — (*bdag gyi gźi*), 209
Grub-chen (*mahāsiddha*), 11
Gtsaṅ-nag-pa, 89
Gtsaṅ-stod, 11
Gtsug tor nag mo, 119
guhya (Secret), 272, 311, 321, 328
guhyakādhipati (Master of the Secret Folk), 206
guhyayoga, 214
Guide (*guru*), 17
guṇa (Merit), 236
Guṇamati, 87
Guṇaprabha, 83, 85
Guṇaśrī, 87
gur rigs bsdus (Concise Pañjarā Family), 255
guru (Guide), 17, 73, 163, 278, 285, 291-

295, 299, 303-307, 311, 315, 319-325; Tibetan —, 293, 303
gżi (see Ground)
Gzuṅs grva, five (Mahāmayūrī, Mantrānudhāriṇī, Pratisarā, Sāhasrapramardanī, and Śītavatī), 113, 145, 167, 169

H

Hand, 230; — Gesture, 233, 271; — Symbols (*hasta-cihna*), 184, 233, 245, 290, 291, 295
Happiness, 184
Happy band of five (*pañcaka-bhadravargiya*), 41-45
Haribhadra, 91, 97, 99
Harśadeva, 79
hasta-cihna (see Hand Symbols)
Hatred (*dveṣa*), 57, 221, 222, 230, 231
Hayagrīva, 123
Ḥchiṅ bu ma, 85
Head, 259, 261, 326
Heart (*hṛdaya*; sometimes a Syllable Incantation), 29-35, 161, 162, 187, 195, 197, 209, 211, 218, 221, 229, 237, 243, 247; — Hevajra, 296; with and without attribute, 237
Heat, 36
Heaven (of the Thirty-three Gods), 107, 115, 117
Hedin, Sven, 284
Hell, 329
Heretic (*tirthika*), 71
Heruka, 100, 304, 305, 316
hetu (see Cause)
hetu-vidyā (see Logic)
Hierophant (*vajra-ācārya*), 141, 271-279, 283, 287, 309-313, 316, 317, 321, 323, 329
Higher (see Cognition, Comprehension, Goal, Morality, Insight, Vision)
Hīnayāna (Vehicle, lower), 17, 21, 53, 57
Hindu Yoga, 220
hita (Benefit), 155
Ḥjam-dbyaṅs-bźad-paḥi-rdo-rje, 84
ḥjog sgom (Stoppage Contemplation), 201
Ḥod gsal ma, 109
homa, 191, 214, 275
Holders of the Teaching (*śāsana-dhara*), 111
Holding (of Wind; *ālaya*), 157
Honey, 48
Horn, hare's, 51
Ḥphags-pa śes-rab, 129
Ḥphaṅ thaṅ, 96; — *ma*, 85
hṛdaya (Essence or Heart; the briefest *dhāraṇī*), 116, 117, 161, 177, 179, 214, 218, 237, 270, 277; General — (of the three Families), 177; *-hevajra*, 296, 297; *-mantra*, 118
Hūṃkāra, 118, 316
hūṃ phaṭ (a *dhāraṇī* conclusion understood to drive away evil spirits), 118

I

Icon, 81, 107, 111, 113, 119
Identification, 230
Illusory Body, 37, 39
Illumination, 25
Illustrious Lives, 25
Image (*pratibimba, nimitta*), 81, 206, 228, 245
Immersion, 187; in heart, in sound, 209
Impermanent (*anitya*), 85
Incantation (*dhāraṇī, mantra*), 171, 199, 202-205, 237, 281, 283, 301, 321; see Syllable
Incense, 177, 183
Incomparable (*anuttara*), 39
Indian Continent (Jambudvīpa), 23; — Mythology, 329; — Teacher, 295; — School, 295
Indifference (*upekṣā*), 184
Individual, a kind of Characteristic, q.v.
Indra, 18, 23, 43, 93, 75, 115, 117
indranīla (Sapphire), 115
Indrabhūti, 102
Indravyākaraṇa (a grammar), 73
indriya (Sensory organ, Faculty), 173, 219
Infant (*bala*), 79
Initial Training (*prathama-prayoga*), 273
Initiation (*abhiṣeka, seka*), 12, 21, 26, 36-39, 101, 109, 119, 133, 135, 137, 140-145, 149, 153, 155, 163-171, 207, 237, 271-279, 285, 287, 291, 295-305, 309-331; — in the four Tantras, 141; — of the Flask (common and uncommon, eleven and fivefold), 313; Inner —, and Consecration (or Unction) of Kingdom, 291, 316; seven Lower, 329, and three Higher, 145, 147, 317, 318, 329; Hierophant's —, 140-155; Wisdom (Vidyā) — (five in number), 143, 147, 149, 313; a category in Yoga-tantra, 214, defined on 236
Insiders, 79
Insight (*prajñā*), 111, 142-3, 168, 185,

200-1, 219, 223, 261-265, 296, 329; Discriminative — (*pratyavekṣaṇa-prajñā*), 211; Insight-Knowledge (*prajñā-jñāna* = *prajñā-bhaga* and *jñāna-bindu*), 37, 39, 272, 318, 321
Instant (*kṣaṇa*), 21
Instigation, 243
Instruction (in Higher Morality, Meditation, and Insight), 57
Instructive Personal Discourses (*nidāna*), 55
Instructor (*ācārya*), 43
Intermediate State (*antarābhava*), 156-7, 264, 295, 332-3
Internal, 228, 230, 233
Intrinsic Purity (*svabhāva-viśuddhi*), 29; intrinsically pure, 53, 259, 328
Invitation, 177, 179, 236
Iron hook (*aṅkuśa*), 224
īryāpatha (Posture, bodily), 247
Īśvaraprabha (the King), 127

J

jaḍā-svabhāva (Substance, unconscious), 93
jagad-vinaya (Training of Living Beings), 217
Jalandhari-pā, 276
Jambhala, 113; the yellow —, 133
Jambudvīpa (Indian Continent), 23, 333
jāpa (Muttering), 159, 214, 218-9; *jāpa-aṅga* (Members of muttering, four), 187-193
jarā (Old Age), 79
jarāyu-jā (Birth from a Womb), 330
jātaka (Bodhisattva Lives of the Buddha), 55
Jayadeva, 79
Jetāri, 113, 145, 167, 276
Jewels (*ratna*), 61, 49, 175, 208, 236; three —, 147, 151, 186, 203; four —, 45; seven —, 44
jina (Victor), 103
Jinajik (a certain mantra-deity), 179
jñāna; *ādarśa-*, *kṛtyānuṣṭhāna-*, *pratyavekṣaṇa-*, *samatā-*, and *viśuddhadharmadhātu-*, see Knowledge and five —; *prajñā-jñāna*, see Insight-Knowledge; *jñāna-sattva* and *jñana-cakra*, see Knowledge Being and Circle of —; also: *jñāna-cakṣus* (Eye of Knowledge), 241; *-kāya* (Knowledge Body), 26; *-skandha* (Knowledge Aggregate), 101; *-sūtra* (Knowledge Line), 285
Jñānadeva, 72-3
Jñānagarbha, 91, 93
jñānamaya-kāya (= *jñāna-kāya*)
Jñānapāda School, 35
jñānaprasthāna (Entrance into Knowledge), 83
Jñānavajra, 168
Jñānavatī, 312
jñāpti-caturtha-karma (three proposals followed by one decision), 311
jñeya (Knowable), 53, 236; *jñeya-āvaraṇa* (Obscuration of the Knowable), 37
Johnston, E. H., 24, 48, 50, 52
Joy (*ānanda*), 291, 322-3; four — (Joy, Super Joy, Extraordinary Joy, and Together-born Joy), 169, 323; — of Gazing, Laughing, Embracing, and Coitus, 169
Joyous Impersonal Utterances (*udāna*), 55
Jujube fruit, 39
jvalita (a kind of Omen, q.v.), 202

K

kakṣa (Armpit), 281
Kāla, 63
kalā, sixty-four, 320
Kalāpa (Collection of Parts), 77
kalaśa; *karma-*; *vijaya-*; see Flask; Action —; Victorious —
kali-yuga (Strife, age of), 79, 277
kalpa (see Aeon)
kalpa-vṛkṣa (Wish-granting Tree), 175
kalpana (= *vikalpa*; Discursive Thought, q.v.), 328
kāma, Arts of, 321; *-kalā*, 321
Kāmadeva, 169, 323
Kamalaśīla, 91, 211
Kanjur, 12, 124
Kaṅkana-dhāraṇī, 123
kanyā (Virgin), 195
kapāla (Skull Bowl), 287
Kapila, 107, 123
Kapilacandra, 107
Kapilavastu, 123
kāraka (Agent), 217
kārikā (Stanza), 83, 85
karma (Action, Act, Rite), 21, 26, 103, 201, 217, 221, 225, 231, 247, 321; *karma-kalaśa* (see under Flask); *-mūdra* (see under Seal); *-sūtra* (see under Line); *-vajra* (see under Thunderbolt).
karmic hindrances, 115

Kārttikeya, the Six-faced Youth, 75, 77
karuṇā (Compassion), 184, 328
Kashmir, 63; — Śaivism, 210
Kāśyapa, 41, 59, 63, 67
Katyāyana, 69
Katyāyaniputra, 83
kāvya (Poetics), 77
kāya (see Body), 77, 79, 223, 225; *mahāsukha-* (Body of Great Bliss), 296; *dharma-*, *nirmāṇa-*, *rūpa-*, *saṃbhoga-*, *svabhāva-*, *vipāka-*, see under Body; *-viveka*, see under Body; *-cakra*, see under Circle; *-cittapraśrabdhi*, see under Cathartic (of Body and of Mind)
kāyavākcitta (Body, Speech, and Mind), 297
khaḍga (Sword), 211
Khaṇḍarohā, 304
Khri-sroṅ-ldeḥu-bstan, 25, 91, 96-7
Khyuṅn gśog ḥbar ba, 133
kīla (Magic Nail), 272, 283
King, the four Great, see under Great; — Degenerate Heart (= Ajātaśatru, the King), 131; — of the Law (*dharmarāja*), 67; — of the Law of the Three Worlds (*traidhātukadharmarāja*), 315
kleśa (see Corruption)
Kleśamara, 18
Kloṅ-rdol-bla-ma. See under Index of Works Cited
Knowable, 53, 236
Knowledge (*vidyā*), 19
Knowledge (*jñāna*), 16-7, 21, 53, 102, 162, 185, 217, 222-3, 228-233, 261-265, 296-7, 321-2; five Knowledges, 34, 236: Discriminative — (*pratyavekṣaṇa-jñāna*), 31, 222-3, 232, 214, 223; Equality — (*samatā-jñāna*), 31, 222-3, 232; Mirror-like (*ādarśa-jñāna*), 29, 34, 214, 222-3, 232; Natural-realm — (*dharmadhātu-jñāna*), 35, 222; Procedure-of-Duty — (*kṛtyānuṣṭhāna-jñāna*), 33, 214, 222-3, 232, 247; also: Divine—, 43; Non-discursive —, 315; Spontaneously generated —, 43; Tathāgata —, 30; Insight-Knowledge, 272, 311, and Wisdom-Knowledge, 315; — of Bliss-Void, 319; — of Great Bliss, 333; — of the Indissolubility of Beatitude and Void, 265; — Born Together with Great Beatitude, 261, 263; Knowledge Being (*jñāna-sattva*), see under Being
koṣṭhaka (a Square portion), 247
krama (Steps); *niṣpanna-krama* or *saṃpanna-krama* and *utpatti-*, see under Steps
kriyābandham akārṣuḥ (*Lalitavistara* 407.18), 43
Kriyā-tantra, General, 135,ff.; and see under Tantra
krodha (Wrathful Deity), 272, 283
kṛṣṇa-dharma (Natures, black), 153
Kṛṣṇasamayavajra, 155
kṛtyānuṣṭhāna, a kind of *jñāna*; see under Knowledge
kṣaṇa (Instant), 21
kṣatriya (the Class), 69
Kṣemendra, 79, 305
kṣetrapāla (Field Protector), 279
kṣetravyūha (Field Array), 109
kṣitipati (Field Protector), 281
Kubjita, 65
Kukkuṭapāda (Chicken-foot Mountain), 59
kula (Family, Progenitor), 37; *anurāga-* (Passion Family), *laukika-* (Family of the Worldlings), *maṇi-* (Wealthy Family), *pañcaka-* (Family of the Five), *pauṣṭika-* (Prosperity Family), *tathāgata-* (Tathāgata Family), and so on, see under Family, Tantric
Kuladatta, 282
kulaputra (Family, Son of), 43
kuleśa, 103
kulika (Progeny), 103
kumāra (Youth), 185
kūrma (Tortoise), 280
kuśa, 73, 177
kuśala-mūla (Merit, roots of), 193
Kuśinagara, 59
Kusumapura (= Paṭaliputra), 67
Kusumatalagarbhālaṃkāra, 205
kūṭāgāra (Palace, eaved building), 105, 175, 207, 215

L

Labrang, 13
lakṣman (Sign), 228
lakṣaṇa (Characteristic); *sāmānya-* (Universal-) and *sva-* Individual -), and so on, see under Characteristic
lakṣaṇa (the 32 Characteristics), 30, 61
lug rjes (Signature), 211
laghu-tantra, 165
Lalou, Marcelle, 300
Lāmā, 304

Lamotte, Etienne, 16, 66
Lamp, 19, 181, 185, 197
Lamp-black, 216
Language(s), four, 67
Last Life (*caramabhavika*), 105
las tshogs (Set of Magical Acts), see under Action (= Acts)
laukika (Mundane), 103, 219
laukika-kula (Family, Mundane, q.v.)
Law (*dharma*), 67, 151, 183, 243; — of the Three Worlds, 317
Lay Buddhists, 203
layana (Residence), 281
Lcags mchu nag po, 133
Legends (*itivṛttaka*), 55
Legs ldan, 119; — spun gsum, 119
lekha (Letters), 93
Lessing, F. D., 13-4, 119, 284
Letters, 161, 187; Set of — (*vyañjana-kāya*), 77; Male, Female, and Neuter —, 79; — of the *dhāraṇī*, 193
Levi, Sylvain, 272, 328
Lexicography (*abhidhāna*), 77, 79
Lexicon, 317, 321
Lhasa, 13
Licchāvi, 61
Light (*āloka*), 21, 71, 105, 117, 133, 161-2, 209, 265, 296, 326-7; Clear — (*prabhās-vara*), 37, 39, 265, 297, 301, 312, 323-327; Culmination-of-Light (*ālokopalab-dhi*), 265, 327; Spread-of-Light (*ālo-kābhāsa*), 71, 265, 327
Lin Li-Kouang, 169
Līlavajra, 127
Limb, 171
Line (*sūtra*), 281, 285, 331; eight chief —, 284; two kinds: Action Line (*karma-sūtra*), 284-5, 299, 303, and Knowledge Line (*jñāna-sūtra*), 284-287, 291, 299, 303; two kinds: Dry Line and Wet Line, 287; see Thread
Lion, 105, 215
Lion's Throne (*siṃhāsana*), 215
Lightning Flash (*vidyut-prabhā*), 36
Liquid Gold, 161
Locanā, 192-3, 313, 319
Logic (*hetu-vidyā*), 73, 83, 85
lokadhātu (World system), 105, 133, 205
lokottara (Supramundane), 103
Lokeśvara, 22, 75
Lord, 161-2, 191, 221, 255, 259, 261, 270, 275, 277, 287-291, 295-299, 311; — of the Diamond Realm (Vajradhātvīś-vara), 243
lotsāva (Translator), 91
Long (*dīrgha*), 161; — Living (*ayuṣmat*), 43
Lotus, 28, 48, 69, 175, 181, 193, 209, 245, 297, 319, 321; Blue — (*utpala*), 69, 175; Red — (*padma*), 69, 175, 243, 319; — Pods, 187; — Seat, 113; — Sitting Posture, 179
Love (*maitrī*), 328
Lower Vehicle (*hīnayāna*), 57
Lucid Exposition, 193
Lui-pā, 256
Lust (*rāga*), 221-2, 230-1
Lva-ba-pa (= Lwa-ba-pa), 29, 149, 289, 314

M

Madhyadeśa, 41
Madhyamaka, 99
Mādhyamika, 53, 87, 89, 97, 99, 211, 335; -Prāsaṅgika, 91-99; -Svātantrika, 91-99
Madhyāntika, 63
Magadha, 41, 105
Magical apparitions, manifestations, and metamorphoses, 59, 215, 224; Magical tricks, 67; Magical power, success, and talent (*ṛddhi, siddhi*), 41, 65, 75, 163, 200, 206, 216. For Set of Magical Acts, see under Action (= Acts)
Mahābala, 118
mahādaṇḍa, 119
Mahākāla, 119
mahākalpa (Great Aeon), 201
Mahākāśyapa, 57-61, 69
Mahākauṣṭhila, 83
mahākrodha (Great Wrathful Deity), 133
Mahāmayūrī, 113
Mahānāma, 41
Mahāpadma (the King), 67
mahārāga (Great Passion), 289
Mahāsammata, 85
Mahāsaṅghika, 69
mahāsattva (Great Being), 218, 296-7
mahāsiddha (Great Master), 273, 289 293, 295
Mahāsudarśana, 63
mahāsukha (Great Beatitude or Bliss), 261, 267, 312, 328
Mahāśvāsa, 134
mahātmaka, 296
Mahāvajradhara, 39

Mahāvibhāṣā, 81, 83
Mahāyāna (see Vehicle, Great or Upper), 152, 210, 216, 331; — Doctrine, 70; — Scriptures, 69; — *sūtra*, 49; two kinds: *pāramitā-* and *mantra-mahāyāna*, 169
mahāyoga, 214
Mahāyoga-tantra, 22, 100
Maheśvara, 75
Maitreya, 59, 69-70, 95, 97, 105, 225; — Expositions, five, 95, 97
maitrī (Friendship or Love), 184, 328
Māmakī, 192-3
māna (Pride), 222
manas (Mind), 217; *manas*-face (*yid ṅo*), 210-1
maṇḍa (Pith), 270
maṇḍala (= *maṇḍa-la* 'seizing or enclosing the essence,' p. 270), 13, 105, 109, 117-125, 137, 145-151, 186-7, 198, 204, 207, 211, 214, 216, 223-227, 233, 236, 255, 259, 261, 270-289, 293-313, 318-321, 327-333; *maṇḍala* varieties, 271; Formless and Form *m.*, 273, apparently equal to Absolute and Relative *m.*, 270, 318; Relative *maṇḍala* of two varieties, Intrinsic Nature (or Self-Existent, *svabhāva*) *m.*, 270, a kind of Meditation *m.*, 271, 303, and Reflected-image *m.*, 236, 270, equal to External *m.*, 273 (cf. explanation of *mahāmudrā*, p. 228); External *m.*, of two varieties, Powdered Colors (*rajo-m.*), 105, 271, 273, 279, 285, 291-301, 307, 311, 313, 329, 331, and Painted on Textile (*paṭa-m.*), 271, 273, 279-303, 311, 313, 331; Body (*deha*) *m.*, 271, 273, 279, 303-307. Also, of three kinds, two *bodhicitta-m.* and *bhaga-m.*, 318-321; of four kinds, *mahā-m.*, 223-225, 230-1, *dharma-m.*, 225, 230-1, *dhāraṇī-m.* = *samaya-m.*, 224-5, 230-1, and *karma-m.*, 225, 231; another four kinds, 117; when *maṇḍala* = *cakra*, three *maṇḍalas*, *kāya-*, *vāg-*, *citta-*, 256, 275, 304; as well as four Element *maṇḍalas* at four corporeal Centers, 211. Accomplishing the *m.*, 293; *m.-vidhi*, 119, 147, 151, and *m.-sādhana*, 275; Preparatory *m.*, 287, 293-299; *m.* of Self Generation, 282-3; Merger of *maṇḍalas*, 293-299; *m.* of Residence (*ādhāra*), 236, 291, 318, 333; and *m.* of Residents (*ādheya*), 236, 291, 313, 318, 333, which are Lord of *m.* (*m.-nāyaka*, *cakreśa*), 105, 275, 311, and *m.* Retinue (*māṇḍaleya*), 271-2, 275, as well as *maṇḍalas* of Attributes, Flowers, Hand gestures, Syllables, or Useful images, 271. Also: — of the Anuttara Tantra, 261, 273-277, 283; of the Families, 117. Named *maṇḍalas*: — of Be-coṅ-maṅ-po, 119; Dharmadhātu-216; Māyājāla-, 261; Samāja-, 261; Sambara-, 256, 304; Vajradhātu-, 145, 216; Vimala —, 117. Triumphant (*vijaya*) *m.*, 295, is one of the three *samādhi*, q.v.
māṇḍaleya, see preceding
maṇi-kula, 102-3
Manifest Complete Buddha. See under Buddha
mañjari, 169
Mañjuśrī, 22, 69-70, 105, 109, 111, 119, 123, 127, 185, 213, 235
Mañju-vajra, 147
manovijñāna (Perception, mind-based), 51
manomaya-kāya (Body, mental or made of mind), 27, 142
mantra, 12, 29-33, 55, 103, 109, 111, 116-118, 121, 125, 136, 151, 160, 198, 214, 237, 272, 275; — Category, Path, Vehicle (*yāna*), see under Path and Vehicle; Heart (*hṛdaya*) —, 118, 286 (for list, see under Syllable); — Deities, 102; *-dhāraṇī*, 191; — Vows, q.v., 309; *upahṛdaya-mantra*, 118
Manu, 74, 329
Māra, 18-9, 23-27, 35, 39, 67, 131
mārga (Path, q.v.), 45
Mārīci, 113, 145
Marks, Minor (*anuvyañjana*), 18-9, 21, 30, 35, 49, 156, 162
Marpa, 91
Marvel (*prātihārya*), 26, 29, 35
Marvellous, The (*adbhutadharma*), 55
Mathura, 61, 85
Mātṛceṭa, 78-9
mātsarya (Avarice), 221
Maturation, 271; — Body (*vipāka-kāya*), 27
Maudgalyāyana, 61, 81, 105
Master (*ācārya*), 311, 328
maula (= *maulī*; Body, or Main Part, of the Rite), 139, 303
mauliseka (Diadem Initiation), 313
Māyā, the Queen (*mahādevī*), 22-3
māyā-deha (Body, illusory), 321

Māyājāla-maṇḍala, 261
Meaning (*artha*), 79; Evident — (*nitārtha*), 219, 259; Final — (*nītārtha*), 49-53; Hinted — (*neyārtha*), 219, 259, 261; Provisional — (*neyārtha*), 49
Means (*upāya*), 71, 168, 216, 261-266, 269, 296
Medicine, 121, 183; Science of — (*cikitsā-vidyā*), 73, 79, 93
Meditation (*dhyāna*), 27, 162, 167, 195-200, 220, 291; Objects of — (*ālambana*), 145, 161-3, 173, 187, 189, 193, 195, 199, 217, 333-4; three, beginning with "Dwelling in the Fire," 139
Members (*aṅga*), 269; — of Muttering, 158; Upper —, therapeutic investigation, 79
Memory (possibly context meaning of *dhāraṇī*), 225
Men of the Middle of the River, 63
Mental elements (possibly *tarka*), 173
Mental series (*saṃtāna*), 227, 249
Merger (of *maṇḍalas*), see under *maṇḍala*
Merit (*puṇya*), 16, 185, 203, 214, 228, 236, 244; Root of — (*kuśala-mūla*), 193
Messengers, 121
Metamorphosis, 209
Mgon po beṅ, 118-9
Mi-pham-tshaṅs-sras-dgyes-paḥi-rdo-rje, 11
Middle, 335
Midnight, 19, 37, 39, 152, 193, 276
Milk, 160, 175, 177
Millet, 277
Minaeff, I.P., 126
Mind (*citta, manas*), 33, 55, 149, 156, 161-167, 171, 187-191, 194, 197-200, 205-209, 217, 224-227, 230-235, 239-245, 268, 272, 291, 295-297, 304, 311-2, 317-327; — Compassion, — Samādhi, and — Truth-Force, 55; also: Arcane — (*citta-viveka*), 312, 320-1, 327; Tathāgata's —, 205-6; True Nature of — (*citta-dharmatā*), 267; Mind-based Perception (*manovijñāna*), 51; Mind-Only (*citta-mātra*), 264, 321, 325, 327; for Mind of Enlightenment, see *bodhicitta*
Mingled Frose and Verse (*geya*), 53
Mirage, 195
Mirror, 181, 209, 210, 289; -like (*ādarśa-*), 34, 223
miśra (Mixture), 77
mithyā-dṛṣṭi (Views, wayward), 221
Mkhas-grub-rje, 11-23, 30, 34-38, 44, 58. 70-2, 84-5, 100, 112, 117, 132, 140, 150, 153, 157-8, 163, 169, 173, 194, 200, 210-1, 217, 222-225, 242-4, 254, 274, 298, 304, 312, 316-8; other names of —, 11, 337
mkhaḥ ḥgro (Sky Walker), 255
moha (Delusion), 57, 221
Moisture, birth from (*saṃsveda-jā*), 330
Momentary reproduction risen (*abhyudita*), 209
Monastery (*vihāra*), 281
Monk, 155
Moon, 19, 29-37, 59, 74-5, 139, 161, 187, 189, 195, 197, 209, 243, 297
Morality, 155
Mother (*yum*), 319; Great —, 109; — Tantra (see under Tantra); Mothers and Sons, 47; Mothers of the Three Families, 192-3
Mountains, 329
Mouth, 172
Mrgadāva, 41
Mrtyumāra, 18
Mtsho-skyes, 288-9
muditā (Joy, sympathetic), 184
mudrā (Seal, q.v.); three kinds, *mahāmudrā* (Great Seal), *dharmamudrā* (Law Seal), *samaya-mudrā* (Symbolic Seal), to which a fourth is added, *karmamudrā* (Action Seal); a different classification, *karmamudrā* (Action Seal) and *jñānamudrā* (Knowledge Seal); also: *mudrādarśana* (Exhibition of the Seals), 179; *mudrānyāsa* (Application of Seals), 163; *mudrā* also Gesture, Hand Gesture
mudryate (is sealed), 102
mukuṭa-abhiṣeka (Diadem Initiation), 27
mūla-mantra, 117
mūlāpatti (Transgressions, fundamental), 329
mūla-tantra, 125
muni, 63; *muni-muni* (an incantation), 109
mūrtijā, 107
Mustard seed, 179, 281
Muttering (*jāpa*), 31, 157-161, 187-203, 207-9, 216-219, 240-243, 272-3, 278, 293, 299; four Members of Muttering (Ground, Objective and Subjective; Immersion in Mind; Immersion in Sound), 187-193; Rosary —, 216
Mysteries, the three, 205

N

nāḍī (Vein), 257, 321; *avadhūtī* (Middle Vein), 321, 327; *lalanā* (Left Vein), 321, 327, *rasanā* (Right Vein), 327
nāga (Serpent, Snake), 55, 59, 103, 121, 220; *nāgarāja* (Serpent King), 280
Nāgabodhi, 295
Nāgārjuna, 77, 85, 89, 91, 96 ,109, 162, 167, 326, 335
Nail, magic, 272, 283
Nairañjanā River, 27, 39
Nairātmyā (the Goddess), 36, 256-7
nairātmya (Selflessness, q.v.), 89
nāmakāya (Set of Names), 77
nāmaseka (Name Initiation), 313
Name, 33-4, 141, 313
Nanda (the King), 67
nanda (Joy), 169
Naro-pā, 267
Nartakapara, 133, 135
nātha, 335
Natural Abode (*svābhāvika-sthāna*), 293, 297
Nature, intrinsic (*svabhāva*), 209, 211, 222, 229, 234, 259, 268, 270, 283, 323, 333-4; Devoid of — (*niḥsvabhāvatā*), 222, 234, 261, 267
Natures (*dharma*, q.v.); All Natures (*sarvadharmāḥ*), 28, 85, 93, 102, 261; Matrix of — (= Source of —; *dharmodaya*), 217, 294-297, 318, 333; True Nature (*dharmatā*), 331; four Black — (*kṛṣṇa-dharma*) and four White — (*śukla-dharma*), 152-3
nāṭya (Drama), 77
Navel, 161, 172-3, 177, 322-3
ñe rgyu (Convergence), 268
Near-essence (*upahṛdya*), 161
Nebesky-Wojkowitz, 18, 118
Neck, 161, 237, 322-3
Neophyte, 323
neya (Drawing, Suggestive), 261, 265
neyārtha (a kind of Meaning, q.v.)
nidāna (Instructive Personal Discourses), 55; (Initial Summary), 215
niḥśabda (Silence), 198
niḥsvabhāvatā (Devoid of Nature, Intrinsic, q.v.)
Ni Khri, 97-7
Nīladaṇḍa, 118
nimitta (Attribute), 228, 234; *-devatā* (Attribute Deity), 291
Nirgrantha, 71
Nirmāṇa-kāya, see under Body
Nirmāṇarati (a class of Desire Gods), 169
nirmita (Magical apparition), 23, 35, 215
nirodha (Cessation), 45; *nirodha-samāpatti* (Cessation Equipoise), 65
Nirvāṇa, 19, 23, 25, 55-63, 67, 69, 85, 105, 111, 156, 184, 216, 222
nirvikalpa-jñāna (Knowledge, non-discursive), 315
niṣpanna-krama (Steps of Completion; see under Steps)
nītārtha (a kind of Meaning, q.v.)
Nobel, Johannes, 110
Noble one (*ārya*), 228; Nobility, 203
Noble Truth (*ārya-satya*), 45
Non-concrete, 53
Non-duality, 263, 268
Non-interruption, 267
Noon, 152, 191, 193, 276; — Arhats, 63
Noose, 233, 236
Nose, 244-5; Nostrils, 172
Nothingness (*akiñcanya*), 297, 301
Nyagrodha, 123

O

Obermiller, E., 16-7, 46, 50, 72
Object (*artha*, *ālambana*): Interior —, 217; see also Absolute Object and Meditation
Objective, 217, 221
Oblation (*bali*, *arghya*), 123; 177-183
Obscuration (*āvaraṇa*), 53, 81, 161, 273
Odor, fragrant, 177, 203
Offering (*pūjā*), 37-9, 113-4, 159, 161, 165, 171, 175-187, 191, 194, 218-9, 236-7, 247, 272, 283, 287-9, 293-299, 313; of two kinds, internal and external, 218; *maṇḍala*-Offering, 186-7, 283, and *sādhana*-Offering, 285, include Mental —, 183, Locational —, 186-7, Procedural —, 187; materials for offering are: — Utensils, 291; Burnt — (*homa*), 139, 191, 195, 273-277; Food — (*bali*), 123, 272, 285; also: — of five Goddesses, 114
Oṃ'd, two and three, 125
Omen, 115, 202-3; including Smoke (*dhuma*), Blazing substance (*jvalita*), and Warmth (*uṣma*)
One-hundred and eight, 121, 123, 131
Ordinary person (*pṛthagjana*), 19
Ordure, 220
Orifice, unclean, 172

Ornament, 181, 209, 228
Outer (see Treatise, School, Science)
Outsider (= non-Buddhist), 79, 89

P

Pa-tshab, 89, 91
pada, 83; *-kāya* (Set of Phrases), 77
padma (Lotus, red), 69, 103, 175, 221, 319
Padmanarteśvara, 100
Padmāṅkuśa (the paṇḍita), 119, 147
Padmasaṃbhava, 25, 67, 91, 109
Padmavajra, 25, 101, 116, 214, 296
padya (Verse), 77
Pair combined beyond Learning (*aśaikṣa-yuganaddha*), 267-9
Pair combined with Learning (*śaikṣa-yuganaddha*), 266
Paiśācika, 69
Palace (*vimāna*), 156, 161, 175, 207, 215, 223, 236, 281, 289, 297-9, 302-3, 333
Palms, 175-7; Palmist, 75
Paṇ-chen Lamas, 11
pañca-rakṣā, 113, 145
pañcaka-bhadravargiya (Happy Band of Five), 41
pañcaka-kula (Family of the Five), 103, 135
Pāṇḍarā, 192-3
Pandey, K. C., 210
Paṇḍit (Expert or Wise man), 295
Pāṇini, 75
pañjarā Family, concise, 255
pāpa-deśanā (Confession of Sins), 185; *pāpadeśanādika* (the Series beginning with Confession of Sins), 185
Parables (*avadāna*), 55
paramabodhi (Highest Enlightenment), 229, 247; *-cittotpāda* (Generation of the Mind towards Highest Enlightenment), 31
paramārtha (the Absolute), 91, 204, 217, 270, 318; *-deva* (1st of the six Gods), 160; *-dharma*, 204; *-satya* (Absolute Truth), 279
Paramārthasamudgata (name of a Bodhisattva), 51
paramārtha-viniścaya-cakra (Wheel of Absolute Certainty), 47
Paramāśva, 118
pāramitā (Perfection), 162; three in Yoga-tantra, perhaps with literal meaning 'Gone Beyond', *dāna-* (perhaps 'Gone Beyond through Giving'), *-vīrya-* (ditto through Striving), *prajñā-* (ditto through Insight), 223, 232; for Paramītā School, Vehicle, or *yāna*, see under Vehicle; for — Path, see under Path
Paranirmitavaśavartin (a class of Desire Gods), 169
Parasol, 291
paratantra (Dependency; see under Characteristic), 49, 51
parāvṛtti (Transmutation, Revolution), 29
parijñeya (to be Recognized or Known), 45
parikalpita (Imaginary; see under Characteristic), 49
pariniṣpanna (Absolute; see under Characteristic), 49, 51
parivāra (Retinue), 36, 161
parivrājaka (Perigrinator), 41
Parṇaśavarī-kalpa, 127
pāśa (Noose), 233
Passion (*rāga*), 57, 169, 203, 319
paṭa (Cloth), 301
pātāla (the Underworld), 79
Pāṭaliputra, 65, 67
Patañjali, 75
Path (*mārga*), 16-19, 45, 89, 101, 150, 171, 207, 215, 221, 227-231, 269, 271, 309, 321, 325, 327, 331-335; two basic Paths: *pāramitā* —, 39, and *mantra* —, 39, 149, 273, 275, 291, 311, 329, 331, 335; *pāramitā* — has five Paths: (1) — of Equipment (*saṃbhāra-mārga*), (2) — of Training (*prayoga-m.*), (3) — of Vision (*darśana-m.*), (4) — of Intense Contemplation (*bhāvanā-m.*), (5) — Beyond Training (*aśaikṣa-m.*), 16, 19, 21, 42, 45; *mantra* — has Common — (*sādhāraṇa-m.*), 321, and Uncommon — (*asādhāraṇa-m.*), 271; *mantra* — includes Anuttara —, 333, of two degrees, — of Production and — of Completion, for which see under Steps; also: —, Action, 230; —, Bodhisattva, 70, 310; — of Entrance, 151; — of Equipment, 16, 21; —, Initiation, 271; — of Liberation (*vimukti-m.*), 184, 331, which is Path (leading to the Realization), 45; — of Maturation (*vipāka-m.*), 331; — of Passion, 169; —, Purification, 231
pātra (Bowl, begging), 43
pauṣṭika (Prosperity), 177; *-kula*, 103

Peacock, 77
Peregrinator (*parivrājaka*), 41
Perfection (*pāramitā, sampad*), 102, 156-7, 169, 171, 194; — of Giving, Striving, Insight, 223; five of resultative Complete Buddha (of Body, Merit, Retinue, Place, and Affiliation), 156-7; of Body, also 266
Perfume, 181, 183, 285
Permission (*anujñā*), 141, 272, 279, 281, 309
Personality (*pudgala*), 335; — Aggregates (*skandha*), 36, 101, 234, 243, 257, 334
Persons (like a Jewel, Red Lotus, White Lotus, Sandlewood, and Blue Lotus), 218-221; Jewel-like Person, also 267-,9, 319; Consciousness or Mental Series of Persons (Lust, Hatred, Delusion, Avarice), 221, 227, 230; — Pledged, 234
Petals, 322
Petitioner, 257
Pha-Khol, 78
phala (Fruit), 214, 266
Phase, Increasing (of the moon), 18; — with Signs, 173, 201; without Signs, 157, 173
Phoneme, 233
Piling-up (of Beings), 297
piṇḍagrāha (Contraction), 327
Pingala, 79, 134-5
piṭaka (Collection, Basket), 53
Pith (*maṇḍa*), 270
Planets, nine, 114
Pledge (*samaya*), 30, 137, 142-3, 155, 177, 207, 215, 220, 229, 309, 328-331; — of Bell (*ghaṇṭa*), of Seal (*mudrā*), of Thunderbolt (*vajra*), 142-3
Poetics (*kāvya*), 77
Poetry, 77-79
Poison, 57, 221
Pore (of Head and of Body hair), 172
poṣadha, 67
Possessions (*bhoga*), 203
Posture, bodily (*īryāpatha*), 247; —, five stances, 273, 282; —, Lotus-sitting, 179
Potala (Mt.), 125, 127
Poussin, de la Vallée, 18
Powdered Color (*rajas*), 301
Power of Truth (*satya-bala*), 55
prabandha (Continuous Series), 266
prabhāsvara (Clear Light), 265
prabhu (Lord), 161
Practices, 21,000, 57
prahelikā (Riddle), 79
praheya (to be Removed), 45
Praise, Praising, 37, 45, 175, 179-185, 272-3, 287, 289, 293, 296-7
Pratyekabuddha, 36, 41
prajñā (see Insight), 71, 143, 168, 319, 261-3, 296; *-buddhivardhana* (Expanding Insight and Cognition), 111; *-svabhāva* (Source, or Self-Existence of Insight), 328; for *-jñāna* see under Insight
Prajñā-pāramitā literature, *sūtras*, or texts, 16, 47, 85, 96-99, 195, 223, 232, 263
Prajñapti (= Prajñaptiśāstra), 81, 83
prakaraṇa, eight, 95, 99
Prakaraṇapāda (Organized Presentation), 83
prakriya, 113
prakṛti (Ground), 69, 266, 275; *-siddha* (produced by fundamental Ground), 93
prāṇa (Wind), 209, 264; *-āyāma*, 172-3, 175, 187, 189, 214, 244, 320
prāṇidhāna (Fervant Aspiration), 185; *-saṃvara*, 147
Prāsaṅgika, 93, 335; -Mādhyamika, 13
praśrabdhi (Cathartic, q.v.), of Mind (*citta-*) and of Body (*kāya-*)
praśvāsa (Encouragement), 141
prathama-prayoga (Initial Training), 273
Pratibhānavatī (name of a Devī), 111
pratibimba (Image), 107, 228
prātihārya, 26-7
pratiloma (Backward), 327
Prātimokṣa, 12
pratipatti-pūjā (Procedural Offering), 187
Pratisarā, 113
pratiṣṭhā (= *pratiṣṭhāna*; Consecration), 235, 272, 275
pratītya-samutpāda (Dependent Origination), 31, 107, 331
pratyāhāra, 320
pratyālīḍha, 282
pratyanta-janapada (Border Countries), 69
pratyavekṣaṇa (Discrimination), 29, 223
pratyaya, 105
Pratyekabuddha, 16
pravacana (the Sacred Word), 53, 55
praveśa (Entrance), 157
praveṣaṇa (Drawing-in), 214, 237
Precept, 155
Preceptor (*upādhyāya*), 169, 313

Preparation, 285, 301, 303; — of disciple, 285, 291, 309; of Flask, 285, 287; of *maṇḍala*-deities and of Earth Goddess, 283
preraṇa (Instigation), 243
preta, 121, 123
Pride (*māna*, *garva*), 160, 165, 167, 203, 222, 243, 293, 299
Prince, 291
Procedure (*anusthāna*), 29, 159; of Duty (*kṛtyānuṣṭhāna*), 34, 223, 247; of evocation, 283
Produced (*siddha*), by Fundamental Ground and by Individual Characteristic, 93
Profound (the mental component), 245, 247, 268; see also Concentration, profound
Progenitor (*kula*), 37, 255
Progeny (*kulika*), 103
Promulgation, 43, 47-57, 71, 81, 85, 95-99, 213, 253, 259
Prophecy (*vyākaraṇa*), 53, 61, 63, 69, 75, 107, 111, 141, 315
Prosody (*chandas*), 77, 79
Prosperity (*pauṣṭika*), 177
Protective Circle (*rakṣā-cakra*), 293
Provisional, a kind of Meaning, q.v.
pṛthag-jana (Ordinary Person), 19
pṛthivī (Earth or Earth Goddess), 281, 285, 332
pudgala (Personality), 335; *-ātman*, 85; *-nairātmya* (Selflessness of Personality), 87, 335
pūjā (Offering), 214, 218-9, 237; *pūjāstutyādika* (Offering, Praising, and so on), 179
puṇya (Merit), 16, 185, 214
Pure Abode, 119, 121
Purification (*viśuddhi*), 156-7, 207, 227-233, 257, 283, 295, 301, 331, 333; — of Attendants (*anucāra-viśuddhi*), 255, 257; Sphere of Purification, three, 157, 295, 331, 333
Purity, two, 53
Pūrṇa, 83
Pūrṇacandra, 77
Pūrṇavardhana, 83
pūrva-sevā (Preliminary Service), 207

Q

Quarter(s), Protectors of (*dik-pāla*), 272
Queen of the Diamond Realm (Vajradhātvīśvarī), 242
Quicksilver, 160

R

Radiance (*tejas*), 43
rāga (Passion, Lust), 57, 221
rahasya paramaṃ rame, 253
Rahder, J., 19
Rāhula, 22, 69
Rāhulabhadra, 135
Rāhula-śrī-kalyāṇamitra (= Rāhula-śrī-mitra), 141-2, 301
Rājagṛha, 41, 59, 63, 69, 121, 135
rajas (Powdered Color), 301; *rajomaṇḍala* (*maṇḍala* of —), 105
rakṣa! (Protect!), 293; *rakṣā-cakra* (Protective Circle), 159, 283
rākṣasa, 135
rasa (Sentiment), 79
ratna (Jewel), 69, 103, 221
Ratnākaraśānti (= Śānti-pā, q.v.), 79
Ratnakīrti, 109
Ratnamati, 77
Ratnarakṣita, 149
Ratnasaṃbhava, 31, 34, 37, 100-1, 217, 221, 264, 286, 313
Ratnaśikhin, 19
ṛddhi (Magical Power), 65
Rdo rje lcags mchu, 133
Rdo-rje-rin-chen, 304
Real Production, 53, 91
Reality, 199, 263, 301; Deity —, 209; Self —, 159, 163, 195, 197, 207; — of Void, 335
Realm (*dhātu*), 257, 334; three: of Desire (*kāma-dhātu*), of Form (*rūpa-dhūtu*), and Formless (*arūpa-dhātu*), 22, 169, 205; also: Diamond or Thunderbolt — (*vajra-dh.*), 204, 217, 221, 225, 242; Nature — (*dharma-dh.*), 204, 206, 222; — of the Reality 'Clear Light', 301; — of Space (*ākāśa-dh.*), 292, 294; Worldly — (*loka-dh.*), 105, 205, 236; — of Void, 316
Reason (*yukti*), 85
Receptacle, worthy and unworthy, 145
Recitation, 189,-193, 209, 243-4, 277; 197, — whispered, 189; — mental, 189, 209
Red-mdaḥ-pa, 86
Referent (*upalakṣaṇa*), 228
Refuge, taking of (*śaraṇa-gamana*), 147, 153; — Formula, 185
Rejection (*spaṅs pa*), 268

Relative (*saṃvṛti-*), 270, 318, 334
Releases, or Liberations, the eight (*aṣṭau vimokṣāḥ*), 63
Relic, 107, 111
Renou, Louis, 320
Residence (*layana*, *ādhāra*), 175, 267, 281, 291
Resident(s) (*ādheya*), 37, 175, 177, 223, 291
Retinue (*parivāra*), 161-2, 236, 255, 259-263, 270, 275, 277, 289, 291
Revelation-Enlightenment (*abhisaṃbodhi*), 29-35, 39, 227, 305
Ri-bo-Dge-ldan-pa, 243
ri-lu, 220
Rice, parched, 177
rigs ḥdra (Affiliation, q.v.), 332
Rin-chen-bzaṅ-po, 24
Rising for leaving (*utthāna*), 157
Rite, Ritual (*vidhi* or *karma*), 101, 107, 113, 117-123, 127, 129, 135, 149, 151 155, 177, 187-193, 201, 203, 223, 237, 241, 266-7, 272, 277, 281, 295, 297, 311, 317; generally in three phases, Preliminary or Preparatory — (see Preparation), 137, 151, 273, 279, 283, 301, 303, Body of the —, 301, 303, Concluding Acts, 139, 193, 273; — of Prophecy, Encouragement, and Permission, 145, 159; also: — of Blessing, 301; Cemetary —, 193; Consecration —, 309, 325; — of the Fierce Act, 272; — of *dhāraṇī*, 109; — of Initiation, q.v., 137, 139, 309; — of *maṇḍala*, q.v., 279-283, 291, 301; — of Oblation, 123; — of Protecting, 301; Purification or Bathing —, 159, 281; — of two Reversals, 272; Seven-membered — (*saptāṅgavidhi*), 153; — of the Site, 278, 286, 295, 299, 301; Soil —, 137, 145; — of "tearing apart" the *saṃpuṭa*, 272; Thread —, 288 (see Line and Thread); — of Vimala Offerings, 117; of taking the Vow, 155. For Set of Magical Acts, see under Action (= Acts).
Rje Rin-po-che (= Tsoṅ-kha-pa), 97
Robes, waist (*saṃghāṭī*), 59, 69
Rouse, W.H.D., 152
ṛṣi, 61
Rṣipatana, 41
Rtogs par sla ba, 91
rudrākṣa (Berries of Elaeocarpus Ganitrus), 187
rūpa (Form), 93; *rūpa-kāya* (see under Body)
Rupiṇī, 304

S

Sa-skya, 304-5; — *paṇḍita*, 129, 131
Sabari-pā, 128, 145
Sabbath (*upoṣadha*), 109
śabda (Sound), 79, 93; *-vidyā* (Grammar, science of), 73
sāccha (Tile Buddha), 117
Sacral place, 322
Sacred Word (*pravacana*), nine and twelve groupings of, 53-57
Sacrifice (*argha*), 289
ṣaḍaṅga-yoga (six-part *yoga*, q.v.), 37
Saḍbhuja, Śrī, 123
sādhana (Evocation procedure), 101, 105, 111-115, 123, 129, 167, 214, 283, 285; — of five Goddesses, 113; — of Mañjuśrī, 111; — of the "Partnership Family", 123; — of Pratisarā, 113; — of Sarasvatī, 111; — of Vaiśravaṇa, 109
sādhāraṇa (Common or Shared), 147, 151, 219, 313; *sādhāraṇa-nīti-śāstra*, 95
Safflower, 195
Saffron, 111, 195
sahaja (Born together with), 261
Sahajalalita, 117
sahā-lokadhātu (World-systems of Tribulation), 23
sāhasracūḍika, 105
śaikṣa-yuganaddha. (see under Union)
Śakra, 209
sākṣātkareya (to be Realized), 45
Śākyamitra, 24-27, 30, 214, 217, 227, 235, 241
Śākyamuni, 16-19, 23, 35, 69, 105, 109, 113, 205, 209
Śākyaprabha, 85
śalya (Sharp Points), 79
samādhi (Concentration, profound), 21, 26-7, 37, 39, 121, 162, 197, 199, 205, 210, 213-4, 217-220, 223, 225, 231, 237, 273, 294, 320, 321; set of three *samādhis* common to the Yoga and Anuttara Tantras, *prathama-prayoga* (Initial Training), *vijaya-maṇḍala* (Victorious *maṇḍala*), and *karma-vijaya* (Ritual Victory), 223, 294-5; two types (see under Concentration) also: *āniñjyo-nāma-* (Unstirring *samādhi*), 27; *āsphara-ṇaka-* (Space-filling *samādhi*), 27, 37,

39; *vajropama-* (Adamantine *samādhi*), 21, 37, 39; *samādhi-saṃskāra* (the Impression of *samādhi*), 210; *samādhi-sattva* (see under Being)
samāna (name of a Wind, q.v.), 264
Samantabhadra, 22, 30-1, 102, 162
sāmantaka (Preparation, Threshold), 285
Samantālokopalabdhiprabhā, 312
Samantaprabhā, 312-3
samapāda (a kind of Stance), 282
samāpatti (Equipoise, Equal entrance, a meditative attainment), 19, 29, 263
samatā (Equality, q.v.), 223; *samatā-jñāna*, 214
śamatha (Calming), 57, 199, 210
samaya (Pledge, q.v.); *-sattva* (see under Being); *samayas tvaṃ* (You are the Pledge!; a frequent *mantra*), 229
Samaya-saṃgraha, 155
Samayavajra, 155
samayin (a person pledged, having the *samaya*), 234
Sambara (= Śrīcakrasaṃvara), 256, 304-5
saṃbhāra (Equipment), 17, 273
Saṃbhoga-kāya (see under Body)
saṃdhi-bhāṣā (Twilight Language), 219
Saṃgha (the Congregation, the Virtuous Host), 59, 65, 67, 185, 203
Saṃghabhadra, 83
saṃghāṭi (Waist Robe), 59
Saṃgītiparyāya (Well-sung Terminology), 83
Saṃjñāya, 111, 135
saṃkleśa (Corruption), 227
Saṃmatīya, 69, 85
saṃpanna-krama (see under Steps), 36
saṃpuṭa, 156, 266-268, 272, 283, 325, 327
saṃsāra (Cycle of Life, Transmigration), 23, 203, 256, 267
saṃskāra (= *preraṇa* as Instigation), 243; (Constructed thing), 85; (as a Hand Gesture), 233
saṃsveda-jā (Birth from Moisture), 330
saṃtāna (Stream of Consciousness, Mental Series), 21, 45, 149, 221, 266, 273, 321; *ekasaṃtāna*, 249
saṃvara (Vow, q.v.)
Saṃvara (= Sambara, q.v.), the Black 277
saṃvṛti (see Conventional and Relative); *saṃvṛti-māyā*, 321
samudaya (Source), 45
samyaksaṃbuddha, 23, 312, 333
Sāṇavāsa, 59-63
Sandlewood-like, 219
śaṅkha (Conch, q.v.)
Śāntarakṣita, 25, 91, 93, 109, 117, 139
Śānti-pā, 53, 97, 113, 145-149, 167, 267, 335
Śāntideva, 91, 153
śantika (Rite, appeasing), 177
Sapphire, 175
saptāṅgavidhi (Rite, seven-membered), 153
sāra, 270
śara (Arrow), 224
Saraha, 270, 298
śaraṇa-gamana (Refuge, taking of), 147, 885
Śaraṇamukta, 109
Sarasvatī, 79, 111
Śāriputra, 22, 61, 81, 105
sarvabhāvāḥ, 49
sarvadharmāḥ, 85, 93, 211, 261
Sarvajña, 11
Sarvajñāna, 72
Sarvakāmin, 63, 65
Sarvanivaraṇaviṣkambhin, 22, 107
Sarvārthasiddha, 27-31
sarvaśūnya (Universal Void), 37
Śarvavarman, 75, 77
sarvayoga, 214
śaśa-viṣāṇa, 51
śāsana-dhara, 111
sāsrava, 85
śāstra (Treatise, q.v.; an Expository Text)
Śāsvatavajra, 301
Śatakratu, 73
ṣaṭkoṭi (Alternatives, six), 219
sattva (Beings, q.v.)
satya-bala (Truth, Power of), 55
Śavari-pā, 169
Sautrāntika, 16, 21, 83, 85
Schools, 'Inner' (Buddhist) and 'Outer' (non-Buddhist), 75; 'Inner' includes: Cittamātra School, 334-5; Jo-naṅ-pa (= Jo-mo-naṅ-pa), 49, 51, 97, 99; Mādhyamika (both Prāsaṅgika and Svātantrika), 335; Mūlasarvāstivādin, 69, 82; Śrāvaka Schools, the eighteen, 68, 85; division of Mahāyāna into Pāramitā, 19, 21, 25, and Mantra, 21, 24-5 (see Vehicle); Mantra School includes Yoga —, 25, 269, and Anuttara —, 35; Anuttara — includes Ārya

and Jñānapāda Schools of the *Guhyasamāja*, 35, 173, and Kālacakra —, 329
Science (*vidyā*, *vidyāsthāna*), five, 73; Inner and Outer —, 73, 77, 81
Scripture (*āgama*), 91
Seal (*mudrā*), defined as 'joyous' and a 'seal', 228; 85, 102-3, 121, 142, 159-165, 171, 177-183, 192-3, 205, 209, 214, 225-237, 241-247, 254-5, 273, 291, 295, 297, 319, 321; four main kinds, Great Seal (*mahāmudrā*), 142-3, 199, 225-239, 243-247, 254, 263, 291; Law Seal (*dharmamudrā*), 225-235, 239, 243, 245, 291; Symbolic Seal or Seal of Pledge (*samayamudrā*), 225-243, 291; Action Seal (*karmamudrā*), of two kinds, Bound or Binding and Imagined, 229, and 227-232, 235, 239, 245; two main kinds, when *mudrā* means the female partner, Action Seal (*karmamudrā*) and Knowledge Seal (*jñānamudrā*), 319-323; Seal creating Body of Deity, 103, 228; Application of the — (*mudrā-nyāsa*), 163-167; Exhibition of the — (*mudrādarśana*), 179; also: — of Akṣobhya, 247, 249; Complete Universal —, 102; — of Equipose (*samāpatti-mudrā*), 209; of Feet-cooling Water, 181; of the Flask (*kalaśa-mudrā*), 193; Flower —, 181; of Food for the Gods, 183; of making Gifts, 181; of Great Symbol (*mahāsamaya*), 179; of Invitation, 177; of Lamp, 183; of Lotus-sitting Posture, 179; of Perfumed Incense, 183; of the Sphere of Purification (including — of the Path and of the Fruit of Purification), 229, 231; of taking Refuge, 181; Symbolic Thunderbolt — (*samayavajramudrā*), 179; of Vairocana, 247; of Washing the Body, 181
Seat (*āsana*), common and uncommon, 177, 297
Secret (*guhya*), 272, 311, 321, 328-9; — Form, 228; see Mysteries
Secret Folk (*yakṣa*), 103, 228; Master of — (*guhyakādhipati*), 206
Sects, division into four and then eighteen, 67, 69
Seed (*bīja*), 48, 295, 297; — Syllable (*bīja-akṣara*), 291; see Syllable
Self-existence (*svabhāva*, q.v.), 247, 234-5; Self-existent (*svabhāvin*), 234
Self-generation, 105
Self Reality (*ātma-tattva*), 139, 195, 197, 207
Selflessness (*nairātmya*), of Personality (*pudgala-n.*) and of Natures (*dharma-n.*), 87, 89
Semen, 195, 220, 319
Semi-circle, 294
Sense Base (*āyatana*), 57, 163, 257, 334
Sensory Organ (*indriya*) and Sensory Domain (*viṣaya*), 173
Sentiment (*rasa*), 79
Serpent (*nāga*), 103; — King (*nāga-rāja*), eight, Ananta, Karkoṭaka, Kulika, Mahāpadma, Padma, Śaṅkhapāla, Takṣaka, and Vāsuki, 280
Servant, 123
Service (*sevā*), equivalent to Muttering (*jāpa*) of *dhāraṇī*, 167, 200-1; as Preliminary or as Concluding, 139, 191, 207, 211, 275-279; through Self Generation, 159, 161, 169, 173, and through Generation in Front, 173; exclusive of the main part of rite, e.g. Meditation, 139, and *maṇḍala*-acts, 277, 279; in Anuttara Tantra, of two kinds, Common and Superior, 200-1
Śeṣa, 75
Sesamum, 177; Sesame Pastry, 75; Sesame Seed, 39
Set of Reasons (= Set of Principles), the Tibetan abbreviated reference (*rigs tshogs*) to the Mādhyamika Nāgārjuna's basic works, 86-7, 335
sevā (Service, q.v.)
Seven: Hierarchs of the Teaching, 63; Logical Treatises, 73; Mountains, 101; *skandhas*, 101; sections of the Abhidharma, 81, 83
Sex organ, male and female, 172
sgra la gźol ba (Immersion in Sound; a mystical Meditation), 209
Shingon sect, 204, 216
Shoulder, 161
Siddhānta, 83, 87, 328
Siddhārtha, 19-23, 217
siddhi (Magical Power, — Success, — Talent), 111, 114, 159, 163, 165, 171, 177, 193, 195, 200-203, 206-7, 211-221, 245, 266, 277, 329; two kinds: Mundane (*laukika*), accruing from Steps of Production, Lower Tantras, 219, referred to as Common (*sādhāraṇa*), 221, including the *mahāsiddhis* (eight), 220-

1; and Supramundane (*lokottara*), 220, concerned with Buddha-nature; *siddhi* defined, 216; see also Magical acts
Signature, 211
Sign (*lakṣman*), 228
śīla (Morality), 155
Silence, 198
Silk, 209
śilpakarmasthāna-vidyā, 73, 95
Silver, 175, 177
siṃhāsana (Lion's Throne), 215
Siṅgala (= Ceylon), 89
Sin, 153, 161
Sitātapatrā, 117, 119, 145
Site, 45, 279-287, 295
Six-handed One (Śrī Ṣaḍbhuja), 123
skandha (Aggregate), 328 (see Personality Aggregates); *dharma-* (Aggregate of Doctrines), 57; *rūpa-* (Personality Aggregate of Form), 257; a seventh —, 101
skandhamāra, 18
skar ma sa gaḥi ña ba, 58
Skill, 264-5
Skull bowl (*kapāla*), 287
Sky (*ākāśa*), 220, 283, 287, 292-3, 297, 299, 303
Sky Walker (*ḍāka, ḍākinī*), 254-5
śloka(s) in various numbers, 57, 75, 77, 83, 113, 119, 329
Smṛti, Paṇḍita (= Smṛtijñānakīrti), 77
Smoke, 203, 268
sṅags btu, 121
Snellgrove, D.L., 18, 28, 34, 142, 256, 319
Sñiṅ po mdor bsags, 275
Soil, 281
Solitarily Enlightened Being (*pratyekabuddha*), 16
Somendra, 79
Son, 47; — of the Gods (*devaputra*), 43; — of Vajrapāṇi, 137; — of Vaiśravaṇa, 135; — of Viśrama, 133
Sorcika Flower, 69
Sound (*śabda*), 93, 137, 161, 167, 187, 189, 193-199, 209, 243-4, 247; — God, 117
Source (*samudaya*), 45
Sow (Vārāhī), 304
Space-filling *samādhi*, 37, 39
Species (*gotra*), 50
Speech (*vāk*), 33, 55, 79, 131, 171, 199, 204-206, 224-235, 241, 244, 291, 295-297, 312, 317; Arcane — (*vāg-viveka*), 312, 321-2, 327
Spine, base of, 322
Spirits, elementary and inimical, 135-6
Square, 294
Śraddhākaravarma, 24
śrāddhasattva (Believer), 328
śrāvaka (Disciple, q.v.), 16-7, 36, 53-57, 329
Śrāvastī, 59, 65, 123, 125
Śrīcakrasaṃvara, 304; — Cycle, 100
Śrīgupta, 91
Śrī Hayagrīvasaptati, 127
Śrī Mahādevī, 111
Śrī Maṇibhadra, 102
Śrī Ṣaḍbhuja (Esteemed Six-handed One = Mahākāla), 123
srod-añjana (Tib. *srod* + Skt. *añjana*), 216, 221
Sroṅ-btsan-sgam-po, 91
sta gon gyi cho ga (Rite of Preparation), 137
Stage(s) (*bhūmi*), 19, 21, 27, 35-39, 48, 70, 105, 162, 205, 227, 235, 312-3, 317; Ten —, listed, 19; Tenth —, 21, 205; 227, 313, 316; seventeen —, 95; also see Steps
Stance, 282-3; Male —, 273; also see Posture
stava-kāya (Collection of Eulogies), 93
Stcherbatsky, Th., 335
Steps (*krama*), 323, 325; — of Birth State, 227 (presumably = *saṃvṛti-māyā* portion of Steps of Completion, 321); — of the Path, 87, 89, 215, 229, 325; — of Revelation-Enlightenment (*abhisaṃbodhi*), 37, 39; —, three (= the Councils), 189, (= Meditative Objects), 189; in Anuttara Tantra, two main —: — of Production (or Generation; *utpatti-krama*), and of Completion (*saṃpanna-krama* or *niṣpanna-krama*), 36-39, 113, 127, 150-1, 157, 173, 198, 201, 219-223, 253-257, 267-269, 294, 296, 312, 317, 320-327, 331, 333, 337
sthavira (Elder), 59, 69
Sthāvira Subhūti, 11
Sthiramati, 85, 87, 316, 335
sthūlāpatti (Transgression, gross), 329
Store Consciousness (*ālaya-vijñāna*), 51, 168; Basis of the — (*ālayavijñāna-āśraya*), 29
Stream of Consciousness (*saṃtāna*), 21, 42, 45, 49, 51, 57, 71, 155-6, 205, 249,

266, 273, 277-291, 309-312, 321, 327-331
Strife, age of (*kali-yuga*), 277
stūpa(s), 59, 63, 105-109, 113-117, 175, 195, 228
Subāhu, 137
Subduing (*vaśīkāra*), 237, 240, 243, 249
Subject matter (*vācya*), 253
Substances, 301
subhāṣita (the Well-Expressed = the Buddhist Teaching), 63
śuddhāvāsa (Pure Abode), 105
Śuddhāvāsāḥ (Gods of the Pure Abode), 23
Śuddhodana (the King), 19, 23-4, 27, 29, 39
śūdra, 69, 291
Suffering (*duḥkha*), 21, 43, 45, 85, 117, 161, 184-5, 267; — beings, 23, 25
Sugata (epithet of Buddha), 281, 328
sukha (Bliss, q.v.), 317; *mahāsukha* (Great Beatitude), 261, 267; *-śūnya* (Bliss-Void), 263, 317
Sukhāvatī, 115
śukla-pakṣa (Phase, increasing, of the Moon), 18
sūkṣma-vajra (see under Thunderbolt), 245
Sumeru (Mt.), 27, 29, 35, 105, 131, 175, 215
Sun, 139, 153, 208, 280
śūnya (Void, q.v.); *śūnyatā* (Voidness, q.v.)
Superior (*upādhyāya*), 63, 65, 69
Supramundane (*lokottara*), 103
Śūraṃgamavarma, 117
Sūryagupta, 127
Sūryakānta, Dr., 305
Susiddhikarin, 136-7
Susthira, 115
Sūtra (Scripture, Aphorism), grouped under three Promulgations, 45-53; *-piṭaka* (one of the three *piṭakas*), 59, 69; the ten *tathāgata-garbha* —, 48-51; — as a category contrasting with Mantra (= Tantra), 109, 111, 277 (see also Pāramitā Vehicle under Vehicle)
Suvāgīśvarakīrti, 300
svabhāva (Own-being, Intrinsic Nature, Self-existence), 160-1, 232, 234, 247, 259; *-viśuddhi* (Intrinsic Purity), 29, 53, 259, 328; *-siddha* or *-siddhi* (Produced or Production by Intrinsic Nature), 93, 209; *niḥsvabhāva* (devoid of Intrinsic Nature), 261; *-kāya*, see under Body; *-maṇḍala*, see under *maṇḍala*; *-śūnyatā* (Voidness of Intrinsic Nature), 28; *jaḍā-* (Unconscious Substance), 93
svābhāvika-sthāna (Natural Abode), 293
svabhāvin (Self-existent), 234
svadevatā (one's own Deity), 203
svāhā (a final in many *dhāraṇīs*, understood to both conclude the mystic incantation and to continue its silent influence), 175, 179-183
svalakṣaṇa-siddha (Produced by Individual Characteristic), 93
svara-nimna (Immersion in Sound), 187
svarūpa ('Formal Cause'), 241
Svātantrika, 91, 93, 335
svarga (Heaven), 79
Sword, 211, 220
Syllable (*akṣara*), 105, 187-191, 195-199, 209, 229-230, 233, 243, 271, 288-291, 325, 333; Forty Introductory —, 69; Germ —, 294; Heavy and Light —, 79; Hundred — (*śatākṣara*), 105; Shape of the —, 187-189, Sound of the —, 189; Seed — (= Germ —; *bīja-akṣara*), 291, 295-297, 325; Three —, 288; see also Heart (*hṛdaya*). Individual Germ Syllables by page location: A, 127, 209; Ā, 209; Aḥ, 209; Āḥ, 286, 288; Aṃ, 209; Baṃ, 289; Bhū, 281; E, 333; Hā, 286; Hoḥ, 236, 240, 243; Hrīḥ, 243; Hūṃ, 118, 236, 240, 243, 286, 288; Jaḥ, 236, 240, 243; Khaṃ, 281; Laṃ, 294; Oṃ, 31, 33, 35, 195, 236, 281, 286, 288; Raṃ, 294; Svā, 286; Vaṃ, 236, 240, 243, 294, 333; Yaṃ, 294
Symbol(s), 197, 233, 243, 290, 295; Symbolic Meaning (*brda*), 71; Symbolized Object, 233; Symbolizer, 230; Symbolizing Agent, external and internal, 233
Sympathetic Joy (= Sympathetic Delight; *muditā, anumodanā*), 184-5

T

Takakusu, Junjiro, 204
Ṭakkirāja (God of Love), 142
Taṃbura, 79
Tanjur (the translation into Tibetan of commentarial Buddhist texts and scientific treatises), 12
Tantra (Buddhist), defined, 266; 12-3, 18, 24, 71, 93, 95, 100-1, 137, 168, 213, 220,

241, 265-6, 272-275, 289, 317, 321, 333; classification of Tantra into groups: for standard division into four groups, Kriyā, Caryā-, Yoga-, and Anuttarayoga-, see under Contents, pp. 6, ff.; for other divisions, seven groups, *Ubhayatantra*, 100; Anuttara texts speak of two higher Tantras, Yoga- and Anuttarayoga-, 147, 161, 163, 187, 199, and of three lower Tantras, Kriyā-, Caryā, Yogā-, 157, 173, 175, 273; Kriyā-: Chapters Three and Four, and 207, 209, 219, 235, 277; Caryā-: Chapter Five, and 100-105, 139, 147, 149, 155, 157, 163-168, 171, 173, 179, 199, 235; Yoga-: Chapter Six, and 24-5, 27, 29, 35, 100-1, 141-149, 155, 157, 167-8, 179, 199, 251; Anuttarayoga-: Chapter Seven, and 24-26, 100-1, 113, 127-8, 141, 143, 147, 151, 155, 165, 168, 173, 175, 179, 194-5, 198-200, 219, 223-4, 227, 234, 242, 273, 311, 317, 319, 333, 335; basic division in Anuttarayoga-: portion in common with Yoga- called *yoga-tantra*, 251, and portion exclusive of Yoga- called *mahāyoga-tantra*, 155, 251; also Anuttarayoga divided into Father (*pitṛ*) = Means (*upāya*) = Dāka = Mahāyoga, 100, 251-267, 284, and into Mother (*mātṛ*) = Insight (*prajñā*) = Dākinī = Yoginī, 47, 100, 251-267, 284, 318-9, while all Anuttarayoga- labelled Non-dual — (*advaita-tantra*), 253-259, 263; Anuttarayoga- further divided into Promulgating Sound and Meaning of Subject Matter, 267, and the latter divided into Tantra of Cause = — of Ground; — of Means = — of Path; and — of Effect, 266-7, 269; while Tantra of Path further divided into four classes, 269. An individual Tantra may have forms called *kalpa-tantra*, 100, 125, or *kalpa-laghu-tantra*, 165, contrasted with *vaipūlya-tantra*, 165; and forms called Basic (= Fundamental) Tantra (*mūla-tantra*), 25, 70, 125, 131, 147, 206, 215-219, 225, 253, 266, 335; Continuation Tantra (*uttaratantra*), 48, 97, 131, 206-7, 216-219, 237, 262, 266; Continuation of the Continuation (*uttarottara*), 216-219; and Explanatory Tantra (*vyākhyā-tantra*), 25, 70, 145, 147, 165, 215, 253, 257, 266, 313, which can be Shared or Unshared, 253. Tantra as practically equivalent to *saṃtāna* (Stream of Consciousness), 266, 321

Tārā, 102, 127; — Cult, 192; Samaya-, 192; Twenty-one Salutations to —, 127

Tāranātha, 79

tarka (Mental element), 173

Tathāgata(s), 30, 34-5, 50-53, 63, 103, 106, 109, 183, 186, 209, 214-218, 221, 224, 244, 255, 313-315; — as Progenitor, 217; *sarvatathāgata-samatā* (Equality with all the Tathāgatas); *tathāgata-dhātu* and *tathāgata-garbha*, 49-51; named —: Dīpaṃkara, Ratnaśikhin, Śākyamuni, Vipaśyin, 17, 19

tattva (as Categories), 214, 273; (as Reality), 199, 263; *ātma-* (Self Reality), 159, 163, 195, 207; *devatā-*, 209; — Chapter, 99

Technique (*prakriyā*), 113

tejas (Radiance, Fire), 43, 332; *tejo-dhātu* (Element of Fire)

Temple (*devakula*), 281

Tenet(s), argued set of (*siddhānta*), 83, 87, 328

Term, Terminology, either Standard (*yathāruta*), or Coined (*na-yathāruta*), 219, 259, 261; Conventional — (*vyavahāra*), 91, 157

Thatness, 245

Therapy, 79

Thirty-three Gods (*trayastriṃśat*), 107

Thought (*citta*), 81, 83; —, belittling (*cittadūṣaṇa*), 328; — Only (*citta-mātra*), 97, 99; —, discursive (*kalpana*), 328

Thread, in five colors (= *jñāna-sūtra*; see Line), 285-287

Threefold or triadic groups: three Collections (*tripiṭaka*), 57, 61; Garments, yellow-red (*trikaṣāyacīvara*), 43; higher Initiations, 145; Jewels, 186, 203; Meditations, 139; Mountains, 59; Persons, religious order of, 87; Pledges, 143; Poisons, 57, 221; Realms (= Worlds), 102, 142, 185, 205, 221; Secrets, 142; Tiers (representing Body, Speech, and Mind), 206-7; Vehicles (*śrāvaka*, *pratyekabuddha*, and *bodhisattva*), 51; Vows, 155; Wheels, 53

Throne, 228; Lion —, 105

Thunderbolt (*vajra*, q.v.), 31, 35, 102, 162,

179, 215, 224, 229, 233, 243-245, 293, 296, 315, 317; Crossed — (= Four-mouthed —; *viśva-vajra* or *karma-vajra*), 229, 247; Firm — (*dṛdha-v.*), 31; First (= Primordial; *ādi-vajra*), 31, 33, 243, 247; — Fist (*vajra-muṣṭi*), 229, 244-247; — Gem, 323; Great —, 142; — of Mind (*citta-v.*), 259; — Tie (*vajrabandha*), 241, 293; Tiny — (*sūkṣma-v.*), 245
Tibetan gurus, 293, 303
Tīkṣṇavajra, 119
tīkṣṇendriya (Faculties, keen), 317
tilaka, 304-5
Tilottamā (Best of Drops, a goddess), 36-39
tīrthika (Heretics), 71
Tongues, 319
Tooth of the Tathāgata, 59
Tortoise (*kūrma*), 280
toya (Water), 332; *-seka* (Water Initiation), 313
Trailokyavijaya, 118, 217, 316
traidhātukadharmarāja (King of the Law of the Three Worlds), 315
Training *(vinaya)*, 261; — of Living Beings *(jagad-v)*, *217*
Transgression(s) (*āpatti*), Basic or Fundamental — (*mūlāpatti*), Gross — (*sthūlāpatti*), and Ancillary, 153, 155, 274, 328-9, 331
Transmigration (*saṃsāra*), 201
Transmutation (*parāvṛtti*), 29
Trāyastriṃśat (the thirty-three God Heaven), 107, 169
Treatise (*śāstra*), 48, 57, 71, 73, 87, 201, 273, 275; — of Inner Science (= Buddhism), divided into those of Doctrinal Part (*darśana-bhaga*) and Practical Part (*caryā-bhaga*) for each of the Three Wheels, starting 81, 83; 87, 93; 96ff.; — of Outer Science (non-Buddhist or profane science), 71ff.
Tree, Wish-granting (*kalpa-vṛkṣa*), 175
Triangle, 294
trikaṣāyacīvara, 43
Tripartition, 253-257
tripiṭaka (Three Collections of Scripture), 61; Abhidharma-, 57, 59, 69; Sūtra-, 57; Vinaya-, 57, 69
Trisāhasramahāsahasra, 105, 205
Truth (*satya*), Absolute and Conventional 278; Power of —, 55; — of Cessation, 53; Four Noble Truths, 19, 45, 81
Tsoṅ-kha-pa, 11-13, 36-38, 42, 78, 86-7, 96-100, 124, 152, 156-160, 168-9, 200, 206, 210-1, 220, 223, 244, 240, 254, 264, 272-3, 276-7, 281-2, 286, 288, 295, 298, 304, 316-318, 326, 328, 332
Tucci, Giuseppe, 11, 304
turīya-abhiṣeka (the Fourth Initiation), 311
Tuṣita, 23, 25, 115; Tuṣitāḥ (the Deities of Tuṣita), 169
Twilight, evening, 276; — Language (*saṃdhi-bhāṣā*), 219
Tying (*bandhana*), 237, 240, 243, 249

U

udaka (= *toya*; Water), 289; *udakābhiṣeka* (Water Initiation), 313
udāna (Impersonal Utterance), 45, 55
udāna (name of a Wind, q.v.)
Udayana, 75
uddeśa (High Goal), 171, 221; *uddeśa-vineya* (Candidate for the High Goal), 45
uddhṛta, 113
Ugly-Eyes, the King (Virūpākṣa), 123
Ugrabhūti, 77
Ulkāmukha, 115
Uncommon or Unshared (*asādhāraṇa*), 147, 263, 309, 313
Unconditioned (*asaṃskṛta*), 49, 53
Unconscious Substance (*jaḍā-svabhāva*), 93
Underworld, 221
Union (*yoga*), with *dharmadhātu*, 217; — of Body, Speech, and Mind, 297; — or Coupling (*yuganaddha*), 199, 320, 325; — or Coupling with Learning (*śaikṣa-yuganaddha*), 266, 325; — or Coupling beyond Learning (*aśaikṣa-yuganaddha*), 37, 39, 266-7, 325, 327; — as Bliss-Void, 143, 162, 296, 321, 323; — as Father-Mother, 259, 287, 289, 304-5, 319-325
Unwisdom (*avidyā*), 315
upacāra (Tib. *ñe rgyu*; Convergence), 268
upādhyāya (Superior of a Monastery, Preceptor), 63, 313
upadeśa (Explanation), 55, 57
Upagupta, 61, 63
upahṛdaya (Near-essence, a kind of *mantra*, q.v.), 116-7, 161
upalakṣaṇa (Referent), 228

Upāli, 59, 69
upapādukā (Birth, spontaneous), 330
upoṣaḍha (Sabbath), 109
upāya (Means, q.v.); *-deha* (Means Body), 157
upekṣā (Indifference, a Boundless State), 184
uraga (Breast-goer), 280-1
ūrdhvāṅga (Upper Member of Body), 79
Urine, 177, 220
ūrṇā (= *ūrṇā-kośa*; a ringlet of hair in middle of forehead), 18, 36, 119, 161, 237
uṣma (a kind of Omen), 202
uṣṇīṣa (= *uṣṇīṣa-śiraskatā*; protuberance upon crown of Buddha), 18, 115, 117, 119, 315; also personified as goddesses, the Uṣṇīṣa of the Family, Uṣṇīṣavijayā, 28, 115, and Vimaloṣṇīṣa and Uṣṇīṣa-Sitātapatrā, 115
utpala (Lotus, blue), 69
utpatti-bhava-krama (Steps, q.v. of Birth State)
utpatti-krama (see under Steps)
Uttarīya, 85
utthāna (Rising for Leaving), 157

V

vācakāna (Promulgation, q.v.), 253
vācya (Subject Matter), 253
vāg (= *vāk*; Speech, q.v.), 225; *vāg-viveka* (see under Speech)
Vāgbhata, 78
Vāgīśvarakīrti, 267, 301
Vaibhāṣika, 16, 21, 81-85
Vaidarbha, 79
vaipulya (Grand Scripture), 55
Vairocana, 34-37, 100-1, 205-209, 214-217, 221-227, 231, 233, 241-243, 247, 249, 264-5, 286, 313, 335
Vaiśākha, 18-9, 58-9, 282
Vaiśālī, 47, 61-67, 105, 109
Vaiṣṇava, 282
Vaiśravaṇa, 111, 133, 135
Vaiśya, 69
vajra (the invariant original of Tibetan *rdo rje*, meaning either Diamond, q.v. or Thunderbolt, q.v., but occasionally the intended meaning is indeterminate, as in the case of *vajrayāna* which is ordinarily taken as 'Diamond Vehicle' but feasibly is also 'Thunderbolt Vehicle'); 31, 33, 102-3, 131, 221, 223, 233, 283, 291, 315; *-ācārya* (Hierophant), 141, 273; *ācārya-abhiṣeka* (Hierophant's Initiation), 313, 315; *-seka* (Diamond Initiation), 313; *-śiṣya-abhiṣeka* (Neophyte's Initiation), 313; also: *-dṛṣṭi* (a *dhāraṇī*), 240-1; *-āsana*, 89, 91, 119, 127, 129, and *-jñāna*, 229, 243, belong to the 'Diamond' interpretation
Vajracaṇḍa, 117
Vajradaṇḍa, 117
Vajradhara, 37, 100-103, 169, 171, 263-267, 297, 316-7, 333, 335
Vajradhātvīśvara (Lord of the Diamond Realm), 142-3, 242
Vajraghaṇṭa-pā, 89, 271
Vajragarbha, 256-7, 262
Vajrakīla, 117-8
Vajramudgara, 117
Vajrapāṇi, 69-70, 102, 107, 109, 117, 127-131, 135-137, 145, 185
Vajrasattva, 22, 37, 100, 143, 241, 243, 296-7, 312, 316
Vajravārāhī (Diamond Sow), 36, 257, 304-5
Vajravega, 283
Vajravidāraṇa, 131, 145, 169
Vajraviḍāraṇa-vaipūlyatantra, 165
Vajrayāna (see Vehicle), 159, 271, 291, 335
vajrin, 297
vajropama-samādhi (see under *samādhi*)
Vajroṣṇīṣa-tantra, 137, 165
viśva-vajra (see under Thunderbolt)
vāk, 256; *-samaya*, 296
Varabodhi, 139, 167, 171, 173, 179, 193
vārāhī (Sow; see Vajravārāhī), 304
Vararuci, 77
Varmavajra, 119, 147
Vārāṇasī, 19, 41
varṣa ('Summer Session'), 59
varṣaśatopasaṃpanna (Lalitavistara 409.19), 43
vāsanā (Disposition), 149
Vasanta (Spring-time), 305; -tilaka (Drop of Spring-time), 36, 305
vaśīkāra (Subduing), 214, 237
Vāṣpa, 41
vastra-abhiṣeka (Garment Initiation), 27
vastu (Ground), 187
Vasubandhu, 57, 95, 97, 316, 334-5
Vasuṃdharā, 113
Vasumitra, 83

Vātsīputra, 67
Vātsīputrīya, 85
vāyu (Wind, q.v.)
Veda, 74
Vehicle (*yāna*), two main kinds, of Upper or Great — (*mahāyāna*) and Lower — (*hīnayāna*): Sūtra-, Vinaya-, and Abhidharma-piṭakas of both Vehicles, 57, and of Mahāyāna, 69; Asaṅga's *Abhidharmasamuccaya* belongs to both —, 95; Lower —, 17; Upper or Great —, 17-21, 53, 57, 69, 85, 95, 99; Asaṅga's *Mahāyānasaṃgraha* belongs to Upper —, 95; Upper — divides into Pāramitā — or School, and Mantra — (*mantrayāna*) or Category and also called Diamond — (*vajrayāna*, q.v.): Pāramitā, 21, 35, 37, 151, 199, 335; Mantra, 35, 41, 95, 101, 109, 111, 151, 199, 334-5
Verse(s) (*gāthā*), 53, 70-1, 105; Versification, 79
Vessel, offering, 177, 195; metaphorical for the Candidate, q.v., called fit Vessel, 236, 321-327, 335, unfit —, 335, good —, 317, outstanding —, 273
vibuddha (fully expanded), see under Buddha
vibhaṅga, 83, 85, 95, 97
Vibhūti (presumably = Vibhūticandra), 280-1
Victor, 103; Victorious over the Three Worlds (trailokyavijaya, q.v.)
vidhi (Rite, q.v.), 101, 119
Vein(s) (or Petals; *nāḍī*), 237, 321, 333; Central — (*avadhūtī*), Right — (*rasanā*), Left — (*lalanā*), 321, 323, 327; their local numbers at Centers (*cakra*), q.v., Crown of Head, Middle of Forehead, Neck (= Speech Vein), Heart, Navel, Sacral Place, Tip of Gem, 321-323
vidyā (Knowledge, Wisdom, Science; sometimes = *mudrā* as Female partner), 19, 102, 116-7, 133-136, 143-149, 160, 181, 214, 237, 268, 317-325; *cikitsā*-, 73; *vidyābhiṣeka* (= *vidyāseka*; Wisdom Initiation), 313-4; *-dhara* (= *-dharin*), 89, 183, 201, 211; *-devī*, 314; *-jñāna* (Wisdom-Knowledge), 314-5; *-jñānacakra* (Circle of Wisdom-Knowledge), 270; *-rāja* (King of the Mystic Science), 177-8, 185; *-rājñī* (Queen of the Mystic Science; sometimes = *pañcarakṣā*, the Gzuṅs grva), 113, 175, 177
vidyut-prabhā (Lightning Flash), 36
vihāra (Monastery), 281
Vijaya, 118
Vijñānakāya (Set of Perceptions), 81
vikalpa (Discursive Thought), 162, 172
vikurvāṇa, 29, 224
Vimala (a City), 105
Vimalamaṇisāra, 115
Vimalaprabha, 105
Vimalasvabhāva (a Mountain), 69
vimāna (Palace), 161, 289, 303
vimukti-mārga (Path of Liberation), 331
Vinaya (one of the three Scriptural collections; also used in its basic meaning of discipline, training), 65, 69, 85, 261, 265; four Defeats of the —, 331; — texts, 82
Vinayakārikā (alternate name of a Vinaya text), 85
vineya (Candidate, q.v.), 219
Vinītadeva, 59, 67, 83
vipāka (Maturation; a kind of Body, q.v.), 232; *-mārga* (Path of Maturation), 331
vipaśyanā (Higher Vision), 57, 199, 210-1
Vipaśyin, 19
Virgin (*kanyā*), 195
Virūpākṣa, 123
Viśākhadeva, 85
visarga, 191
viṣaya (Sensory Domain), 173
Viśrama, 133, 135
Visualization (*abhisamaya*), 309, 317, 321, 323
viśuddhadharmadhātujñāna, 214
vitāna (Canopy), 175
Voice, 230-233, 239; Vocal Expression (*abhilāpana*), 247
Void (*śūnya*), 12, 37, 39, 49, 161, 204, 209-211, 263-265, 268, 301, 317, 319, 321-323, 326, 335; nomenclature of three Voids, 39, means: Void (*śūnya*), Further Void (*atiśūnya*), Great Void (*mahāśūnya*), 37, 39, 71, to which a fourth is added, Universal Void (*sarvaśūnya*), 37; the four Voids are equivalent to four Lights, q.v.; Bliss-Void (*sukha-śūnya*), 277, 333; Void in the sense of real production (*tāttvikasiddhyā śūnya*), 49
Voidness (*śūnyatā*), 12, 28-31, 53, 71, 87,

157, 160-162, 165, 167, 195, 199, 207, 222, 243, 247, 283, 296, 299, 317, 323-327, 334-5; list of sixteen, 28; Knowledge of — (*śūnyatā-jñāna*), 214; Knowledge Diamond of — (*śūnyatā-jñāna-vajra*), 160; — of the Natural State, 157; — of the Void (*śūnya-śūnyatā*, perhaps = *śūnyatā-śūnyatā*, 28), 333
Vow(s) (*saṃvara*), 12, 101, 141, 145-155, 185-6, 207, 275, 283, 309-311, 316, 328-331; *bhikṣu* —, 311; Bodhisattva — (including Aspiration —, and Entrance-), 12, 147, 151-155, 810; Common (*sādharaṇa*) and Uncommon (*asādharaṇa*) —, 147-151, 309; — of five Families, 147, 149; Initial —, 16; Laymen's —, 155; Mantra —, 12, 153, 155, 275, 309, 311, 329; Prātimokṣa — (= Vinaya —), 12, 155, 331; Vidyādhara, 147
Vowel(s), 30-1, 191
vrata, 214
vṛṣa (Vigor), 79
vyākaraṇa (Prophecies), 53, 141
vyāna (a kind of Wind, q.v.),264
vyavahāra (Conventional Term), 91, 157
Vyavahāra-siddhi, 87
vyañjana-kāya (Set of Letters),77
vyūha (Array), 205

W

Watch (as a time or portion of Day and Night), 18, 43, 102, 152-3, 191-195, 259, 261, 276-7
Water (*toya*, *udaka*), 34, 121, 123, 160, 177, 181, 185, 211, 230-1, 281, 289, 295, 299, 313, 317, 332; — Disk or Center in Body, 211; — Drops, 17; Perfumed —, 117, 121; 'Water' (*udaka*) as a *mantra*, 289
Wayman, Alex, 37, 70
Wayward views (*mithyā-dṛṣṭi*), 221
Wealth, 123
Wicked (*duṣṭa*), 328
Willow Leaves, 133
Wheel (*cakra*), 36, 69; — of the Law (*dharmacakra*), 19, 23, 25, 41-47, 57, 81, 85, 95, 101, 185; Three Wheels in terms of Hīnayāna and Mahāyāna, 53
Wind (= Air, vital; *vāyu*), 157, 172-3, 189, 191, 211, 230-1, 264-5, 284, 295, 321, 323, 333; the Winds *prāṇa*, *apāna*, *udāna*, *samāna*, *vyāna*, 264; upper vital Air (*ūrdhva-vāyu*) and lower vital Air (*adhas-vāyu*), 272-3
Wisdom (*vidyā*, q.v.); Wisdom Holder (*vidyādhara*), see under *vidyā*.
Woman, 321, 328
Womb, 25, 48, 330; Birth from a —, 333
Word categories, *svarga*, *pātāla*, and *bhūmi*, 79
Worlds, three (= Realms, three, q.v.), 221; World Emperor (*cakravartin*), 291; — Systems (*lokadhātu*), 133; — Systems of Tribulation, 23
Worship, 273
Wrath, 283

Y

yab-yum (Father-Mother), 259, 304; see also Union
yakṣa, 18, 55, 59, 103, 109-115, 121, 135
Yama, 18, 115
Yamāntaka, 119
Yamāri, red and black, 265, 277, 295
Yaśas, 63, 65
Yaśodharā, 22, 118
Yaśomitra, 83
yathāruta (see under Term, Terminology)
yauvarāja (Crown-Prince), 316
Ye-śes-sñiṅ-po, 104
yid ṅo (*manas*-face), 211
yoga (Union, q.v.; Praxis), defined as Union with the *dharmadhātu*, 217; 71, 127, 157, 206, 210, 214, 220, 224, 245, 263, 265, 289, 329; sequence of four, *yoga*, *anuyoga*, *atiyoga*, and *mahāyoga*, 214, 223; also *guhyayoga*, *sarvayoga*, 214; two kinds, *yoga* with Images or Signs (*sanimitta-y.*), 157, 173, 197, 201, 207, 210-1, and *yoga* without Images or Signs (*animitta-y.*), 157, 199-201, 210-1; — of Contemplation, 157; — of the Deity (*devatā-y.*), 203, 207, 247, 273, and two kinds, rough and fine, 199, fine (= subtle —, *sūkṣma-y.*, 255, 257); — of Heat (*caṇḍā-y.*), 36; — of the Wind, 157; also — of six parts (*ṣaḍaṅga-y.*), 37, 223, 320; — of inner *samādhi* contrasting with outer ritual, 219; *-tantra* as Chapter Six
yogin (one engaged in the Praxis or Union), 162-3, 218, 234, 236, 256, 261-2, 296, 326; *yoginī* (Female *yogin*), 261-2, 263, 304-5, and a kind of Tantra, q.v.

yojana, 175
Yoshimura, Shūki, 202
Youth, 220
yuganaddha (Pair Combined, or Coupling), of two kinds, *śaikṣa* -(with Learning) and *aśaikṣa*- (beyond Learning); see under Union; Yuganaddha-krama, verse 12 (from Nāgārjuna's *Pañcakrama*), 157
yukti (Reasons), 85
yum (Mother), 319
Yung-ho-kung, 13
Youth (*kumāra*), 185

Z

Zaṅs-dkar (a place name), 129
Zenith of the Sun, 63
zur bkaḥ, 112-3